The New York Times

THE TIMES OF THE SEVENTIES

The New York Times

THE
TIMES
OF THE
SEVENTIES

The Culture, Politics and Personalities
that Shaped the Decade

Edited by Clyde Haberman

BLACK DOG
& LEVENTHAL
PUBLISHERS
NEW YORK

Copyright © 2013 The New York Times

All rights reserved. No part of this book, either text
or illustration may be used or reproduced in any form
without prior written permission from the publisher.

Published by
Black Dog & Leventhal Publishers, Inc.
151 West 19th Street
New York, NY 10011

Distributed by
Workman Publishing Company
225 Varick Street
New York, NY 10014

Manufactured in Malaysia

Cover design by Evan Gaffney Design
Interior design by Pauline Neuwirth, Neuwirth &
Associates, Inc.

Interior images courtesy of Getty Images.

ISBN-13: 978-1-57912-945-3

h g f e d c b a
Library of Congress Cataloging-in-Publication Data on file.

Contents

Introduction

A soldier coming home to New York in early 1970 after 16 months of overseas duty felt as if he had entered a strange land. Sixteen months is not a long time, yet in that stretch the world seemed to have somehow tilted 15 degrees, rendering it all but unrecognizable. People even looked different. Many men suddenly wore their hair long. They sported beards and mustaches. They wore wildly colored clothes. Sure, long hair and psychedelic outfits had been part of the scene for a while. But those fashions were largely the province of political radicals and kids referred to, not always kindly, as hippies. Now, stockbrokers and insurance agents went around like that. "There's something happening here," ran the lyrics of a popular Buffalo Springfield song. That there was. The returning soldier sensed that this decade, still in its infancy, would usher in a thorough break from much of the past.

The Sixties, for all its acclaim, did not begin as a true departure from the Fifties, notwithstanding the election of a young president; what most people call the Sixties, meaning an era of turmoil and rebellion, did not really begin until 1964 or 1965. But the Seventies lost no time asserting itself as a decade when many of the old verities no longer applied. Clothes and facial hair were one indication. They were also the least of it. In May 1970, students at an Ohio school unfamiliar to most Americans, Kent State University, staged several days of demonstrations denouncing the Nixon administration's expansion of the seemingly endless Vietnam War into Cambodia. The protests were rowdy at times. There was vandalism and rock-throwing. But nothing prepared the students, or the rest of the nation, for what would happen on May 4. After crowds of unarmed demonstrators ignored orders to disperse, Ohio National Guardsmen opened fire. They killed four students and wounded nine others, one of whom was permanently paralyzed. There would be investigations and endless recriminations. But there was no escaping a fundamental, haunting reality of the new decade: What did it say about a country when those who were in charge would shoot their children for doing little more than speaking up?

Mutual trust between the governors and the governed, an essential component of a democracy, had broken down. It would be thus through much of the decade. At the dawn of the 1960s, most Americans believed their government to be honorable and truthful. Not so at the dawn of the 1970s. More and more, people felt they could no longer accept on faith what their leaders said. That returning soldier, for example, went back to his old job as a newspaper reporter in New York. It fell to him in September 1971 to write about inmates at the maximum security prison in Attica, N.Y., who rioted, took prison employees hostage and then turned the chaos into an extraordinary rebellion stretching across four days. It ended with dozens of inmates and their hostages being killed when state policemen stormed the rebels, firing indiscriminately as they retook control. The authorities insisted that the troopers moved in only after the insurrectionists had begun slashing hostages' throats, even castrating one of them. A day later, autopsies showed that not a single hostage had been killed by the inmates. No one had been castrated. The troopers did all the killing. The young reporter could not shake off a question that would stay with him and with many others forever: If officials could lie so blatantly about something like that, when the falsehoods could be scientifically discredited in short order, was there anything they said that could be taken at face value? All too often in the '70s, the answer was no. It was an era when doubting authority became, for many, a default position.

This was the decade of the Pentagon Papers, a government history that fell into The New York Times's hands and traced a trail of deceit that had drawn the United States ever deeper into an unpopular war in Vietnam. It was the decade of slain Israeli athletes at the Munich Olympics, when the self-absorbed, tone-deaf head of the International Olympic Committee publicly fretted not about the deaths but about the inconvenience they created for his precious Games. It was the decade of oil embargoes and soaring gasoline prices, with many in the West convinced they were being taken for a ride by OPEC and Big Oil. It was the decade when the mad-dog Khmer Rouge took control in Cambodia and slaughtered two million or more of their countrymen in a genocidal frenzy. And it was, to be sure, the decade of Watergate, the catch-all word for an assortment of government misdeeds, lies and cover-ups that forced a president to resign and left little doubt that Americans could not take for granted that those who led them were men of honor.

Not that it was all bleakness. Hardly. Medical breakthroughs and new technologies, like computers that grew in use, made life better. There were glorious improvements in the food people ate, daring writing in the movies and television shows they watched, exciting new records set by the athletes they cheered. But an abiding cynicism took root, one captured well by the decade's "Godfather" films, widely regarded as among the greatest of all time. Though set in the 1940s and '50s, they offered insights into latter-day corruption in government and business, as much as in organized crime. Michael Corleone, son of the supreme mob boss, says to the woman he would marry, "My father is no different than any powerful man, any man with power, like a president or senator."

"Do you know how naïve you sound, Michael?" she says. "Presidents and senators don't have men killed."'

"Oh," he replies. "Who's being naïve, Kay?"

As the 1970s wore on, Americans lost whatever innocence they still had about the questionable ways in which power was often exercised. But they also resigned themselves to life as it was. That weariness was captured in another '70s movie set in an earlier era, a brilliant work about a private eye in 1930s Los Angeles who stumbles upon deeply embedded corruption. He is forced to accept his helplessness in changing things when a colleague says to him, "Forget it, Jake. It's Chinatown."

In **many ways,** the seventies took a back seat to its more celebrated cousin, the sixties. But what many Americans think of as part of the tumultuous sixties in fact reached fulfillment in the seventies. From the decade's start, the wheels seemed about to come off the wagon.

View of the large crowd with a sympathetic banner that had gathered in front of the State House at Boston Common to protest the Kent State University shootings, 1970.

This was what 1970 alone looked like in the United States:

Five defendants in the so-called Chicago Seven trial were found guilty of seeking to promote a riot at the 1968 Democratic National Convention in Chicago. An Army lieutenant, William L. Calley Jr., was found guilty of war crimes: the premeditated murder of 22 civilians at My Lai, South Vietnam. A band of radical leftists known as the Weather Underground resorted to bombings, though often incompetently and self-destructively. National Guardsmen in Ohio fired on student protesters at Kent State University, killing four of them.

Law enforcement personnel wearing gas masks wait to storm hostage-holding prisoners during the Attica riots.

Matters did not then improve. In 1971, inmates at Attica state prison in upstate New York staged a full-throated rebellion to protest shoddy conditions and demeaning rules. By the time the uprising was put down four days later, 43 inmates and prison employees they had taken hostage were killed, nearly all by state troopers who went in with guns blazing on orders from Gov. Nelson A. Rockefeller. It was one of the bloodiest one-day encounters between Americans since the Civil War.

Nor did political assassination, which in part defined the 1960's, show signs of fading. George Wallace, Alabama's segregationist governor, was shot and left paralyzed in 1972 while campaigning for president outside Washington. Twice in 1975, unhinged women in California shot at President Gerald R. Ford, but missed. Three years later, a San Francisco politician, Dan White, flipped out, drew a revolver and killed Mayor George Moscone and then Harvey Milk, the city's first openly gay elected official.

But if anything could be said to define the '70s in America, it was not political killing so much as political corruption. It reached spectacular levels.

In 1971, The New York Times published documents that came to be called the Pentagon Papers, a history tracing the mendacity and misjudgments that led America into the Vietnam War. President Richard M. Nixon tried to suppress its publication on dubious national-security grounds, but the Supreme Court rejected his arguments and affirmed a newspaper's right to publish in the face of government attempts to impose "prior restraint."

Gerald Ford being sworn-in by Chief Justice Warren Burger, with wife Betty between them, hours after President Nixon resigned.

The U.S. Supreme Court Building.

er, it was Nixon's turn to quit, done in by the multi-tentacled scandal lumped under the heading of Watergate. It all seemed unthinkable. It was all too real.

The Supreme Court, too, contributed to the turmoil. In 1972, it declared the death penalty unconstitutional. A year later, in *Roe v. Wade*, it struck down restrictions on abortion before the final trimester. As everyone knows, those rulings settled nothing. Abortion continues to divide the country bitterly. So does capital punishment. The Supreme Court itself was torn, reversing its own decision in short order and reinstating the death penalty in 1976.

The decade's end brought no relief. It had less than two months to go when dozens of American diplomats in Tehran were taken hostage by Iranian militants. There was no way to anticipate that this would become a crisis lasting an excruciating 14 months. But the phrase "America held hostage" had entered the language, and a mighty nation was pained to its soul.

Nixon's troubles—and the country's—were only beginning. In October 1973, Vice President Spiro Agnew's corrupt past caught up with him, forcing his resignation. Ten months lat-

A demonstration at the American embassy in Teheran, Iran, where hostages were taken, in November, 1979.

FEBRUARY 19, 1970

CHICAGO 7 CLEARED OF PLOT; 5 Guilty on Second Count

J. Anthony Lukas

American social and political activist and Yippie co-founder Abbie Hoffman speaks to a crowd gathered to protest the "Chicago 7" conspiracy trial, Chicago, Illinois.

CHICAGO, Feb. 18—All seven defendants in the Chicago conspiracy trial were acquitted today of plotting to incite a riot here during the 1968 Democratic National Convention, but five of them were convicted of seeking to promote a riot through individual acts.

The five men, David T. Dellinger, Rennie C. Davis, Thomas F. Hayden, Abbie Hoffman and Jerry C. Rubin, were found guilty of crossing state lines with intent to incite a riot and then giving inflammatory speeches for that purpose. The two other defendants, John R. Froines and Lee Weiner, were acquitted on both the conspiracy and the individual counts.

After nearly 40 hours of deliberation, the jury returned its verdict at 12:20 p.m. in the brightly lit courtroom on the 23rd floor of Chicago's Federal Building, where the four-and-a-half-month trial took place.

William M. Kunstler, one of the defense attorneys, said later that the five convicted defendants would appeal. They face possible penalties of five years in prison, $10,000 fines or both.

It was an ambiguous end to the marathon trial, which has aroused passions on all sides. Each side won something. For the defense, it was the Government's failure to persuade the jury that any conspiracy existed among demonstrators here during the convention. For the Government, it was the failure of five of the defendants to establish to the jury's satisfaction that their intent was innocent.

The defendants were apparently stunned, not so much by the verdict, but by the jury's capacity to produce it.

When the defendants were taken from their cells at Cook County Jail, where they had begun serving sentences for contempt of court, they believed they were to attend a hearing on the defense's motion to discharge the apparently deadlocked jury.

So they, their attorneys and most of the newsmen were astonished when Marshal Ronald Dombrowski announced to the hushed courtroom: "The jury has reached a verdict, Your Honor."

Before the jury was brought in, Richard G. Schultz, Assistant United States Attorney, asked Judge Julius J. Hoffman to exclude all spectators and the defendants' families from the courtroom to prevent the sort of disorders that often erupted during the trial's tensest moments.

Mr. Kunstler argued strenuously that at least the defendants' wives and girlfriends should be allowed to remain.

"It would be the last crowning indignity of this trial," he said, "to make these men face this moment in a courtroom surrounded only by marshals and lawyers. At this moment, no man should be alone. I beg and implore you to reject the Government's motion."

But Judge Hoffman quickly approved the motion, and Federal marshals promptly moved towards four young women seated in the third row of the press section: Abbie Hoffman's wife, Anita; Mr. Rubin's girlfriend, Nancy Kurshan; Mr. Weiner's girlfriend, Sharon Avery; and Mr. Dellinger's 13-year-old daughter, Michelle.

As a marshal reached for Anita Hoffman, she stood and shouted at the defendants: "You will be avenged."

Then, as marshals propelled her down the aisle, she spun towards the judge and shouted: "We'll dance on your grave, Julie."

F.B.I. SPURS HUNT FOR WEATHERMEN

John Kifner

CHICAGO, April 3—The Federal Bureau of Investigation has begun a nationwide hunt for the 12 Weathermen indicted in Chicago on charges of conspiracy and violation of the Federal antiriot act.

Marlin Johnson, the agent in charge of the F.B.I. offices in Chicago, said that the search began almost immediately after indictments were handed down yesterday charging the 12 young men and women, who make up most of the central leadership of the violence-oriented faction of the Students for a Democratic Society, with planning and staging rioting here last October.

But the Weathermen have virtually dropped out of sight in the last three months and former associates and other radicals say they have no idea where members of the group are and believe they will be difficult to find.

The national office of the Students for a Democratic Society, which had been the faction's headquarters, is closed, and the S. D. S. newspaper New Left Notes, renamed Fire by the Weatherman, is no longer published.

The Weathermen, estimated to number around 300 persons, have reportedly gone "underground." They have broken up into small, secret groups, living in several cities with almost no contact with other radical organizations.

The 12 being sought under yesterday's indictment are:

Mark Rudd, 22 years old; William Ayers, 25; Jeffrey Jones, 22; Bernardine Dohrn, 27; Terry Robbins, 22; John Jacobs, 22; Linda Evans, 22; Howard Machtinger, 23; Kathy Boudin, 26; Michael Spiegel, 23; Judy Clark, 21, and Lawrence Weiss, 22.

The police are already searching for a number of Weathermen who have forfeited bail in several cities and are seeking Miss Boudin and Cathy Wilkerson for questioning in connection with an explosion that destroyed a New York City townhouse owned by Miss Wilkerson's father.

Miss Wilkerson was named as an unindicted co-conspirator in yesterday's charges.

The Chicago police are also searching for Miss Boudin, Miss Dohrn and Dianne Donghi, 21—also named as an unindicted co-conspirator—in connection with the discovery of an alleged bomb factory in an apartment on Chicago's North Side Monday night.

The police say they found 59 sticks of dynamite; blasting caps; bottles of liquid explosives, and guns and ammunition in the third-floor apartment. ■

4 KENT STATE STUDENTS KILLED BY TROOPS

John Kifner

National Guard troops on the Kent State University grounds on May 4, 1970.

KENT, Ohio, May 4—Four students at Kent State University, two of them women, were shot to death this afternoon by a volley of National Guard gunfire. At least 8 other students were wounded.

The burst of gunfire came about 20 minutes after the guardsmen broke up a noon rally on the Commons, a grassy campus gathering spot, by lobbing tear gas at a crowd of about 1,000 young people.

In Washington, President Nixon deplored the deaths of the four students in the following statement:

"This should remind us all once again that when dissent turns to violence it invites tragedy. It is my hope that this tragic and unfortunate incident will strengthen the determination of all the nation's campuses, administrators, faculty and students alike to stand firmly for the right which exists in this country of peaceful dissent and just as strongly against the resort to violence as a means of such expression."

In Columbus, Sylvester Del Corso, Adjutant General of the Ohio National Guard, said in a statement that the guardsmen had been forced to shoot after a sniper opened fire against the troops from a nearby rooftop and the crowd began to move to encircle the guardsmen.

This reporter, who was with the group of students, did not see any indication of sniper fire, nor was the sound of any gunfire audible before the Guard volley. Students, conceding that rocks had been thrown, heatedly denied that there was any sniper.

At 2:10 this afternoon, after the shootings, the university president, Robert I. White, ordered the university closed for an indefinite time, and officials were making plans to evacuate the dormitories and bus out-of-state students to nearby cities.

Students here, angered by the expansion of the war into Cambodia, have held demonstrations for the last three nights. On Saturday night, the Army Reserve

Officers Training Corps building was burned to the ground and the Guard was called in and martial law was declared.

Today's rally, called after a night in which the police and guardsmen drove students into dormitories and made 69 arrests, began as students rang the iron Victory Bell on the commons, normally used to herald football victories.

A National Guard jeep drove onto the Commons and an officer ordered the crowd to disperse. Then several canisters of tear gas were fired, and the students straggled up a hill that borders the area and retreated into buildings.

A platoon of guardsmen, armed—as they have been since they arrived here with loaded M-1 rifles and gas equipment—moved across the green and over the crest of the hill, chasing the main body of protesters.

The guardsmen moved into a grassy area just below the parking lot and fired several canisters of tear gas from their short, stubby launchers.

Three or four youths ran to the smoking canisters and hurled them back. Most fell far short, but one landed near the troops and a cheer went up from the crowd, which was chanting "Pigs off campus" and cursing the war.

A few youths in the front of the crowd ran into the parking lot and hurled stones or small chunks of pavement in the direction of the guardsmen. Then the troops began moving back up the hill in the direction of the college.

As the guardsmen moved up the hill in single file, they suddenly turned, forming a skirmish line and opening fire.

Some of the students dived to the ground in terror. Others stood shocked or half crouched, apparently believing the troops were firing into the air. Some of the rifle barrels were pointed upward.

Near the top of the hill at the corner of Taylor Hall, a student crumpled over, spun sideways and fell to the ground, shot in the head.

When the firing stopped, a slim girl, wearing a cowboy shirt and faded jeans, was lying face down on the road at the edge of the parking lot, blood pouring out onto the macadam, about 10 feet from this reporter.

The youths stood stunned, many of them clustered in small groups staring at the bodies. A young man cradled one of the bleeding forms in his arms. Several girls began to cry. But many of the students who rushed to the scene seemed almost too shocked to react. ∎

JULY 10, 1970

NIXON PROPOSES 2 NEW AGENCIES ON ENVIRONMENT

James M. Naughton

WASHINGTON, July 9—President Nixon called today for a major reshuffling of Government agencies to coordinate efforts to understand, protect and enhance the nation's environment.

In separate reorganization plans he sent to Congress, Mr. Nixon proposed transferring most pollution control activities to an independent Environmental Protection Agency and combining air and sea research under a new National Oceanic and Atmospheric Administration. The latter would be in the Department of Commerce.

Both plans will take effect automatically unless either branch of Congress objects within 60 days.

There were no new functions or powers suggested in the message today, but the President said that consolidation of activities now spread throughout the Government would permit a more effective assault on despoilers of the environment.

"Our national Government today is not structured to make a coordinated attack on the pollutants which debase the air we breathe, the water we drink, and the land that grows our food," Mr. Nixon said. "Indeed, the present governmental structure for dealing with environmental pollution often defies effective and concerted action."

Under the reorganization, the Environmental Protection Agency—reporting directly to the President—would take over responsibility for clean air and water programs, pesticide research and standard-setting, and radiation monitoring.

The new agency would have 5,650 employees and an estimated budget of $1.4 billion in the fiscal year 1971. Both the manpower and the funds would be transferred from sections of the Departments of the Interior, Agriculture, and Health, Education and Welfare, and other separate agencies now charged with pollution abatement.

The National Oceanic and Atmospheric Administration (whose acronym, N.O.A.A., already is being pronounced "Noah" by officials here) would have a $270 million budget and 12,000 employees. Again, both the manpower and the funds would be transferred from a variety of agencies.

The President said that the ultimate objective should be "to insure that the nation's environmental and resources protection activities are so organized as to maximize both the effective coordination of all and the effective functioning of each." ∎

John A. Green, seated, Environmental Protection Agency regional administrator, with eight other agency officials in 1971.

CALLEY GUILTY OF MURDER OF 22 CIVILIANS AT MYLAI

An American soldier stokes a fire of burning houses during the Mylai massacre on March 16, 1968, in My Lai, South Vietnam.

Homer Bigart

FORT BENNING, Ga., March 29—First Lieut. William L. Calley Jr. was found guilty today of the premeditated murder of at least 22 South Vietnamese civilians at Mylai three years ago.

He faces a mandatory sentence of death or life imprisonment. Arguments in mitigation will be heard tomorrow by the same jury of six officers that sentenced him today, and the punishment will probably be announced tomorrow afternoon.

An appeal is automatic within the military court system and could consume months.

The verdict in this protracted war crimes trial, the longest in the history of American military justice, was announced at 4:31 p.m. after 79 hours and 58 minutes of deliberation stretching over 13 days.

Lieutenant Calley, a short, stocky 27-year-old who led his platoon on a sweep through an undefended hamlet called Mylai 4 March 16, 1968, was escorted before the jury box. Silence fell in the courtroom.

He stiffly saluted the president of the jury, Col. Clifford H. Ford, a partly gray, 53-year-old veteran of World War II and Korea with three rows of ribbons on his chest. The colonel returned the salute and, in a gentle voice, began reading the verdict.

The Government had charged Lieutenant Calley with four specifications of premeditated murder involving at least 102 men, women and children. The first specification charged that he killed at least 30 noncombatants along a trail at the south end of the village.

Colonel Ford announced that the jury had found Lieutenant Calley guilty of the premeditated murder of "an unknown number, no less than one."

The second specification charged Lieutenant Calley with the murder of at least 70 civilians in a ditch outside Mylai. Colonel Ford announced that the jury had found Lieutenant Calley guilty of the premeditated murder of "an unknown number, no less than 20" in this incident.

In the two remaining counts, the jury found Lieutenant Calley guilty of the premeditated murder of a South Vietnamese male in white robes, possibly a monk, and of assault with intent to commit the murder of a small child.

In the case of the child, the original charge was murder, but the judge told the jury, in his charge, that a verdict on the lesser charge was permissible.

One reason Lieutenant Calley was convicted of murdering 22 persons, rather than 102 as charged, was that witnesses disputed the number of dead at Mylai, some saying they had counted fewer than 100. The jury's finding, therefore, reflected its effort to reconcile the contradictions in the testimony.

As he heard the verdict, Lieutenant Calley stood ramrod stiff, his face flushed. His eyes, normally half-closed, were wide open as he stared at Colonel Ford.

A crowd of about 100 spectators stood outside the red brick courthouse. As Lieutenant Calley emerged, surrounded by military policemen, a woman yelled: "We're with you, Calley."

Lieutenant Calley was not handcuffed when driven to the stockade.

He is expected to be flown to the Army Disciplinary Barracks a Fort Leavenworth, Kan., immediately after he is sentenced. Meanwhile, he is confined in a separate officers' cell at the stockade, rooms normally used by the chaplain as an office.

"This boy is a product of the system," said Calley's attorney George Latimer, a 70-year-old retired judge of the Court of Military Appeals. "He was taken out of his own home, given automatic weapons, taught to kill. And then the same Government tries him for killing and selects the judge, the court and the prosecutor. From now on, parents will be less willing than ever to send their boys to Vietnam and soldiers will be less likely to obey orders in the field." ■

JUNE 13, 1971

Pentagon Study Traces 3 Decades of U.S. Involvement

Neil Sheehan

A massive study of how the United States went to war in Indochina, conducted by the Pentagon three years ago, demonstrates that four administrations progressively developed a sense of commitment to a non-Communist Vietnam, a readiness to fight the North to protect the South, and an ultimate frustration with this effort—to a much greater extent than their public statements acknowledged at the time.

The 3,000-page analysis, to which 4,000 pages of official documents are appended, was commissioned by Secretary of Defense Robert S. McNamara and covers the American involvement in Southeast Asia from World War II to mid-1968—the start of the peace talks in Paris after President Lyndon B. Johnson had set a limit on further military commitments and revealed his intention to retire.

Though far from a complete history, even at 2.5 million words, the study forms a great archive of government decision-making on Indochina over three decades. The study led its 30 to 40 authors and researchers to many broad conclusions and specific findings, including the following:

- That the Truman Administration decision to give military aid to France in her colonial war against the Communist-led Vietminh "directly involved" the United States in Vietnam and "set" the course of American policy.
- That the Eisenhower Administration's decision to rescue a fledgling South Vietnam from a Communist takeover and attempt to undermine the new Communist regime of North Vietnam gave the Administration a "direct role in the ultimate breakdown of the Geneva settlement" for Indochina in 1954.
- That the Kennedy Administration, though ultimately spared from major escalation decisions by the death of its leader, transformed a policy of "limited-risk gamble," which it inherited, into a "broad commitment" that left President Johnson with a choice between more war and withdrawal.
- That the Johnson Administration, though the President was reluctant and hesitant to take the final decisions, intensified the covert warfare against North Vietnam and began planning in the spring of 1964 to wage overt war, a full year

before it publicly revealed the depth of its involvement and its fear of defeat.

- That this campaign of growing clandestine military pressure through 1964 and the expanding program of bombing North Vietnam in 1965 were begun despite the judgment of the Government's intelligence community that the measures would not cause Hanoi to cease its support of the Vietcong insurgency in the South, and that the bombing was deemed militarily ineffective within a few months.

The Pentagon study also ranges beyond such historical judgments. It suggests that the predominant American interest was at first containment of Communism and later the defense of the power influence and prestige of the United States in both stages irrespective of conditions in Vietnam.

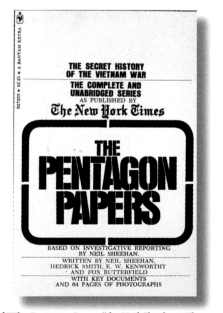

The cover of "The Pentagon Papers" by Neil Sheehan. The papers published in the New York Times revealed government deceit over the conduct of the war in Vietnam.

JULY 1, 1971

Supreme Court Upholds Publication of Pentagon Papers

Fred P. Graham

WASHINGTON, June 30—By a vote of 6 to 3, the Supreme Court freed The New York Times and The Washington Post today to resume immediate publication of articles based on the secret Pentagon papers on the origins of the Vietnam war.

In a historic test—the first effort by the Government to enjoin publication on the ground of national security—the Court declared that "the Government has not met that burden."

Chief Justice Warren Burger was one of the dissenters along with Associate Justices Harry A. Blackmun and John M. Harian, but because the decision was rendered in an unsigned opinion, the Chief Justice read it in court in accordance with long-standing custom.

The case had been expected to produce a landmark ruling on the circumstances under which prior restraint could be imposed upon the press, but because no opinion by a single Justice commanded the support of a majority, only the unsigned decision will serve as precedent.

Alexander M. Bickel, the Yale law professor who had argued for The Times in the case, said in a telephone interview that the ruling placed the press in a "stronger position." He maintained that no Federal District Judge would henceforth temporarily restrain a newspaper on the Justice Department's complaint that "this is what they have printed and we don't like it" and that a direct threat of irreparable harm would have to be alleged.

All nine Justices wrote opinions in a judicial outpouring that was described by Supreme Court scholars as without precedent. They divided roughly into groups of three each.

The first group, composed of Hugo L. Black, William O. Douglas and Thurgood Marshall, took what is known as the absolutist view that the courts lack the power to suppress any press publication no matter how grave a threat to security it might pose.

The second group, which included William J. Brennan Jr., Potter Stewart and Byron R. White, said that the press could not be muzzled except to prevent direct, immediate and irreparable damage to the nation. They agreed that this material did not pose such a threat.

The third bloc, composed of the three dissenters, declared that the courts should not refuse to enforce the executive branch's conclusion that material should be kept confidential—so long as a Cabinet-level officer decided that it should—on a matter affecting foreign relations.

Paramount among the responsibilities of a free press, said Justice Black, "is the duty to prevent any part of the Government from deceiving the people and sending them off to distant lands to die of foreign fevers and foreign shot and shell."

Justice Marshall's position was based primarily upon the separation-of-powers argument that Congress had never authorized prior restraints and that it refused to do so when bills were introduced in 1917 and 1957.

Chief Justice Burger blamed The Times "in large part" for the "frenetic haste" with which the case was handled. He said that The Times had studied the Pentagon archives for three or four months before beginning its series, yet it had breached "the duty of an honorable press" by not asking the Government if any security violations were involved before it began publications.

Arthur Ochs Sulzberger, president and publisher of The New York Times, said yesterday that his reaction to the Supreme Court's decision was "one of complete joy and delight." ■

JULY 1, 1971

THE STATES RATIFY FULL VOTE AT 18

R. W. Apple Jr.

WASHINGTON, June 30—The 26th Amendment to the Constitution, lowering to 18 years the minimum voting age in local and state as well as Federal elections, was ratified tonight.

Ohio became the 38th state to approve the Amendment when the state's House of Representatives, meeting in an extraordinary evening session, gave its assent, 81 to 9. The Ohio Senate had approved the measure yesterday, 30 to 2.

The ratification of at least 38 states, or three-quarters of the total, is required for constitutional amendments.

An atmosphere of near-panic attended Ohio's climactic vote. The Republican Speaker of the House, Charles F. Kurfess, had planned to let a number of members, both Republicans and Democrats, speak on the issue before calling for a vote.

But after only three short speeches, the Republican floor leader, Robert E. Leavitt, interrupted to warn:

"I've just been informed that the Legislature of Oklahoma has gone into special session tonight. The time for debate and

A young woman during at an Equal Rights demonstration in the 1970s.

J. EDGAR HOOVER, 77, DIES; WILL LIE IN STATE IN CAPITOL

Fred P. Graham

WASHINGTON, May 2—J. Edgar Hoover, who directed the Federal Bureau of Investigation for 48 years and built it into a dominant and controversial force in American law enforcement, died during the night from the effects of high blood pressure.

Mr. Hoover, who at 77 years of age still held the F.B.I. firmly within his control, died in his bedroom after working a full day in his office yesterday. He was found by his housekeeper at 8:30 this morning, slumped on the floor beside his bed.

Dr. James L. Luke, Washington's Medical Examiner, attributed the death to "hypertensive cardio-vascular disease." He said that Mr. Hoover had been suffering from a heart ailment for some time.

He said that death could have been caused by heart failure associated with high blood pressure, but that no autopsy would be performed because the death was known to be due to natural causes.

Acting Attorney General Richard G. Kleindienst announced the death at 11 a.m., after F.B.I. offices around the world had been given the news and reports of it began to circulate here. Congress promptly voted its permission for his body to lie in state in the Capitol Rotunda—an honor accorded to only 21 persons before, of whom eight were Presidents or former Presidents.

Hoover presided over the F.B.I. from the day—May 14, 1924—when he took over a small, politics-ridden bureau, through the eras of its most famous exploits. These included the solution of the Lindbergh kidnapping, the battles against gangsters like John Dillinger in the thirties when "G-man" became a byword, the capture of spies in World War II and the campaign against Communists in the postwar period.

Yet toward the end of his reign, he became the target of critics from both the left and the right, from those who thought he rode roughshod over civil liberties and those who thought he was slighting the old F.B.I. role of spy-catching.

His death is expected to touch off a major political debate about the proper purposes and functioning of the agency, which has been accused by critics on the political left in recent years of devoting too much effort to pursuing radicals and alleged subversives and too little to combating organized crime and white-collar offenders.

In recent years, Mr. Hoover had come under periodic pressure to resign, usually after some widely publicized public quarrel with figures on the political left. He exchanged insults with the late Rev. Dr. Martin Luther King Jr., accused the late Senator Robert F. Kennedy of ultimate responsibility for the F.B.I.'s wiretapping when he was Attorney General and called former Attorney General Ramsey Clark "a jellyfish."

His most recent controversy grew out of his charge that the Rev. Philip F. Berrigan and other antiwar activists were plotting to kidnap Henry A. Kissinger, the President's top foreign policy adviser. ∎

---

discussion is over. The time for action is here."

Ratification means that millions of young voters will be able to participate in elections this year, including contests for Governor in Mississippi and Kentucky, mayoral elections in Boston, San Francisco and other large cities and scores of races in towns and counties.

In addition, it removes the legal cloud that had hung over the right of young voters to cast their ballots in Presidential primaries next year.

Political commentators have gradually arrived at the conclusion, which runs counter to their earlier thesis, that the Democrats will be aided by the enfranchising of the young. But one issue, still unresolved, could blunt the effect of the change: the question of where students can register—where they live or where they attend school. Most states have forbidden students to register at school, and experience indicates that they will not vote heavily if forced to resort to the absentee ballot.

Local politicians have expressed the fear that they could be voted out of office, particularly in college towns, by students with no proprietary interest in the towns. Their view is already under challenge in State courts and will soon be challenged in Federal courts in several states as well.

Ratification has come with a rush as opposition to youth voting collapsed. It has been only two months and seven days since the process of getting the requisite 38 assents began—by far the shortest time in which the process has ever been accomplished.

When notified of the ratification, President Nixon said at the White House, "Some 11 million young men and women who have participated in the life of our nation through their work, their studies and their sacrifices for its defense now are to be fully included in the electoral process of our country.

"I urge them to honor this right by exercising it—by registering and voting in each election." ∎

MAY 21, 1972

AGAIN A GUN ALTERS THE POLITICS OF THE REPUBLIC

James T. Wooten

SILVER SPRING, Md.—George Corley Wallace, the 52-year-old segregationist governor of Alabama, lies paralyzed in a hospital in this Washington suburb, a bullet in his spinal canal—and in his mind, a grim prognosis that he will never again use the legs that supported him over a remarkable 26-year climb from the obscurity of a Southern state legislature to the glories of national prominence.

(cont'd. on next page)

(cont'd. from previous page)

His insurgent campaign for the Democratic Presidential nomination had brought him on Monday to Laurel. He finished his speech and moved to a roped area separating him from the hundreds who had come to see him.

"Hey, George!" a voice bellowed from his right. "Hey, George! Come here. I want to shake your hand." He turned toward the voice. The shots rang out and the Governor fell backward, his arms akimbo, his legs motionless. Cornelia, his 33-year-old wife of less than 16 months, rushed to his body and crouched over it. Her chic, yellow suit was splotched with the dark stains of his blood.

The terror was complete. Police and members of the hysterical crowd pummeled Arthur Herman Bremer, the 21-year-old busboy accused of the shooting. Some eyewitnesses said the suspect was savagely kicked in the groin and ribs.

The Governor and three other persons wounded—a Secret Service agent, an Alabama state trooper and a Maryland woman working in his campaign—were rushed to the hospital; the young man from Milwaukee, whose head was bleeding, was hustled off by state and local police.

Bremer, a moody, withdrawn man, had apparently been tracking the Wallace campaign for several days through several states, including his native Wisconsin. As a sketchy portrait of his personality and background emerged, there were numerous contradictions. He had pasted Wallace bumper stickers on his car and apartment door and he had kept Wallace pins and brochures in his unkempt apartment. Writings in notebooks found in his apartment ranged from illegible scribbling to paradoxical political epigrams. One passage referred to himself: "Once in America here lived a pig named Arthur Herman."

The wounded Governor underwent five hours of emergency, exploratory surgery on Monday night. One bullet was removed from his abdominal cavity and he had wounds in his right forearm and upper arm as well as two superficial wounds in his back.

Physical therapy began for Governor Wallace on Thursday, and at week's end doctors said he was making good progress. But the paralysis below the point of the bullet's impact on the spinal cord, from the hips down, remained constant.

What role George Wallace will now play in the politics of this election year must to some extent depend upon the effects, physical and psychological, of his injury. Some commentators have suggested that, as a candidate, he might win the kind of sympathetic support accorded Franklin Roosevelt. But the full extent of Governor Wallace's paralysis has not been made clear.

He had collected 206 Democratic convention delegates in eight primaries, three of which he had won. Although there was only a slim possibility that he could amass the kind of delegate strength that would make him a realistic candidate for the nomination, there were few politicians who could or would say just what the extent of his power at the convention would be.

He has told his wife that he will continue his campaign from a wheelchair if necessary and his staff is smilingly predicting that their man will be in Miami Beach when the convention convenes in mid-July. ■

Aides assist George Wallace during the Democratic National Convention.

JUNE 25, 1972

WATERGATE CAPER

Tad Szulc

Exterior view of the Watergate apartment and hotel complex in 1972.

WASHINGTON—The affair has become popularly known in the capital as the "Watergate Caper." But what it means no one is quite sure.

It all began at about 2 a.m. Saturday, June 17, when three Washington policemen answered what they thought was a burglary call to the elegant hotel and business Watergate complex overlooking the Potomac River. In the offices of the Democratic National Committee on the sixth floor of the Watergate Office Building the police surprised five men carrying electronic listening devices and special cameras. Upon being questioned they proved to have unusual political links and Central Intelligence Agency backgrounds.

One of them was James W. McCord, a former C.I.A. official and the security expert for the Republican National Committee and the Committee to Re-Elect the President. The others were Bernard L. Barker, a wealthy Cuban-born Miami realtor (equipped for the job with walkie-talkie radios, canisters of Mace, burglar tools and 53 sequentially numbered $100 bills which the F.B.I. later discovered were part of the proceeds of four checks drawn on a Mexi-

can bank deposited in a Miami Beach bank and then withdrawn in an $89,000 lump by Mr. Barker in May); a Florida notary public of Cuban origin; a onetime Havana barber and locksmith; and an American soldier of fortune.

And looming behind the group was an even more adventurous figure—E. Howard Hunt Jr., a former top C.I.A. official who planned the abortive 1961 Bay of Pigs invasion of Cuba. Mr. Hunt until last March had been a $100-a-day White House consultant and has worked as a writer for a Washington public relations firm connected with efforts to raise funds for President Nixon's re-election campaign. He is also a prolific author of spy novels.

Mr. Hunt, who would not talk with the F.B.I., vanished from sight. Mr. Barker would not talk with the F.B.I. either. But various sources said he had recruited three of the operatives arrested at the Watergate Office Building, plus four others who escaped.

What was the reason for the job?

Judging from the equipment found on the suspects when they were arrested in the office of Lawrence O'Brien, national chairman of the Democratic party, Mr. Barker and his companions were trying to install a secret transmitter in the ceiling and photograph Democratic files.

The incident apparently was not an isolated event. This commando team or its associates were suspected of having pulled off several other jobs recently. One of them was a burglary at the Chilean Embassy, during which documents were apparently microfilmed. And there was an earlier attempt on the Democratic headquarters.

For the Republicans the affair was, of course, an embarrassment. They deplored it, officially, as un-American. President Nixon told a news conference last Thursday that the White House had "no involvement whatsoever." But neither he nor any of his staff explained why Mr. McCord—who was later freed on bail—was among the raiders captured. Nor was there any explanation of the relationship between Mr. Hunt and Charles W. Colson, a special counsel to the President who had recommended hiring Mr. Hunt as a part-time White House consultant.

For the Democrats the affair produced some satisfying anti-Administration publicity. "I wish it had happened in October instead of June, but I don't want to sound ungrateful," one Democrat said. The party moved to exploit the case by filing a million-dollar suit against the Republican National Committee and the Committee to Re-elect the President. That could keep the topic alive through the summer. ■

13

NATIONAL

HURRICANE AGNES LEFT DEATH AND MISERY

Grace Lichtenstein

Flooding in Alexandria, Va., after Hurricane Agnes in 1972.

It was one of the worst storms in half a century—and the most widespread flood disaster in the nation's history. The toll: 18 dead in Florida…more than 95 dead in the North…scores missing…thousands of homes and offices evacuated in Virginia, Pennsylvania, New Jersey, Westchester and the southern tier of New York…damage in the billions.

The impact was particularly severe along the Susquehanna River in Pennsylvania. Harrisburg was virtually cut off—its airport was under water and its major roads were blocked. Thousands of persons fled from their homes with nothing but the clothes they wore. Said Franklin L. Bradley, a Harrisburg car salesman: "When my bed started floating around the room, I decided to leave. When I came back later I couldn't even see my house."

In Virginia, the James River crested at more than 35 feet, breaking the record of 30 feet set in 1771. In downtown Richmond, two-story buildings were nearly submerged and a 200-block section of this city was evacuated.

In New York, thousands were forced to flee their homes. Water from septic tanks and large sewage treatment plants washed into reservoirs and wells and residents were told to boil all water before using it.

President Nixon, accompanied by newsmen, made a helicopter tour yesterday of the devastated areas. He declared five states to be disaster areas—Florida, Maryland, Pennsylvania, New York and Virginia—thus making them eligible for Federal funds in relief and recovery efforts.

Actually, the disaster was the result of three different storms. They began Sunday night. As an early bird hurricane named Agnes bustled into the Florida panhandle, another deluge, swept inland by a high-pressure area off Labrador, drenched the New York metropolitan area in more than 10 inches of rain.

For those not preoccupied with pumping out cellars, replacing power lines or getting drinking water, the most persistently asked question was: why a hurricane now, in the first week of summer, when they're supposed to happen in September?

The Weather Bureau's answer was to blame the storm on air currents—for the layman, about as helpful as blaming rainfall on moisture. An "influx of upper air currents" pushed the storm east. When it pulled onto the traditional hurricane highway north, it was picked up by a westerly air current that fed the storm's intensity rather than allowing it to weaken and break up, as hurricanes often do when they move over land.

Capital Punishment Ruled Unconstitutional

Fred P. Graham

WASHINGTON, June 29—The Supreme Court ruled today that capital punishment, as now administered in the United States, is unconstitutional "cruel and unusual" punishment.

The historic decision, came on a vote of 5 to 4.

Although the five Justices in the majority issued separate opinions and did not agree on a single reason for their action, the effect of the decision appeared to be to rule out executions under any capital punishment laws now in effect in this country.

The decision will also save from execution 600 condemned men and women now on death rows in the United States, although it did not overturn their convictions. Most will be held in prison for the rest of their lives, but under some states' procedures some of the prisoners may eventually gain their freedom.

The decision pitted the five holdovers of the more liberal Warren Court against the four appointees of President Nixon, who dissented.

Three Justices in the majority, William O. Douglas, William J. Brennan Jr. and Thurgood Marshall, concluded that executions in modern-day America necessarily violate the Eighth Amendment's prohibition against "cruel and unusual punishments."

The other two in the majority, the two "swing men" of the Court, Justices Potter Stewart and Byron R. White, reasoned that the present legal system operates in a cruel and unusual way, because it gives judges and juries the discretion to decree life or death and they impose it erratically.

As the dissenters pointed out, this alignment means that no death sentence can pass muster before the present Supreme Court unless it satisfies the objections voiced by Justices Stewart and White.

In any event, Chief Justice Burger said,

NOVEMBER 8, 1972

AT VICTORY CELEBRATION, NIXON VOWS TO MAKE HIMSELF 'WORTHY'

Robert B. Semple Jr.

WASHINGTON, Wednesday, Nov. 8—President Nixon summoned the nation last night "to get on with the great tasks that lie before us" and, in a later statement to a crowd of cheering supporters, pledged to make himself "worthy of this victory."

Mr. Nixon made two statements, both televised.

The first of these was a brief statement from his desk in the Oval Office of the White House in which he pledged himself to secure not only "a peace with honor in Vietnam" but also "a new era of peace" throughout the world; to "prosperity without war and without inflation" at home, and to an America in which all citizens will have "an equal chance."

The President then sped by limousine to the Shoreham Hotel, where a boisterous victory celebration had begun much earlier in the evening.

After thanking Vice President Spiro Agnew and other major figures in his campaign, the President, on a more sober note said that while he might have achieved the "greatest victory in American political history," much would depend "on what we do with it."

Although the scene at the Shoreham was predictably noisy and joyous, the mood among the President's aides at the White House was one of a quiet vindication. The President had campaigned little in the traditional sense this year, but in another sense he had been working for this victory for four years.

In the last few weeks, he and his associates had concluded that victory would be theirs. So the final result tonight was perhaps a bit anticlimactic. ∎

U.S. President Richard Nixon (left) with Vice President Spiro Agnew at a Washington reception after their re-election in 1972.

Congress and the state legislatures will be required to "make a thorough re-evaluation of the entire subject of capital punishment," including a serious inquiry into whether it serves as a deterrent.

The gist of the dissenters' position was that the Eighth Amendment has been in effect for 191 years and has not, until today, been held to rule out executions. They charged that the majority had usurped the prerogative of the legislatures in the decision today.

Justice Lewis F. Powell Jr. said the action would have a "shattering effect" upon the rule that prior decisions should be followed, as well as on the principles of "Federalism, judicial restraint, and—most importantly—separation of powers." ∎

JANUARY 23, 1973

ABORTION GUIDELINES SET BY 7-TO-2 VOTE

Warren Weaver Jr.

WASHINGTON, Jan. 22—The Supreme Court overruled today all state laws that prohibit or restrict a woman's right to obtain an abortion during her first three months of pregnancy. The vote was 7 to 2.

In a historic resolution of a fiercely controversial issue, the Court drafted a new set of national guidelines that will result in broadly liberalized anti-abortion laws in 46 states but will not abolish restrictions altogether.

Establishing an unusually detailed timetable for the relative legal rights of pregnant women and the states that would control their acts, the majority specified the following:

- For the first three months of pregnancy the decision to have an abortion lies with the woman and her doctor, and the state's interest in her welfare is not "compelling" enough to warrant any interference.

(cont'd. on next page)

(cont'd. from previous page)

- For the next six months of pregnancy a state may "regulate the abortion procedure in ways that are reasonably related to maternal health," such as licensing and regulating the persons and facilities involved.
- For the last 10 weeks of pregnancy, the period during which the fetus is judged to be capable of surviving if born, any state may prohibit abortions, if it wishes, except where they may be necessary to preserve the life or health of the mother.

Today's action will not affect existing laws in New York, Alaska, Hawaii and Washington, where abortions are now legally available in the early months of pregnancy. But it will require rewriting of statutes in every other state.

The basic Texas case decided by the Court today will invalidate strict anti-abortion laws in 31 states; a second decision involving Georgia will require considerable rewriting of more liberal statutes in 15 others.

Justice Harry A. Blackmun wrote the majority opinion in which Chief Justice Warren E. Burger and Justices William O. Douglas, William J. Brennan Jr., Potter Stewart, Thurgood Marshall and Lewis F. Powell Jr. joined.

Abortion law being protested in a Denver demonstration in 1971.

Dissenting were Justices Byron R. White and William H. Rehnquist.

The Court's decision was at odds with the expressed views of President Nixon. But three of the four Justices Mr. Nixon has appointed to the Supreme Court voted with the majority.

The majority rejected the idea that a fetus becomes a "person" upon conception and is thus entitled to the due process and equal protection guarantees of the Constitution. This view was pressed by opponents of liberalized abortion, including the Roman Catholic Church. ■

MARCH 24, 1973

At Wounded Knee, Two Worlds Collide

John Kifner

WOUNDED KNEE, S.D., March 21—In a scrubby valley here in this empty, windswept plains country, a band of young Indians and their allies are dug in, armed and painted for war, while on the hillsides around them a Federal force of armor and automatic weapons stands nervously.

The impasse at Wounded Knee has already lasted more than three weeks. But behind it lies a century-long clash of values between a defeated Indian culture and a dominant white culture.

It is a tragic and twisted history, and it takes in both the tribal officials in nearby Pine Ridge, with their closely cropped hair and triplicate Government forms, and the long lines of Indian men who sit at the crossroads in the early spring sun blankly watching the dust as white Justice Department officials, marshals, lawyers and newsmen rush by.

To the occupiers of this tiny hamlet, led by members of the militant American Indian Movement, it is a struggle to overthrow the elected government headed by Richard Wilson, which they contend is dictatorial and corrupt. Mixed in is a deeply felt will to return to a tribal purity that they never really knew.

Today, the Pine Ridge Reservation is a bleak picture of some of the worst poverty in America. Abandoned, rusted cars cluster around tumble-down shacks and litter the prairie hills, the best acres of which are grazed by white men's cattle. The unemployment rate stands at 54 percent and goes up to 70 percent in the winter months.

More than half the families are on welfare, and every index of social disorder and decay is higher than among the nation's black population. Hopeless, drunken men lurch about the streets at mid-morning.

At the heart of the situation lies the concept that the white man's government, in exchange for the land, will be the provider for the Indians. In the early days, rations were used as a kind of bribe to keep the Indians in line, and the tradition continues today, with a limited Government largesse that seems only to induce a resentful dependency. Both dissident Indians and those allied with the authorities say that treaty promises have not been kept.

The thrust of Federal Indian policy has been toward acculturation—the integration of Indians into white society—and B.I.A. officials here say that at times this has included deliberate, conscious attempts to destroy Indian culture.

AGNEW MAKES DEAL TO AVOID PRISON

James M. Naughton

WASHINGTON, Oct. 22—The collapse of Spiro T. Agnew's career was a negotiated decline and fall.

The dimensions of the bargaining were even broader than the public record suggested. President Nixon sent a messenger to the Vice President in early September to seek his resignation. The Vice President consented at that time, but fought to obtain a guarantee that he would not go to prison. The Attorney General encouraged the bargain because he feared that fate might elevate a felon to the Presidency.

The details behind Mr. Agnew's bartered resignation and disgrace were as fascinating as the event was stunning. They produced a game of legal chess in which constitutional issues were pieces and the Presidency itself was a pawn.

The drama began with a luncheon conversation late last year. It culminated 12 days ago as a result, in part, of a speech by Secretary of State Kissinger about war and peace.

And in between, over barely 10 months, were ingredients more suited to a novel than to a national trauma: A President who could not bring himself to tell his heir apparent, to his face, to quit. A Vice President inviting his own impeachment in order to threaten a President with the same prospect. Lawyers for the nation's second-ranking official taking steps to guard against Government wiretaps of their telephones. Prosecutors discussing the mental health of the President.

The outcome became history when Mr. Agnew stood before United States District Judge Walter E. Hoffman in a Baltimore courtroom. He resigned, pleaded no contest to one charge of income tax evasion and permitted the Government to publish evidence that he had extorted bribes for a decade. In return, his plea left him technically free to proclaim his innocence of any wrongdoing and the Government settled for a sentence of three years of unsupervised probation and a $10,000 fine.

Not until the last few days have central figures been willing to describe the steps that led up to that momentous result. Some of the elements are matters of dispute. Years from now, scholars may debate the causes and consequences.

Vice President Spiro Agnew the day after resigning his office, October 10, 1973, in Washington, D.C.

Older men, for instance, remember being beaten in school for wearing Indian garb and being forced to chew pieces of soap if they spoke in Lakota, the Sioux language. And, in a traditionally masculine culture, men no longer have their roles as hunters, warriors and providers. ∎

Leaders of the American Indian Movement (A.I.M.) Dennis Banks, Russell Means and an unidentified third man, give a press conference to make demands on the Federal Government for an increase in financial aid for the town of Wounded Knee, Custer, South Dakota, March 16, 1973.

WHITE HOUSE AIDS WATERGATE INQUIRY

Anthony Ripley

The Senate Watergate Committee investigation during the Watergate Scandal hearings.

WASHINGTON, Dec. 21—Leon Jaworski, special prosecutor for the Watergate investigation, said today that the White House agreed to let his investigators search through its files in looking for information tied to the Watergate scandals.

The White House confirmed the arrangement. It is a measure of cooperation unprecedented in the long Watergate criminal investigations.

President Nixon had repeatedly stressed the need for confidentiality, asserted executive privilege and gone to court to try to block attempts to force him to hand over tapes and documents.

The arrangement for inspection of the files was worked out in the last few days. Watergate investigators will describe to White House aides the documents they are seeking and the aides will then go with the investigators to the files to help look for the papers, according to Mr. Jaworski's staff.

"I think we're getting the kind of cooperation I'd hoped we'd get," Mr. Jaworski told reporters outside the courthouse.

A staff member will go over the documents one by one, Mr. Jaworski told the Senate committee. If his aide sees other papers there related to the Watergate investigations, the special prosecutor added, "I would expect him to tell me about it."

There was no immediate explanation from either the White House or the special prosecutor as to why the change of attitude had taken place.

In other Watergate developments today, Judge Sirica signed an order for a third Watergate grand jury to be assembled on Jan. 7.

The first grand jury, which indicted the men caught inside the Democratic national headquarters at the Watergate hotel and office complex on June 17, 1972, is still sitting. It has been considering the break-in and subsequent cover-up.

The second grand jury, impaneled last August, has handled the other four main areas of the investigation: campaign sabotage, illegal campaign contributions, the International Telephone and Telegraph Corporation, and the White House special investigation group called the "plumbers."

The new grand jury is needed to help the second grand jury, which the special prosecutor's office said was overburdened. It will deal particularly with illegal campaign contributions. ∎

HEARST KIDNAPPING LINKED TO TWO ESCAPED CONVICTS

Earl Caldwell

SAN FRANCISCO, Feb. 15—Two escaped convicts were reported today to be providing the leadership for the mysterious Symbionese Liberation Army, the group that kidnapped 19-year-old Patricia Hearst.

The two convicts were identified as Donald David DeFreeze, 30, who escaped from Soledad Prison last March, and Thero M. Wheeler, 29, who escaped from the California Department of Corrections medical facility at Vacaville in August, 1973.

Meanwhile, the victim's father, Randolph A. Hearst, a newspaper executive, said that he was still attempting to meet the kidnappers' demands that he provide some $350 million in free food to the state's aged and poor as evidence of good faith toward negotiating his daughter's release.

A letter purportedly from the Symbionese Liberation Army was received by a Berkeley

This file photo from a security camera shows Patricia Hearst during a bank robbery in San Francisco on April 17, 1974.

radio station, KPFA, but both the F.B.I. and Mr. Hearst said it was bogus, United Press International reported. The letter said that Pepperdine College in Southern California, "a college of genocide," should be turned over to the black community. It also said, "The next time you see a bullet like this it will be filled with cyanide in the head of Patricia Campbell Hearst." However, no bullet was enclosed with the letter.

A New York Times investigation has shown that in the summer of 1972 at Vacaville State Prison a group of young Maoist radicals were linked with black convicts in what is now believed to be the birthplace for the Symbionese Liberation Army.

It was an unlikely vehicle, the Black Culture Association, that was used to bring the two groups together. But it gave the radicals access to the prison and it provided revolutionary-minded convicts with valuable outside contacts.

What the motives of the two groups were in 1972 is still unclear. However, Mr. DeFreeze has since surfaced as an S.L.A. leader and many of the young radicals in that program have been identified as S.L.A. members.

In 1972, Mr. DeFreeze was intimately involved at Vacaville in the activities of the Black Culture Association.

Among the young radicals involved was Russell J. Little, a 24-year-old white who was arrested last month and identified by the police as a member of the S.L.A. He was later charged with involvement in the slaying of Dr. Marcus A. Foster, the Oakland Superintendent of Schools.

It was just after the Nov. 6 election night slaying of Dr. Foster that the Symbionese Liberation Army first came to public attention. In letters to a Berkeley radio station and Bay Area newspapers, the group said it was responsible for the Foster killing.

The group struck again some three months later, this time with the kidnapping of Miss Hearst.

One source said that the aims of the radicals soon began to conflict with those of the group as a whole. Mr. DeFreeze was described as one of the most dynamic members of the group. He was recognized as being sharp, intelligent and articulate. At one point, he designed his own program, a course dealing primarily with the black family.

Although he had a long criminal record at the time, Mr. DeFreeze was not described as being either militant or revolutionary in his writing and lectures inside the prison.

Mr. DeFreeze, who grew up in Cleveland, first got into trouble back in 1965 in Newark, N.J., when he was arrested for possession of a bomb.

He moved to California in either 1966 or 1967 where he again came to the attention of the police, who said that he was involved in firebombings. ∎

AUGUST 8, 1974

NIXON RESIGNS; FIRST TO QUIT POST

John Herbers

continued . . .

President Richard Nixon holds back a tear as he makes his final speech at the White House.

(cont'd. from previous page)

NIXON RESIGNS

Washington, Aug. 8—Richard Milhous Nixon, the 37th President of the United States, announced tonight that he had given up his long and arduous fight to remain in office and would resign, effective at noon tomorrow.

At that hour, Gerald Rudolph Ford, whom Mr. Nixon nominated for Vice President last Oct. 12, will be sworn in as the 38th President, to serve out the 895 days remaining in Mr. Nixon's second term.

He acknowledged that some of his judgments had been wrong.

Less than two years after his landslide re-election victory, Mr. Nixon, in a conciliatory address on national television, said that he was leaving not with a sense of bitterness but with a hope that his departure would start a "process of healing that is so desperately needed in America."

He spoke of regret for any "injuries" done "in the course of the events that led to this decision." He acknowledged that some of his judgments had been wrong.

The 61-year-old Mr. Nixon, appearing calm and resigned to his fate as a victim of the Watergate scandal, became the first President in the history of the Republic to resign from office. Only 10 months earlier Spiro Agnew resigned the Vice Presidency.

Mr. Nixon, speaking from the Oval Office, where his successor will be sworn in tomorrow, may well have delivered his most effective speech since the Watergate scandals began to swamp his Administration in early 1973.

"I would have preferred to carry through to the finish whatever the personal agony it would have involved, and my family unanimously urged me to do so," he said.

Conceding that he did not have the votes in Congress to escape impeachment in the House and conviction in the Senate, Mr. Nixon said, "To continue to fight through the months ahead for my personal vindication would almost totally absorb the time and attention of the President and the Congress in a period when our entire focus should be on the great issues of peace abroad and prosperity without inflation at home."

Mr. Nixon expressed confidence in Mr. Ford to assume the office, "to put the bitterness and divisions of the recent past behind us."

Further, he said he was leaving "with no bitterness" toward those who had opposed him.

Mr. Nixon's announcement came only two days after he told his Cabinet that he would not resign but would let the constitutional impeachment process run its course, even though it was evident he would be removed from office after a trial by the Senate.

In the next 48 hours the pressures for him to resign and turn the reins of the Government over to Mr. Ford became overwhelming.

His chances of being acquitted were almost hopeless. Senator Barry Goldwater, the Arizona conservative who was the Republican Presidential candidate in 1964, told him that he had no more than 15 votes in the Senate, far short of the 34 he needed to be sure of escaping conviction. Members of his own staff, including Gen. Alexander M. Haig Jr., the White House chief of staff, strongly recommended that he step down in the national interest.

In the end only a small minority of his former supporters were urging him to stay and pledging to give him their support. It was his friends, not his legions of enemies, that brought the crucial pressures for resignation.

It was exactly six years ago last night that Mr. Nixon was nominated on the first ballot at the Republican National Convention to be the party's nominee for President, a note of irony that did not escape members of the President's staff.

Secretary of State Henry Kissinger gave a number of assurances that the nation's "bipartisan foreign policy" would remain firmly in place. The Defense Department announced that American military forces around the world would continue under normal status. And across this city thousands of Federal employees performed their chores as if nothing was happening. ∎

Ford Pardons Nixon, Who Regrets 'Mistakes'

John Herbers

Washington, Sept. 8—President Ford granted former President Richard M. Nixon an unconditional pardon today for all Federal crimes that he "committed or may have committed or taken part in" while in office, an act Mr. Ford said was intended to spare Mr. Nixon and the nation further punishment in the Watergate scandals.

Mr. Nixon, in San Clemente, Calif., accepted the pardon, which exempts him from indictment and trial for, among other things, his role in the cover-up of the Watergate burglary. He issued a statement saying that he could now see he was "wrong in not acting more decisively and more forthrightly in dealing with Watergate."

the "act of mercy"

Phillip W. Buchen, the White House counsel, who advised Mr. Ford on the legal aspects of the pardon, said the "act of mercy" on the President's part was done without making any demands on Mr. Nixon and without asking the advice of the Watergate special prosecutor, Leon Jaworski, who had the legal responsibility to prosecute the case.

Reaction to the pardon was sharply divided, but not entirely along party lines. Most Democrats who commented voiced varying degrees of disapproval and dismay, while most Republican comment backed President Ford.

However, Senators Edward W. Brooke of Massachusetts and Jacob K. Javits of New York disagreed with the action.

Mr. Buchen said that, at the President's request, he had asked Mr. Jaworski how long it would be, in the event Mr. Nixon was indicted, before he could be brought to trial and that Mr. Jaworski had replied it

U.S. President Gerald Ford signs his pardon of Richard Nixon from the Oval Office in The White House, September 8, 1974.

HOFFA REPORTED MISSING; POLICE FIND HIS CAR

DETROIT, July 31—James R. Hoffa, the former president of the International Brotherhood of Teamsters, was reported missing by his family this morning after he failed to come home last night.

Mr. Hoffa, who has been seeking to again become head of the 2.1 million-member union, the nation's largest, was reported missing to the Bloomfield Township police.

They found Mr. Hoffa's 1974 Pontiac in the parking lot of the Machus Red Fox Restaurant in Bloomfield Township this morning.

Detective Robert Bloom said that there was no evidence of struggle and that the

(cont'd. on next page)

would be at least nine months or more, because of the enormous amount of publicity the charges against Mr. Nixon had received when the House Judiciary Committee recommended impeachment.

This was one reason Mr. Ford cited for granting the pardon, saying he had concluded that "many months and perhaps more years will have to pass before Richard Nixon could obtain a fair trial by jury in any jurisdiction of the United States under governing decisions of the Supreme Court."

Mr. Ford's decision was not unexpected, in light of his previous statements that he thought the former President had suffered enough by being forced from office. Yet the unconditional nature of the pardon, taken without the recommendation of Mr. Jaworski, was more generous to Mr. Nixon than many had expected.

The only adverse aspect of today's action from Mr. Nixon's point of view is that he can now be more easily forced to testify in the forthcoming trial of several of his former aides accused of obstruction of justice in the Watergate case.

Mr. Ford's action today was a sharp reversal from the position his aides conveyed as he ascended to the Presidency on Aug. 9.

However, since taking office, there have been several changes. Mr. Nixon, in seclusion in San Clemente, has been reported by his friends to be deeply depressed and some have said that the legal troubles he faced were causing him so much anguish that his health was in jeopardy.

The way for a Presidential pardon was further prepared when Mr. Ford came out for conditional amnesty for Vietnam draft evaders and deserters as an act of mercy and as a means of uniting the nation.

After announcing the pardon, Mr. Ford went to the Burning Tree Country Club and played a round of golf. At the White House, switchboard operators said, "angry calls, heavy and constant," began jamming their boards soon after Mr. Ford's announcement. ∎

Reflection of former Teamster boss Jimmy Hoffa in a rear-view mirror of truck he's driving.

(cont'd. from previous page)

police had no immediate clues to Mr. Hoffa's whereabouts.

The Oakland County Prosecutor, L. Brooks Patterson, said, however, that the police suspected foul play since Mr. Hoffa "never stayed out this long without reporting in."

Mr. Hoffa does not smoke or drink and has very close ties to his family.

James R. Hoffa, Jr., the former labor leader's son, said that his mother, Josephine, called him after Mr. Hoffa had not returned to their home in Lake Orion, Mich.

Leonard Boudin, Mr. Hoffa's attorney, in his attempt to lift the restrictions on union activity that were attached to the commutation of his prison sentence, said he hoped that Mr. Hoffa had not been kidnapped or injured.

Mr. Hoffa's disappearance comes at a time when a series of incidents in the last several months, including car bombings and beatings, have left the local teamster organization here shaken and divided.

On July 10, a Lincoln Continental used by Richard Fitzsimmons, the vice president of teamster Local 299, was destroyed by a bomb outside a bar where he was having a drink. Mr. Fitzsimmons is the son of Frank E. Fitzsimmons, who succeeded Mr. Hoffa as president of the International Brotherhood of Teamsters and who is seeking to prevent Mr. Hoffa from regaining office within the union.

Hoffa and Fitzsimmons factions have been vying with each other for control of local 299.

The elder Fitzsimmons had been a close associate of Mr. Hoffa, and was instrumental in persuading the Nixon Administration to commute Mr. Hoffa's 1-year prison sentence for jury tampering and mail fraud in 1971.

As a provision of the commutation, however, Mr. Hoffa was prevented from seeking union office or engaging in any union activity for 10 years.

Mr. Hoffa has since charged and sought to prove in court that after the Watergate disclosures, it was evident that Mr. Fitzsimmons had made a deal with the Nixon Administration.

Mr. Hoffa had served nearly 5 years of his 13-year prison term when he was released from a Federal penitentiary in February 1972.

Before his conviction on conspiracy and fraud charges in 1967, Mr. Hoffa had been on trial in Federal court four times in five years. He was acquitted twice, and one trial ended with a hung jury.

Ever since he took over the teamsters union in 1954 from Dave Beck, Mr. Hoffa had been the object of nearly constant investigation by the Federal Government.

The late Senator Robert F. Kennedy, as counsel to the Senate rackets committee and later as Attorney General, was a longtime adversary. He called Mr. Hoffa's handling of the union a "conspiracy of evil." ∎

PATRICIA HEARST IS SEIZED BY F.B.I.; LONG HUNT ENDS

Wallace Turner

SAN FRANCISCO, Sept. 18—Patricia Hearst, the wealthy kidnapping victim who proclaimed herself a revolutionary and was accused of being a bank robber, was captured here this afternoon by the Federal Bureau of Investigation.

The 19-month drama of the 21-year-old granddaughter of the legendary newspaper owner, William Randolph Hearst, involved holdups, a reported kidnapping and the deaths of six of her alleged associates in a Los Angeles gun battle and fire. But it ended quietly today when she told F.B.I. agents, "Don't shoot. I'll go with you."

Seized with Miss Hearst in the lower middle-class Mission district was Wendy Yoshimura, 32, who had apparently joined Miss Hearst after she had gone into hiding.

An hour earlier, F.B.I. agents arrested William and Emily Harris, members of the self-styled Symbionese Liberation Army that kidnapped Miss Hearst and apparently converted her to its beliefs.

Miss Hearst was charged with bank robbery, the Harrises with two counts of possession of illegal firearms and possession of automatic weapons. Each was held in $500,000 bail for hearings tomorrow, according to an F.B.I. spokesman.

Miss Yoshimura was remanded to the custody of the Alameda County authorities. She was taken to Oakland, where she faces charges on an indictment brought three years ago. It is based on an arms cache found in a garage that she rented.

The arrests capped a bizarre criminal case that began on the night of Feb. 4, 1974, when Miss Hearst was dragged screaming from her apartment in Berkeley, where she lived with Steven A. Weed while both attended the University of California.

As the weeks passed, she made tape recordings for her captors in which she gradually shifted from victim to member of the S.L.A. and allegedly took part in a bank robbery here on April 15, 1974. From that time on, the F.B.I. had sought her as a fugitive.

"I don't think very much is going to happen to her, because she was a kidnap victim, you will remember," said Charles Bates, the agent in charge of the F.B.I. investigation.

At the urging of Patricia Hearst, who spoke through tape-recorded messages, Mr. Hearst gave away $2 million worth of food to poor people to comply with the demand of her captors that he show good faith before Miss Hearst was released.

On April 2, 1974, the S.L.A. promised to release Miss Hearst in 72 hours. The next day, a tape was delivered to a bi-weekly newspaper here in which she said, "This is Tania," which was the underground name she had taken. She said, "I have chosen to stay and fight."

Within two weeks came the bank robbery, in which $10,960 was taken, and two passers-by were shot. Miss Hearst was photographed by an automatic security camera during the robbery. Some suggestions were made that she had been coerced. But on April 24, she said in a recorded message that she had willingly taken part and was a full member of the S.L.A.

Miss Fromme Gets Life in Ford Attack

SACRAMENTO, Calif., Dec. 17—Lynette Alice Fromme, 27 years old, was sentenced today to life imprisonment for attempting to kill President Ford in Capitol Park here on Sept. 5.

In a courtroom session in which Miss Fromme hit the United States Attorney with a thrown apple, Federal District Judge Thomas J. MacBride termed Miss Fromme unfit for a lesser sentence that would have involved possible rehabilitation.

Dwayne Keyes, United States Attorney, was struck on the right side of his head by the apple after he had told Judge MacBride that Miss Fromme's punishment should be "severe" because she has shown herself to be full of "hate and violence."

As she hurled the apple at Mr. Keyes, Miss Fromme shouted, "He's the one to talk about hate."

John E. Virga, Miss Fromme's court-appointed attorney in the stormy trial that began Nov. 4 and ended Thanksgiving Eve with a jury verdict of guilty on a charge of attempting to assassinate the President, asked for a lesser sentence.

He told Judge MacBride that Miss Fromme's action on Sept. 5 had been an attempt to draw attention to a concern about the environment and he urged that he not consider a life sentence but one that would give the defendant a chance for rehabilitation.

"I can't be rehabilitated because I haven't done anything wrong," Miss Fromme told Judge MacBride in a short pre-sentence plea.

"I want Manson out, I want a world at peace. I know no one can bring it. You only have 10 years of air and water."

In an incoherent, rambling manner, she repeated earlier threats that the world court of retribution would avenge her and the so-called family led by Charles M. Manson to which she belonged. He is serving a life term in California in the murders of seven persons in Beverly Hills, including Sharon Tate, an actress.

Miss Fromme, who was given the nickname "Squeaky" by Manson family members, repeatedly interrupted Judge MacBride as he gave his reasons for imposing a life sentence.

Under the law Miss Fromme would be eligible for parole in 15 years.

Judge MacBride told Miss Fromme that he was "convinced that you would murder or cause another to commit murder in the false and distorted belief that only terror and violence can save our environment and natural resources."

Judge MacBride went on: "I suggest that the most precious natural resource in the world is a human life and to casually and coldly and consciously take a life solely for the purpose of calling attention to a cause is to me the most reprehensible and despicable crime that a person can commit.

"Had John Kennedy, Robert Kennedy or Martin Luther King been allowed to live out their lives rather than having fallen at the hands of a person like yourself, they could have accomplished more for our environment and for all mankind than all the terrorists in the history of the world—you and Charles Manson included." ■

Lynette Fromme being led away by police in Sacramento, Calif, 1975.

Miss Moore Given Life Prison Term For Attack on Ford

SAN FRANCISCO, Jan. 15—Sara Jane Moore was sentenced today to life in prison by a Federal district judge who said that she would not have tried to kill President Ford here on Sept. 22 "if we had in this country any effective capital punishment law."

The judge, Samuel Conti, calling the 45-year-old defendant "a product of our times, a product of a permissive society," said that he was giving her the maximum sentence prescribed by law.

She was the second woman within a month to be given a life term for having tried to kill the President in California. Lynette Alice Fromme received a life sentence for pointing a gun at Mr. Ford in Sacramento on Sept. 5.

Under Federal law, Miss Moore will be eligible for parole in 15 years.

Miss Moore, who pleaded guilty on Dec. 12, fired a shot at the President as he walked out of the St. Francis Hotel. The bullet missed him by several feet.

Today, in a 10-minute statement in court, Miss Moore asked, "Am I sorry I tried" to kill the President?

"Yes," she said, "because it accomplished little except to throw away the rest of my life.

"And no, I'm not sorry I tried, because at the time it seemed a correct expression of my anger, and, if successful, the assassination combined with the public disclosures of this Government's own activities in this area just might have triggered the kind of chaos that could have started the upheaval of change."

After Miss Moore read her statement, the judge said that he was disturbed because it was indicative of "how calloused we have become to crime and violence, and

(cont'd. on next page)

(cont'd. from previous page)
we have accepted it as an ingredient of our daily life."

Miss Moore, a one-time F.B.I. informer and would-be revolutionary, told how in two years she changed from a "relatively normal, middle-aged suburbanite to a would-be assassin." Today, she asked rhetorically, "Would I counsel anyone else to attempt such an assassination?" Then she answered "No," and there was no further discussion of the point.

Miss Moore expressed dismay at what she said she learned when she was working as an F.B.I. informer in 1974 and 1975. She said that the left in this country "seemed disorganized, strife-ridden and weak," but predicted that this would change.

She said that it would be "a revolution that will change the Government from one of the politicians, by the docile puppets or the corporate interests, to a 'government of the people, by the people and for the people.'" ∎

JULY 3, 1976

Death Penalty a 300-Year Issue in America

Warren Weaver Jr.

WASHINGTON, July 2—The Supreme Court decision reinstating the death penalty is the latest chapter in a controversy that stretches back more than 300 years into American and Colonial history.

Ever since the 1650's, when colonists could be put to death for denying the true God or cursing their parents, advocates and opponents of capital punishment have clashed almost continuously, in the forum of public opinion, in state legislatures and, most recently, in the courts.

Generally, those seeking to curb or abolish the death penalty gained ground over the years in times of peace and internal security, while proponents of capital punishment advanced their cause in wartime and during periods of national concern over crime and subversion.

The earliest laws of the American colonies, reflecting their British heritage, were harsh by modern standards but more lenient than those in most of Europe. In Virginia from 1612 through 1619, the death penalty could be imposed for stealing grapes, trading with Indians or killing farm and household animals without permission.

The founding of the new nation in 1776 did not rouse any stirrings of reform against the British criminal justice system for some years.

In the early 19th century, some people began speaking out for abolition, but the chief legislative result was the enactment, in the 1830's, of statutes barring public hanging by Rhode Island, Pennsylvania, New York, Massachusetts and New Jersey, more an issue of taste and order than of conscience.

In 1837 Maine became the first state to declare, in effect, a moratorium on capital punishment. The decision was made in part because of riots that had accompanied a public hanging in Augusta.

In the 1840's, abolition of capital punishment became a major public cause, with editors, writers, professional reformers and, above all, clergymen participating.

From the beginning of the Mexican War in 1846 through the slavery controversy, the Civil War and its aftermath, there was little activity on the issue, with the nation preoccupied by self-preservation.

National interest in the issue was revived when New York adopted electrocution as an instrument of capital punishment and, in 1890, made William Kemmler the first victim of the electric chair. From then until World War I there was a new wave of reform.

In 1897 Congress reduced the number of Federal capital crimes. Then, abolition of the death penalty was voted by Kansas in 1907 and Minnesota in 1911, followed by Washington, North Dakota, South Dakota, Oregon, Arizona and Missouri.

By 1917, twelve states, or a quarter of the nation, had adopted such a ban, and six others had gotten one through at least one house of their legislatures.

The advent of World War I reversed this trend. Rising hatred of foreigners and fear of radicals plus anticipation of a crime wave induced four states to reinstate capital punishment.

Through the Roaring Twenties, the Depression, World War II, the McCarthy era and the Korean War, attempts to abolish the death penalty continued, but with little success beyond the propaganda level.

Still, states executed fewer criminals after World War II than they had before. In 1950 the number was 82 and in 1955 only 76, down from 199 in 1935.

Abolishing or limiting capital punishment in the 1960's, in addition to New York, were Iowa, Vermont, West Virginia and New Mexico. But referendums with that goal were voted down in Colorado and Massachusetts, and inaction was the general rule.

Then the opponents of the death penalty shifted their attention to the courts, with civil rights lawyers moving into the forefront because of the number of blacks involved.

The NAACP Legal Defense and Educational Fund Inc. began by defending blacks convicted of rape in Southern courts but rapidly expanded their effort. Successful class action suits won stays of execution for all inmates on death row in Florida, then California.

The resulting statistics were startling. There were seven executions in the entire country in 1965, one in 1966, two in 1967. Then they stopped altogether. Meanwhile, the fund's chief trial counsel, Anthony Amsterdam, was bringing lawsuits in an effort to force the courts to declare the death penalty unconstitutional as cruel and unusual punishment.

Finally, in 1972, the Court struck down, by a 5 to 4 vote, the death penalty as then imposed as unconstitutional, setting off attempts by many states to enact new statutes that they hoped would pass legal muster. Today three of the statutes did.

BICENTENNIAL SPIRIT LINGERS IN NEW YORK

Fireworks around the Statue of Liberty during New York's bicentennial celebration, 1976.

Richard Severo

The morning after, the euphoria was still there.

Japanese seamen visited British ships, Scandinavians drank Irish beer on Eighth Avenue, hundreds of thousands of tourists from Connecticut, New York and New Jersey and points west converged on vessels from Sweden, Italy, Germany and points east.

The waterfronts were jammed and, somehow, the momentum that developed over the weekend—when the ships in Operation Sail '76 and the International Naval Review were on parade and when the fireworks exploded—continued on the streets of New York yesterday.

Thanks mostly to the older vessels, the piers looked much the way they must have at the turn of the century: freshly swabbed decks of teak dried in a bright sun; flags of yellow, red, blue and white swooped down from rigging and cascaded over taffrails.

By mid-afternoon, the crowds swelled to many hundreds of thousands of people.

Although there were traffic jams and long lines by the middle of the afternoon, and some of the discomfort that comes with the crush of New York-size crowds, there was evidence of good will everywhere.

"New York is absolutely different, such a spirit of joy and celebration," said Jack Lickowski, who had come with his family from Wayne, N.J. "I've never seen the city like this. Everyone feels so united."

Perhaps because it was such a grand day, perhaps because the weekend's events reminded many that New York City is on the water, those portions of it closest to the sea were mobbed. By mid-afternoon, the police estimated, there were at least 150,000 people in and around Pier 88 alone.

Farther north, the stretch of grass between 72nd and 74th Streets in Riverside Park was like beachfront without sand. Thousands of people stretched out on blankets, picnicked, read books and newspapers and listened to transistor radios. At the 79th Street boat basin, people gathered to look at the two tall ships—Tovarishch and Kreuzenshtern—from the Soviet Union that were anchored offshore.

And last night, long after visiting hours were over, hundreds of onlookers still clustered by the piers in the West 40's to see the tall ships, their masts dramatically illuminated. ∎

CARTER, IN VICTORY, HAILS 'NEW SPIRIT'

R. W. Apple Jr.

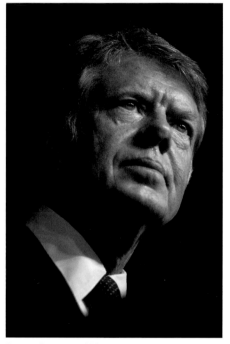

Jimmy Carter in 1976.

James Earl Carter Jr., his improbable dream of attaining the White House finally fulfilled, fought back tears yesterday as he told his fellow citizens of Plains, Ga., and the United States that he saw "a beautiful new spirit in this country."

Several hours later, Gerald Rudolph Ford, the man Mr. Carter defeated Tuesday in one of the closest Presidential elections of the century, conceded defeat in a voice ravaged by his vain campaign to avoid becoming the first President to lose since Herbert Hoover was swept away in the Great Depression.

The 52-year-old President-elect, the first son of the Deep South to win the Presidency since the Civil War, returned to his hometown at dawn, shortly after his narrow electoral-vote majority was assured with the four votes of far-off Hawaii.

Mr. Carter talked by telephone with Mr. Ford, then announced that their staffs were already at work on the transition from one Administration to another.

Having won no more than 303 electoral votes and perhaps as few at 272, Mr. Carter

(cont'd. on next page)

(cont'd. from previous page)

failed to win the mandate he had appealed for in the waning days of his 22-month campaign. But strong Presidents often create mandates after the fact, and Mr. Carter could argue that anyone who defeats a sitting President has profoundly moved the electorate. He was only the eighth man to beat an incumbent in the nation's 200 years.

The slight, soft-spoken Georgia Democrat will take office along with a solidly Democratic Congress and as the leader of a party in ascendancy. The Democrats will control the Senate by 3 to 2 and the House of Representatives by 2 to 1, almost exactly the same margins as before the election, and they will hold 37 governor's chairs, an advantage of 3 to 1.

It was the closest electoral-vote contest since 1916, when Charles Evans Hughes went to bed thinking himself the President-elect, only to awaken the next morning to find that he had lost California and the election to Woodrow Wilson. And it was the third tight race in the last five elections.

Mr. Carter, who will bring to the White House an extraordinarily unusual professional background—that of a naval officer, nuclear engineer, peanut farmer and small-business man—won the election by reassembling most of the elements of the New Deal coalition. The pattern of his victory resembled that of 1960 more than that of more recent elections such as 1968.

It was the closest electoral-vote contest since 1916

As in his campaign for the Democratic nomination, the single most important fact about Jimmy Carter was that he came from the South—an area of rising economic and political power. ∎

The New York Times THE TIMES OF THE SEVENTIES

MAYOR RICHARD DALEY OF CHICAGO DIES AT 74

Paul Delaney

CHICAGO, Dec. 20—Mayor Richard J. Daley, head of this city's Democratic machine and one of the most powerful Democrats in the country for more than two decades, died today of a heart attack.

The 74-year-old Mayor, last of the big-city bosses, was stricken after 2 p.m. and collapsed on his way to lunch on the Near North Side. He was taken to the office of his private physician, at 900 North Michigan Avenue, where he was treated as emergency equipment and vehicles stood by. He was pronounced dead at 2:55.

Earlier in the day, Mayor Daley attended the annual Christmas breakfast for department heads, where they surprised him with round-trip tickets to Ireland for him and Mrs. Daley. At noon, during dedication ceremonies for a new gymnasium on the Far South Side, he was asked to shoot the first basketball. He sank the shot on his first try.

The portly, red-cheeked Irish-American was elected in 1975 to his sixth four-year term. The previous year he had suffered a stroke that kept him from his civil duties for four months, leading to speculation, even among close associates and friends, that he would not be able to run again. He not only won, but scored overwhelming victories in the primary and general elections, as usual.

From the day in 1953 when he seized its controls until he died, Mr. Daley drove the Cook County machine, and the machine directed virtually every municipal function performed for the people of Chicago and many of those offered residents of the suburbs in Cook County that surround Chicago on three sides.

He understood every bolt and gear in the machine, and how to utilize its power. No detail of its functions was too small for him to bother with, even after 20 years at its head. He understood the block by block development of the machine, beginning with the precinct captains, who held card files on every resident in their precinct and who called on every one of them before Election Day to make certain that each understood whom the organization was supporting.

He knew the workings of the ward committeemen, who directed the precinct captains and stood ready to see that the garbage of the faithful voters was picked up and the potholes in their streets were filled.

For almost all of those 20 years, Mr. Daley was also the dominating force among Illinois Democrats. And with his tight grip on the state's large convention delegation, he had been one of the most potent figures in the selection of the Democratic Party's Presidential candidates.

"Daley means the whole ball game," the late Senator Robert F. Kennedy once said when assessing the deciding factors in Democratic conventions.

The Mayor did indeed play a major role in gaining the Democratic Presidential nominations in 1952 and again in 1956 for Adlai E. Stevenson, whose election as Governor of Illinois had depended heavily on Mr. Daley's efforts.

The Mayor will be immediately succeeded by Alderman Wilson Frost, president pro tem of the City Council. Mr. Frost, who is black, will serve until the council convenes a special meeting to elect an acting Mayor from among the Aldermen. Then, a special election will be set within three months for the remaining two-and-one-half years of Mayor Daley's term. ∎

the dominating force among Illinois Democrats

DRAFT EVADERS PARDONED;
Deserters' Fate Uncertain

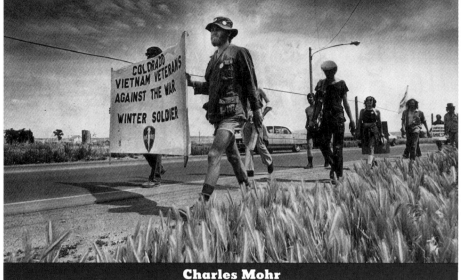

Charles Mohr

Veterans march in search of amnesty for deserters and draft evaders in the 1970's.

WASHINGTON, Jan. 21—President Carter granted a pardon today to almost all draft evaders of the Vietnam war era, but he left unsettled the status of those who deserted the armed forces in the long Asian conflict.

In effect, the first major act of the new President offered immediate, full legal relief to a relatively small number—estimated by the Justice Department at about 10,000—of predominantly white, middle-class and upper-class young men who either fled the country or refused to enter military service.

For the nearly 100,000 men who entered but then deserted the armed forces, many of whom were black, poor or disadvantaged, Mr. Carter postponed action but said that he would "immediately" initiate a study of a process that might accelerate the review of their cases with a view toward upgrading less-than-honorable discharges.

The President's actions drew protests, some of them vehement, from some veterans organizations and from some conservative politicians. There was mild praise from some pro-amnesty groups but also complaint that his decision was too grudging.

The pardon was the most important action in a day largely occupied with hours of White House social events to mark the arrival at the mansion of Mr. Carter and his family.

Avoiding, as he had in his political travels, the word "amnesty," President Carter this morning signed a pardon proclamation and an Executive order instructing the Attorney General to put the action into effect.

A Justice Department spokesman said today that most of those affected by the pardon are about 8,700 people who have been convicted of draft violations, at least five of whom are still in prison. About 1,800 others, he said, are fugitives, about 1,600 of them in foreign countries such as Canada.

The two documents granted a "full, complete and unconditional pardon" to all persons who "may have committed any offence between Aug. 4, 1964, and March 28, 1973, in violation of the Military Selective Service Act . . . with two exceptions: cases alleging acts of force or violence "deemed to be so serious by the Attorney General as to warrant continued prosecution" and cases involving employees of the Selective Service System.

The American Veterans Committee said in a statement that if the President "wishes to fulfill his inaugural promises of compassionate justice" his pardon should include deserters.

Today's pardon will permit draft evaders in exile abroad in such nations as Canada, Sweden and France to return home. ■

Coal Strikers: Mountain Men Are Clannish, Combative

Ben A. Franklin

CHARLESTON, W.Va.—Twenty-five years ago, a coal miner made an eloquent plea for tougher safety enforcement underground, to a Congressional committee that heard him politely—and then did the mine operators' bidding. Congress cleared such cream puff amendments to the Federal Mine Safety Act in 1952 that President Truman was embarrassed to sign them into law. "Loopholes were provided to avoid any economic impact on the coal mining industry," the President noted. But he signed. As much as the countless other cynical abuses that have befallen them before and since, this Truman-era episode illustrates why 160,000 Appalachian and Midwestern coal miners have found the angry strength to press their strike to its 90th day today.

The grievances are ancient. As perceived here in the coalfields, the strike is an inevitable triennial, apolitical case of "us against them"—now against the hapless leadership

(cont'd. on next page)

Unidentified male miner in the 1970's.

(cont'd. from previous page)

of their own United Mine Workers union, as well as against the coal operators. It happens every three years. And if the miners reject the contract proffered them with union and industry approval, perhaps next against the Government. "Us against them" is still powerful stuff in Appalachia.

A mountain man's endurance is such that even John D. Rockefeller IV, an immigrant (to West Virginia) heir to millions of dollars who is now the Democratic governor of the Mountain State, predicted two weeks ago that the miners could hold out another two months. "Their credit people continue to extend credit," Mr. Rockefeller explained on a television panel show. The culture of coal is a clannish combination of economic beholdenness to, and fear of, the mines together with well-placed fatalism about anyone's doing anything more than bare political or legal necessity to abate hazards that have killed an average of 100 miners a month for more than a century.

The original miners in the 1870's and 80's were here when the coal companies came. The locals were long rifle pioneers, the descendants of Anglo-Saxon immigrants who had fled the crowded coastal plains west through the first row of mountain gaps. They had settled in hardscrabble country. They were the isolated subsistence farmers whose heirs still dominate the demographics of the highland coalfields of Tennessee, eastern Kentucky, southwestern Virginia and southern West Virginia.

It is in southern West Virginia where hostility to the mine operators and militancy about the union are greatest. The history is older. Preceded by city slicker land buyers on horseback, who euchred many of the illiterate settlers out of their mineral rights with an "X" on deeds that yielded them a pittance, coal mining came into the southern Appalachian frontier culture at its most innocent and vulnerable time. It was a period in which Edgar Allan Poe was writing about the mountain region's "fierce and uncouth race of men," and President Lincoln's promise of post-Civil War aid to an abolitionist people "whom the world…has long since passed by" had been broken by an assassin.

Coal did not pass the Appalachian people by. It colonized them. It used them up. In the 1920's and 30's there were union-busting company police, evictions from company houses, and debts owed to company stores and company doctors. And after the World War II boom in the mines, there were massive layoffs and unemployment as the United Mine Workers, under the late John L. Lewis, acceded to mechanization to keep coal cheap and competitive in a fuel market that was suddenly afloat in oil. Hundreds of thousands of miners were simply cast aside.

Even if the contract is ratified, the jarring legacy of this strike seems an invitation to three more years of trouble.

By its own ineptitude, the coal industry may have recreated the top-hat-and-spats ambience of George Baer, a 1902 coal baron. He replied to a suggestion that he make peace with his workers, who were on strike seeking union recognition, by writing: "The rights and interests of the laboring man will be protected and cared for not by the labor agitators but by the Christian men to whom God, in His infinite wisdom, has given the control of the property interests of the country." If deadlock this weekend is followed by temporary Federal seizure of the mines, Big Coal may wonder whose interests it served in this year's negotiating overkill. ■

NOVEMBER 28, 1978

SUSPECT SOUGHT JOB
MOSCONE AND MILK SHOT DEAD

Wallace Turner

SAN FRANCISCO, Nov. 27—Mayor George Moscone was shot to death in his office at City Hall this morning, and a few minutes later Supervisor Harvey Milk, the city's first acknowledged homosexual official, was shot and killed in an office on the other side of City Hall.

About an hour after the killings, Dan White, who stepped aside Nov. 10 as a Supervisor but sought to withdraw his resignation and remain in office, surrendered to the police. He was booked on two counts of murder.

Dianne Feinstein, President of the Board of Supervisors, was sworn in as Mayor and will serve until the board selects a replacement for Mr. Moscone.

Mr. Moscone had scheduled a news conference for 11:30 a.m., when he was to announce the selection of Don Horanzy, a real estate broker, bank analyst and former Federal employee, to replace Mr. White as Supervisor.

When Mr. White came into the reception room of the Mayor's suits this morning and asked to see Mr. Moscone, the Mayor came out personally to greet him and said that of course he would see him, witnesses recalled.

Mr. Moscone escorted Mr. White down the long corridor past the offices of the staff and into the public office, a large room about 30 feet square where mayors usually meet reporters and visitors. Then, witnesses said, the two men went into a smaller, private meeting room accessible only through the public office.

The secretary heard noises shortly afterward and nervously went to a window, she said, expecting to see a truck that had backfired. She and others in City Hall were nervous because of the possibility of assassination connected with the People's Temple, which had had a controversial history in this city.

At 11 a.m., Deputy Mayor Rudy Nothenberg went to the Mayor's private office and found Mr. Moscone dead, shot three times in the head and arm.

The four cooling towers at the Three Mile Island nuclear power plant stand inactive after a cooling system leak had caused a shutdown on March 28, 1979.

Mr. White was next seen some distance away, near Room 250.

Stan Yee was working in Room 250, which is the work area for the supervisors' staffs. He had his back to the door, he said, and, "I heard Dan White come in here screaming for a key to the supervisors' offices."

Mr. Yee said the next thing he knew, sheriff's deputies with rifles were running up the stairs.

Peter Nardoza, an aide to Supervisor Feinstein, said she had told him earlier today that she wanted to see Mr. White. "I happened to meet him in the hallway outside the Mayor's office," Mr. Nardoza said. "I asked him if he were ready to see and talk with Supervisor Feinstein, and he said, 'In a couple of minutes. I have something to do right now.'

"Later I saw Dan run back down the hall to his aides' offices," Mr. Nardoza said. "And then I learned that White came into the area where the supervisors' offices are and asked Harvey Milk to come into White's old office for a couple of minutes. After a while I looked into that room, and I could see Harvey Milk face down on the floor."

Mr. Milk was elected at the same time as Mr. White. The slain Supervisor was a declared homosexual who walked in parades with his male lover and even sought to introduce him to the audience on the day the new board was sworn in. The lover has since committed suicide.

Whether Mr. White knew that he would not be reappointed was unclear. As Supervisor, Mr. White made it clear that he saw himself as the board's defender of the home, the family and religious life against homosexuals, pot smokers and cynics. ∎

Radiation Released At Pennsylvania Nuclear Plant

Donald Janson

MIDDLETOWN, Pa., Thursday, March 29— An accident at a three-month-old nuclear power plant released above-normal levels of radiation into the central Pennsylvania countryside early yesterday.

By last night, officials of the Nuclear Regulatory Commission had still not determined the full extent of the radiation danger, but they said the amount of radiation that escaped was

assassin

no threat to people in the area. Major amounts were released into the building housing the reactor, but workers were not believed to have been endangered.

Still, the accident at the Three Mile Island nuclear power plant, on an island in the Susquehanna River about 11 miles south of Harrisburg, was described as the worst ever at an American nuclear generating plant.

The precise cause of the accident was not determined. A Federal nuclear expert suggested last night that it stemmed from problems with filters in the plant.

Officials of the Nuclear Regulatory Commission said radiation outside the plant was far less than that produced by diagnostic X-rays.

Some of the 60 employees on duty were contaminated, a plant spokesman said, but they did not require hospitalization. And the 15,000 people living within a mile of the plant were not evacuated, although a "general emergency" was declared.

The commission said that "low levels of radiation" had been measured up to a mile from the plant and that traces had been found in the air up to 16 miles away. The amount in the immediate area was described as above normal for the plant site but below what is considered dangerous to health.

William Dornsife, a nuclear engineer with the State Bureau of Radiation Protection, confirmed that the radiation was not expected to pose a serious health threat, but there was some concern that radioactive iodine, one of the isotopes detected by the monitors, could show up in cows' milk in a week or two.

Details of the accident were in dispute almost immediately. Commission spokesmen first said it appeared to involve not just radioactive steam from the cooling system, but "direct radiation coming from radioactive material within the reactor containment."

Whatever the initial cause, a cutoff of the flow of water in the primary cooling system appears to have resulted in uranium pellets in the fuel rods melting or cracking, releasing radiation before control rods could be inserted to stop the nuclear reaction.

In Washington, Senator Gary Hart, chairman of the subcommittee on nuclear regulation, said that "some human error seems to have been involved in responding to the emergency situation." The commission informed him, he said, that "the emergency core cooling system was turned off prematurely, resulting in a partial blockage of water needed to cool the nuclear core and keep it under control."

Part of the confusion over the exact chain of events was due to the inability of the monitoring team to inspect the reactor because of the high levels of radiation within the reactor dome. Based on readings taken outside, some N.R.C. officials said that levels inside the building were between 5,000 and 6,000 roentgens—more than 10 times the lethal level.

However, company officials said those figures were too high.

As company, state and Federal officials converged on the site, there were expressions of concern about the long-range effects of the radiation release.

Company officials took pains to reassure the public.

"This is not a 'China Syndrome' type situation," said Blaine Fabian, a plant spokesman, referring to the possibility of a massive meltdown—with an uncooled nuclear reactor core burning hundreds of feet into the earth. The title of a current movie is derived from this slang expression used by scientists. ■

No decade is free of despair or devoid of hope, and the 1970's were no exception. They began badly enough for the United States and North and South Vietnam, locked in combat that seemed endless. Secretly, in Paris in 1970, negotiations on a ceasefire were begun by the Nixon administration and the Communist leadership of North Vietnam. They would produce a peace accord, but it took them three years of hard bargaining, while many thousands more died in the Vietnam War. Nor did that agreement end the fighting right away. The conflict—till then, America's longest and one of its deadliest—was not truly over until North Vietnamese forces overran Saigon, South Vietnam, in 1975 and united the long-divided country.

U.S. Marines guard the evacuation of civilians at Tan Son Nhut airbase in South Vietnam while under Viet Cong fire, during the fall of Saigon, April 15, 1975.

Neighboring Cambodia had seemed a side show to Vietnam, but a true horror unfolded there mid-decade. It would take a few years before the world learned the extent of this nightmare.

The Khmer Rouge, a fanatical Communist party, took control of the country and began purges on a scale comparable to the worst of the Nazis and Soviet Stalinists. Executions reached genocidal proportions. While no one can say for sure how many were killed, the death toll is widely believed to have been about 2 million, if not more. This in a population of maybe 7 million. The crimes against humanity did not end until the Khmer Rouge was driven from power by Vietnamese invaders in 1979.

As ever, the seething Middle East provided scant reason for cheer.

Palestinian nationalists—some call them terrorists—repeatedly hijacked airplanes to call attention to their cause after the Six-Day War of 1967 left Palestinians either under Israeli control or in exile. One hijacking with a potential for mass death, in 1976, was the trigger for perhaps the most spectacular rescue mission ever conducted: a raid by Israeli commandos at Uganda's Entebbe airport that saved dozens of hostages and caused few deaths. In 1972, Palestinians even hijacked the Summer Olympics. They invaded the athletes' village in Munich, and took Israelis hostage. The siege ended badly for the Israelis, with 11 of them being killed.

Khmer Rouge soldiers are cheered on by a crowd of youngsters after the fall Phnom Penh in 1975.

Members of the Israeli Olympic team mourn during a memorial ceremony held September 6, 1972, on the field of the Munich Olympic stadium, their countrymen killed after being held hostage by Palestinian terrorists.

Arab countries also licked their wounds after their 1967 debacle. Seeking revenge, Egypt and Syria attacked an unprepared Israel in October 1973, for a while regaining territory they had lost six years earlier, until the Israelis pushed back, aided mightily by emergency military supplies from Washington. Uncertainty plagued another corner of the Middle East at decade's end when Islamic revolutionaries overthrew the Shah of Iran, a staunch ally of the United States, now denounced as the Great Satan.

But as is the case often enough, hope can emerge from despair. Israel and Syria reached a truce in 1974, and it has held with few breaches ever since. In 1977, a brave Egyptian president, Anwar al-Sadat, took it upon himself to journey to Israel, a stunning act of statesmanship that spawned a peace treaty in 1979 (and, sadly, set the stage for Sadat's assassination by Islamic extremists two years later).

Israeli Prime Minister Menachem Begin greets Egyptian President Anwar Al-Sadat November 21, 1977, in Jerusalem, Israel.

There were other favorable signs. Long-entrenched dictatorships were toppled in Spain and Portugal. President Richard M. Nixon traveled to China in 1972 and ended more than two decades of abiding enmity. That same year, Nixon became the first American president to visit the Soviet Union.

And something important was developing at the Vatican. In 1978, a Polish cardinal became pope, the first non-Italian pontiff in centuries. The significance that the ascension of John Paul II had for the world at large was not evident at first, but over time his moral force helped sustain anti-Communist resistance in his homeland. When Communist regimes finally tumbled in Poland and across Eastern Europe, it was in no small part thanks to him.

Pope John Paul II makes his first public appearance of his papacy, Vatican City, October 16, 1978.

BONN LOOKS TO EAST BLOC AFTER MOSCOW TREATY

David Binder

West German Minister for Foreign Affairs Walter Scheel and Soviet foreign minister Andrei Andreyevich Gromyko signing the accord between West Germany and the USSR, August 10, 1970.

BONN—For years, German politicians have been telling each other that "the key to the German problem lies in Moscow." By this, they meant that the Soviet Government was chiefly responsible for the hardships of division burdening this nation ever since World War II.

With the signing of a treaty in Moscow last week, that key was turned and the heavy lid on the German problem opened a crack.

The spirit of conciliation and cooperation expressed by the Soviet-West German pact is not restricted merely to their bilateral relations. Rather, the accord specifically intends that spirit to imbue West Germany's relations with the rest of Eastern Europe, including the hitherto spited and spiteful Government of Communist East Germany.

The accord states: "There exists accord between the Government of the Federal Republic of Germany and the Union of So-

cialist Soviet Republics that the agreement to be concluded by them (the Moscow treaty) and corresponding agreements of the Federal Republic of Germany with other Socialist countries, especially the agreements with the German Democratic Republic, the Peoples Republic of Poland and the Czechoslovak Socialist Republic, form a unitary whole."

That is to say that the Government of Chancellor Willy Brandt is now committed, with Moscow's express approval, to carry its eastern policy to its logical conclusion. It will do this by negotiating "goodwill" treaties with those European Communist states still awaiting the fulfillment of Bonn's new diplomacy. In addition to Poland, Czechoslovakia and East Germany, there are Hungary and Bulgaria, both willing candidates.

But Poland is highest on Bonn's priority list, not the least because Chancellor Brandt

has long believed and repeatedly declared that reconciliation between Germany and Poland is "equal in importance" to reconciliation between those other arch-enemies of yore, Germany and France.

Bonn and Warsaw have already made considerable progress toward negotiating a "normalization treaty." This was accomplished in preliminary talks that started last winter. The next round is scheduled to open in Bonn Sept. 10 and, after the success of the Moscow parley, virtually everyone here expects an accord with Warsaw to follow directly.

Talks with Czechoslovakia have yet to open. However, Bonn was already prepared to negotiate a "normalization" package with Prague two years ago, including the juridical issue of the 1938 Munich pact, which the Czechs want declared null from the outset. The talks were postponed because of the Soviet bloc invasion of Czechoslovakia. ■

What to Do About the Palestinian Refugees?

James A. Michener

The civil war in Jordan, like the hijacking and destruction of four international airliners by Palestinian refugees following the Maoist line, grew out of the fact that after 22 years the world has failed to find a solution to one of its thorniest problems: how to provide justice for the Palestinian refugees.

Any successful peace negotiations would require the United States to pick its way through the claims and counterclaims of Arab and Jew. To do so we shall require a special wisdom, for each proposal we sponsor will be lined with booby traps and we shall be lucky to avoid them.

Prior to the Six-Day War of 1967, I spent some time in a refugee camp near Jericho, a short distance northeast of Jerusalem. It was a huge-sprawling collection of tents and lean-to shacks. It had no paved roads, no organized water system, no sewage disposal, no acceptable schools or hospitals. It was a hideous place, filled with ragamuffin children and distraught mothers. I asked one mother of four how long she had been in this camp. "Nineteen years," she said. Her children had been born here and she supposed they would live here for the rest of their lives.

I have rarely seen a spot so desolate, so without hope. And then I met the oldest son, a bright-eyed youngster of 15. He took me to where a score of boys his age were sitting under a tree, doing nothing, and their conversation terrified me.

"In two years or three years, we are going to march into Israel and slaughter every Jew. We shall go directly to Haifa and drive into the sea any who have escaped. Then my father will take back the mansion he used to own, before the Jews drove him out, and Palestine will again be free."

If the camps are as horrible as they have been described, why have they been tolerated? It seems probable that the four Arab states who received the refugees, especially if richer ones on the periphery had helped, could easily have absorbed them. The deci-

sion not to do so was a conscious political gamble, the Arab leaders calculating that if the refugees were kept in camps as an undigested mass they would always be at hand as a force to exert pressure on Israel.

Is it possible for the American observer to isolate the truth in this inflammable situation? What follows is as free from special pleading as it can be made.

Who are the Arab refugees? They fall into two groups. The first comprises those Arabs who for two years prior to 1948 lived in that part of British Palestine which subsequently became Israel. In the course of the 1948 Israeli war for independence, they left their homes and became refugees. Twenty-two years later they are still living in refugee camps in four nations which share common boundaries with Israel: Egypt, Jordan, Syria, Lebanon.

The second group comprises those Arabs who prior to 1967 lived in lands which Israel occupied in the Six-Day War of 1967. This group is less significant than the former in that the solution of their problem is simpler. Any reasonable peace treaty that will be worked out between the Arab states and Israel will provide for the immediate return of these refugees to their homes.

Could the refugee problem have been avoided? Ironically, the United Nations Partition Plan for Palestine, adopted Nov. 29, 1947, took into account the desirability of insuring a homeland for the Palestinians. The plan was generous in concept and if it had been accepted by the Arab states, the boundaries which Israel ultimately occupied would have been much reduced. Jews would have been restricted to areas that were already predominantly Jewish and, most important, the Palestinians would have held in 1947 more than what they can reasonably hope to attain in 1970. On the other hand, it was not unreasonable for the Palestinians to cry, "Who has the authority to *give* us anything? All of Palestine belongs to us and we'll take it all." So the Arabs went to war and in the resulting peace settlement the Palestinians lost everything that had been awarded them, a portion going to Israel, the bulk to Transjordan. Today, among the fanatical groups, the all-or-nothing philosophy still prevails, but among most Arabs it is generally recognized that the best the Palestinians can attain is an approximation of what they already held in 1947. ∎

OBITUARY

NOVEMBER 10, 1970

DE GAULLE, 79, DIES OF HEART ATTACK

Charles de Gaulle in 1960.

PARIS, Tuesday, Nov. 10.—Gen. Charles de Gaulle died last night of a heart attack, the French Government announced today. He would have been 80 years old on Nov. 22.

The General, the French hero of World War II, took over the government on 1958 when France was near civil war and the army was in revolt in Algeria. For 11 years he ruled as a strongman, a number of times going to the people in referenda to make certain he had their backing. Each time he won until the spring of 1969, when he lost what he considered a crucial referendum on administrative reform.

He also withdrew entirely from French political life and refused to comment or make his thoughts known on current political affairs. ∎

UGANDA'S NEW MILITARY RULER
IDI AMIN

Maj. Gen. Idi Amin, Uganda's new head of state, was the Ugandan army's heavyweight boxing champion for nearly 10 years.

He retired undefeated. And he has promised to try to do the same thing in the presidency: retire unbeaten and hand over control to an elected government. General Amin—a large, bluff informal man known to almost everyone as "Idi"—led the military coup that deposed Milton Obote Monday.

He made it clear, however, that in doing so he was not changing his role: "I'm a professional soldier," he said on the Uganda radio 14 hours after starting the coup, "and I've always emphasized that a country's military should support a country's government while that government has the support of the people. I have not changed my views about this."

Idi Amin (the name is pronounced EE-dee ah-MEEN) was born about 1925 in the village of Koboko in the northern section of Uganda, then a British protectorate.

In 1944, he enlisted in the Fourth (Uganda) Kings Africa Rifles. He was promoted to corporal in 1949, and took part in punitive expeditions against tribal marauders in Northern Uganda. In 1953, he saw action in the forests of Kenya against Mau Mau terrorists. General Amin, who is an enthusiastic rugby player, is reported to have described hunting Mau Mau as "the finest physical training a footballer could have."

By the end of 1963, he was a major and by 1964 a colonel and deputy commander of Uganda's Army and Air Force.

General Amin and Mr. Obote were close friends; General Amin's fourth wife—as a Moslem he can and does have four wives, who have borne him seven children—is a member of Mr. Obote's Langi tribe. But General Amin has never tried to conceal his distaste for politics.

General Amin's growing disaffection with Mr. Obote's policies became increasingly public, and Mr. Obote worked in a variety of ways to weaken General Amin's position.

But General Amin, heavier now than in his championship days maintains his popularity with the ranks. "I am not an ambitious man," he was quoted as saying earlier this week, "I am just a soldier with a concern for my country and its people."

Idi Amin, the third President of Uganda from 1971 to 1979.

dictator

FOE'S TROOP FLOW IS REPORTED CUT BY DRIVE IN LAOS

Craig R. Whitney

SAIGON, South Vietnam, Tuesday, Feb. 16—
Military officials asserted yesterday that the sweep westward into the Laotian mountains, where thousands of South Vietnamese troops are trying to block the Ho Chi Minh Trail network, had already succeeded in cutting off the flow of enemy supplies and troops into the northernmost province of South Vietnam.

The officials also said that the South Vietnamese advance had denied to the enemy all but two of the most important southbound sections of the trail, diminishing although not halting the movement of North Vietnamese traffic farther south.

The Americans have maintained since they started the operation Jan. 30 with a push as far as the western border of South Vietnam that their objective was to counter an enemy build-up in the northernmost military region of South Vietnam.

From 11,000 to 12,000 South Vietnamese troops are said to be in Laos. Their advance has been a slow, cautious one, with little progress over the last four days. But besides caution, the reason for the slowness, their spokesman here said yesterday, is "the discovery of so many supply caches we have to have time to search."

The United States command here reported that American forces killed eight enemy soldiers Sunday evening 10 miles north-northwest of Khesanh.

With the 24,000 South Vietnamese and 9,000 American troops strung out over about 75 miles of road between Quangtri and the deepest South Vietnamese positions inside Laos, the supply problems could quickly become critical if the flow is interrupted. ∎

South Vietnamese forces gathering for an invasion of Laos in 1971.

NIKITA KHRUSHCHEV

Nikita Khrushchev died a second time yesterday. His first, a political death, took place in 1964 when he was unceremoniously ousted from power, plunging overnight from the status of one of the world's key leaders to an unperson in the land he had ruled. His continued disgrace seven years later was emphasized by the fact that most Soviet citizens first learned of his passing from broadcasts to the Soviet Union by Radio Liberty and other foreign transmitters.

Yet the petty vengefulness of the present Kremlin rulers, many of whom were originally his protégés, cannot obscure the fact that Khrushchev was a giant in Soviet and world history. A complex and colorful figure, he must rank with Lenin, Trotsky and Stalin in any honest account of Soviet history.

His greatest accomplishment was the break with Stalin and Stalinism. In 1956 and 1961, his blows to the Stalin cult were so effective that even the strong Stalinist forces now in the Kremlin have found it impossible to turn back the clock completely, although the Soviet Union has retrogressed signifi-

Nikita Khrushchev with Fidel Castro in Moscow in 1963.

CONGO CHANGES NAME TO ZAIRE REPUBLIC

KINSHASA, Zaire, Oct. 27 (Reuters)—The Congo, a former Belgian colony, changed its name to the Zaire Republic today. The new name was taken from the original name of the Congo River, which in Zaire will be called the Zaire River.

This country became independent in 1960. Its capital, Kinshasa, was formerly known as Leopoldville.

Across the river to the west is the Congo Republic, a former French colony once known as the Middle Congo, which gained independence in 1960. Its capital is Brazzaville. ∎

CANADIANS HOLD A-TEST PROTESTS

Jay Walz

OTTAWA, Nov. 2—Protests against the United States nuclear test on Amchitka Island are spreading across Canada.

Tomorrow, many university and college classes will close in a number of cities. Protest marches, with United States consulates as the main objective, are planned in Ontario, Quebec, Alberta and British Columbia.

In Ottawa, Prime Minister Pierre Elliott Trudeau has been under pressure to voice Canada's "concern" directly to President Nixon. So far, he has refused to do so, stating that a House of Commons resolution condemning the test has expressed Canada's concern in the most emphatic way.

This week, a number of adult organizations joined what had previously been largely a student protest.

Roger Tobin of Local 1520 of the United Automobile Workers at Talbotville, Ontario, proposed a one-day embargo against goods from the United States and the closing of the border to United States tourists.

Meanwhile, the Greenpeace 2, a motor vessel carrying a protest mission to the Amchitka area, continued her voyage westward despite adverse weather conditions.

Capt. Hank Johansen reported to The Canadian Press by radio that he had been forced back to the British Columbia coast but would try to get through on a changed course tomorrow. The object is to place the vessel inside the danger zone charted by the Atomic Energy Commission at the time the underground device is detonated.

In Ottawa, meanwhile, it was learned that Canada had joined Japan and the United States in mobilizing a special network to warn coastal communities of any dangers that might follow the Amchitka test. ∎

politics

IDEOLOGY

cantly from the peak of Khrushevian liberalism. He was not a free believer in free speech and other civil rights as the West understands those concepts, but he appreciated the no nation could continue to live in the Stalinist atmosphere of terror and lies.

At the time he was purged, the Soviet press was full of accusations about his "subjectivism" and "hare-brained scheming." It is true that many of his historic gambles were poorly received and boomeranged. Yet, much of the fault lay in the totalitarian nature of the Soviet system, which permitted Khrushchev to embark upon these and other rash gambles without adequate debate.

And it was Khrushchev, too, who made Soviet ideology come to terms with the facts of the thermonuclear era. By declaring war between Communism and capitalism was not a "fatal inevitability," he reversed a fundamental tenet of Leninist theology. His understanding of the suicidal potentialities of nuclear war helped avoid disaster when the United States discovered his October 1962 effort to install Soviet missiles in Cuba.

In both his accomplishments and his failures, Nikita Khrushchev was a giant. In different times and different areas, he was both this nation's friend and its enemy. Yet now, conscious of the years he spent in disgrace and loneliness, many here and around the world will mourn his passing. It is sad that Soviet leaders could not find the vision yesterday to surround the announcement of his death with the dignity that his contributions and career deserved. ∎

China Joins U.N. Council, Assails Superpowers

Henry Tanner

UNITED NATIONS, N.Y., Nov 23—China took her seat as a permanent member of the Security Council today and charged that "one or two superpowers" continued to commit aggression and subversion against other countries.

Huang Hua, Peking's permanent representative, in his first statement to the Council said that "colonialists and neo-colonialists and particularly the one or two superpowers have not ceased their activities in practicing power politics and in carrying out aggression, interference, subversion and control against other countries and their people."

(cont'd. on next page)

(cont'd from previous page)

His allusion was unmistakably to the United States and Soviet Union. Both are also permanent members of the Council, along with Britain and France. All five hold the veto.

Diplomats specializing in Chinese affairs said that ever since the Soviet-led invasion of Czechoslovakia in August, 1968, the Chinese have maintained that the attitudes of the two big powers toward smaller nations were essentially the same.

George Bush, the United States representative, said that "all of us in the United States Mission look forward to cooperating with the members of this new Chinese delegation in any efforts to find constructive solutions to the important issues of peace and security that concern us all."

The Assembly also elected China to the Economic and Social Council, along with Chile, Poland, Burundi, the Soviet Union, Finland, Britain, Bolivia and Japan. ■

The leader of the Chinese delegation to the United Nations, Huang-Hua, arriving at U.N. headquarters in New York in November, 1971.

JANUARY 12, 1972

EAST GERMANY RECOGNIZES BANGLADESH

Sydney H. Schanberg

NEW DELHI, Jan. 11—East Germany granted recognition today at Bangladesh, the nation proclaimed by Bengali secessionists in East Pakistan.

The announcement—marking the first recognition by any government outside the Indian subcontinent—was made by Foreign Minister Otto Winzer.

Until today, only India and a sister state, the Himalayan Kingdom of Bhutan, had recognized the new Bengali government.

The East German step heightened expectations in diplomatic circles here that the Soviet Union and other members of its East European bloc would also recognize Bangladesh very soon. Many diplomats believe that the East Germans acted at the urging of the Russians.

The East German move could have a side effect—Indian establishment of full diplomatic relations with East Germany. Such a step by India, under consideration for some time, has been strenuously opposed by the United States, just as Washington opposed India's establishment of full diplomatic relations with North Vietnam, a step New Delhi took last Friday.

India's latest diplomatic moves serve in part to rebuff the United States for its support of Pakistan during the Indian-Pakistani war last month, while rewarding the Soviet Union for its firm backing of New Delhi.

Some Western countries, Britain among them, have already established working relationships with the Bangladesh government, and several members of the Communist bloc, including the Soviet Union, Poland, Bulgaria and Czechoslovakia, have been negotiating agreements with Dacca.

FEBRUARY 6, 1972

'Faith In the System Is Shattered'

Bernard Weinraub

LONDONDERRY— An icy rain fell on the bleak hilltop overlooking Londonderry.

One by one the 13 coffins were borne from St. Mary's church, the name's of the dead echoing through the streets from loudspeakers. "Patrick Doherty . . . William Mash . . . Michael Kelly . . ."

The sight of frenzied children weeping, women shrieking in the agony of loss, men trembling and bereft—somehow the tragedy of Northern Ireland reached a brutal peak with the burial of the men who were killed by British soldiers last Sunday during a massive demonstration by Roman Catholics.

Londonderry is a site of Catholic power (over 60 percent of the citizens are Catholic), of Irish Republican Army strength and now, of sullen, total fury at the political Establishment. After "Bloody Sunday," the situation, in effect, is one of war against the British Army and the Northern Ireland Government.

"People are stunned and angry, people are hopeless," said the Rev. George McLaughlin, a 39-year-old priest standing inside the packed

40

church where requiem mass for the 13 dead was held. "This tragedy is the final blow."

To the Catholic minority the deaths of the 13 symbolize the death of Northern Ireland in its present political form. Virtually all Catholics have withdrawn from government. Catholic lawyers are seriously discussing a boycott of the courts. Thousands of families have stopped paying rents and electricity bills.

The demand for civil rights has been overtaken by a surge of feeling that both the Belfast and London governments are no longer tolerated in the Catholic community, which forms one-third of the population in Northern Ireland.

To the Protestant Union Government the prospect of unity is abhorrent because it would mean being swallowed up by the Catholic majority to the south. The Protestants have offered housing and voting reforms, but Catholics insist these measures came too late and offered too little. ∎

IRA terrorist suspects are rounded up by British soldiers on Bloody Sunday in Londonderry, Northern Ireland, when 13 Roman Catholics were killed, January 30, 1972.

FEBRUARY 24, 1972

Nixon Talks Further With Chou

Max Frankel

PEKING, Thursday, Feb. 24—President Nixon logged four more hours of private conversations with Premier Chou En-lai yesterday and went off this morning to view the Great Wall of China and the historic Ming tombs.

Mr. Nixon said that one result of his trip "may be that walls erected—whether like this physical wall or whether other walls, ideological and philosophical—will not divide peoples of the world, that peoples regardless of differences in philosophy and background will have an opportunity to communicate with each other and know each other. As we look at this wall, what is most important is that we have an open world."

The formal talks were followed by yet another kind of social experience here— the Premier's display of his guests before 18,000 spectators in the indoor Capital Stadium for a dazzling exhibition of gymnastics and a dozen fierce rounds of racket combat that go by the name of badminton and table tennis but bear no resemblance to the lazy paddling that most Americans associate with these games.

U.S. President Richard Nixon toasts with Chinese Premier Chou En-lai during his trip to China in February 1972.

There has been speculation among the press corps that the conferees have already reached "tentative" agreement on exchanges of tourists, cultural attractions, students and news bureaus. The White House had no comment last night on such reports.

Whatever the basis of the reports, a prediction of more trade, more tourists and more exchanges of scientists and students and correspondents seems safe.

The chances are that Mr. Nixon and Mr. Chou are concentrating not on the details of such exchanges but on how far they might go beyond people-to-people contact toward some kind of unofficial diplomatic dealing while they lack embassies in each other's capitals.

Beyond that, the talks must deal with the main obstacle to such contacts—the United States' continuing recognition of the Chinese Nationalist Government in Taiwan and China's claim to sovereignty over the island. ∎

MAY 16, 1972

JAPANESE CELEBRATE THE RETURN OF OKINAWA

Tillman Durdin

TOKYO, May 15—The return of the Ryukyu Islands, with their one million people, to Japanese rule was marked today with a ceremony in Tokyo attended by high Japanese and American officials and with other festive observances throughout the country.

Vice President Agnew was President Nixon's representative at the solemn Tokyo ceremony, which was attended also by Emperor Hirohito and Premier Eisaku Sato. The island group, which extends south from southwestern Japan, has become Okinawa Prefecture, or province, as it was before its capture by United States forces in 1945.

An amnesty for many categories of persons serving prison terms freed several thousands throughout Japan. The United States High Commissioner on Okinawa, Lieut. Gen. James B. Lambert, proclaimed a similar amnesty there before he turned over control at midnight last night.

Satisfaction over Okinawa's return was for some Japanese diluted by dissatisfaction with the terms of reversion, which permit a continued large-scale American military presence on the islands.

But in general, the day passed without major violence as thousands of special policemen parried attempts of demonstrators to reach official buildings.

Okinawa's return was a particular triumph for the 71-year-old Premier Sato, who had worked for years to bring it about. Mr. Sato has said he would retire after the reversion agreement was carried out, and now the ruling Liberal-Democratic party must resolve rivalries over a new leader.

Late in the day, President Nixon and Premier Sato exchanged greetings to mark the inauguration of a hot line telex connection between Washington and Tokyo.

Mr. Nixon, extending congratulations to Mr. Sato on the occasion, said that a hot line was generally regarded as a crisis communications system but said it "can also be used to carry messages of hope and conciliation." ∎

MAY 21, 1972

NIXON HOPES TO CELEBRATE A DOUBLE TRIUMPH

Max Frankel

U.S. President Richard Nixon and Russian leader Leonid Brezhnev watch as U.S. Secretary of State Henry Kissinger (left) Russian Minister of Foreign Affairs Andrei A. Gromyko (right) sign the SALT treaty.

WASHINGTON—In Richard Nixon's melodramatic vision of the world, Communists and crisis are synonymous. Encounters with them are battles and he believes that they, like he, aspire to win victories and inflict defeats.

In that spirit, the President flies toward the Soviet Union this weekend to celebrate a triumph—a victory, as he sees it, over the fates of history, which have denied Presidents Eisenhower, Kennedy and Johnson their journeys to Moscow (also envisioned for election years), and a victory, as he also sees it, over the endemic Soviet habit of preferring tactical gains by confrontation to strategic advances by negotiation.

Mr. Nixon goes as the first peace-time President to visit the Soviet Union. He goes to proclaim the first arms limitation of the nuclear era. He goes to demonstrate that in the triangular competition of the United States, the Soviet Union and Communist China, he alone is on good bargaining terms with the other two.

He goes, therefore, to celebrate a double triumph, one diplomatic, one personal.

Diplomatically, Mr. Nixon thinks he has succeeded where all his predecessors, back to Franklin Roosevelt, failed. He thinks he has orchestrated a summit conference that will dwell on concrete agreements instead of mere atmospherics, capped by a major undertaking to limit the deployment of nuclear weapons and supported by a dozen other cooperative ventures so that a growing circle of Americans and Russians will have a continuing stake in collaboration. The taste of this impending achievement is even sweeter this week than last, for it has been sealed by the Russians' willingness to sit still for the American mining of North Vietnam's harbors and the bombing of North Vietnamese cities.

Personally, the President expects respect and tribute where in the past he has been alternately challenged or rebuffed, and always disliked. He has carefully plotted his climb to the summit through the rebellious Communist capitals of Rumania, Yugoslavia and China, timing it so as to extract maximum political and strategic advantage.

Although the danger of Soviet-American confrontation around Vietnam still lurks in the background, and although North Vietnam's army remains poised to embarrass the high-level collaboration in Moscow, the President hopes that this week's journey will at least and at last win a great deal of time—years, and not merely months—for the evolution of a more mature and stable relationship between the two superpowers.

The President will address the Russian people on Soviet television and, on a less elaborate schedule than during his China visit, will be widely covered on American screens.

On the eve of his departure, Mr. Nixon said the principal objective of his trip was to establish "a different relationship" between the two countries so that they "work together rather than against each other."

The Soviet approach to the arms and trade talks suggests a basic decision to concentrate on the economic development of the country now that strategic security seems assured, and now that Japan and Western Europe as well as the United States are booming competitors. In the Soviet view, it is undoubtedly the United States that has had to resolve the ambiguities of its policies in favor of retrenchment and concentration on domestic development. But whatever the motive, the Russians obviously set a high priority on their new friendship treaty with West Germany and other accords with the United States.

What the nuclear stick can no longer accomplish, Nixon hopes the economic carrot can now assure. ∎

23-HOUR DRAMA AT MUNICH OLYMPICS

David Binder

One of the defining images of the Munich Olympics in 1972: This Palestinian is one of a group that had taken Israeli athletes hostage.

MUNICH, West Germany, Wednesday, Sept. 6—Eleven members of Israel's Olympic team and four Arab terrorists were killed yesterday in a 23-hour drama that began with an invasion of the Olympic Village by the Arabs. It ended in a shootout at a military airport some 15 miles away as the Arabs were preparing to fly to Cairo with their Israeli hostages.

The first two Israelis were killed early yesterday morning when Arab commandos, armed with automatic rifles, broke into the quarters of the Israeli team and seized nine others as hostages. The hostages were killed in the airport shootout between the Arabs and German policemen and soldiers.

The bloodshed brought the suspension of the Olympic Games and there was doubt if they would be resumed.

In addition to the slain Israelis and Arabs, a German policeman was killed and a helicopter pilot was critically wounded. Three Arabs were wounded.

The bloodbath at the airport that ended at 1 a.m. today, came after long hours of negotiation between Germans and Arabs at the Israeli quarters in the Olympic Village where the Arabs demanded the release of 200 Arab commandos imprisoned in Israel.

Finally the West German armed forces supplied three helicopters to transport the Arabs and their Israeli hostages to the airport at Fürstenfeldbruck. From there all were to be flown to Cairo.

Two of the terrorists, carrying their automatic rifles, walked about 170 yards from the helicopters to the plane. And then they started back to pick up the other Arabs and the hostages.

As the Arabs were returning, German sharpshooters reportedly opened fire from the darkness beyond the pools of light at the airport. The Arabs returned fire.

How the hostages were killed was still in doubt. One theory was that an Arab threw a

(cont'd. on next page)

(cont'd from previous page)

grenade into a helicopter in which some or all of the hostages were bound hand and foot.

Before the bloody end, tense negotiations had gone on all day yesterday between Germans and the commandos. The games were halted and the German police, wearing bulletproof vests beneath track suits, had closed in on the Olympic Village building invaded by the Arabs.

The bloody interlude in the Olympic games, international symbol of peace and sportsmanship, began about 4 a.m. yesterday when the Arabs climbed a fence into the lightly guarded compound that is housing more than 10,000 athletes.

About an hour later, according to witnesses, the commandos broke into the three-story structure where 26 Israelis were staying.

As they tried to rush the Israelis, they were halted at the door by a coach. He held the door against them, shouting to other athletes to flee.

Recalling the episode later, Tuvia Sokolsky, a weight-lifting coach, said, with traces of fear in his eyes and voice:

"I heard this shout: 'Boys get out!' I jumped to my feet and locked the door. My room is opposite the apartment entrance and I saw a strange picture—one of the men on the team trying to keep the door shut. Because of the warning, I was able to escape from the room." ∎

SEPTEMBER 24, 1972

Mass Arrests and Curfew in Philippines

MANILA, Sept. 23—President Ferdinand E. Marcos followed up his declaration of martial law in the Philippines today by announcing the mass arrest of what he said were Communist conspirators plotting to overthrow the Government. He also announced plans for economic reforms.

In a nationwide radio and television address Mr. Marcos imposed a curfew from midnight to 4 a.m. daily and announced controls on newspapers, radio stations and foreign correspondents. He banned travel of Filipinos abroad except those on official missions and barred rallies and demonstrations.

The President said that civil authorities would remain in power and that all national and local government officials would continue to function.

"This is not a military takeover," the President said.

"I have proclaimed martial law in accordance with the powers vested in the President by the Constitution of the Philippines," Mr. Marcos said.

"I as your duly elected President use this power, which may be implemented by military authorities, to protect the Republic of the Philippines and our democracy, which is endangered by the peril of violent overthrow of the duly constituted Government."

There was no immediate indication how many persons had been arrested. Friends and relatives of those detained said those arrested included at least three senators, several journalists and a number of delegates to the constitutional convention.

In his address, Mr. Marcos announced a cleanup of "corrupt and sterile government officials," a proclamation of land reform throughout the Philippine archipelago, establishment of a military commission to try and punish military offenders and a ban on the carrying of firearms by civilians and unauthorized persons, with violation punishable by death.

OBITUARY

MAY 28, 1972

THE DUKE OF WINDSOR DIES AT 77

The Duke and Duchess of Windsor in 1967.

LONDON, Sunday, May 28—The Duke of Windsor, who gave up the British throne in 1936 to marry an American divorcee, died in his home near Paris early today a Buckingham Palace spokesman announced here.

The Duke, who reigned for 10 months as King Edward VIII before abdicating, had been ill for some time.

The Duke defied the British establishment to marry Mrs. Bessie Wallis Warfield Simpson, a twice-divorced American.

He remained in virtual exile from Britain ever since, estranged from the royal family until recently. It was not until 1965 that Queen Elizabeth II met the Duchess of Windsor at the bedside of the Duke while he was in London for eye operations.

Two years later, the Duke and Duchess were formally received by the Queen at a ceremony for Edward's mother, Queen Mary. Last May 18, Queen Elizabeth visited her ailing uncle at his Paris home.

After the abdication, the Duke and Duchess attracted wide publicity as they traveled about. They often attended charity balls and other events in New York, where they stayed at the Waldorf-Astoria. ∎

VIETNAM CEASE-FIRE AGREEMENT: 'PEACE WITH HONOR'?

U.S. National Security Adviser Henry Kissinger (right) shakes hand with Le Duc Tho, leader of North Vietnam delegation, after the signing of the Paris Peace Accords on January 23, 1973, in Paris, France.

After all the death and destruction, the settlement finally written simply codified the military stalemate of the long war. The United States agreed to depart without a guarantee of the survival of an independent, anti-Communist South Vietnam. North Vietnam agreed to stop fighting without a guarantee of a Communist-dominated coalition government in Saigon. Both sides agreed to leave the South's future to a political contest among Vietnamese.

So that when President Nixon announced the cease-fire agreement on television Tuesday night, he could justly claim to have won "peace with honor" as he had previously defined it—a peace that would give the Saigon regime a "decent chance" of survival in the years ahead. Yet given the uncertainty of Saigon's prospects without the support of American fire power, no one could be sure whether the President's phrase was just a formula to enable the United States to extricate itself from a continuing conflict or a promise to see to it that the Communists abided by the new rules—even if it meant a reintroduction of American power.

In Saigon, President Nguyen Van Thieu was plainly nervous. Even if the Communists abide by the terms of the agreement, he said in a radio address, the struggle for South Vietnam will be entering a political phase "just as dangerous" as the military one.

In Hanoi, news of the accord was celebrated in the streets, and at a Paris news conference Le Duc Tho, the North Vietnamese negotiator, spoke jubilantly of a "great victory for the Vietnamese people."

In New York, the bells of Trinity Church that are rung only on "great occasions" pealed across deserted Wall Street after Mr. Nixon's night-time announcement, but the general reaction in the country was subdued. Both for those who had supported the war, only to find its ultimate costs too heavy to bear, and those who had opposed it, only to despair of its ever ending, the experience was too painful to permit more than exhausted relief.

The signing ceremony in the gilt ballroom of the former Majestic Hotel in Paris yesterday was a complex compromise in itself. To avoid even implying that they recognized each other's legality, Saigon and the Vietcong signed on separate pages a document that referred only to "the parties" to the negotiation. The settlement was fragile and ambiguous. But there are no neat ends for stalemated wars, and this ending seemed to give peace a chance. ∎

45

LONDON SHAKEN BY TWO BOMBINGS LAID TO THE I.R.A.

Alvin Shuster

LONDON, March 8—Terrorists struck in London today, setting off two large explosions, near Trafalgar Square and at the Old Bailey, the Central Criminal Court. One man was killed and 243 were injured.

Not since World War II had London seen such chaos. Windows in scores of buildings shattered, ambulances and fire engines screamed through London all afternoon and casualty wards in several hospitals quickly filled with the injured. By tonight, most of the injured had been treated for shock and cuts and released. About 20 remained for further treatment, some for severe injuries.

Both bombs, planted in automobiles, were believed by authorities to be the work of the Provisional wing of the Irish Republican Army. Officials said the blasts had clearly been timed to coincide with the referendum today in Northern Ireland, on whether the province should remain under British control. The I.R.A. opposes the referendum.

Two more car bombs were found and defused. "They were all aimed at the military, police and the courts," an official said. "Our clear feeling is that it is the I.R.A."

The casualties would have been greater if there had not been telephoned warnings. A caller, said to have a slight Irish accent, gave The Times of London the location of three of the automobiles 45 minutes before the first blast.

All four bombs, including the two that were defused, had been set to go off an hour before Mr. Heath was scheduled to meet Liam Cosgrave, the new Prime Minister of the Irish Republic and a firm opponent of the Irish Republican Army, which supports unification of the predominantly Catholic Republic with the Province of Northern Ireland, where Protestants are in the majority.

The I.R.A. is intent on serving notice to the British Government that despite the blows it has taken from security forces, it still has the power to strike. So far during the recent troubles, it had confined its terrorism to Northern Ireland, with one exception. ∎

AFTER SIX BITTER YEARS, THE ARABS ATTACK

Henry Tanner

CAIRO—"It was not possible for the Arabs to gaze across the cease-fire line indefinitely at their own land," Sir Alec Douglas-Home, the British Foreign Secretary said Friday in a bit of hindsight. Yet this was precisely what the Egyptians and the Syrians had been doing for the last six years and what they thought the world powers had condemned them to forever.

To be sure, over the six years since the 1967 defeat, the Arabs made both military and diplomatic moves to escape their predicament.

Some time this spring, Mr. Sadat decided to fall back on Arab support. He found King Faisal of Saudi Arabia ready to back him. From then on, everything was changed.

On Saturday Oct. 6, at 1:30 p.m., the Egyptians and Syrians stopped gazing at their lost lands and went across the cease-fire lines. War is never pretty or something to be exalted. But the depth of the humiliation and frustration in which the Arabs had been immersed could be gauged only by someone who saw the joy that gripped simple young Egyptian soldiers as they rode their trucks across the pontoon bridges on the Suez Canal.

Last week it was as if Egypt had finally rid herself of a collective inferiority complex. In spite of the tension and the worry about the days ahead, people have been more serene and kinder to each other and to foreigners, even Americans, than before. If they had agreed on a common exclamation it would have been, "We did it! Nobody thought we could."

As the Egyptian leaders see it, they have destroyed two pillars of American policy in the Middle East. One is the assumption that the oil-rich Persian Gulf states could be kept separate from the Arab-Israeli conflict. The other is that the Israeli armed forces, with Iran, as America's "surrogates," in Senator Fulbright's phrase, would police the Middle East for Washington.

As the Egyptians also view it, the achievement of the Egyptian army in crossing the Suez Canal, which was supposed to be one of the world's great tank barriers, and in reconquering a wide strip of Egyptian territory in the Sinai, has destroyed the myth of Israeli invincibility. That being done, a Cairene said last week, "Nothing will ever be the same again in the Middle East." ∎

Israeli howitzer pounds enemy positions in the Sinai Desert during the Yom Kippur War.

Le Duc Tho Rejects Nobel Prize, Citing Vietnam

Flora Lewis

PARIS, Oct. 23—Le Duc Tho has rejected the Nobel Peace Prize awarded to him jointly with Secretary of State Kissinger for the Vietnam agreement they negotiated, Hanoi announced today.

He said that "peace has not yet really been established in South Vietnam. I will be able to consider acceptance only when the Paris accord is respected, the arms are silenced and real peace is established in South Vietnam."

Mr. Tho's reaction clearly reflected a careful decision of the North Vietnamese leadership. There had been no comment on the subject from Hanoi from the time the prize was announced until the publication of his letter, but the rejection was not surprising to observers familiar with North Vietnam's view of the war and of existing conditions.

There was no mention of Mr. Kissinger at any point in the letter, nor that the prize offered to Mr. Tho was to be shared with Hanoi's former enemy.

The North Vietnamese have consistently taken the position that the Paris agreement was not a compromise settlement but a victory over the United States. They could not therefore, have been expected to be pleased at equal honors granted to their representative and that of the belligerent they feel that they defeated, Mr. Kissinger.

Further, they maintain that the United States holds responsibility for continuing violation of the cease-fire and failure to implement any of the accord's political clauses. Hanoi has invariably considered the Government of South Vietnam as a puppet of the United States, and therefore insists that the United States should account for Saigon's deeds.

It was not at all clear whether Mr. Tho was suggesting that the prize would be acceptable once South Vietnam was actually at peace.

Hanoi's decision posed a dilemma for the Nobel committee. It could leave Mr. Kissinger as the sole recipient of the 1973 Nobel Peace Prize, or the committee could meet again to reconsider the initial decision. ∎

President Pompidou Dead After Almost Five Years as De Gaulle's Successor

For over a year, President Georges Pompidou faced an agonizing personal and political choice. He knew he was gravely ill, although he forbade any official confirmation of the fact.

He was quoted saying: "perhaps I can't elect the candidate of my choice but I can defeat whom I don't want."

By clinging to office despite his fatal disease, he lost that chance and the chance to set the course of the Gaullist party and of France beyond his own term of power.

Now, whoever is elected, broad changes in French policy are widely anticipated.

The most likely candidate of the Gaullist party is Jacques Chaban-Delmas, the 59-year-old ex-Premier whom Mr. Pompidou removed from office in the summer of 1972 ∎.

APRIL 28, 1974

A Joyful Lisbon Celebrates Coup with Flowers

Richard Eder

Mario Soares during the Carnation Revolution in Lisbon, Portugal, in May, 1974.

LISBON, April 27—The Portuguese were saying it with flowers today. Just what they were saying was not quite clear, even to themselves, except that they were very happy.

Carnations have become the symbol of Thursday's coup and there were carnations all over Lisbon. The soldiers, country boys most of them, with ill-fitting brown uniforms, looked like walking bouquets. One soldier assigned to direct traffic on a steep hill leading down to the port, signaled with great sweeping gestures, a brunch of red flowers in each hand.

It is hard not so much to describe the euphoria here as to describe it believably. Everyone in Lisbon is talking, and what is more—to their own incredulity—talking politics. In the streets, on the squares, a man will hold up a newspaper, another man will look over his shoulder and soon a dozen people are talking like old friends, each trying to tell the other just exactly what was wrong with the authoritarian regime under which the country has lived for more than 40 years.

"Everyone is laughing. We always said the day the regime fell there would be rivers of blood, and it was almost nothing."

In a country with the formidable economic and political backwardness of Portugal any celebration is almost bound to end in hangover. Today's mood of hilarity feeds in part on the rather dangerous fact that nobody knows very much about the captains and majors who are the real force behind the coup.

A student who is active in what has up to now been an illegal left-wing group worried about Gen. António de Spínola.

"Our people are sentimental and they have no political experience," he said. "They could make Spínola a dictator out of sheer gratitude that he overthrew the dictatorship."

But whatever may happen next week and in the weeks to come, this weekend is a time for trust and display. The column in the center of Rossio Square was occupied by 30 students who spent the morning making speeches about the next revolution to a crowd that watched benevolently but quietly, clearly determined to enjoy the fruits of this one. ∎

MAY 19, 1974

INDIA BECOMES 6TH NATION TO SET OFF NUCLEAR DEVICE

Bernard Weinraub

NEW DELHI, May 18—India conducted today her first successful test of a powerful nuclear device.

The surprise announcement means that India is the sixth nation to have exploded a nuclear device. The others are the United States, the Soviet Union, Britain, France and China.

A brief Government statement said that India's Atomic Energy Commission had carried out "a peaceful nuclear explosion experiment." The underground blast took place "at a depth of more than 100 meters," or about 330 feet, the statement said.

In exploding the device, India was entirely within her rights in international law, Government officials said. India is a signatory of the Moscow test-ban treaty of 1963, forbidding explosions on land, in the air or underwater in the seas. In exploding the device beneath the ground, officials say, India adhered to the treaty.

Although India is a party to the nuclear test-ban treaty, she did not sign the 1968 treaty to bar the spread of nuclear weapons. She declined to subscribe to it on the ground that it divided the world into countries with nuclear weapons and those without such weapons and, India said, imposed obligations on nonnuclear states without imposing similar obligations on nuclear states.

The Government announcement of the nuclear explosion gave few details but one Indian scientific analyst told a news agency here that "it can be inferred" that the explosion was as powerful as the atomic bomb dropped by the United States on Nagasaki in World War II. That bomb had a force equivalent to 20,000 tons of TNT.

The disclosure today strengthens India's powerful military position on the subcontinent and provides firmer leverage over the nation's major rival, Pakistan. Government officials insisted, however, that the nation's nuclear program was intended solely for peaceful purposes.

Asked if the explosion would raise India's prestige among developing nations, Prime Minister Indira Gandhi said: "I never bother about prestige. It is nothing to get excited about. We are firmly committed only to the peaceful uses of atomic energy."

The blast immediately aroused discussion about the uses of nuclear energy here. There was some belief that it was likely to revolutionize mining operations, especially in regions containing large amounts of mineral resources, especially copper, that would take a long time for exploitation by conventional methods.

India spends about $40 million a year on the development of atomic energy. ∎

JUNE 1, 1974

A PACT THAT COULD RESHAPE THE ARAB WORLD

Henry Tanner

CAIRO, May 31—The Syrian-Israeli disengagement agreement will have long-range repercussions throughout the Arab world, affecting the domestic and foreign policies of almost every country and deciding the shape of changing alliances.

The leaders of the Palestinian movement face the vital choice of defying the most powerful Arab governments or taking part in the move toward a negotiated settlement of the Arab-Israeli conflict that these governments now advocate. This perhaps is the most important single result of the agreement.

In Cairo, not unnaturally, the agreement is seen first of all as a vindication for President Anwar el-Sadat, who gambled on the success of Secretary of State Kissinger's personal diplomacy and persuaded the Syrian President, Hafez al-Assad, to do likewise.

Mr. Sadat and Mr. Assad emerge politically strengthened at home and in the Arab world. Their alliance—which had its moments of strain since last October—is thought to be very close again.

The westward trend in the area has been further enhanced. The Soviet Union, which was only marginally involved in the negotiations in spite of Foreign Minister Andrei A. Gromyko's last-minute appearance in Damascus, suffers a further loss in power and prestige.

The United States, which had been virtually absent from the Arab world for more than 20 years, is riding higher than ever.

In general, the agreement has increased the influence of the moderate Arab leaders who favor a negotiated settlement with Israel.

It has deepened the isolation of Col. Muammar el-Qaddafi of Libya and the Baathist regime of President Ahmed Hassan Al-Bakr of Iraq, both of which reject all accommodation with Israel.

Syrian-Israeli disengagement has left King Hussein of Jordan once more exposed to danger of isolation. The King is once more on a collision course with Syria and Egypt over the Palestinian issue.

Jordan would like to see some kind of Israeli withdrawal from the West Bank, following the pattern of disengagement agreements with Egypt and Syria. At this stage this would mean that the Israelis would give a part of the West Bank back to Jordan. This is not what the Palestinians—or the Egyptians and Syrians—want.

Yasir Arafat, head of the Palestine Liberation Organization, and other moderates among the Palestinians have been maneuvering to set up "a national Palestinian authority" on the West Bank and in Gaza, over which the Palestine Liberation Organization would claim sovereignty. The idea is that any area left by the Israelis would go to the Palestinians, not to Jordan.

In recent weeks the heads of the various groups that make up the Palestine Liberation Organization have been meeting in Beirut. A majority is understood to be in favor of going to Geneva if the Palestinian delegation is invited by the co-chairmen, the United States and the Soviet Union, and is given the same rights as the national delegations from Egypt, Israel, Jordan and Syria. The Palestinians also want the terms of reference of the conference changed to take in discussion of "the legitimate rights of the Palestinian people."

No one here expects quick action on these conditions. The Soviet Union has recognized the Palestine Liberation Organization. The United States has not, and will find it hard to do so in view of Israel's fierce opposition to such a step. ∎

PERON DEAD; WIFE TAKES OVER DIVIDED ARGENTINA

Jonathan Kandell

Isabel Perón succeeded her husband, Juan Perón, after his death in 1974 but was ousted by a military coup in 1976.

BUENOS AIRES, July 1—President Juan Domingo Perón of Argentina, one of the most remarkable and controversial political figures in Latin-American history, died today at the age of 78. His death left his politically divided country in a state of deep uncertainty.

The announcement of his death, reportedly of heart disease, was made this afternoon by his wife, Vice President Isabel Perón, 43. She assumes her husband's office, becoming the first woman chief of state in the Americas.

General Perón rose to power through a bloodless military coup in 1943. Over the next decade he won the presidency twice, riding a crest created by his popular appeal and the economic and social benefits that he showered on Argentina's working class.

With the late Eva Duarte Perón, his second wife, General Perón, in his first era, built one of the strongest labor movements in Latin America, broke the back of the landed aristocracy and presided over a vast internal resettlement that made most Argentines urban dwellers.

Despite the progressive reforms that, for the first time, socially integrated the rural poor and the "shirtless ones," as he called the urban proletariat, General Perón angered his opponents by his early admiration for Fascist Italy, the corruption of government officials around him, the widespread use of arbitrary detentions that brought charges of torture, and by extravagant economic programs that drove the country close to bankruptcy.

General Perón aroused fears of deep social change in the leadership of the armed forces and other groups who saw the basic stability of Argentina threatened. These forces, which included the Roman Catholic hierarchy, came together after the death of Eva Perón of cancer at the age of 33 in 1952. She had been regarded as almost a secular saint, but the effect of her political force diminished with her death, and the general's fortunes slid disastrously. He was easily overturned in the military coup of 1955.

He staged a stunning comeback and returned to the country from an 18-year exile, capturing more than 60 percent of the vote in the election last September.

But during the nine months of his third presidential term, the aging, ailing general was unable to keep his country on a promised course of national unity and stable economic progress.

His wife was given full presidential powers on Saturday, shortly after Government officials publicly disclosed the seriousness of the President's illness. Despite her political inexperience, she has received immediate and full expressions of support from political, military, labor and business leaders.

100,000 MARCH THROUGH NEW DELHI IN ANTI-GOVERNMENT PROTEST

NEW DELHI, March 6—At least 100,000 people surged through the heart of New Delhi today in a demonstration against the Government, the biggest such march here in years.

Led by Jaya Prakash Narayan, the 72-year-old follower of Mohandas K. Gandhi, the noisy and festive march and rally was marked by fierce attacks on the policies of Prime Minister Indira Gandhi and the Congress party, which has dominated India for 27 years.

"Today's march will change India's history," Mr. Narayan said in a quavering voice. "It is the beginning of a new chapter. The rulers will be forced to listen to the people's voice."

As the throng applauded and shrieked on the sun-drenched field near Parliament, Mr. Narayan shook his fist and said in Hindi: "There is corruption all around, mismanagement, poverty, illiteracy. In any other country the situation would have exploded into a revolution. We are a peaceful people. But democracy does not mean that people will tolerate corruption and misrule."

Mr. Narayan, an ailing figure who has emerged as the most powerful anti-Government force in years, announced "a month-long agitation" across India to press demands for the dismissal of corrupt ministers, an overhaul in the education system and an austerity program.

The march and demonstration were, perhaps, the most sweeping and bitter protest against Mrs. Gandhi since she became Prime Minister nine years ago.

More than 15,000 policemen and security troops were deployed around the center of the city, which was quiet and sultry during the day. Thousands of people—office workers, hawkers, shopkeepers—lined the four-mile route, applauding and waving at the marchers.

J. P., as virtually everyone calls Mr. Narayan, rose in the center of the procession, standing in a jeep, waving and emotionally lifting his hands as the demonstrators and bystanders applauded. The mood seemed at once friendly and bitter.

There were signs in Hindi reading: "Vacate the throne, the people have come," "The Government which cannot provide food and clothing is worthless." A group of lawyers walked arm in arm along the Janpath in the heart of the city, chanting, "Indira Gandhi will not last."

Mr. Narayan, who arranged the march with a group of opposition figures, addressed the rally from an area called the Boat Club, a park with a thin stretch of water for rowboats. He referred several times to the freedom struggle and Gandhi, the spiritual founder of India.

"We should not lose patience, we should be aware of the dangers ahead," said Mr. Narayan. "The danger is that Mrs. Gandhi and her party want violence to impose dictatorship. Twenty-seven years after independence the people have lost their patience." ■

OBITUARY

Aristotle Onassis, 69, is Dead of Pneumonia in France

PARIS, March 15—Aristotle Onassis, the Greek shipping magnate, died today at the American Hospital in nearby Neuilly-sur-Seine.

Mr. Onassis was taken to the hospital by special plane from Athens last Feb. 7 and underwent an operation to remove his gall bladder two days later. Although the operation was successful, he was also suffering from myasthenia gravis, a debilitating neurological disease, which had affected his heart.

Dr. Maurice Mercadier, one of his physicians, said death was due to bronchial pneumonia, which "resisted all antibiotics." Mr. Onassis had been receiving cortisone treatment, which, the doctor said, lowered his resistance to infection and made the pneumonia "uncontrollable."

Mrs. Onassis, the former Jacqueline Kennedy, was in New York today but left for Paris by air in the evening. Mr. Onassis had not left the hospital since he arrived five weeks ago, and his wife had taken to commuting between Paris and New York. ■

Jacqueline Kennedy Onassis and Aristotle Onassis in New York City in 1970.

DEATHS NEAR 100 IN BEIRUT BATTLE

Juan De Onis

BEIRUT, Lebanon, April 15—Gunfire, rockets and bombs took a deadly toll here today as Palestinian guerrillas battled for the third day with the right-wing Phalangist party's armed militia.

Palestinian sources said 11 persons had been killed by nightfall in sectors under their control. This raised the unofficial count of the dead to close to 100, many of them bystanders.

The survival of Lebanon's coalition Government, headed by Premier Rashid al-Solh, was uncertain tonight as the sound of guns reverberated through the dark and deserted streets while families huddled in their homes.

After a Cabinet meeting that ended at 9 p.m., Premier Solh said he hoped there would be "a settlement tonight," but the shooting continued.

Young men, some in camouflaged combat dress, crouched in doorways and behind automobiles in the predominantly Moslem Chia sector. They were armed with submachine guns: At intersections

(cont'd. on next page)

CHIANG KAI-SHEK IS DEAD IN TAIPEI AT 87; LAST OF ALLIED BIG FOUR OF WORLD WAR II

TAIPEI, Taiwan, Sunday, April 6—Chiang Kai-shek, the President of Nationalist China and the last survivor of the Big Four Allied leaders of World War II, died of a heart attack here last night. He was 87 years old.

An announcement by the Government said Generalissimo Chiang suffered a heart attack at 10:20 p.m. and was taken to the Taipei Central Hospital, where he died at 11:50 p.m.

General Chiang will be succeeded automatically as President by Vice President C. K. Yen, but the real power in the Government is expected to remain in the hands of Premier Chiang Ching-Kuo, 65, who assumed control when his father fell ill and was incapacitated nearly three years ago.

With Roosevelt and Stalin, Chiang was known in World War II as one of the Big Four leaders of the Allies in the war against Germany, Italy and Japan.

His Nationalist Government was driven from the mainland by the Communists in 1949 and has been in exile here since then.

The death of General Chiang is not ex-

pected to have any significant impact on the policies of the Nationalist Chinese Government or on the political morale of the people here.

The President had not taken an active role in governmental affairs for nearly three years, and was seen in public only rarely after he fell ill with pneumonia in the summer of 1972. ■

MILITARY TAKING OVER IN CAMBODIA AS LAST AMERICANS ARE EVACUATED

Sydney H. Schanberg

PHNOM, PENH, Cambodia, April 12—Premier Long Boret announced tonight that a "summit committee" dominated by generals had been formed to run the Government and continue the fight against the insurgents until peace can be achieved.

This announcement, made in a radio broadcast, came several hours after the American Embassy had been closed and Ambassador John Gunther Dean together with the last remaining staff members were evacuated by helicopter.

In his broadcast, the Premier said the new governing committee had been given full powers for three months. He appealed to the people "to remain calm and cooperate with the military."

To fill this "leadership vacuum," the Premier said, he called together today the main generals and political leaders as well as the Cabinet and other key Cambodian figures.

The Americans, who had scaled down their embassy staff a week ago from its original 285, had the last remaining foreign mission in the capital and were the only foreign support of the Phnom Penh Government.

With the evacuation, that support in effect ended. In fact, the American supply airlift that has been keeping this Government alive for two months ended with yesterday's flight. The airlift, from South Vietnam and Thailand, had been bringing in up to 1,400 tons of ammunition, fuel and food every day.

Although the airlift built up some stocks, it seems unlikely that the Government can now last for more than a few weeks.

The insurgents are less than three miles from the airport and Government lines all around are thin.

The shelling of both the airport and Phnom Penh continued during the day.

The former acting president had apparently been privately recommending an appeal to Prince Norodom Sihanouk, nominal leader of the insurgents, to come back from exile in Peking and lead the country. It was the overthrow of Prince Sihanouk in 1970 by Marshal Lon Nol and others that led to this civil war. ■

(cont'd. from previous page)

leading into the Phalangist party neighborhood of Ashrafiya, armed men turned back reporters who tried to enter.

"It is hell at night with all the shooting," said a driver for a foreign embassy who lives in the vicinity of the Tell al-Zattar Palestinian refugee camp. This sector has been under fire for three days by the Phalangists who have been firing rockets into the crowded housing.

Banks, schools, offices and most stores have been closed since the fighting erupted Sunday, when members of the Phalangist militia opened fire on a bus loaded with Palestinians returning to the Tell al-Zattar camp through Beirut's Christian district of Ain al-Rummaneh.

The Phalangist leader met with Mahmoud Riad, Secretary General of the Arab League, who has been sent by President Anwar el-Sadat of Egypt to mediate in the crisis.

The Phalangist party grew out of a Christian youth movement in the nineteen-thirties that fought for Lebanese independence from France. It was officially recognized in 1952. It has a strong base, traditionally one of the two or three parties that form the coalition governments.

The roughly equal Christian-Moslem division of the Lebanese population makes the Palestinian issue a critical issue in the country's political relations.

"It is hell at night with all the shooting."

The future of the Palestinian guerrillas, who were driven out of Jordan in 1970 and 1971, when they challenged the authority of King Hussein, is the main issue in the conflict here.

President Franjieh, a Christian, and Premier Solh, a Moslem, are under strong pressure from other Arab countries to avoid intensifying the conflict and bringing the Lebanese Army into the fighting.

In 1973, Syria sent troops across the border to support the Palestinians.

A Syrian military delegation arrived here today with instructions from President Hafez al Assad to consult with the Lebanese military on a solution to the current crisis. ∎

APRIL 30, 1975

Evacuation From Saigon Tumultuous at the End

George Esper

SAIGON, South Vietnam, Wednesday, April 30—With American fighter planes flying cover and marines standing guard on the ground, Americans left Saigon yesterday by helicopter after fighting off throngs of Vietnamese civilians who tried to go along.

Eighty-one helicopters from carriers in the South China Sea landed at Tan Son Nhut airport and on roofs at the United States Embassy compound to pick up most of the approximately 1,000 remaining Americans and several thousand Vietnamese.

But large groups of other Vietnamese clawed their way up the 10-foot wall of the embassy compound in desperate attempts to escape approaching Communist troops. United States marines and civilians used pistol and rifle butts to dislodge them.

The final stage of the evacuation, which stretched over 19 hours, brought to an end an American involvement in Vietnam that cost more than 50,000 lives and $150 billion. Four marines died during the final evacuation.

While most Americans were pulling out, some newsmen and missionaries chose to remain.

Communist forces, meanwhile, pressed closer to Saigon. The Vietcong said they had captured the large Bien Hoa air base, 15 miles northeast of the capital. Earlier, fighting had been reported less than 10 miles west of Saigon along Route 1.

One of the last civilians to leave was Ambassador Graham Martin, who boarded the final regular lift of 19 helicopters that had flown out about two hours earlier.

After the last marines had left, hundreds of civilians swarmed into the compound and onto the roof. On the roof of a nearby building that had also served as an emergency helipad, several hundred civilians huddled together, hoping there would be more helicopters to carry them away.

The American involvement ended in tumultuous scenes at both airport and embassy, Marines in battle gear pushed all the people they could reach off the wall, but the crush of people was so great that scores got over.

Some tried to jump the wall and landed on barbed wire strung along the top. A middle-aged man and a woman were lying on the wire, bleeding. People held up their children, asking Americans to take them over the fence.

During the airport evacuation, two Vietcong rockets whistled overhead and exploded behind the United States defense attaché's compound, sending marines and evacuees diving for the pavement. ∎

Fleeing Americans board a U.S. Marine helicopter at Tan Son Nhut airbase in Saigon April, 1975.

FORD BIDS NATIONS LIVE UP TO SPIRIT OF HELSINKI PACT

James M. Naughton

British Prime Minister Harold Wilson, U.S. President Gerald Ford, French President Valery Giscard d'Estaing and German Chancellor Helmut Schmidt in August, 1975.

HELSINKI, Finland, Aug. 1—President Ford, declaring that the summit meeting here will be judged "not by the promises we make but by the promises we keep," joined leaders of the Soviet Union and 33 other nations today in affirming a broad charter for peace and human progress throughout Europe.

"Peace is not a piece of paper," the President said in an address that carefully tempered hope with caution.

A few hours later each of the presidents, prime ministers, chancellors, Communist party chiefs and the envoy of Pope Paul VI sat at a long, blue-draped table in Finlandia House to sign the 30,000-word "final act" of the Conference on Security and Cooperation in Europe.

In blunt phrases unmistakably directed at the leaders of Eastern Europe, President Ford called détente an "evolutionary" process that must produce a better life for those on opposite sides of the line frozen across Europe in the cold war.

"Our presence here offers them further hope," Mr. Ford said; "we must not let them down."

Even as the three-day meeting was ending, however, old divisions were creating new tensions among some participants.

Premier Suleyman Demirel of Turkey, who was to meet here tomorrow with Premier Constantine Caramanlis of Greece to explore possible solutions to their dispute over Cyprus, canceled that meeting and re-turned to Ankara. This was described as a reaction to the refusal of the House of Representatives late last night to consider lifting its embargo on arms aid to Turkey.

The smaller nations of the European Economic Community expressed dissatisfaction that their large partners, France, West Germany and Britain, were proceeding on their own to arrange for a possible summit meeting with the United States and Japan on international monetary problems.

President Francisco da Costa Gomes of Portugal, who arrived here at midnight from troubled Lisbon, appealed publicly for respect for his country's right to settle its own fate without interference.

President Nicolae Ceausescu of Rumania, who will be Mr. and Mrs. Ford's host when they travel tomorrow to Bucharest, rose after Mr. Ford addressed the meeting to declare that Rumanian "democracy" was superior to that mentioned by some other speakers.

Addressing the conference yesterday, the Soviet Communist leader Leonid I. Brezhnev intimated strongly that the charter reaffirmed the "Brezhnev doctrine," under which Soviet-led troops entered Czechoslovakia in 1968 to put a stop to liberalization of the Communist Government there.

But Mr. Ford, in the most forcefully delivered address of his year in the Presidency, said that every signer would be held to account for the charter's promises of a freer flow of ideas, information and people across ideological frontiers. ∎

Franco Is Dead in Madrid at 82: Juan Carlos to Take the Oath as King Within 48 Hours

Henry Giniger

MADRID, Thursday, Nov. 20—Generalissimo Francisco Franco died early today after 36 years of dictatorial rule over Spain. He was 82 years old.

The death of the Chief of State, who led rightist military forces to victory in the Spanish Civil War that ended in 1939, came at 4:30 a.m. at the La Paz Hospital on the northern edge of Madrid. He had been rushed there on Nov. 7 from the Pardo Palace for surgery to stop internal bleeding.

Although his designated successor, Prince Juan Carlos de Borbón, 37, had been acting Chief of State since Oct. 30, interim power upon the general's death passed formally to the three-member Council of the Regency, headed by Alejandro Rodriguez de Valcárcel, the Speaker of Parliament.

General Franco, stricken on Oct. 21 by acute heart diseases, withstood a long series of crises complicated by kidney failure and severe bleeding from multiple ulcers. In his final days, his fight for physical survival was linked in the mind of many Spaniards to the political survival of the authoritarian regime he grounded. Even before his death, the Spanish political world was focusing discussion on what the post-Franco era under Juan Carlos might be like. ∎

JUNE 17, 1976

6 Die in South Africa Riot After Black Student Protest

John F. Burns

JOHANNESBURG, June 16—At least six people died today when a demonstration by 10,000 black students against instruction in the Afrikaans language turned into a riot.

The deaths came only a week before the South African Prime Minister, John Vorster, is scheduled to meet with Secretary of State Henry A. Kissinger in West Germany. Apartheid will be on the agenda of the talks, which South African officials have described as the country's most important diplomatic encounter in decades.

Mr. Vorster had no immediate comment, but a prominent black leader, the Very Rev. Desmond Tutu, Anglican Dean of Johannesburg, said that black leaders "have been warning the Government about something like this happening for a long time."

More than 70 people were injured, 19 with bullet wounds, when the riot erupted in the black township of Soweto, 10 miles from Johannesburg. It continued from midmorning until after dusk, with army units standing ready to intervene. The area was sealed off to whites.

It was the worst riot between the races in South Africa since the Sharpeville massacre on March 21, 1960, when police fired on a crowd of more than 5,000 demonstrating black Africans, killing 72 and wounding more than 170.

Soweto, a sprawling township of 700,000 people, is the most populous urban concentration in southern Africa. Despite its nearness to Johannesburg, it is as separate from it as apartheid can make it.

The trouble began when the students gathered to protest a government regulation requiring the use of Afrikaans as the language of instruction for some subjects in the township's schools.

The students complained that the regulation required them to cope with a third language, in addition to English and the African language

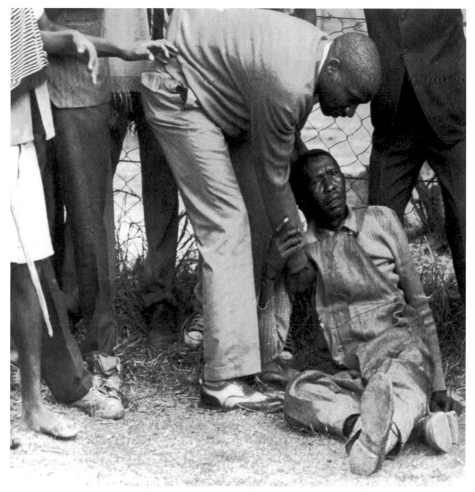

An injured man is helped away from a riot scene in the South African township of Soweto during tribal conflicts in 1976.

most of them speak as a mother tongue. But the strikes had broader political overtones since Afrikaans is the language of South Africa's ruling Nationalist Party, the architect of apartheid.

Describing the scene immediately before the gunfire, the minister said the students "were aggressive, shouted inflammatory slogans, carried banners and attacked and stoned police as well as private vehicles."

"Two police dogs were hacked to death and set on fire," he went on. "Ten police vehicles were damaged and set on fire."

In a radio interview later, he added: "Of course some shots were fired. But the police used as little force as possible."

A reporter for The Johannesburg World, a newspaper aimed at black readers, gave a somewhat different account. The reporter, Sophie Tema, said that the students were ap-

proaching the school, singing black nationalist songs, when police vehicles pulled up. Most of the policemen were black, but only the white officers were armed, two with submachine guns and the rest with revolvers.

The reporter said that the police had given no warning to the students to disperse. Once the rock-throwing began, a white policeman pulled out his revolver, pointed it and fired, she said. Other policemen followed suit, and one student, hit in the chest, fell to the ground.

Under fire, the students started running, throwing more rocks as they went, Miss Tema's account continued. The police continued firing, and a second boy, aged 6 or 7, was hit. ∎

conflict

JUNE 18, 1976

3 in Beirut Confess to Slaying of U.S. Ambassador

James M. Markham

BEIRUT, Lebanon, June 17—Palestinian security agents said today that three Lebanese men had confessed to involvement in the slaying yesterday of the American Ambassador, Francis E. Meloy Jr., the embassy's economic counselor and their chauffeur.

Mahmoud Labady, an official of Wafa, the Palestinian press service, said at a news conference that the three Lebanese were arrested by security agents of the Fatah guerrilla organization early this morning.

Mr. Labady, who provided few details about the identity of the men, said they were still being interrogated and would be turned over to an Arab League peacekeeping force when it arrived in Lebanon.

All sides in the 14-month Lebanese civil war denounced the murders. A Palestinian communiqué called them "a flagrant crime," and there were suggestions from many quarters that the killings might have been an attempt to roil the military situation in the country, which has begun to quiet down.

At his news conference, Mr. Labady suggested that the arrested men had been working for what he called an "outside power." He cited as possibilities Israel, Syria, Lebanon's right-wing Christian Phalangist Party or the United States Central Intelligence Agency.

"We don't think it's an isolated action for sure," Mr. Labady said.

While Mr. Labady announced that three men had been arrested in the slayings, he said that the Ambassador's armored Chevrolet Impala had not been recovered. He said the three prisoners belonged to no identifiable political organization but had been apprehended in the western, largely Moslem quarters of the city, where Mr. Meloy, Robert O. Waring, his economic counselor, and their driver, Zoheri Moghrabi, were apparently seized.

Since the Beirut airport has been closed for 11 days, it was not clear how the embassy intended to transport the bodies of the two Americans out of the country. However, an evacuation convoy organized by the British Embassy is leaving by road for Damascus tomorrow.

For months, the United States Embassy has encouraged Americans not having pressing business here to get out. Even so, the embassy estimates that there are 1,800 American citizens in Lebanon, some Lebanese born.

Mr. Meloy, who took up his post here a month ago, was on his way to his first meeting with President-elect Elias Sarkis when he, Mr. Waring and Mr. Moghrabi were seized.

All sides denounced the murders

The Beirut daily An Nahar reported that at 3:15 p.m. a car without license plates was seen stopping near the garbage dump in the Ramlet al-Baida section and that three bodies were rolled onto the pavement wrapped in woolen blankets.

A crowd reportedly gathered and soldiers from the Palestine Liberation Army were said to have taken the bodies to a nearby makeshift hospital run by the International Red Cross.

At 6:25 p.m., according to Mr. Ross, an official from the Red Cross contacted the embassy, which sent Lebanese employes to the tent hospital, where they identified the murdered men. They were said to have been fully clothed, though their wallets and other papers had been removed.

DRAMA IN HIJACKING OF JET TO UGANDA

JERUSALEM, July 10—Legends of heroism have emerged from the week of drama that began with the hijacking of an Air France jet airliner over Greece June 27 and ended with the rescue of 103 hostages in a daring Israeli commando raid into Uganda July 3.

It was shortly after noon, Sunday, June 27, when the white Air France airbus lifted off the runway at Athens airport, climbed through a thin layer of smog and banked westward over the shimmering blue waters of the Gulf of Corinth.

The seat-belt sign was still lighted eight minutes later when a woman's scream pierced the air. In the first-class section, a man and a woman sprang to their feet, each brandishing a pistol in one hand, a grenade in the other. While the woman trained her gun on the startled cabin attendants, the man stepped toward the pilot's cabin. Behind the insulated door, Capt. Michel Bacos heard the scream and the commotion in first class.

"First I thought there was a fire on board," he said later. "The chief engineer opened the door and found himself nose to nose with the German hijacker."

The West German, later identified as 27-year-old Wilfried Böse, pushed his way into the cockpit and took the microphone of the plane's intercom.

"My name is Achmed el-Kibesi," he was quoted as having said in English with a heavy German accent. "The Popular Front for the Liberation of Palestine, the Guevara group, Gaza Brigade, is in complete control of this flight. If you stay still and do nothing suspicious, no one will be hurt." The el-Kibesi name is believed to be that of a slain guerrilla from Gaza regarded as a martyr by the Palestinians.

The hijacking, which began like so many others, was the start of a harrowing week for the 244 passengers and 12 crew members aboard the Tel Aviv–Paris flight. It was a week in which the hijackers flew their hostages first to Benghazi, Libya, for refueling, and then to Entebbe Airport in Uganda, where they were held for

(cont'd. on next page)

(cont'd. from previous page)

six days in a dusty, unused old passenger terminal.

The ordeal came to an end last Saturday night when three planeloads of Israeli commandos flew into Entebbe under cover of darkness, surprised and killed the hijackers and escaped back to Israel with the remaining hostages and crew.

The passengers aboard Air France Flight 139 out of Tel Aviv were a mixture of Jews and non-Jews, young and old. Their occupations included pharmacist, doctor, welder, teacher, gas-station owner, lawyer, microbiologist, economist, nurse, student and computer engineer, in addition to many retired people.

The hijacking operation actually began Sunday morning when four passengers who had disembarked from Singapore Airlines Flight 763 from Bahrain at 6:17 a.m. entered the transit lounge at Athens Airport.

Two were Arabs, apparently in their early 20's, wearing sport shirts and slacks. They were later described as nervous and unsure of themselves. The other two were non-Arab: the tall, fair-haired, husky Mr. Böse, who wore a brown suit and green shirt, and a woman who has still not been positively identified.

The hijackers' hand luggage apparently was not examined when they joined the 52 other passengers boarding the Air France flight at Athens.

En route, one of the passengers, a Mr. Har-Tuv, recalled later, the passengers were generally quiet. "The atmosphere was very, very tense," he said, "but there was no shouting, no hysterics."

After circling Benghazi about 10 times, the big plane finally bumped down on the runway.

Böse officially informed the passengers that they had landed at Benghazi and he promised to take off as soon as possible.

After six hours on the ground, they left Benghazi. The "commander" announced that they were now heading for their "last destination." Five and a half hours later, at 3 a.m., Monday, the airbus touched down at Entebbe.

MONDAY

The plane wandered about the runway for an hour or so before it came to a halt. Uganda soldiers surrounded it and the passengers were told that President Idi Amin would be arriving soon.

The French stewardesses served fruit juice, beer and soda. About three hours after the landing some of the hostages peeking out the windows saw the towering figure of the Uganda President.

French hostages and crew members, who were among the hostages held for a week at the airport of Entebbe in Uganda during the highjack of an Air France plane in 1976.

Böse came on the intercom and explained the purpose of the hijacking. He attacked France for helping Israel with Mirages and nuclear weapons, mentioned various Palestinians assassinated in Europe, talked about the "international revolutionary movement" and called Israel a fascist state that engaged in genocide.

It was now 24 hours since the plane left Athens. As the passengers debarked they were startled by the sight of Uganda soldiers lining their path, rifles at the ready.

TUESDAY

Listening to their radios, the hostages heard that Israel had refused to negotiate with the terrorists, who threatened to blow up the plane and the passengers. At 3:30 in the afternoon, the terrorists read out to the hostages their demands, which called for the release of 53 prisoners, 40 of them in Israel. The deadline was Thursday at noon.

THURSDAY

At noon President Amin, appearing in battle dress with his son, announced an extension of the deadline until Sunday.

FRIDAY

General Amin and his wife arrived at 7 a.m. He told the hostages that they had the wrong information, that Israel had not responded to the terrorist demands. He said he was on his way to Mauritius for a meeting of the Organization of African Unity and would talk about the problem there.

SATURDAY

By 11:30 p.m., most of the hostages had settled down for another uncomfortable night. Mr. Har-Tuv had just removed his slippers when he heard a burst of gunfire, a pause, then another burst. He ducked into a hallway for protection and fell to the floor. From there, he could see that the hijackers were being fired at and were firing back. He concluded that the Israeli Army had come to save them.

In fact, several Israeli units had arrived at the airport and were fanning out across the runways, securing the entire area.

Uganda soldiers opened fire from several points including the airport control tower.

The exchange of fire with the hijackers guarding the terminal was short but fierce. All but one of them apparently was cut down outside the terminal. Only Böse, the German, rushed inside, machine gun in hand.

For a hair-raising few seconds, the hijacker looked at his hostages sprawled in front of him.

"I couldn't believe my eyes when I realized he wasn't going to shoot us," Mr. Har-Tuv said.

The three hostages who were killed during the operation were caught in this initial crossfire as the Israelis stormed the terminal.

The hostages arrived back in Israel Sunday morning, exactly a week after their takeoff from Lod Airport. A huge crowd welcomed them exuberantly. ■

JAPANESE ARREST FORMER PREMIER IN LOCKHEED CASE

Andrew W. Malcolm

TOKYO, Tuesday, July 27—Former Prime Minister Kakuei Tanaka was arrested this morning for alleged involvement in the multi-million-dollar Lockheed Aircraft bribery scandal.

For now, he is accused of having violated Japan's foreign exchange and currency regulations by accepting money that was illegally brought into Japan. Other charges could come later.

Mr. Tanaka is the highest-ranking Japanese politician to be arrested since 1948, when Hitoshi Ashida, a former Prime Minister, was arrested for bribery.

The move is sure to have profound political implications in the domestic politics of Japan, the United States' chief Asian ally and the non-Communist world's second largest economic power.

The powerful Mr. Tanaka controls the largest combined factions of the governing Liberal-Democratic Party in the Parliament, and his long experience in government has earned him legions of influential supporters in the powerful government bureaucracy and the industrial establishment.

In recent months Mr. Tanaka has been a major behind-the-scenes mover in struggles within the Liberal-Democratic Party to oust its present leader, Prime Minister Takeo Miki, who is 69.

In Senate testimony there, officials of the Lockheed Aircraft Corporation said they had spent $12.6 million in fees, commissions and bribes to promote the sale of their aircraft in Japan. Since many of those intense secret sales efforts went on during Mr. Tanaka's tenure as Prime Minister, there was immediate suspicion that he would be implicated.

Prosecutors did not release details of Mr. Tanaka's alleged crimes. But it is believed they have evidence that he accepted almost $2 million from Hiro Hiyama, former president of the Marubeni Trading Corporation, Lockheed's official sales agent here. ∎

DELAYED DISCLOSURE OF CHAIRMAN MAO'S DEATH

PEKING, Sept. 9—Mao Tse-tung, the pre-eminent figure of the Chinese Communist revolution and the leader of his country since 1949, died today at the age of 82.

His death, at 12:10 a.m. after a long illness, left uncertain the question of who was to succeed him. There is no designated heir, nor is there anyone among his subordinates who commands the awe and reverence with which he was regarded among the 800 million Chinese.

The party leadership delayed the announcement of Chairman Mao's death for about 16 hours until 4 p.m. [4 a.m. Thursday New York time]. The announcement included an appeal to the people to uphold the unity of the party that he had headed.

Funeral music followed today's announcement broadcast over the Peking radio, and 2,000 people gathered in the vast Tien An Men Square, many wearing black armbands, some weeping. Flags fluttered at half staff.

Eight days of memorial ceremonies were scheduled to begin Saturday and end Sept. 18 with the entire nation standing in silent tribute for three minutes but with trains, ships and factories sounding sirens.

The announcement said that no foreign leaders would be invited to Peking during the period of mourning.

Peking Radio and Hsinhua, the Chinese press agency, said Mao's body would lie in state in the Great Hall of the People.

While the announcement did not specify the illness, which had kept Mao out of the public eye for months, it was widely believed that the chairman had been suffering from Parkinson's disease, which causes progressive rigidity of the body's muscles.

Mao last appeared in public on May Day 1971.

The last foreign leader to see him was Prime Minister Zulfikar Ali Bhutto of Pakistan on May 29. He said that Mao had a bad cold and was frail, but that he "was very quick on the uptake and grasped everything."

President Ford visited him last December.

"All victories of the Chinese people were achieved under the leadership of Chairman Mao," a statement said in eulogizing the man who led the Communist takeover in 1949 and then dominated the nation as he guided it from backward isolation to the status of a nuclear power with a burgeoning industrial base, purging rivals, defying Soviet ideological leadership, opening a relationship with the United States and winning a seat in the United Nations. ∎

Picture released by the Chinese official news agency with following caption: "The Party and state leaders standing vigil before the remains of the great leader and teacher Chairman Mao Tse-tung."

Brezhnev Is Made Soviet President, First Party Chief to Take the Title

Christopher S. Wren

Soviet leader Leonid Brezhnev in 1977.

MOSCOW, June 16—Leonid I. Brezhnev, the head of the Soviet Communist Party, was also named chief of state today, becoming the first person in his country to hold both posts simultaneously.

His election by the Supreme Soviet, the nominal Parliament, came at the outset of a two-day session. The move had been expected following the removal last month of President Nikolai V. Podgorny from the party's ruling Politburo, the main policy-making body, and the creation of a new post of First Vice President under the proposed new constitution.

The conferring of the Presidency on the 70-year-old Mr. Brezhnev appeared to confirm his political power. The honor also seemed calculated to add luster to his reputation as a statesman at a time when he has been the subject of increasing adulation at home.

Mr. Brezhnev previously served as President under Nikita S. Khrushchev, from May 1960 to June 1964. Because the post is largely ceremonial, it then represented something of a setback since he had been closer to the seat of power in the previous four years as one of Khrushchev's national party secretaries. When Khrushchev was overthrown in October 1964, Mr. Brezhnev assumed the party leadership.

With his authority now at its apogee, Mr. Brezhnev has sought to avoid comparisons with the personality cults surrounding Stalin and Khrushchev. Even now, he is likely to maintain a semblance of consensus in the decisions made in the Politburo.

By also holding the post of President, Mr. Brezhnev resolves his protocol problems with elected Western leaders. He is expected to wield his new title when he visits France next week. Until now, he has had to sign international treaties with his party title which has no counterpart in the West.

Mr. Brezhnev was elected President with a predictably unanimous vote and a standing ovation from the delegates at the Supreme Soviet session.

Nobels Go to 2 Ulster Women And Amnesty International

Robert D. Hershey Jr.

OSLO, Oct. 10—Two women who ignored danger in campaigning for peace in Northern Ireland were today belatedly named winners of the 1976 Nobel Peace Prize. At the same time, Amnesty International was named winner of the 1977 prize.

The two Northern Ireland women, Mairead Corrigan and Betty Williams, were awarded the 1976 prize jointly for organizing a broad-based movement to end the violence between Roman Catholics and Protestants in the British province.

"Their initiative," the Norwegian Nobel Committee said, "paved the way for the strong resistance against violence and misuse of power which was present in broad circles of the people."

Amnesty International, the London-based human-rights organization, was cited as a "bulwark" against increased brutality and the internationalization of violence and terrorism.

"Its efforts on behalf of defending human dignity against violence and subjugation have proved that the basis for peace in the world must be justice for all human beings," the committee said.

Mrs. Williams and Miss Corrigan, who will share a prize of $140,000, launched their peace movement after Mrs. Williams saw three children killed by the getaway car of fleeing Irish Republican Army guerrillas in Belfast. Miss Corrigan was an aunt of the dead children.

The campaign met with widespread support in Northern Ireland, where sectarian strife has claimed more than 1,700 lives since 1969, and also attracted a tide of international sympathy.

This is the first time since the early 1960s that two Peace Prizes have been announced at the same time.

Amnesty International, which was founded 16 years ago in London as a voluntary group to assure human rights around the world, now has 100,000 members in 33 countries who seek to promote human rights through public reports citing violations of those rights. ∎

SADAT WELCOMED IN ISRAEL; BRINGS PEACE PROPOSALS

William E. Farrell

JERUSALEM, Nov. 19—The leaders of Egypt and Israel, two nations that have fought four wars in 29 years, met on Israeli soil tonight.

President Anwar el-Sadat of Egypt stepped aground at Ben-Gurion International Airport, creating Middle East history as the first Arab leader to visit Israel since its founding in 1948.

He was greeted by Prime Minister Menahem Begin and President Ephraim Katzir, who have lauded Mr. Sadat in recent days for his bold move in deciding to come to Israel despite growing antipathy and violence in the Arab world caused by his tacit recognition of Israel's existence.

After his arrival at the King David Hotel, President Sadat met for a half-hour with Mr. Begin, Mr. Dayan and Deputy Prime Minister Yigael Yadin for what was described as a courtesy call.

"I have already had a private discussion with him," Mr. Begin said to reporters, referring to the Egyptian leader, "and I can say that we like each other."

As Mr. Sadat walked with Mr. Begin and Mr. Katzir, the Egyptian leader was applauded by Israeli dignitaries and other officials, who were as stunned as their fellow countrymen in recent days as the Egyptian's declaration that he would come to Israel came to fruition.

Theaters canceled performances, shops were shuttered and hundreds of thousands of Israelis sat glued to television sets to watch proceedings that were unthinkable here two weeks ago.

While the overwhelming response here to the Sadat visit was positive, some extremists in the occupied territories tried to get Palestinians to call a general strike. But the call, by the Palestine Liberation Organization, fizzled.

Extraordinary security measures attended the Sadat visit. Thousands of Israeli soldiers, policemen and security officials will be on constant alert during the visit.

Mr. Sadat's arrival time was arranged, at his request, so that it would not conflict with the Jewish Sabbath, which ended at sundown. As his plane flew low over Tel Aviv hundreds of bystanders in the streets applauded.

Tomorrow morning, Mr. Sadat will pray at Al Aksa Mosque, a sacred shrine, in the ancient walled city. He will take part with his Arab co-religionists in Id al-Adha, or Feast of Sacrifices.

Afterward, he will visit a Christian shrine, the Church of the Holy Sepulcher. He is then scheduled to visit Yad Vashem, Israel's intensely emotional memorial to the six million Jews killed by Germans during World War II.

Later in the day, Mr. Sadat will address the Israeli Parliament, and he is also expected to have private meetings with Mr. Begin.

The visit has had a tremendous impact on Israelis. At a soccer game today, a peanut vendor shouted, "Sadat shalom," a play on the traditional Jewish Sabbath greeting of "Shabbat Shalom," or "Peaceful Sabbath."

Whether the Sadat visit will mean substantive progress toward the convening of a Middle East peace conference at Geneva to settle the protracted and bitter Arab-Israeli impasse is not known. ■

ITALIAN PARLIAMENT APPROVES LAW PERMITTING ABORTION

ROME, May 18 (UPI)—The Italian Parliament today legalized abortion for the first time in this nation's history.

The bill was approved in the Senate by a vote of 160 to 148. The Chamber of Deputies had approved it last month by 308 votes to 275, despite a fierce campaign by the Vatican, which termed abortion "as grave an offense as homicide."

The new law permits state-subsidized abortion on demand in the first 90 days of pregnancy for any woman 18 years old or older who says childbirth would endanger her physical or mental health.

(cont'd. on next page)

Egyptian President Anwar el-Sadat (top left) waving to a crowd greeting him on arrival in Israel in 1977.

(cont'd. from previous page)

A medical certificate is required after more than 90 days, and girls under 18 must have the approval of a parent or guardian.

Passage of the legislation in the homeland of the Roman Catholic Church left only four Western European countries—Spain, Portugal, Ireland and Greece—that do not allow any form of abortion.

The Archbishop of Ravenna, Ersilio Tonini, reflected the church's anger over the new law by writing in the Vatican newspaper L'Osservatore Romano: "No vote can transform homicide into a right."

The small Radical Party had also fought the measure from the beginning—but for a different reason than the Vatican. The Radicals wanted to permit abortion at any stage of pregnancy and were pushing for a June referendum on the issue.

The governing Christian Democratic Party opposed the law but decided against a full-scale fight because it wanted to avoid a politically disruptive vote at a time of worsening terrorism, unemployment and inflation. ∎

Egyptian President Anwar el-Sadat, U.S. President Jimmy Carter, and Israeli Prime Minister Menachem Begin join hands after the Camp David Accords on September 17, 1978, in the East Room of the White House in Washington, DC.

NOVEMBER 6, 1978

After Camp David Summit, A Valley of Hard Bargaining

Hedrick Smith

WASHINGTON—"This is one of those rare, bright moments of human history," President Carter declared as President Anwar el-Sadat of Egypt and Prime Minister Menachem Begin of Israel embraced in celebration of the accords they signed Sept. 17, after 13 days and nights of negotiations at Camp David.

The brilliance of that moment was darkened almost at once by the angry reaction of most of the Arab world, the resignation of the Egyptian Foreign Minister, and a dispute between Mr. Carter and Mr. Begin over just what the agreement was on future Israeli settlements on the West Bank. Syrian President Hafez Assad patched up his quarrel with ultraradical Iraq and all the Arab states—except Egypt—met in Bagdad Nov. 2 to protest the Camp David accords, though they sounded less stridently anti-Sadat than expected.

But for all the nagging difficulties, the diplomatic momentum of Camp David persists. As a result, it appears that the political landscape of the Middle East will be irrevocably altered. For the central fact that has emerged is President Sadat's determination to sign a separate peace treaty with Israel. After he and Prime Minister Begin won the Nobel Peace Prize, diplomats began stage-managing peace negotiations so the treaty could be signed just before the Nobel ceremonies in Oslo Dec. 10.

Mr. Sadat's demand that Israel give back every inch of Egyptian soil put Mr. Begin under fire initially from hardliners in the Knesset. "I do not trust you," angrily shouted Moshe Shamir, long a close Begin ally. But Mr. Begin countered that peace with Cairo diminished the chance of war on all fronts. "If Egypt signs," he argued, "Syria cannot attack us because Syria knows it would be suicide." And ultimately, after 17 hours of debate ending at 4 a.m. on Sept. 28, that logic prevailed. By 84 to 19, the Knesset approved the Camp David accords, including the Egyptian demand that all Israeli settlements in Sinai be dismantled.

This cleared the way for the final round of peace negotiations. They opened with a colorful ceremony in the East Room of the White House Oct. 12. President Carter himself broke the chilliness among the negotiators. "You all look like you're at war instead of peace," he joked, and the diplomats relaxed. With the Americans pushing hard, the two sides moved ahead, then stalled over two issues—"thickening" of Israeli settlements on the West Bank and a link between the peace treaty and the future of the West Bank. Then the talks edged slowly toward initialing a treaty.

But that is only half—the easy half—of the promise of Camp David. The American strategy, echoing President Sadat's, is to count on the momentum of the Egyptian-Israeli negotiations to lure moderates like King Hussein of Jordan, West Bank Palestinians, and ultimately Saudi Arabia and possibly Syria into the peace process either directly or indirectly, leaving the militants of the Palestine Liberation Organization, Iraq and Libya out in the cold.

So far, however, that remains what Mr. Carter termed "the impossible dream." The Camp David accords call for a five-year period of interim self-rule on the West Bank and Gaza Strip with the Israeli military presence restricted to military strongpoints, establishment of a Palestinian self-governing authority and Jordan and the Palestinians joining the negotiations. ∎

After Two Conclaves, a Polish Pope

Pope John Paul II, 58, former Polish cardinal Karol Wojtyla, after being named the head of the Catholic Church in 1978.

The election of Pope John Paul II, a strong-willed, vigorous Polish prelate and the first non-Italian head of the Roman Catholic Church in 455 years, has given a new dimension to the Vatican's global political role.

By word and manner the new Pope, chosen on Oct. 16, has convinced church and foreign officials that he will be an "activist pope." "We have got a boss now, we haven't had one in a long time," one priest said.

Under a succession of Italian popes the Vatican leadership had become parochial and politically remote, tied to Italian issues and Italian politics.

John Paul I, who reigned only 33 days from Aug. 26 to Sept. 28, radiated warmth and simplicity, but was regarded as "politically naïve," a provincial Northern Italian prelate whose simple ambition was to become the Good Shepherd of Christendom.

Paul VI, who reigned from 1963 to last Aug. 6, was an intellectual, also from Northern Italy, and in the end old age and failing health made him distant and withdrawn. Even Pope John XXIII, for all his earthiness and his reforms, remained very Italian.

The new Pope, by contrast, on his inauguration day addressed the world's Catholics in 11 languages including Ukrainian and Lithuanian which significantly are languages of restless minorities in the Soviet Union.

The new Pope clearly is a "maximalist" in church terms. In his first statements he emphasized the role of the clergy and of the church as a militant organization. This is in the Polish tradition. By contrast, his predecessors stressed the universal community of the faithful—a sort of general Christian togetherness rather than the militancy of the Catholic institutions.

Theologically, the new pontiff is considered a conservative. His conservatism showed on the day of his election when he twice invoked the Virgin Mary. Liberal Catholic theologians have lately attenuated the cult of the Mother of Jesus to spare Protestant feelings. The new Pope also has backed such conservative positions as the ban on artificial contraceptives.

But he strongly backs the reforms of Vatican II, the great church assembly held from 1962 to 1965. The reforms include acceptance of the concept of freedom of conscience, celebration of mass in local languages instead of Latin and decentralization of the church government by giving a greater voice to national bishops' conferences.

At 58, the new Pope is younger than any of his predecessors since 1846 when Pius IX was elected at 54. At his inauguration he exuded physical vigor. At times, as he walked, he was swinging his crozier like an alpenstock. He is an athlete, a hiker and skier. There is talk of building a tennis court in the Vatican.

He has announced he will be a travelling pope. A visit to Poland next May is almost scheduled. Like Paul VI, he may want to spend his first Christmas as a pope in the Holy Land, and there will almost certainly be trips to Africa, Asia and Latin America. "It will be busy around here," a Vatican prelate said. ∎

THE AGONY OF CAMBODIA

Henry Kamm

BANGKOK– "The Cambodian no longer exists," said Hen Soth, speaking the soft French of the educated Indochinese. "Another animal—yes, animal—that I cannot recognize has taken his place."

The gentle, 38-year-old agronomist, pouring out for the first time his thoughts about the country from which he had just escaped, grew more melancholy as he thought about his wife and five children, the youngest only 1 month old, whom he had left behind. "We do not dare tell our children what Cambodia once was," he continued after a moment. "My oldest boy asked me to continue to teach him to read and write, now that there are no more schools. But I did not dare, and there are no books. I just told him to work harder, just a little harder, in the fields, so that he will survive." His oldest boy, Hen Soth said with an apologetic smile for saying something so sad, is 10 years old.

"We grow ignorance," the former head of a district agricultural extension service said. "No schools, no books, no newspapers, no radio, no television, no pagodas. There are no more traditions, no festivals. I don't know how it will continue. My culture is finished, I think."

"The ignorant have become an honorable and inviolable class," said Seng Hurl, a 38-year-old former Phnom Penh high-school French teacher and law student. "Ignorance is good for the country, they believe. Our children learn only to work, and most of the work they do is gathering dung and digging ditches."

Seng Hurl and Hen Soth are refugees from the pitiless class war that has transformed Cambodia, which the present regime has resumed Democratic Kampuchea, into a vast forced-labor camp. They fled because this class war is systematically killing those who are educated—and, in increasing number, their families with them. But they are a tiny minority among Cambodian refugees. Most are illiterate, and have fled simply because every Cambodian is constantly aware of death near at hand,

(cont'd. on next page)

61

INTERNATIONAL

(con'd. from previous page)

whether it be by summary execution, hunger or overwork.

With the country almost hermetically sealed off from the world, except for rare and carefully guided tours for carefully selected visitors, refugees who cross the heavily mined and closely guarded borders to Thailand and Vietnam are the only reliable source of information about life in Cambodia since the Khmer Rouge troops strode into Phnom Penh on April 17, 1975.

Their accounts of the forced evacuation of all Cambodian towns, of the herding of perhaps three million of Cambodia's seven million people into the countryside, of mass slaying and starvation, of mindless hatred and destruction, of orgies of book-burning, fires fed by musical instruments, television sets, radios and Buddha images, seemed incredible when I first heard them from refugees near the Thai border town of Aranyaprathet a few weeks after the Khmer Rouge victory. ∎

300 DEAD AT RELIGIOUS SECT'S JUNGLE TEMPLE

GEORGETOWN, Guyana—Information Minister Shirley Field Ridley reported that 300 to 400 bodies had been found today in the Guyana jungle camp of a California religious sect. Five Americans, including Representative Leo J. Ryan of California and three newsmen who had gone to investigate the group, were killed nearby on Saturday night.

Miss Ridley said the bodies had been found by troops who invaded the camp of the People's Temple at Jonestown in northwest Guyana. She said there were no marks of violence on the bodies, and that no living persons had been found in the camp so far.

About 1,100 persons, all of them Americans, were reported to have been living in the camp.

Stephen Katzaris, a psychologist from Potter Valley, Calif., who accompanied Mr. Ryan to Guyana in a futile attempt to get his daughter out of Jonestown, said the inmates of the camp had had mass suicide rehearsals and had signed undated suicide notes before leaving California for Guyana.

"They will all be dead by tomorrow," said Mr. Katzaris, whose son Anthony, 23 years old, was critically wounded in the attack in which Mr. Ryan was killed.

The Guyanese Government flew troops and policemen into the remote jungle area

Dead bodies lie around the compound of the People's Temple cult on November 18, 1978. The number of those who commited suicide by drinking cyanide-laced Kool Aid was initially reported between 300 and 400, but eventually was raised to approximately 900.

near the Venezuelan border. Officials and witnesses said the ambush was carried out by members of a California religious sect, the People's Temple, whose activities Mr. Ryan was investigating.

The 53-year-old Representative, a Democrat from California, was also trying to negotiate the release of some of the sect's members from what California constituents—including parents of sect members—had charged was "slave-like" bondage in which young men and women were held against their will in the jungle and subjected to bizarre sexual practices. The attack occurred about 115 miles northwest of this city, the capital, at the dirt airstrip of Port Kaituma, a small rural community about eight miles from Jonestown, a jungle commune of the People's Temple.

Survivors spoke about the terrifying violence of the incident, in which men emerged from a trailer truck with rifles blazing. One of the survivors from Mr. Ryan's party, Robert Flick, a producer for NBC, identified the assailants as being from the United States.

"They killed only the Americans," he said, his body shaking with shock. "When the people would fall wounded, the men would come and shoot them point blank in the head. There was absolutely no doubt. The people doing the shooting were all Americans."

"I did not see Congressman Ryan being killed, but I did see his body later, on the ground at the airstrip," Mr. Flick added.

Mr. Flick said Guyanese troops arrested nine people after the killings. A Guyanese Government spokesman in New York said that there had been one arrest, of Larry John Leyton, an American.

The Guyanese Government promised a "full investigation" and expressed its regret at the deaths of Representative Ryan and the others. ∎

OBITUARY

DECEMBER 9, 1978

GOLDA MEIR, 80, DIES IN JERUSALEM
ISRAELIS ACCLAIM 'STALWART LIONESS'

Paul Hofmann

Golda Meir in 1969.

JERUSALEM, Dec. 8— Golda Meir, a one-time teacher in Milwaukee who became Prime Minister of Israel, died this afternoon at the age of 80.

Mrs. Meir had been in Hadassah Hospital since August for treatment of an undisclosed back ailment. Early this week a hospital spokesman said she had also been suffering from liver infection and jaundice.

Hadassah Hospital doctors said later that Mrs. Meir had had leukemia for 12 years, including the years 1969-74, when she was Prime Minister. The hospital spokesman said that the illness was kept under control until recently, when viral hepatitis developed.

Death came at 4:30 p.m. The news was broadcast to the nation an hour and a half later, after strict observance of the Sabbath had begun.

There was little public reaction in the largely deserted streets of Jerusalem and other cities. Israelis who heard the news expressed deep grief and said the country had suffered a grave loss.

President Yitzhak Navon conveyed his sympathy and that of the nation to the family. "Your sorrow is that of all Israel," he said.

Shimon Peres, chairman of the Labor Party, in which Mrs. Meir had long been a leading figure, described her in a statement as "one of the great women in Jewish and world history" and as a "stalwart lioness." He recalled tributes paid to her by President Anwar el-Sadat of Egypt during his visit to Israel in November 1977 and added that "the Labor movement is in deep mourning." ∎

Khomeini Calls Shah 'Dethroned,' Vows to Take Over

NEAUPHLE-LE-CHATEAU, France. Jan. 19— Contending that today's demonstrations in Iran had "already dethroned" the Shah, the Ayatollah Ruhollah Khomeini said that "we will take power through the legitimate referendum of the streets.

"The arrival of the Shah on the throne was illegal. With a popular referendum the Shah has been dethroned. With pressure from the people we will take power."

As reports of the demonstrations came in by telephone and radio, aides at the Ayatollah's headquarters outside Paris were elated by the size of the turnout, which they saw as an important victory in their struggle to overthrow the Bakhtiar regime.

Asked whether he would agree to see the head of the regency council, Sayed Jalaleddin Tehrani, who is in Paris as an envoy of Prime Minister Shahpur Bakhtiar, the Ayatollah said he would "entertain no relations whatsoever with the regency council."

While holding out more strongly than ever for a complete political victory in Iran, the Ayatollah again tried to allay Western fears about the kind of government he wants to install in Iran, which he has done frequently in the recent past.

The Ayatollah said an Islamic government would favor "a modern Iran." But he said it would be a different kind of modernization from that pursued by the Shah, which he charged had "taken the country backward toward heroin, immorality and prostitution and which has killed the economy." ∎

Mohammed Reza Shah Pahlavi, the Shah of Iran, with his third wife Farah Diba and their son Reza in 1974.

A MILLION MARCHERS RALLY FOR KHOMEINI

R. W. Apple Jr.

Iranian religious and political leader Ayatollah Ruhollah Musavi Khomeini greets a group of his followers, Iran, 1979.

TEHERAN, Iran, Jan. 19—A great river of humanity flowed down Teheran's main street today as the people of the Iranian capital demonstrated their support for Ayatollah Ruhollah Khomeini's crusade for an Islamic government to replace the Government of Prime Minister Shahpur Bakhtiar.

But Dr. Bakhtiar insisted that he would carry on despite the evident hostility of much of the population. According to British reporters, Dr. Bakhtiar said in an interview that if Ayatollah Khomeini tried to set up an alternative government he would tell army commanders they had no further obligation to refrain from political action—apparently meaning that they would be free to mount a coup.

Although Shah Mohammed Riza Pahlevi left the country three days ago, probably forever, the demonstrators again sounded their familiar battle cry, "Marg bar Shah"—"Death to the Shah."

The Government of Prime Minister Bakhtiar was all but ignored, with only an occasional chant calling him the Shah's puppet. The crowd's enmity was evident, nevertheless, in slogans of support for an Islamic government and in tens of thousands of pictures of Ayatollah Khomeini, who has proclaimed the Bakhtiar regime illegal and has vowed to replace it with an Islamic republic.

Members of the committee that organized the procession said that the revolutionary council, a direct challenge to the nine-member regency council appointed by the Shah to act in his absence, would be named either tonight or tomorrow morning.

The procession in Teheran, which was accompanied by smaller demonstrations in provincial cities, again showed the tactical skill and the discipline of the opposition religious leaders. No injuries, indeed no untoward incidents of any kind, were reported during the six-hour parade.

The leaders had three purposes: to insure that the Shah would never return, to help bring down the Bakhtiar Government and to show support for Ayatollah Khomeini's plans for an Islamic republic.

The rich rubbed elbows with the poor, and radicals mingled with moderates. Three elegantly dressed women, each clutching a bag from an exclusive Paris shop, walked beside a group carrying placards honoring dead guerrillas of the Mujaheddin. The Mujaheddin, a non-Marxist urban guerrilla group that has claimed responsibility for killing eight Americans here since 1977, made a strong show of force.

Led by mullahs using portable loudspeakers, the demonstrators accompanied their words with clenched fists. They chanted such slogans as "God, Khomeini, the Koran—this is our national motto," "The monarchy is the root of corruption," and "Dear Ayatollah, we anxiously await your return."

One man, dressed in black, carried a miniature scaffold from which dangled a hangman's noose marked "The Shah."

Europe's Currency Ties to Start; Exchange Rates To Be Set Today

PAUL LEWIS

PARIS, March 12—A new monetary system for Europe will begin operation at the start of business tomorrow, leaders of the European Economic Community announced today at the outset of a two-day summit meeting here.

The system, whose inception had been delayed by France until last week, will lock currencies together in an attempt to create a more expansionary economic climate and lay the basis for Europe's eventual monetary unification with a single currency and a common economic policy.

The countries involved will intervene on the markets to defend their new fixed exchange rates against speculative attack by borrowing from a new $32 billion stabilization fund, financed by pooling 20 percent of all the Common Market members' gold and dollar reserves. The fund, which is designed to become the basis for a single European currency, could in time become a powerful gold-backed rival to the dollar as a medium for international trade and payments.

Britain is the only Common Market country that will not link its currency to the others at this time, but it will subscribe to the stabilization fund and enjoy limited borrowing rights.

Since all Common Market currencies have been fairly stable for the last few months, Europe's return to fixed exchange rates is unlikely to have any immediate impact on foreign exchange markets. ∎

MARGARET THATCHER IS PRIME MINISTER

R. W. Apple Jr.

Conservative leader Margaret Thatcher, the first woman to hold the office of prime minister of Great Britain, next to a campaign poster in 1979.

LONDON, May 4—Margaret Thatcher, who lived above her father's small-town grocery store for the first 18 years of her life, took office today as the Prime Minister of Britain.

For a nation that still thinks of Pitt and Churchill, Gladstone and Disraeli when it thinks of Prime Ministers, the election of a woman, the first to be Prime Minister in any European country, somehow came as a surprise even though it had been widely expected.

Mrs. Thatcher and the Conservative Party had swept to a solid victory in yesterday's general election, piling up a majority over all other parties combined of 43 seats in the House of Commons and dooming the Labor Government of James Callaghan.

Those who voted Mrs. Thatcher into office look to her to correct what they see as the errors and the excesses of socialism; those who opposed her see her as a sower of discord. As soon as the trend to the Tories was established early today, trade union leaders began warning of possible confrontations over restrictive new laws and cuts in job subsidies.

It was a day of high political drama, partly because of the novelty of having a woman as Prime Minister, and partly because of her pledges to set Britain on a new course by cutting income taxes, scaling down social services and reducing the role of the state in daily life.

Although Mrs. Thatcher won a mandate solid enough to keep her in power for a full five-year term, the swing to the Tories was not large enough to suggest a national demand for immediate action. Some politicians expected her to proceed cautiously at first.

For the Liberals, it was a frustrating election. They failed in their attempt to put together a centrist bloc of 20 to 50 members that would prevent the major parties from gaining an overall majority.

Their share of the national vote, however, was the third best they had achieved in the last 50 years, and they at least avoided the decimation that befell the Scottish National Party. The Nationalists, who two years ago seemed on the verge of winning a majority of the Scottish seats, lost nine seats, retaining only two.

In national terms, the swing to the Tories since the October 1974 election was 5.2 percent. But this was an exceptional British election in that there was no uniform voting pattern. Tory strength was concentrated in southern England; the further north the contests, the weaker they were, until in Scotland there was actually a swing to Labor.

Mrs. Thatcher used one of her favorite phrases before crossing the threshold of No. 10 today. "Now there's work to be done," she said. ∎

LORD MOUNTBATTEN KILLED AS HIS FISHING BOAT EXPLODES; I.R.A. FACTION SAYS IT SET BOMB

William Borders

MULLAGHMORE, Ireland, Aug. 27—Earl Mountbatten of Burma, one of the heroes of modern British history, was killed today when his fishing boat was blown up in the sea, apparently by terrorists of the Irish Republican Army.

The 79-year-old World War II hero died instantly in the explosion, which occurred a quarter mile off the coast, near his summer home here in the northwest of Ireland. A 14-year-old grandson and a 15-year-old passenger were also killed and four other passengers in the 29-foot boat, including a daughter, Lady Brabourne, were seriously injured.

The explosion this morning reverberated like thunder through this peaceful little seaside village. A witness who saw it from the shore said, "The boat was there one minute and the next minute it was like a lot of matchsticks floating on the water."

In Belfast, Northern Ireland, the Provisional wing of the Irish Republican Army issued a statement taking responsibility for the killing, which it called "an execution," and vowed to continue the "noble struggle to drive the British intruders out of our native land."

Lord Mountbatten, who never had any particular connection with the sectarian battle over Northern Ireland, was an uncle of Prince Philip, a cousin of Queen Elizabeth, and former chief of the British defense staff and the last Viceroy of India. His murder, probably the boldest and most dramatic act of the long terrorist campaign here, sent waves of shock and indignation across both Britain and Ireland.

Prince Charles, discussing Lord Mountbatten earlier this year, said, "I admire him almost more than anybody else I know."

Although the Irish Government immediately expressed its outrage and promised a diligent investigation, which was promptly begun, the killing was likely to strain further the relationship between Britain and Ireland. It also raised new concerns for the security of the Pope, who is scheduled to visit Ireland next month on his way to the United States.

The goal of the terrorists is a united Ireland. The almost exclusively Roman Catholic I.R.A. and its splinter groups are struggling to end British rule in the Protestant-dominated north. The majority in Northern Ireland is

The Funeral of Lord Louis Mountbatten (Earl Mountbatten of Burma) in Westminster Abbey, in 1979.

loyal to Britain and resists reunification with Ireland, which is 96 percent Roman Catholic.

In recent years, the Irish Republican terrorists have concentrated their attacks on the police, the army and other Government figures. ■

MOTHER TERESA WINS PEACE PRIZE

Frank J. Prial

STOCKHOLM, Oct. 17—Mother Teresa of Calcutta, a Roman Catholic nun of Albanian stock who has cared for the poor and sick in India for more than 30 years, was named the winner today of the 1979 Nobel Peace Prize.

"I am unworthy," Mother Teresa said in Calcutta on hearing that she had been selected by the five-member Nobel Committee of the Norwegian Parliament in Oslo.

But, she said, because she is "more aware of the condition of the poor," she plans to use the prize money, the equivalent of $190,000, to build more homes for the destitute, "especially for the lepers."

The Nobel Committee's announcement said:

"This year, the world has turned its attention to the plight of children and refugees, and these are precisely the categories for whom Mother Teresa has for many years worked so selflessly."

Mother Teresa, who is 69 years old, has been a candidate for the Peace Prize ever since her work first gained worldwide recognition more than two decades ago. Even so, she was a surprise winner today.

Mother Teresa refuses direct financial assistance from the Indian Government but has accepted an occasional gift of land for a new project.

The Nobel Committee said today that it had decided to honor her as much for her organizing and managerial skills as for her compassion and dedication to the poor. ■

Mother Teresa in 1979.

A U.S. hostage (blindfolded) November 8, 1979, is paraded by his captors in the compound of the U.S. Embassy Teheran, Iran.

NOVEMBER 5, 1979

TEHERAN STUDENTS SEIZE U.S. EMBASSY AND HOLD HOSTAGES

TEHERAN, Iran, Nov. 4—Moslem students stormed the United States Embassy in Teheran today, seized about 90 Americans and vowed to stay there until the deposed Shah was sent back from New York to face trial in Iran.

There were no reports of casualties in the takeover of the embassy building, although witnesses said some of the several hundred attackers were armed.

A student spokesman told reporters at the embassy that 100 hostages had been taken and that 90 percent of them were Americans. He said the embassy staff was being treated well.

In the holy city of Qum, a spokesman for Ayatollah Ruhollah Khomeini said the occupation of the embassy had the revolutionary leader's personal support.

Iranian Revolutionary Guards at the embassy gates did not intervene during the attack, which came as tens of thousands of people marched through the streets of the Iranian capital on the first anniversary of the shooting of students at Tehran University by the Shah's security forces.

The students who invaded the embassy compound wore badges with the portrait of Ayatollah Khomeini, and they put up a banner saying: "Khomeini struggles, Carter trembles."

The embassy takeover followed a series of strongly anti-American speeches by Ayatollah Khomeini, who said recently he hoped reports that the former Shah, Mohammed Riza Pahlevi, was dying of cancer were true. The Shah, who was deposed in the revolution led by the Ayatollah last January, is being treated for cancer at New York Hospital-Cornell Medical Center.

The official Iranian radio broadcast a statement by the Islamic Society of University Teachers and Students commending the embassy takeover. "We defend the capture of this imperialist embassy, which is a center for espionage," the statement said.

This was the second time the embassy has been taken over since the revolution. Gunmen believed to be dissident revolutionaries invaded the embassy last Feb. 14, killing one Iranian and taking 101 people hostage, including Ambassador William H. Sullivan and 19 Marine guards.

The takeover came when both the Iranian and United States Governments appeared to be seeking improved relations. ■

67

INTERNATIONAL

DECEMBER 2, 1979

THE BLUNT CASE:
A LIFE DEVOTED TO BEAUTY AND TREACHERY

Hilton Kramer

A mong the art historians of our time, only a very few have attained the eminence of the British scholar and connoisseur Anthony Blunt. For many years the director of the Courtland Institute of Art and professor of art history at the University of London, Surveyor of the Queen's Pictures at Windsor Castle, occupant of many other positions of high academic distinction and author of numerous works in the fields of French, Italian and British art history, Mr. Blunt has long been regarded as a model of his profession, and he has wielded a considerable influence on several generations of art historians on both sides of the Atlantic.

It therefore came as a special shock to those who have followed his work—and that would include just about everyone with a professional interest in the history of European art since the Renaissance—to discover that this distinguished figure had served for some years as a secret agent of the Soviet Union and had thus been a traitor to his own country. Even in a century as much given over to political treachery as ours, Mr. Blunt's is an unusual, if not indeed a unique, case. Certainly nothing like it has ever before occurred at this level of distinction in the international community of art historical scholarship.

Most of us are inclined to suppose that a lifetime devoted to humanistic study carries a certain meaning—that, at the very least, it represents a certain commitment to the free and open life of the mind, and to the fundamental ethos of the liberal culture that supports it. On the other hand, an allegiance to Soviet totalitarianism, with its well-known history of coercion and terror, and its total debasement of all intellectual standards, is clearly understood by most of us to be incompatible with such a commitment. Yet, the revelations of the past few weeks have shown that Mr. Blunt—now identified as the so-called "fourth man" in the Burgess-Maclean-Philby spy ring in the employ of the Comintern—has for most of his professional career lived on remarkably easy terms with this fundamental contradiction. Inevitably, the effect is to put into question—and ultimately, I think, to diminish—our sense of what it means to be a great art scholar. It suggests, at the very least, that this vocation need have nothing to do with either moral intelligence or personal probity.

It had long been known, of course, that Mr. Blunt was a Marxist of some sort. In the 1930s, when he served as art critic for the weekly Spectator, he wrote openly from a Marxist point of view. And when "Art and Architecture in France, 1500-1700" was published in this country in 1954, Clement Greenberg—reviewing the book in The New York Times Book Review—observed that "surprisingly, he spells out the political and social background in Marxist characters." But Marxism of this sort has been a commonplace of intellectual discourse in this century, and few readers had any reason to suppose that, in Mr. Blunt's use of it, it was anything but a disinterested instrument of historical analysis.

Not that he was exactly above suspicion even before last month's revelations. But what were such suspicions worth when weighed against the "benignly approving" glance of Kenneth Clark? It was simply assumed—incorrectly, as we now know—that a man of Mr. Blunt's social and intellectual credentials could not conceivably be guilty of a criminal or even a dishonorable act against his own country.

That he is guilty—and not only of his own treachery but of recruiting others for the same detestable purpose—is now established, and we are all obliged to adjust ourselves to this phenomenon of a first-class mind so thoroughly divided against itself, and make what sense of it that we can.

Anthony Blunt, ca. 1979.

Through much of the 1970s, it was the winter of economic discontent. The decade didn't start off that way. On May 27, 1970, the Dow-Jones industrial index registered what was then its largest one-day surge on record: 32.04 points, a 5 percent gain that in early 2013 would have been equivalent of a 700-point rise. The increase left the stock market still well below its peak from four years earlier. But at least it suggested that investors were ready to shake off a gloom that had Wall Street bears ascendant for an uncomfortably long stretch.

An unemployment line in the early 1970s.

Optimism proved short-lived. With inflation clinging stubbornly to a disturbing 6 percent a year—a legacy of Vietnam War miscalculations that Americans could have both guns and butter, and endure no pain—President Richard M. Nixon took drastic action. In August 1971 he imposed a new economic order, most conspicuously in the form of a 90-day freeze on wages and prices. It put a cap on pretty much everything, from worker salaries to apartment rents, with corporations asked to impose the same discipline on shareholder dividends. That these restrictions were imposed by a Republican president made them all the more remarkable. So much for cherished concepts of the free market's inviolability.

The Nixon measures helped in the short run. Inflation dropped to a more bearable 3 percent or so. But it didn't stay down there for long. The economy, both America's and the world's, would soon be jolted by one-two punches known as "the oil shocks."

The first wallop came in 1973 when Saudi Arabia, the world's largest oil producer, imposed an embargo on the United States as punishment for its having rearmed Israel during the so-called Yom Kippur War, which erupted in October that year. The second energy blow fell in 1979 after an Islamic revolution unseated the Shah of Iran, who had effectively been installed by the Americans a couple of decades earlier.

In each instance, the result was immediate dislocation. Crude oil prices rose sharply, as did those at gasoline pumps. Across the country, pumps ran dry, though many people were unsure if the shortages were genuine or the result of oil-company manipulations. In any event, nerves frayed. Gas stations limited customers to a few gallons each. Many operators had to close for lack of fuel deliveries. Blocks-long lines formed at those that remained open. Panic buying was epidemic. Fist fights became routine.

Looking down at the interior of the New York Stock Exchange in the 1979.

Customers stock up on gas at a station in Suffolk County, N.Y., while an attendant at a station in Chestnut Hill, Mass. uses flags to indicate the level of supply.

By decade's end, the economy was reeling, and President Jimmy Carter seemed flailing in his search for a semblance of normalcy. Unemployment was distressingly high. Inflation and interest rates both ran to double digits. While many Americans felt that Carter had fallen victim to circumstances beyond his control, they were in an unforgiving mood. Polls in mid-1979 showed that barely one in four voters approved of his performance.

The marquee at the Whittier Towers in Detroit, Michigan, in the late 1970s.

His undoing—indeed, he failed to win re-election the following year—was reflected in a phrase that entered common usage in the '70s. This was an economic indicator that added up the inflation rate and the unemployment rate. At its 1970's worst, it exceeded 20 percent. "The misery index," it was called, and it clung to the president no less disastrously than if a cruel prankster had slapped on his back a sign that said, "Kick me."

STOCKS SET SINGLE-DAY RECORD

Leonard Sloane

Stock brokers at the New York Stock Exchange in the early 1970s.

The stock market, struggling to fight its way out of one of the deepest slumps in history, soared yesterday to the largest one-day advance ever recorded.

As measured by the most closely-watched indicator—the Dow-Jones industrial index of 30 blue-chip stocks on the New York Stock Exchange—stock prices spurted 32.04 points to 663.20. The previous record gain had occurred on Nov. 26, 1963, the Tuesday after the funeral of President John F. Kennedy, when the index leaped 32.03 points.

Bond prices, which had been declining almost without interruption for about eight weeks, also rose, although not as impressively as Big Board stocks. Stocks on the American Stock Exchange turned in their best daily performance in almost eight years, while over-the-counter issues moved sharply higher, too.

Despite all the gains achieved yesterday, the gain was only a small step forward in the midst of a severe bear market. For the 32.04-point advance just managed to recover the 31.01-point loss registered on the index during the first two days of this week.

Until yesterday's bullish performance on the corner of Wall and Broad Streets, many leaders in the investment field had been attributing the decline to such factors as the war in Vietnam and Cambodia, the social unrest at home and the apparent lack of Washington's success in curbing inflation.

Within the financial community, a variety of possible reasons were widely put forward to explain the surge, which came at a time when investor and broker morale was low. The first reason was hopes had been raised during the day that last night's meeting between the President and business and financial leaders would produce a major announcement on economic controls of foreign-policy changes.

Whether the day's dramatic recovery will start the market back on the long path upward remains to be seen.

Yesterday's activity, as welcome as it was by most Americans involved in the stock market, still represents only a partial return to the level around the time of the President's inauguration. The upward movement was broad-based, with both investment-grade issues and glamour stocks involved. All of the issues on the Dow-Jones industrial index advanced, with 25 of the 30 rising more than a point.

GENERAL MOTORS AND UNION REACH TERMS FOR PACT

Jerry M. Flint

United Auto Workers President Leonard Woodcock shaking hands with a worker during a tour of the Terex Division plant of General Motors in the early 1970s.

DETROIT, Nov. 11—The United Automobile Workers and the General Motors Corporation agreed today on a package of money and fringe benefits designed to end the union's eight-week strike.

The union, however, delayed approval of the pact, and there was some rank-and-file opposition to the agreement.

Details of the three-year agreement were not disclosed by the union, but the following provisions became known:

- A first-year raise, for the typical worker, of 13 percent, or 51 cents an hour, and a raise of 3 percent, or 14 cents an hour, in each of the second and third years.
- A cost-of-living escalator clause without a ceiling, with pay adjustments annual at first but quarterly starting in March, 1972.
- An early retirement program that gives a $500-a-month pension to workers with 30 years of service at the age of 58 years at the start of the contract, with the age dropping to 56 by the end of the contract.

The raise, not counting the inflation protection, will increase wages about 20 percent over the three years, and the inflation protection could raise pay 10 percent more.

Earl Bramblett, the company's chief negotiator, said that the contract cost was "substantially more than the anticipated increase in productivity of the country"—which averages 3 percent a year—and was thus by definition inflationary.

There were other benefits reported, such as a fourth week of vacation for workers with 20 years of service, but there was no dental care plan, one of the union's goals.

The heart of worker opposition comes from the union's failure to win a full "30 and out" retirement, meaning retirement with a $500 monthly pension after 30 years of work with no age minimum.

Jack Wagner, president of U.A.W. Local 599 at Flint, Mich., who is a leader in the 30-and-out movement, said he would ask his local to reject the contract. "This is an old game. They keep you out eight weeks and they think you're going to buy anything," Mr. Wagner complained.

It will be at least several weeks before

General Motors is back in full production.

Contracts with the Ford Motor Company and the Chrysler Corporation are still to be negotiated, but they usually follow the pattern of the contracts of the strike target company, which was General Motors this year.

The strike has been the costliest in the industry's history. In terms of production, wages, taxes and supplier contracts, the 130,000 cars and trucks lost each day totaled $164 million, or about $7 billion over the eight weeks. ∎

280,000 Miners Strike in Britain

Alvin Shuster

LONDON, Jan. 9—Britain's coal miners, most of whom earn less than $80 a week, went on their first national strike in 46 years today.

Some 280,000 miners, whose leaders demanded pay increases of up to 47 percent, decided to strike after the National Coal Board, which runs the nationalized industry, refused to offer more than just under 8 percent. Officials of the Coal Board and the National Union of Mineworkers predicted a long strike.

The coal miners, part of a declining but still important industry here, have seen their ranks drop over the years as Britain turned increasingly to oil, gas and electricity for fuel. In the last 10 years, for example, the number of miners has dropped from 536,000 to 280,000 and the number of working pits from 669 to 290.

About half of the nation's coal production is now used to produce power. Much of the rest goes to industry, with only about 10 percent of the output being used in private homes.

Not since 1926 has Britain faced a strike by all her coal miners, although there have been many local strikes since then, usually lasting a few days. Resentment has been rising among the miners, who feel it is time the Government rewarded them for cooperating without serious complaint over the years as pits closed and men were dismissed.

Striking miners march on Westminster to lobby Parliament in 1971.

"Our men spend all day in dangerous and unhealthy jobs underground," said a union official. "Yet their daughters, working as secretaries, earn nearly as much as they do. It is no wonder the men are angry."

The union says it is striking not only for the miners but also for the trade union movement. So far, however, other unions have withheld decisions on whether to back the strike by refusing to transport coal already mined.

The union has demanded a raise of $20.80 a week for the lowest-paid surface worker, and $13 a week more for the highest-paid men underground. The Coal Board has offered about $5.20 a week for virtually all miners, with $2.60 more a week later if productivity increases.

So far, there has been no panic among coal users. A spokesman for the Central Electricity Generating Board said that coal stocks at the power stations have never been higher at this time of year. In general, the estimate is that the impact of the strike will not be felt for from four to eight weeks. ∎

AUGUST 16, 1971

Nixon Orders 90-Day Wage-Price Freeze

James M. Naughton

WASHINGTON, Aug. 15—President Nixon charted a new economic course tonight by ordering a 90-day freeze on wages and prices, requesting Federal tax cuts and making a broad range of domestic and international moves designed to strengthen the dollar.

In a 20-minute address, telecast and broadcast nationally, the President appealed to Americans to join him in creating new jobs, curtailing inflation and restoring confidence in the economy through "the most comprehensive new economic policy to be undertaken in this nation in four decades."

Some of the measures Mr. Nixon can impose temporarily himself and he asked for tolerance as he does. Others require Congressional approval and—although he proposed some policies that his critics on Capitol Hill have been urging upon him—will doubtless face long scrutiny before they take effect.

Mr. Nixon imposed a ceiling on all prices, rents, wages and salaries—and asked corporations to do the same voluntarily on stockholder dividends—under authority granted to him last year by Congress but ignored by the White House until tonight.

The President asked Congress to speed up by one year the additional $50 personal income tax exemption scheduled to go into effect on Jan. 1, 1973, and to repeal, retroactive to today, the 7 percent excise tax on automobile purchases.

He also asked for legislative authority to grant corporations a 10 percent tax credit for investing in new American-made machinery and equipment and pledged to introduce in Congress next January other tax proposals that would stimulate the economy.

Combined with new cuts in Federal spending, the measures announced by Mr. Nixon tonight represented a major shift in his Administration's policy on the economy.

The program issued tonight at the White House came with an unaccustomed suddenness, reflecting both domestic political pressures on the President to improve the economy before the 1972 elections and growing international concern over the stability of the dollar.

"Prosperity without war requires action on three fronts," Mr. Nixon declared in explaining his new policies. "We must create more and better jobs; we must stop the rise in the cost of living; we must protect the dollar from the attacks of international money speculators."

Political pressures for some form of an incomes policy have been building for weeks. Public opinion polls have certified concern over unemployment and prices as the No. 1 domestic issue.

HIGH POLITICS OF MONEY

Leonard Silk

U.S. Secretary of the Treasury, John B. Connally, in 1971.

"Whenever money is involved, gemütlichkeit disappears," says Walter Scheel, the West German Foreign Minister, who has been seeking to rebuild a spirit of cooperation among the Common Market nations—toward each other and toward the United States. The Europeans are prepared to move a considerable distance to meet Secretary of the Treasury John B. Connally's terms—provided that the United States is prepared to make its own contribution to a monetary settlement. To the Europeans, the American contribution must involve two elements: a devaluation of the dollar in terms of gold by 5 to 7 percent, and an American agreement to drop the 10 percent surcharge as soon as currencies are realigned.

The Europeans insist that they are really not asking too much. They need the dollar devaluation, they say, to quiet public opinion at home. But the real reason they need it is to satisfy the French Government, which has planted its feet in concrete against changing the value of the franc in terms of gold.

The French have said, however, that they would hold still for a moderate American devaluation.

The Europeans think it is only fair that the United States remove its import surcharge, since it was adopted unilaterally in violation of American commitments to the General Agreements on Tariffs and Trade—and was described by President Nixon as a temporary measure.

Of all the European governments, the West German Government is ready to move fastest and furthest to end the threat of a monetary and trade war with the United States.

The Germans regard the economic issue as too important to be left to their economic and finance ministers—especially since Karl Schiller and Valéry Giscard d'Estaing are involved in a bitter dispute, which has become personal.

"We cannot continue our détente with Eastern Europe," says Foreign Minister Scheel, "unless Europe's ties with the United States are strengthened."

Fears are expressed in a number of European capitals these days that a withdrawal of American forces from Europe will be the prelude to a "Finlandization" of Europe.

Willy Brandt, Chancellor of Germany is determined to do all he can to prevent a trade war from breaking out between Europe and the United States. In this he has the support of German industry. Aides to Mr. Brandt say that the German Government has felt no pressure from industry for retaliation against the United States.

They need the dollar devaluation . . .

The Germans are willing to go far to oblige the Americans on the monetary, trade, and burden-sharing fronts to avoid serious damage to their foreign policy.

However, some American observers in Germany believe that the Germans are delaying unwisely in proposing increases in their offset arrangements to help support United States troops stationed in their country.

The Germans are seeking to avoid an open quarrel with the French. Mr. Scheel says, "France's first aim is to expand industrial production. Here in Germany, our main aim is economic stabilization—the checking of inflation. This yields differences in monetary policy. But we shall try to come to a common position."

Lacking an American move to devalue the dollar, it will be difficult or impossible to achieve that common position.

The international monetary game of "chicken" is growing too risky on all sides.

U.S. ACTS TO PROP VALUE OF DOLLAR

H. Erich Heinemann

In a major change of policy, the United States Government intervened in the foreign exchange markets yesterday to protect the value of the dollar.

The Government's action, which was not announced, took the form of heavy selling by the Federal Reserve Bank of New York of the German mark at declining prices.

At the same time, the Government indicated that, as needed, it would reactivate its reciprocal borrowing arrangements with foreign central banks, which have been suspended for almost a year.

The sales of German marks represented the first significant intervention of this type since last Aug. 15, when President Nixon formally severed the link between the dollar and gold, and set in motion the events that, in time, led to the devaluation of the dollar.

The move, which represented a reversal of the policy followed by former Secretary of the Treasury John B. Connally, appeared to be designed to provide a show of cooperation among the major financial powers, and thus to calm the recent turmoil in world financial markets.

As part of his new economic policy, President Nixon suspended agreements last Aug. 15. At the time, there were some $11.7 billion in credit lines available under these arrangements, of which about $3 billion was actually in use.

Arthur F. Burns, the Federal Reserve chairman, said that "we are moving to play our part in restoring order in the foreign exchange markets and to do our part in upholding the Smithsonian Agreement. We are doing this entirely on our own initiative and not at anybody's request."

To allay any doubts in the foreign exchange markets, he added that the selling of German marks yesterday was "on the account of the United States Government, not the Bundesbank"—which is the West German central bank. Foreign exchange traders in the New York market estimated that the equivalent of at least $50 million was involved in yesterday's selling of German marks.

The sales had the effect of depressing the price of the German currency—which was already under some downward pressure even before the Federal Reserve acted—and thus increasing the value of the dollar in relation to the mark.

But market analysts said that the importance of the Federal Reserve's selling transcended by far the amount of money involved.

In recent months, foreign governments have countered successive waves of dollar weakness in part by erecting an ever-widening net of direct controls over the movement of international capital. Washington's move yesterday appeared to be as concerned with forestalling the further spread of these controls—which could harm the growth of world trade—as with maintaining the value of the dollar.

Since last August, the official attitude of the United States—at least in rough paraphrase—has been that the international value of the dollar was a matter primarily of concern to foreigners.

Should the dollar depreciate in relation to foreign currencies, the Administration has in effect argued, so much the better, for this would provide a long-run advantage for American exports.

But the passive role that the United States has assumed has become a source of irritation to other governments, and of unsettling in the foreign exchange markets.

Most importantly, it has cast doubt on the willingness of the Nixon Administration to take the initiative in the pending long-range negotiations for reform in the international monetary system.

The effect of the Federal Reserve action was to give additional momentum to a downward move that had already started in some of the major European currencies. ■

Kissinger Fails to Sway Saudis from Oil Embargo

Juan De Onis

RIYADH, Saudi Arabia, Nov. 9—Secretary of State Kissinger has been unable to obtain a relaxation of Saudi Arabia's oil embargo on the United States but he has reportedly convinced King Faisal of his sincerity in the search for peace in the Middle East.

During a 15-hour stopover here yesterday and early today, according to Saudi officials and American diplomats, Mr.

Kissinger was told by King Faisal and other Saudi officials that oil production cuts imposed since Oct. 17 would not be relaxed until there was a physical withdrawal of Israeli forces from Arab lands occupied during the 1967 war.

The American and Saudi sources said that correction of the cease-fire lines in the Sinai would not in itself be sufficient to bring resumption of Saudi Arabia's major oil production at prewar levels.

No Saudi Arabian crude oil is being shipped to the United States or to refineries anywhere in the world that supply American customers, including the United States Navy's Sixth and Seventh Fleets, in the Mediterranean and the Far East.

While Saudi Arabia, the oil giant of the Arabian peninsula, has seen her long-standing friendship with the United States go into a severe crisis as a result of the war

(cont'd. on next page)

King Faisal of Saudi Arabia in 1973.

(cont'd. from previous page)

that broke out last month, from all indications here there has been no irreparable breach so far.

And there is a strong desire for an agreement that will save a relationship in which the United States has large economic and security interests. The billion-dollar Arabian-American Oil Company here is the largest single United States overseas investment.

The conservative, anti-Communist Saudi Arabian monarchy, which receives an annual income from oil exports of close to $5 billion, has been a major moderating influence against revolutionary Arab movements. The

armed forces are primarily equipped and trained by the United States.

The crisis in relations came when the news reached here during the fighting between Israel, Egypt and Syria last month that President Nixon was asking Congress for $2.2 million in purchasing funds to resupply Israel, followed by a publicized airlift to Israel.

King Faisal is reported by a member of the royal family to have reacted with "bitter disappointment." An American source said the United States move "drove the Saudi Arabians up a wall."

Since this desert kingdom is the world's largest oil exporter, her oil cuts led the way

in reducing Arab oil supplies by more than five million barrels a day.

In its use of "oil weapons," Saudi Arabia has acted in close cooperation with President Anwar el-Sadat of Egypt, with whom King Faisal planned the Arab strategy for the Middle East war.

The political calculations of the Arabs were that the outbreak of war, involving the Soviet Union in support of Egypt and Syria, and the crisis produced in industrial countries by oil production cutbacks would generate enough alarm in Western countries to put pressure on Israel to withdraw from occupied Arab lands. ∎

DECEMBER 2, 1973

U.S. OIL 'SELF SUFFICIENCY' BY 1980 UNFEASIBLE

Ernest Holsendolph

The elements that make up today's energy emergency have been around for some time, but it took the Arab oil embargo to reveal them starkly and cause broad concern from Main Street to the White House.

Put simply, the United States uses far more energy daily than it produces domestically. President Nixon, launching what he calls Operation Independence, has promised to move toward what he calls "self sufficiency" in energy by 1980.

But most experts feel that, despite our best efforts, the United States is likely to remain dependent upon oil imports to make up the gap between domestic supplies and sharply rising demand.

The nation, of course, remains richly endowed with energy-producing natural resources. The United States has the world's largest coal reserves, which will come increasingly into use as environmentally sound ways to use coal are found.

Still the world leader in petroleum production, this nation is also likely to find new supplies of oil and gas in hard-to-reach places, such as off-shore.

The United States grew up on a diet of cheap and plentiful energy that fueled industrial expansion and contributed directly to a quality of life unequaled in history.

This has led to a wasteful attitude toward natural resources: Homes are heated

to 80 degrees in the winter, then cooled below 70 in the summer. Office buildings are lit up all night so that the cleaning staff can tidy up one room at a time. Ten-mile trips are made in gasoline-devouring cars to buy a pack of cigarettes.

But all this may change. Undoubtedly the sudden need for more efficient use of energy, which had been preached by analysts for months and now is a national priority, may affect habits and long-term energy consumption.

A sign at a gas station announcing temporary fuel rationing, 1974.

In a study of energy supply and demand, published since the Arabs announced their embargo, A. G. Becker & Co. points out that future demand may be related to four major variables: economics activity or growth in the gross national product, the cost of energy, population growth and environmental controls.

Other variables depend on how swiftly efficient use may be brought about. It Is reasonable to expect better insulation for buildings, improved heating and cooling systems and more efficient industrial plants and equipment—particularly as the cost of fuel rises.

One of the most prominent areas where greater efficiency may be realized is in transportation, which uses fully 24 percent of consumed energy. Here smaller and more efficient cars, already in public demand, seem sure to moderate projected gasoline demand.

A medium projection of the economy's growth has been 4.2 percent, which would indicate a consumption of 102.6 quadrillion B.T.U.'s by 1980.

"We are confronted for the first time with a world where demand may be constrained by supply," said Paul F. Donovan, director of the Office of Energy Research and Development Policy of the National Science Foundation.

To meet growing energy needs, the nation's experts foresee a sharp growth in nuclear power supply sometime after 1980, and expanded, sophisticated use of coal, an abundant national resource. These growing sources of energy must largely compensate for an anticipated decline in domestic oil production in the 48 contiguous states and sluggish expansion of domestic natural gas production.

Dr. Donovan of the National Science Foundation said he foresees no breakthrough that can quickly bring into play the newer sources of energy; solar energy, coal liquefaction, coal gasification, shale oil or even nuclear power.

In the long run, especially as the price of energy continues to climb, coal liquefaction and gasification, the extraction of heavy oil and the use of tar sands and oil shale seem certain to pay off.

But nearly no one sees an era in the offing when the nation can be fully independent of imported energy. ∎

OCTOBER 9, 1974

Franklin Found Insolvent by U.S. and Taken Over

John H. Allan

The Franklin National Bank was declared insolvent yesterday in the largest bank failure in American banking history.

The institution was immediately taken over by the European-American Bank and Trust Company, a New York State-chartered entity owned by six of the largest banks in Europe.

Under the take-over agreement worked out with regulatory authorities, no depositor will suffer any losses.

Franklin, in effect, was pressed to insolvency by the Federal Reserve Bank of New York, which had lent it almost $1.77 billion. On Monday, the Federal Reserve told James E. Smith, Controller of the Currency, that it "would not be in the public interest" to continue to lend the Franklin money.

For the Franklin National Bank, once the pride of Long Island with some $4.5 billion in assets that made it the 20th largest bank in the country, the action yesterday ended a five-month effort to remain alive and independent.

The Franklin National Bank's fundamental problem, Government officials said yesterday, was bad management. This fault was exacerbated this spring when the bank incurred large foreign-exchange trading losses that eventually were estimated at nearly $46 million.

Yesterday's take-over, rumored for weeks, was effected swiftly during the afternoon after the bank closed at its normal 3 p.m. hour.

Basically, European-American agreed to take over slightly more than $1.7 billion, mostly comprising Franklin deposits, plus $1.58 billion of loans and securities. For this package it paid a combined premium of $125 million.

The F.D.I.C. took over loans to Franklin from the Federal Reserve Bank of New York—borrowings that had reached more than $1.7 billion, the reserve bank disclosed yesterday. The deposit insurance agency will also take over about $2 billion of less-desirable Franklin loans and securities and repay the $1.7 billion to the Federal Reserve Bank over a three-year period.

This agreement avoids any need for payments to Franklin's 620,000 depositors by the F.D.I.C. and it avoids financial loss or delay to approximately 6,000 Franklin depositors whose accounts exceed the $20,000 deposit insurance limit. ∎

OCTOBER 21, 1975

U.S. AND RUSSIA AGREE ON 5 YEARS OF GRAIN EXPORTS

William Robbins

WASHINGTON, Oct. 20—The White House announced today a five-year agreement with the Soviet Union, effective next Oct. 1, under which the Russians would buy six to eight million tons of American grain a year.

At the same time, President Ford lifted a two-month moratorium on further grain sales to the Russians this year. Representatives of United States companies are in Moscow even now seeking to close additional deals, according to trade sources.

The White House also disclosed a letter of intent, signed today in Moscow, to conclude an agreement to buy up to 200,000 barrels a day of Russian oil and petroleum products.

It was clear that a price for the Russian oil was continuing to hold up agreement. The United States had sought a discount to put pressure on the Arab producing countries, and the Russians have reportedly continued to refuse such concessions.

Frank Zarb, administrator of the Federal Energy Administration, said the price remained among the "major" features to be worked out and that the United States would insist on "favorable" rates.

(cont'd. on next page)

(cont'd. from previous page)

President Ford, in a statement, praised the conclusion of the grain agreement, asserting:

"The long-term agreement signed in Moscow today promotes American economic stability. It represents a positive step in our relations with the Soviet Union."

The grain agreement accomplishes an objective of the United States, which sought to minimize the impact on consumer prices of erratic Russian buying on the world grain markets while realizing the foreign-exchange benefits of further exports to the Soviet Union.

While the consumer price effect of the long-term agreement could not be determined, William L. Seidman, the President's economic counselor, said it would be "negligible."

The Joint Economic Committee of Congress said in a study released today that sales made thus far could raise consumer prices 1 percent and that further sales of grain and soybeans could have an additional impact of 1.4 percent.

Under the terms of the agreement, the United States is committed to supply the Russians up to eight million tons a year unless the total United States grain crop should fall below 225 million tons. American production has not fallen that low in the last 15 years, not even during the drought of 1974.

In a briefing at the White House, Secretary of Agriculture Earl L. Butz said the agreement would have a stabilizing effect on the American economy. He said it would allow farmers to plan for full production and to make investments more confidently in machinery and labor.

Mr. Butz said that amount was well within the United States capacity after allowing for both domestic needs and commitments to regular export customers. He said the possible effect on United States consumer prices would be "negligible." ∎

PEUGEOT RAISES CITROEN HOLDING

The Peugeot automobile and industrial group announced in Paris yesterday that it had increased its holdings in Citroën, S.A. by 90 percent through the purchase of the Michelin tire group's majority interest. Peugeot, in an agreement concluded in 1974, was due to extend its 38.2 percent interest in Citroën, S.A. to 51 percent this month. At Michelin's request, Peugeot acquired all of Citroën's shares, constituting 53.2 percent of the total.

Under the 1974 accord, Peugeot already had technical and commercial direction over Citroën, backed by French Government financial aid.

The takeover gives Peugeot and Citroën a combined output and sales capacity to compete with the state-owned Renault company.

Last year, Peugeot produced 660,000 vehicles, Citroën 692,000 and Renault 1,293,000.

Peugeot announced that the two companies planned to maintain their individuality on trade marks and sales networks.

Peugeot announced a net profit of $450 million in 1975 and Citroën is believed to have lost $92 million. In the preceding year, Citroën's loss was $230 million. ∎

Grain-reaping machine during wheat harvest in Djizak, Uzbekistan.

The Peugot logo.

80

agriculture

BankAmericard to Get a New Name:
VISA

The BankAmericard is headed for extinction—at least in name. Starting some time next year, according to National BankAmericard Inc., the name of this credit card will be changed all over the world to Visa, a word expected to be universally acceptable.

The reason is that the BankAmericard system has a multiplicity of names in foreign countries, usually featuring local banks and logotypes. Moreover, it is felt that cards issued in the United States will prove to be more widely accepted overseas if they bear the same name as overseas cards. So Visa it will be. The word is recognized in all languages, because of its connection with passports and border-crossing.

Another possibility, unconfirmed by National BankAmericard, the organization behind the card in this country, is that the word "America" on a credit card could inspire unfavorable reactions in some parts of the world, whereas "visa" is entirely neutral.

Master Charge is still the most widely used bank credit card, although BankAmericard is closing the gap. In terms of retail outlets, however, BankAmericard has passed Master Charge, with 1,239,824 at the end of the first quarter, a shade ahead of Master Charge's 1,239,119. In terms of gross dollar volume, Master Charge did $2.88 billion in the first quarter, compared with BankAmericard's $2.35 billion. Both cards experienced strong growth over the first quarter of 1975, in terms of the number of participating banks, merchant outlets, cardholders, dollar volume and overall measures of activity. Both card systems listed substantially lower delinquency rates. ∎

WHY HOLLYWOOD FINDS PROFITS OUT OF THIS WORLD

Star Wars action figures.

Ben Bova

The millennium has arrived early. Science fiction is now big business in the entertainment industry. Long lines of ticket-buyers circle theaters all over the nation (and soon, all over the world) to see "Star Wars." And now Columbia is bringing out Steven Spielberg's $18 million "Close Encounters of the Third Kind."

Grown men and women have gone to see "Star Wars" eight or nine times. University students halt their studies to watch the 50th re-run of "Star Trek" episodes on TV. Even the stock market is affected by science-fiction films. 20th Century-Fox's stock soared as "Star Wars" took the nation by storm this summer. Columbia's stock sagged when the first verdicts on sneak previews of "Close Encounters" were less than ecstatic.

Psychologists and social philosophers are bending their pet theories into pretzels in attempts to explain the "science-fiction phenomenon." But to a veteran science-fiction writer and editor, there appear to be three major reasons for the new-found success of SF in the cinema. (And please note that it is abbreviated "SF," not "Sci-Fi," which is a linguistic barbarism used only by ignorant disk jockeys and desperate headline writers.)

The first reason for science fiction's booming popularity is excitement. In an era when almost every new film is a remake of an earlier film, science fiction offers bold

(cont'd. on next page)

81

(cont'd. from previous page)

new visions for a jaded audience. SF has something called "a sense of wonder." With all of the starry universe and all of time to play in, science fiction spreads a huge canvas, on which are painted stories of epic scope and sweep.

The second reason is morality. We think we're too sophisticated for old-fashioned virtues like honesty and courage. Even Westerns are riddled with neurotics. But the basic concepts of good and evil still underlie every tale, and in science-fiction films, the good guys are easily distinguished from the bad guys. The audience is encouraged to act on its simple, fundamental instincts, cheering for the heroes and hissing the villains. And, as Al Capp's Mammy Yokum often put it, "Good always wins over evil—'cause it's nicer."

The third reason is our growing concern about the future. Call it future shock, technology assessment, or whatever, we are now a future-oriented society. We demonstrate against SST's, nuclear power plants, and recombinant DNA experiments because of the damage they might do in the future.

Escapism? Certainly. But as Isaac Asimov has said, science fiction is "escape into reality." Instead of watching Fred Astaire tap-dancing his way through the Depression, we are now seeing films that emphatically tell us that to live is to change and that tomorrow will be vastly different from today.

Small wonder that directors such as Steven Spielberg and George Lucas have turned to science fiction to express themselves—and to make money.

For economic reasons, films and TV productions must be aimed at mass audiences. This means that heavy demands on the audience's intelligence are usually taboo in SF films. Producers go for spectacular special effects, weird-looking alien monsters and skimpy skirts on the women.

Spielberg says that "Close Encounters" is an "adventure thriller." Lucas described "Star Wars" as "space fantasy." Both draw on science-fiction themes that date back to the 1930's: invasion of earth by alien intelligences, an old-fashioned "space opera," complete with flashing ray guns and dashing interstellar spaceships.

There will be a galaxy of new science-fiction films as a result of the success of "Star Wars" and the likely success of "Close Encounters." Most of these films will also be firmly embedded in the blood and thunder traditions of science fiction's younger years.

But maybe, if we are very, very lucky, intelligent directors such as Spielberg or Lucas will work up the courage to try some of the best SF from later years, and deal with themes that make published science fiction so vital. Imagine big-budget motion pictures made of Frank Herbert's "Dune" trilogy, with its theme of survival in the face of ecological disaster; or Robert A. Heinlein's "Stranger in a Strange Land," which examines our entire religious myth-making apparatus.

That's something worth looking forward to!

MAY 16, 1978

Philip Morris Offer Is Accepted by 7-Up

Anthony J. Parisi

Philip Morris Inc. and the Seven-Up Corporation jointly announced yesterday that they had reached an agreement to combine the two companies under the control of Philip Morris.

The announcement brought to an abrupt end a takeover struggle that started just two weeks ago.

Under the agreement, Philip Morris increased its most-recent cash tender offer by $2, to $48 a share, for all 10.7 million shares of Seven-Up outstanding. The offer expires May 22.

Philip Morris made its first offer, of $41 a share, on May 1, when Seven-Up stock was selling at about 31. The stock closed yesterday at 47¼.

Ben H. Wells, chairman of Seven-Up, stated that the company's directors had approved the latest offer and recommended that Seven-Up shareholders accept it. Members of the Grigg, Ridgeway and Gladney families, who founded the Seven-Up Company in 1920 and who today hold about 45 percent of the outstanding shares, intend to tender their holdings to Philip Morris, the joint announcement said.

At the price of $48 a share, Philip Morris will pay about $231 million for the three families' interest and almost $514 million for all of Seven-Up's stock. Seven-Up's assets of record as of Dec. 31, 1977, were $145.7 million. Current assets were listed at $97.2 million, with current liabilities at $29.6 million.

Yesterday's statement quoted Joseph F. Cullman III, chairman of Philip Morris, as saying the addition of the Seven-Up line of products was a "further constructive step in the Philip Morris diversification program." In addition to being the nation's second-largest tobacco company—producing such major brands as Marlboro, Benson & Hedges 100's, Merit, Virginia Slims and Parliament cigarettes—Philip Morris also owns the Miller Brewing Company and Lowenbrau beer's United States operations.

Philip Morris has been growing at a fast pace of late. In 1977, the company reported net income of $334.9 million on revenues of $5.2 billion, up from $265.7 million on revenues of $4.3 billion in 1976. The company also made some important marketing advances in the period from 1976 to 1977, particularly with its Miller Lite beer, a low-calorie product.

Seven-Up's performance has been lackluster in comparison. In 1977, the company reported net income of $25.8 million on revenues of $251 million, barely higher than its 1976 income of $24.8 million on sales of $233.3 million.

Although Seven-Up reported record sales and earnings for the first quarter, analysts of the beverage industry say Seven-Up's share of supermarket sales, a key sector of the market, has been slipping since 1971.

In February, the company announced that it would switch its advertising from the J. Walter Thompson Company after 36 years as a client. Seven-Up gave as a reason the need for "long-term development of the company's overall position in the soft-drink industry." Its chief product, 7-Up, is the third best-selling soft drink, behind Coca-Cola and Pepsi, despite an extensive advertising campaign promoting the "Uncola" over its cola rivals. ■

DECEMBER 7, 1978

ROSE SETS OFF BASEBALL SALARY RIPPLE

Murray Chass

ORLANDO, Fla., Dec. 6—Reaction to the Pete Rose signing left no question today that from now on players, beginning with Dave Parker of Pittsburgh, will look at their futures through Rose-colored glasses. They should, however, also look through glasses that have a tinge of Blue.

When Rose signed with the Philadelphia Phillies yesterday, he was believed to have made a breakthrough in baseball salaries. However, a source familiar with the negotiations said today that Rose's four-year contract would average $750,000. That is not significantly greater than the $700,000 Vida Blue could average with the San Francisco Giants for six years beginning next season.

Players will look at their futures through Rose-colored glasses.

Rose, who will be 38 years old in April, acquired his wealth in a national spotlight yesterday. The 29-year-old Blue, on the other hand, quietly signed a new contract last summer that could bring him about $800,000 in 1979 if he pitches a certain number of innings, which the source described as very reachable.

Rose, meanwhile, could earn more than $3 million if he plays a certain number of games in his fourth season, 1982. That number, however, might not be so easily reached by a 42-year-old player, the source said.

Blue, who was unhappy and relatively impoverished playing for Charlie Finley in

Pete Rose in 1979.

Oakland, could have become a free agent at the end of next season. However, he was delighted with his trade last March to the Giants and more delighted with his lucrative contract.

Meanwhile, the Yankees offered Jerry Grote, the former Met and Dodger catcher turned free agent, a one-year contract last night with a one-year option. But Grote, 36, telephoned Al Rosen, the Yankee president, this evening and told him he was pleased with the offer but had decided to retire.

"It was a family decision," Rosen reported. "He said he had been away from his family long enough and wanted to begin spending more time with them."

The Yankees won't necessarily trade for a backup catcher, Rosen said. If they don't, 23-year-old Jerry Narron would be No. 2 to Thurman Munson.

As for making trades during these winter meetings, Rosen said, the Yankees have two chances, "slim and none." ■

DECEMBER 20, 1978

Coca-Cola to Go on Sale in China

N. R. Kleinfield

A Coca-Cola advertisement sign in Canton, China.

Coca-Cola, probably the one product most symbolic and symptomatic of the American way of life, is going to China.

The Coca-Cola Company said yesterday that it would start selling the world's most popular soft drink in China next month. Coke says it will be the first American consumer product to hit the market there since the Communist regime took power.

Although the disclosure of the exclusive contract follows by less than a week President Carter's announcement of the Jan. 1 normalization of relations between the United States and China, the Coca-Cola Company said there was no link between the two developments.

But in other indications of the growth of commercial ties with China in recent weeks, the Boeing Company announced yesterday that it had signed a $156 million agreement with Peking under which the Chinese are to buy three of the American company's special-performance 747 aircraft. Also, Pan American World Airways petitioned for permission to fly between San Francisco and Peking.

The supply of Coca-Cola to China has not been decided on but is expected to be, by Coke standards, relatively small. It will be aimed chiefly at the tourist trade, and thus will be for sale at restaurants and hotels in principal Chinese cities and tourist spots such as Shanghai, Peking, Kwangchow and Hangchow.

The accord specifies that Coke will be the only cola drink sold in the country, an arrangement similar to the one Pepsico Inc. has with the Soviet Union.

How do you pronounce Coca-Cola in Chinese? Curiously enough, pretty much the same way you say it in English. What do the Chinese characters mean? Translated literally, they work out to "Can mouth, can happy," or, by extension, "tastes good, tastes happy."

There are about 900 million people in China, around a quarter of the world's population. If they take to Coke, the impact on Coca-Cola could be huge.

Coca-Cola does not release figures on how much Coke it sells, though analysts figure some four and a half billion cases are sold worldwide. Roughly 40 percent of that is in the United States.

"In the near future, this isn't going to do anything for Coca-Cola's financial standing," one analyst said. "But eventually—and eventually may mean a couple of decades—you could have a market there bigger than this country."

Pepsico, marketer of Coke's arch-rival Pepsi-Cola, had no comment on the China accord, though it said that it has been trying to get into that market, too. "We try to get in anyplace we can," a spokesman said.

Pepsi did beat Coke into the Soviet Union. In 1973, Pepsico won exclusive rights to sell cola drinks there until 1984, with the exception of the Olympic Games. Coca-Cola is going to sell its Fanta orange drink in the Soviet Union beginning next year, and it will sell Coke too, but only at the Olympics.

Pepsico was helped into the Soviet Union by the good friendship between its chairman, Donald Kendall, and Richard M. Nixon, under whose Presidency the arrangement was ultimately struck.

Besides Coca-Cola, McDonald's is known to be discussing with China the possibility of marketing on the mainland. That could provide another outlet for Coca-Cola, as Coke is a primary supplier to the fast-food company. ■

JUNE 15, 1979

TO RATION OR NOT TO RATION

Leonard Silk

Does gasoline rationing make sense or not? The latest New York Times/CBS News Poll shows that most Americans now favor rationing as the way to handle a gasoline shortage.

One question put to 1,422 voting-age people around the country was: "If people have trouble getting gasoline, would you rather the Government set up a system to ration gasoline, or would you rather take your chances in getting gasoline yourself?" Sixty-two percent favored Government action.

Virtually an identical majority favored rationing by Government rather than by market price when asked the following question: "President Carter and others have said we need to use less gasoline. To get people to drive less, would you rather have gasoline rationed, or would you rather let gasoline prices rise until people drive less?"

The results were all the more startling in that only 42 percent said they expected the rationing system to be fair.

What people fear most is uncertainty. They want to know: "Can I get home if I drive or will all the gas stations be closed?" "How long will I have to wait in line to get gas before I go to work, and can I get to work at all?" Many insist they would rather do with less gasoline if they could be sure of getting the amount they are entitled to by their ration coupons, so that they can plan their lives more securely.

This position may be understandable, but it can be a poor guide to public policy. The fundamental question is not how to live with a shortage but how to get rid of the shortage. If there is one sure finding that centuries of economic analysis has made, it is that holding a price below the market level will create a shortage, as demand exceeds supply at the controlled price. It does not matter whether it is a gasoline shortage, a housing shortage or a shortage of nylon stockings. Conversely, it does not matter how scarce a commodity is—diamonds, emeralds or moon rocks—at a market-determined price, there will be no shortage, at least not for those willing to pay the price.

Oil companies can and do sometimes make mistakes in inventorying oil, and hence can interrupt supply, contributing to shortages and distorting gasoline prices (note the plural; they vary all over the place). Indeed, an article in The Journal on Wednesday explains in detail how some oil companies have erred recently, first in over inventorying and then in under inventorying, thereby contributing to the crunch. "In retrospect," as the chief economist of the Standard Oil Company (Indiana) has been quoted as saying, "we screwed up."

Nevertheless, a market-determined price (even a not-completely-free market price) is still the best means of wiping out a shortage. On the demand side, if prices reflect genuine economic costs, consumers will buy only to the point where costs are matched by received values; on the supply side, producers can afford to expand production as long as the fuels (petroleum or other) they produce yield returns in excess of their costs. ∎

GAS SHORTAGE SPURS CARTER DECLINE IN POLL

Spreading gasoline shortages, persistent unhappiness with the economy and doubts about President Carter's judgment under pressure have continued to erode his public support, the latest New York Times/CBS News Poll shows.

Approval of Mr. Carter's handling of his job declined in a month from 30 percent to 26 percent, and the breadth of his problem was reflected in the fact that some of his sharpest declines were measured among groups that have not had serious gasoline problems. Moreover, the declines were not spotty but were shown in almost every population group.

Despite the immediate focus of public and White House attention on energy, Mr. Carter's general decline was not accompanied by any increase in number of people blaming him for the energy problem, and the share of Americans who thought any "effective President" could solve the problem dropped.

OIL COMPANIES UNDER ATTACK

American oil companies continued to be considered the principal villains in the energy situation, but blame for Middle East oil-producing nations increased significantly, a development that squared with public statements by the Administration. But only one American in four accepted Mr. Carter's argument that the shortage was real.

There was also one particularly menacing political signal: Mr. Carter ran an effective dead heat with Gov. Edmund G. Brown Jr. of California when Democrats were asked their preference for a 1980 nominee. Senator Edward M. Kennedy of Massachusetts, who insists he is not a candidate, continued to lead them both by wide margins when his name was included.

The poll, of 1,192 Americans of voting age interviewed by telephone on Monday, Tuesday and Wednesday, carried with it mixed signals on public attitudes toward some of the alternatives Mr. Carter is considering as he prepares for Sunday's energy speech. Support for gasoline rationing, which was backed 2 to 1 in a June Times/CBS News Poll, declined from 62 to 52 percent. And when the real likelihood of a 10-gallon-a-week limit was included, only 45 percent said they favored rationing, while 47 percent said they would rather take their chances finding gasoline.

While there was an increase, compared with a 1977 poll, in public willingness to support energy production at the expense of the environment, the two sides were about evenly divided, with 41 percent preferring energy, 43 percent the environment.

Strong support, 77 percent, was expressed for keeping air conditioning at temperatures no lower than 78 degrees, the level set by Mr. Carter Tuesday. But a similarly lopsided majority opposed letting gasoline prices rise until people drove less, in what amounted to rejection of the price decontrol measures urged on the President by some in his Administration.

The persistent distrust of the oil companies appeared to be shown when the public expressed a slight preference for having the Government, not the oil companies, undertake a major program to make synthetic fuels. Forty-four percent supported a Government program, while 36 percent wanted the oil companies to do it.

Whatever the answers on specific programs he might propose, the basic political problem of energy remained to drag at Mr. Carter's efforts to develop effective public backing: The public still does not believe his argument that the oil shortage is real.

BROWN PREOCCUPIED AT HOME

The Brown-Carter results appeared more likely to be reflecting the President's

decline than any surge in support for the Californian, who is expected to get busy on campaign activities later this summer. In the last month, Mr. Brown has been preoccupied with California matters and has made no significant national splash.

But the findings were still dramatic. Forty-two percent of the Democrats polled preferred Mr. Carter, while 39 percent said they wanted Mr. Brown, a lead within the margin of error of the Democratic sample of 518 persons.

That showed a significant falloff for Mr. Carter when compared with earlier polls. In March an ABC News/Lou Harris Poll gave Mr. Carter a 59 to 36 percent edge. In late June a Gallup Poll put Mr. Carter ahead, 51 percent to 34.

Mr. Brown outdid Mr. Carter among young Democrats, liberal Democrats and, perhaps most important, Roman Catholic Democrats. The latter group carries significant weight in several states that choose national convention delegates early— among them, Iowa, New Hampshire and Massachusetts. ∎

Top Banks Lift Prime to 11¾%

Robert A. Bennett

The nation's major banks increased their basic lending rate from 11½ percent to 11¾ percent yesterday on the apparent belief that the growth of the money supply will be restrained.

The shift marked the first time since last Nov. 24 that the major banks in the United States moved with unanimity in a single day to change their prime rates. The only money market bank that moved earlier was the First National Bank of Chicago, which acted on Monday.

All the major New York City banks raised their prime rates yesterday, as did the Bank of America in San Francisco, the world's largest. Other banks across the nation followed quickly.

A clear perception that money will become less available and interest rates will move still higher was at least partly responsible for the herd-like move yesterday, according to a number of money market analysts. The current rate is just one-quarter of a percentage point below the 12 percent peak set during the 1974 credit squeeze.

"Banks don't like to have to change their prime rates every few weeks," said Frederick W. Deming, vice president and senior economist of the Chemical Bank. Some economists and bankers believe rates will decline in the not-too-distant future, he said, but added that most agree a decline is unlikely within the next few weeks.

Citibank's decision to raise its prime rate yesterday underscored the different tone of the market. Citibank pegs its prime rate to a formula based on the interest rate being paid by banks on large certificates of deposit. When Citibank's money management committee met yesterday morning the formula called for a prime rate of 11.61 percent, which is closer to 11½ than to 11¾ percent. But the bank, which moves its prime in quarter-point steps, chose to increase the rate to 11¾ percent despite the formula.

Bankers pointed to rising short-term interest rates, high loan demand, the continuing high level of inflation, downward pressure on the dollar in the foreign exchange markets and the appointment of a "conservative" as chairman of the Federal Reserve Board as reasons for the mass movement to the higher rate.

Earlier this year, predicting the trend of interest rates, even for brief periods, was unusually difficult. G. William Miller, then the chairman of the Federal Reserve, described the Fed's monetary policy as one of restraint, yet bankers were puzzled by the abundance of short-term funds. Thus they were reluctant to change the prime although money conditions were much easier than the Fed's avowed policy would suggest.

This doubt was overcome this week, however, with the nomination by President Carter of Paul A. Volcker, president of the Federal Reserve Bank of New York, to succeed Mr. Miller, whom the President has nominated to become Secretary of the Treasury. Mr. Volcker is expected to be less wary than Mr. Miller in restraining the growth of the money supply.

Other factors that economists say point to high interest rates have been heavy corporate borrowing from banks, which Mr. Deming says has been increasing at a pace of about 30 percent, and the stubborn double-digit rate of inflation. The Federal Reserve, they say, is likely to keep the supply of money tight, and thereby drive up interest rates, to get inflation under control.

New York

In the 1970s, New York suffered what might be fairly called a near-death experience. Decades of fiscal gimmickry brought the local government to the brink of bankruptcy. By 1974, the city had trouble paying its workers. It was shut out of the borrowing markets. Things got so bad that City Hall went begging the federal government for a bailout. Eventually, Washington did help, but not before telling New York's political leaders to go fly a kite, a national humiliation best captured in a 1975 *Daily News* headline that endures as a classic: "Ford to City: Drop Dead."

Martin Scorsese on the corner Hester and Baxter Streets in lower Manhattan, one of the locations he used in his film "Mean Streets." 1973.

The crime scene where the body of Virgina Voskeritchian, a victim of Son of Sam, was found, 1977.

Storefront gates failed to keep out looters in Brooklyn in 1977.

The acrid smell of failure enveloped far more than the municipal treasury. A disease of the spirit infected the very marrow of civic life. For many, Martin Scorsese's 1976 film "Taxi Driver," with its hellish vision of New York, might well have been a documentary. In perhaps no other modern decade did New Yorkers think as badly of themselves as in the '70s.

Several Fortune 500 companies, like American Airlines, decamped to other parts of the country. Much of the South Bronx went up in flames. Crime rose sharply. A serial killer who went by Son of Sam spread terror. Bombings took lives in Manhattan and at La Guardia Airport, precursors to the far more deadly terrorism that would strike at the dawn of the 21st century. In 1977, a blackout led to widespread looting in heart-of-darkness contrast to an earlier blackout, in 1965, that was a model of we're-all-in-this-together camaraderie. So sorry was the state of affairs that Broadway theaters moved up the evening curtain by an hour so suburbanites could make it home before the night stalkers entirely took over Times Square.

The police? They didn't seem much help. They even did the unthinkable in January 1971 by going on strike for a few days, part of widespread labor unrest that included walkouts by garbage collectors and doctors at municipal hospitals. Fortunately, it was so cold during the strike that muggers, like everyone else, didn't venture outdoors; crime actually went down.

Even when officers were on the job, they commanded far less than universal respect, in good part because of revelations about police corruption from Frank Serpico, who became a household name, and from a city commission that concluded the rot was systemic.

It wasn't all dismal, though. Several events suggested that the city was not about to collapse, no matter how much its knees had buckled. The Yankees rebounded from years of despondency to World Series triumph. A bicentennial spectacle of tall ships known as Operation Sail sent hearts soaring. The 1977 election of a new mayor, the ebullient Edward I. Koch, hinted of better days to come.

And New York still retained enough glamour for the Democrats to hold their national convention at Madison Square Garden. That was in 1976, the year that it was the turn of American voters to tell Gerald Ford, politically, to drop dead.

New York Yankees manager Billy Martin with the World Series trophy, after his team defeating the Los Angeles Dodgers, 4 games to 2 in the 1977 World Series.

TWO FIGURES IN 'VILLAGE' BLAST LINKED TO LEFT

Lawrence Van Gelder

The demolished Wilkerson townhouse at 18 W. 11th Street in New York City.

Two of the individuals involved in the mysterious explosion that demolished a Greenwich Village townhouse last Friday have been linked by sources close to the investigation with the world of New Left politics.

Theodore Gold, the 23-year-old former leader of the student revolt in 1968 at Columbia who was found dead in the demolished house, was reportedly a founder of the Mad Dogs, a splinter group formed last year.

The Mad Dogs came into being after the Weathermen faction emerged last June as the dominant force in Students for a Democratic Society, an event that factionalized adherents of the organization.

Catherine Wilkerson, the 25-year-old Swarthmore College graduate whose father, James, owned the townhouse, was reportedly a Weatherman—a small, uncompromisingly revolutionary group. The Weathermen faction shares a background of white, middle-class America, college and families that range from comfortable to wealthy.

The organization owes its name to a line in a Bob Dylan song—"Subterranean Homesick Blues"—that says: "You don't need to be a weatherman to know which way the wind blows."

When the S.D.S. held its national convention last June, the Weathermen—also known as the Revolutionary Youth Movement I—emerged as the dominant force controlling the S.D.S. national office, which subsequently became known as the Weather Bureau. ∎

Millions Join Earth Day Observances

Joseph Lelyveld

A banner at the inaugural Earth Day depicting the Earth crying in pain, New York City, April 22, 1970.

Huge, light-hearted throngs ambled down autoless streets here yesterday as the city heeded Earth Day's call for a regeneration of a polluted environment by celebrating an exuberant rite of spring.

If the environment had any enemies they did not make themselves known. Political leaders, governmental departments and corporations hastened to line up in the ranks of those yearning for a clean, quiet, fume-free city.

For two hours, except for crosstown traffic, the internal-combustion engine was barred from Fifth Avenue between 59th and 14th Streets: the only wheeled vehicle to go down the avenue during this period was a horse-drawn buggy carrying members of a Harlem block association.

Fourteenth Street between Third and Seventh Avenues, left free for pedestrians between noon and midnight, became an ecological carnival.

The Consolidated Edison Company, identified by many environmentalists as a prime enemy, draped orange and blue bunting from the lampposts. And balloons stamped with the slogans of the peace and population-control movements—"War is the worst pollution" and "Stop at two"—drifted over the crowds.

Union Square, the focus for scores of Earth Day observances and teach-ins throughout the metropolitan area, saw the kind of crowds it had rarely seen since the turbulent days of the thirties, when it was a favorite arena for leftists.

Each visitor to the square had to improvise his own Earth Day, by deciding where to spend his time. Some resolved the range of choices by taking part in a nonstop Frisbee game on Union Square Park's piebald lawns. Thousands crowded into a block-long polyethylene "bubble" on 17th Street to breathe pure, filtered air; before the enclosure had been open to the public for a half an hour the pure air carried unmistakable whiffs of marijuana.

Mayor Lindsay, in a brief speech, helped set the general theme of the day. "Behind the complex predictions and obscure language," he said, "beyond words like ecology, environment and pollution there is a simple question: Do we want to live or die?"

But for its sponsors and its youthful participants, Earth Day was less a demonstration than a secular revival meeting. The hope was that citizens would pause and consider what they could do as individuals to fight pollution. To this end, the Environmental Action Coalition sold a "New York Pollution Survival Kit" with a list of 40 actions that individuals could take to fight noise, waste and dirt.

Governor Rockefeller was greeted in Union Square with scattered cries of "Fascist pig!" Earlier he spoke in Prospect Park and rode a bicycle there.

POLICEMAN SERPICO TELLS TRIAL OF PAYOFFS

David Burnham

A decorated New York policeman testified in court yesterday that gamblers paid bribes of $700 to $800 a month to individual patrolmen assigned to suppress gambling in part of the Bronx.

The witness who gave this picture of systematic and entrenched corruption was Patrolman Frank Serpico, a 34-year-old City College graduate who has been on the force for more than 10 years.

Patrolman Serpico, who now is with the Narcotics Division, testified that he first related the picture of corruption to a high police official in January, 1967, more than two years before any of the policemen involved were indicted.

He said a plainclothes man who arrested a gambler in New York was normally expected to give a $5 tip to the police lieutenant who processed the arrest.

The witness said the lieutenants were convinced the plainclothes men making the arrests were getting a great deal more than the $5 from the gamblers.

Patrolman Serpico testified that a plainclothes man told him that if he did not want to take bribes from the gamblers, "we can put up some money" for friends at headquarters and "I would be transferred."

Many aspects of the testimony about police corruption previously were reported in a New York Times survey of the problem published on April 25. As a result of this survey Mayor Lindsay has formed a special five-man commission to investigate police corruption and develop ways of preventing it.

Patrolman Serpico said he was assigned to the 7th Division plainclothes unit in December, 1966. This unit, which at the time included 15 patrolmen, 2 lieutenants and 2 inspectors, was responsible for enforcing the gambling laws in a four-precinct area of the Bronx with more than a half a million inhabitants.

The patrolman said that within a month he became convinced the unit was corrupt and he reported to that effect to an old friend, Inspector Cornelius J. Behan, now in charge of the Police Department's planning division.

Patrolman Serpico said Inspector Be-

han told him that as a result of that report he would be assigned to do "undercover work" for Deputy Police Commissioner John F. Walsh, the second highest police commander in the department and the man bearing direct responsibility for fighting police corruption.

Patrolman Serpico testified that some time in October, 1967—about four months after he had talked with Arnold G. Fraiman, then Commissioner of Investigation and now a State Supreme Court jus-

tice—he reported the corruption in the 7th Division plainclothes unit to Supervising Assistant Chief Inspector Joseph McGovern, then as now the Police Department's top uniformed internal investigator.

After a long investigation, eight policemen were indicted on perjury charges in connection with alleged protection payoffs by number racketeers.

Patrolman Serpico's testimony yesterday came during the trial of one of these eight policemen. ■

Frank Serpico at right with his lawyer, Ramsey Clark, testifying before the Knapp Commission on police corruption, December 15, 1971.

FIREMAN IS FIRST TO FINISH IN MARATHON

Al Harvin

Gary Muhrcke, a 30-year-old fireman running for the Millrose Athletic Association, finished nearly a half-mile ahead of his nearest competitor as he won the first New York City Marathon in 2 hours 31 minutes 38.2 seconds in Central Park yesterday.

Of 126 runners who started in front of the Tavern on the Green at 11 a.m., 55 finished. The first 10 received wrist watches, the next 35 clocks and everybody who competed got commemorative trophies.

The lone woman in the race—unofficially—was Mrs. Nina Kuscsik. She went home empty-handed, having dropped out after the third circuit, covering 14.2 miles in 1:39. Her husband, Richard, did not finish either.

"I wanted to finish very badly," said Mrs. Kuscsik, who completed the Boston Marathon in 3:11 unofficially earlier this year. "But I had a virus earlier this week and I just couldn't. I can't accept any awards and, by dropping out, I avoided any problems with the A.A.U. [Amateur Athletic Union]."

Moses Mayfield of Philadelphia, running unattached, led on every lap, but started to feel dizzy on the last. He fell behind and finished eighth in 2:49:50.

"This is a nice, easy course," said Mayfield, who finished 23rd in the Boston Marathon. "I don't know why I got dizzy. I'm in very good shape. I'm going to a doctor to check it out."

"I knew Moses was going to fade," said Muhrcke. "He always starts fast. I passed him around 90th Street with about three miles to go." ■

BROADWAY CURTAINS TO GO UP AT 7:30

Louis Calta

In an effort to lure more patrons, all Broadway stage shows will raise their curtains at 7:30 p.m., an hour earlier than usual, beginning Jan. 4.

A 2 p.m. curtain time, already in effect for midweek matinees, also will be instituted for Saturday-afternoon performances.

The change was unanimously voted by the governing board of the League of New York Theaters, Richard Barr, the group's president, said.

Mr. Barr noted that the changes were made "because it's clear that the vast majority of Broadway playgoers prefer an earlier curtain time. It will reduce the time span between the end of the business day and the start of performances, and it will allow our audiences to get home an hour earlier."

SUBURBANITES IN MIND

The earlier curtain time also is intended to revive theater interest among suburbanites, according to Mr. Barr. "It will make it less difficult for many of these people to engage baby sitters who prefer getting home before midnight," the league official said.

Angus Duncan, executive secretary of Actors Equity Association, said that the early curtain would be an improvement from an actor's point of view since it would permit him to "kill less time between shows on Wednesdays and Saturdays."

However, news of the projected early evening curtain was viewed with some misgivings by Broadway and East Side restaurateurs.

Knicks Spotlighted in Sport's Boom

Leonard Koppett

Willis Reed of the New York Knicks holding the MVP trophy for the 1970 N.B.A. finals.

The melodramatic triumph of the New York Knickerbockers, who won the National Basketball Association championship despite an injury to their key player, Willis Reed, was only one facet of the most eventful, most prosperous and most extensive season professional basketball ever had.

Partly because of the excitement generated by the Knicks, whose 18-game winning streak early in the 1969-70 season caught the country's attention, but also because of many converging lines of growth, 1970 was the year in which pro basketball finally achieved an economic breakthrough comparable to that enjoyed by professional football a decade before.

A three-year national television contract, worth $17-million, not only gave the N.B.A. new resources but established its prestige in the sports marketplace. The Knicks, repeatedly selling out the 19,500-capacity Madison Square Garden, drew nearly a million customers at the highest price scale in basketball history. The league, in its 24th season, drew more than five million fans, 2½ times its total of only five years ago.

Meanwhile, the rival American Basketball Association played through its third season, and established itself firmly enough to create serious negotiations about a merger.

This, in turn, prompted the players of the N.B.A. to take legal action to block such a step, on antitrust grounds, and a court order was obtained limiting such negotiations to the preparation of a request to Congress for permission to merge.

The merger possibility, however, did not eliminate competition between the two leagues for talent. The most publicized college star, Pete Maravich of Louisiana State, was signed by Atlanta of the N.B.A. for a multi-year package worth, supposedly, $2 million.

Lew Alcindor, the major prize of the preceding college season, won instant stardom with the N.B.A. Milwaukee Bucks, a publicly held corporation immediately turned into a profit-maker by his presence, even though he had a four-year $1.4-million contract. As the 7-foot-2-inch Alcindor became acclimated, the Bucks, who had been a distant last as an expansion team the year before, ran a strong second to the Knicks and were beaten by New York in the semifinal round of the playoffs.

In the final against the Knicks, the Los Angeles Lakers, despite Jerry West, Wilt Chamberlain and Elgin Baylor, were beaten for the championship for the seventh time in nine years. ■

'Attention Must Be Paid!' Say Policemen On Strike

Richard Reeves

New York's Finest began a wildcat strike on Thursday. At least 85 percent of the city's 27,400 patrolmen refused to go out on the streets Friday after the New York Court of Appeals delayed a final decision on a Patrolmen's Benevolent Association suit seeking a $100-a-month retroactive raise for each man.

Law and order? "There is no such thing—we have to use muscle!" an angry patrolman screamed at a P.B.A. meeting last summer when pressure was building for a strike over the complicated pay issue that led to Thursday's court decision.

Order? There was as much order as there ever is in New York for the first 36 hours. It was mercifully cold and the few

people on windy streets occasionally saw a police car or two as a very thin blue line of 6,500 sergeants, detectives, lieutenants and captains, working 12-hour shifts, patrolled on a haphazard basis—and many patrolmen indicated that they would hit the streets again if there was real trouble.

Perhaps the calm was temporary. In any event, the Mayor's office believed that the desk officers and detectives could provide minimal protection for "a few days." Beyond that, there were contingency plans to call in National Guard or Army protection if necessary. Last night Federal marshals were moved into the city to guard diplomatic establishments.

But the crisis involving the city's policemen, firemen and sanitationmen is not temporary. It is a two-level thing—the complex money issue erupting on the surface and class and racial issues seething below.

The wildcat strike—P.B.A. President Edward J. Kiernan has urged his men to keep working and let the courts handle parity—really fits into the fabric of frustration of the

Americans President Nixon has called his "silent majority." The cops are median Americans—$10,950 a year, mostly white in a department welded together by the values of its Irish Catholic heritage, family men with flag decals on a two-year-old car still owned by the bank. The firemen and sanitationmen are pretty much the same.

There are two men standing starkly against this smoldering background. Mayor Lindsay, who must try to force the patrolmen back onto their beats. Mr. Kiernan seems almost a pathetic figure, after holding off younger and more militant patrolmen who wanted to strike six months ago by convincing them they couldn't lose in court. Although they distrust each other, the mayor and the union leader seem to be on the same side at the moment. Both have to figure out something to calm down the patrolmen before Mr. Kiernan has to face his delegate assembly with recommendations on Tuesday—that's what the "around the clock" negotiations this weekend are about. ■

OFFTRACK BET SHOPS SWAMPED ON FIRST DAY

Steve Cady

A $2 bet made by Mayor Lindsay on a pacer named Money Wise helped get the country's first system of legal offtrack wagering onto the track here yesterday.

"It's a small wager and I had my wife's permission," said the Mayor, holding up a validated ticket on his choice to win last night's seventh race at Roosevelt Raceway.

The Mayor's bet, made at 10:53 a.m. in the main concourse of Grand Central Terminal, set off a day-long outpouring of action that proved too heavy for the city's Offtrack Betting Corporation to handle. Eventually, OTB had to ration tickets to five a customer.

Money Wise didn't win, finishing out of the money in fourth place at odds of 4-1. But the performance of offtrack betting was more encouraging.

Despite the failure of the manual ticket-selling operation to provide adequate service, the so-called "New Game in Town" generated a combined total of $66,098 in offtrack wagers on nine races, a daily double and four exactas. Howard J. Samuels, president of OTB, had predicted an opening-day handle of $10,000.

All the bets were relayed by the public benefit corporation to Roosevelt Raceway via teletype for insertion into the track's totalisator to help determine odds.

Under the OTB system, designed to raise revenue primarily for New York City, offtrack wagers are taxed at the same basic 17 percent as ontrack wagers. However, the "take" is divided differently: ½ percent off the top to the state, 1 percent to the track and the remaining 15½ percent to OTB. After OTB expenses are met, 80 percent of the net revenue goes to the city, 20 percent to the state.

By 4 p.m., horseplayers were standing in lines that stretched the width of the Grand Central concourse. As clerks at the 10 betting windows there struggled with OTB's painfully slow manual system of ticket-selling, it was taking as long as two hours to move up 50 places in a line and make a bet.

The slowness of the manual system appeared to be the major bug in the operation. Hundreds, perhaps thousands of would-be bettors went home without betting or were prevented from getting a bet down.

Among those on hand was former Mayor Robert Wagner, whose citywide referendum on offtrack betting was approved by a 3 1 ratio in 1963.

"It looks good," he said. "It's going to have some problems to work out, but every new venture has problems."

Even as OTB struggled into reality, subsidiary industries appeared to be springing up around it. For example, 10,000 copies of an elaborate eight-page tipsheet billing itself as "America's first daily for the offtrack bettor" appeared on 2,500 newsstands around the city. The 35-cent publication, called "The Off-Track Bettor," contained brief past-performance records of last night's horses, the code letters, and comments on the participants.

There were also reports of messenger services being formed to take people's bets to an offtrack shop for a fee.

YO-YO MA, NOW 16, PERFORMS AN ENVIABLE RECITAL

Allen Hughes

Yo-Yo Ma is said to have been a prodigy when he was a child, and although he is growing older now—he is all of 16—one can well believe it. The cello recital he gave at Carnegie Recital Hall Thursday night was of a quality to make many an older man green with envy.

He played Locatelli's Sonata in D, Beethoven's Sonata in A (Op. 69) and Hindemith's Unaccompanied Sonata with remarkable technical control and musical authority. Then, for lighter fare, he added Fauré's "Elegy," Chopin's Polonaise Brillante, the Paganini-Silva Bravura Variations (for one string) and Popper's "Elfentanz."

This youth's skill and musicality did not spring from nowhere. His father, Hiao-Tsiun Ma, is a violinist and composer and the founder-director of the Children's Orchestra, which benefited by this recital.

Yo-Yo Ma, a Chinese born in Paris, began studying at 4 and gave his first recital at 6. Since 1964, he has studied with Leonard Rose at the Juilliard School.

It would be a disservice to him to suggest that he has already reached his full artistic maturity. Time will probably mellow the tone he produces from the cello at present, and there will be a deeper penetration of musical meanings.

If all goes well, however, he will not lose the joy he radiates when he plays and the engaging abandon with which he tosses off things like the Paganini variations and the "Elfentanz." ∎

AIR AND GROUND ATTACK FOLLOWS REFUSAL OF CONVICTS TO YIELD

Mattresses, crates and other rubble litter the yard after the uprising at Attica state prison in 1971.

Fred Ferretti

ATTICA, N.Y., Sept 13—The rebellion at the Attica Correctional Facility ended this morning in a bloody clash and mass deaths that four days of taut negotiations had sought to avert.

Thirty-seven men—9 hostages and 28 prisoners—were killed as 1,000 state troopers, sheriff's deputies and prison guards stormed the prison under a low-flying pall of tear gas dropped by helicopters. They retook from inmates the cellblocks they had captured last Thursday.

In this worst of recent American prison revolts, several of the hostages—prison guards and civilian workers—died when convicts slashed their throats with knives. Others were stabbed and beaten with clubs and lengths of pipe.

Most of the prisoners killed in the assault fell under the thick hail of rifle and shotgun fire laid down by the invading troopers.

A volunteer doctor who worked among the wounded after the assault said the prison's interior was "like a war zone." Standing in front of the prison in a blood-stained white coat, he said that many more of the wounded "are likely to die."

Late today a deputy director of correction, Walter Dunbar, said that two of the hostages had been killed "before today" and that one had been stabbed and emasculated.

Of the remaining seven, five were killed instantly by the inmates and two died in the prison hospital.

Mr. Dunbar said that in addition to the 28 dead inmates, 8 other convicts of the total of 2,237 were missing. Two of the dead prisoners, he said, were killed "by their own colleagues and lay in a large pool of blood in a fourth-tier cellblock."

He said he considered the state's recapture of the prison an "efficient, affirmative police action."

The recapture of the maximum-security prison was hampered by trenches dug by the convicts, filled with burning gasoline and ignited in cellblock corridors; by electrically wired prison bars separating detention areas; by homemade bombs and booby traps hidden in underground tunnels and conduits; by barricades and by salvos of Molotov cocktails and bursts from captured tear-gas guns.

The attack began before 10 o'clock and ended four hours later as troopers fought hand to hand with stubborn knots of prisoners in the second tier of cellblock D, the portion of the prison that the prisoners had completely controlled since the riots on Thursday.

Members of a citizens' observers committee, which had been called to Attica by the state at the request of the inmates, were locked in an Administration Building office inside the prison walls during the assault. Those who cared to speak expressed deep regret that no way had been found to avert the killings. ■

Lennons Love U.S.

Albin Krebs

"New York City is the center of the earth," said John Lennon, explaining why he and his wife, Yoko Ono, will fight deportation on charges that their visas have expired. Their deportation hearing was adjourned until April 18 to give them time to apply for permanent residence.

The chief stumbling block to that application is Mr. Lennon's 1968 conviction, in England, on possession of marijuana charges. He told the immigration hearing officer that he was trying to have the conviction expunged from his record.

"We were shocked" on learning of the deportation order, Miss Ono said. "We are looking for my child, Kyoko, who has been taken off by her father. The court in Houston gave us temporary custody of Kyoko, on condition we keep her in this country. If we are deported, it is synonymous to our losing our child. That is why we are so desperate about it."

Even if it weren't for Kyoko, the Lennons said, they want to remain in this country because "we love it."

John Lennon and Yoko Ono on the streets of New York, 1979.

Joe Gallo poses with his wife, Sina Essary, at their wedding reception in New York City, three weeks before he was killed in 1972.

Gallo: This Time, The Gang Shot Straight

Joseph (Crazy Joe) Gallo had spent the evening of his 43rd birthday sipping champagne at the Copacabana. At 4 o'clock Friday morning, he and his wife of three weeks and her 10-year-old daughter, his sister, his bodyguard Pete Diapoulas and Pete's date had adjourned to Umberto's Clam House, a new restaurant on Mulberry Street in Little Italy. Sitting around two butcher-block tables, they drank soda and ate Italian delicacies. Gallo, in a relaxed and expansive mood, ordered a second helping.

Then the side door opened. Women screamed. Customers ducked to the floor. The intruder wore a tweed coat and a .38-caliber revolver blazed in his hand. Gallo was hit three times, Diapoulas once. Diapoulas and an unknown man seated at the bar returned the fire; more than 20 shots were exchanged. Gallo staggered out the front door, collapsed and died in the middle of the street. His killer, firing as he went, fled out the back door, hopped into a waiting car and sped from the scene.

Said New York City Chief of Detectives Albert A. Seedman: "The assassin walked in with just one thing in his mind—to get Gallo." Why? Police weren't getting any help from Pete Diapoulas. "I don't want to give you a hard time," he told them, "but I'm not going to give you information." He wouldn't even tell police his name.

But well-placed informants offered a motive: Bad blood between the Gallo gang and the Colombo Mafia family. The rivalry goes back to 1960, when Gallo and his followers challenged the power in Brooklyn of the boss of their Mafia family, the late Joseph Profaci. Before the Gallo-Profaci war was finally settled, with Joseph A. Colombo Sr. taking over the reins of the family, more than a dozen gangland murders had been committed and Gallo was in jail, serving a term for extortion. ∎

INQUIRY ON 1971 ATTICA REVOLT BLAMES GOVERNOR

Michael T. Kaufman

The New York State Special Commission on Attica concluded in its final report released yesterday that New York State Governor Nelson Rockefeller should have gone to the upstate prison before ordering an armed assault on rebel inmates.

This determination, as well as a variety of others on the origins, development and aftermath of the uprising, was conveyed by the commission in its 518-page report issued to coincide with today's anniversary of the assault, in which 30 inmates and 10 hostages died. Over-all, 11 prison employees and 32 inmates lost their lives as a result of the uprising, the bloodiest in American prison history.

In addition, the report made the following judgments:

- The eruption of violence by inmates was not planned, but occurred spontaneously. Like the disturbances in the slums in the 1960's, it "was the product of frustrated hopes and unfulfilled expectations after efforts to bring meaningful change had failed."
- The highly organized inmate society in the captured prison yard also developed spontaneously.
- The assault plan itself was faulty since it could not have saved hostage lives if inmates were in fact set on killing.
- No nonlethal weaponry was available to the state police and the guns and ammunition used were such that they made inevitable the death and injury of innocent people.

Special attention has been focused on those aspects of the report dealing with the Governor's actions.

Mr. Rockefeller has declared that he rejected the requests of his aides that he journey to Attica because "I was trying to do the best I could to save the hostages, save the prisoners, restore order, and preserve our system without undertaking actions which could set a precedent which would go across the country like wildfire." ∎

GOVERNORS DEDICATE TRADE CENTER

Frank J. Prial

The Twin Towers, New York, 1973.

The $700-million World Trade Center, its two 1,350-foot towers the largest buildings in the world, was dedicated formally yesterday by Governors Rockefeller and Cahill.

In a message read at the ceremonies in the purple-carpeted lobby of the northernmost of the twin, 110-story towers, President Nixon hailed the center as "a major factor for the expansion of the nation's international trade."

Mr. Nixon's message was to have been read by Secretary of Labor Peter J. Brennan. However, Mr. Brennan refused to cross a picket line of Railway Carmen who are striking PATH, the commuter railroad of the Port Authority of New York and New Jersey, which also built and owns the World Trade Center.

His speech was read to an audience of city, state and foreign officials by James Kellogg III, chairman of the Port Authority.

Governor Rockefeller termed the dedication a "really thrilling and exciting occasion" and called the twin towers a "great marriage of utility and beauty. He noted that New York State would be the principal tenant of the South Tower. ∎

MAY 18, 1975

20% RISE IN FIRES ADDS TO DECLINE OF SOUTH BRONX

Firemen fight a three-alarm fire in the Bronx in the 1970s.

Joseph B. Treaster

Twenty, thirty, forty times a day the cry of fire sirens and clouds of acrid smoke rise above the stretch of decay and poverty that is the southern third of the Bronx.

"It sounds like an air raid up here sometimes," said Eric Kaiser, a 25-year-old social worker.

More than 12,300 sirens raged through the five-story and six-story tenements and small stores there last year, an increase of 20 percent over the previous year, in what fire department officials say has been the most intense concentration of fires in the city. There were nearly 4,100 fires in the first four months of this year, and with the months in which most fires occur still ahead fire officials anticipate another record total for the year.

High-ranking fire officers conservatively estimate that more than 30 percent of the blazes have been intentionally set—more than three times the national norm for arson.

The fires, which have been steadily increasing for several years, have been killing 30 to 40 persons a year. They have uprooted thousands of poor families, scattered them as refugees throughout the city, and accounted for millions of dollars in property losses. Whole city blocks are in ruins, with only the charred hulks of buildings left standing.

"If this keeps up there will be no South Bronx," said the Right Rev. Paul Moore, Episcopal Bishop of New York. Bishop Moore, along with several clergymen and community leaders, says that city, fire and police officials are making no serious effort to curtail the destruction by fire.

"It looks like they've red-lined the South Bronx as an area not worth saving," the Bishop said in an interview.

(cont'd. on next page)

(cont'd. from previous page)

Fire Commissioner John T. O'Hagan said in an interview that he realized that, "What we've done in the past isn't satisfactory." But, he said: "We're going to put additional effort into this problem until we get results."

The Rev. Louis R. Gigante, a City Councilman from the South Bronx, says, "They say they don't have the manpower and I say that's baloney. If there's something wrong and bad and crippling you put your forces there and take care of the problem. Let the other problems go for a while."

Assistant Chief Francis Cruthers, the Fire Department commander in the Bronx, and others familiar with the area cite a number of possible motives for the widespread arson. Among them are revenge, insurance fraud by landlords and the desperation of tenants who set fire to their decrepit apartments to qualify for priority admission to public-housing projects.

Of the fires deliberately set to settle grudges, one marshal said: "It's easier than buying a gun." About 90 percent of the 430 arson arrests in the city last year were related to this type of fire, fire officials say, because the arsonist and the victim knew each other. ∎

DECEMBER 31, 1975

LA GUARDIA BLAST YIELDS NO LEADS IN INVESTIGATION

Peter Kihss

Investigators were reconstructing yesterday a locker area where one of the most lethal bombs ever exploded in New York City killed 11 persons and injured about 75 at La Guardia Airport's main terminal Monday evening. But they appeared still to be without a clue to the bomber or to the motive.

Lieut. Kenneth W. O'Neil, commander of the police bomb section, estimated the force of the explosion as equivalent to 25 sticks of dynamite, compared with estimates of 10 sticks for the explosion that killed four persons and injured 58 at Fraunces Tavern last Jan. 24.

Scores of investigators from the Police and Fire Departments were engaged in the reconstruction efforts and interviewing of potential witnesses, along with a force of 15 assistant district attorneys and 40 investigators set up by District Attorney Nicholas Ferraro of Queens. The Federal Bureau of Investigation said that it had deployed "many" of the 1,000 agents in its New York office and brought in bomb experts from Washington with the Federal Aviation Administration.

President Ford declared that "we must do something in the area of terrorist control," and that "we are going to do what is necessary to make certain that this tragedy does not happen again," just before he flew back from Grand Junction, Colo., to Washington.

It was the worst death toll from a bomb explosion in the city since a bomb went off in a horse-drawn wagon at Wall and Broad Streets Sept. 16, 1920, killing 40 persons and injuring about 300.

The explosion occurred near the gate of a baggage area used jointly by Trans World Airlines and Delta Air Lines, where there are conveyor belts for baggage coming off arriving aircraft and tiers of lockers used for depositing personal effects.

The powerful explosion destroyed the entire inside area, shattered plate glass windows

---

NOVEMBER 7, 1975

Beame and Carey Decry 'Bailout' Talk

Steven R. Weisman

The debate over what the Federal Government should or should not do for New York City has begun to take on the hazy quality of supposition and speculation that has enshrouded so much of the city's fiscal crisis. Advocates of a Federal rescue to avert municipal default, and advocates of planned default and bankruptcy, agree that they are arguing essentially about potential risks and not certain outcomes for either course of action.

One side issue that illustrates the hypothetical nature of the discussions is the question of what a Federal rescue would "cost" the Federal Government and the taxpayers of America.

On the one hand, Mayor Beame and Governor Carey say they are seeking "neither a bailout nor a handout"—simply the chance to have the city restore stability to its fiscal affairs in an orderly fashion by having the Federal Government guarantee city borrowing so that it can work to balance its budget by 1978.

On the other, President Ford has said that the city's proposals would mean that the "working people" of the country would have to "support" New York City, with all its high salaries, pensions and other expenses—and with no assurance that the city would mend its profligate ways.

In the narrowest terms, a Federal loan guarantee does not have to cost anything for the Federal Government—in fact, it is designed to actually generate revenues for the Government.

The prime bills being considered in Congress would have the United States Treasury guarantee a certain amount of municipal borrowing over a period of years, one of them as much as $7 billion worth.

Because the lenders would not be paying any taxes on the yields of the guaranteed New York City notes, their interest rates are expected to be roughly equivalent to the rates of Treasury notes, or about 4.5 or 5 percent.

But the bills being considered in Congress would require the city to pay an additional 3.5 percent interest surcharge to the Federal Government—a sum that might be increased if it is delinquent in its budget reforms. The surcharge, according to one estimate, would yield the Federal Government an additional $140 million in revenue. Mayor Beame

bailout

30 feet high, sprayed glass over a length of 125 yards of roadway and hurled metal from shattered lockers and baggage carousels and window-glass shards like shrapnel.

Killed 11 persons and injured about 75

The upward force smashed open a hole about 12 feet in diameter in the second-story six- to eight-inch floor of reinforced concrete and affected the upper-story ceiling.

The injured were quickly evacuated. The Health and Hospitals Corporation said its Emergency Medical Service, with 20 ambulances, four mobile emergency rooms and two paramedic unit vehicles, took 60 patients to hospitals. ∎

Pieces of broken glass are everywhere as cops motion vehicles to positions outside a terminal at La Guardia Airport where a bomb went off in 1975.

and Governor Carey say that they would never allow the city to default, and that there would be no fear of a default after the guarantee because of the city's commitment to balance its budget and keep a tight rein on expenses and borrowing.

But Federal officials, led by President Ford, warn that these sound like promises that have been heard before. Against the possibility of default, the authors of the loan-guarantee measures have arranged for the Government to pay off any municipal obligations by issuing 20-year United States bonds.

Since President Ford has pledged to keep vital services going in the city, Washington may have to pump funds—through loans, advances or outright appropriations—to do so. These would cost the Government as much, if not more, as predefault guarantees, the city says.

But to both President Ford and city and state officials, the ultimate "cost" of averting default in the city, or of rescuing default with Federal loan guarantees, lies in the precedent being set. ∎

JULY 4, 1976

Warshps of 22 Nations Arrive for Bicentennial

End of Free Tuition Hurts Women

Georgia Dullea

The day they voted to end free tuition at the City University of New York was the day the dinner table debates began in modest middle-class homes, debates that threaten to heat up as the summer wears on.

On one side of the table sits mother, the part-time undergraduate, who is expecting the first in a series of hefty tuition bills this fall and feeling somewhat guilty about it.

On the other side is father, the primary breadwinner, who may not be convinced that the family budget could—or even should—be stretched to finance mother's education.

"A lot of us are getting hassled at home about money. I guess I'll get hassled, too," said Kathleen Titolo, a 30-year-old mother with 75 credits toward a psychology degree at Richmond College on Staten Island.

In the next breath, though, Mrs. Titolo vowed to have her tuition check by September "if I have to beg, borrow or steal it."

It's not unusual to hear older women talk that way about college. They are, after all, a determined breed, part of a growing national phenomenon. Thousands of such mothers have made the leap from kitchen to campus in recent years. Many have walked off with degrees, some with honors.

Now money looms as a large, possibly insurmountable hurdle for some women in families whose taxable income hits the $15,000 mark—not that high by today's standards, yet high enough to exclude them from the Community University Assistance Program for part-time students.

As a result, they face tuition bills of $35 to $40 a credit next fall. This, added to the babysitting and other expenses that go with a mother's college career, may mean the end of some careers.

And in at least one community, Staten Island, women are searching for alternatives.

Rosalyn Ruggiero and Kathleen Titolo, slim, dark-haired sisters who wore gold chokers that spelled out their first names, came to a lounge at Staten Island Community College where a meeting of the newly formed Women for Education was under way the other night.

"These are not active feminists. They do not have that kind of support group," said Sandi E. Cooper, associate professor of history at Richmond. "These are women who are angry and frightened that they won't be allowed to finish the educations they started."

"Many are driven by poverty," Professor Cooper said. "The emotional poverty of being around small children all day long has gotten to them. They're like sponges soaking up ideas."

Some women's lives are further complicated by full-time jobs. This was the case with Helen Ferrarese.

"I'm so interested in school that I came with the flu," Mrs. Ferrarese said. "I wish my children had the enthusiasm I have for school. I feel younger, like a new person. I feel important. When I put down on my job application that I went to college… me…I felt so proud."

A few weeks ago the women loaded up their station wagons with placards and children and converged on the St. George Ferry Terminal where they demonstrated before crowds of commuters. They are also starting workshops to learn how to lobby.

As more than one wife admitted, the problem may not always be the husband.

"If it comes down to a bike for my child's birthday or tuition money for me, I think I'm going to choose the bike," Marie Schiavo said. "I have too much guilt on my back. It's hard to shake it when you're brought up like that." ■

Dem Convention Raises Issue of Watergate

James M. Naughton

Jimmy Carter and wife, Rosalynn, wave to the delegates at the 1976 Democratic National Convention in New York.

Mr. Carter need not mention Watergate or the Nixon pardon. Other Democrats are willing to do so, with or without his encouragement.

They have done so all week at Madison Square Garden. Watergate is at once the target of the Democrats' National Convention rhetoric and the wellspring of the party's enthusiasm for a Nov. 2 contest with President Ford.

There was symbol enough in Mr. Carter's choice of Peter W. Rodino Jr., the New Jersey Representative who directed the Nixon impeachment inquiry, to nominate him for President last night. Even so, the Carter staff encouraged Mr. Rodino's allusion to a national faith "shaken by the resignation in disgrace of a President and his Vice President and by the issuance of an untimely pardon that outraged the American sense of equal justice."

In the aftermath of the blackout in 1977, firemen battle an arsonist's handiwork on Marmion Avenue in the Bronx.

It was not accidental that Barbara C. Jordan, the black Texan with slate-like self-assurance and eloquence with the ring of fine crystal, delivered a convention keynote address and that Paul S. Sarbanes of Maryland presented a platform plank on law enforcement by vowing never to tolerate "lawlessness in govern-

pardon

ment." Both served with Mr. Rodino on the House Judiciary Committee that helped drive Mr. Nixon from office and then inquired formally into the pardon.

If Watergate subverted their last bid for the White House, the Democrats are clearly trying to make it a foundation for this one.

"The American people," said Robert S. Strauss, the Democratic national chair-

man, "can forgive and forget many things, but they cannot and will not pardon an Administration and a governmental philosophy which has undermined our nation for eight painful years.

Senator John Glenn's otherwise bland opening night speech was enlivened by a reference to "the unprecedented disgrace of Watergate." The Democrats' unsuccessful nominee of the Watergate election year, Senator George McGovern, felicitously reminded the convention of a line that emerged from Ronald Reagan's camp: "Congressman Ford couldn't pardon Nixon; President Ford did."

Senator Hubert H. Humphrey, the "happy warrior," roused the Garden audience to a roar with a declaration that, under the Republicans, "crime has reached into the highest offices in the land."

"They took it off the streets," he said. "They put it in the White House." ∎

JULY 14, 1977

State Troopers Sent into City as Crime Rises

Lawrence Van Gelder

Thousands of looters, emboldened by darkness and confusion, ranged through the city last night and early today in a wave of lawlessness.

Amid shattering glass, wailing sirens and the clang of trashcans used to demolish metal storefront barricades, thieves and vandals ravaged store after store.

Governor Carey ordered the state police into the city to assist the local police.

At the same time, other people left their homes to help direct traffic in the suddenly darkened streets. Often armed with flashlights, they took up their impromptu stations at intersections and guided drivers and pedestrians.

By 2 o'clock this morning, the police reported a total of 880 arrests, almost all for looting in Manhattan, the Bronx, Brooklyn, and Queens. In downtown Brooklyn and in East Harlem, where looting and rock and bottle-throwing were reported, several policemen were listed as casualties.

"It's a lot different from 10 years ago," said Daisy Voight, referring to the blackout of 1965 as she emerged from a meeting in Harlem. "Last time people were helpful. This time people are scared. They are running for buses or bars. Everybody's afraid to go out."

So accelerated was the police effort against the onslaught of looters in Brooklyn that officers bringing prisoners into the central booking facility in the 84th precinct stationhouse, at 301 Gold Street, did not wait as usual to fill out papers.

Some vandals invaded apartments. Here and there, there were reports of gunfire. In Harlem, Diane Dickens of Norfolk, Va., said: "I heard about five shots up there and I started running. This is the first time I ever saw anything like this."

"As soon as the lights went out, the people went for the stores," said Patrolman Paul Migdalen at the 23rd Precinct stationhouse, on 102nd Street between Third and Lexington Avenues, where a score of black and Hispanic women and children had taken refuge. ∎

103

AUGUST 12, 1977

SON OF SAM ON KILLINGS: 'It Was a Command...I Had a Sign'

Howard Blum

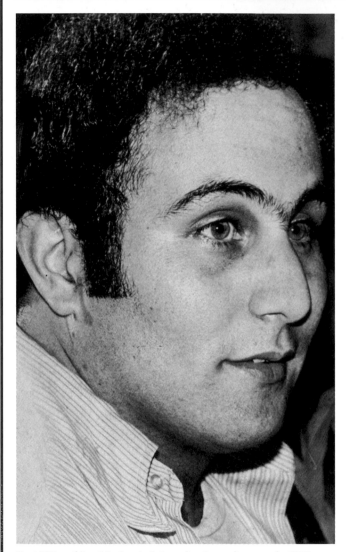

David "Son of Sam" Berkowitz being taken into police custody, 1977.

"For more than a year I had been hoping for just one thing—a chance to talk to the 'Son of Sam,' a chance to ask him why," said Detective Gerald Shevlin. He was part of the special homicide task force that had conducted the search for the .44-caliber killer, the largest manhunt in New York's history.

At a little after 2 o'clock yesterday morning, Detective Shevlin had his chance.

Ten detectives who had been assigned to the task force headed by Inspector Timothy Dowd since its formation after the .44-caliber killer claimed his fourth and fifth murder victims in April, crowded into Room 1312 in Police Headquarters and for one-half hour "fired every question we could think of" at the 24-year-old suspect, David Berkowitz of Yonkers.

"Why? Why did you kill them?" a detective asked the suspect.

"It was a command," a detective reported Mr. Berkowitz as responding. "I had a sign and I followed it. Sam told me what to do and I did it."

Sam, the 24-year-old postal worker explained in a passive voice, is Sam Carr, a neighbor in Yonkers, "who really is a man who lived 6,000 years ago."

"I got the messages through his dog," Mr. Berkowitz said. "He told me to kill. Sam is the devil." Mr. Carr is a neighbor whose dog Mr. Berkowitz is accused of having shot.

Earlier, the detectives had Mr. Berkowitz reconstruct each of the .44-caliber killer's eight attacks.

The suspect, according to officers at the interrogation, said he was "out driving every night since last July [1976] looking for a sign to kill."

"The situation would be perfect," the suspect was quoted as having said. "I would find a parking place for my car right away. It was things like that which convinced me it was commanded."

"Then when I got a calling," he said, "I went looking for a spot."

Mr. Berkowitz, who said a "buddy in Houston" had bought the gun for him, reportedly told the police he had the Charter Arms Bulldog revolver, the .44-caliber weapon the police say was used as the murder weapon, "for about a month" before the first shooting.

Speaking in terse sentences, the suspect explained how he always parked about a block and a half away from the scene of each attack "and then ran like hell to my car."

The constant hurling of questions at the suspect was interrupted, however, as Mr. Berkowitz explained what he had planned to do on the night when he was captured.

"I was going out to kill in the Bronx," he allegedly explained. "I was going to look in Riverdale."

And then Mr. Berkowitz for the first time posed a question: "Do you know why I had a machine gun with me tonight?"

"I'll tell you," he said. "I wanted to get into a shootout. I wanted to get killed, but I wanted to take some cops with me."

When asked if he had any remorse, he reportedly said, "No, why should I?"

Fortune's 500 Go to Connecticut

Eleanor Charles

Over the last 10 years more than 100 corporate executive offices have relocated in Connecticut, virtually all from New York City, and concentrated for the most part in lower Fairfield County. According to David Driver, executive assistant to the State Commissioner of Commerce, 104 such companies were listed as of February 1976, "and at least a dozen more have come in since."

Mr. Driver said that Fairfield County was possibly second after New York as the home of "Fortune 500" companies. "The last time I looked, Chicago was second with 33, but Fairfield now has 33, so unless Chicago acquired more, it may be a tie," he said.

As the saturation point approaches, companies are looking farther up in the state. Union Carbide, which will employ between 3,500 and 4,000 people (at least 1,000 of them from the local area) has announced that it will build a substantial blood-diagnostic facility in Wallingford, providing production jobs for that area.

"That's an offshoot we're very glad to have," remarked Mr. Driver. "We are finding that once a company builds a corporate headquarters they begin to consider Connecticut for factory operations and they bring a plant in later."

Stamford has acquired the largest number of corporate headquarters of any community in the state.

Said Mr. Driver, "We are actively trying to pinpoint Connecticut as the place from which to serve the Northeast market, whether it's as far down as Washington or as far north as Montreal. The Governor is one of our top salespeople—she often meets with executives. We don't really go out and raid. We usually hear from them first—they tell us they might be interested in Connecticut, and then we ask them how we can help." ∎

Reggie Jackson, 'Mr. October,' helped defeat the Dodgers in the '77 World Series.

YANKEES TAKE FIRST SERIES IN 15 YEARS

Joseph Durso

With Reggie Jackson hitting three home runs in three straight times at bat, the New York Yankees swept all those family feuds under the rug last night and overpowered the Los Angeles Dodgers, 8-4, to win their first World Series in 15 years.

They won it in the sixth game of a match that had enlivened both coasts for the last week, and that rocked Yankee Stadium last night as hundreds of fans poured through a reinforced army of 350 security guards and stormed onto the field after the final out.

For a team that already had made financial history by spending millions for players in the open market, the victory in the 74th World Series also brought new baseball history to the Yankees: It was the 21st time that they had won the title, but the first time since they defeated the San Francisco Giants in 1962 toward the end of their long postwar reign. And it marked a dramatic comeback from the four-game sweep they suffered last October at the hands of the Cincinnati Reds.

But for Jackson, the $3 million free agent who led the team in power hitting and power rhetoric, this was a game that perhaps had no equal since the World Series was inaugurated in 1903. He hit his three home runs on the first pitches off three pitchers, and he became the only man in history to hit three in a Series game since Babe Ruth did it for the Yankees twice, in 1926 and again in 1928.

But nobody had ever before hit five in a World Series—let alone five in his last nine official times at bat—a feat that the 31-year-old Pennsylvanian accomplished during the last three games in California and New York.

"This is very rewarding," Manager Billy Martin said later, referring to the quarrels his team had surmounted while beating the Kansas City Royals for the American League pennant and then the Dodgers for the World Series. "We had to beat two great teams. I'm proud of our players and what they accomplished this year. What made them overcome all those obstacles? We had five or six guys help patch things up during the season. Reggie? He was sensational." ∎

KOCH'S NARROWED WIN

Douglas E. Schoen and Mark J. Penn

The real story of the mayoral election is not so much that Edward I. Koch won but that his margin of victory was so small. Mr. Koch, who began the general-election campaign with a 30 percent lead in the polls, sank to as low as 4 percent last weekend and managed to win by only a relatively narrow 50 percent to 42 percent margin over Mario Cuomo.

The precipitous decline in Mr. Koch's position was not the result of any change in his campaign strategy or rhetoric during the eight-week general-election campaign. He continued to say and do exactly what he had done during the primary and runoff campaigns. Moreover, his campaign was better organized and financed than Mr. Cuomo's during the general election, and on that basis alone he should have been expected to increase his lead rather than see it shrink so dramatically.

Why did Mr. Koch win so narrowly? The answer lies not so much in the details of the day-to-day campaign but rather in the nature of the electorate.

New York City voters now have a deep suspicion of candidates supported by the political Establishment, and by Election Day Mr. Koch found himself surrounded by a disparate group of political, labor and business leaders who were united in just one thing: They sensed a Koch victory.

And while Mr. Koch went to great lengths to maintain his independence, nevertheless by Election Day he appeared to the electorate like a man allied with the same forces that were behind Abraham Beame four years ago.

Mr. Cuomo had twice the budget Mr. Koch did in the initial primary because of Governor Carey's fundraising help. But Mr. Carey's support proved to be such a liability for Mr. Cuomo that it probably cost him victory in the first primary and in the runoff.

While Mr. Cuomo may have appeared the less independent candidate in the runoff, Mr. Koch probably made more ad hoc alliances during that period. And Mr. Cuomo tried to point this out. Unfortunately for him, his charges made no impact during the 10-day campaign, and Mr. Koch mitigated the potential damage by announcing that he did not want the county leaders' support.

In his victory speech, Mr. Koch joked that governing would be easy compared to campaigning. But he now faces a more difficult task. On one hand he must seek accommodation with established business and labor leaders. But he cannot lose his independent posture, or his popular support will be severely jeopardized. ∎

Westway's Liabilities

John B. Oakes

The fate of Westway, the colossal interstate highway-and-landfill proposal for lower Manhattan's Hudson River waterfront, is now hanging in the balance somewhere between Mayor Koch, who doesn't want it, and Governor Carey, who does.

The Mayor would "trade in" the $800 million (more or less) in available Federal highway funds for urgently needed mass-transit improvements, as the law specifically allows. The Governor, whose consent is necessary for the proposed "trade-in," seems bemused in this election year by what could well turn out to be a billion-dollar boondoggle, reminiscent of Albany Mall and World Trade Center, as unnecessary as it is uneconomic.

The fundamental point is that the city does not have to assume the burden of the air- and water-polluting Westway project in order to achieve the universally accepted goal of opening up the Hudson waterfront, rehabilitating those piers worth saving, providing access to the river, and accelerating (without increasing) north-south traffic along Manhattan's western rim.

A program to improve the rapidly deteriorating mass transit system, by all odds the principal artery of New York's economy, seems more directly responsive to the long-term economic and social requirements of the city than does the alternative choice of pouring the same Federal funds into what Mayor Koch long ago described as the "economic and environmental disaster" of Westway. ∎

Manhattan's Hudson River waterfront is now hanging in the balance

'IN' CROWD AND OUTSIDE MOB SHOW UP FOR STUDIO 54 BIRTHDAY

Leslie Bennetts

Liza Minnelli and club owner Steve Rubell (right) at Studio 54 in 1978.

Outside it was chaos: Pushing, shoving mobs squashed against the barricades at the front and back entrances, shouting and pleading to be let in by the harried sentries at the door.

Inside, however, the scene was something else entirely. "It's like the end of the Roman Empire," marveled one wide-eyed young woman. "It's like being inside a Fellini film," remarked a curly-haired man. "It's the best floor show in town," giggled Truman Capote. "It's show business," purred Bianca Jagger.

It was, in fact, the first anniversary of Studio 54, and the birthday party Wednes-day night marked what seemed, in the short and racy life span of the disco, a ripe old age indeed. One year old this week, Studio 54 is still drawing the kind of night people "everyone said wouldn't last more than a couple of months," recalled Steve Rubell, the owner, with a grin.

Lasted they have, and the beat goes on. The fierce music throbs like a pulse in the brain, strobe lights flicker over hundreds of seething bodies, the air is musky with the fragrance of marijuana, and the spectacle is so riveting a lot of people never get around to dancing at all. Up in the balcony, a black-leather-clad Truman Capote simply stood and watched, looking blissful. "I've been to an awful lot of nightclubs, and this is the best I've ever seen," he said happily, waving a tiny hand at the cavorting multitudes below. "This is the nightclub of the future. It's very democratic. Boys with boys, girls with girls, girls with boys, blacks and whites, capitalists and Marxists, Chinese and everything else—all one big mix!"

That it was, and rather an exotic mix, too: close to three thousand people of assorted (and sometimes indeterminate) gender, looking a bit like the effluence of a time warp machine gone berserk. There were gorgeously

(cont'd. on next page)

(cont'd. from previous page)

rouged half-naked boys dressed as slaves; there were emperors with capes of gold and silver lamé; there were courtesans and vamps, denims and furs, leathers and feathers, sequin-spangled faces and wild hair shot through with glitter. Heads bobbed in cowboy hats, monks' cowls and jewel-encrusted skullcaps, flowered bonnets and fluorescent antennae, top hats and Mouseketeer ears.

"I think Studio 54 brought a glamour back to New York that we haven't seen since the 60's," mused Liza Minnelli. "It's made New York get dressed up again."

Those who made it through the barricades ranged from Diana Vreeland to Reggie Jackson, Andy Stein, Margaret Trudeau, David Brenner, Bob Tisch, Kenneth Jay Lane, Peter Allen, Clive Davis, Geoffrey Holder, Bill Boggs, Francesco Scavullo, Carrie Fisher and David Geffen, Princess Diane de Beauveau, Lucie Arnaz and D. D. Ryan.

The party was still going strong as a pale dawn crept into the sky, but everything must eventually come to an end— eventually, one suspects, even Studio 54, despite its current state of prosperity. Discos tend to self-destruct long before they can claim a second birthday, but Steve Rubell seemed unconcerned about the future of his phenomenon. "Nothing lasts forever," he agreed. "But I'm going to try my darnedest to keep it going as long as possible. You just keep on hustling." ∎

MAY 16, 1978

Gambling Board Gives Go-Ahead to First Atlantic City Casino

Donald Janson

ATLANTIC CITY, May 15—Resorts International was granted a temporary license today to operate the first legitimate gambling casino in the country outside Nevada, and it appeared likely that the casino would open on the Boardwalk here May 26.

The vote of the five-member commission, following a four-day public hearing that ended today in Convention Hall, was unanimous. The decision was greeted with loud applause by spectators at the hearing.

The temporary license is for six months. The Casino Control Act was amended earlier this year to permit this during investigation into any possible criminal associations or criminal records of company officials.

Robert Martinez, director of the Division of Gaming Control of the Department of Law and Public Safety, is in charge of the ongoing investigation into possible criminal backgrounds. He said the investigation had turned up nothing that would prevent issuance of a license. If it does, he said, "We will bring it before the commission post haste."

The commission also approved "test runs" at the casino, using play money at the roulette, blackjack and craps tables Wednesday and Thursday for 700 invited guests, to be followed by test runs the next three nights for 2,000 guests who could also play slot machines with real money and keep winnings.

The commissioners and their staff applauded when acrobatic dancers performed for them as they reached the Superstar Theater, a big, terraced black, silver and green nightclub above the casino, when Steve Lawrence and Eydie Gorme have been booked as the first headliners, to be followed by Bill Cosby, then Don Rickles.

"This room is a conspicuous improvement over Las Vegas," Mr. Merck said. "The chairs are big enough to sit on and the tables are far enough apart to have a drink and enjoy the show."

NOVEMBER 6, 1978

THE TIMES AND NEWS RESUME PUBLICATION
Resolution of Labor Disputes Ends 88-Day Shutdown of Papers

Damon Stetson

The New York Times and The Daily News resumed publication today after the resolution of a pressmen's strike and other labor disputes that had shut down operations at the two newspapers for 88 days and had prevented The New York Post from publishing for 56 days.

The windup was complicated during a hectic weekend of negotiations when the Times unit of the Newspaper Guild of New York, representing news and business employees at the newspaper, suddenly put up picket lines as its bargaining talks dragged on Saturday night.

With other unions pressuring for a return to work, the guild agreed yesterday to remove its picket lines at The Times and to hold a meeting to permit members to vote on the publisher's final proposal.

Early today, the guild members approved the pact, 226 and 121.

Members of Printing Pressmen's Union No. 2, who walked out Aug. 9 after the publishers of the three newspapers unilaterally posted new work rules, formally ratified a new six-year contract late yesterday that assures job security during that period for 1,508 regular pressmen, but that also allows management to reduce manning through attrition and to eliminate costly overtime. Management officers say they won most of their goals of cutting pressroom costs over the next six years, but concede that they had miscalculated how long and costly the shutdown would be.

Unions ratifying new agreements included the paperhandlers' and the machinists' at both newspapers and the truck mechanics' at The News, all of whom had been on strike, and the stereotypers'. The deliverers' union, a key group because of

---

the indispensable role of its members in distributing newspapers, reached a new agreement with the publishers of The Times and The News last Friday.

The long strike officially ended at 3:34 P.M., when George E. McDonald, the president of the Allied Printing Trades Council and also of the mailers' union, announced that the unions on strike, with the exception of the guild, had settled their disputes and that the papers would be able to publish today's editions.

Wages were never a major issue in the dispute, since a pattern for increases of $23 a week in the first year, $23 a week in the second and $22 a week in the third had been established in earlier negotiations between the publishers and the deliverers' union. The basic weekly pay for pressmen working five shifts had been $261.41, but management sources said many pressmen made substantially more as a result of extra shifts and overtime.

Wages were never a major issue

During the long strike, radio, television, local magazines and suburban newspapers experienced a boom in advertising, listeners and readership. The papers that were struck face possible long-term damage in the loss of readers and advertisers who may not return. Some of these losses could be to cost-efficient newspapers in the suburbs, such as Newsday on Long Island, The Newark Star-Ledger, The Record in Hackensack, N.J., and eight Westchester County dailies published by the Gannett chain.

The strike also saw the emergence of four interim tabloids published in the city in an effort to cash in on advertising revenues and to fill the news void. Many bylines familiar to readers of the struck papers appeared in these papers—The City News, The New York Daily Press, The New York Daily Metro and The Graphic. ■

NELSON ROCKEFELLER: BORN TO WEALTH BUT THE WRONG PARTY

Warren Weaver Jr.

Nelson Rockefeller picutred here in 1974, died on January 26, 1979 at the age of 70.

The stocky man in the well-worn double-breasted suit took a deep breath, strode over to a cluster of farmers, held out his right hand and said: "Hi there, I'm Nelson Rockefeller. I'm running for Governor, and I'd like to hear about your problems." The time was 1958, the scene a field at the edge of Savanah, N.Y., where something called a Potato Festival was in progress. The moment

(cont'd. on next page)

(cont'd. from previous page)

in history: the political debut of Nelson Aldrich Rockefeller, the first of uncountable handshakes, his first face-to-face with the American electorate—that group he was never able to persuade to grant him their highest confidence.

At a routine ground-breaking ceremony, he insisted on mounting a bulldozer, got the operator to give him instructions, then maneuvered the machine down the field. He was, all agreed, made for television.

He also proved to be made for New York. After disposing of Averell Harriman, a distinguished public servant but a dull and doctrinaire campaigner, Mr. Rockefeller brushed aside over the next dozen years challenges by three Democrats who remain footnotes in history. Within a year after his first victory, he was campaigning for President.

Nelson Rockefeller was a politician of enormous resources, great ambition and very considerable natural skill, but he was born, by fate unkind, into the wrong party. Later the rules changed, but members of his family and the Dartmouth Class of 1930 simply did not become Democrats. And public figures who counted loyalty among their assets did not switch parties—not in the 1950's. With the wisdom of hindsight, it can be said with near-certainty that no convention of the Republican Party was ever going to nominate Nelson Rockefeller for President.

It was not that they didn't like him; a great many of them did. It was not that he was really too radical; he publicly professed conversion to almost every Republican orthodoxy. It was that he symbolized all the things that heartland Republicans disliked and distrusted: the East, the Ivy League, internationalism, big government, social consciousness. To the last, when Gerald Ford felt compelled to push him aside as Vice President to appease his centrist constituency, he was unwelcome not because of what he said or did but what he stood for.

He was a fascinating, charming, complex and sometimes confounding figure. Long before the fundamentalism of Jimmy Carter, Mr. Rockefeller brought a measure of Baptist faith into politics.

Mr. Rockefeller was one of the first national politicians brave enough to risk divorce while still an active campaigner. He was demonstrably attractive to women, a political as well as personal asset. His personal generosity was great. And although he largely kept it under control in public, he had a temper. He once interrupted a speech to berate, by name, a reporter who had been whispering to a companion rather than paying strict attention. The public reprimand was before an audience of editors; an apology was private.

The cultural gap between Mr. Rockefeller and much of his party was exemplified when he hung part of his modern art collection in the executive mansion in Albany and invited the Legislature over for drinks. Staring at an abstract work that was an explosion of vivid colors, one upstate Assemblyman said: "That's the way the world looked to me on the day I discovered sex." ∎

Science, Technology
and Health

There was this new device that a store clerk waved over a coded tag and thus automatically recorded a sale. There was another gizmo, too, that let a person compose letters, contracts, the great American novel, whatever, and store the material for easy retrieval. Its name wasn't terribly appealing: word processor. Not many writers thought of themselves as in the business of processing words. But the machine had its uses. So did a gadget with the funny name of Apple II, introduced by a fellow called Steve Jobs. It was just the thing for playing games, displaying color graphics or even doing sophisticated mathematical computations.

The Apple II computer, designed and built by Steve Jobs and Steve Wozniak.

Many of the technological inventions that the world now takes for granted had their birth in the 1970s, often without a widespread appreciation for their revolutionary potential. "No one could say for sure why people might need a computer at home," a Times article said in 1977. " 'For fun' seemed the most honest answer." The personal computer, it continued, "seems to be a spectacular toy in search of a use."

In fact, the '70s were in a many respects a golden age of technology, even if new inventions were often designed for entertainment purposes. Video cassette recorders first ap-

peared on the market; by decade's end, 800,000 of them had been sold. Sony introduced the Walkman, which provided two-way privacy—for the listener, who had a band in his ears as if it were live, and for everyone else, spared from having to put up with his musical tastes. Electronic games offered new forms of relaxation, like the bouncing dot that went back and forth, an imitation of table tennis called Pong.

The computer tennis game Pong being played on the Videomaster games console.

But if such machines were only for fun, they wouldn't merit discussion for long. Far more substantively, technology in the '70s charted new territory in medicine and in the applied sciences.

To cite but one example, a machine introduced in 1973 made it possible for doctors to see the human brain in cross section, just as in their illustrated anatomy textbooks. The rest of us took a little longer to appreciate the wonders of CAT scan technology.

In 1978, a girl named Louise Brown was born in England. Nothing unusual there—except that sperm from Louise's father did not fertilize an egg cell from her mother in the tried-and-true manner of old. Louise was conceived in a Petri dish, with the fertilized embryo then injected into the uterus of the mother, whose fallopian tubes were blocked. Thus we had the first test-tube baby, an inelegant description for a perfectly normal infant who would otherwise have not come into being.

Louise Brown, the first 'test-tube' baby at age 3 with her parents, John and Lesley Brown.

SCIENCE, TECHNOLOGY AND HEALTH

Not all innovations required machines and laboratories. Choking on food was a leading cause of death in the United States. A Cincinnati surgeon named Henry J. Heimlich discovered that if you sharply pressed against a person's upper abdomen, you could expel whatever was blocking the windpipe. Now, in New York and other cities, one cannot dine in a restaurant without gazing at a poster that explains how the Heimlich maneuver works.

But for heroic discoverers it would be hard to top Norman E. Borlaug, a crop expert whose work earned him a Nobel Prize in 1970. Dr. Borlaug's experiments in plant breeding led to an agricultural movement called the Green Revolution. He never much liked that term. But it was indeed nothing short of a revolution, enabling high-yield wheat and rice to be bred. Habitually famine-plagued countries in Asia and Latin America could finally feed themselves. In the second half of the most blood-soaked century ever known, Dr. Borlaug was credited with saving hundreds of millions of lives.

Let it be noted that he did not win in one of the science categories. He was awarded the Nobel Peace Prize.

Nobel Prize–winning biologist, Dr. Norman Borlaug, holding up stalks of his specifically crossbred wheat, designed to be more disease resistant to produce maximum yields.

FEBRUARY 3, 1970

Bertrand Russell is Dead; British Philosopher, 97

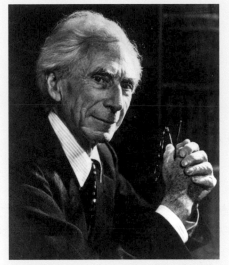

Welsh philosopher and mathematician Bertrand Russell in the 1950s.

LONDON—Bertrand Russell, the philosopher and mathematician, died at his home in Wales last night. He was 97 years old.

The winner of the Nobel Prize for literature in 1950, Russell, was best known in recent years for his campaign against war, nuclear bombs and racial discrimination.

Advancing years did not diminish Lord Russell's fervor. In December he appealed to Secretary General U Thant of the United Nations to support an international war crimes commission to investigate alleged "torture and genocide" by Americans in Vietnam.

"Three passions, simple but overwhelmingly strong, have governed my life; the longing for love, the search for knowledge and unbearable pity for the suffering of mankind."

In those words Bertrand Arthur William Russell, the third Earl Russell, described the motive forces of his extraordinary long, provocative and complex life.

Possessing a mind of dazzling brilliance, he made significant contributions to mathematics and philosophy for which alone he would have been renowned. Two works "The Principles of Mathematics" and "Principia Mathematica," both published before World War I, helped to determine the direction of modern philosophy. Russell's name, as a result, was linked with those of such titans of thought as Alfred North Whitehead and Ludwig Wittgenstein.

Largely for his role as a philosopher, Russell received the Nobel Prize for Literature in 1950.

Unlike some progressive thinkers, Russell epitomized the philosopher as a public figure. He was the Voltaire of his time, but lacking in the Sage of Fernay's malice. From the beginning to the end of his active life, Russell engaged himself with faunlike zest in the great issues of the day—pacifism, rights for women, civil liberty, trial marriage, new methods of education, Communism, the nuclear peril and war and peace—for he was at bottom a moralist and a humanist. ∎

APRIL 15, 1970

CRIPPLED APOLLO 13 STARTS BACK; MEN APPEAR CALM

John Noble Wilford

Apollo 13 astronauts James Lovell, John Swigert and Fred Haise after their rescue.

(cont'd. on next page)

(cont'd. from previous page)

CRIPPLED APOLLO 13 STARTS BACK

HOUSTON, Wednesday, April 15—With the lives of its three astronauts hanging in the balance, the crippled spaceship Apollo 13 swung around the moon last night and rocketed toward an emergency splashdown in the Pacific Ocean Friday.

After the craft looped the moon, a crucial four-minute and 24-second rocket firing sent the astronauts on a fast and more accurate course—a drastic change of plans caused by Monday night's massive power failure aboard the moon-bound spacecraft.

The rocket blast started at 9:41 p.m. Eastern standard time as the astronauts, depending on their attached lunar landing craft as a back-up return craft, pulled away about 6,000 miles from the right side of the moon.

"That was a good burn," Mission Control radioed after the lunar module's descent rocket shut down on schedule.

Though its success sent the first ripple of relief through Mission Control in 24 hours, Capt. James A. Lovell Jr. of the Navy and Fred W. Haise Jr. and John L. Swigert Jr., both civilians, were still a long way from home and not yet out of trouble.

The three astronauts were calm, despite the fact that they were racing time, trying to reach the earth before their severely limited reserves of oxygen, electricity and water ran out.

Grim-faced flight directors here called it "the most critical situation" in the history of the American space program. But, barring any further trouble, they said the chances of the astronauts' safe return were "excellent."

Dr. Thomas O. Paine, head of the National Aeronautics and Space Administration, said at a news conference that the exploration of the moon would continue despite the Apollo 13 crisis.

The U.S.S. Iwo Jima, the primary recovery ship, is steaming toward the splashdown site, about 600 miles southeast of American Samoa.

The three astronauts appeared calm, though a little weary, as they turned their backs on the moon and their chances for making the nation's third manned landing there. The original mission plan was for Captain Lovell and Mr. Haise to land on the moon tonight.

What would have been their landing craft, the lunar module, was now their "lifeboat." Still attached to the command ship, it was providing their oxygen, electricity and propulsion for getting home. ∎

OCTOBER 22, 1970

U.S. Agronomist Gets Nobel Peace Prize

Bernard Weinraub

OSLO, Norway, Oct. 21—An Iowa-born crop expert who has sought to ease the world's hunger with research into improved strains of wheat and rice was awarded the Nobel Peace Prize for 1970 today.

Dr. Norman E. Borlaug, who heads a team of scientists from 17 nations experimenting in Mexico with high-yield grains, was given the prize, valued at $78,000 for his "great contribution" in spurring food production, especially in Mexico, India and Pakistan.

He is director of the International Maize and Wheat Improvement Center of Mexico, a research organization operated by the Rockefeller Foundation in cooperation with the Mexican Government.

"Dr. Borlaug, as the prime mover in the 'green revolution,' has made it possible for the developing countries to break away from hunger and poverty," said the chairman of the five-member prize committee, Mrs. Aase Lionaes, who is president of one of the segments of the unicameral Norwegian Parliament.

"Dr. Borlaug, through his improvement of wheat and rice plants, has created a technological breakthrough which makes it possible to abolish hunger in the developing countries in the course of a few years," she said.

Dr. Borlaug, 56 years old, the son of Norwegian immigrants and a resident of Mexico City, said during a visit to Norway in August: "The world's population problem is a monster which, unless tamed, will one day wipe us from the earth's surface."

The most recent award of the Nobel Peace Prize to an American was made to Dr. Martin Luther King Jr. in 1964. Other recent American peace laureates were Dr. Linus C. Pauling in 1962, Gen. George C. Marshall in 1953 and Dr. Ralph J. Bunche in 1950. Last year's winner was the International Labor Organization.

The 1970 laureate—one of 38 nominees—was born in Cresco, Iowa, and educated at the University of Minnesota. Since 1944 he has worked on plant pathology and agricultural projects, mostly in Mexico, to increase food production in countries where hunger remains a searing problem.

The award was announced in a third-floor board room of the green stone Norwegian Nobel Institute, which is across the street from the United States Embassy.

Mrs. Lionaes, seated before television cameras and reading in Norwegian and later in English, said:

"The Nobel Committee of the Norwegian Parliament has decided to award the Nobel Peace Prize in 1970 to Dr. Norman E. Borlaug for his great contribution toward creating a new world situation with regard to nutrition."

After taking note of his efforts to improve wheat and rice strains, she said:

"By his work he has also contributed to the solution of another main problem of today, namely the population explosion.

"The kinds of grain which are the result of Dr. Borlaug's work speed economic growth in general in the developing countries. In short, we do not any longer have to be pessimistic about the economic future of the developing countries."

MARINER 9 PLACED IN ORBIT OF MARS

John Noble Wilford

PASADENA, Calif., Nov. 13—An unmanned American spacecraft, the television-equipped Mariner 9, rocketed tonight into an orbit of Mars.

It thus became the first manmade object to circle another planet—the first to get a close-up view of the Mars of fanciful dreams, of legendary civilizations and, in reality, of reddish deserts and craters, polar caps and occasional dust storms.

Mariner was apparently set for months of monitoring the planet with television and remote sensing instruments. The mission's primary objectives are to return mapping photographs of 70 percent of the surface and to study the planet's thin atmosphere, clouds and hazes, surface chemistry, and seasonal changes.

Confirmation of the successful maneuver came 6 minutes 43 seconds after it happened. That is the time it takes for a radio signal to travel from Mars to the earth.

The robot explorer first swung into orbit over the planet's southern hemisphere, about 940 miles over Sirenum Sinus, which is a Martian feature that appears dark to viewers on the earth.

The first to get a close-up view of the Mars of fanciful dreams, of legendary civilizations

---

A 15-minute firing of the spacecraft's small rocket slowed Mariner from a speed of nearly 11,000 miles an hour to about 8,300 miles an hour, slow enough to be captured by the Martian gravity.

Mariner's planned orbit should take the vehicle as close as 800 miles from the surface and as far out as 10,700 miles twice daily. Following this course, at a 65-degree angle to the equator, the spacecraft should weave between the planet's two tiny moons, Phobos and Deimos, and maintain enough altitude to keep it from plunging to the Martian surface for at least 17 years. This was planned so as to avoid contamination of the planet before studies are conducted on the surface by landing spacecraft.

Two Soviet spacecraft, each five times larger than Mariner, are approaching Mars and, according to reports from Moscow today, are intended to make landings. It was not clear, however, if the Soviet craft carry any life-detection instruments. ∎

Protecting Ocean Mammals

To the Editor:

Your excellent Feb. 16 editorial, "Incidental Slaughter," eloquently lamented the fact that dolphins and porpoises are being slaughtered by the hundreds of thousands each year by the U.S. tuna fleet, which drowns these animals in their huge nets used to catch tuna. Your editorial was much appreciated by all of us who have been engaged in the legislative battle to save not only the porpoises and dolphins, but all ocean mammals from killing for fun and profit.

You mention with favor a bill introduced by my colleague Senator Harrison Williams of New Jersey. I am familiar with this bill and its proposals. However, on Sept. 19, 1971, The Times editorially endorsed the Ocean Mammal Protection Act, introduced by Representative David Pryor and myself in March, 1971. Our bill, which had about 100 co-sponsors in the House and 27 co-sponsors in the Senate, is a tougher bill than any introduced so far. It is a bill which basically calls for a ban on the imports of ocean mammal products into the United States, a moratorium on all killing of marine mammals by U.S. citizens except for treaty obligations and native hunting, and a directive to our Secretary of State to stop "fearing to negotiate," but to immediately initiate negotiations for protective treaties for all species of ocean mammals worldwide.

Hearings are presently being held before Senator Ernest Hollings' Oceans and Atmosphere Subcommittee, and I am supporting an amendment to my bill introduced by Senator Hubert Humphrey which deals with the dolphin situation in a more specific way. Money would be allocated to the U.S. tuna fleet to help it switch over to new types of nets, and after a one-year period, it would be illegal to kill dolphins in the course of catching tuna.

The U.S. Government estimates that between 250,000 and 400,000 dolphins are being killed annually in one area of the Eastern Pacific, and some scientific estimates go as high as 900,000. Unless the Oceans and Atmosphere Subcommittee takes immediate steps to end the killing of dolphins—perhaps the most intelligent and friendly of all animals—several species of these mammals will soon be threatened with extinction.

Fred R. Harris
U.S. Senator from Oklahoma
Washington, March 7, 1972

DDT BANNED IN U.S. ALMOST TOTALLY

E. W. Kenworthy

William D. Ruckelshaus of the Environmental Protection Agency, in 1972.

WASHINGTON, June 14—William D. Ruckelshaus, administrator of the Environmental Protection Agency, banned today almost all uses of DDT, the long-lived toxic pesticide that lodges in the food chain of men, animals, birds and fish.

After almost three years of legal and administrative proceedings, reports by scientific bodies and public hearings, Mr. Ruckelshaus declared in a 40-page decision that the continued use of DDT over the long term, except for limited public health uses, was an unacceptable risk to the environment and, very likely, to the health of man.

Mr. Ruckelshaus's order is effective Dec. 31, 1972. In the meantime, he explained, growers of cotton, peanuts and soybeans—the three crops that account for almost the total domestic use of DDT—will get instruction in the handling of a substitute pesticide, methyl parathion. The substitute is toxic, but unlike DDT, it degrades quickly.

Samuel Rotrosen, president of Montrose Chemical Corporation, sole United States manufacturer of DDT, immediately asked the United States Court of Appeals for the Fifth Circuit in New Orleans to set aside the order.

Mr. Ruckelshaus's order represented a major victory for environmental groups that in October, 1969, petitioned the Secretary of Agriculture to begin the proceedings that would lead to cancellation of DDT for shipment in interstate commerce. The organizations, which later took their cause to the Federal courts, were the National Audubon Society, the Izaak Walton League, the Sierra Club, the Western Michigan Environmental Council and the Environmental Defense Fund, which also supplied legal counsel for the plaintiffs.

The decision came 10 years after Rachel Carson, the biologist, set off the controversy over DDT with her book "The Silent Spring," in which DDT was called "the elixir of death" for birds, mammals, fish, insects and perhaps for man if it proved to have cancer-causing properties.

The order represented a defeat for the maker and the 31 formulators of DDT; for the Department of Agriculture, which had entered the case on their side, and for Representative Jamie L. Whitten, Democrat of Mississippi, chairman of the House Appropriations subcommittee that handles funds for the environmental agency. Mr. Whitten, a cotton-state Congressman, has maintained that DDT is necessary to combat the boll weevil and boll worm. ∎

English Cow Gives Birth to Calf From Embryo

LONDON, June 7—A calf grown from an embryo that was removed from its mother and frozen for a week before being implanted in another cow was born at an agricultural research unit near Cambridge today.

The calf, a Hereford bull, was the first large animal to be developed from an embryo held in a frozen state. Previously, only mice have been born this way, in experiments in the United States.

In the Cambridge experiment, conducted at the Agricultural Research Councils Unit of Reproductive Physiology and Biochemistry, two fertilized eggs were removed from the mother, frozen, and then implanted in a Friesian-Hereford crossbred cow. One embryo failed to develop, but the other grew into a calf that was born naturally and in good health.

A spokesman for the Agricultural Research Council, which is financed by the Government, said it was too early to say whether the process would cause genetic change.

The freezing technique, which the spokesman stressed is a long way from commercial application, could prove of great value in livestock breeding.

Breeds of cattle not of current commercial interest could be maintained as embryos until required, since fertilized eggs could be stored long after the parents were dead, and valuable cattle could be transported easily in an embryonic state.

According to L. E. Rowson, deputy director of the Cambridge unit, the process could also help improve the quality of beef cattle. Some dairy cows—because of their higher grade milk—produce better quality calves than beef cattle, and would make excellent host mothers for embryos from beef cows.

The embryos, removed from the mother 10 days after she was fertilized by artificial insemination, were stored in liquid nitrogen at a temperature of minus 196 degrees Centigrade for six days.

A major problem in the process is to prevent the death of the egg from the breakdown of tissues when ice crystals are formed. For this reason, some of the water in the eggs was replaced with an antifreeze agent and the eggs cooled slowly, at one-fifth of a degree Centigrade a minute.

Surgery was used to remove the eggs from the mother and implant them in the host mother. ∎

Scientists Envision Tapping Power of 'Black Holes'

Walter Sullivan

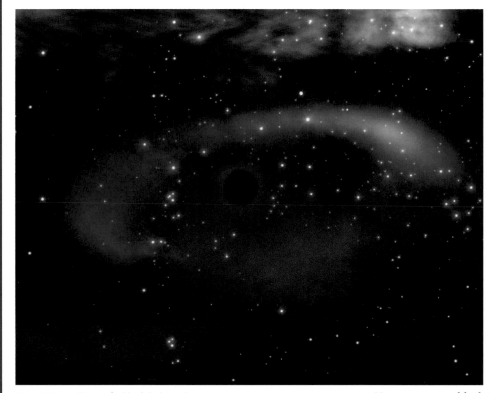

An artist's rendition of a black hole in the universe.

What probably qualifies as the most far-out proposal yet advanced to meet the world's future energy needs—harnessing hypothetical "black holes" within the solar system—was presented here Thursday to an international audience of physicists.

This elicited gasps and chuckles from the scientists. However, it was offered in all seriousness by a three-man team from the Lawrence Livermore Laboratories, which are operated for the Atomic Energy Commission by the University of California.

As pointed out by Dr. Lowell Wood, who presented the paper by the Livermore scientists, the conditions required for fusion are provided in stars by "gravitational confinement"—that is, by the vast pressure generated by gravity in the core of such objects, including the sun. In the proposal that he described, gravity would also provide the compression, but its source would be a "black hole."

It is widely suspected that here and there in the universe there are assemblages of matter that have been crushed to such density that they have lost almost all the characteristics of atomic particles.

Such an object would generate gravity so intense that no light could escape it or pass close to it, producing, in effect, a black hole in the sky.

In 1971, Stephen Hawking, a young British theorist, proposed that during the earliest, most chaotic, superdense phase of the universe's explosive birth some areas were forced, by the turbulence, to contract, rather than expand. This could have generated a multitude of black holes, great and small, that may still exist, including some within the solar system or even in orbit around the earth.

If the earth were squeezed enough to become a black hole it would be no larger than a table tennis ball. However, a black hole exerting gravity comparable to that of the earth could not have remained unobserved within the inner solar system.

For such an object to have been undetected so far within the orbit of the moon, it would have to be less than one millionth the earth's mass, according to the Livermore group.

However, some black holes, they said, may be so tiny that their effects would not be evident beyond a few hundred yards. If such an object were discovered, they continued, a power plant would be placed in orbit to accompany the moving hole (also in orbit), but remain at a discreet distance from it.

Fusion fuel would then be fired from the power plant to plunge into the hole. As the fuel was squeezed toward the vanishing point by the hole's extremely powerful, close-in gravity, the fuel would fuse, releasing vast amounts of energy. The radiated energy would be collected by the plant and then beamed to the earth at microwave radio frequencies.

Dr. Wood and his co-authors, Thomas Weaver and John Nuckolls, cited arguments that more than half the matter of the universe may be in the form of black holes.

It has also been suggested by some scientists that the catastrophic Tunguska explosion that blew down forests in Siberia in 1908 may have been the impact of a small black hole. The conventional explanation is that the earth collided with a comet head.

While exploiting black holes "may appear to be enormously more difficult" than more conventional approaches to fusion, the three Livermore scientists said, the difficulties "may have been overestimated."

EAST AFRICA FOSSILS SUGGEST THAT MAN IS A MILLION YEARS OLDER THAN HE THINKS

Boyce Rensberger

Fossil remains of early man discovered over the last two years in East Africa are causing a major upheaval in the study of human evolution by suggesting that man's origins lie more than twice as far into the past as had been supposed from earlier evidence.

The new evidence is beginning to suggest that relatively intelligent human beings originated at least three million years ago in the plains of Africa, living in complex societies and inventing stone tools. Hitherto the earliest evidence of man was about 1.75 million years old.

The latest fossils also indicate that the early ancestors of modern man may not have been the only manlike creatures alive at that time. It now appears that early man coexisted with at least two and perhaps three or more other species of "near man" whose physical appearance may have been largely human but whose brains had remained apelike.

Until recently these "near men," called Australopithecus, were almost universally accepted as ancestors of modern man. Now there is evidence that they were merely smaller-brained contemporaries who died out as their larger-brained cousins continued to evolve.

Some authorities also believe that for early man to have attained the level of advancement inferred from certain three-million-year-old fossils and stone tools found over the last two years in Kenya and Ethiopia, the human lineage must have begun sometime between four and six million years ago.

These emerging views of man's evolution and the fossils upon which they are based are forcing a major rethinking of what was once considered a fairly straightforward interpretation of human origins.

Although these new views are not widely accepted among paleoanthropologists, who study human evolution, they constitute a revolution in the effort to learn where man came from. The more conservative experts who do not yet accept the new views concede only that the latest fossils, which are significantly different from previously known finds, have thrown the field into a disarray that may take years to sort out.

One of the basic difficulties now confronting paleoanthropologists is the lack of wide agreement as to what physical traits qualify a creature to be considered human. All manlike creatures, whether ancestral to modern man or not, are called hominids. "True man," given the genus name Homo, is considered but one branch of the hominid family tree.

At a recent meeting of fossil man experts in London, Dr. F. Clark Howell of the University of California at Berkeley said many new fossil finds possessed such perplexing anatomic features that it was almost impossible to put them into any coherent evolutionary sequence.

The current reassessment of man's evolution began in the spring of 1973 when Richard Leakey, a Kenyan scientist, announced the discovery of a 2.9-million-year-old form of man with a brain that was unexpectedly large for its antiquity.

It is now generally agreed that there were at least two types of Australopithecus, a large "robust" form and a smaller "gracile" form.

From the bones it is known that Australopithecus "man-apes" had short-statured bodies proportioned very much like those of modern man, walked erect or nearly so, had teeth adapted for a mixed diet of meat and vegetation, but had a brain of only 450 cubic centimeters, approximating that of chimpanzees. In modern human beings brain size ranges from 1,200 to 1,800 cubic centimeters. ∎

UPDATING DARWIN ON BEHAVIOR

American sociobiologist E. O. Wilson holds an ant at Harvard University in 1975.

The tightly organized societies of bees and ants, the mating rituals of birds, the hunting tactics of lion prides, the social hierarchies of monkey troops—these and dozens of other examples of animal behavior have long fascinated people. But they have rarely been offered as anything more than intriguing evidence for the remarkable variety of nature.

Lately, however, some of the biologists who study animal ways have come to believe that their findings point to a far more profound conclusion. Beneath the superficial aspects of social behavior that vary so across the animal kingdom, the scientists assert, there lie common behavioral patterns governed by the genes and shaped by Darwinian evolution.

This belief—the product of a new field of scientific inquiry called sociobiology—carries with it the revolutionary implication that much of man's behavior toward his fellows, ranging from aggressive impulses to humanitarian inspirations, may be as much a product of evolution as is the structure of the hand or the size of the brain.

The greatest impact outside of animal research is expected to be on sociology and psychology, which, some forecast, will eventually be forced to modify their theories and practices.

Sociobiology is the study of the biological basis for social behavior in every species from the lowliest ameba colony to modern human society. It seeks to explain the origin of that behavior in terms of how it improves an individual's or a society's fitness to survive.

Sociobiology's key contribution is the integration of Darwinian theory with the observations of animal behavior research, which have largely been descriptive.

"Sociobiology, The New Synthesis" by Edward O. Wilson, a widely recognized zoologist at Harvard University, is not due to be published until late June, but word of its preparation has spread far among biologists. Among those scientists who have seen advance copies of the book, which comprises 700 oversize pages, it has already stimulated considerable excitement.

Perhaps the most startling assertions of sociobiology have to do with the origins of altruism, a type of social behavior once regarded as uniquely human but which biologists have observed in many animal species, even down to microorganisms.

For example, when a predator breaks into a nest of termites or ants, members of the colony's "soldier caste" instinctively rush to place themselves between the intruder and the rest of the colony.

Like virtually all insect behavior, this act is believed to be governed by inherited instinct. But how could behavior that reduces an individual's chances for survival have evolved if natural selection favors only traits that improve the ability to survive?

Several species of birds and mammals will give warning signals to others of their kind if they see predator's approaching. In the process they draw the predator's attention to themselves, diminishing their own chances of survival.

Among birds, such as the Florida scrub jay, yearling offspring commonly remain with their parents for two or three more years to help feed the hatchlings of succeeding seasons.

That parents should help their offspring fits conventional evolutionary theories because they are ensuring the survival of those directly inheriting their own genes. The puzzle is why brothers and sisters should tax themselves to help those who are not their direct descendants. ∎

CREWMEN EAT LUNCH— BREZHNEV, FORD PRAISE LINK-UP

John Noble Wilford

HOUSTON, July 17—Astronauts of the United States and the Soviet Union united spaceships today and then joined hands in the first international meeting away from earth, a symbolic gesture of the two nations' expressed desire to cooperate in the exploration of space.

The American Apollo made physical contact with the Soviet Soyuz at 12:09 p.m., Eastern daylight time, about 140 miles over the Atlantic Ocean, 620 miles west of Portugal. Then, three and a half minutes later, the two ships achieved a firm link-up.

The Soviet and American crews met face to face more than three hours and two orbits of earth later. The linked spaceships were passing over Amsterdam at the moment.

Peering through the opened hatches into the Apollo's connecting module, Colonel Leonov welcomed General Stafford with the English words, "Glad to see you."

General Stafford, replying in Russian, said:

"A, zdravstvuite, ochen rad vas videt!" ["Ah, hello, very glad to see you."]

The two astronauts then shook hands through the hatches, an event that would have been all but unthinkable a few years ago when the two nations were rivals in space, as in most other affairs.

The 16-ton Apollo and 7½-ton Soyuz are scheduled to remain docked for two days, until Saturday morning. During that time, the astronauts will exchange gifts, share meals and conduct some scientific experiments.

Back on earth, in Moscow and Washington and at the Johnson Space Center here, officials of both nations offered congratulations to the crews and expressed the oft-repeated hope that this historic meeting would lead to further cooperation.

President Ford told the astronauts:

"Your flight is a momentous event and a very great achievement not only for the five of you, but also for the thousands of American and Soviet scientists and technicians who have worked together for three years to insure the success of this very historic and very successful experiment in international cooperation."

Leonid I. Brezhnev, the Soviet Communist leader, said in a message to the astronauts: "The successful docking proved the correctness of the positions which were carried out in joint cooperation and friendship between Soviet and American designers, scientists and cosmonauts."

U.S. Astronaut Thomas Stafford (left) with cosmonaut Alexei Leonov meeting in padded hatchway of the docking module that connects their spacecrafts.

LAST OF APOLLOS RETURNS SAFELY

John Noble Wilford

HOUSTON, July 24—The three Apollo astronauts returned safely to earth in the Pacific Ocean today, successfully concluding the first international manned space flight and ending an era of American space exploration that began in 1961.

No further manned space trips are planned by the United States until 1979 at the earliest.

The cone-shaped spacecraft, suspended from three parachutes, hit the calm waters at 5:18 p.m., Eastern daylight time. It was almost precisely on target, about 6.2 miles from the U.S.S. New Orleans, a helicopter carrier, and 330 miles northwest of Hawaii.

Within 45 minutes, after recovery teams hauled the spacecraft out of the water and onto the carrier deck, the three astronauts emerged from the vehicle that had been their orbital home for nine days.

Brig. Gen. Thomas P. Stafford of the Air Force, Vance D. Brand and Donald K. Slayton were reported in excellent physical condition. They walked briskly, with no apparent stiffness, to a platform for the formal welcoming ceremonies that included a telephone call from President Ford at the White House.

Mr. Ford noted that the splashdown marked the conclusion of the Apollo program, which included the landings of men on the moon, the operation of an orbital space station for periods of up to 84 days at a time and the first Soviet-American mission.

A week ago, General Stafford, Mr. Brand and Mr. Slayton flew the Apollo spaceship to a rendezvous and link-up with a Soviet Soyuz spaceship 140 miles out in space. It was the first cooperative space venture between the two nations, once bitter rivals in space exploration. The two ships remained docked in earth orbit for 44 hours, while the two crews visited each other's craft and conducted some joint experiments.

A principal objective of the Apollo-Soyuz project was to test compatible rendezvous and docking systems being developed for future United States and Soviet manned spacecraft and stations under the agreement on space cooperation signed in May, 1972, by President Nixon and Premier Aleksei N. Kosygin.

At a news conference here after splashdown, Dr. James C. Fletcher, administrator of the National Aeronautics and Space Administration, said:

"By going into space together we have shown a sometimes skeptical world that perhaps there is a real chance for world unity. It is my belief that we should hang on to this chance and expand our efforts into more extensive cooperation both on earth and in space." ∎

Nobel Winners Explain the Asymmetry of Atomic Nucleus

Walter Sullivan

Three physicists—an American and two Danes—who a quarter of a century ago showed that the atomic nucleus can be grossly asymmetrical and explained why, have been designated 1975 winners of the Nobel Prize in Physics.

The winners are Dr. James Rainwater of Columbia University, Dr. Aage N. Bohr of the Institute for Theoretical Physics in Copenhagen and Dr. Ben Mottelson of Nordita, the Nordic Institute of Technology, also in Copenhagen.

Dr. Bohr's father, Niels, one of the foremost physicists of this century, founded the institute with which his son is now associated. Dr. Mottelson, a former American, has acquired Danish citizenship. The three winners were closely associated in their efforts to explain perplexing features of some atomic nuclei that had come to light in the late 1940's.

It had long been believed that the electrons surrounding the atomic nucleus, while moving at high velocity in a seemingly random manner, can be considered to be arranged in concentric shells. Each shell has "slots" for a specific number of electrons.

When this concept was applied to the nucleus, the protons and neutrons of which it is formed were likewise seen as arranged in shells. In some cases the outermost shell had its full complement of these nuclear particles. In others it did not.

In the latter case it was noted that the electric charge on the nucleus was not spherically symmetrical. Since the other shell was incomplete, a departure from electrical symmetry was not surprising, but in the heavier nuclei—those with numerous "slots" in their outer shells—this asymmetry was far greater than expected.

Dr. Rainwater told yesterday of a colloquium given at Columbia in 1949 by Dr. Charles H. Townes, himself to become a Nobel laureate, describing this puzzling discovery.

"It seemed obvious." Dr. Rainwater said, that it could be explained if the nucleus was far from being spherical—if some nuclei for example, were cigar-shaped.

There was, however, "enormous reluctance" on the part of physicists to abandon the idea of a spherical nucleus. It occurred to Dr. Rainwater, though, that interactions between the swiftly moving particle or particles of an incomplete outer shell with particles churning about deep inside the nucleus might distort the entire nucleus.

Dr. Rainwater, according to Dr. Havens's recollection, replied that he was an experimenter, not a theorist. At the time, however, he was sharing an office at Columbia with Dr. Aage Bohr, then a visiting fellow in physics.

Dr. Bohr returned to Copenhagen with Dr. Mottelson and worked out a more detailed explanation for this "collective" effect within the nucleus in terms of the various forces at work between particles there.

Since the work that is being honored was done so long ago, Dr. Rainwater said the announcement took him by surprise. ∎

MARGARET MEAD IS DEAD OF CANCER AT 76

Alden Whitman

Margaret Mead, the anthropologist, author, lecturer and social critic, died yesterday at New York Hospital after a yearlong battle with cancer. She was 76 years old.

The slight but sturdy Dr. Mead was possessed of virtually boundless energy, an unquenchable curiosity, a tenacious memory and a genius for organizing her time.

She often gave the impression of being ubiquitous because she was rarely at rest in any one place for very long and because she could not permit a moment to pass unutilized. In all this she had a zest that even in her 70's confounded friends and colleagues of lesser verve.

The American Museum of Natural History, with which she was associated for most of her professional life, once drew up a list of subjects in which she was "a specialist." The list read:

"Education and culture; relationship between character structure and social forms; personality and culture; cultural aspects problems of nutrition; mental health; family life; ecology; ekistics; transnational relations; national character; cultural change and cultural building."

The museum might well have added "etcetera," for Dr. Mead was not only an anthropologist and ethnologist of the first rank but also something of a national oracle on other subjects ranging from atomic politics to feminism. She took on (and dismissed with disdain) Dr. Edward Teller,

Anthropologist Margaret Mead studying a decorated Tchambul skull in 1968.

the hydrogen bomb advocate, and she was once described as "a general among the foot soldiers of modem feminism." Insofar as anyone can be a polymath, Dr. Mead was widely regarded as one.

Although she could be lacerating, she was more often gentle and witty. She believed civilized mankind to be often ill-informed and pigheaded, yet she usually displayed great compassion for its individual members.

From the publication of her first book, "Coming of Age in Samoa," in 1928, in which she described the values of adolescent lovemaking in Samoan society, Dr. Mead's name became associated with sexual theory. A good deal of her subsequent writing contended that sexual repression worked against healthy maturation of the young and against successful marriages.

The book was descriptive rather than statistical. It also included two chapters that daringly applied her findings to modern society, in which she proposed that

straitlaced sex attitudes might be relaxed without "accepting promiscuity."

The book has often been attacked in scientific circles as too subjective and lacking the data for verifiable behavior. However, her conclusions were based on detailed observation, and if she did not conduct anthropometric tests or produce statistical surveys she did convey her subjects graphically.

Dr. Mead settled down with the people she was studying. She ate their wild boar, wild pigeon and dried fish; helped to care for ill children, and gained the confidence of her informants. At one time she built a wall-less house so she could observe everything around her.

She possessed a trait unusual in anthropologists of her time, an ability to shed her Western preconceptions. She would sit on the ground for hours without moving as she watched tribal peoples. "She knows how to use her eyes, how to see," said Kevin Heyman, a fellow scientist. "She has an uncanny perception for different cultural styles." ∎

Man Stood Up First and Got Smart Later

Stephen Jay Gould

Longfellow exhorted us to "make our lives sublime" by leaving "footprints on the sands of time." Metaphor sometimes turns concrete (literally in this case), for the oldest signs of human activity have been reported from Tanzania—footprints 3.6 to 3.8 million years old pressed into volcanic ashes that cemented within hours after an array of creatures from centipedes, to hu-

man ancestors, to elephants passed by.

Those who have seen the footprints say they can scarcely find words to express the stunning visceral impact these fossils have had upon them. Two protohumans walked north for about half a city block; one paused midway, turned west for a moment and then proceeded on. To discover evanescent

(cont'd. on next page)

(cont'd. from previous page)

activity, a frozen moment, seems almost miraculous.

Yet the discovery extends far beyond esthetics; it resolves a crucial issue that could not be decided from the scrappy bones thus far discovered at this oldest of fossil hominid sites. From the orientation of the prints and the inferred morphology of the foot, with its well-developed arch and strong big toe parallel to the other toes, we know that these earliest hominids had developed fully upright posture—long before the brain began its major episode of enlargement. These early hominids had larger brains than any ape—but not much larger. Yet they walked upright.

The truly amazing thing is that scientists have known this fact for so long, yet it continues to elicit astonishment at every rediscovery. Eugen Dubois even recognized this fact in the name he gave to the first human fossil,

discovered in Java in the 1890's—Pithecanthropus (now called Homo) erectus. But Homo erectus, at nearly 1,000 cubic centimeters, had a brain already closer to human than to great-ape size. When the African australopithecines were discovered in the 1920's, their equally upright posture, this time in a creature with a brain only slightly larger than an ape's, sealed the case. Upright posture evolved first. The standard texts of anthropology have carried this message for 50 years.

Yet it is a message that many people do not want to hear. Humans are so tied to an old philosophical prejudice for elevating the brain above all other parts (in importance, not only in mere anatomical position) that they tend to assume that its increase must have guided historical evolution as well.

A motley group of idiosyncratic and eminent scholars defended the primacy of upright posture for more than 100 years before

bones were found to verify their suspicions. Lorenz Oken, the oracle of a German romantic movement known as *Naturphilosophie*, wrote in 1809: "Man by the upright walk obtains his character. The hands become free and can achieve all other offices. With the freedom of the body has been granted also the freedom of the mind."

So let it be recorded once again, this time from the volcanic ash of Tanzania—upright posture was the trigger of human evolution. It also represents the most radical anatomical alteration experienced during human evolution—a major restructuring of the pelvis and foot. An enlarged brain, by contrast, requires little more than a prolongation of rapid fetal growth rates to later stages of our life cycle. ■

Paleontologist Stephen Jay Gould next to drawers filled with fossils at Harvard University.

JANUARY 11, 1970

COMPUTERS TAKE STEP TO MATURITY

Dr. John C. Porter

Office workers learning a new computer system in 1970.

A generation ago, there were no electronic computers. By 1960, 6,000 had been installed; and by today, 60,000. Midway through the 1970's, that number could double.

Neither the number of computers nor their "gee whiz" technology are likely to be the most dramatic aspects of this young and burgeoning field in the new decade. We are beginning to accept and understand the computer's incredible computation speeds, measured in billionths of a second; its ability to transmit information across continents and to process many different jobs simultaneously, and man's ability to communicate directly with the machine on his own terms.

In the seventies, the most dramatic innovations will not be in the tools themselves, but in the results from thoughtful and timely application of these tools.

The computer today holds enormous potential for people determined to find solutions to mankind's most pressing problems.

Medical applications are high on the list of socially beneficial applications beginning to emerge for the seventies. Computer-based systems will process information between patient wards and laboratories, freeing doctors, nurses and laboratory personnel from time-consuming paperwork. Continuous monitoring of critical patients will spot potentially serious conditions earlier than ever.

Psychiatry and psychology will turn to the computer for assistance. Computers linked directly with testing instruments can help detect abnormalities and analyze how the brain responds to different kinds of stimuli. They will also be used in matching transplants and in helping to classify chromosome images, separate certain ones from their neighbors and allow detailed study.

As computer memories get larger, our cities will be able to plan more intelligently for water distribution systems, air pollution controls, fire, ambulance and police deployment, traffic flow and controls, urban renewal projects and airport facilities.

The natural environment is another application. We have begun to study earthquakes by mathematical simulation to enable man to predict them.

Increasingly more accurate mathematical models of our economy will be developed with the aid of computers. Federal, state and local governments will be able to try new ways of dealing with economic and social problems, testing alternative solutions before they are implemented.

The fight against hunger is beginning to enlist the help of the computer in developing better cereal grains and livestock. Test data from breeding experiments in many parts of the world are beginning to be fed into a central computer and analyzed. The results will help the individual grower to match available varieties of hybrid seed to his special growing conditions.

Much still needs to be learned about the learning process itself. The new decade will see more widespread experimentation with computers in an effort to find out how people learn, and how the computer can be used to help them learn.

In the decade just ended, technology has developed the means for another form of man-to-computer interaction. Relatively low-cost terminals and communications links now allow hundreds of users to take advantage of the power of the same computer. "Time-sharing" techniques will expand rapidly in the seventies.

We have not yet learned how to take full advantage of the technology we have at our disposal today. The decade of the seventies will be one of developing the applications that will have the greatest beneficial impact on man and his future. ∎

FEEDING WHILE FLYING

JULY 4, 1970

Stacy V. Jones

WASHINGTON, July 3—The job of serving meals promptly to all the passengers in a large modern aircraft has challenged the manufacturers of the planes.

The Lockheed Aircraft Corporation's answer is given in a patent granted this week to Richard L. Vernon, a consultant on passenger accommodation. Mr. Vernon's plan for the L-1011, a three-engine jumbo jet, or air bus, called the Tri-Star, which will roll out in September, has already been demonstrated in a full-scale ground mock-up at the plant in Burbank, Calif. There, 250 people have been served within an hour.

In the arrangement broadly covered by Patent 3,517,899, carts partly loaded in a land commissary are stored in a galley below the passenger compartment. At meal time, they are raised to the cabin floor in elevators. Each Lockheed food cart has 27 trays, and hot entrées are kept in 27 casseroles in an oven on top of the cart. The stewardess puts the hot entrées onto the trays, which usually carry a dessert such as pastry.

First-class passengers who rate ice cream can be served from a special refrigerated cart. The L-1011 will have 18 carts, 10 for food and 8 for drinks. The company estimates that one stewardess can serve 30 passengers. ∎

PRICE TAGS 'READ' BY CASH REGISTER

SEPTEMBER 16, 1970

Isadore Barmash

A new electronic cash register and information system for stores that uses an optical "wand" to read credit cards, price tags and other coded tickets was introduced here yesterday by the National Cash Register Company.

Describing the system as "our most important program in 85 years of service to the retail industry," Robert S. Oelman, chairman, said that it virtually eliminated salesclerk errors, improved customer service and speeded up sales transactions.

The new system, known as NCR 280, sells for from $25,000 to $1-million, depending upon the complexity of the installation. A company official said that the system was applicable to department stores, discount stores and large specialty and apparel stores but "most likely could not be used by smaller retailers."

A hand-held wand, which looks like a penlight extending from a cable, is used to speed the process of recording the sale at the same time that the system amasses information.

The wand scans color-coded bars on credit cards, price tags or identity cards, with the cash register recording the information in the same general manner as a mechanical register would. This process, as a demonstration at the New York Cultural Center showed, takes seconds. Since it is not necessary to remove tags from merchandise in order to be scanned, there is little chance of tags being misread by the cashier and errors being recorded.

But the wand, which uses the principle of fiber optics, or wire fibers that respond electronically to different colors in the code, does not need to be used exclusively to operate the system. The register keyboard can be operated by the salesclerk's or cashier's fingers, except that this takes longer than the use of the wand would.

The Dayton, Ohio-based business machines company unveiled its new retail accounting system at a time when a number of other equipment manufacturers were also demonstrating either new or recently introduced point-of-sale devices. ∎

SPEED

French Jet Doubles Speed of Sound

NOVEMBER 5, 1970

Clyde H. Farnsworth

PARIS, Nov. 4—Sud-Aviation, builder of the French prototype of the Concorde supersonic airliner, announced today that its plane flew at twice the speed of sound, achieving its design cruise speed for the first time.

Concorde's inaugural flight in France on May 8, 1971.

I.B.M. Expands Capacity Of Computer

The International Business Machines Corporation announced yesterday that it had expanded the data storage capacity of its System/7 and provided a new custom-designed console. The System/7, introduced last fall, is I.B.M.'s lowest-cost computer, renting for as little as $352 a month.

The disk storage module is housed within the System/7 and contains either one fixed disk, or a fixed disk and a removable disk cartridge on a single drive. Storage capacity is either 1.23 million or 2.46 million 16-bit words with an average access time of either 126 or 269 milliseconds. The data transfer rate is 99,500 words a second.

The custom console, available on special order, permits users to display the status of a process, convey instructions to the computer or make inquiries.

The IBM Building in Chicago, October 1972.

André Turcat, the chief test pilot, took the plane to Mach 2 (about 1,320 miles an hour) 10 miles over the Atlantic. It flew at that speed for 53 minutes before returning to the Toulouse-Blagnac Airdrome an hour and a half later on its 102nd test flight.

The supersonic Soviet transport, the TU-144, flew 1,336 miles an hour—a little more than Mach 2—on May 26, Tass, the official press agency, announced. The TU-144 is remarkably similar in design to the Concorde.

The British Aircraft Corporation, the joint builder with Sud-Aviation of the controversial craft, also has a prototype in a testing program. The two planes made a dramatic flight over Paris in May, 1969, during the Paris Air Show.

Mr. Turcat said in an inflight interview with Radio Luxembourg that the plane handled beautifully and that he was satisfied. He told newsmen in Toulouse that the success went beyond expectations and marked the beginning of a new stage in the testing program.

He said he could not tell the exact noise level in the cockpit because he was wearing a flight helmet. "But I can tell you as soon as we fly at supersonic cruising speed," he added. "The cockpit is altogether quiet."

The French and British Governments are spending $100-million a year on the supersonic program and have been at pains to deny rumors that it may be scrapped. It has been denounced, mainly in Britain, as a diversion of resources needed for urgent social problems and as an atmospheric pollutant and noisemaker.

When he came to power in 1964, Prime Minister Harold Wilson weighed pulling out of the venture. He was persuaded to continue only after President Charles de Gaulle, the project's leading backer, threatened a suit against Britain in the International Court of Justice at The Hague.

Najeeb Halaby, president of Pan American World Airways, which has options on 8 of the first 24 production Concordes (British Overseas Aircraft Corporation and Air France share the others), told The Financial Times this week that a small group of airlines should be allowed to fly the plane in passenger service before it goes into quantity production. He said the airline industry had to be careful about so complex and expensive a plane. ■

sonic

LAND ACHIEVES HIS DREAM WITH NEW POLAROID

Robert Reinhold

American scientist and inventor Edwin Herbert Land with a Polaroid camera—model SX-70, October, 1972.

CAMBRIDGE, Mass., Oct. 29—It has been nearly three decades since Edwin H. Land, the physicist who reigns over the Polaroid empire, first dreamed of producing a totally automatic camera that would instantly print vivid color pictures.

Now at 63 years of age, the shy but friendly inventor-industrialist believes he has finally achieved his dream of "absolute one-step photography."

Unlike previous Polaroid Land cameras, Dr. Land's new SX-70 requires nothing more of the user than to focus and snap the picture. There are no sticky caustic negatives to peel off. A second and a half after exposure, a dry blank film card pops out automatically. At once it begins to develop and print itself in daylight. Moreover, the final, richly colored picture is said not to fade or darken with time.

Dr. Land, describing the technology in his cluttered office here last week, said that the new film process required an elaborate chemical balancing act performed by dozens of ingredients. They migrate, react, dissolve, oxidize, reduce and combine with precision—then all activity ceases when the picture is finished.

Asked how he knew the idea would work, Dr. Land recites his philosophy about scientific creativity. "If you can state a problem, then you can solve it," he said, meaning that the most important thing is to visualize what has to be done. "From then on it's just hard work.

"There is no such thing as a simple invention," he continued. "It has to be supported by a whole chain of equally difficult ideas. There were 100 places where most people would have said, 'There is no point in going on.'" ■

New Brain X-Ray Device May Transform Therapy

Lawrence K. Altman

LONDON, Aug. 25—Radiologists in five British and American hospitals are X-raying patients' heads with a new machine that for the first time allows doctors to see the brain in cross section, just like an illustration in Gray's textbook of anatomy.

Preliminary results suggest that the technique could have a major impact on the health industry by reducing cost, risk and length of hospitalization for patients suffering from a wide variety of brain disorders.

The machine has become a main topic of discussion in international medical circles. Some doctors regard the new technique, which provides far more detail than conventional skull X-rays, as the most revolutionary advance in radiology since Wilhelm Röntgen discovered X-rays in 1895.

By the end of 1973, seven more hospitals will be using the $350,000 scanner, developed by EMI, Ltd., a British company, largely out of American parts and British know-how.

Among the neurologists optimistic about the machine's potential is Dr. Roger Bannister, who, while a medical student in 1954, was the first to run a mile in less than four minutes. Dr. Bannister, now a specialist in brain diseases, said in an interview here that the new method was "terrific" and "fulfills a long-standing need."

DECEMBER 8, 1974

Shakeout Time for Calculators

Nathaniel C. Nash

Consumer delight with pressing the little buttons and reading the lit-up numbers on pocket calculators is reflected in the fact that 1 out of 10 Americans now owns one.

A look behind the scenes, however, where these quietly efficient instruments are made, discloses nothing less than a fierce struggle for survival.

Most consumer products have suffered from the squeeze of inflation and recession, but pocket calculators defy such economic pressures. Their unit sales have increased 80 percent over last year while prices have decreased 40 percent.

This still immature industry had its beginnings in 1971, when the first calculators sold for $300 and up. Today the cheapest one retails for $17. Almost 5 million units were sold in 1972, the first full year of production and officials estimate that the worldwide market this year will total 25 million units with revenues of $2 billion.

By 1977, they predict, the market will reach its saturation point of 160 million units.

During the last three years dozens of companies have jumped into the calculator field. At one point last year, close to 90 American and Japanese companies were producing and marketing their own brand-name calculators. Fierce competition and price cutting flourished, and a substantial market shakeout has resulted, and it's not over yet.

Of the 90-odd companies, some 20 have already dropped out. After the new year begins, analysts say, 20 or 30 more could easily leave. Eventually fewer than 10 viable companies are expected to remain in the industry.

"There was a time when a calculator manufacturer or assembler couldn't do anything wrong," commented Edward A. White, chairman of the Bowmar Instrument Corporation. "Everything he came out with sold. Now things have changed. Prices have come down so much that he has to make especially his own chips and other components to keep costs down and remain competitive."

Texas Instruments is the giant in the industry, and analysts expect it to stay that way. The company was a large semi-conductor manufacturer when it entered the consumer market with its first calculators in September, 1972. ■

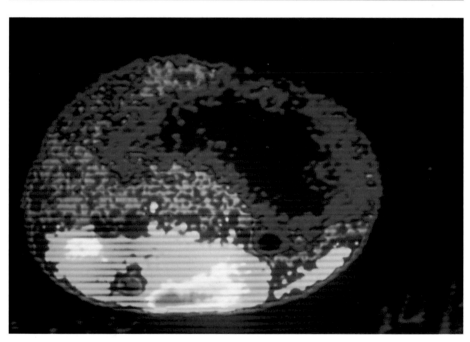

The first CAT scan of brain, 1973.

In less than 30 minutes, doctors can get precise information about a wide variety of brain disorders from the machine, which combines conventional X-ray tubes with computers and a Polaroid camera. The disorders include strokes and other effects of arteriosclerosis, cancers, benign brain tumors, birth defects such as cysts, and some skull injuries resulting from accidents.

The new technique, in which a fully conscious patient lies flat on his back while an X-ray tube moves across his head, allows doctors to film the brain directly from above, getting a view that was previously unobtainable. As a result, a technician can select the level at which doctors wish to obtain horizontal cross section pictures of the brain.

In some cases, the new machine can provide more information than can be extracted from all the existing sophisticated X-ray techniques. In others, it can provide the same information but at less X-ray exposure and without the sometimes fatal risks involved in the special techniques used in medical centers throughout the world.

Enthusiasm among radiologists and neurosurgeons reflects the difficulties of accurately diagnosing brain diseases through present techniques, which require several hours from a team of highly trained medical specialists and anesthesia in some cases. ■

The "Executive" calculator by Clive Sinclair in 1972.

ELECTRONIC GAMES BRING A DIFFERENT WAY TO RELAX

William D. Smith

Pong being played on an original Magnovox Odyssey 200.

The delighted cries of young children this Christmas morning will be punctuated in many homes by "blips" and "pongs" as families settle down to the latest craze—electric games.

The games, which are played on the family television set, to which electronic-game logic has been added, are the bestselling indoor entertainment item in years, according to some stores.

Odyssey, an electronic game by the Magnavox Company, has been on the market since 1972 but began taking off last Christmas. This year a new competitor has entered the home market, Atari Inc., which has specialized in selling coin-operated electronic games to amusement parks and penny arcades.

Stanford J. Zimmerman, chairman of Abraham & Straus, commented, "The Odyssey game is going very good with us, as it is around the country."

"Pong is one of the strongest items we have this Christmas," a spokesman for Sears, Roebuck & Company said. "Pong," the Atari game, is an electronic version of table tennis with the black electronic dot flashing back and forth between the electronic paddles.

The electronic games, which sell at $100 and more, are based on modern electronic circuitry that allows an electronic designer to infuse any kind of desired logic to the television screen.

Both companies' production lines were working full time until the Christmas holiday.

While Magnavox and Atari have the field to themselves at the moment, a number of competitors are expected next year.

Why have electronic games suddenly become popular?

Mr. Zimmerman of retailer Abraham & Strauss suggests that "people want new ways in which to spend their leisure time. It's part of a trend of looking for different ways to relax."

A Sears spokesman commented, "It is part of the consumer desire to get away from harsh realities. The success of citizen-band radio systems in the market is part of the same syndrome."

A retail analyst said, "It's part of the growing trend toward participation. Warm-up suits, jogging, power hockey, electronic games in which you have to use your reflexes. We may be leaving the spectator era for the participation era. For my part I don't plan to watch the Super Bowl this year."

JULY 10, 1976

CB INTERFERENCE BRINGS F.C.C. 'HORROR STORIES'

Les Brown

The explosive growth in citizens band radio in the last 18 months, with new enthusiasts emerging at the rate of 500,000 a month, has been accompanied by a voluminous catalogue of complaints to the Federal Communications Commission about interference with other electronic devices, ranging from church organs to automobile ignition systems.

Among what the commission describes as "CB horror stories" are reports of automatic garage doors responding to the spill-over energy from citizens band transmissions, phonographs and public-address systems picking up from the CB sets, and television pictures suffering severe disturbances.

Despite these problems, the F.C.C. is expected next month to expand the number of channels available to CB users from the present 23 to as many as 40 or even 45. This would be done ostensibly to alleviate the congestion on the available citizens band channels, a traffic jam that worsens week by week as thousands more join the 12 million who are already caught up in the two-way radio craze.

But the commission believes that the addition of channels may actually be the key to reducing the capricious interference caused by the four-watt CB units.

In the view of the commission's engineering experts, much of the interference problem stems from equipment manufactured under the F.C.C. technical standards for CB radio that were adopted in 1958, when the boom was not foreseen.

"Expansion could bring in a whole second generation of equipment. This would be the time to tighten up our specifications," said Robert A. Luff, engineering assistant to Richard E. Wiley, chairman of the F.C.C.

"When CB radio took off, it caught the manufacturers as well as ourselves by surprise. Everyone started cutting corners for mass production and lowered their quality control. But even if everyone conformed to the standards, there would still be an interference problem," Mr. Luff remarked.

Mr. Luff said the commission was not convinced that the interference problem was wholly the fault of the CB radio sets. Many of the electronic products that are affected by the frequency energy radiated by CB units are susceptible to interference because they were built without the necessary shielding parts, he pointed out. Recognizing this problem, a bill has been introduced in Congress that proposes to give the F.C.C. regulatory authority over all electronic equipment.

The channel expansion is expected to set off an even greater explosion in CB radio usage than now exists, because of the aggressive promotional campaigns that are likely to be waged by the major domestic manufacturers for a share of the market.

Thus, the F.C.C. considers the increase to 40 channels only a temporary solution to the problems of overcrowded airways and electronic interference. When the present number of CB radio users doubles or triples, the commission expects to confront the present problems again. ∎

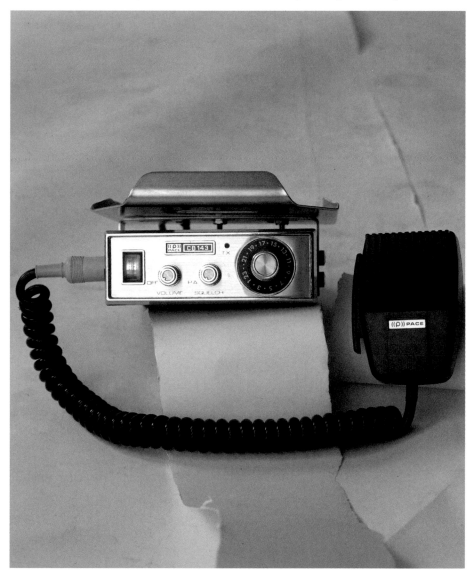

A Pace brand CB radio, model CB143, with an under-dashboard mount, 1977.

Computer Power Applied to Processing Words in Offices

Victor K. McElheny

Evelyn Berezin is a computer designer and entrepreneur who has lived a revolution for the last 25 years. Now she finds herself in the thick of another revolution: applying the powers of the computer to processing words in offices.

Still concerned by hindrances to her own career because she is a woman, Miss Berezin says she expects that easier measurement of productivity in the office with the new equipment should raise women's status and pay rather than lower them.

Up to 90 percent of the more than $500 million in sales of "word processing" equipment in the United States each year are made by the International Business Machines Corporation, some of whose engineers in West Germany invented the term a decade ago.

But the next largest enterprise in the field, with 1975 sales of nearly $20 million, is the Redactron Corporation of Hauppauge, L.I. Miss Berezin founded Redactron in 1969 and still heads the enterprise which was sold to the Burroughs Corporation last January.

With capital from Burroughs, Redactron is adding to its sales force and preparing for the first shipments in March of its Redactor II system, equipped with a cathode ray tube for text-editing. The system was introduced at a trade fair in Hanover, West Germany, last May. The introduction came as competition in the word processing industry was heating up.

I.B.M., continually adding to its word processing line since the introduction of typewriters equipped with magnetic cards in 1969, reached a climax last June with the announcement of a combined word and data processor using its System 32 computers.

The vague, catch-all term, "word processing," describes the use of a computer's ability to store and process electronic information in composing and producing the paperwork of an office: letters, contracts, reports, statistical tables and the like.

The computerized word processing system, flowering in a period when electronic components were becoming dramatically smaller and cheaper, transcribes the words that an author or a secretary writes onto magnetic cards, tapes or disks.

Word processors call up documents, page by page and line by line, on cathode ray screens for editing. They print out finished versions automatically or send them via telephone lines to distant points. Similar systems are penetrating the newspaper business rapidly.

After studying such other applications of the computer as point-of-sale terminals, cash registers hooked up to computers, and rejecting them because too much capital was involved, the founders of Redactron, including Ed Wolf, who died at the age of 36 in 1974, turned to word processing.

The business was expanding because of an explosion in office paperwork, a shortage of secretaries that drove up salaries, and the development of much cheaper electronic components.

Describing the $9 million in capital raised by Redactron from 1969 to 1972 as "keeping the wolf from the door," Miss Berezin said, "Not bad for somebody who grew up under the El in the Bronx." ■

COMPUTER SHOW'S MESSAGE: 'BE THE FIRST ON YOUR BLOCK'

Lee Dembart

Apple Computer co-founder Steve Jobs with Apple II computer. A chess game is displayed on screen.

BOSTON, Aug. 25—The computer revolution seems endless. Every six months, a new product comes along that outdates everything before it. The latest is the microcomputer, based on the same technology as the pocket calculator but capable of putting a powerful computer into homes and small businesses.

Several thousand people, many of them students or businessmen, turned out here today for "Computermania," a major explosion of microcomputers carrying price tags of $300 to $3,500. The displays were extensive, the exhibitors excited and the computer enthusiasts eager to study everything new.

But no one could say for sure why people might need a computer at home. "For fun" seemed the most honest answer. Some manufacturers said a home computer could balance a checkbook, although a $15 calculator could do the same thing. The personal computer seems to be a spectacular toy in search of a use.

"Sometimes it is difficult to explain to somebody what they need it for just as it would have been difficult to explain to someone in 1850 what they needed an automobile for," said Dave Armitage, president of Computer Power Inc. of Warwick, R.I., who was demonstrating a Sol terminal computer. "The uses of a machine like this are limited only to the user's imagination."

At another booth, Steve Jobs was demonstrating the Apple II computer, which is the

Some Good Teachers Never Get an Apple

Evan Jenkins

FREEPORT, NY—The poster outside the activities room at the Archer School acclaimed a couple of celebrities. It read: "Congratulations! Computer Wizards—Cathy Esopa—Olentha Von Redden—You've TOPPED OUT in Math at 8.0."

What it meant was that the two had mastered the mathematics curriculum at a level considered standard for the eighth grade, and were working to finish ninth-grade math. Olentha volunteered that he needed "nine more points to top out of junior high"—nine more 100's on tests. Cathy said she needed 10 more.

Olentha and Cathy are in the fourth grade. They are obviously bright children, but their work is not all that remarkable in the Freeport public schools, where computer terminals at which children learn have apparently been the key to a dramatic reversal of educational performance.

In 1970, the year Freeport began a pilot program using eight computer terminals, 29 percent of its third-graders and 40 percent of its sixth-graders performed "below minimum competence" in mathematics as measured by the New York State Pupil Evaluation and Progress Tests. Twenty-nine percent were below the minimum in reading in the third grade, 31 percent in the sixth.

In 1977, with all 8,000 Freeport students having access to instruction at a total of 200 computer terminals, only 6 percent of third-graders and 11 percent of sixth-graders tested below the minimum in math. The figures for reading were 9 percent in the third grade and 16 percent in the sixth grade. In the same seven-year span, the Freeport percentages in the "superior range" soared—in math from 21 to 40 percent in the third grade and 13 to 34 percent in the sixth; in reading, from 20 to 28 percent in the third grade and 13 to 26 percent in sixth.

"Target children" spend about two and a half hours a week at the terminals doing drill and practice exercises to supplement classroom instruction. Average and above-average children are required to spend only about 40 minutes a week, but so many use the terminals at lunchtime and after school, Mr. Holbrook said, that the average for each child in the district comes to about an hour and a half a week.

"It allows the talented child to surface by the second, third or fourth grade," Mr. Holbrook said. "Without computation, we could never give them the math they're getting. A really talented kid will learn by the ninth grade what I learned in the first or second year of college.

"Everybody in our district uses these things," he said. "It may not be the be-all and end-all, but it sure is a hell of a tool."

---

size of a portable typewriter and hooks up to a regular television set. It plays games, displays color graphics or does sophisticated mathematics. Mr. Jobs suggested that amateur radio operators could use the $1,300 device to figure frequency skips and that investors could use it to chart stock prices or do commodity spreads.

But, Mr. Jobs agreed, "most people are buying computers not to do something practical but to find out about computers. It will be a consumer product, but it isn't now. The programs aren't here yet."

Three years ago, there were no microcomputers. People who wanted computers at home had to rent or buy a terminal and plug in to a large computer somewhere, frequently at a university, where they would be one of a hundred other users in a time-sharing network.

The personal computer industry, which is estimated to total $30 million a year (up from $5 million two years ago) thinks its biggest market today is not the same hobbyist but the small business with sales of $250,000 a year or less. Up to now, computer time was too expensive for such enterprises. ■

Digital Dawn For Telephony

Peter J. Schuyten

WAKEFIELD, VA.—Since February the sleepy eastern Virginia town of Wakefield—once described as the kind of place you would like to live in on a Sunday—has been playing host to a steady stream of curious visitors from telephone companies in such distant places as Sunburst, Mont., Clinton, Ark., the Bahamas and even Hong Kong.

What they have come to see is a windowless, 30-by-100-foot red brick building that resembles nothing so much as it does a utility substation.

Yet this central office, owned and operated by the Continental Telephone Company of Virginia and serving 900 telephone customers, is in the forefront of what has been called the quiet revolution in telecommunications.

Inside, it contains the inner workings of a new and rather special telephone system, one that processes calls not in their original analog waveform but rather digitally, a technology that telephony experts say will someday be the standard for telephone switching systems of the future.

Digital switching technology, in use by the military for more than 20 years, not only is cheaper to manufacture and operate (taking up considerably less floor space when installed) but also extends telephone technology's most advanced features such as speed dialing, call forwarding and call waiting to even the most rural telephone company customer.

More important, when adopted on a large scale it will also mean substantial savings through a reduction in telephone company costs. These are savings that can be passed on to the consumer. The residents of Wakefield are already benefiting from this—Continental Telephone will not

(cont'd. on next page)

SCIENCE, TECHNOLOGY AND HEALTH

(cont'd. from previous page)

be asking for another rate increase for at least five years. Before the installation of the new system, rates were going up about once every two years.

For more than 75 years, ever since the birth of the telephone itself, voice signals have been transmitted in continuous electrical analog waves. In digital transmission, these sound waves are translated into the binary language of 1's and 0's understood by computers. In operation the digital equipment samples the voice about 8,000 times a second. The samples are then translated into digital characters that express the height of the analog wave form. Technically a digital signal is stronger than its analog counterpart, and it does not pick up interference or crosstalk. But the big advantage of digital use lies in both the initial and maintenance cost of the equipment.

Today such equipment manufacturers as Northern Telecom Inc. of Nashville, a subsidiary of Northern Telecom of Canada, are looking at a market of $700 million to $750 million a year, excluding Western Electric's portion. And by 1982 that figure is expected to reach $1 billion.

The Bell System, for its part, started converting to digital technology several years ago. Unlike the independents, who are starting at the local office level and working upward, Bell is starting at the top by converting its largest intercity toll offices to digital as well as some of its short-haul intracity transmission facilities at a cost of about $1 billion a year.

Today A.T. & T.'s manufacturing arm, Western Electric, is installing about 18 new digital toll switches a year. By the late 1980's it expects to have a nearly all-digital toll switching network in place, says Frank S. Vigilante, Western Electric's vice president for engineering.

A.T. & T. has been criticized over the years for not making the conversion sooner, but Mr. Vigilante says that it is strictly a matter of economics. Typically a local switch depreciates over a period of 30 to 40 years and, unlike the small independents, Bell's operating companies for the most part are using very reliable analog equipment. "Right now we have too big a capital investment to make such a conversion," Mr. Vigilante says. ∎

Videotapes for Homes

Philips V2000 video recorder, 1979.

Les Brown

Along with cable television, pay television and new networks distributed by satellite, the 80's promise a burgeoning of the home video market. The key components of this new field are to be video tape-recording units and phonograph-like devices that play video disks.

If industry projections are correct, 12 million to 16 million households will have one or both kinds of playback equipment by 1985, and this will foster a multibillion-dollar home video market in prepackaged programming: movies, concerts, stage productions, sports classics, children's fare and instructional, or how-to, presentations.

The disk technology has been slow in developing for the mass consumer market and is still in the test-market stage. But the home video recorders, known as VCR's, have in the last three years proliferated sufficiently to create a separate programming industry, with more than 100 companies already engaged in the production or distribution of prerecorded programs, the most popular of which are old movies selling from $39.95 to $70 each.

According to industry surveys, 800,000 video recorders have been sold at the retail level. Kalba-Bowen Associates, a research and consulting concern, estimates that last year 400,000 prerecorded cassettes were sold, totaling $24 million.

The June issue of Videography, a magazine of television technology, lists 10 best-selling programs for the previous month, all movies.

The No. 1 seller was "M*A*S*H," the 20th Century-Fox film on which the CBS-TV series is based. The others, in order, were "The Sound of Music," "The Story of O," the 1933 version of "King Kong," "The Wild Geese," "Patton," "Those Magnificent Men in Their Flying Machines," "Deep Throat," "Fantastic Voyage" and "The Devil in Miss Jones."

"Americans aspire to own film libraries," John S. Lollos, vice president of the Video Tape Network, a distribution company, said.

Attempts are being made to expand the market by offering cassettes on a rental basis, by mail order, at rates from $9 to $14 for a seven-day period. An attempt to make a permanent copy of a rental tape will result in a scrambled picture.

Two companies—the Video Corporation of America and Time-Life Films—have formed videotape rental clubs in the manner of book and record clubs.

Video Corporation established its Vid America Club after acquiring exclusive rights to distribute on cassettes a group of United Artists and Embassy Pictures titles, including "Carnal Knowledge," "The Graduate," "Darling" and "A Lion in Winter."

Time-Life entered the field a week ago after reaching an agreement with Columbia Pictures to offer about 20 of its features on a rental basis. Another Time Inc. subsidiary, the Book-of-the-Month Club, will be the distributor. ∎

JULY 10, 1979

SKYLAB AND OTHER MISHAPS TARNISH TECHNOLOGY'S IMAGE

John Noble Wilford

WASHINGTON, July 9—These are not good times for those who want to press forward with technological advances in the name of progress. So many things have been going wrong with man's shining symbols of technology, it seems, that they have lost their luster. The imminent fall of Skylab is only the latest example.

In March there was the accident and near disaster at the Three Mile Island nuclear power plant in Pennsylvania. No one needed to be reminded that splitting atoms could be dangerous, but the accident brought the hazard frightfully close to home at a time when there is an urgent need to develop energy sources as alternatives to petroleum.

Then a DC-10 crashed while taking off from O'Hare International Airport in Chicago when an engine tore away from a wing; 273 persons were killed in the worst domestic aviation accident in United States history. The resulting investigation revealed design and structural shortcomings in the jetliners, suggesting that the system for making aviation technology as safe as possible may have been wanting in the case of the DC-10.

And now Skylab, the 77.5-ton American space station, the largest craft ever put into earth orbit, is expected to come crashing back to earth Wednesday. Its fragments could rain down over an area 100 miles wide and 4,000 miles long, and the National Aeronautics and Space Administration—which is associated in the public mind with precision and success and 10 years ago this month was responsible for one of technology's crowning achievements, man's walk on the moon—can do very little about it.

The space station Skylab orbiting around the Earth.

Even though NASA keeps insisting that the risks of injury are slight, that Skylab will more than likely drop in the ocean out of harm's way, these assurances have not stemmed the rising tide of the-sky-is-falling anxiety. It does not seem to matter that, according to NASA, the odds of a particular individual being injured are 1 in 600 billion. Many people seem to be in a mood these days to expect the worst of technology—not the best, as was the case throughout most of American history.

Yet there is little evidence that Americans want to turn back the technological clock. They may now have a more realistic and less optimistic idea of progress. They are no longer willing to give carte blanche to inventive genius, as evidenced by the decision to kill the supersonic transport project. But even as Skylab was about to fall they were watching pictures transmitted from an incredible machine, Voyager 2, which is flying by Jupiter, and they were building the space shuttle for further exploration and exploitation of space. There may be deep concerns, but there is no technological paralysis.

> there is little evidence that Americans want to turn back the technological clock

Dr. Frank Press, President Carter's science adviser, said in answer to a recent question that he did not think that the public had turned against science and technology. He cited four recent opinion polls that asked, "What institutions do you expect will contribute most to the solution of the nation's serious problems?" Science and technology were at the top of the list of answers each time. ■

DECEMBER 20, 1979

Sound System in Your Pocket

Hans Fantel

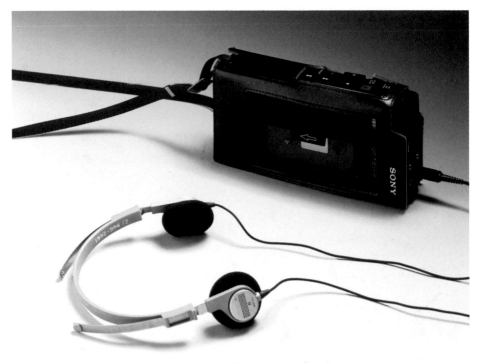

The Sony Soundabout showed that big sounds could come in a small package.

Like most last-minute Christmas shoppers, I'm rushing to beat Santa to the chimney, gathering small items for audio-minded friends. One splendid item literally small enough for a stocking-stuffer is actually a complete sound system. Just introduced by Sony, it is a stereo-cassette player hardly bigger and not much heavier than a pack of cigarettes and it plays through a special set of earphones hardly larger than those of a hearing aid. Called the Soundabout, it measures 3½-x-5½-x-1¼ inches and weighs less than 14 ounces including batteries, yet the sound rivals a quite respectable stereo system in clarity and fullness—an unusual feat for anything so small and light. You can just stick the player in your pocket and, if you put on a hat, hardly anyone will notice that you're wearing the earphones.

The Sony Soundabout (model TPS-L2) makes an ideal gift for commuters traveling by train, giving them the same chance to sweeten their daily trek as is enjoyed by automobile travelers riding to the tunes of their car stereo. What Sony has achieved is the first portable personal sound equipment with musically adequate fidelity. Unlike the raucous boxes carried nowadays by indefatigable rock fans, it affords privacy both ways: Though heard at full volume by the listener, the music disturbs no one else. Conversely, the listener is sonically isolated and psychologically removed from his surroundings.

Schubert on Conrail unquestionably helps in traversing the South Bronx.

The benefits of the TPS-L2 naturally aren't confined to music. A friend of mine, suffering toward a doctorate, commutes to Yale and uses his pocket sound system to review taped lectures and seminars on the way to New Haven. And I have used the machine on the Second Avenue bus, catching up on Dick Cavett's interviews from the night before. To my surprise, I found that the fidelity of this little gizmo contributes greatly to the enjoyment of spoken programs as well as music. I have yet to try it while riding a bicycle, but I'll wait for that till the weather gets warmer.

The motion of walking doesn't affect the steadiness of tape speed, and power consumption is kept low enough to make a pair of alkaline penlight batteries last about eight hours. Considerable development work has also gone into the design of the earphones to enable them to handle ample power levels despite their small size. In toto, the TPS-L2 represents something unusual in audio: a personal portable stereo system of astonishing musical capability yet small enough to leave the listener fully mobile and unencumbered.

At $200, the Sony would most likely be reserved for someone at the very top of your Christmas list. ■

136

APRIL 7, 1970

LONG-STUDIED DRUG LICENSED FOR TREATMENT OF MENTAL ILLNESS

Harold M. Schmeck Jr.

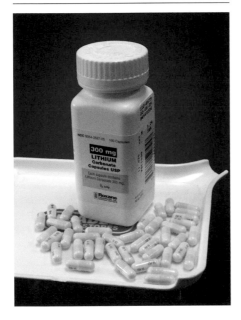

WASHINGTON, April 6—The Food and Drug Administration has licensed the much-discussed drug lithium carbonate for treatment of a common form of mental illness, the manic phase of manic-depressive psychosis.

Some experts consider the drug to be far the most effective treatment for the condition. Lithium is widely used for that purpose elsewhere in the world, but has not previously been licensed in the United States because of concern over its potential dangers.

The action by the drug agency indicates that its officers have decided the drug is too useful to be barred any longer, although it must be used with caution.

In a telephone conversation today Dr. Frederick Goodwin of the National Institute of Mental Health said the treatment of the manic-depressive patient had been particularly discouraging in the past. Two main avenues of treatment for the manic state have been electroshock and heavy doses of tranquilizers. Neither has been entirely satisfactory.

Dr. Goodwin said lithium seemed to treat the manic symptoms. In contrast, tranquilizers have only a sedative effect, leaving the patients subdued but still manic, he said, and electroshock treatment is usually temporary and sometimes results in severe side-effects.

The person in the manic state is usually overactive, talks too loudly and too rapidly, has grandiose ideas of his own abilities and is likely to undertake entirely impractical schemes often with the foolish spending of large sums of money. The other side of the coin is the depressive state, in which the same person may be suicidal.

Since the drug is simply the carbonate salt of the metallic element lithium, it is not patentable. The fact that it cannot be patented is considered one probable reason for the long delay in licensing it in the United States. Many drug companies have presumably not considered the effort and expense of preparing the case for it to be economically worthwhile.

The dose range at which toxic effects may occur is only three times the normal treatment range. That gives substantially less margin of safety than most tranquilizers.

The early symptoms of toxicity from lithium include diarrhea, vomiting, muscular weakness and lack of coordination and drowsiness, according to the required labeling. It is not recommended for use in children nor in women of child-bearing age unless the alternative methods of treatment have been tried without success.

Dr. Goodwin, whose group has studied about 50 patients over a five-year period, said a great potential value of the drug is in prevention of both manic and depressive episodes in patients subject to them. ∎

JUNE 22, 1971

HERPES TREATMENT CALLED FAVORABLE

ATLANTIC CITY, June 21—A research team from Baylor College of Medicine reported here today that it had obtained favorable preliminary results with a new treatment that reduced individual occurrences of herpes simplex, the viral infection most commonly known as cold sores or fever blisters.

"It is with some caution that we suggest yet another approach to treatment of herpes virus," said Dr. Troy D. Felber, a dermatologist who presented his findings at the 120th annual meeting of the American Medical Association here.

The method, known as photodynamic inactivation, involves the rupturing of early lesions, treating them with neutral red or proflavin dye and exposing them to a 15-watt daylight-type fluorescent light for 15 minutes from a distance of six inches.

With the new treatment, the lesions rapidly formed painless crusts and fell off in three to four days.

After the treatment proved successful on guinea pigs, it was tried on 60 patients, 20 of whom had occurrences of herpes simplex more than four times a year.

Although several separate outbreaks had to be treated before a reduced rate could be seen over a one- to two-year period, 80 percent of all patients tested said their occurrences were cut in half. ∎

virus

Commission Endorses Controversial Technique to Save Choking Victims

Jane E. Brody

A commission of the American Medical Association has concluded that the controversial Heimlich maneuver is "a most important addition" to the emergency care of persons who cannot breathe because they are choking on food or other objects.

Choking on food is estimated to cause between 2,500 and 3,900 deaths in the United States each year, making it the sixth most common cause of accidental death. Deaths from choking are more common than those from air crashes or firearms.

The Heimlich maneuver, conceived and publicized by Dr. Henry J. Heimlich, a surgeon at The Jewish Hospital in Cincinnati, involves an abrupt upward squeeze of the choking victim's upper abdomen to expel the object that is blocking the windpipe.

Controversy has surrounded the question of whether laymen can be taught to recognize a person who is choking and to correctly and safely apply the Heimlich maneuver in an emergency.

There has also been some debate as to whether the Heimlich maneuver is the safest and most effective emergency remedy to dislodge foreign objects blocking the windpipe.

If the windpipe is completely blocked, death from choking may occur in four or five minutes. Among the first-aid measures that have been advocated to rescue a choking victim are forcing a cough, bending the person over and slapping him hard between the shoulder blades, attempting to remove the stuck object with one's fingers or a specially designed plastic tweezers and cutting a hole through the neck into the windpipe with any available object—knife, fork or ballpoint pen—to create an emergency airway.

The medical group's Commission on Emergency Medical Services, writing in the issue of the Journal of the American Medical Association published today, did not discuss these alternative methods. But while seeming to endorse the Heimlich

---

Drug Agency Keeps Ban On Birth-Control Shield

Harold M. Schmeck Jr.

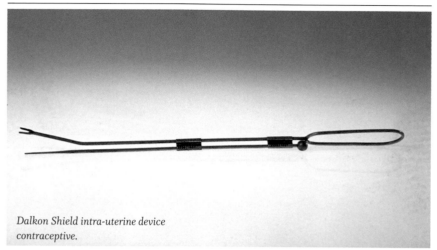

Dalkon Shield intra-uterine device contraceptive.

WASHINGTON, Jan. 28—Dr. Alexander M. Schmidt, Commissioner of Food and Drugs, said today that a moratorium was continuing on the use of a contraceptive device called the Dalkon Shield.

The device has been the subject of much controversy because of 14 deaths and numerous lesser ill effects reported in recent years among women using it.

He said the F.D.A. would allow distribution of a modified type of shield in the future, but only under a tightly controlled system similar to that imposed on drugs in the clinical research stage.

His statement did not mention a requirement that the device be modified, although the drug agency said the manufacturer was planning such a change.

In December and again today, Dr. Schmidt denied that his decision about the device was contrary to the experts' recommendations.

Dr. Richard Dickey of Louisiana State University School of Medicine, who had written to Dr. Schmidt in protest, said today that he considered the plan for a registry, designed and maintained by the manufacturer, to be of dubious scientific value and that it would endanger additional women.

It has recently been discovered, according to one scientific report, that a multi-filament tail on the Dalkon Shield is capable of harboring bacteria. Some specialists believe this bacterial contamination may be an important factor in the risks associated with the device.

A spokesman for the company said today that none of the devices with the multi-filament tail have been distributed since the moratorium began in June, 1974. Last week the company began to recall existing on-the-shelf stocks of the old model. It does not expect the new type to be available until sometime in the second half of this year.

protection

THE HIDDEN HEALTH BOMB

George B. Jacobs, M.D.

Over the last two years, my personal observations have convinced me that the tick population in Suffolk County is increasing without any control. Ticks are responsible for carrying the organisms that cause Rocky Mountain spotted fever and various forms of encephalitis.

At different times, after strolling along the beach areas, I have collected more than 20 ticks from my own person and larger numbers still from my dog. I am now taking the precaution of not letting my dog out at all in any grassy area and preventing my children from walking or playing on dune grass near any beach of Suffolk County to protect them from infestation.

The ticks and the diseases for which they are vectors constitute an enormous health hazard to the residents and vacationers of Suffolk County as well as to domestic animals. Manifestations of tickborne diseases can be devastating.

I have been corresponding with both the State and County Public Health Commissions without success on this matter, and it is very difficult for me to understand the seemingly complete lack of attempts on their part to control this hazard. Since protection of the

public against health hazards is one of the most important functions of local government, it would seem to me that legal liability might be asked of the county and state by any patient who becomes a victim of diseases communicated to them by anthropod vectors whose population is not controlled.

While I fully recognize that environmental protection makes the use of certain pesticides undesirable, the hazard of permanent defects or death in the population should certainly be considered as an urgent reason for using approved pesticides or finding acceptable substitutes instantly.

Immediate action must be taken by the county and the state to protect its residents and the environment from this serious hazard. ■

maneuver, the commission hedged on the question of whether this technique should be widely taught to the public.

The American Red Cross will meet today to discuss the Heimlich maneuver and is expected to announce a decision in a few days on whether the technique should be taught as a Red Cross first-aid measure.

In the same issue of the journal, Dr. Heimlich described 162 reports of lives saved by the maneuver in the nine months since he described it.

Dr. Heimlich recommends the adoption of a universal signal—grasping the neck between thumb and index finger—to indicate that a person is choking on something and is unable to talk or breathe. ■

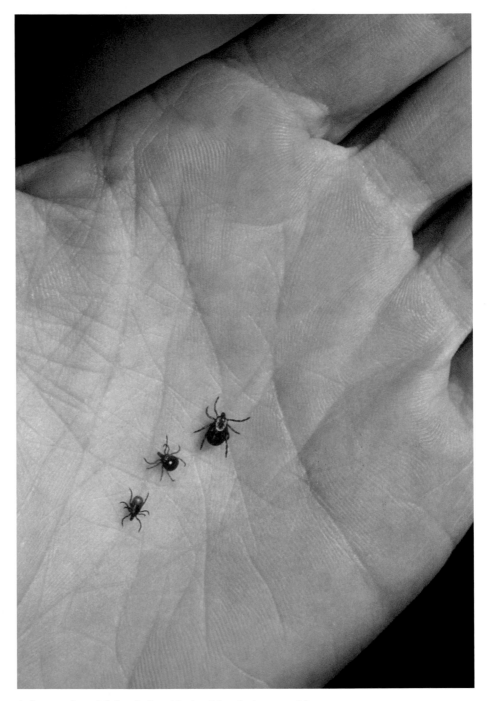

A close-up of an adult female deer tick, dog tick and a lone star tick.

FLU-LIKE DEATHS STRIKE LEGIONNAIRES

Lawrence K. Altman

HARRISBURG, Pa., Aug. 3—The death toll from an explosive outbreak of a mysterious flu-like disease in Pennsylvania rose to 20 today as teams of Federal and state epidemiologists intensified their search to identify the cause of the illnesses.

An additional 115 people, some in serious condition, were hospitalized throughout the state with high fevers, generalized malaise, muscle aches, respiratory complaints and headaches—the symptoms most commonly associated with the disease.

Pennsylvania health officials said at a news conference here that autopsies of four persons in different hospitals indicated that they had died of a severe viral pneumonia.

All the victims had attended a state American Legion convention in Philadelphia July 21–24. There are no reports thus far of the disease's spreading to anyone who was not among the 10,000 people attending the convention.

Swine influenza is among a long list of many possibilities, according to Dr. Leonard Bachman, the Pennsylvania Secretary of Health, who said, "As long as we don't have the cause, no cause is ruled out."

The lack of secondary spread does not necessarily preclude the possibility that the disease is infectious or contagious. ∎

"As long as we don't have the cause, no cause is ruled out."

Scientists Construct Functional Gene

Boyce Rensberger

A group of scientists in Cambridge, Mass., has constructed a gene, the basic unit of heredity, complete with its regulatory mechanisms.

And by implanting it in a living bacterial cell, where it functioned as if it were a natural part of the cell's heredity, they have proved that the gene they constructed works.

Although several researchers in recent years have synthesized the main portion of genes—the part of the long-chain molecule bearing the genetic code for the structure of a molecule of protein or other substance—the synthetic genes did not include the molecular "start," "stop" and other control messages needed to make the gene work. The latest achievement does.

Many scientists believe that a better knowledge of gene functions, particularly of the regulatory mechanisms that govern the gene's rate of operation, will some day yield a better understanding of a wide variety of diseases, such as cancer and many birth defects.

Scientists will now be able to use the methods developed to alter the synthetic gene's message at any point in the sequence of 199 genetically coded "words." Then they will observe how these artificial mutations influence what the gene does.

The Massachusetts Institute of Technology group's approach has been to take the four basic units of the genetic code, each of which is commercially available in purified form, and assemble them into a double-stranded DNA molecule whose sequence of units is identical to that known for a natural gene. All of the genetic instructions coded into all the genes of living things can be written with various sequences of the four letters of the genetic alphabet.

Geneticists know that the genetic material in living cells comprises much more than simply the blueprints for the structure of the various protein molecules that make up the cell. Most of the genetic material is there to regulate the synthesis of the proteins. Collectively, these regulatory portions of the genes govern the cell's metabolism and, therefore, affect the health of the whole organism.

Massachusetts Institute of Technology, Cambridge, Massachusetts.

F.D.A. BANNING SACCHARIN USE ON CANCER LINKS

Richard D. Lyons

Some popular grocery store items that contained saccharin in the 1970s.

WASHINGTON, March 9—The Food and Drug Administration announced today that it would ban the use of saccharin in foods and beverages, because the artificial sweetener had been found to cause malignant bladder tumors in laboratory animals.

Agency officials said that the ban was based on findings of a study sponsored by the Canadian Government, which found that large amounts of saccharin fed to rats caused cancer.

With no other artificial sweetener even in the development stage, products such as diet soft drinks, artificially sweetened fruits and sugar substitutes for coffee will disappear from the market when the saccharin ban goes into effect.

The ban will not take place immediately. A proposed suspension order will be issued in the next month, and the food and drug agency will allow 60 days for public comment and reaction. After that the order should become effective within a few days.

"We have no evidence that saccharin has ever caused cancer in human beings,"

Dr. Sherwin Gardner, Acting Commissioner of Food and Drugs said. "But we do now have clear evidence that the safety of saccharin does not meet the standards for additives established by Congress."

The artificial sweetener, which is 350 times sweeter than sugar, was first introduced in the United States about 1900, and its use has steadily increased.

Saccharin is the only artificial sweetener now permitted in the food supply. Another, cyclamate, was banned in 1969. Americans used about five million pounds of the substance in 1974, about three-quarters of which was used in diet soft drinks. It is also an ingredient in dietetic foods such as canned fruits and ice creams.

Dr. Gardner told newsmen there had been no recent requests from pharmaceutical companies to market a new artificial sweetener. This leaves somewhat unclear what effect the ban will have on products needed by diabetics, and others besides dieters, who cannot tolerate sugar. ■

Researcher Asserts Nuclear Magnetic Technique Can Detect Cancer

Lawrence K. Altman

A New York City medical researcher announced yesterday at a news conference that he had developed "a new technique for the nonsurgical detection of cancer anywhere in the human body." However, in an interview later in the day, he retracted a contention that he had already used the technique on a cancer patient.

And other cancer experts expressed skepticism that the technique had reached the stage where it could be used in diagnosing cancer.

The researcher, Dr. Raymond V. Damadian of the State University of New York Downstate Medical Center in Brooklyn, held a news conference there to announce the new technique that he calls FONAR, for field focusing nuclear magnetic resonance.

A spokesman for the National Cancer Institute said that it had spent $225,000 in contracts with Dr. Damadian over a two and one-half year period but that the Federal cancer agency was no longer financially supporting Dr. Damadian or anyone else for the nuclear magnetic resonance type of research.

"We don't look on nuclear magnetic resonance as a promising area of diagnosis" in cancer, Larry Blaser, an N.C.I. spokesman, said. He said that the agency would not issue a formal statement about Dr. Damadian's research claims.

Dr. Damadian said that the FONAR technique had been under development since 1971 with the ultimate aim of pinpointing cancers in the human body that could not be detected by X-ray or other techniques, and determining their chemical makeup.

The idea of applying the technique to cancer arose in part because of the observation by other scientists that the water content of cancerous cells can be up to 90 percent whereas it is about 66 percent in normal cells. Dr. Damadian said that his technique utilized this point in distinguishing between normal and cancerous human tissues in the test tube.

To test it in humans, Dr. Damadian said, he had built a one and one-half ton, 10-foot-high unit with a 53-inch magnetic diameter that he described as the world's largest magnet. He said that he held the news conference because he had developed "the first instrument for the chemical imaging of the normal human."

But later in the interview, after repeated questioning, Dr. Damadian said that he retracted as "not accurate" the contention that his device had diagnosed cancer anywhere in the body. He expressed hope that it would do so someday. ■

nuclear

CALIFANO CALLS SMOKING 'SLOW-MOTION SUICIDE'

Richard D. Lyons

WASHINGTON, Jan. 11—Joseph A. Califano Jr., the Secretary of Health, Education and Welfare, today announced a series of actions and proposals designed to reduce the number of Americans who smoke, a figure estimated at 53 million.

"Last year, smoking was a major factor in 220,000 deaths from heart disease, 78,000 lung cancer deaths and 22,000 deaths from other cancers," he said.

Mr. Califano's antismoking package includes a proposal to see if the Federal cigarette tax, now 8 cents a pack, can be increased; a suggestion that cigarette smoking be banned on commercial planes, and a plan to increase to $6 million from $1 million the funds that his department spends each year on antismoking educational efforts.

There was also a proposal to ban smoking in most areas of Federal buildings and a plan to ask the broadcasting networks to increase radio and television spot announcements against smoking.

Mr. Califano's package leaned more on voluntary action than on compulsory directives and would not, at least for the next two years, invest significant new amounts of Federal money in antismoking efforts.

His proposals won immediate support from some legislators from states that do not grow tobacco, such as Senator Birch Bayh, Democrat of Indiana, and Senator Gary Hart, Democrat of Colorado.

However, Senator Walter Huddleston, a Democrat from the major tobacco state of Kentucky, accused Mr. Califano of "putting the cart before the horse" for starting "a massive propaganda campaign" against cigarette smoking without having sufficient scientific evidence to justify it. ∎

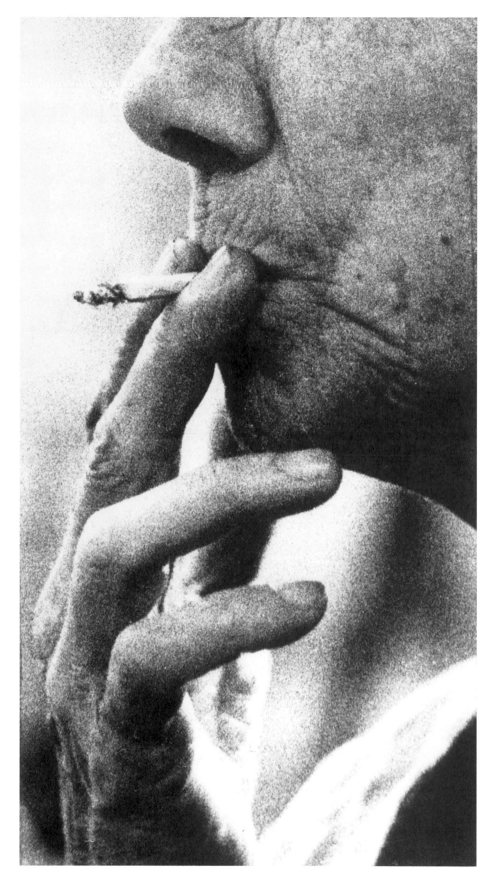

142

A TOUR OF EXERCISE CLASSES

Anne Anable

An exercise class at the Y.M.C.A. in Denver, Colorado, in the 1970's.

Interest in physical fitness and exercise has been growing nationally, but nowhere with greater enthusiasm than in the suburbs, where it's difficult to find a truly sedentary being.

Availability of public courts has contributed to the tennis boom in the summer and the popularity of paddle tennis in winter.

More traditional exercise classes are held at the Y.M.C.A.'s, Y.W.C.A.'s, and Y.M.H.A.'s. Yoga remains a staple, along with ballet, Slimnastics and figure conditioning. Fencing, too, is increasing in popularity.

Senior citizen fitness classes include swimming and floor exercises. Many Y's hold special co-ed evening classes, so husband and wife may exercise together.

In New Jersey, many people are more concerned with changing their bodies than their life styles, and the newest magic word is aerobics, stemming from Dr. Kenneth H. Cooper's exercise program for the Air Force, designed to benefit the cardio-respiratory system.

Nine years ago an enterprising professional dancer and choreographer, Jacki Sorensen, developed a dance program incorporating the movements best suited to achieving cardiovascular fitness. Her carefully trained instructors spread the word via Y.M. and Y.W.C.A. classes, and now, 750 strong, they have branched out on their own, under Mrs. Sorensen's control.

Students are kept from the boredom of repetition by being introduced to new dance material every 12 weeks. There's a "Star Wars" number in the current repertoire that manages to combine robot movements with jogging that even R2-D2 would approve.

At Stockton State College, outsiders are welcome at the weekly folk dance lessons given by Arthur Rosenfeld. Linda and Claude Epstein, who live in Ventnor, have been involved in square-dance clubs since Mr. Epstein's undergraduate days at Brown University. He is now with Stockton's Environmental Studies Department and has run folk-dance clubs in the past for the college.

"Folk dancing is a wonderful way to combine vigorous exercise with informal socializing," said Mrs. Epstein, who noted that Balkan dances seem most popular at the moment, although English dances are second on the list and some clubs devote themselves entirely to dances from a given country or region.

Exercise fans who cannot or will not settle for prescribed days and hours of exercise tend to gravitate toward the spas, which usually hold out total flexibility as a drawing card. If time and stamina permit, it's wise to shop around. ■

143

It's a Healthy Girl!

Louise Joy Brown, the first test-tube baby, with her parents Lesley and John Brown, in England in 1979.

LONDON, Wednesday, July 26—The first authenticated birth of a baby conceived in laboratory glassware and then placed in the uterus of an otherwise infertile mother occurred last night, apparently without complications.

Reports from Oldham General and District Hospital in Lancashire said the baby, a girl, was delivered by Caesarian section, appeared normal and weighed 5 pounds 12 ounces.

The birth culminated more than a dozen years of research and experimentation by Dr. Patrick C. Steptoe, a gynecologist, and Dr. Robert G. Edwards, a Cambridge University specialist in reproductive physiology.

The parents are Mrs. Lesley Brown, 31 years old, and her husband, John, 38, a railway truck driver from Bristol.

Mrs. Brown in more than 10 years of marriage had been unable to conceive a child because of a defect in the oviducts, or fallopian tubes, which each month carry egg cells from the ovaries to the uterus. It is during this passage that the egg cells are fertilized.

In the procedure that culminated in last night's birth, an egg cell was removed surgically from Mrs. Brown's ovaries last Nov. 10 and fertilized with sperm from her husband in a petri dish. After two or more days in a laboratory culture, the fertilized embryo was injected into Mrs. Brown's uterus.

There have been previous reports of so-called "test-tube babies" but none have been authenticated. While the experimenters have often been frowned upon, they also are highly regarded by many in the field of obstetrics.

Working with a succession of patients, Dr. Edwards has gradually improved his ability to manipulate the hormones that control the reproductive cycle.

Dr. Steptoe has used a surgical procedure known as laparoscopy to enter a woman's abdomen at the appropriate moment in her monthly cycle to retrieve one or more egg cells. Once the egg cells have been exposed to sperm, and once microscopic examination after a few days has shown that an embryo is developing normally, the embryo is placed in the uterus with a tube inserted through the cervix.

It is estimated that one-fifth to one-half of women who are sterile are unable to bear children because of absent, defective or blocked oviducts. Because of that, it can be assumed that there will be considerable pressure on physicians to repeat the performance of Drs. Steptoe and Edwards, even though their work is still at a very experimental stage.

Reports from the hospital this morning said that the baby was born just before midnight and that her condition was "excellent." Mrs. Brown and her husband were reported to be jubilant.

Once the fetus began developing, its own hormonal signals generated all the effects of a normal pregnancy. Mrs. Brown is reported to have experienced the sort of cravings often reported by pregnant women—in this case, a yearning for mints.

If **you were** a newlywed in the 1970s, it was almost a dead certainty that your wedding gifts included a fondue pot. Chances were good that you received two or three of them. Across the land, young couples invited friends over, so that they could all plunk down around coffee tables, spear chunks of bread with long forks and dip them into pots of melted cheese. It may not have qualified as haute cuisine, but it did seem oh so continental.

Fondue, a party staple in the 1970s.

And then, poof, the fondue fad faded. Those pots and dipping forks were stored in a remote corner of the basement—unmourned relics of that era, maybe along with the Marimekko couch and the three-piece white disco suit. Yet a revolution in American eating habits had begun, one that would endure far longer than the vats of molten Gruyère. In Berkeley, Calif., a woman named Alice Waters opened a restaurant, Chez Panisse, that relied on organically grown ingredients and on a supply chain of local farmers and other producers. Today's inescapable embrace of the organic food movement is testament to her success.

She was not alone in changing Americans tastes. A cook-

book by Marcella Hazan introduced this country to Italian classics, prompting Craig Claiborne, the eminent New York Times food writer, to rhapsodize that "no one has ever done more to spread the gospel of pure Italian cookery in America." "The Silver Palate Cookbook" was another indispensable reference work for many, offering instruction in boldly seasoned dishes from France and Southern Europe. Garlic became a valued ingredient, as did fresh produce of all kinds. In New York, greenmarkets opened and flourished, perhaps none more so than one in Union Square, where farmers sold their produce directly to consumers. It's still going strong. Perhaps it was no

Marcella Hazan introduced many Americans to Italian cuisine.

146

Alice Waters at her restaurant, Chez Panisse, in Berkeley, California.

coincidence that a palace of traditional, sauce-laden French cuisine, Le Pavillon in mid-Manhattan, closed its doors in the early '70s for want of enough customers interested in grande luxe dining.

Sadly, it is hard to muster that sort of enthusiasm for fashions and furnishings in those days. Dress and skirt designers, and the women they served, seemed unable to make up their minds where they wanted their hemlines. Mini, midi, maxi—sounds like something Julius Caesar might have said had he been a garment-industry executive—all had their day and their eclipse. Maybe you know some people who get dewy-eyed nostalgic for hot pants, platform shoes, mile-high shag carpeting, indoor rattan furniture, leisure suits and palazzo pants, not to mention the Annie Hall look. Bet you don't know many of them. But a nose-in-the-air attitude in no way extends to the wrap

Miniskirts and platform shoes were must have fashion items in the 1970s.

Artist Andy Warhol with fashion designer Diane von Furstenberg, who is wearing one of her signature designs, a leopard print wrap-dress, 1974.

dress, introduced by Diane von Furstenberg in 1972. It hugged a woman's curves and, to not put a fine point on it, was as sexy as could be without really trying. Regardless of age, shape or size, women looked great in it. Naturally, it became a raging success. Nor was it a great surprise when the dress had a rebirth of popularity three decades later.

Then again, cheese fondue also made a mild comeback in the early 2010's. You never know about crazes in food and fashion. *De gustibus non est disputandum.* That, too, is something Caesar might well have said.

Cold Duck Drinkers Sought

AUGUST 12, 1971

Leonard Sloane

Wanna buy a duck? A cold duck, that is.

Cold duck, in case there's any confusion, is a mixture of extra dry champagne and sparkling burgundy. In recent years, it has been one of the fastest growing categories of sparkling wines in the United States and ambitious plans are being laid for its future.

"With cold duck, we're getting a new type of wine drinker," says Paul M. Schlem, chairman of Gold Seal Wineyards, which produces the Henri Marchant brand. "These are the people who formerly drank only wine and soda."

The drink called cold duck dates back to the post-World War I era in Europe and was even mentioned in some of the novels written at that time. Its origins are based on the cold cuts—or cold ends, called "kalte ende" in German—served at that time.

Bartenders vied with each other to mix the best combination of champagne and burgundy from the leftover bottles after the parties in which the lost generation dissipated throughout the night. Their various versions were termed "kalte ende," or cold duck, and the duck name stuck.

It wasn't until the middle of the 1960's that bottled cold duck came to the United States. Henri Marchant brought out its version—which carries a label picturing a duck on the ice—in 1965 and sold 6,000 bottles that year.

Cold duck is now sold in the United States by both the premium producers like Henri Marchant and Paul Masson and by the bulk process producers like Gallo and Italian Swiss Colony. Mr. Schlem says that his company alone sold about three million bottles in the year ended July 31.

APRIL 19, 1973

Indian, Italian and Inexpensive Food

Raymond A. Sokolov

Culinary bibiliomaniacs of America, you have certain treats in store for you. The season's cooking stars will show you new and clever and authentic ways to cook meals that are Indian, Italian and inexpensive.

Madhur Jaffrey's "An Invitation to Indian Cooking" is the most useful and interesting introduction to Indian food that I have ever seen. Although Miss Jaffrey, who is an actress living in New York City, does not pretend to be giving us a comprehensive rundown on subcontinental cuisine, she tells us much, nevertheless, by focusing thoroughly on a compact number of favorite recipes, most of which represent the practice of her native Delhi.

The recipes come directly from her mother, but she has translated them with great facility into American terms. Perhaps most important of all, she provides lucid and informal and gently authoritative explanations of why and how Indians eat the way they do.

This background is particularly necessary because we cannot acquire an Indian culinary education eating in the almost universally degenerate Indian restaurants in this country. Anyone who has ever had the good fortune to eat in an Indian home will agree with this and with Miss Jaffrey, who hereby embarks on a laudable crusade against the monotony of that pidgin spice, curry, and in favor of the fabulous galaxy of Indian home-ground spice mixtures.

With Italian food, we stand on surer ground. Everyone can at least cook spaghetti and also knows the proper taste of some dishes. We still await an encyclopedic

(cont'd. on next page)

149

(cont'd. from previous page)
and usable handbook of Italian cuisine, but Marcella Hazan offers us a fine stopgap: 250 North Italian recipes, unusual and intricate, which she has perfected for American consumption in her New York cooking classes.

"The Classic Italian Cook Book" extends one's already large admiration for Italian ingenuity. People bored with just plain creamy fettucine can now try it spiked with gorgonzola, for instance. Mrs. Hazan knows unusual (to us) ways of cooking artichokes, garnishing risottos and pan-frying steaks with fennel-flavored sauce. She fries asparagus, sautés broccoli with garlic and roasts lamb with juniper berries.

The budget-conscious will find much that is helpful and discover a feast of ideas, too, in Miriam Ungerer's "Good Cheap Food."

It can also be said that this is a most appealing group of international recipes, none of them lavish. And Miss Ungerer is a pleasure to read. ■

JULY 30, 1974

Convenience Dinners: How Quick? How Convenient?

Jean Hewitt

Those convenience dinner mixes such as Hamburger Helper that the instant food industry is pushing with such zeal are giving homemakers somewhat of a windfall these days: After dinner, there's only one pot to wash.

The quick dinner—about 25 minutes on the stove is all that's needed—doesn't add up to such a plus in other areas, however. The quick dinner isn't significantly less jarring on the pocketbook than its homemade equivalent (which, it turns out, can be prepared without taking much longer).

As for the taste, a test showed that, like the products, it's at best a mixed bag.

Hamburger Helper—there are 13 flavors—is one of an assortment of prepared convenience dinner mixes that attempt to expand "real" food into an entire meal rather than replace it. You provide the base (hamburger meat, a can of tunafish), and the product provides the rest of the meal. The idea has caught on so that there are now at least four major companies producing two dozen varieties of such dinner mixes as hamburger stew and creamy rice and tuna.

Are they tasty? That depends on who is asked. People who are used to eating made-from-scratch casseroles, sauces and the like are repelled by the odor of hydrolyzed (chemically broken down) plant protein, dried and canned vegetables and some of the seasonings. The odor is strongest when the ingredients hit the water but persists in the finished dinner.

Besides the odor, many users report they find the taste flat, synthetic and often objectionable. Picking out individual ingredients by taste alone was found to be difficult. In a blindfold test, sliced and diced potatoes as well as dried and canned vegetables were recognized by texture and sometimes smell, but not taste. The flavor of the sauce tended to mask everything.

And in a blind test, nine people (including four school-age children), compared four dishes made from dinner mixes (with hamburger added) with four homemade, look-alike versions.

In three of the four cases, all nine testers preferred the homemade dinner. The exception was Hamburger Helper's Cheeseburger Macaroni dinner, which rated higher than a made-from-scratch look-alike.

Acceptable homemade versions of 10 add-meat packaged dinners were made for an average of 10 cents less than the store-bought product and required only 5 to 10 minutes extra preparation time when cooked in one skillet. How long does it take to chop an onion, scrape a carrot or open a can of tomato sauce?

Simple, homemade alternatives that are good-tasting, inexpensive and attractive are abundant if you start with a pound of ground beef, have a minimum of fresh ingredients and seasonings and are willing to spend 15 to 20 minutes putting them together. True, it does take extra thought and planning, but to help you there are entire cookbooks devoted to the subject.

There isn't even a pot to wash when you fix tuna fish salad and you'll be avoiding the possibility of eating monosodium glutamate, artificial colors and flavors, preservatives and other chemicals whose value may be questionable.

On the other hand there are people who eat, and seem to enjoy, soups, sauces and gravies made from dry mixes, airline food, canned vegetables, dinner at fast food hamburger stands, canned ravioli and coffee cream substitutes.

And among those who find the mixes helpful are campers, the handicapped, elderly persons, baby-sitters, bachelors and college students, with only a hot plate to cook on. They are often more concerned with satisfying hunger quickly and easily than in creating superior tasting, economical and nutritious meals. ■

HAUTE CUISINE BEATS HIGHER LEARNING

Liza Bercovici

BERKELEY, Calif.—Robert Flaherty rarely reflects on the fact that his B.A. from Georgetown, his law degree from Michigan, his year of study at the London School of Economics or his three-year stint with one of San Francisco's more prestigious corporate law firms never really equipped him for his current profession: waiting on tables in Berkeley.

Mr. Flaherty waits on tables because he likes to wait on tables.

"Law was boring," he said the other day. But he concedes that his decision to abandon law four years ago was a little unusual, even in a city like Berkeley with its well-known reputation for tolerating the unusual.

As in other cities in the nation, this campus town across the bay from San Francisco is experiencing a renaissance in restaurants and specialty food stores. Unlike other cities, however, these restaurants and food stores are being manned by former graduate students and professionals who are finding "la cuisine" more satisfying than white-collar work.

And at Il Pavone, one of the newest places on Berkeley's dining scene, the dishwashers are still finishing high school, but the sous-chef has an M.A. in English and the third cook an M.A. in philosophy. Four years ago, disillusioned by academe, the principal chef, Maurice Kuku, abandoned work on his master's thesis in philosophy at Rochester ("Can there be a set of laws in a nonspace?") and went to Europe to study cooking.

Patty Unterman had been working as press secretary to a Berkeley city councilman since 1972 when it occurred to her that the "perfect fantasy" was to run a restaurant. Her partner, Melissa McCloud, a Stanford graduate, was doing accounting work. In the Berkeley tradition of self-taught amateurs, neither had any professional cooking experience.

The first night the two, working with just one waiter, were "totally unprepared," but since then Beggar's Banquet has moved to new quarters in Berkeley, with double the seating area, 15 waiters, and no more 16-hour work days for the two partners.

When Chez Panisse opened four and a half years ago, the total professional restaurant experience consisted of the jobs in Indi-

ana drive-ins and a London pub that the manager, Alice Waters, had held. The restaurant's other owners are Tom Guernsey, now the bartender, before that a Peace Corps worker; Lindsay Shere, now the pastry chef, before that a housewife; Jerry Budrick, now the head waiter, before that a person who had been "just cruising;" and Jeremiah Tower, who had been completing his graduate degree in architecture at Harvard.

"If you know the taste you're trying to achieve, you can get there one way or another," Mr. Tower said as he nibbled on a plate of smoked Big Sur mountain trout. "It's a very simple thing we do here. Buy the food every day, cook it simple and to order and charge a reasonable price—$10—for it. That combination is a huge success."

How do the newest members of Berkeley's restaurant scene feel about switching from textbooks to cookbooks?

"Some of my old lawyer friends actually feel embarrassed to have me waiting on them," Mr. Flaherty recalled recently, "but I never think about it. It's stupid to do so when I'm enjoying it." ∎

JUNE 9, 1976

California Labels Outdo French in Blind Test

Frank J. Prial

Several California white wines triumphed over some of the best Burgundy has to offer in a blind tasting in Paris recently. More startling: The judges were French.

The tasting was arranged by Steven Spurrier, an Englishman who runs a wine shop and the Académie du Vin, a school for tourists and Frenchmen alike, in Paris. The wines were limited to two types, chardonnay, the grape that makes the best whites in California and France, and cabernet sauvignon, the grape that makes the best reds in both areas.

The French judges voted the 1973 chardonnay from Chateau Montelena and the 1973 cabernet sauvignon from Stag's Leap Wine Cellars the two best bottles in the tasting. Both wineries are in California's Napa Valley.

(cont'd. on next page)

LIFE & STYLE

(cont'd. from previous page)

Each judge was asked to evaluate the wines as to color, bouquet, palate and balance and to give each a numerical rating on a scale of 20 possible points.

Regular readers will recall several other similar comparisons in which the American chardonnays bested their French rivals. In both instances, the latest only six months ago here in New York, champions of the French wines argued that the tasters were Americans with possible bias toward American wines. What is more, they said, there was always the chance that the bur-gundies had been mistreated during the long trip from the wineries.

What can they say now? The judges included some of the leaders of the French wine establishment and there is always the chance that the American wines suffered during their long trip to France.

The fact is that the best American vineyards and wineries can produce extraordinary wines. Admittedly the wines in this tasting are from the premium wineries, are in extremely short supply and cost a great deal of money— anywhere from $6 to $20 a bottle. But the same is true of the burgundies. ∎

JULY 11, 1976

Cheese, Cheese Everywhere

Frank J. Prial

***Fromagerie, Ridge Road and Avenue of the Two Rivers, Rumson, New Jersey. (201) 842-8088.

The only problem with the Fromagerie is that it can't possibly be as good as its adherents claim. And it isn't. It is very good, but not that good. For what it worth, though, it is probably the best restaurant in this corner of New Jersey.

The ambiance here is Swiss, with a not-unexpected emphasis on cheese and fondue. There is the traditional fondue Neuchateloise, which is made with Swiss cheese, kirsch and red wine. and there is a fondue formidable, which is made with Gruyere and Emmenthal, purportedly blended in chablis and flavored with bourbon.

Also on the menu arc a quiche Valaisanne, a cheese soup and an onion soup with, hopefully, a lot of cheese in it. One fondue has no cheese in it. It is a dessert fondue made with chocolate. But there is certainly some cheese in the homemade cheesecake.

The menu is not without its cliches. Shrimp Scampi Fromagerie is just another scampi: good, but nothing new. Then there is something called a "Skipper's Sampler," which is just an inane as its name: a melange of clams, shrimp and frozen lobster tail. Hardly a great Swiss delicacy.

A surprise on the card recently was chicken a la Hongroise: half a sauteed chicken served with a tasty cream sauce flavored with paprika. Another excellent selection on a recent visit was the pork chop in a wine sauce flavored with mustard and onions. It was one of the few original pork chop dishes around.

Service is good at the Fromagerie when one of the owners is around. When they disappear, which is often. things seem to wind down. The waitresses are pleasant, but not exactly dedicated. The dining room is pleasant and very European.

Dinner for two, with wine, will cost $30 or more. ∎

GREEN MARKET AT UNION SQUARE

The Green Market in Union Square, New York.

The second city-sponsored Green Market will open tomorrow at the northern end of Union Square, where farmers will truck in fresh fruits and vegetables for sale directly to consumers—a practice almost forgotten by most city dwellers here.

Farmers are expected to bring in varieties of lettuce, onions, peppers, cabbage, pears and apples as well as leeks, chives, cucumbers, celery, peaches and melons. The first Green Market began five weeks ago at Second Avenue and 59th Street, and the Council on the Environment of New York City, the sponsors, said it was a success. This week, at 59th Street, a farmer is scheduled to bring in organic produce.

The Union Square market will be on 17th Street between Broadway and Park Avenue South. ∎

CHANGES PROPOSED IN U.S. WINE LABELS

Frank J. Prial

A series of sweeping changes in the labeling of United States wines, including a new Government seal to be awarded to wines meeting the highest standards, was proposed yesterday by the Treasury Department's Bureau of Alcohol, Tobacco and Firearms.

The proposals, which call for strict definitions of grape-growing regions and tough new limitations on what winemakers can say on their labels, are expected to meet with considerable industry opposition.

The most radical change would be the introduction of the "ATF Seal." It would indicate to the consumer that 95 percent of the grapes used in a bottle of wine had come from the region specified on the label. It would indicate, too, that 85 percent of the wine in the bottle had been made from the grape variety listed on the label.

At present there are no Federal laws governing the use of area names on wines, a wine sold as having been made from a specific grape may contain as little as 26 percent of wine from that variety.

Under the proposal, only an ATF Seal wine could qualify as "estate bottled." These wines would have to be produced entirely from grapes grown in a recognized vineyard or viticultural area, on property owned or controlled by the bottling winery. Also, the winery and grape-growing area would have to be in the same state.

ATF Seal wines presumably would include only a small portion of the nation's annual production. But the laws governing the nonseal wines would be stiffened, too. A varietal wine from any part of the country would have to contain at least 51 percent of the wine of the grape listed on the label, and all wines would have to indicate the state, county and grape-growing area from which they had come.

Most industry observers, whether they oppose or favor tougher labeling restrictions, view this as an almost impossible task. "Where does the Napa Valley begin," asked one veteran grower, rhetorically. "Even people who have lived there all their lives aren't sure." ∎

Perrier, the Snob's Drink, Soon to Come in Six-Packs

James F. Clarity

VERGEZE, France—Perrier, the gaseous mineral water that has been bubbling up from an underground spring near this southern village for at least 2,000 years, is about to lose some of its chic on the American drinking market.

The people who put the Perrier in green bottles shaped like Indian clubs say they are grateful to the handful of Americans they call "Perrier freaks" who have been buying several million bottles a year. But the freaks, most of whom are said to be in the top five percent in American income, are going to be spared some of the work of hunting down the water in gourmet shops and expensive bars, paying sometimes more than a dollar to take home 23 ounces.

The snob value of Perrier will drop because the price should fall by 20 to 30 percent. The company, through an aggressive United States distributor, intends to start filling up the shelves of supermarkets—on the East and West Coasts for a start—with three-packs and six-packs of the water, beginning early in the summer.

Perrier is going to compete with soft drinks such as Coca Cola and Seven-Up and with diet drinks that Perrier officials feel will soon lose their appeal, and possibly disappear from the beverage aisles, due to what they call, without a trace of bitterness, "the saccharine situation" in the United States.

"We think the love affair France has had with Perrier for the last 30 years is being duplicated now in the United States," said Gustave Leven, the Perrier chairman. ∎

Zinfandel: A Favorite of California Wine Lovers

Frank J. Prial

We had a merlot fad, we almost had a petite sirah fad and cabernet sauvignon is always a bit faddish, but there is one red wine grape that is constantly popular with the true California wine enthusiasts: the zinfandel.

The only place in the world you will find the grape is in California and how it got there nobody really knows. For almost a century, everyone was convinced that it had been brought here by Agoston Haraszthy, the improbable Hungarian who founded Sauk City, Iowa, Buena Vista Vineyards in Sonoma County and later allegedly was eaten by crocodiles in Costa Rica.

There are some indications that the grape was here before Haraszthy in the mid-1800's, but, whatever its origins, it has become one of the best-known grapes grown in this country. That has to be at least partly because it produces such good wine.

The zinfandel grows well in any region *(cont'd. on next page)*

(cont'd. from previous page)

suitable for the true European wine grape varieties—and in a lot of hotter regions where other varieties, such as cabernet sauvignon, do not. Thus, zinfandel can be found in almost every wine-growing section of California, from the blazing-hot Central Valley around Bakersfield to the coolest vineyards of Mendocino County, hundreds of miles to the north.

For many years, the zinfandel was considered a lesser grape and was used for jug wine, for blending into other wines, and for ship-ping east, as fruit, for the home wine-makers of New York and Boston. Today, zinfandels are vinified with all the skill and care of the finest cabernet and the results show it.

Most wine lovers, including the oenologists at the University of California, say the zinfandel flavor at its best is reminiscent of blackberries. In any case, it should be about halfway between the cabernet sauvignon and the pinot noir grape in terms of tannin—that astringent taste that is part of any great wine—and the wine should be fruitier than the best cabernets.

If anything, it is too early—by about 20 years—to say where the best zinfandels come from. Ridge makes one entirely from grapes from the Shenandoah Valley in the foothills of the Sierra Madre. Sutter Home, which makes only zinfandels, brings many of its grapes from the Deaver Ranch in Plymouth, 120 miles east of the Napa Valley winery.

David Bruce makes magnificent zinfandels from Monterey County grapes, and Bernard Fetzer has a little gem of a light zinfandel made entirely from grapes from Lake County, east of his winery in Mendocino. ■

AUGUST 7, 1977

Frothy Profits in Light Beers

Ann Crittenden

The fastest-growing and most profitable segment of the $6 billion brewing industry is low-calorie beer, a liquid cornucopia of Lites, Natural Lights, Extra Lights and Lights promising Rabelaisian satisfaction and waistline retention as well.

Consisting of only a handful of regional labels with a fraction of the market five years ago, the low-calorie brands took 4 percent of the market last year and are expected to account for 6 to 7 percent this year. Within a few years, many industry experts believe, they could account for 10 percent or more of all beer sold.

The popularity of light beer is part of the whole evolution of consumer taste toward less fattening, less filling and more natural products, demonstrated in the success of everything from low-calorie soft drinks to low-tar cigarettes and natural cosmetics. Old-timers in the beer industry say the trend has been evident in their products for years, and that today's brews in general are far less "heavy" and viscous than the average post-Prohibition beer.

Some even go so far as to admit that light beer is not really all that different from what was already on the market. Unlike low-calorie soft drinks, for example, which have virtually no calories, most of the light beers have only one-third (about 50) fewer calories than regular beers, hardly enough to save the silhouette of a serious drinker.

Worse, in the eyes of old-school brewers, is the fact that for every calorie they take out of a beer, they have to take alcohol out as well. Most of the light brands have only 2 to 3.2 percent alcohol by weight, versus more than 4 percent for average beers.

Still, the light beers have an undeniable appeal, both to heavy drinkers who like to be able to put down a six-pack without feeling like they've swallowed a bale of cotton, and among younger people and women, who may be lured by the lights into drinking beer for the first time.

Miller Lite, an instant hit, now accounts for approximately 60 percent of all low-calorie beer sold. According to John A. Murphy, president of Miller Brewing, the company has filed roughly a dozen lawsuits seeking to prevent other brewers from using the word "light" to describe their low-calorie beers. ■

OCTOBER 24, 1979

A TINY FOOD SHOP WITH BIG IDEAS

Patricia Wells

It started small. Very small. The pocket-sized shop measures only 11 by 16 feet, and when the Silver Palate opened at 274 Columbus Avenue at 72nd Street just two years ago, the offerings were traditional and modest. A selection of tiny sausages, French cheeses, an elegant, take-out entree of the day. The young entrepreneurs, Sheila Lukins, a one-time graphic artist, and Julee Rosso, formerly in advertising, wanted a simple, Upper West Side shop, where the food was fresh, the atmosphere homey, the quality exceptional.

But then, about a year ago, things began to mushroom. Customers didn't want just the asparagus-in-blueberry-vinaigrette salad. They also wanted to buy the blueberry vinegar that went into the dressing. The regulars liked the tomato-apple chutney that Sheila Lukins served with the sliced cold beef, but why couldn't they buy a whole jarful of the bright red relish?

Then the two shopkeepers took a trip to Paris, eyeing all the lovely bottled confitures, herb-flavored vinegars, nut-enriched oils that sparkle in the shop windows of France.

They returned to New York with a "we can do that" sort of attitude, and quickly set about bottling a small, select assortment of their specialties, all in elegant,

French-style canning jars, under the Silver Palate label.

"People are dying for foods that look like what their grandmother used to make"

This year, buoyed by encouraging customers and sparks of interest from gourmet shops around the country, they have taken their fledgling canning business one step further. In June they contracted with a local food packager, multiplied ingredients for their favorite recipes, and expanded the Silver Palate line to more than 30 products, including chutneys and conserves, cookies and chocolates, sweet sauces, hot sauces, pickled cherries and cornichons.

"People are dying for foods that look like what their grandmother used to make," said Miss Rosso, a cheery Middle Westerner who never dreamed she'd spend her 30's in Manhattan, putting up jars of zucchini pickles or tins of chocolate chip cookies.

And while the Silver Palate could hardly be credited with reviving the American practice of preserving, the shop and its owners are doing their best to elevate the homey art to the European level of elegance and quality.

"Whenever possible, we use American ingredients, local ingredients," explained Mrs. Lukins, who had spent the previous week "on the line," in their local factory, overseeing the hand packaging of the season's final batch of chili sauce.

Although the Silver Palate is going national, the owners note that they started small and insist they will stay small, for quality's sake.

Next year they hope to hold the line on production costs by contracting directly with local farmers for fruits and vegetables. They also hope to find molds for old-fashioned American bottles, then find a factory to manufacture those bits of history. ∎

DECEMBER 9, 1979

THE WORLD ACCORDING TO GARLIC

Jean Strouse

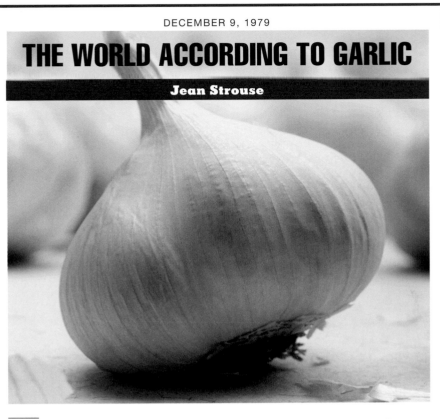

Garlic has been claimed to be good for everything from complexions and posture to sibling rivalry, impotence, tuberculosis, whiplash, cancer and scorpion bites.

Whether or not it is one of nature's medicines, its prodigious taste is of the essence in the cooking of France, China, Italy and Spain. But garlicky breath does offend, and the innocent herb has probably been the object of greater ambivalence than any other food in the history of civilization.

Garlic was a food staple in the ancient and medieval worlds. Herodotus claims that the Egyptians building the Pyramid of Cheops refused to work without daily portions of garlic. The Israelites wandering with Moses in the desert wept recalling "the fish, which we were wont to eat in Egypt for nought; the cucumbers, and the melons, and the leeks, and the onions, and the garlic; but now our soul is dried away; there is nothing at all." The ancient Greeks thought the odor of skorodon was vulgar, and barred garlic eaters from worshipping at the Temple of Cybele. But the Romans cooked with great quantities of the herb, primarily because they thought it was an aphrodisiac.

In socially fastidious eras, garlic has been relegated to condiment shelves or excluded from the kitchen arts entirely. And where it was popular with peasants it was often despised by lords. The Elizabethans, like the Romans, believed in garlic's aphrodisiac powers, but like the Greeks they thought its odors coarse: Shakespeare has Bottom in "A Midsummer Night's Dream" tell his actors to "eat no onions nor garlic, for we are to utter sweet breath"; and in "Measure for Measure," Lucio, "a fantastic," slanders the Duke by saying that "he would mouth with a beggar, though she smelt brown bread and garlic." Seventeenth-century English literature is full of fine ladies turning up their delicate noses at garlic's "intolerable rankness." And in Victorian England, where the predominant style was a genteel decorous propriety that would admit no strong odors or passions, Mrs. Beeton wrote in her 1861 "Book of Household Management" that "the smell of this plant is generally considered offensive, and it is the most acrimonious in its taste of the whole alliaceous tribe . . . It was in greater

(cont'd. on next page)

(cont'd. from previous page)

repute with our ancestors than it is with ourselves, although it is still used as a seasoning or herb."

Garlic did not find its way into French haute cuisine until the early 19th century, but it has always been a central ingredient in the cuisine bourgeoise of the south of France, where the noon meal in homes and restaurants on winter Fridays is called aioli after the garlic mayonnaise it features.

The vicissitudes of belief in garlic's medicinal and mystical properties constitute another kind of social history. One of the herb's common names is "heal all," and garlic has almost always been seen as having some sort of curative power.

Eleanor Roosevelt took three chocolate-coated garlic perles every morning, on the advice of her physician, to improve her memory. Russian newspapers in the 1960's advised citizens to chew raw garlic in order to protect themselves against an epidemic of the flu. In May 1978, subscribers to Blue Cross/Blue Shield of Greater New York received with their bills a leaflet called Health Talk, informing them that garlic and onions help reduce cholesterol levels and blood clotting.

And, according to a recent book titled "Medical Botany," the files at the National Cancer Institute in Bethesda, Md., contain a number of reports about possible uses of garlic in the fight against cancer. Clearly, garlic is a powerful folk remedy. Belief in its healing capacities has persisted for an astonishing 5,000 years, and its potent odor and taste have made it something of a cultural Rorschach test: it is seen as a remedy for whatever ill-nesses people are particularly anxious about, usually those that conventional medicine can't cure. Yet folk remedies are not just wishful thinking. They frequently work, whether or not science can find a reason, and they are based as often on trial and error as they are on superstition.

In the 1950's, middle-brow aspirations to gourmet exoticism produced the semichic of garlic bread, usually accompanying pots of spaghetti or chili and often made with salts or powders rather than fresh cloves. But part of the experience of the 1960's was an expansion of the boundaries of American taste. We are somewhat less finicky than we used to be about odors, and definitely more interested in cooking and eating well. In Berkeley, Calif., a French nouvelle cuisine restaurant called Chez Panisse celebrates garlic for a week in July, leading up to a Bastille Day feast in which every course of the dinner is made with garlic. And a group called the "Lovers of the Stinking Rose" in Berkeley publishes a newsletter called The Garlic Times.

The current penchant for nature and good food may not last, but for the time being at least the volatile garlic clove seems to be on the way to securing for itself a respectable place in American life. Whether or not garlic is, as the advertisement says, good and good for you, it is an essential ingredient in the world's great cuisines and a wonderful addition to our own. And whatever the demonstrable physical effects of Allium sativum turn out to be, several thousand years of belief in its powers probably won't come to an end even if scientists in Bethesda decide that it can't cure cancer

HOME & GARDEN

AUGUST 23, 1970

HOME-SEWING BOOM

A woman attending a sewing class in 1971.

Producers of man-made fibers are jumping aboard the home-sewing band wagon and the ride will cost them millions of dollars. The leading companies in the field have plans for extensive promotion campaigns starting this fall and extending through next spring.

Home sewing provides a market of almost $1-billion-a-year worth of textiles, and while this may be only 10 percent of all fabric sales, it is a market that presents lucrative possibilities.

Home sewing has grown steadily since World War II and it is now estimated that between 42 million and 44 million American women and girls are actively making their own clothes and home-furnishing items. Higher costs of apparel and complaints about manufactured textile items have stimulated home sewing.

E. I. du Pont de Nemours & Co., Inc., the largest producer of man-made fibers, will start a home-sewing promotion this fall for one of its newest products, Qiana. It will be backed by an active campaign in print and television advertising and spot TV announcements in 60 markets, and in Vogue, McCalls and Simplicity pattern books and special interest magazines.

The Celanese Fibers Marketing Company will start a spring and summer fashion promotion in February. It will include spot TV commercials in 30 major market areas, point-of-sale advertising with automatic photographic slide machines, print advertising in pattern books and demonstrations in retail stores. Textile manufacturers providing fabrics with Celanese fibers will include Ameritex, Blends Cohama and Rosewood Fabrics, Inc.

Celanese will provide retail stores with patterns and literature that can be distributed to local schools that have sewing classes.

The Allied Chemical Corporation's fiber division will back up its Touch nylon in an assortment of prints manufactured by J. P. Stevens & Co., Inc., in nearly 500 Singer sewing machine centers. This will be part of Singer's "Two Million Dollar Promotion Week" from Sept. 28 through Oct. 3. ∎

APRIL 29, 1973

'Sharing' Homes Is Popular in Suburbs

Paula R. Bernstein

CHAPPAQUA, N.Y.—For single, widowed or divorced people it can be expensive as well as depressing to live alone in the suburbs.

So three middle-aged women move into a neat Colonial on a quiet street. A divorced dentist advertises for men to share his rambling farmhouse on the edge of town. Nine young people pool their paychecks to rent a 15-room, gingerbread-trimmed mansion overlooking a new superhighway.

Domestic arrangements like these are frequent—and illegal—in most Westchester towns. A typical zoning code allows "no more than two people unrelated by blood or marriage" to occupy a home in a one-family area. Another version specifies only two "nontransient roomers or boarders."

In the eyes of the law, those three, five, or nine friends who live together as a family are operating a boarding house without the required special permit.

Real estate values in northern Westchester continue to climb, with a small house in most towns selling for about $45,000, and the few apartments available usually renting for $250 to $300 a month. This shortage of moderate-priced housing helps propel more people into group living. "Believe you me, it's happening here!" declared John A. Lombardi, Supervisor of North Castle, an affluent town that, he said, has a $55,000 price tag on the average house, no apartment zoning and several group homes.

Mr. Lombardi is somewhat sympathetic to groups. "If they are peaceful and there are not too many of them, I can understand it because of the economics. The big problem is a need for conventional housing for young people and young married couples. Eventually it will have to change."

Growing interest in group living has been noticed by some homeowners advertising their houses for rent during temporary

(cont'd. on next page)

LIFE & STYLE

157

(cont'd from previous page)
job transfers or long summer vacations. Homeowners who rent out their houses to three or more people usually do so on their own, without a real estate agent to warn them of possible zoning violations.

Someday, such violations may be only memories. A Federal Court of Appeals has ruled unconstitutional the antigrouper ordinance in Belle Terre, L.I., near Port Jefferson.

The New York Civil Liberties Union has vowed to defend similar cases, and Mr. Lombardi concedes that there is a good possibility of a challenge to the local ordinances.

The attitude of neighbors is a key factor in the survival of a group home, according to North Castle's Town Clerk, Joseph T. Miller. "All you need is two or three persons signing a complaint about a group home on a nuisance charge. Then they're in trouble."

"We're not hippie freaks, like some people assume," said Bernadette Adams, a research technician who lives with a married couple and five other single women, all working full-time in hospitals and schools at salaries ranging from $4,500 to $7,900.

For $125 a month, each member of the group has a private room in an ivy-garlanded stone house high on a hill. The home-cooked meals are served family style at the polished oval dining-room table, and the domestic chores are shared.

Group life "can be a financial advantage," said Karen Holtslag, one resident of the house, "but it is more than that for us. Everybody cares about everybody else." ■

Dressed-Up Vans Are a New Way of Life

Iver Peterson

BOWLING GREEN, Ky., July 27—Vantasy, Vantastic, Moby Van. Chiquita Vanana and Van on the Run were all here this weekend.

They rolled in from every state in the Union except Alaska—giant, brightly painted shoeboxes rolling along on fat tires, choking the narrow lanes and wide campgrounds of Beech Bend Park with a throbbing cacophony of rock music, the burble and hiss of their engines, the odor of marijuana and their shaggy, long-haired and sometimes naked young owners, their wives and girlfriends, all here to celebrate their affection for a kind of truck. The van.

It was the Third Annual Truck-in of the National Street Van Association, a gathering of more than 5,000 gaudy, customized street vans that couldn't help raising, for an outsider, the question, What is this all about?

To the devotee, a van is the only way to travel, to live in sometimes, to put your money into (usually most of it). Vans go where cars go, get as good mileage, and provide a miniature version of the comforts of home done up in styles ranging from legendary Turkish bordello to early American Colonial. Vanners live in their trucks, sleep in them, cook and watch television in them, and do things that have earned the street van a variety of nicknames, including "sin bin."

Street vans are the offspring of a marriage of the working class hot rod and the counterculture, middle-class Volkswagen camper of the 1960's. The cradle of vanning, as the latest automotive craze is called, was California, where young people, at the turn of the decade, began noticing the practical possibilities of the ordinary delivery van.

If it can carry plumbing or electrical supplies, they reasoned, why not a couple of bicycles or a surfboard? Why not spiff up the inside with a bed and some interior decorating, add some "killer sounds"—an ear-splitting hi-fi whose large speakers would not fit in a car—re-work the body a little, add a little paint and art work, and make it something special?

As a million-dollar business that is still growing, the major manufacturers are watching this development closely, and each is already putting a larger share of its production into vans that are basically built for personal and recreational use rather than commercial purposes.

The style of the vans and the experience they provide will probably become the subjects of psychiatrists trying to figure out young people again. In a windowless, hermetically sealed and air-conditioned van with a hi-fi system that seems to operate only at the threshold of pain, a passenger sees nothing, hears nothing and smells nothing of the passing scene.

It could be considered the environment for people who are withdrawn and yet restless. The most common murals on the outside panels depict eerie, desolate landscapes illuminated by pale suns and moons reflected from vast, still oceans. The most common legend to be found on the back on vans is "just passin' thru." ■

The comforts of home, in miniature.

WHAT'S HAPPENED TO THE CLEAN SWEEP?

Broom sales are collapsing. Last year about 27 million brooms were sold, down 20 percent from the number sold a decade before, when there were fewer floors and fewer potential sweepers.

Why aren't brooms selling? "That's something the broom industry would like to know," says Jack Springer, executive director of the National Broom and Mop Council in Chicago.

He theorizes that the "advent of all this indoor-outdoor carpeting," or the use of vacuum cleaners or electric brooms might be hurting the traditional broom business. But the advent of the vinyl floor may be helping the broom makers find another niche.

"A lot of broom people have started to make mops," he explains. ■

PATTERNED SHEETS: Where Will It All End?

Enid Nemy

Helen Gurley Brown, editor of Cosmopolitan, showing off her patterned bedspread and sheets.

Some years ago, a few avant-garde decorators and a few creative real people took a second look at patterned sheets—and their prices—and a new decorating concept was born.

Since then, the use of sheets for home decoration has proliferated. Now almost every textile company involved in the manufacture of bed linens considers it a challenge to find new and more ingenious ideas for sheets.

Many ideas are translated into reality in model rooms, in department store decorating and, frequently, in do-it-yourself booklets.

Price—very often six yards of fabric for well under $8—and sturdiness are not solely responsible for the increasing use of sheets as a decorating fabric. They are, in

(cont'd. on next page)

159

(cont'd. from previous page)
truth, of secondary importance. The fact is that sheets today include some of the best fabric designs available anywhere, and fashion trends are picked up while they are still whispers in the wind.

"The best value in terms of design is sheets," said Sue Morris, a decorator who has used sheets for everything from bedrooms to dining rooms. "They are also the best value economically—they are practical and they always look fresh."

Although bedrooms have provided the most popular backgrounds for sheets used for purposes other than bed linen, an increasing number of dining and living rooms are being covered and/or upholstered in some of the more sophisticated patterns.

Such women as Carol Farkas, who have had whole walls covered in shirred sheeting, are pleased with the practicality. And women who have taken to using sheets on round dining tables and for chair cushions have discovered that matching or contrasting 22-by-22-inch napkins—from sheets, of course—are not only attractive but also particularly useful for buffet parties.

JANUARY 11, 1977

After a Decade of Shag, the Close-Cropped Rug Comes Back

Rita Reif

CHICAGO, Jan. 10—After a decade of tangling with everyone's toes, shag wall-to-wall is out, and close-cropped rugs with Oriental designs, folk motifs and geometric patterns are in.

Thousands of store buyers are reviewing acres of crushed velvets, twists, loops and a lustrous, thick construction called Saxony. But these shoppers are not exposed to the llama look that once spelled status in this country.

The change is sweeping and dominates the collections of all of the giants and the smaller trend-setting producers showing at this market. Stark Carpet Corporation, for instance, the Francophile house that once produced subtle wall-to-wall designs, has now made a deep commitment to stocking period Orientals and its own copies of these.

"The area rug business is growing at a much faster rate than broadloom," Francis X. Larkin, president of Karastan, reported.

Mr. Larkin said that Orientals continue to dominate area rugs, noting that 65 percent of the rug business is in Orientals or designs that look as if they were woven in the East.

That emphasis may now be changing with the intro-

duction at this market of several collections of geometric patterned rugs and carpets, and the spread of interest in folk patterns and Egyptian designs. Karastan offers all these looks. Its Cathay Medallion is rich in such Taoist and Buddhist symbols as knots, lotus buds, clouds, flowers and lutes.

The broadloom binge that America has been on for a decade is far from over, according to Walter Guinan, the retired president of Karastan, who spoke to buyers and manufacturers this morning. He said that the carpet industry, which was the fastest-growing consumer goods industry in the country in the 1960's, growing 12 times in a decade, is still on the upswing with homeowners more willing to spend money on carpeting than on furniture. ∎

MEN NOW MAN WELCOME WAGON

Ruth Rejnis

It may be possible to leave town like a thief in the night, but move in that way? Slim chance—at least where Welcome Wagon is in operation.

Before the last cup is unwrapped, a hostess—or, these days, a host—will appear on the newcomer's doorstep with gifts from local merchants and a snappy patter about the new community. The new resident will be soothed and feeling at home. The hostess will be paid and so will Welcome Wagon. Everybody's happy.

But then Welcome Wagon International is a cheery organization, and an enduring one. Next month it begins its 50th year of operation in this country and abroad.

The organization, owned by the Gillette Company, is the only nationwide greeting service, with more than 8,000 greeters dispensing its successful combination of good will and commerce.

The newcomers' program is the best known Welcome Wagon service. That is where a hostess brings a basket of goodies around to the new folks in town. It works this way: The hostess is responsible for wooing local businesses into supporting the program. Each merchant who places his product in the basket pays about $1.30 a call. The greeter keeps 45 percent of that amount and the balance is turned over to the company.

Gifts can range from a ballpoint pen with a store's imprint to small pieces of jewelry, hardware, plants, and coupons worth merchandise or services at community shops. An average basket brings the homeowner about $60 worth of notions.

Hostesses average $200-$300 a month in commissions for the part-time job.

There have naturally been changes in the company's activities over the last 50 years.

Not all greeters are women these days. "We're actively seeking men," said Jane McNaught of Saddle River, N.J., a regional manager whose territory encompasses much of the Middle Atlantic states and close to 900 hostesses. ∎

House Paint Turns Colorful

Ruth Rejnis

Colorful row houses in Washington, D.C.

As any Sunday driver has probably observed, there is a new style in house painting these days: color—lots of it, and in interesting, sometimes bold, combinations.

Painting a house white was—and in many parts of the country still is—Americana: the Midwest farmhouses, homes in New England hamlets, and, perhaps the most famous of the genre, the White House in Washington.

But the explosion of color in other arenas and the heightened interest in decorating that began in the late 1960's has seen an increasing interest in experimentation in house painting.

"White is still our best seller," said Clayton Lange of the Sherwin-Williams Company. "But there is a definite trend toward color."

The company's most popular hues are brown and autumn red (no, not on the same house).

Simple frame houses and those in Victorian styles dating to the 19th century were usually painted originally in muted colors. In the late 19th and early 20th centuries brighter colors and a greater use of white were introduced.

"They would use, say, green with maroon shutters," explained Amy Flowerman of the Victorian Society of America, which is based in Philadelphia. "And peach, and olive green and beige-grey with a rose trim. White wasn't terribly popular."

Today, the prime example of Victoriana—the gingerbread houses of San Francisco—are an artist's palette of color. Many of those tones date back to the 19th century, but San Francisco's colors are hardly all muted. There is sunshine yellow and sea blue and pink. No one knows quite why the city by the bay wandered from true Victorian colors, but one theory advanced is that it has a Mediterranean look—bright sunlight, few street trees—that lends itself to pastel colors.

Being by the water, too, allows the houses to carry off strong colors. The Victorian houses in Cape May, N.J., are also brightly, not always subtly, painted.

Will the trend toward color last? Paint manufacturers have special "color stylists" within their companies, so they feel it will. But a spokesman for the Heritage Foundation, a San Francisco preservation group, wonders.

"Different paints weather at different rates," she explains. "People may just get fed up with having to keep up these colors. I have my eye on a navy blue house here and I'm just wondering what it will look like a year or two from now."

"Paint can always make an ugly house interesting," said Joan Hoonhout, a real estate broker in Upper Montclair, N.J. "There's one house I particularly admire now that was painted a rich chocolate brown with persimmon trim. It's very smart looking and a sophisticated buyer would appreciate it. And, all things being equal, it probably would bring more money now." ∎

Punk Furniture Makes Itself Felt

John Duka

The 1950's gave us skinny ties, pegged pants and Elvis Presley. The 1970's, in a quantum leap forward, have so far given us skinny ties, pegged pants and Elvis Costello. The important difference is that what was then dismissed as a fad is currently deemed a movement—pure punk. Now, another manifestation of the punk movement is upon us—punk furniture, designed by a young man named Richard Mauro.

Mr. Mauro, a second-generation Italian who is 30 years old and once studied to be a priest, zigs and zags around his spacious Brooklyn loft pointing to the various pieces of punk furniture he has developed over the last two years. He is dressed in black. His hair is now shortish, cut, he said, by the same person who cuts Divine's hair.

The furniture he has designed, variations on standard contemporary pillow furniture, lies in complacent anomie on the floor like strange house pets waiting to be fed and stroked. There is a mat—made of glued-together sheets of uncut baby bottle nipples—that quivers like some primordial protozoan. There is an amoeboid shape, as long as a man and covered with 1,000 No. 3 safety pins. In a corner, an ottoman made of clear vinyl stuffed with newspapers quietly disintegrates. Something that could easily pass for a Claes Oldenburg soft sculpture gone punk, but which is really a punk chair made of a 150-yard-long industrial zipper sewn to itself in widening concentric circles, pulsates invitingly. The punk designer *(cont'd. on next page)*

(continued from previous page)

sat on it and explained the evolution of his work.

"We've always seen a zipper on jackets or trousers, but I'd never sat on one, or on safety pins," said Mr. Mauro. "When these were taken out of their contexts and multiplied, they seemed to take on a violence and force that I didn't know they had. But the pieces are comfortable. And they're not dangerous. I wanted to create a pause in the function of sitting and lounging, a refreshing confusion."

"Punk was a great influence on me," he said. "I'd read about it in punk magazines like Slash. Then I went to London to see how the punks lived there." Two other influences on Mr. Mauro were the furniture designer Joseph Rykwert and the architectural historian Charles Jencks, author of "Adhocism: The Case for Improvisation."

The zipper chair is stuffed with discarded zippers. The clear vinyl ottoman is filled with newspapers that he bought from a man who stores undelivered newspapers in a warehouse. The Discus ottoman is covered with aluminized nylon; inside, a quilted canvas bag is filled with broken plates that Mr. Mauro bought on the Bowery for a penny apiece. "What I like about the Discus is that the more you sit on it, the more crumbled the dishes get until there's nothing left. You see, my furniture is not art. It is an exercise, things for now that won't last."

"I think vinyl slipcovers shouldn't exist," said Mr. Mauro, "so I guess I'm making some sort of statement. What I'm really doing is mocking the things we take for granted. But I'm not making furniture that is negative. What I consider to be negative furniture is contemporary reproductions of traditional designs, like the Chippendale chairs made today." ∎

MAY 28, 1978

Furniture Moves Off the Porch

Lisa Hammel

The country has come to the city. Go into the furniture department of almost any of the large stores, and you'll see such rustic items as Windsor chairs, rush seat ladderbacks, trestle tables, Welsh dressers and lots of pieces in pine. But more than anything else, you'll find rattan—in all its variety of forms.

Maybe it has something to do with our current fondness for the "natural look"; or the back-to-the-land movement come back to the city; or the more casual way many people now prefer to live and dress.

Whatever it is, the wherewithal for turning an urban apartment or a suburban house into a country cottage is very much there.

At Bloomingdale's, one sees the charms of country décor in evidence all over the fifth floor, peeking out between the chrome and glass or the more staid traditional.

In addition, two of the room settings are done mostly with rattan furniture, are there are other touches in the model rooms that intensify the rustic effect, such as white stucco walls, painted furniture, jute rugs, plants—and baskets, baskets everywhere.

The store has also done a number of good country furniture reproductions, modified a bit to suit more contemporary tastes.

At Lord & Taylor, one can also find a good selection of rattan. And in one room setting, a woven bamboo console table, desk and étagères share space with peach-colored modular seating, for an unusual, urbane look.

At Altman's, a country shop in one corner of the furniture floor offers reproductions in oak, pine, painted and stenciled finishes.

Macy's contribution to rusticity are some natural pine cupboards, dressers and drop-front desks tucked away among the traditional furniture, and Gimbels has two small groups of rattan furniture that include chairs, sofas, table bases and ottomans, as well as a bar cart with a built-in ice bucket and wine storage racks.

All that seems to be missing among the wide selection of rustic furnishings now in the stores is the sound of crickets. ∎

Rattan furniture comes indoors.

LIFE WITH TV

Suzanne Slesin

What to do with the living room eyesore?

Often it seems designers would rather forget that there is such a thing as a television set. If a client insists on having one (and almost all do), a designer or architect will often stash the set in a bookcase, or slip it behind a sliding cabinet door. Basically, the architect is just as happy not to have to deal with an object that he more often than not finds aesthetically unappealing.

When the architect Peter Wilson and his associates, Jon Evans and Barbara Weinstein, were hired by television-loving Allen Schwartz to redesign his two-bedroom apartment, they knew they were being presented with a special challenge. Mr. Schwartz made that quite specific:

"I want the TV's near me and visible, but I don't want them to stick out," he told them at the first design consultation.

Mr. Wilson and Mr. Evans, who had been a student of Mr. Wilson's at Pratt Institute, studied the way their client likes to use television in different rooms at different times of the day.

They found that the bedroom television was for early-morning or late-night viewing, the kitchen/dining area set was for early evening news programs and the living room large-screen set was strictly for sports and movies. The designers divided the space into three zones that match the viewing spheres.

"Allen doesn't watch TV all the time," Mr. Evans said, "but when he's home at least one of the TV's is always on, sort of like background music."

The first step in the renovation was to take down the wall between the kitchen and the living room so that a banquette and a dining table could be installed. The television was placed on an above-eye level pull-out drawer and swiveling base, so that the set can be turned to face the sofa in the kitchen, or swiveled to face the dining room banquette.

The designers visually tied the kitchen, dining area and living room together with tile. The tile border starts off as the kitchen counter, snakes around the dining area and turns into a handrail as it follows the steps down into the living room. There, above the sleek black marble fireplace is the room's focal point—a 52-inch-by-70-inch Advent TV screen, majestically framed by the room's pair of floor-to-ceiling niches and plants. The television projector is enclosed in a cabinet that doubles as a coffee table.

At a flick of a switch, Mr. Schwartz can turn on a 26-foot-long double strip of neon and transform his living room into what he calls a "party room."

"For Allen," said the architect, "the living room is a social thing, a movie theater, a stadium."

In the master bedroom, there is only room for the bed—and a television. Placed on a swiveling base at the foot of the bed, the television is the room's most important presence. "Everything in this room moves," said Mr. Evans. "Doors slide open, the bed rises up and down, the TV swivels, but the overall feeling is meant to be restful."

Real Estate 101

Enid Nemy

There are three kinds of people at dinner parties these days: Those who didn't buy a house or apartment two or three years ago, those who did, and those who know they can't afford anything now but are still looking. Members of the first group are miserable, mad (as in you fool you), and inclined to spend most of the evening verbally kicking themselves. Members of the second group are insufferably complacent, inviting more than a verbal kick. And those in the third group are more to be pitied than censured.

Occasionally, an oddball who knows and cares nothing about real estate gets into such a party and lives to regret it. The evening is a total loss, with no fascinating light conversation about the latest doings of Bianca Jagger and Farrah Fawcett and not even any heavier discussion as to what's going on with Jacqueline Onassis, Woody Allen and Joan Baez.

The situation is sad and serious, and it could well herald the breakdown of, if not all dinner parties, at least fashionable dinner parties. Fashionable dinner parties are not going to survive ignoring Jackie for very long, even with Rosalynn acting like a member of the Government, Miss Lillian doing whatever she does, and real estate.

Dinner party real estate is actually a concentrated short course in numerous

(cont'd. on next page)

LIFE & STYLE

(cont'd from previous page)

subjects, ranging from property, money, banking and sociology to architecture and interior decorating. The topics aren't new; there's always been desultory talk about them, but never before with such fervor and intensity. The disinterested oddballs are becoming fewer and fewer. The only people left who might like to get off the subject are foreigners who don't plan to settle here, and have no money to invest, and members of that happy group who pay $250 a month for 10-room, rent-controlled apartments and therefore bought their country homes 20 years ago.

The renter didn't have brains enough to snap up a co-op bargain when the going was good

Other than people who own both a Manhattan apartment and a country house, both bought some years ago, it's a no-win situation at these parties. The apartment renter, who pays going rates, is regarded with a mixture of pity and disdain. Pity at the idea of forking out all that money, with no "equity or tax deduction," and disdain that the renter didn't have brains enough to snap up a co-op bargain when the going was good. Which brings up the subject of financing. One end of the table says borrow from the bank, mortgage to the hilt, the dollars one repays get cheaper each year. Not so, says the other end, interest rates are high, pay the whole thing off as quickly as possible. How much does the bank charge? That depends if you get the prime rate. Who gets the prime rate? Big customers. Is a $500 checking account a big customer?

What kind of a degree do you get after a dinner like this? ■

OCTOBER 21, 1979

SPENDING ALL DAY IN BED

A day in bed in Pittsburgh, 1976, with essentials at hand: books, beer and yes, cigarettes.

Enid Nemy

So it isn't everyone's idea of heaven. Still, for a lot of busy people, it's an awfully nice way to spend the day. Let those who will jog, cycle or roller skate in the park, window-shop the avenue, do the museums, drive to the country. The sybaritic, some say the smart, stay in bed.

"I'm highly disciplined and when I stay in bed all day on a Sunday, I have the feeling I'm playing hooky, but my conscience doesn't hurt me much or long," said Melanie Kahane.

Miss Kahane, the president of the interior design concern of Melanie Kahane Associates, spends a weekend day in bed whenever she can, and she couldn't care less whether it's sunny, raining or snowing outside.

"It's like a religion and I'm devoted to it," Miss Kahane said. "Anyone who disagrees is a heretic."

If the housekeeper is working, breakfast and lunch are brought up to her; if she's alone, she goes down, makes her own meals and brings them up herself. But the eating is done in bed, propped up on Porthault bed linen ("my one fierce extravagance") with lots of pillows, and surrounded by more books and papers than she can possibly get through, a telephone and directory, paper for notes and lists, some work and the television set.

"I'm like a child with all my toys around me," she said. "The next morning, I feel divine, and wish it was Sunday again."

Anita Tiburzi remembers when she could spend a Saturday or Sunday in bed whenever she wished. Now, with a 3½-year-old son, she stays in bed only when he's visiting his grandparents in Florida.

"My whole bedroom is set up for such days," she said. "I have a stereo, telephone, television and bookcases within reach."

The morning begins with orange juice, a croissant, sweet butter and cafe au lait and progresses to the newspaper, books, music and old movies.

"Somewhere in between," she said, "I do all that good stuff like milk pads on my eyes, giving myself a manicure, and aside from breakfast, fasting."

The fasting is accomplished with the help of a 23-ounce bottle of Perrier, placed beside the bed and "swigged down, at room temperature, right out of the bottle." Miss Tiburzi characterized swigging from the bottle as "too gauche," but as director of corporate communications for Perrier, she's sensitive to such things.

And what about the men? Don't they ever spend lazy days in bed? Impeccable sources—wives and friends—say yes, they do. But most of the men refuse to admit it.

"It's that whole jock thing," said the wife of one. "They think that it gives them the wrong image to admit that they're human—and lazy." ■

MAY 30, 1970

FIJIAN OR AFRO, THE COMB MAKES SENSE

Robert Trumbull

SUVA, Fiji—The image projected by Fiji, a British colony of several hundred beautiful islands that will become an independent state on Oct. 10, has to include a magnificently proportioned race of tall, robust, smiling women with a distinctive bushy hair style.

"You trim it like a hedge," said Josafeen Naulu, a vivacious 25-year-old desk clerk at the Travelodge Hotel in this capital city of 55,000 people.

Once universally worn by Fijians of both sexes, the traditional bouffant hair style still adorns nearly all females but only a few men of the predominantly Melanesian race indigenous to these islands.

"In World War II, when many Fijians joined the British forces, we found it awkward to pull a helmet quickly over bushy hair," a middle-aged Fijian said. One who has conspicuously retained the old style is Leone Lesianawai, a retired policeman who has become a familiar figure in Suva as a tourist guide.

Achieving a proper puffiness takes careful preparation of the hair with a solution of lime and clay, Miss Naulu explained. When dry, the stiffened locks are painstakingly teased with a long-toothed wooden comb.

"In the old days, the hair was kept in place overnight by sleeping with the neck supported on a wooden rack called a kali," said Miss Naulu. "Nowadays, we just tie up the hair with a cloth."

Almost never seen any more are young girls wearing side locks often falling to the waist. That style denoted virginity, and the locks were cut upon marriage.

An American is said to have discovered that the Fijian comb is also ideal for the Afro haircut. According to curio dealers, Afro-wearing crew members of American tour ships coming through Suva buy the combs in quantity and send them home to friends. ■

The Afro hairstyle was very popular in the 1970s.

SEPTEMBER 25, 1970

MORE THAN YOU WANTED TO KNOW ABOUT THOSE HEMLINES...

Enid Nemy

Fashion and protest are no strangers to each other, but never has a new fashion encountered as much hostility or been embroiled in as much controversy as the midi hemline, a length that hovers around the calf.

If the midi, with almost every major designer and manufacturer behind it, is not a resounding success, it will be the fashion industry's first major defeat.

The controversy this year has arisen not on the basis of good or bad fashion, as was the case with the mini, but rather on peripheral issues and circumstances. All of them will contribute to the midi's eventual fate. Among them are:

- A hard-sell promotion led by Women's Wear Daily, a fashion trade publication, fashion magazines and many stores, that many women call dictatorship.
- More women confident of their own judgment, accustomed to the great choice and relative fashion freedom of the late 1960's, less willing to accept a single trend and the dicta of designers, fashion leaders and movie stars. This new feeling of liberation is widely discussed and generally underrated.
- A business recession coupled with inflation.

(cont'd. on next page)

165

(cont'd. from previous page)

- Almost universal male disapproval and hostility, from husbands and beaux to television talk show hosts and syndicated columnists heard and read by millions.
- A viable alternative in pants.
- Unseasonably hot weather.

Who are the women who have taken the plunge into a sea of controversy and uncertainty? They cut across economic brackets, size ranges, age groups and occupations. They eat in fashionable restaurants and at hot-dog stands; they pound typewriters and play bridge in the afternoons; they are busy dating and busy looking after grandchildren.

Many of them are likely to be women who want to be first in fashion and will accept anything pushed with sufficient vigor. They have gone through the chemise, the mini, the maxi, the poor girl, the peasant, the gypsy, La Belle Epoque and the Moroccan look.

Others are women with the time, money and inclination to change wardrobes seasonally and, in some cases, even more frequently.

There is, too, a not inconsiderable group of older women who have never felt dignified or comfortable in shorter skirts, as well as career and college girls whose interest in pure fashion is minimal and whose look changes from day to day. These girls are buying the midi, but they are also buying the mini and anything that pleases them at the moment and is labeled as "fun."

Perhaps the largest pro-midi group comprises the women involved in fashion—the models, buyers, designers, showroom assistants, copywriters and publicists—and the women married to men in fashion. In a random survey last week, 80 percent of the women with a completely coordinated and well-accessorized midi look were involved in the industry. ■

A viable alternative in pants.

Modeling denim hot pants.

JANUARY 31, 1971

IS THAT A WAY TO SAVE FACE? SELL HOT PANTS?

Judy Klemesrud

Hot Pants…Les Shorts…Shortootsies… Happy Legs. Suddenly the fashion industry, badly burned by its effort to foist the midi on resisting womankind, has counterattacked. Its chief weapon: shorts.

At the Rome and Paris fashion showings this month, shorts were all the rage. Already last week New York fashion plates were braving the icy weather to be the first on the block to wear shorts to lunch, to fashion shows—even to black tie parties.

The midi, of course, was rejected by a thumping majority of American women, many of whom joined midi protest groups with catchy acronyms like GAMS (Girls Against More Skirt) and FADD (Fight Against Dictating Designers). So far, nobody's fighting hot pants.

William M. Fine, president of Bonwit Teller, who suggested that his employees wear midi-skirts last fall so customers would feel more comfortable, believes the shorts are a reaction "to all the seriousness that invaded the fashion business last fall. We got into so many damn debates and it turned out to be the most publicized fashion election in history. This is the reaction. It's a game."

And who won the length debate? "Everybody won," he said. "Women can now wear the length they're in the mood to wear."

Women's Wear Daily, the fashion industry trade paper, had pushed the midi, or the "Longuette," as they called it, last fall. Demonstrating its resilience, Women's Wear

AUGUST 14, 1971

SWAZILAND'S NEWEST EXPORT:
Hot Pants and Maxis

Kathleen Teltsch

UNITED NATIONS, N.Y.,—Now it's hot pants from Swaziland, a pocket-sized kingdom in southern Africa.

The pants, along with maxidresses, shirts and trouser suits, are being turned out by a new enterprise set up with funds and help from the United Nations and its affiliate, the International Labor Organization.

The Swazis do not wear the kind of mod apparel they're making. It's strictly for the export trade.

G. Alan Major, the I.L.O. business export who put Swaziland in the fashion business, explains that the idea of adapting the Swazi designs for the Western fashion trade developed last year when Mrs. Kosi Noge walked into his office in Mbabane, the Swazi capital, looking for help in starting a workshop.

"I told her we had no workshops built, but that she was welcome to use the kitchen in our office building and dry her materials on the veranda," he recalls.

In the kitchen, Mrs. Noge began adapting the Swazi patterns, sometimes using the tie-dye technique teenagers are using these days to color their T-shirts. She also used the potato printing technique—cutting a design into a potato, dipping it in dye and then applying it to the fabric.

When Swaziland secured its independence from Britain in 1968, the new Government gave priority to the encouragement of small enterprises, and Mrs. Noge's plan fit smoothly into the program.

In one year, the one-woman operation has grown into a profitable enterprise employing 24. When her Swazi Flame Company turned out its first collection, Mr. Major carried the samples in suitcases to I.L.O. headquarters in Geneva.

There, on the lawns of the I.L.O. building, youthful staff members staged an outdoor fashion show to display the new sports apparel and Mr. Major modeled a favorite Swazi shirt. The I.L.O. staff members tried to buy the clothes, but Mr. Major had to refuse. The entire line was packed off to London for viewing by British buyers.

has now espoused shorts, coining the term, "hot pants," and last week it showed another new fashion that it said could be worn interchangeably with the shorts. To most observers it looked like the old mini, but to Women's Wear it was a "hot skirt."

Most Manhattan stores that sell hot pants reported last week that they were sold out almost as soon as new shipments came in.

"They are an expression of the female's new freedom," said Dr. Jason Miller, a Manhattan psychiatrist, "and they mean she's no longer willing to be submissive to convention. They also show that she is on a serious mission to relate to other people—especially men. She may not be wearing them just to be sexually provocative, but because she desires to get attention as a prelude to a genuine relationship."

But some fashion historians think the shorts fad is firmly rooted in nostalgia. "It's the look of the 30's and 40's," said Dorothy Tricarico, fashion and textile coordinator at the Design Laboratory of the Brooklyn Museum. "That's when Ruby Keeler and Deanna Durbin and Betty Grable were always seen in short shorts. And some of our other fashions now come directly from that period, too—hair ornaments, chokers, deep red lipstick, soft fluid fabrics, and a wide shoulder look.

"But hot pants are a first in one sense," she added. "In no other time in history have shorts been accepted for street wear and business as they are right now." ∎

APRIL 23, 1972

Women Shun the 'Dress-Dress' Sportswear, However, Finds Ready Market

Isadore Barmash

American women are not buying dresses.

Consumers across the country are buying television sets, furniture, carpets, appliances, automobiles, hardware and building materials, as well as sportswear—but not dresses.

"Dresses are simply selling to a smaller number of people," reported William M. Fine, president of Bonwit Teller. "Spring was a lethargic season for dresses, but summer looks much better based on our reorders," said Sy Cohen, vice president, sales, for R & K Originals, the largest dress producer in the moderate-priced field.

Women became so used to pants-suits, pants and sportswear that they neither need, want nor desire as many dresses as they once bought.

The midi-length fiasco of 1969-1970 created such confusion among American women that they lost faith in their own ability to select lengths. In the midst of this, however, a demand grew for knit dresses and "sporty" dresses, and it made inroads into the regular dress departments.

A relatively new approach in sportswear, the "layered look," has become popular among all age levels. The "look" refers to sweaters and other knitted tops that can be worn over blouses and with different slacks or skirts.

Regardless of whether all will agree on the impact of these elements, the effect on Seventh Avenue, which in recent years has developed skill as a "survival area," has nonetheless been near-traumatic.

"Consumers continue to be sluggish in their buying, and this, plus the imports problem, has hurt dress production. It appears to be stagnant in the latest weeks or possibly drifting somewhat lower."

An odd element in the total dress picture is that retail sales in New York appear to be more depressed than in other cities. Abe Schrader, a dress producer, said last

(cont'd. on next page)

(cont'd. from previous page)
week that his concern's orders were running about 25 per cent under last year at some New York stores but were up that amount with his retail accounts in other cities.

While dresses may not bear the big price tickets of furs, coats, television sets or even men's suits, they represent a key element in the sales total of many stores. In a cross-section of many stores, women's, misses' and juniors' dresses represent an average 3 percent of total store sales. This is about 1 percent more than women's, misses' and juniors' coats and suits represent of the total store business.

Will this be the year-of-the-dress, as many hope? Will the "dress-dress" make a comeback? No one really knows at this stage. But one thing is certain. The old industry truism, "When fashion is right, it supersedes all seasons," will be severely tested this year. ∎

AUGUST 6, 1972

THE LEVI LIFESTYLE

Milton Moskowitz

SAN FRANCISCO—When Levi Strauss, a Bavarian Jewish immigrant, came here in 1850 to join the California Gold Rush, he didn't exactly discover gold. But he did come up with an idea that has proved to be golden both to the corporation bearing his name and the relatives who have succeeded him at its helm.

The glitter is bright for Levi Strauss & Co. Its Levi's label is one of the best known in this country. (In the public mind, Levi's has become a generic name like Kleenex, Coke or Xerox.) And today Levi Strauss & Co. is probably the prime beneficiary of the jeans revolution that has swept the world.

"Of course we recognize that we have been lucky," said Walter A. Haas Jr., chairman of Levi Strauss and a great-grand-nephew of the founder. "We happen to represent a lifestyle that is being adopted by a growing part of the world."

This lifestyle, highlighting informality and casualness, has helped to make jeans an essential part of the wardrobe of young people everywhere. Beginning on college campuses in the mid-1950's, jeans have been in the center of the world-wide fashion hurricane for male apparel ever since. Now Levi Strauss's strongest overseas market is Amsterdam, which has become an international meeting turf for the counter-culture.

The kind of blue denim jeans made by Levi Strauss and other producers, furthermore, have become the symbol of the freedom associated with clothing today, not only for youth but for everyone. As Charles A. Reich put it in "The Greening of America":

"Jeans make one conscious of the body, not as something separate from the face but as part of the whole individual. Consciousness III believes that a person's body is one of the essential parts of his self, not something to be ignored while one carries on a conversation with his face and mind."

Other observers have viewed jeans as a medium of protest, defiance and political-social engagement. Still others regard tight-fitting jeans—for young men and women alike—simply in terms of sex appeal.

Corporate responsibility, like jeans, has a faddish tone these days, but this theme has been threaded into Levi Strauss for many years.

The Bay Area is honeycombed with cultural contributions from members of the company's founding family, ranging from the Sigmund Stern Grove to the Strawberry Canyon recreation area at the University of California.

Inside a Levi Strauss factory, 1972.

The multimillion-dollar international corporation that Levi Strauss now consists of is a far cry from the dry-goods peddling business begun by the 20-year-old Mr. Strauss 122 years ago. Arriving with a roll of heavy tent canvas from his brother's clothing store in New York, he had a pair of pants

AUGUST 23, 1972

Doctors Predict a Broken Foot

Mary Ann Crenshaw

There's a new fashion malady afoot these days: the broken-bone syndrome. It's the summertime version of skiing's broken leg and this time it's a direct result of those stilt-like platform shoes that are teetering all over the sidewalks of New York. Dr. Monroe Jacobs, president of the Podiatry Association of the State of New York, says that "the platform shoe is supremely dangerous."

He maintains that "the normal reflex pattern of walking is interrupted by the rigidity of such a thick sole and the shape of the platform, which is not conducive to the normal function of walking." He goes on to explain that these problems are compounded by the open back of many clog shoes which gives even greater instability to the foot.

As for those platform shoes with high, high heels (often towering to 4 inches), Dr. Jacobs points out that they are easily caught on a curb or a step. And the sudden stop is similar to that in a skiing accident.

After a tumble last March while wearing a pair of much-advertised clog-soled sandals, Gay Morris, sportswear editor of Seventeen magazine, spent eight weeks in a cast.

Every bone in her foot was broken, she says. Miss Morris returned the shoes to Bendel's Shoe Biz., where they were purchased, and was eventually given credit for the $32 she had spent for the shoes, along with a note of apology from Super Shoe Biz president, Jerry Miller.

Mr. Miller feels that some people are prone to falls, though he does concede that some safety measures, such as instep straps, are being added to his new clogs.

Laura Tosato, designer for I. Miller, doesn't really approve of clogs or platforms and says that "the fear of getting hurt takes the fun out of the design."

"the platform shoe is supremely dangerous"

"With the speed of life what it is today," says Miss Tosato, "clogs are dangerous because they don't hang on." And Miss Tosato says that super-high-heeled shoes are bad for the younger generation that was brought up on low-heeled shoes. "Learning to walk in them is the new gymnastics," she says.

With all this shoe-fashion furor raging, one of the prime promoters of the platform shoe has given them up. Norma Kamali, owner of the avant-garde Kamali boutique at 229 East 53rd Street, maintains that by autumn the platform shoe will be passé. She has ordered all her fall shoes with just plain soles. And as for herself, she swears by sneakers. ∎

Catalogue Fashions Have Come a Long Way

Angela Taylor

It was a great day at the George Hurd household in Brooklyn when the Sears, Roebuck catalogue—all 5½ pounds of it—arrived last month.

"We always sit around at night and fight over it," Mrs. Hurd said. She and her married daughter have already bought their fall wardrobes from the book, plus things for the 5-year-old Hurd grandson.

Scenes similar to the one around the Hurd dining table are repeated twice a year in millions of American homes as Sears, Montgomery Ward and J. C. Penney blanket the country with their major fall and spring books. (Smaller catalogues are issued in between: back-to-school, Christmas or special sales.)

Despite the fact that all three chains have been opening a good many retail stores in shopping areas convenient to suburban communities, catalogue sales are on the increase, the companies say. And customers are a far cry from the farm families on R.F.D. routes who shopped by lamplight for overalls and gingham yardage from Montgomery Ward's four-page, 394-item mailer 100 years ago.

If Montgomery Ward is the oldest company, Sears, Roebuck claims to be the largest general merchandiser in the world. Company sales last year were $10.9 billion, of which 22 percent were catalogue sales. Sears, Roebuck's book is the biggest—1,587 pages—and the only one of the three that shows a dress, rather than pants, on its cover.

J. C. Penney is a Johnny-come-lately in the catalogue business. The company, whose 1972 sales were $5.5 billion, was founded in 1902, but didn't go into cataloging until 10 years ago. The gamble paid off—$388 million in catalogue sales last year. The 4½-pound fall book shows a girl in a battle-jacket and wide-legged pants on the cover of the 1,308 pages, many of them devoted to clothes. (Fashion accounts for 40 percent of Penney's catalogue business.)

How high style are the catalogues? Not very. Their strength is that their clothes are safe and not fads. "I know that what I buy from Penney's is not about to go out of style in a year," says a New York secretary. "The sportswear is very good and it's classic."

Quality control is the big stress at all three houses. Manufacturers' samples are checked for size, wear and washability. "All the size 10's will be the same," says Ida Shalit, Ward's dress stylist. "And if it's washable, we wash everything, including the belt."

The catalogues have come a long way from the poorly sketched or photographed early ones. Clothes are photographed on the same models used by the leading fashion magazines. But shooting catalogues is different from the arty photography of the magazines, Virginia Sorem of Penney's explained.

"The customer must see a garment exactly as it is. You can't pin it or stuff it to make it fit better. You have to minimize accessories because they hide the garment. You don't show three-quarters or seated views. The models can't be too tall or exotic. They have to look like the all-American girl, even though the ideal American look seems to be found on Swedish or German models these days."

What will the American catalogue fan find this year? More dresses than last season, particularly if she shops at Sears. (Hemlines are just above the knee.) Good-looking wrap coats, well priced: $50 at Penney's; $62 at Sears. A Wardrober for $24.88, made up of a sweater with a built-in dickey, plaid pants and a plaid skirt.

And, for those who don't want the newfangled stuff, the black and white pages of the books feature warm winter underwear, nice, firm corsets and padded bras. ■

A Message for Rock Fans— SEQUINS ARE OUT

Bernadine Morris

David Bowie, circa 1974.

The game in any part of the fashion world is to keep one step ahead. When the players are leaders of the glitter-rock brigade, it has to be a giant step. How they look is, after all, about as important as how they sound.

So it is of some significance that among the fashionable, decadent, liberated subculture, the word at the moment is: sequins are out. So, for that matter, are feathers, satin and the outrageous colors that have inspired hordes of teenage fans to deck themselves out in outlandish costumes, following the pattern set by their rock idols.

"The audience, even in places like Minneapolis, outshine the stars these days," said Freddie Burretti, the other day. He had a hand in shaping the glitter. Now he's changing the image.

Mr. Burretti, 23, is the personal designer for David Bowie, a front-runner in the fashionable rock crowd. As with Mick Jagger, another British rock leader known for his dazzling dress, Mr. Bowie was not averse to leather boas, eccentric make-up and lots of glitter.

But these days he strides onto a stage wearing a jacket, trousers that often match it, and a shirt.

"He looks played down, as if he just walked off the street," his designer said.

Suiting Up for Leisure

Leonard Sloane

A typical 70s leisure suit.

The most talked-about written-about, sketched, photographed and analyzed category of men's clothing these days is the "leisure suit." Essentially this is a casual suit for wearing almost anywhere but in the office or on formal occasions—and, for the very casual man, perhaps in the office and on formal occasions, too.

It is being made and sold in virtually every fabric, every jacket length, every form of clothing construction.

Perhaps the best way to define a leisure suit is to say what it is not. It is not a traditional business suit, and it is not a sport-coat-and-pants combination. For one thing, the jackets of these outfits have normal coat collars, whereas leisure suits have a collar more like a shirt.

this is a casual suit for wearing almost anywhere

A leisure suit is less expensive than a comparable business suit. Seymour Schimel, executive director of the National Association of Men's Sportswear Buyers, says: "The key price range is under $100. And you can use the shirt or jacket or pants as separate items, too."

As is the case with most fashions, it is impossible to date the beginning of the leisure suit precisely. It evolved during the last decade or so.

The name and the concept did not really register on the public consciousness until last year. By the spring of 1974 the leisure suit had become the "hot item" of the wholesale market place. And now it is in all the department and specialty stores—and is being heavily advertised.

The three most important styles are:

The Safari—the biggest seller. This suit is made in various popular fabrics. The jacket is typically 30 or 31 inches long, with a shirt-type collar. Among the variations are military epaulets and short sleeves.

The Battle Jacket—the Eisenhower jacket from World War II brought up to date with a longer length and matching trousers. Some manufacturers are turning out twill products that are designed to be worn with a shirt and tie.

The Shirt Suit—a suit using shirt-weight fabric in both the top and the bottom. A wide variety of shirt suits are in the stores now and are being produced for next spring for the jeans generation as well as luxury customers.

Although producers of everything from dungarees to tailored clothing are turning out leisure suits, some retailers—in middle America and elsewhere—are not yet convinced of their long-range versatility.

Nevertheless, the actual and projected sales figures for leisure suits at the wholesale and retail levels indicate that they have made their mark. What happens in the years ahead, of course, is up to the public. ∎

Mr. Burretti exaggerates. This is not exactly ordinary street wear, but not glittery either.

"A real clean look," as Mr. Burretti explains it. "Shoulders squared, waist sharp, everything neat and crisp."

Mr. Burretti said that he himself "dropped sequins a year ago." "When you're into things early, you get bored with them by the time everybody else starts wearing them," he said.

Mr. Burretti's mother designs clothes and taught him to sew before he went to school. "I was terrible as a child—I wouldn't go out of the house unless my cuffs were turned back properly," he recalled. "If the trousers weren't neatly pressed or the hems weren't right, I would scream. I guess I get that from my mother, because she was always perfectly turned out, but my father thought it was strange."

"Four years ago, after I made a couple of outfits for him, David asked me to work with him and I've been doing it ever since," he said.

Now he's preparing to broaden his scope. For the last few months, along with Susi Craker, another young British designer he's been working on a loft on 18th street, preparing a collection of clothes for both men and women. It is, of course, based on ideas he's been developing with Mr. Bowie. "Older people will be able to wear them too," he said. "The gap is narrowing now that clothes will be more tailored." ∎

style

'I'M THE BIGGEST MODEL, PERIOD'

Great face, great figure, great personality, the supergirl next door insists she's more than just the biggest black model in the business.

Ted Morgan

Beverly Johnson modeling a Halston gown, 1975.

The first thing I learned about women who model is that they can be washed up at 25. The second thing I learned about women who model is that there are exceptions to the first thing I learned.

Runway models last longer than photographers' models. They earn less and they have slack periods between collections, but some keep working into their 40's, by which time the only way a print model might still be active would be in the "matron" category.

Like the houses of Lancaster and York, these two branches of the modeling profession conduct a running feud. When I decided to focus this inquiry on Beverly Johnson, her press agent, Bryna Millman, warned me: "Don't lump Beverly together with runway models. There's no comparison."

Of the various kinds of models, the photographic or print model has the best chance of becoming a highly paid star, with a name and face familiar to millions. This is what happened to Beverly Johnson, a 23-year-old black girl from Buffalo whom Horatio Alger, if he were writing today, could have made the subject of an inspirational tale. Beverly is a triple threat—she has been a runway model for Halston; on TV, she has sung "Come On and Fly Me" for National Airlines, and danced around a huge can of deodorant; and in the high-fashion field, she became the first black girl to appear on the cover of Vogue.

Beverly has interesting blood lines: Her father, a machine operator, is part Blackfoot Indian, and her mother, a surgical technician, is a Louisiana Creole. She looks, in the words of another black model, "like a white woman dipped in brown paint." She has straight hair, a classic nose, lips that are not too full, and flawless skin that stretches like a drumhead over her face. Five feet, 8 inches tall and 115 pounds, she fits all the correct high-fashion measurements. When she visited Senegal, President-poet Léopold Sédar Senghor told her that she reminded him of the Queen of Sheba, who came not from Africa but from Southern Arabia.

Beverly likes to tell the ugly-duckling story on herself: "I was tall and awkward. My little sister was the beauty. She had all the boyfriends. I was into sports." She just missed qualifying for the 1968 Olympics in the 100-yard free style. When she was

swimming, she learned a lesson that she applies to modeling: "If you look around to see where everyone else is going, you lose the race. The trick is to keep swimming."

In two years, Beverly was on the cover of Glamour six times. "Glamour loved the image I was projecting," Beverly recalled. "The first issue I was on set records. Their circulation doubled."

A market-research company tests reader response to each Glamour cover. "How would you like to know this person?" they ask. "How would you like to be this person?" Readers from the Midwest and the Deep South replied that they would like to be Beverly Johnson. Affluent young white women in the heartland were identifying with a black cover girl.

When the word got around that Glamour was on to something special, Eileen Ford, who with her husband, Jerry, operates New York's foremost model agency, recruited Beverly. Under Eileen Ford's tutelage, Beverly became a star model.

Beverly makes between $100,000 and $200,000 a year. She is on her way to becoming a "millionette." But she knows that a top fashion model lasts about six years, even though she says, "I could go on modeling forever."

"You've come a long way, baby," says the captain for the Virginia Slims ad that shows Beverly next to a package of cigarettes. Beverly recently appeared on Jack O'Brian's radio show. "You're the biggest black model in the business," O'Brian said. "No, I'm not," Beverly said. "I'm the biggest model—period."

On one recent day, Beverly booked out, giving up $800 in fees to play a two-line speaking part in a movie called "Troubled Times," starring James Earl Jones. Roughly a hundred atmosphere persons, as extras are known these days, were waiting, garishly garbed, in the orchestra of the Theatre de Lys, where a party scene was about to be filmed on the stage. Beverly, in a long, cream-colored evening gown, was humming, "I want to be in pictures."

"I saw Beverly on the cover of Vogue," the Hungarian-born director Ivan Nagy remarked, "and I said, 'Let's get her.' She's got great warmth, which is unusual for models. They're usually distant. Very seldom is there a successful crossover . . . somehow, it seldom works." Noticing, Beverly's crestfallen look, Nagy added tactfully, "Maybe this time it will." ■

A Flavor of Peasantry With a Feminine Flair

Bernadine Morris

The peasants are from Guatemala or Peru, which gives them something other than European ancestry.

They're given more to cotton than silk taffeta, but they still wear skirts that are full enough to flounce and blouses that fall off the shoulder and are gathered like smocks. Occasionally they wrap their waistlines snugly.

It's the new direction of clothes, according to Donna Karan, who, with her associate, Louis Dell'Olio, put the New World peasants for resort and spring on stage at the Anne Klein showroom yesterday. The generous proportions provide a new sense of luxury, she explained, and the soft construction makes the clothes comfortable.

What gives the clothes more than average significance is that they represent a turning point for the Anne Klein company, which helped inaugurate the present vogue for sportswear in the late 1960's. The company's emphasis then, and until recently, was on tailored separates, as typified by mannish blazer, straight leg pants and a turtleneck sweater.

Typical today would be an off-the-shoulder printed blouse over a big skirt in another print. The skirt is designed with an apron or overskirt that makes the underlayer suggest a petticoat.

The pants are no longer the sleek mannish-tailored affairs that once pre-dominated. They're now gathered at the waistline with drawstrings and they have soft folds about the hips. They're more female than mannish.

Besides these, there are culottes and Bermudas, both cut with more fullness than expected.

Separates, which are practically synonymous with sportswear, haven't been outmoded. They've simply changed their gender, and the effect is exhilarating.

relax

MINISKIRTS—
Surprise, Surprise

DECEMBER 1, 1976

Bernadine Morris

Kenzo's miniskirts are turning up in New York, but even the women who wear them don't think they're going to take over the fashion scene.

"Who needs the aggravation?" asks Dawn Willis, who works in the accounting department of Penthouse Magazine, speaking of the attention that miniskirts attract from the men in the street. "There's a thin line today," she went on in a serious tone, "between wearing minis and being a hooker."

Miss Willis's mini is a black turtleneck that she wears with ribbed black stockings "because black is my color." Usually, she wears the minidress over a long black skirt, "Sonia Rykiel style."

"People always get violent about the way I dress—they take it as a personal threat," said Miss Willis who is 26. She modeled a bit when she was 16, went to art school and left it a few years later to go to Europe.

"I figured, what could I paint if I never went anywhere?" she said.

She doesn't think minis will take over because "American women are too into pants." She wears pants once a week, when she goes to art school—in jeans. ∎

The Princess Who Is Everywhere

Joyce Maynard

Belgian-born American fashion designer Diane von Furstenberg in 1970.

Diane von Furstenberg—princess, author, dress company president, cover girl and mother of two—meditated for a moment. The secret to life, she said, is organization.

And she should know. In the week just past, Diane von Furstenberg had put in an appearance on the "Today" show to promote "Diane von Furstenberg's Book of Beauty," met with chemists to discuss the new von Furstenberg cosmetic line, which joins the von Furstenberg eyeglass frames and the von Furstenberg perfume and the von Furstenberg lingerie and the von Furstenberg wrap dress. She had flown to Boston for a morning talk show and returned in time to tuck her children into bed, studied fabric designs and checked inventories for her new dress lines. None of which, of course, had kept her from her 29 minutes of exercising every morning.

She said she has not always been organized. When she was Diane Halfin, an upper-middle-class girl growing up in Belgium, her mother used to despair, "How will you ever get a husband, you're so lazy?"

Then, when she was 18, and living in Geneva, she met Egon von Furstenberg. At 22, and three months pregnant, she married von Furstenberg and headed for America.

"The minute I knew I was about to become Egon's wife, I decided to have a career," Miss von Furstenberg said. "I had to be someone of my own, and not just a plain little girl who got married beyond her deserts."

The marriage ended shortly after the birth of Diane's daughter—and perfume namesake—Tatiana. Meanwhile, the career that started seven years ago "as a little joke," with a $30,000 investment, has turned into a $100-million business that is still growing.

Just turned 30 and wearing no makeup (an act of "bravery" the old Diane could not have mustered, she said) she is a striking—if not precisely pretty—woman with "good bones" and the kind of hollowed cheeks some models have their rear molars extracted to attain. She wore her hair a few inches beyond her shoulder and her nails were short and unpolished. The handshake was businesslike and firm.

"Just because a woman's smart doesn't mean she has to look like a truck driver," she said, speaking with what seemed like a blend of accents, identifiable only as exotic. "You use what you have, and that includes your looks. You have to work at beauty."

"You have to accept yourself as you are," she added (self-improvement books like her own notwithstanding). "And after a while, the nose starts to fit the face."

But more than insecurity about looks, Miss von Furstenberg contended that many women were plagued by the insecurity that comes from being financially dependent on their husbands.

"The more you are in control of your life, the better," she said. "All your days, until you die, you have only one constant companion—yourself. Depend only on yourself and you won't be disappointed."

"I'm not the normal, average type of mother in an apron," Diane von Furstenberg admitted. "But I have a very close relationship with my children. There's nothing I don't talk about in front of them—they're very mature. I just sat them down once and said, 'Listen, I have to work, and you'll have to understand,' and they did."

Sometimes Tatiana and Alexandre travel with her ("as my little helpers," Miss von Furstenberg said), but as for their possible careers the children's interests, so far, appear not to lie in the dress designing business.

"Alexandre wants to be a farmer," said his mother, laughing gaily. "And Tatiana says she wants to be a mother just like the one on the Brady Bunch on television. She says she wants 10 babies and a big house for baking cookies." ∎

ALL ABOUT:
Sneakers

Sneaker selection a few years ago rarely troubled anyone. Girls got white sneakers, boys got black, and both usually bought the cheapest in the store. These days, the sneaker seeker is confronted with nearly 40 styles in many stores and you can spend up to $40 on one pair. It's enough to make you want to cancel your tennis lessons.

But while the range of styles may be a little overwhelming, it is beneficial because today sneakers are being designed for specific uses.

"We even have sneakers for parachute jumping," said Matt Zale of The Athlete's Foot, a store in Greenwich Village that recently opened just to sell sneakers. Mr. Zale also displayed sneakers designed for discus throwers, javelin tossers, fencers and bicyclists.

"Consider the sport you will be playing," counsels John Weiss, owner of Runner's World, a Manhattan sporting goods store. "And then get the best shoe available."

Good sneakers will cost a minimum of $20, according Weiss. He advises beginners to get the more expensive sneakers, because their superior construction provides better support.

Leather or suede provide the most support because they conform to the foot, while canvas and nylon stubbornly retain their original shapes. Nylon is not without its advantages, though. It is said to "breathe" better, dry faster and resist the decaying effects of perspiration longer.

But whether it's leather or canvas, the primary factor to consider is what you will be doing when you wear the sneakers.

And if you find that your sneakers are wearing down but you're too attached to them to throw them out, a number of shoe stores will resole them for you. Some sneaker buffs recommend the sole restorations at Harvey's Sporting Goods Store in Sheepshead Bay for $10 to $12. A partial replacement of toes and heels costs about $4. The replacement takes about three days and is supposed to last as long as the original parts.

Farrah Fawcett's famous hair style.

A New Crimp in Old Styles: It's All in the Curls and Flips

Angela Taylor

Will two highly visible stage stars do for their hairdos what Dorothy Hamill, the skater, did for the "wedge" cut last year? Miss Hamill's crisp, short hair at the Olympics sent what seemed like half the women in this country scurrying to hairdressers to be done just like her.

Now two new images are threatening to cause waves in beauty shops. On the one hand, there's the new Barbra Streisand in "A Star is Born," all frizzly curly and peeking through bangs like a French poodle.

Then there's television's new sex symbol, Farrah Fawcett-Majors of "Charlie's Angels," she of the flipped-back, streaked-blonde mane. So far the Farrah flip hasn't made much of a splash on New York streets, but she seems to have an army of imitators in the Middle West and South. The Crimpers salon in Chicago had to retrain it staff because of the demand, and Kenneth, who has a branch salon in Atlanta, says it's popular there.

New York hairdressers are resisting the Farrah fad. Among trend-setting hair stylists here, the vote this week was a qualified "yes" for Barbra, a resounding "no" to Farrah. (Among six men queried, only one, Xavier, voted the other way.)

All of the stylists point out that both hairdos are dated. But while the current trend to curly hair is an evolution of the hippie "naturals" of the 1960's, the Fawcett mane is a copy of the Cinandre flip, which swept the country about seven years ago.

(cont'd. on next page)

175

LIFE & STYLE

(cont'd. from previous page)

Andre Martheleur, who owns Cinandre, might be said to be prejudiced. He has done Miss Streisand's hair, but not Miss Fawcett's. Kenneth Battele, who usually likes longish, loose hair, says that curly hair makes sense in some instances but that copying Miss Fawcett "may be leading a lot of women down the garden path."

Andre says that for Barbra Streisand, the frizz has given her a whole new outlook. Her hair is incredibly fine and straight, he explained. "Now that she has a permanent, she can do it herself."

Which is ironic, since Miss Streisand has Jon Peters, a former hairdresser, sharing her house. He apparently is tired of doing her hair: He called in a California hairdresser for the original Streisand hairdo, then asked Andre to take over when she was in New York.

the frizz has given her a whole new outlook

As for Miss Fawcett, both Kenneth and Andre are pleased that she may speed a trend to longer hair. They feel it's on the way.

"That hair may look carefree," said Kenneth, "but it's very hair-dressered. You know there was a hairdresser there five minutes before the picture was taken. You've got an extreme difference in lengths. And the growing out of that kind of hair would be awfully difficult." ■

JULY 12, 1977

THE HALL-MARKS OF THE ANNIE LOOK

Enid Nemy

Diane Keaton at the Academy Awards in 1976.

Take a hat—slouchy, too big for the head it's on, and slightly punchy looking. Better still, take a man's hat that pulls down deep and covers the forehead. The hat is a crucial ingredient, one of the keys to the Annie Hall look.

Annie Hall is, of course, the name of Woody Allen's newest film. Annie Hall is also Diane Keaton, who, in the film, has the kind of flung-together look that belies the infinite care and thought that went into creating it. Almost everything she wears is a curious mixture of raffish tomboy and femininity.

"The look was designed for a girl who didn't quite know who she was," said Ruth Morley, the costume designer for the film. "The girl is a little confused but not a hippy; she's unusual, she's trying to find herself."

The Annie Hall look is now popping up on the streets with amazing frequency—men's shirts, several sizes too big, odd vests, loose, wide-leg trousers or full, longish skirts. The mix of pieces is worn with an off-hand nonchalance; part of the nonchalance is a wrinkled effect that gives one the impression that the clothes have never seen a hanger.

Despite the influence of men's haberdashery, the look—perhaps because so much of it is oversized—often gives the wearer an appearance of fragility. It is tenderized men's wear, slightly waifish, frequently romantic. Old-fashioned shawls often cover the floppy shirts and little vests; bouquets of tiny flowers are sometimes tucked into necklines, and almost always hair is long, with stray tendrils or masses of waves. Occasionally, the hair is gathered and tucked under the hat.

The Annie Hall ingredients aren't new; they simply had never before been brought together in a clearly definable way. Now that they have, the betting is that jeans and T-shirts will be in for some pretty stiff competition this fall.

AUGUST 2, 1977

Navy Reviving the Bell-Bottoms

WASHINGTON, Aug. 1 (AP)—The Navy announced today that it was returning the traditional uniform of bell-bottomed trousers and white caps to its lower enlisted ranks.

The decision follows findings of an official poll earlier this year that the new uniform of coats, white shirts, black ties and peaked caps is widely unpopular among sailors.

The more formal uniform became compulsory two years ago after Adm. Elmo Zumwalt Jr. in 1971 ordered a transition to it with the announced aim of enhancing morale and presenting "the concept of one Navy."

But his decision apparently achieved the opposite effect, drawing complaints from sailors about the difficulty of keeping the new uniforms crisp and clean, and complaints from others, who simply preferred the traditional look.

The return to bells will be made gradually under the decision of Adm. James L. Holloway III, who is Admiral Zumwalt's successor as Chief of Naval Operations.

Sailors have said that they do not have space to hang the new uniforms, and that they are a bother to keep in presentable condition, particularly aboard smaller ships

---

The Uniquitous Hair Dryer—Everybody's Got One

Wendy Schuman

When Steve Hope and his wife split up, she took the blow dryer, which put the 34-year-old film editor in something of a quandary. "I went through two months of dripping into my shirt collar before I broke down and bought my own. I had to admit it was no longer a luxury, but a necessity, like my toothbrush or razor."

Blow dryers—the hand-held, hot-air guns that have revolutionized hair styling—are becoming essential grooming aids for both sexes and all ages. Jockey Steve Cauthen used one in the Belmont locker room after riding Affirmed to a Triple Crown victory. Twelve-year-old Doris Ramos, a sixth grade student at P.S. 64 on Manhattan's Lower East Side, has been using one since she was 8. Now she takes more than an hour each Saturday to feather and curl her long brown hair into a Farrah Fawcett style for church socials.

The evolution of the hair dryer from a luxury product for women to an essential grooming tool for all segments of the American population is underscored by that fact that some schools, including Greenwich High School in Greenwich, Conn., provide stationary wall hairdryers in gymnasium locker rooms so students can emerge dry and stylish after sports activities.

Back in the early 1960's, when the prevailing hairstyle for women was a rigid bouffant, hair had to be set in rollers and dried for hours under stationary hood-type dryers. "Women looked like dolls, with

heavy makeup and all that teased hair," recalled Pierre Ouaknine, owner of the fashionable Manhattan hair salon Pierre Michel. Gradually a more natural, unset look freed women from reliance on rollers. By 1968 the hand-held dryer, once found primarily in beauty salons, was gaining wide consumer use as well.

Despite the popularity of blow dryers, some people refuse to have one in the house. One housewife says her two hours a week at the hairdresser are "my one luxury—I can sit under the dryer, have my nails done, do the crossword puzzle or just daydream. And I can't hear a word anyone is saying." ■

that lack cleaning and pressing facilities.

And some chief petty officers have been bothered by the fact that the distinction they once enjoyed when wearing coats and peaked caps disappeared when all enlisted men began dressing the same way.

Before Admiral Zumwalt's order, bells were worn by grades E-1 through E-6. Admiral Holloway said that the coat and tie uniform would continue to be worn by grades E-5 and above. ■

PANTS:
NEW LIFE AND A NEW LOOK

Bernadine Morris

"Is it still all right to wear pants?"

After "What shall I do about hemlines?" that's the question designers hear most frequently when they meet the customers on their visits to stores, or even at dinner parties.

The answer, of course, is that even without designers' approval, it's perfectly all right to wear anything you feel is comfortable and appropriate.

But pants are a special case. After invading all kinds of sacrosanct precincts, from offices to elegant eateries, for a decade, they've taken a back seat in recent seasons to the resurgence of skirts, dresses and even coats and suits.

But it's not yet back to the garden for trousers.

"I feel very strongly that the whole thing about shorter skirts will give pants new authority," says Bill Blass. He was referring to the predilection of many designers, including himself, to raise hemlines just below the knee for spring—and the resistance of some women who have recently become accustomed to longer skirts.

Pants, he believes, are a logical alternative, just as they were in 1970 when the mini was superseded by the longer midi skirt.

"Having known the comfort of pants, women would be foolish to give them up," says Geoffrey Beene, who is especially enthusiastic about pants for evening.

To prove they mean what they say, designers have done what they can to vary the design of pants and thereby make them more intriguing. While the basic shape for day remains tapered and narrow, and the lengths have shortened from the floor-sweepers of a few seasons back, there is an explosion of new shapes for leisure hours.

The key to the new casual attitude is the turned-up cuff. Not the carefully pressed variety. The ends of the pants legs are now simply rolled up, so that the effect is similar to sleeves that are just pushed up. It breaks the pall of solemnity that hangs over many of the new spring fashion collections and suggests the carefree attitude that is fact disappearing: Everyone seems to be taking clothes much too seriously.

ROLLER-DISCO FASHIONS:
Stretch Fabrics on a Runway to the 80's

The Inferno, at 5 West 19th Street, was the sprawling discotheque chosen by the designer Betsey Johnson as the site to roll out her wares—her spring and summer clothing, in a show that was traditional right down to the bridal gown finale and up to the minute in choice of fabric and presentation: Lycra spandex and disco and rock-and-roll music and 56 roller skaters to do the modeling.

The clothing concept? "Interchangeable, nonseason, stretchy, striped, bright, bodywear shapes plus other shapes that go over and under them," said the designer.

She said: "It's really the 1980's look about clothing. I think it's the next type of clothing to happen."

Faye Dunaway in a late '70s look

Jogging Suits, Too, Are Off and Running in a Race for Style

Bernadine Morris

The brilliantly colored velour tops with the tiny images of polo players, attesting to the fact that they were designed by Ralph Lauren, are as pure in design as sweatshirts. But instead of battleship gray, they are in such colors as yellow, red, green or cyclamen pink, set off by white bands.

Once limited to gray sweatsuits, the lexicon of jogging fashions has expanded greatly since the sport began to capture the popular fancy. There are styles to wear when the weather is hot as well as when it's brisk, and there is a wide choice of colors and fabrics.

"When I started to run a while back, I wore a gray sweatsuit, but I got tired of it,"

Ralph Lauren explained. "It made me feel dreary. That's when I started to get into color."

Like many of the jogging fashions, the Lauren velour styles began with tennis warm-up suits.

"I don't call them tennis clothes any more," the designer said. "People wear them for squash, paddle ball or racquet ball—and a lot of the things are suitable for jogging or running. The clothes for these sports are all interchangeable."

Not only for active sports. People are also wearing them to cocktail parties, even if the glass they hoist is filled with nothing more lethal than Perrier water.

"Ever since tennis became a social event, women have been wearing their warm-up suits for marketing, driving the children to school and even when they go to someone's house for a drink after a game," said Janice Watts, of Loomtogs. "When they pay $100 for a velour warm-up suit, it becomes as valuable as a cocktail dress." ■

Arts & Entertainment

The 1930s—in particular 1939, perhaps the most dazzling year in Hollywood history—is understandably held by many film scholars to be the apex of cinematic excellence. But the 1970s could go toe to toe with any decade, and prevail.

"Best" lists are hardly a reliable guide in any field. Nonetheless, it is worth noting that in the American Film Institute's most recent roster of the 100 greatest movies of all time, no decade had more entries than the '70s, with 20. In contrast, the '30s had 12.

Such numbers aside, the breadth of '70s films was astounding. Having fully shaken the shackles of Hollywood's arthritic studio system and its censorship codes, directors flourished

Mark Hamill and Carrie Fisher as Luke Skywalker and Princess Leia in George Luca's Star Wars trilogy, 1977.

in ways that had long eluded them. The result was as exciting a lineup as ever seen, one that included, to name but a few works, Francis Ford Coppola's elegant "Godfather" epics (the first two parts, anyway), Sidney Lumet's gritty "Dog Day Afternoon," Woody Allen's bubbly yet insightful "Annie Hall," Roman Polanski's forbiddingly noir "Chinatown" and Hal Ashby's destined-for-cult-status "Harold and Maude." By decade's end, the first of what would become half a dozen episodes in the blockbuster "Star Wars" series left no doubt that the force was with American filmmakers.

It was truly a celluloid renaissance. Nor was it the only area of the arts enjoying a rebirth.

By the early '70s, a death knell seemed in order for the Broadway musical. Then along came a director-choreographer named Michael Bennett and a songwriter named Marvin Hamlisch. Mid-decade they produced "A Chorus Line," as fresh and vibrant a musical as the theater had seen in years. At the same time, the extraordinarily productive machine known as Stephen Sondheim was emanating brilliance almost yearly, from "Company" in 1971 to "Sweeney Todd" in 1979.

Dramatists were in full flower as well. It was a decade of Tom Stoppard and John Guare, David Mamet and Sam Shepard, Arthur Kopit and Peter Shaffer, not to mention the rise of two very different Wilsons: August and Lanford. Female playwrights came into their own as well, arguably none more so than Wendy Wasserstein and Beth Henley.

The punk rock band the Sex Pistols on tour in 1978. From left, Johnny Rotten, Sid Vicious, Steve Jones and Paul Cook.

Marvin Hamlisch at the Academy Awards in 1974.

"Ragtime" author E.L. Doctorow.

By comparison, the fields of literature and of art and architecture may not strike some people as equally game-changing. But that is only by comparison. No decade that produced some of the finest works of William Styron ("Sophie's Choice"), E. L. Doctorow ("Ragtime"), John Updike ("Rabbit Redux") and Thomas Pynchon ("Gravity's Rainbow"), or of cultural palaces like the Kennedy Center for the Performing Arts and the Sydney Opera House need hang its head.

Still, breakthroughs and change seemed more spectacular in other areas, like popular music. Take for better or for ill, pop music. This was the decade when, alas, the Beatles broke up and when Jimi Hendrix, Janis Joplin and Jim Morrison succumbed to drug-induced hazes. It was when Elvis Presley died, Diana Ross left the Supremes and John Lennon had to fight attempts to deport him from the United States because his visa had expired. (He would be murdered in December 1980.) But the music itself never died. It just went in new directions, often quite divergent. What did Billy Joel and his ballads, Sid Vicious and punk rock, Donna Summer and disco have in common? Other than coexisting, not a heck of a lot.

ARTS & ENTERTAINMENT

Carroll O'Connor (left), as Archie Bunker, and Mike Evans, as Lionel Jefferson, in an episode of "All in the Family."

Television was where change was inescapable. Gone were the domestic coziness and artistic timidity of shows like "Father Knows Best" and "My Three Sons." Now we had "All in the Family," whose central figure was an unreconstructed, albeit at heart likable, bigot. A spinoff of that program, "The Jeffersons," introduced America to a highly successful African-American family led by a man, George Jefferson, who was no less bigoted, if more high-spirited, than Archie Bunker.

HBO came into being in the '70s, a relatively small operation that seemed to offer viewers little more than a chance to watch recycled movies they may have missed. There was no hint then of the economic powerhouse and creative force that this cable network would become.

There was also no way to anticipate in 1975 the future for a late-night weekend comedy show that had just begun on NBC. It was topical and irreverent, with a bunch of performers few viewers had ever heard of. Nearly four decades later, "Saturday Night Live" is still going strong. It may, for all anyone knows, be immortal.

Chevy Chase at the Weekend Update desk on "Saturday Night Live."

OBITUARY

FEBRUARY 26, 1970

Mark Rothko a Suicide at 66

Grace Glueck

The Mark Rothko Room at The Phillips Collection, Washington, D.C.

Mark Rothko, a pioneer of abstract expressionist painting who was widely regarded as one of the greatest artists of his generation, was found dead yesterday, his wrists slashed, in his studio at 157 East 69th Street. He was 66 years old. The Chief Medical Examiner's office listed the death as a suicide.

Mr. Rothko had suffered a heart attack last year, and friends said that he had been despondent in recent months.

Like most American artists of his generation, Mr. Rothko's early career was marked by struggle and was untouched by recognition. His fortunes rose with those of the American brand of painting known as abstract expressionism, in whose development he had played a crucial role along with Jackson Pollock, Willem de Kooning, Robert Motherwell, Adolph Gottlieb and Clyfford Still.

Today, Mr. Rothko's monumental canvases, in which simple rectangles of glowing color seem to float on the canvas, are known and collected throughout the world. Mr. Rothko's significance as a painter was underscored by a retrospective exhibition of his works in 1961 at the Museum of Modern Art, which at the time only gave such shows to living painters of worldwide reputation.

Yesterday, William S. Rubin, chief curator of painting and sculpture at the museum, said: "The loss to modern art is incalculable. One of the pioneers of abstract expressionism, his work was crucial to the establishment of the whole tradition of recent color-field painting and continued to pose challenges right up to his death."

Mr. Rothko's quiet, contemplative canvases, often described as "painting about the sublime," are in strong contrast to the turbulent imagery of most of his contemporaries. The subdued content of Mr. Rothko's art was described as "empty" by conservative critics; those in favor admire their other-worldly calm.

Starting out as a realist, Mr. Rothko exhibited in a group show in 1929 at the Opportunity Gallery in New York. Later, with many other New York artists hit by the Depression, he worked on the Federal Arts Project in 1936-37.

By the 1940's, his work, which in the previous decade stressed urban themes, began to absorb the surrealist influences of Miró, de Chirico and Max Ernest, artists whom Mr. Rothko greatly admired. In his first important one-man show at Peggy Guggenheim's Art of This Century gallery, the surrealistic direction of his work was already apparent.

In 1951, Mr. Rothko showed for the first time at the Museum of Modern Art, in a now-famous exhibition called "Abstract Painting and Sculpture in America." Later he was represented in museum shows that traveled abroad, and he gave Europeans their first exposure to his work.

With Adolph Gottlieb, Mr. Rothko once stated his artistic credo in a letter that was published in The New York Times on June 13, 1943.

"We favor the simple expression of the complex thought. We are for the large shape because it has the impact of the unequivocal. We wish to reassert the picture plane. We are for flat forms because they destroy illusion and reveal truth." ∎

Top Art Auctions Boom, Though Economy Sags

Grace Glueck

"Haven't they heard of the recession?" asked a non-bidding viewer at Parke-Bernet last month, after a snappy auction in which 53 buyers paid $2.5 million for 66 impressionist and modern paintings.

Apparently not. First-class airplane seats go begging and co-op apartments don't sell. There's been a let-up in yacht buying, and sables have fallen off. But, despite a dip in the general art market, the best-quality works of art continue to topple records at the major auction houses.

Some of the prices have been set under sale conditions that have created controversy in the trade over whether the auction system is indeed a free market. But buyers are still willing to spend freely. This year at the three top houses, for instance, a silver inkstand fetched $187,000, a Chinese porcelain vase brought $226,680, a pear-shaped diamond was knocked down for $1,050,000 and a painting by Velasquez went for a world auction record of $5,544,000.

True, there's been a considerable slackening in sales of middle-quality works of art, running in price between $20,000 and $60,000—the area in which the auction houses make bread-and-butter commissions. But officials of the top houses insist that the recession has not deterred their big-league customers.

"In recent months," points out Peter Wilson, the urbane chairman of Sotheby's Inc., the London-based auction house that is the world's largest, "when stocks were down, the very finest works of art in all categories fetched record prices."

His contention is echoed by I. O. Chance, chairman of Christie's, the world's second largest auction house, also in London.

"Works of top quality are now in global demand," maintains Mr. Chance, in whose salesroom last November the $5.5-million Velasquez was sold, "and therefore, even if there may be a temporary recession in one country, there are enough people in the world competing for comparatively few works to insure continuing high prices."

This year the effect of the recession on middle-range works of art will undoubtedly put a dip in the upward curve. But business slump or no, the houses are expanding. In an effort to increase the popularity of their lively indoor sport, they are, for one, stepping into more specialized markets to reach new categories of collectors.

They are holding special sales of Russian art, Chinese art, Art Nouveau, Art Deco, Chinese snuff bottles, French paperweights and such offbeat items as wine, antique cars, old photographs, musical instruments, antique buttons, minerals and shells.

The reasons for the current strength of the auction market have much to do with widespread uneasiness about the value of money. In periods of inflation, experts have noted, people of wealth tend to put their money into commodities least affected by the economic weather. Over the long haul, the uniqueness of art objects has made them a durable investment, the more so as the number of competing collectors increases. ∎

DIANE ARBUS:
The Subject Was Freaks

Gene Thornton

Photographer Diane Arbus poses for a rare portrait in 1968.

One hears stories of Diane Arbus stalking her prey at a cocktail party or an art opening. A tiny, birdlike woman, freighted with all the baggage of a well-equipped freelance photographer, she tiptoes up to the intended victim and stops just inches away, camera to eye, ready to shoot. The victim, flattered but frightened, is transfixed, but does not forget to adopt a public face. Miss Arbus waits. The victim then adopts another public face. Still no movement from Miss Arbus. The victim adopts a third face. Finally the victim runs through his entire repertory of public faces, and when the last one is gone and he stands revealed, Miss Arbus shoots.

This is the story one hears, and in part I do believe it. "It was a terrifying experience," said one such victim with passionate conviction—a woman no more freakish than you or I—and indeed it must have been. But the pictures by Diane Arbus that people knew best—portraits, mostly, posed rather formally—were not taken at cocktail parties but in private, and they do not show more or less normal people but freaks. I do not believe they could have been taken by force.

The earliest pictures of hers that I have seen, a group that appeared in the magazine Infinity in 1962, include a tattooed man, a fully clothed transvestite and an otherwise ordinary woman who loves to put on false teeth and a wig and live a whole different life as a different person.

The late pictures, including the group shown at the Museum of Modern Art in 1967, have equally bizarre subjects, or subjects that come to seem bizarre in the context of the others: female impersonators, lesbians, burlesque queens, a Levittown living room, twins and triplets, children, nudists and old people. A giant and a dwarf were included in a portfolio published last May in Artforum, and there is, as yet unpublished, an extraordinary series of pictures taken at a home for mentally retarded women in Vineland, N.J.

But most of the later pictures, though bizarre in subject matter, are plain and unadorned in treatment. The subjects simply stand facing the camera against a neutral background, as frontal and unemphatic as in a passport photograph, and the occasional odalisque lies lightly draped on a bare bed.

The curious thing about Diane Arbus's pictures is the ease with which the freakish comes to seem normal and vice versa.

Among the pictures she left behind when she died last month at the age of 48 was one of a successful young Westchester couple. Here, if anywhere, was normality triumphant: the well-fleshed, shapely limbs sprawled on deck chairs in the sun, the generous sweep of expansive suburban lawn, the single child dabbling in a plastic pool. Yet of all the portraits Diane Arbus took, this is one of the few in which the sitters do not look you in the eye. ∎

A LOOK AT THE KENNEDY CENTER

Ada Louise Huxtable

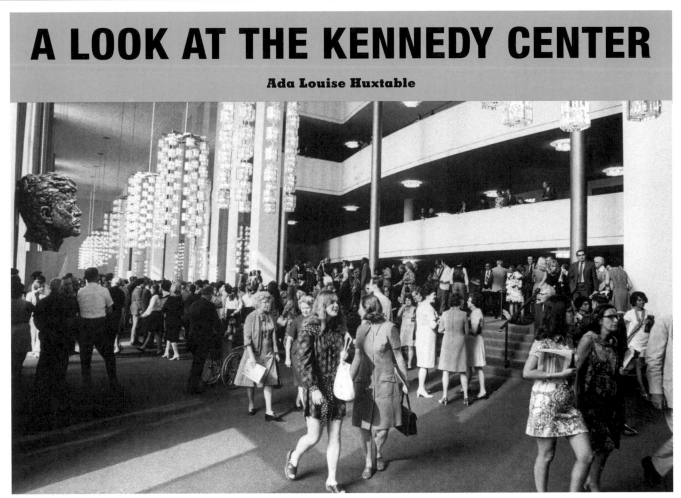

The grand foyer of the John F. Kennedy Center for the Performing Arts.

WASHINGTON, Sept. 6—This capital city specializes in ballooning monuments and endless corridors. It uses marble like cotton wool. It is the home of government of, for and by the people, and of taste for the people—the big, the bland and the banal. The John F. Kennedy Center for the Performing Arts, opening officially Wednesday, does not break the rule. The style of the Kennedy Center is Washington superscale, but just a little bit bigger. Albert Speer would have approved.

It has apotheosized the corridor in the 600-foot-long, 60-foot-high grand foyer (the length of three New York City blockfronts), one of the biggest rooms in the world, into which the Hall of Mirrors at Versailles could be cozily nested. It would be a supertunnel without its saving Belgian gift of mirrors.

The corridor is "dressed up," in the words of the architect, Edward Durell Stone, by 18 of the world's biggest crystal chandeliers, with planters and furniture still to come. There is enough red carpet for a total environment.

There are two other flag-hung, polished marble-walled, red-carpeted, 250-foot long and 60-foot high corridors called the Hall of States, and the Hall of Nations. They are disquietingly reminiscent of the overscaled vacuity of Soviet palaces of culture. They would be great for drag racing.

The two halls separate the three theaters that are the structure's raison d'être: the Opera House, the Concert Hall and the Eisenhower Theater. The grand foyer is the entrance to them all.

The building itself is a superbunker, 100 feet high, 630 feet long and 300 feet wide, on the Potomac. One more like this and the city will sink.

Because it is a national landmark, there is only one way to judge the Kennedy center—against the established standard of progressive and innovative excellence in architectural design that this country is known and admired for internationally.

Unfortunately, the Kennedy Center not only does not achieve this standard of innovative excellence; it also did not seek it. The architect opted for something ambiguously called "timelessness" and produced meaninglessness. It is to the Washington manner born. Too bad, since there is so much of it.

The center sets still another record—for architectural default. What it has in size, it lacks in distinction. Its character is aggrandized posh. It is an embarrassment to have it stand as a symbol of American artistic achievement before the nation and the world.

May all the performing arts flourish. Because the building is a national tragedy. It is a cross between a concrete candy box and a marble sarcophagus in which the art of architecture lies buried.

JANUARY 9, 1972

WILLEM DE KOONING:
EVEN HIS 'WRONG' IS BEAUTIFUL

Peter Schjeldahl

By 1950, Willem de Kooning was enshrined in notoriety, with Jackson Pollock, as one of the two (perhaps mad) geniuses of American avant-garde painting.

In the late fifties, de Kooning was further installed as the sort of combined chef d'école and philosopher king of the wilder "Action-Painting" wing of Abstract Expressionism—a development that accounted for a mild decline in his art-world reputation when, about a decade ago, "his" part of the movement got mangled in the spokes of a sudden revolution of taste that left much of it looking absurdly pompous and incontinent. He was not to blame for the excesses of his followers, but he was blamed. He has since realized, particularly in a series of "Figures in Landscapes," some of his finest work.

A vest-pocket show of seven new lithographs at the Museum of Modern Art would scarcely seem to justify a full-dress review. But such is the controversy and confusion that have always surrounded the career of this, the most refractory of modern masters, that in dealing with his work one seems obliged to be incessantly starting afresh, much as one would in the case of a sensational newcomer. And indeed, a profound kind of "youthfulness" is today as much (if not more) a quality of his art as it was 30 years ago.

The seven large lithographs at the Modern mark only de Kooning's third experiment with lithography (the first two did not come to much), and the variousness of their motifs, no less than the fact that they are all strictly black on white, bespeaks a certain tentativeness. As it is, he drew them on transfer paper or on thin aluminum plates, perhaps feeling that an encounter with the monumental lithographic stone would constrict the full spontaneity he values, it sometimes seems, above all else.

The pictorial element of which de Kooning has been the foremost modern proponent

Willem de Kooning painting a canvas in his studio in Easthampton, Long Island, in the late 1960s.

has been the gesture—the movement of his wrist and arm producing a mark at once "free" and somehow constrained, at once expressive and belonging to the composition.

What lithography seems to have fortuitously granted to de Kooning, and what may account for these works' power and free-wheeling inventiveness, is a fresh experience of his gesture; in effect, a means to re-apply his whole pictorial vocabulary. That the lithograph "freezes" a brushstroke within its perimeters and renders it perfectly flat might seem likely to be intolerable to an artist used to moving thick paint around, but in this case the loss of materiality is more than compensated for, in the peculiar dialectic of de Kooning's inspiration, by the fact that in lithography strokes do not build up on a surface or blend with each other; they stay put, firmly part of the surface however random they may appear.

That de Kooning should produce masterpieces in a medium of which he has no technical mastery is typical of this odd, divided genius, who remains perhaps the most isolated figure in the mainstream of American art. He continues to be disliked by many avant-gardists, who dismiss him for his "traditional" easel-painting esthetics, and by many conservative critics, who wince at his flamboyant emotionality and procedures. And he is still worshipped as a hero by people given to finding, in the quirks of his personality, the system of an ethical philosophy. Truthfully, however, few younger painters are any longer being misled by his example into thinking that, because they have a sense of what he's doing, they can do it, too. There can be only one de Kooning, and by now everybody knows it. ∎

Arrest of a Fifth Avenue Art Dealer

Eric Pace

Posing as polished art lovers, detectives arrested a Manhattan art dealer yesterday and seized seven paintings that they said he had falsely labeled as valuable works of the 18th and 19th centuries.

The raid was conducted by the Police Department's newly formed art identification unit, whose members have been trained at the Sotheby, Parke-Bernet Galleries and the Metropolitan Museum of Art.

"This was a middle-class type of fraud, against people who want to buy paintings but have no expertise," said Detective James Robert, who ran the operation.

The authorities identified the dealer as Andrew Fodor, 64 years old, the proprietor of the Midtown Gallery at 172 Fifth Avenue. He was booked on charges of grand larceny, attempted grand larceny and criminal simulation.

Three years ago Mr. Fodor, who says he has a doctorate from a Hungarian university, sold a 2-by-3-foot oil painting to Mrs. Barbara Ellers Winebright, a sometime actress who lives in Greenwich Village.

Mrs. Winebright paid $580 for the canvas, which shows a man and woman in 18th-century attire playing cards while a second woman serves tea. Mr. Fodor was cited as saying the painting was a unique 19th-century work brought from a European estate.

Mrs. Winebright was upset when she revisited the gallery last March and saw an identical, hand-painted oil painting hanging where her canvas had hung.

Detective Robert and his commander, Lieut. Erasmo Germano, visited the gallery, pretending to be patrons of the arts. They were followed by other incognito detectives and an incognito art expert sent by the Art Dealers Association of America, which has given the squad enthusiastic aid.

The expert examined the paintings and found that almost all of them had been painted within the last 10 or 20 years. They were of "mass-produced quality," in the words of one detective. Mrs. Winebright's work was valued at $100 or less.

Yesterday morning another incognito art squad member, Sgt. Thomas Connolly, put down a deposit on the second painting of the card players, which was signed E. Gibinn—as was the painting that Mrs. Winebright had bought.

Then in strolled Detective Robert, wearing a gray flannel suit of Edwardian cut, instead of his customary sports shirt and cowboy boots.

Three other detectives also came in and Mr. Fodor was served with a search warrant before the seven canvases, all about 2 by 3 feet, were seized, along with books and records.

The authorities said they thought Mr. Fodor had swindled dozens of other would-be art collectors who had not come forward, because of either shame or ignorance. ∎

PICASSO IS DEAD IN FRANCE AT 91

Pablo Picasso in 1971.

MOUGINS, France, April 8—Pablo Picasso, the titan of 20th-century art, died this morning at his hilltop villa of Notre Dame de Vie here. He was 91 years old.

The death of the Spanish-born artist was attributed to pulmonary edema, fluid in the lungs, by Dr. Jean-Claude Rance, a local physician who was summoned to the 35-room mansion by the family. Dr. Rance said that Picasso had been ill for several weeks.

With him when he died was his second wife, the 47-year-old Jacqueline Roque, whom he married in 1961. In the last few years, Picasso rarely left his 17-acre estate, which was surrounded by barbed wire. He had been in exile from his native land since 1939, when Generalissimo Francisco Franco defeated the Republican Government of Spain in the three-year Civil War.

Three years ago, in 1970, 16 of Picasso's paintings and 4 drawings were shown in the Palais des Papes. They constituted Picasso's production from January, 1969, through January, 1970. The pictures were mostly of vibrant men and women, often in close embrace. There were also dozens of goateed, lusty figures, which the artist's friends called "the musketeers."

In 1971, on the occasion of Picasso's 90th birthday, the Museum of Modern Art in New York, which has the world's largest public collection of his works, put on a special exhibition. At the same time, the French Government displayed some Picassos in the grand gallery of the Louvre, the first time the museum had ever exhibited work by a living artist.

As for Picasso, he ignored his birthday, shutting himself up in his villa, even refusing to receive a delegation from the French Communist party, of which he was a member. The group included his old friend, Louis Aragon, the poet.

(cont'd. on next page)

187

ARTS & ENTERTAINMENT

(cont'd. from previous page)

Large crowds thronged about the Picassos at the Museum of Modern Art yesterday afternoon.

Tourists, museumgoers and television camera crews mingled before "Guernica," "Harlequin," "The Card Player" and "The Studio," major works from the middle years of 1913 to 1937. The museum put a large vase of flowers in the main lobby and nearby a strip of cloth with "Picasso" lettered on it in gold.

"Guernica" drew many to the third floor. "I was a small girl when he did this painting," said Margaret Schneider of Brooklyn. Rose Friedman of Huntington, L.I., called it "haunting."

Mya Kroksteron of Stockholm called the reaction at the museum touching.

Following are some of the tributes to Picasso expressed yesterday:

HENRY MOORE, the sculptor: "There's no doubt Picasso was a unique and great person. He was a phenomenon, really."

HENRY GELDZAHLER, curator of 20th-century art at Metropolitan Museum of Art: "His work will live on and cast its spell on younger artists. The implications of what he's done haven't been worked out. His greatness was in throwing out ideas, in never repeating himself."

THOMAS MESSER, director of Guggenheim Museum: "Not only is the art of the first half of this century unthinkable without Picasso, but I suspect the world itself would have been different and quite unimaginable without him." ∎

MAY 7, 1973

Miami's Controversial Bass Museum Closed

George Volsky

MIAMI BEACH, May 6—The Miami Beach City Council, by closing the John Bass Art Museum last week, has moved to "settle once and for all" the most unhappy cultural experience this city has had in its 58-year history.

"The art world has been laughing at us for years," said Councilman Herbert Magnes,

commenting on the art collection at the museum, which opened here 10 years ago and which has been involved in controversy since.

A legal battle still might ensue as the result of the Council's decision because of the 1963 city contract with Mr. Bass, a New York financier. But many local citizens, who have been unhappy over what is called here the Bass Museum affair, applauded the action.

At issue is the authenticity of many West European paintings that are part of the collection.

Donating it to the city in 1963, Mr. Bass represented the collection as having, among others, more than 50 "original works" by such painters as Botticelli, El

Greco, Franz Hals, Rembrandt, Rubens and Van Dyck.

Mr. Bass presented the city with an appraisal by Appraisals, Inc., of New York, which valued the collection at $7.5 million.

In its September, 1969, report, the Art Dealers Association wrote: "We believe that [the Bass collection] comprises the most flagrant and pervasive mislabeling by any museum known to this association." The report added that it was "the duty" of Miami Beach to rectify the situation.

The city has begun looking for a professional curator for the museum to make a re-evaluation of about 500 art items on display, to remove those that are obvious fakes and to identify the mislabeled ones before reopening the museum. ∎

OCTOBER 2, 1973

SYDNEY HAILS NEW OPERA HOUSE

Robert Trumbull

SYDNEY, Australia, Oct. 1—Judging by the enthusiastic response of the first paying customers, as well as local and foreign music critics, the expensive, trouble-plagued Sydney Opera House is a smash hit.

The controversial $150-million edifice, constructed to look like a huge ship under

The Sydney Opera House set sail at last.

OCTOBER 20, 1973

DAVID HOCKNEY GOT START IN BRITISH POP

James R. Mellow

David Hockney in the late 1970s.

Although he rose to prominence as one of the brighter stars of British pop art, in the nineteen sixties, David Hockney has emerged as an artist in a class by himself. In his paintings and prints of the last decade, he has begun to seem more a lively and sometimes caustic observer of the pop scene—a kind of latter-day Hogarth of the pop life-style—rather than a rank-and-file pop artist.

The retrospective showing of Mr. Hockney's prints now on view at M. Knoedler & Co., affords only a limited view of the artist's always engaging the subject-matter—one turns to his paintings and drawings for a more comprehensive look at that—but it does give a very good accounting of his qualities as a draftsman and a graphic artist.

In his graphics, he is not an experimenter for experiment's sake; his technical effects usually serve some visual purpose. In the series of unique prints, "Henry and Christopher," each made on the rejected sheets of a Frank Stella lithograph, for ex-

ample, he uses the Stella work as a painting on the wall of the apartment pictured. It is a nice bit of underplaying.

As a draftsman, despite the childlike scrawling of his illustrations for "Rumpelstiltskin," for example, he is remarkably fastidious and even elegant. His recent color lithograph, "Still Life With Book"—a bouquet of blue-flag irises in a clear-glass vase—is, I think, one of his most spare and beautiful prints to date.

Mr. Hockney has a wonderful facility for underplaying his technique and overstating his imagery—the banal visual clichés he uses in his series of prints on weather effects are marvelously sly and at the same time quite handsome. It gives his work both tension and humor. ∎

sail on the broad Sydney Harbor, opened its glass doors to the public last week for the first time, after nearly 19 years of planning and more than 14 years in the actual building.

It was the structure, more than the first production—the Australian Opera in Sergei Prokofiev's "War and Peace"—that was under review. The verdicts were overwhelmingly favorable, although limitations were noted.

Crowds of Sydneyites who were not attending the inaugural performance strolled around the many-sided edifice. It was a balmy spring evening in Sydney, where the seasons are the reverse of those north of the equator.

"The Opera House is more than an architectural triumph," Prime Minister Gough Whitlam, who occupied center seats with his wife, Margaret, said in a for-

mal statement. "[The opening] marks the beginning of a new era in the cultural life of our country."

"It was hard not to be captivated by this 'war and peace,'" said David Gyger, music critic of the national newspaper, The Australian. "The production often makes brilliant use of the awkward stage area, very narrow but quite deep."

"How to fit such an epic opera of Hollywood proportions on a small stage…and how to fit an orchestra of respectable size into a postage-stamp pit…all this and much more was overcome," said David Ahern in The Sydney Daily Telegraph. There was only praise for the acoustics. ∎

APRIL 28, 1974

Smithson Dreamed of Floating Islands

John Russell

The major artist is the one who carries within himself, and eventually makes visible, the whole history of the human race. As an ambition it's colossal; but someone who got within striking distance of it was Robert Smithson, who was killed in a plane crash in July of last year while prospecting above the site of his "Amarillo Ramp" in what is called the Texas Panhandle.

The current show of Smithson's drawings at the New York Cultural Center is the more welcome in that it is not easy to see a major Smithson at firsthand. Few people get to see the "Spiral Jetty," which runs out into the Great Salt Lake in Utah. The "Amarillo Ramp" stands on a private ranch to which the public is not admitted. Smithson worked in both cases with a disinherited landscape: one that was forlorn, faintly sinister and had long lost all claims to conventional affection.

In his choice of these places, Smithson was inspired not by morbid sensationalism but by a whole complex of motives, some of them rooted in the history of man-made (or man-altered) environments, some of them derived from predilections formed in his own childhood. He was fascinated, for instance, by geological changes and by the sheer magnitude which those changes assumed in North America. He saw it as the role of the artist to make these changes a part of our inmost experience.

Smithson's point of view was based in part on a generous republican instinct. It was also based on close knowledge of what had been thought and said and done in Europe from the days of Edmund Burke onwards to define the potential, and the philosophical implications, of man-made landscape. He rejected, without compro-

(cont'd. on next page)

189

ARTS & ENTERTAINMENT

> Smithson worked . . . with a disinherited landscape: one that was forlorn, faintly sinister and had long lost all claims to conventional affection.

(cont'd. from previous page)

mise, the impulse to sort and tidy and hierarchize which powered so many European experiments; but a European may perhaps be allowed to say that whereas in America local feeling rejected many of his projects out of hand, it was a Dutch community that voted in 1971 to allocate funds for the permanent maintenance of two large-scale works by Smithson.

It is the great merit of the Cultural Center show that it reveals the ferocious vivacity of Smithson's imagination at maximum strength, and with no regard for practicalities. Smithson the master of words is there, in a drawing of 1966 called "A Heap of Language" and made up entirely of written near-synonyms for language arranged in tumulus-form. Smithson the visionary is there, in the project for a map of Atlantis to be carried out with several tons of clear broken glass, and for a floating island, to be towed round Manhattan by a tug and ornamented with trees commonly found in the New York area. Smithson the filmmaker is there also, with drawings that specify requirements easier, perhaps, to draw than to bring about: "dead tarantulas buried in apple sauce," for instance. Visitors who concern themselves with the unity of artistic effort at any given time may also note that the abstract expressionist use of dripping and pouring is paralleled in completed Smithsons like the "Asphalt Rundown" and the "Partially Buried Woodshed." This is an exhibition of the rarest and most intense interest and I could go on about it forever if I were not halted by one of Smithson's rougher remarks. "Judgments and opinions in the area of art," he said, "are doubtful murmurs in mental mud." ∎

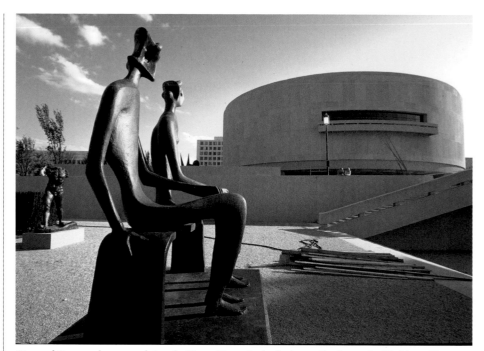

King and Queen, a bronze sculpture by Henry Moore in the Sculpture Garden at the Hirshhorn Museum in Washington, D.C., 1974.

OCTOBER 2, 1974

HIRSHHORN MUSEUM UNVEILED

Grace Glueck

WASHINGTON, Oct. 1—With the pomp befitting a high occasion, the capital's newest cultural treasure, the Joseph H. Hirshhorn Museum and Sculpture Garden, was formally unveiled tonight.

About 2,000 invited guests, including the cream of Washington officialdom, were on hand for the opening, which took place eight years after Congress authorized construction of the controversial building, shaped like a ring molded cake. Its rich holding of 6,000 paintings and sculptures, given by Joseph H. Hirshhorn, the self-made financier and art patron, approaches in scope the unparalleled collection of New York's Museum of Modern Art, and gives Washington the status of a major modern art center,

Among the 300 guests assembled at a private dinner before the opening was Mrs. Lyndon B. Johnson, whose husband, the late President, was instrumental in getting the much-courted collection for Washington. "I very much hoped that it would come here," said Mrs. Johnson, dressed in a black sequined gown. "The fact of its being in the nation's capital is very special to me."

Asked about the controversial exterior, she tactfully replied, "Well, it's by the same architect who has done the LBJ Library in Austin, which we're all very proud of."

Senator Hubert H. Humphrey, Democrat of Minnesota, laughed about the furor over the museum's design. "In Washington, they'd have a controversy over the sky," he said. "There's never been a historical building here that hasn't aroused disagreement. The Hirshhorn is different, as it ought to be. We don't have to put everything in rectangular boxes."

The occasion was considerably enlivened by the presence of the 73-year-old art acquisitor himself, who on a pre-opening inspection tour of the museum's gallery floors expressed delight and admiration with what he—and the United States Government—had wrought.

"It's got space, it's got life, it's got character," said Mr. Hirshhorn of the four-story building, as he walked the circular galleries, pausing to admire works long kept in storage. "I was never able to say it before, but I can say it now with pride—we have a great collection." ∎

JUNE 8, 1975

CHICAGO:
A City of Architectural Excellence

Ada Louise Huxtable

To say that style is important for a city, that it may figure as much in its destiny as the human factor, is a statement that flies in the face of today's more sociological concerns. But this is the city's essence that endures as conditions change. And so I am writing unapologetically about style—the Chicago style—with full awareness that the proper Chicago story must deal also with the conditions of its unredeemed slums, the tenuous health of a rebuilt but urbanistically unreconstructed central business district, the dislocations and pathologies of its functions, and the failure of municipal government to come to grips with the past or the future. That the middle holds in Chicago is no one's fault; that the city has style and life is almost an accident.

What it amounts to, in the narrowest sense, is that Chicago is a city of architectural excellence, which New York is not; it is probably the best city in the country for building quality. That statement, of course, needs to be hedged with all kinds of qualifications. But the good buildings, past and present, still overrode the bad, and they have a unifying power. Chicago does not, like New York, depend on sheer, overwhelming mass and the life force that represents for effect. A visit to Chicago, prompted in part by a desire to see the latest entry in the world's-tallest-building derby, the Sears Tower, turns out to be a richly rewarding experience in the Chicago style—or as the scholars call it, the Chicago School of architecture.

The Sears Tower is there, all right, presiding over the city with an almost nonchalant understatement, if that can be said of a 110-story skyscraper containing five million square feet of space. And Big John, the tapered and cross-braced John Hancock Building, is there too, now cuckholded with a pair of television spires. But Sears indulges in a curious self-effacement that is not unattractive. Beyond its exceptional height and unusual shape—it is made up of a cluster of square "tubes" rising to different heights—it makes no aggressive call for attention. Personally, I think this is fine, but it seems to be a disappointment to those who look for a more monumental "statement."

The structural formula, an ingenious and precedent-setting one by Fazlur Khan of Skidmore, Owings and Merrill, is notable for its economy and strength. Architect Bruce Graham has sheathed the structure in the simplest, cleanest, flattest glass and metal skin.

Mr. Graham has an architectural philosophy which holds that there is no point in overreaching (except in height), overcomplicating, striving for dubious originality, or going gratuitously beyond what amounts to an unbeatable basic solution. And if that makes for the paradox of an unpretentious tall building, so be it. God is still in the details, and SOM has a direct line to heaven.

The building is not as successful at ground level, with a conventional plaza and a dead rear end. Whether the architectural and engineering exhilaration of stunning structural advance and dropdcad size is offset by the kind of economic and spatial efficiency that modern industrialization and urbanism increasingly require, is an endless subject for inquiry and debate.

But there is no debate about the technological achievement. Or the fact that it is in the Chicago building tradition that combines technology and money, art and business for an expression that has created almost a century of architectural history. The skyscraper has a fascination beyond environmental price, and most of its development was written on Chicago's streets. ■

The Sears building (center) dominating the Chicago skyline with the John Hancock Building on the left and the Aon Center on the right, 1974.

shape

WARHOL MEETS WYETH

Hilton Kramer

It may or may not be true, as George Orwell believed, that every man gets the face he deserves at the age of 50, but it is undoubtedly true that certain faces sooner or later—exactly when depends on the vagaries of publicity—get the portraits they deserve.

This particular form of pictorial justice has now been meted out to both James Wyeth and Andy Warhol who, in a rare display of mutual self-sacrifice, have submitted to the ordeal of having their portraits painted by each other.

The results—currently on view at the Coe Kerr Gallery, constitute a notable event, if not exactly in the history of art, then surely in the history of artistic celebrity. Here are two artists who, for the last decade, have seemed to occupy opposite poles in the world where art is preposterously overpraised and sold at ridiculously high prices and where, as a consequence, it acquires a fame and distinction out of all proportion to its actual esthetic merit. Not

surprisingly, they turn out to have quite a lot in common.

Mr. Wyeth, scion of a family of famous artists, represents everything that is retrograde about the old, conservative realism, for his art is little more than a facile rehearsal of academic technique at the service of a moribund "tradition." Andy Warhol, the Pop artist who became the darling of the gossip columnists and the beau monde, represents what, in the discothéque atmosphere of the 60's, it pleased a great many people to mistake for something avant-garde. Each seemed to embody an esthetic principle that negated what the other stood for.

Yet, seeing their work side by side on this occasion, it is clear that both are really skilled illustrators plying a popular trade in the production of easy, ephemeral images. They differ only in the means they employ in reaching a similar end. Whereas Mr. Wyeth offers us a slick parody of the old academic mannerisms, Mr. Warhol gives us a slick variation on modernist reduc-

tionism. In the end, however, it comes to the same thing—a vulgar, vacuous, theatrical art that ministers to a cheap and ready taste.

As an exercise in the exploitation of such taste, this show—consisting of drawings as well as the finished portraits—does have an undeniable, indeed almost an archetypal, interest. For its underlying, unacknowledged scenario is a curious, all-male version of Beauty and the Beast.

The role of Beauty is, of course, reserved for the face of Mr. Wyeth, whose handsome features are rendered by Mr. Warhol in his familiar movie-poster manner.

Mr. Warhol, on the other hand, with his acid yellow hair and red-blotched face and vacant stare, makes the perfect figure of a Beast in this pictorial fable. Mr. Wyeth has been unsparing in depicting this unlovely countenance—so unrelievedly grotesque that one wonders if Mr. Warhol, with his unfailing instinct for theatrical effects, had not got himself "made up" for the part. ■

ALEXANDER CALDER, LEADING U.S. ARTIST, DIES

John Russell

Alexander Calder, whose stabile structures enlivened his Connecticut home.

Alexander Calder died in New York City yesterday of a heart attack at the home of his daughter, Mrs. Robert Howar. He was 78 years old.

More than any other American artist, Calder penetrated the awareness of the public at large. He was known initially for the mobile sculptures that hung in public buildings all over this country and in cities all over the world. Since the late 1950's, he had also become known for the "stabiles"—monumental and motionless structures in sheet metal or steel plate—which can be seen outdoors at Lincoln Center and the World Trade Center in New York, on the

Empire State Plaza in Albany, in the Federal Center Plaza in Chicago, in a plaza in Great Plains, Mich., and in open spaces throughout Europe, Japan, Australia and South America.

Calder was a complete artist and a complete citizen. In his life, as in his art, he never prevaricated. It somehow got through to everyone, irrespective of age, nationality, color or creed, that Alexander Calder was all of a piece, and that for all the irresistible sense of fun that bubbled up in his work, he was a man who could be depended upon to know what was right and to act upon it. ■

MARCH 2, 1977

TRANSAMERICA BUILDING:
What Was All the Fuss About?

Paul Goldberger

SAN FRANCISCO—When plans were announced in 1969 for the design of the Transamerica Building, the pyramid that stabs San Francisco's skyline with a point 853 feet in the air, there was an enormous public outcry. "It is a large and pretentious folly," said Allen Temko, the architectural historian. It is "insensitive, inappropriate and incongruous," wrote Progressive Architecture magazine. It would be "ideal for Las Vegas," complained an angry letter writer to the Transamerican Corporation, which planned the pyramid as its headquarters.

But the building was built—although its 853-foot height is somewhat shorter than what was originally planned—and now that it has been occupied for four years it is a bit difficult to understand what all the fuss was about.

Transamerica may be flamboyant and a little silly, but it is also the most sensible new skyscraper in this city. Its shape may be bizarre, but it does less damage to San Francisco's skyline than almost any other large building that has been erected here in the last few years.

Transamerica's architect was William L. Pereira and Associates of Los Angeles, a commercial firm with a certain leaning to science fiction futurism. That leaning has not always yielded the most sophisticated products, and even at Transamerica, there is a lot to be criticized in the way of details—the huge pyramid meets the ground in a confusing forest of columns, and the windows are precast concrete units that come together to create a façade of crashing mediocrity.

But these problems do not deny the basic validity of Mr. Pereira's idea—that there is reason for creating a skyscraper in a city like San Francisco that emphasizes height but not bulk, and that has an identifiable shape that will add life to the skyline in the way that the elaborately topped towers of the early part of the century did.

Lately the skyline of San Francisco has become a deadened mass of boxes, much as that of the southern tip of Manhattan has; Transamerica's pointed top is the one brightening element.

The Transamerica pyramid in San Francisco in 1971.

Still, the nagging question remains—why, at a time when most intelligent voices are calling for a less flamboyant, more modest architecture, can Transamerica be called acceptable? It draws attention to itself, perhaps too much of it, but if there is a simple answer, it is that the building's flamboyance is more than just architectural narcissism. Its form is derived from the logical desire to be high, yet not to block light and views. And the result of all this is a shape that also enlivens the skyline in a way that benefits the entire city.

towers

BIG HEADS BY CHUCK CLOSE

John Russell

You don't have to have been in a Byzantine church (though it helps) to know that there is something peculiarly disquieting about a very big head. To be stared back at by eyeballs many times larger than our own is an experience that puts us in our place: and who better to do that than the Saviour of mankind?

But Chuck Close isn't the Saviour of mankind, and his enormous heads are not seen in churches. They are on view at this moment at the Pace Gallery.

Mr. Close himself is the most approachable of men. He is big, to begin with: big enough to be halfway on the road to enlargement, one might say. His face meanders this way and that and is so basically convivial as not to lend itself to an intimidating posture. In fact there is no reason why his 80-inch-high self portrait head should scare us.

And it doesn't. What it does do is stretch the experience of looking at another human being. The pictures are also about the concept of identity. Mr. Close toils away month after month, riding high on a Big Joe mechanized chair that goes up and down at will, and he does his portraits piece by piece, with all the rest of the picture bandaged and out of sight. The whole procedure is a long, clearsighted gamble that just happens to pay off in Mr. Close's own terms. ∎

American painter Paul Cadmus poses in front of Chuck Close's portrait of him.

THE REICHSTAG COVER-UP

Grace Glueck

Christo and Jeanne-Claude had to wait until 1995 to cover the Reichstag building with shimmering silver fabric.

The long-running proposal by Christo to wrap West Berlin's historic Reichstag building in 60,000 square yards of synthetic fabric for 14 days has hit a bit of a snag. The packaging artist, whose last project—in the fall of 1976—was a running fence of white nylon that snaked through 24½ miles of northern California landscape for two weeks, reports that after considerable discussion, he has a "nein" from Karl Carstens, the conservative Christian Democratic president of the West German Bundestag, or parliament.

The Bundestag president believes, said a spokesman, that Christo's ministrations to the Reichstag, burned by the Nazis in 1933 and now regarded as a symbol of German reunification, would engender "not useful" discussion among the German people.

Nevertheless, the opposition Social Democratic Party is still gung-ho for the project. Klaus Rosen, secretary to Willy Brandt, former mayor of West Berlin and now head of the Social Democratic Party, says that the pro-party newspaper, Vorwärts, will soon carry an editorial stating that realization of the proposal can prove the Germans have "achieved a certain distance from their own history." And he adds, "We hope that the president can be persuaded to change his mind."

The Centre Georges Pompidou, also known as the Centre Beaubourg.

. . . Christo's ministrations to the Reichstag . . . would engender "not useful" discussion among the German people.

So hot an issue is the Reichstag wrap that it has even drawn fire from Pravda. The Soviet Communist Party newspaper views it as "a means of political propaganda to emphasize West Berlin, which as a result of détente has lost to Bonn as a power center." And it refers to the Bulgarian-born Christo as "a famous American artist"; his project as "a truly American idea."

For Christo, whose big wraps have included a number of buildings and a mile of the Australian coast, and who in 1972 strung a nylon curtain between two peaks in a Colorado valley, the project repre-

sents "a new dimension" in his work. "I've always had a fascination for Berlin, a city with a complex relationship to 20th-century life," he says. "It's the first time I'd be involved in a work of art with a highly political international context."

As usual, he takes a not unhappy view of the current difficulties. "At the moment, the project is a complete mess," he says gleefully, recalling the hassle of persuading 57 ranchers in California's Sonoma and Marin Counties to allow last year's running fence to go through their land. ■

JULY 30, 1977

Tourists Gawk, Parisians Sneer at Pompidou Center

Susan Heller Anderson

PARIS—An immense blue big top in the plaza of the Centre Georges Pompidou welcomes full houses twice daily, but the real circus is in the museum.

Some 2.8 million visitors have invaded the Centre Pompidou, or Centre Beaubourg as it is known, since its opening last February. As a tourist attraction it will shortly overtake the Eiffel Tower, which claims three million visitors a year.

One afternoon, an hour after opening,

(cont'd. on next page)

ARTS & ENTERTAINMENT

(cont'd. from previous page)

lines formed everywhere. Some 400 people queued up in front of the narrow escalator that is the only access to the upper floors where the library and art exhibitions are housed. These escalators are transporting 22,220 people a day and quickly become overloaded. The transparent plastic exterior tubes that house them smell of burning rubber.

According to one guard, most visitors come mainly to gawk at the building. Once they make the trip to the top and take in what is possibly Paris's finest view they tend to leave—the vast exhibition areas are not overcrowded. "The French come to complain about the architecture," said the guard.

A spokesman for the museum expressed astonishment at the crowds. "We originally estimated about 8,000 a day and thought we were being optimistic. Now we've got three times that."

The crowds have been tough on the museum's appearance. Paint is already chipping off the exposed tubes and ducts, windows are filthy, the plaza is littered with cigarette butts and the place looks tacky. But museum officials think they have the problems licked and, beginning Sept. 7, Beaubourg will open an hour earlier.

Meanwhile, a patient guard answered questions in three languages and advised visitors to come back around 7 P.M. when most civilized Frenchmen are in cafes thinking about dinner. ■

OCTOBER 21, 1977

JASPER JOHNS
Packs Them In

John Russell

Jasper Johns at 47 is a lot of people's favorite American painter. More than 4,100 of those people pushed their way into the private view of his exhibition at the Whitney Museum last Monday evening; and ever since the show opened to the public a long, impatient and talkative line has been filing through the doors and keeping the cash register clacking.

These people know what they are doing. It is 13 years since Johns had a museum show of paintings, drawings, prints and sculptures in New York. During that time he has completed a long series of large, complex and difficult paintings that have been shown briefly or not at all. As for the paintings with which he made his name in the late 1950's, they have turned out to have that sure mark of major art—the ability to satisfy a whole set of new needs as one decade follows another.

It is not too much to say in this context that by the time he was 30 Jasper Johns had produced some of the most beautiful pictures ever painted by an American. Anyone who doubts this should drop by at the Whitney and look at the big "White Flag" of 1955, the "Grey Alphabets" of 1956, and the three paintings of numbers, which date from 1958-59. The history of recent art knows of no beginnings more extraordinary than these.

In these paintings, Johns started from subject matter that was "given," plain and impersonal. Every day of our lives we see the flag, we run up the scale from 0 to 9 and down again, and we put the alphabet to work. Advanced American painting in

Jasper Johns (right) talking to American art dealer Leo Castelli and his wife, Antoinette, in the Castellis' home, New York City, where one of John's flag paintings hangs over the fireplace.

the early 1950's had to do with images that nobody had ever made before; and when Johns busied himself with images that we see every time we open our eyes there were people who took it to be a nihilistic put-on.

It was anything but that. Johns was out to reinvent the expressive possibilities of painting. Starting from a contemporary situation, and working primarily in encaustic—a medium slowed and thickened with wax—he built his pictures, as much as painted them; and after 20 years the results have an ageless, timeless, dateless look. They could hang anywhere and in any company and not be discomfited.

Johns could have gone on painting those primary images forever—and indeed he does occasionally allow himself a luxurious reprise—but in general he prefers to sire a whole new family of images every year or two and go back to them from time to time to see how they are getting on.

He can be a most diabolical tease. When people all round him were getting steamed up about "the integrity of the picture plane," he would violate that integrity and see what came of it. There were paintings that had drawers adumbrated within them. There were paintings in which the taut flat skin of the image was tweaked aside to admit the intrusion of two small balls; that intrusion had overtones of discomfort and exasperation that were very characteristic.

To find out whether Johns is what many people take him to be—the most important artist to have emerged in the second half of this century—we have to come to terms with the big symphonic paintings that began with "Diver" in 1962 and are still in full evolution. It may well be a long time before they give up all their secrets.

The major works by Jasper Johns could be discussed forever, and most probably will be. ■

BALTHUS: 'LAST OF THE GREAT EUROPEAN PAINTERS'

John Russell

From time to time the message drifts westward across the Atlantic that Balthus may be the last of the great European painters. Balthus is a French painter of Polish extraction, now in his late 60's. Alone among painters now active on the mainland of Europe, he can take the classic modes of European painting and excel in every one of them. He can paint landscape. He can paint still life. He can paint the nude. He can paint portraits. He can paint interiors with figures. His paintings, once seen, are rarely forgotten.

But the trouble is that, in general, they aren't seen. This being so, the Balthus exhibition at the Pierre Matisse Gallery Is a considerable event. There is no mistaking the catch of the breath with which visitors move from bay to bay, as if hardly able to believe what hangs before them.

The earliest painting in the show is "The Guitar Lesson" of 1934. This has had a clandestine reputation for many years, but it has never been shown in public before. In the "Guitar Lesson" a young girl on the threshold of puberty is being given instruction by an older girl. The lesson in question was initially in the techniques of the guitar; but what with one thing and another, the guitar fell to the floor, the pupil's skirts were pulled up way above her waist, and she ended by having a lesson of quite another kind.

Though mild by the standards of today, the subject matter of "The Guitar Lesson" is undeniably private. No museum would hang it, for instance. Nor would any newspaper reproduce it. "The Guitar Lesson" after 40 or more years looks like something of a sport or freak in his output. The paintings by which his reputation will stand or fall are those in which much is left unanswered.

Balthus still regards the act of reading as primordial to human development: witness "Katia Reading" (1970-1976). He still regards the act of looking at oneself in a mirror as crucial: witness "Nude in Front of a Mantel" (1955) and the two big paintings of a Japanese girl half-lying, half-crawling towards a looking glass. And he still prizes the card game as a metaphor for those decisive upheavals in which a human destiny is settled once and for all: witness "Card Game" of 1967-73.

Balthus, when younger, had a very sharp eye for the townscape of Paris, the landscape of the apple-green uplands on the border between France and Switzerland and the tumult of textures which is likely to have piled up in a country house where people are quite alone and yet do not wish to live like hermits in a cave. It is as if he had taken vows of simplicity and austerity to offset the impact of Rome.

Whereas earlier he re-created a given landscape in terms of Poussin, in his new paintings he is out on his own. The space is completely arbitrary. The anatomy, likewise. Formal invention is the servant of feeling. We have never before seen paintings in which people looked like this, behaved like this, or were integrated into their surroundings in anything like the same way. These paintings persuade us that painting can still tell us the whole truth about a beloved human being in ways which have no precedent.

Norman Rockwell working in his studio in 1974.

Norman Rockwell, Artist of Americana, Dead at 84

Edwin McDowell

Norman Rockwell, the artist whose nostalgic evocations of small-town America appeared in hundreds of Saturday Evening Post covers, died Wednesday night at his home in Stockbridge, Mass., at the age of 84. He had been in failing health for two years.

(cont'd. on next page)

(cont'd. from previous page)

Mr. Rockwell painted in a converted carriage house in Stockbridge, a town whose New England charm he captured in his paintings.

"My worst enemy is the world-shaking idea," he once said, "stretching my neck like a swan and forgetting that I'm a duck." That assessment was characteristically modest, for Mr. Rockwell neglected to add that if he was in fact a duck, he was an important duck in a very big pond.

There is hardly an American adult who at one time or another has not experienced a wave of nostalgia while gazing at a Rockwell magazine cover, Boy Scout calendar or advertisement. "He had been America's most popular artist for half a century," Thomas S. Buechner, director of the Brooklyn Museum, wrote in 1970. "In fact, his big work has been reproduced more often than all of Michelangelo's, Rembrandt's and Picasso's put together."

Mr. Rockwell was best known for his covers for The Saturday Evening Post, 317 of them between 1916 and 1963. Although it sometimes seemed that a Rockwell cover graced the magazine almost every week, his actual output averaged about one every seven. A former Post editor observed that during his experience in the 1950's and early 60's, a Rockwell cover was good for an extra 50,000 to 75,000 newsstand sales.

This was no doubt because a typical Rockwell cover tended to evoke emotions of sentiment, reverence or poignancy: a family gathered in thanksgiving around a holiday table; ample Pickwickian gentlemen singing Christmas carols; freckled boys, barefoot and in tattered overalls, carrying makeshift fishing poles; the kindly doctor preparing to inoculate a wide-eyed child's bare bottom; a run-away boy at a lunch counter confiding in an understanding policeman; a tomboy with a black eye in the doctor's waiting room or shy young couples bathed in the innocence of new love.

This vision of America endeared Mr. Rockwell to millions of his countrymen, but it was not uniformly admired. Critics complained that his serene America—a land unpopulated by ethnic or black Americans, or untroubled by controversy more serious than an occasional youthful peccadillo—existed solely in the imagination.

Art critics also tended to disparage Mr. Rockwell, pointedly referring to him as an illustrator rather than as an artist. They said that his illustration lacked subtlety, nuance and depth.

Mr. Rockwell finally achieved formal recognition as an artist with a 1968 exhibition of 50 of his oil paintings at the Bernard Danenberg Gallery on Madison Avenue that drew large crowds.

Four years later, a Rockwell retrospective at the Brooklyn Museum drew equally enthusiastic crowds. ∎

DECEMBER 22, 1978

Warhol's Gang Pops Back Again

Vivien Raynor

Andy Warhol in 1978.

Jackie and Liz, Marilyn and Mao: they are all riding again, along with Campbell's Soup and the electric chair. In other words, some of the images chosen by Andy Warhol during the period 1960 to 1973 are being paraded in their original form at the Blum Helmann Gallery. The show is an invitation to reflect, yet again, on the confusion which, begun by Duchamp, was brought to a boiling point by one of his brightest descendants.

Pop, as everyone must know by now, took the intimidation out of art (though not out of its prices) and opened the sluice gates for its mass appreciation. However, its prime exponent may, in the end, seem to have been more a politician than an esthetic genius. For Warhol, more than his colleagues or even Duchamp, aimed straight at society itself. He took irony and camp, attitudes that were formerly the prerogatives of the few, and made them available to the many. Thus the public, having mastered a few basic intellectual steps, learned to feel superior to the idols and ideas they once took seriously, while the cultivated found they could be even more so by espousing the kitsch they had previously despised.

Pop art itself scarcely lasted to the end of the 60's, but its effect has lingered on like a stain, seeping into life itself and blurring the lines between fact and fiction, the serious and the fatuous.

Supposedly never meant to be treated as art objects, these prototypical canvases have, of course, lost their shock value and can be viewed only as symbols of an important war. The images are silk-screened, usually in black, and painted by hand, and, when used more than once, are changed enough in color and texture to make each version legally unique. One "Mao" for instance, is dressed in a violet-gray tunic, expressionistically painted, the other in turquoise.

WINNING WAYS OF I. M. PEI

Paul Goldberger

I. M. Pei is pacing his living room floor, and he is talking about the state of architecture. "It is Louis Kahn who I admire most," he is saying. "He will stand the test of time—there is a spirit, a sense of being in a very special place in his buildings. From him I learned that it is not just a concept, but the way that concept is executed that is important. His is the architecture of ideas, and I worry that ideas and professional practice do not intersect enough." He pauses, then adds: "Maybe my early training set me back. Maybe it made me too much of a pragmatist."

That is an unexpected comment from a man like Pei, who runs an architectural office that employs 160 people and numbers among its clients major corporations, real-estate developers and cultural institutions around the world. Yet I. M. Pei & Partners is more than a commercial architectural

Marilyn and Elvis have a picture apiece, Liz Taylor has two. The head of Jacqueline Onassis in the weeds of her first widowhood is repeated 16 times in black and white. And, for anyone who needs it, there's a Technicolor package of 56 Troy Donahues. Directly opposite this is a large single image of the electric chair in black and purple (as distinct from the multiple blue version).

Meant to remind spectators that Warhol's mass produced icons came out of paintings, which, in turn, had come from photographs, the show doesn't settle the question of whether the artist was the finest mind of his time or simply is a sharp operator with good timing. Nor for that matter does it presage his current position as a meek kind of Salvador Dali, hanging out with the nobs and "painting" their portraits. On the other hand, it does prove, sadly, for he had talent—that Warhol was right to make his career in art management rather than its labor. ∎

firm. Its work has always tried to merge serious esthetic ideas with a certain professional business sense, and today it is probably the leader among the few architectural practices in the United States that manage to make a mark both esthetically and commercially.

At the moment, I. M. Pei's star—clear in the firmament for a good two decades by now—is rising higher than ever. He has just been named architect of the New York Convention and Exhibition Center. His drawing boards are full of work from Singapore to Park Avenue, and this fall he will see the John F. Kennedy Library in Dorchester, Mass., a project that has eluded completion for 15 frustrating years, open its doors at last. And next month Pei will receive the gold medal of the American Institute of Architects—the highest award the professional society gives to any architect in the world.

It is a long way to have come since the early 1970's, when I. M. Pei & Partners meant only one thing in the public's mind: the John Hancock Tower, the 60-story skyscraper in Boston whose double-paned glass windows mysteriously fell out. The Pei resurgence is due in large part to Pei himself. He is surely the most gracious and thoughtful of all of American architecture's elder statesmen today. If he lacks Philip Johnson's verbal and architectural flamboyance, or Kevin Roche's painstaking inventiveness, he has a sense of quiet dedication to certain architectural constants which the other two lack.

Pei's approach has won him few friends in academic architectural circles. But with the Hancock stigma gone, corporate clients flock to Pei. They feel he can deliver a building that will impress but not shock their visitors, employees and customers. Similarly, institutional clients such as art museums look to the Pei firm for a kind of strong, yet discreet, modern design; something that will make a statement of quality in both concept and execution.

Several Pei museums have received significant public acclaim, from the Everson in Syracuse of 1968 to the East Building of the National Gallery of Art in Washington. This marble palace opened last year to such fanfare that it can surely be said to have played a major role in and of itself in the recent surge of interest in I. M. Pei.

By now, I. M. Pei & Partners is in a position in this country not unlike that of McKim, Mead & White at the beginning of this century. Their work was so much better than that of most of their competitors that they were able to bring quality architecture to a far broader public than ever saw the designs of those architects more concerned with pure innovation.

So it is with I. M. Pei. Today, the abstract, geometric forms of Pei's modernism are the conservative style, not unlike the neo-Renaissance buildings favored by the McKim firm in its time. His own variations on modernist themes in buildings such as Hancock, the National Gallery, Kips Bay Plaza housing in New York and Society Hill in Philadelphia are among the most studied and discussed buildings of the last 20 years. ∎

"Maybe my early training set me back. Maybe it made me too much of a pragmatist."

I.M. Pei and his wife, Eileen, in 1979.

ARTS & ENTERTAINMENT

American Notebook

Richard Lingeman

SELLING SEX

If you scan the Best Seller List this week you may notice that a book with the seductive title "Everything You Always Wanted to Know About Sex" is now Number One after only six weeks on the list. The book's rapid rise (it is selling at a rate of 5,000 copies a day; there are 130,000 copies in print; and McKay, the publisher, has a standing order with its printer for 20,000 copies per week) apparently indicates that a lot of Americans want to know more about sex than they presently do, which may come as a shock to purveyors of the "sexual revolution."

Asked how the book came about, the author, Dr. David Reuben, said that his own patients had made him aware that "many people have only a rudimentary knowledge of sex—including sophisticated, educated people."

The book is in question-answer form (Q. "Do nymphomaniacs have orgasms?" A. "Yes . . . ."), which Dr. Reuben found more natural—like talking to a patient—and less likely to encounter reader resistance, which tends to occur with conventional sex manuals. The result is a zingy, colloquial book, laced with humor (some of it unintended), which sounds a little like a cross between Sigmund Freud and a young, with-it Reform rabbi. But the book's basic idea—people are often sexually in the dark—and its steadily reiterated sermon—sex is good, natural and pleasurable, not nasty, guilt-ridden and dirty—seems to be right on target, judging from sales and the letters Reuben has been receiving.

Initial reactions to "Everything" were lukewarm; some booksellers were reluctant to stock it, and the major television talk shows were wary of the subject matter, but eventually came around. ("TV hosts want to ask about sex, too," says Dr. Reuben. "They have sexual problems like everybody else.") A favorable review in Life magazine and an appearance on the Dick Cavett show sparked sales.

NUMEROLOGY

In setting the prices of their books, publishers manipulate a variety of cost factors, and sometimes the difference between a 500-page $6.95 book and a 600-page $7.95 book is merely the thicker paper and wider spacing used to make the latter look bigger, though the number of words may be the same. But it has remained for a French publisher to provide his American colleagues with an example of truly inspired pricing. At a recent William Morrow & Co. luncheon at Sardi's to celebrate their forthcoming American edition of "Papillon," a runaway French best seller about a man who escapes from Devil's Island, the publisher, Robert Laffont, confessed he had originally thought of charging 26 francs for the book. That would be the usual price for a book of 500 or so pages. But M. Laffont's lucky number is 28, so on a whim he decided to set the price at 28 francs. Result? Since the book sold over a million copies, Laffont's publishing house was 2 million francs richer than it would have been had sober reason held away.

This winter has been one of discontent in the publishing world. The trouble has already surfaced at two houses. Funk & Wagnalls, owned by Reader's Digest, recently fired its entire editorial staff; while McGraw-Hill, a giant in the business-professional-educational field, is reorganizing its trade department after bidding goodbye to editor-in-chief Frank W. Taylor.

The turbulence has been great in the trade departments of several large, conglomerate-owned or Wall Street-monied houses. Though no heads have rolled, there have been a variety of belt-tightening measures, such as demands for longer hours, increased editorial productivity, slashes in expense account largesse, and the like. ∎

The New English Bible

Robert M. Grant

New York: Oxford University Press and Cambridge University Press.

The New English Bible to be published tomorrow is one of the great translations. It uses fresh, living language to express the religious insights that have meant much and still mean much in the English-speaking world. For our generation this Bible may well become and remain the common version in English. More than a million copies are already in print in this country and abroad.

The New English Bible, like the King James Version of 1611 and the Revised Standard Version of 1946-57, was prepared by committees. The members, who have been at work on the N.E.B. for more than 20 years, were from the British non-Roman churches and Bible societies; there were Roman Catholic observers. The translators were from British universities. They agreed that scholarship did not automatically lead to expression in good English, and they were aided by a panel of literary advisers.

They realized that English is a living language and therefore keeps changing. They knew that modern translators aim not at literalness and sameness but at saying in English what they believe the original authors were saying in their languages. Modern knowledge of Hebrew and Greek

For our generation this Bible may well become and remain the common version in English.

has advanced remarkably, and manuscripts of the Bible unknown in 1611 have been found and critically examined.

Changes always produce problems. Handel's "Messiah" has rooted the words of Job 19:25-26 in American and British memories. But what did Job himself want to say? In the King James: "For I know that my Redeemer liveth,/And that he shall stand at the latter day upon the earth:/And though after my skin worms destroy this body,/Yet in my flesh shall I see God." The New English Bible is strikingly different: "But in my heart I know that my vindicator lives/and that he will rise last to speak in court;/and I shall discern my witness standing at my side/and see my defending counsel, even God himself."

If we want to know what the inspiration (theological or otherwise) of the Hebrew author led him to say and mean, we cannot tinker with his intentions. This is why the N.E.B. is such a remarkable translation. It is boldly accurate. At the same time, the accuracy comes through not in baldly literal or vulgar terminology but in elegant English.

A translation of the Bible can be fully adequate only if it points through itself and beyond its readers to the region of the sacred and the numinous. Its language must not be commonplace, but it must be comprehensible. The language of the New English Bible meets this test. The university presses of Oxford and Cambridge have presented it in a format that assists understanding and gives pleasure to the eye. Form and content work together to stimulate and challenge the reader. ∎

SOLZHENITSYN SHUNS NOBEL TRIP

Bernard Gwertzman

MOSCOW, Nov. 27—Aleksandr I. Solzhenitsyn said today that he had decided "for personal reasons" not to ask official permission to go to Stockholm to accept the 1970 Nobel Prize for Literature.

Mr. Solzhenitsyn's decision put an end to the speculation here and abroad. His friends said that his decision was motivated largely out of concern that Soviet authorities might not permit him to return.

They stressed, however, that the issue of whether to go had become complicated in Mr. Solzhenitsyn's mind in recent weeks as the controversy over the award mounted here.

Mr. Solzhenitsyn, whose most recent works are banned here, had earlier indicated that he hoped to go to Stockholm and receive the award, which carries with it a cash prize of about $78,000.

Swedish sources stressed tonight that his decision not to travel to Sweden in no way deprived him of the prize.

There are several precedents for this, they said. He has not rejected the award, as did the late Boris Pasternak, the winner of the 1958 award for his novel "Doctor Zhivago."

Ironically, Mr. Khrushchev liked the anti-Stalinist aspects of Mr. Solzhenitsyn's writing and authorized the publication in 1962 of his first novel, "One Day in the Life of Ivan Denisovich."

Mr. Solzhenitsyn, who was expelled from the Writers Union last year, has been spared the kind of attack leveled against Mr. Pasternak. The comments have been directed primarily against the Swedish Academy for granting of the award.

But even this relatively mild campaign against the award brought forth a strong denunciation from the cellist, Mstislav Rostropovich, at whose country home Mr. Solzhenitsyn lives. In a statement, never published here, Mr. Rostropovich said that he admired Mr. Solzhenitsyn's writings, and that the writer deserved the Nobel Prize because of his suffering for truth.

Mr. Solzhenitsyn, who regards himself as a Russian patriot, has never contemplated emigrating, his friends said. When he was expelled from the Writers Union, the newspaper Literaturnaya Gazeta suggested that he was free to leave at any time.

Mr. Solzhenitsyn has been attacked by conservatives for painting too black a picture of Soviet life and of being obsessed with the Stalin terror. The current leadership has virtually banned publication of any work that describes in detail the Stalin repressions.

The writer is idolized by many intellectuals and particularly by students, who admire his austere existence, his outspoken attacks on censorship and repression and his writing.

Virtually every Soviet intellectual has read at one time or another most of his works that are banned here, either through smuggled copies printed abroad or in manuscripts. ∎

Russian novelist Alexandr Solzhenitsyn in 1974.

ARTS & ENTERTAINMENT

DECEMBER 20, 1970

LOVE (AND SUCCESS) STORY

Robert McG. Thomas Jr.

If you were born in Brooklyn and your father was a rabbi and you went to Midwood High School and made it into Harvard—where you wrote the Hasty Pudding show and became the first Class Orator in 300 years to be Class Poet too.

And you got your Ph.D. and moved to Yale, where your lectures to the Elis drew overflow attendance and were branded "star performances."

And your first play ran Off-Broadway.

And your first movie was "Yellow Submarine."

And your first novel is "Love Story."

And the paperback edition produced the largest initial print order in the history of publishing—4,350,000 copies that gobbled up 500 tons of paper and no telling how many trees.

And made your publisher so happy he decided to crown your achievement amid all the glamour and excitement of a reception in the rarefied atmosphere of the literary world's favorite salon.

Then, on the Tuesday before Thanksgiving, when you'd scaled the heights at last and finally arrived—on the red carpet of the St. Regis-Sheraton's Library Suite for what is not only your coronation, but your very first New York party—you might find it just a shade disconcerting to discover, well...

The man in the tweeds, pulling reflectively on his meerschaum, is none other than Murray Berk, a stalwart of the New American Library sales force for 25 years. The man to his left on the couch is Ed Zemsky, the head paperback buyer for the 38-store Doubleday chain. He has this very day placed a 10,000-unit order—to replace the original 10,000 "Love Stories" that six days after paperback publication are being rapidly depleted.

It's that kind of party.

Inside, the man with the scruffy muttonchops is Sidney Kramer, the N. A. L. president and a host who keeps a kindly eye on the p.r. women, salesmen, marketing reps, promotion men, jobbers, buyers and the few editors and media types who sprinkle themselves a hundred strong through the three-room suite.

There is a theatrical contingent led by Stanley Jaffe, the young president of Paramount ("Love Story" opened Dec. 17) and Nat Lefkowitz, the head of the William Morris agency (the woman with the cane and the diamond Star of David on her bosom is Mrs. Lefkowitz), as well as a quota of pretty and semipretty unattached girls.

But if the party isn't exactly the event of the season, the guest of honor is. It is, of course, Erich Segal—Yale's answer to Sesame Street, and the self-confessed fulfillment of every Harvard sophomore's dream.

> It has been translated into 17 languages, is number one in France and is required reading at at least one Ivy League college . . .

From the time the wiry, five-and-a-half-foot, 33-year-old Yale classics professor prances in (20 minutes late), wearing the black flap-pocket Italian job he picked up off the rack on "the Strip" (Sunset) and the snowy ribbed shirt with the white clerical collar ("I'm no Tom Wolfe," he apologizes. "No, I don't know him, I just admire him.") to well beyond the party's official 8 P.M. closing more than two hours later, Segal is in constant, booming, animated conversation.

On Feb. 4, Barbara Walters had filled millions of television screens and allowed as how she had liked "Love Story." "It just took off," Segal exclaims, his hand leaping from the launching pad.

It has not come down. The hardcover "Love Story" has been on the Book Review's best seller list for 43 weeks. During 33 of those weeks, it has occupied the number one position. It has been translated into 17 languages, is number one in France and is required reading at least one Ivy League college Segal could name. It's hard to tell just how much over a million his take will run—but, yes, it will be more than Capote made from "In Cold Blood."

This outpouring for a 131-page book The New York Times called "not even semi-serious literature" is more surprising than embarrassing to the author, who admits he was afraid to turn it in because it was so brief. "It takes the average person an hour and a half to read the book," explained the author. "The movie lasts longer." ■

Author Erich Segal in 1971.

The Female Eunuch

Sally Kempton

By Germaine Greer.
349 pp. New York:
McGraw-Hill Book Company, $6.95.

I must admit I approached "The Female Eunuch" with suspicion. I first heard about it last fall from a male magazine editor who had read the British edition and said it was the most brilliant piece of feminist writing he had ever read, and it has since been recommended to me by four different men, not to mention Norman Mailer, who plugged it in the course of his anti-feminist tirade in the February Harper's.

It is Greer's fundamental insight that women have been systematically robbed of productive energy . . .

In fact, "The Female Eunuch" is a great pleasure to read. It is brilliantly written, quirky and sensible, full of bile and insight; if many of its insights are available to us in the work of other feminist writers that does not make the book less interesting.

Greer's book is a conglomeration of fact and speculation and polemic, arranged under chapter headings that follow each other with almost poetic logic, and if "The Female Eunuch" is not in the least confessional, it is highly personal in the sense that the essays of Lamb and Hazlitt and Virginia Woolf were personal.

One felt, reading "The Second Sex," that Simone de Beauvoir was writing al-

Australian writer Germaine Greer with a Dutch edition of her best-known book, "The Female Eunuch," 1972.

ways about other women, that she had singled herself out as the exception to her own rule. Greer's theories about sex and love are stated with such positive assurance that one somehow knows that she has tested her own "right" way of loving, has found it good, and now regards with a little perplexity those women who have not found it out for themselves.

It is Greer's fundamental insight that women have been systematically robbed of productive energy by society's insis-

tence on confining them to a passive sexual role. When all activism is assumed to be male, and femininity is defined as merely receptive (and hence irresponsible), then women must repress their normally human drive toward active sexuality in order to conform with the male supremacist idea of what is feminine. Woman's energy, Greer maintains, is then channeled by the denial of her sexuality into a system of repression which extends into every area of her life. ∎

ARTS & ENTERTAINMENT

NERUDA, CHILEAN POET-POLITICIAN, WINS NOBEL PRIZE FOR LITERATURE

John L. Hess

STOCKHOLM, Oct. 21—Pablo Neruda, the Chilean poet, diplomat and Communist leader, was awarded the 1971 Nobel Prize for Literature today.

The Swedish Academy announced that it was conferring the award with this citation: "For poetry that, with the action of an elemental force, brings alive a continent's destiny and dreams."

Mr. Neruda, whose original name was Neftali Ricardo Reyes Basualto, first published poems at the age of 17 and had won wide esteem by his early twenties. In an old tradition of subsidy to artists, he was given consular posts that allowed him to turn out a huge body of work, which is still growing.

Except for a brief surrealistic period around 1930, his poetry is clear and lyrical, infused with love—and politics. The Spanish Civil War and his friendship with Garcia Lorca sealed his affiliation to the left. He was elected a Communist Senator in 1945 and was forced into hiding in exile from 1947 to 1952.

Neruda's hymns of praise to the Soviet Union and his acceptance of a Stalin Prize in 1950 are thought to have spoiled his very strong chance to have won the Nobel award more than a decade ago. His work is frequently published in Swedish translation, and he has been a leading candidate ever since.

According to literary circles here, the academy's vote last Thursday went to Mr. Neruda by a narrow majority, the runner-up being the Australian Patrick White. ■

MS., A MAGAZINE FOR FEMINISTS, SETS JANUARY DEBUT

Gloria Steinem, feminist leader and founder of Ms. magazine in 1979.

Gloria Steinem will be editor and Elizabeth Forsling Harris, publisher, of a new monthly magazine for women "whose needs and interests go far beyond the limits of home and husband."

Entitled Ms., the form of address preferred by feminists, it is scheduled to hit the newsstands in January with a double issue dated Spring, and regular monthly issues expected by early summer.

Although its founders make it clear that Ms. is an independent publication, it is getting a nice boost from New York magazine, of which Miss Steinem is a contributing editor.

The magazine is the first effort of Majority Enterprises, Inc., a corporation formed last June "to provide products and services to women."

Miss Steinem, writer and feminist, is president. Miss Harris, who is chairman, has been an administrator in the Peace Corps and Girl Scouts and mostly recently a corporate vice president of CRM, publisher of Psychology Today.

UPDIKE GOES ALL OUT AT LAST

Anatole Broyard

RABBIT REDUX. By John Updike. 407 pages. Knopf. $7.95.

When I began this book and found Rabbit Angstrom 10 years older, fatter, softer, settled and no longer even running as he was in the earlier version, I wondered why Updike had locked himself in with this loser, why he had given himself so little elbow room. He has this habit, I thought, of keeping his people small—old, precious or ordinary—so he can write all around them, pin them with his exquisite entomology.

There were many of us who felt that "Rabbit, Run" was Updike's most solid book—or at least until "Bech"—and now it looked as if he was going to fall back on it and try to milk it for whatever was left. A tour de force about a creep—that's about what I expected. And I was never so wrong. "Rabbit Redux" is the complete Updike at last, an awesomely accomplished writer who is better, tougher, wiser and more radically human than anyone could have expected him to be.

Life grows stale, it loses interest, Freud says somewhere, when we stop risking our lives—risking in the sense of staking them on something and holding nothing back, no hedge or insurance. This is what Rabbit is doing now—climbing out on every limb he can find and swinging there. Feeling he has nothing further to lose, he lets himself go wherever the currents of contemporary life carry him. Philosophers and estheticians have talked about the role of chance in life and art, but Rabbit takes chances. He is like a man who is determined to reach the reduction ad absurdum—or sublime—in his life once and for all.

In "Rabbit Redux," Updike's ear is perfect and he has finally put together in his prose all the things that were there only separately. He has sacrificed none of his sensibility—simply translated it into gutsier, more natural but no less eloquent rhythms. He moves now with the sureness, grace and precision of the born athlete.

For God's sake, read the book. It may even—will probably—change your life. ■

Irving: Gulling Experts for Fun and Fame

John Corry

Clifford Irving, his friends and acquaintances say, is full of charm, resolute in his convictions about himself, and eager to be famous, which, of course, he now is. Moreover, if he invited disaster, as the indictment Thursday suggested, he wanted to do it with style.

Lawrence Lipton, a prominent figure from the "beat generation" of writers, who knew Mr. Irving in California in the early nineteen sixties, recalls him then as being more ambitious—torn by an urge to be either a serious writer or simply a celebrity.

"He wanted to meet world literary figures," Mr. Lipton, the author of "The Holy Barbarians," said. "He tried to understand the revolution and the renaissance in the arts, but he was a very strong careerist; he didn't want to endure poverty.

The yearbook of the High School of Music and Art, from which he was graduated in 1947, said that Clifford Irving, "you'll see, the chief of our treasury will be," and an old classmate at Cornell said he had assumed that Mr. Irving would write for a while and then become, say, a stockbroker.

Nonetheless, Mr. Irving persevered as a writer, publishing eight books, and behaving for a while as a romantic and even tragic hero. For one thing, his second wife died in an automobile accident when she was eight months pregnant, and, for another, he was rootless.

He optioned a novel to a Hollywood producer, wrote for television, traveled to India, and lived for a while in Amsterdam, Stockholm and Vienna.

Once he was a crewman on a sailing yacht going from Mexico to Europe. The yacht was late arriving, but on the voyage Mr. Irving got to know Ibiza, a sunny island off the Mediterranean coast of Spain, full of expatriates, where he eventually met his future wife, Edith.

Nonetheless, Mr. Irving was never quite the success that his appetite demanded.

"The publishers pushed Cliff around on every book he did," novelist James Sherwood said. "Cliff said to me, 'I'm the house hack.'" His Autobiography of Howard Hughes, which he admitted to forging in January of 1972, was tremendously commercial. It would make his name well known.

(cont'd. on next page)

Clifford Irving in 1972.

ARTS & ENTERTAINMENT

(cont'd. from previous page)

A friend, Mrs. Christine Geiser, said, "If this Hughes thing is true, it was Edith who was the active person. Clifford may have thought of it as you would think of a plot for a book, but she is the one who all at once says, 'Come, let's try it.'"

The Hughes matter was a mistake, Edith said, an amusing one, but a mistake, nonetheless.

"I've read the Hughes manuscript and it's good, very good," she said. "It's so good it's a shame it's an autobiography."

If Mrs. Irving entranced those around her with her charm, her husband sometimes overwhelmed them with his intensity.

One by one he had dropped his literary agents, charging that they hadn't really furthered his career, and sometimes he had gone into the darkest of rages.

"Cliff threatened to kill me in 1959," his friend James Sherwood said. "I didn't play fair, and it was my fault. He told me that if you're going to be a friend you've got to be a friend you've got to be fair, truthful, honest. For years I was terrified of him. I thought he might kill me."

In 1969, McGraw-Hill, Inc., published Mr. Irving's "Fake," which was the story of an art forger, Elmyr de Hory, another resident of Ibiza.

In a French film documentary about Mr. de Hory, Mr. Irving said:

"All the world loves to see the experts and the Establishment made a fool of. And anyone likes to feel that those who set themselves up as experts are really as gullible as anyone else. And so Elmyr, as the great art faker of the 20th century, becomes a modern folk hero for the rest of us." ■

DECEMBER 24, 1972

Authors Peddle Their Best Sellers From a Pushcart

C. Gerald Fraser

Some of the nation's bestselling authors joined yesterday to peddle their books from a colorful but wet pushcart and bookstalls on Fifth Avenue.

Their actions were to protest what they called the book-publishing industry's "antiquated" and "unimaginative" methods of selling their books.

The authors maintained that the publishers did not get the books into the nation's bookstores with any efficiency. Standing beneath a yellow umbrella that shielded the pushcart, George Plimpton suggested a "massive clearinghouse" where readers could call, "dial something like 'library' and get the book they wanted."

"A few best sellers are displayed in bookstore windows," he said, but most—even those that are significant—are obscure and "disappear onto a miserable void."

Eleanor C. Munro, who wrote "Through the Vermillion Gates," suggested a writers' cooperative bookstore, similar to an artists' cooperative. "Painters don't sit around waiting for galleries to buy their work," she declared.

"It's no way to make a living," said Isaac Asimov, a science-fiction author who had 131 books published.

"I make a living because I write a lot. But not everyone can. And none of my books has ever been a best seller." ■

FEBRUARY 11, 1973

AHH!

Nora Sayre

When did you last have relations with a vacuum cleaner? (Technology may have outmoded Portnoy's slice of liver.) The anonymous authors of "The Joy of Sex," edited by Alex Comfort, warn that numerous (male) accidents in the home have resulted from such intimacies, and that the damage can be devastating. Meanwhile, since it appears that more and more people are feeling like interchangeable spare parts, it's instructive to look back at the self-help manuals which preceded those that focus on the sensuous battery or lamp or chair, and all the other guides which are selling even more hotly in the seventies than they did in the late sixties.

For example, in "The Marriage Art" (Dell, 95 cents, 1961), Dr. John Eichenlaub cautioned that "ineptly arranged intercourse leaves [your clothes] in a shambles, your plans for the evening shot" (a far cry or moan from the latest books, which celebrate impromptu happenings on airplanes, in washrooms, against trees).

Of course the recent manuals push hard to be encouraging, and they do squash some mossy myths, such as the notion that only simultaneous orgasms are acceptable. But you still suspect that they may merely increase the tensions which the authors aim to dissolve. Although they pay lip service to individuality, too many swing on the assumption that "most" members of either sex will enjoy the same experiences as the rest of their gender, that most of their tastes or needs will be the same.

Today, the terrors of squaredom can humble almost any audience. Hence those who aren't impassioned by g-strings or vibrators or ice cubes or being gagged by Jell-O in the tub may fear that they're unsensuous or downright undesirable—even though the text stresses that gimmicks are "not for everyone."

Most of these guides, which are intended as a gateway to freedom, actually suggest a new conformity—or even tyranny—in that you ought to have multiple orgasms at this moment, or at that one. But what if you don't? Meanwhile, the manuals may make one partner much more demanding—and he or she could be outraged if the other doesn't collaborate correctly. Despite the authors' steady protestations, many manuals can sound like rulebooks, and they may be promoting certain styles of sex life which some people just can't manage.

Undoubtedly, some buy manuals for the occasional erotic passages—perhaps they're regarded as porn made respectable. Also, it appears that many are convinced that others are doing brilliantly in the sack: that almost everyone is much more talented than they.

Among those I've read, the most humane is "The Joy of Sex"; it's rather literate too. The lavish illustrations are gripping. But the participants' faces aren't very appealing, so face-fetishists may be disappointed. The aim is "to stimulate your creative imagination"; once stimulated, "you won't need books"—an admission that's scarce in this field. Still, the text is awash with whimsy, and the British author's brisk references may jar your sensibilities now and then: as when they remark that one technique of "slow masturbation" with massage "may be the one good thing America gets out of the Vietnam war." Thank you. The White House was always grateful for any kind of support. ■

GRAVITY'S RAINBOW

Richard Locke

By Thomas Pynchon.
760 pp. New York: The Viking Press.
Cloth, $15. Paper, $4.95.

In America in the late 1950's and early

One of the longest, most difficult, most ambitious American novels in years

1960's there appeared a series of comic apocalyptic novels organized around picaresque anti-heroes or schlemiels and filled with what came to be called black humor. Writers like Joseph Heller ("Catch-22"), John Barth ("The Sot-Weed Factor"), Bruce Jay Friedman ("Stern") and Kurt Vonnegut Jr. ("Cat's Cradle," "Mother Night") became celebrities of sorts, cult figures. In 1963 Thomas Pynchon's first novel "V." was greeted with enthusiasm: Stanley Edgar Hyman immediately identified it with "Catch-22" and "Stern" and called it "powerful, ambitious, full of gusto, and overflowing with rich comic invention." Three years later came Pynchon's second novel, "The Crying of Lot 49," as short and swift as "V." was long; it too received high praise.

Yet as the sixties carried on, Pynchon remained silent; his aversion to publicity (no photographs, no bio, no interviews) was at odds with the times; his failure to rush to the marketplace with another hot masterpiece disappointed the getters and spenders. His two novels remained in print in paperback, but sales never really boomed: the exotic intricacy of his plots and the saturnalian density of his prose attracted covens of fanatics; but in a cultural scene where "a boy's got to peddle his book," silence, exile and cunning don't win the day: "You need exposure, baby."

Looking back, however, it seems to me

that of all the American novelists who emerged with Pynchon in the 1960's only Vonnegut, Barth and Heller are his peers. Pynchon is a much more complex writer than Vonnegut, a less esthetic and narcissistic one than Barth, and works on a larger scale and has a finer prose style than Heller—though he is not a better architect, or "greater" novelist, or bigger heart.

Pynchon's new book is thus an event—it breaks seven years of silence and allays the fear that he might never go beyond his early success. "Gravity's Rainbow" is longer, darker and more difficult than his first two books; in fact it is the longest, most difficult and most ambitious novel to appear here since Nabokov's "Ada" four years ago; its technical and verbal resources bring to mind Melville and Faulkner. Immersing himself in "the destructive element" and exploring paranoia, entropy and the love of death as primary forces in the history of our time, Pynchon establishes his imaginative continuity with the great modernist writers of the early years of this century. "Gravity's Rainbow" is bonecrushingly dense, compulsively elaborate, silly, obscene, funny, tragic, pastoral, historical, philosophical, poetic, grindingly dull, inspired, horrific, cold, bloated, beached and blasted. ■

Kurt Vonnegut in 1975.

MAY 2, 1973

Is Kurt Vonnegut Kidding Us?

Christopher Lehmann-Haupt

BREAKFAST OF CHAMPIONS. Or Goodbye Blue Monday. By Kurt Vonnegut Jr. 295 pages. With Drawings by the Author. Delacorte Press/Seymour Lawrence. $7.95.

You have to hand it to Kurt Vonnegut Jr. In his eighth novel, "Breakfast of Champions, or Goodbye Blue Monday," he performs considerable complex magic. He makes pornography seem like any old plumbing, violence like lovemaking, innocence like evil, and guilt like child's play. He wheels out all the latest fashionable complaints about America—her racism, her gift for destroying language, her technological greed and selfishness—and makes them seem

fresh, funny, outrageous, hateful, and lovable, all at the same time. He draws pictures, for God's sake—simple, rough, yet surprisingly seductive sketches of everything from Volkswagens to electric chairs. He weaves into his plot a dozen or so glorious synopses of Vonnegut stories one almost wishes were fleshed out into whole books. He very nearly levitates. Yet—astonishingly—this fiction is also a factual announcement of his intention to give up fiction. And what mars the book is that one believes the fiction, but not the facts.

Up to a certain point, it is easy to accept what is going on in this "tale of a meeting of two lonesome, skinny, fairly old white men on a planet which was dying fast." It's amusing and charming, yet oddly frightening, to watch Kilgore Trout—the undiscovered science-fiction writer who has kept popping up in Mr. Vonnegut's previous works—hitch-hiking across America to a Festival of the Arts in Midland City, where he has been invited through the lone intervention of that benign-evil millionaire, Eliot Rosewater.

But I began worrying after a while about certain narrative charms that Vonnegut keeps plying. After several repetitions, I got bothered by his repeated use of

(cont'd. on next page)

(cont'd. from previous page)

the exhortation to "Listen" with which he begins so many of his paragraphs, as well as the three little words "And so on" with which he concludes some of his most appalling descriptions. Even those dumb, lovable drawings began to pass after a time. I think I understand what he is getting at—that fictional art simply won't serve any more as he approaches middle age and a deeper insight to his own motives for writing (not to mention the impotence of art to purge the earth of evil); and that the persona who is creating "Breakfast of Champions" is trying to get a last desperate grip on the most simple rudiments of story-telling. But there is a certain coyness in this desperation, especially since it is surrounded by so much polish and inventiveness.

If your fiction must be destroyed, Mr. Vonnegut, then why create more fiction in the process of destroying it? If you must beg comparison to Tolstoy freeing his serfs, or Jefferson his slaves, why not just do the deed? Or are you just kidding us? ∎

Erica Jong in 1977.

OBITUARY

SEPTEMBER 3, 1973

J. R. R. TOLKIEN
Dead at 81; Wrote 'Lord of the Rings'

Special to The New York Times

LONDON, Sept. 2—J. R. R. Tolkien, linguist, scholar and author of "The Lord of the Rings," died today in Bournemouth. He was 81 years old.

Three sons and a daughter survive.

John Ronald Reuel Tolkien cast a spell over tens of thousands of Americans in the nineteen sixties with his 500,000-word trilogy, "The Lord of the Rings," in essence a fantasy of the war between ultimate good and ultimate evil.

Creating the complex but consistent world of Middle-earth, complete with elaborate maps, Tolkien peopled it with hobbits, elves, dwarves, men, wizards and Ents, and Orcs (goblins) and other servants of the Dark Lord, Sauron. In particular, he described the adventures of one hobbit, Frodo son of Drogo, who became the Ring Bearer and the key figure in the destruction of the Dark Tower. As Gandalf, the wizard, remarked, there was more to him than met the eye.

The story can be read on many levels. But the author, a scholar and linguist, for 39 years a teacher, denied emphatically that it was allegory. The Ring, discovered by Frodo's uncle, Bilbo Baggins, in an earlier book, "The Hobbit," has the power to make its wearer invisible, but it is infinitely evil.

Tolkien admirers compared him favorably with Milton, Spenser and Tolstoy. His English publisher, Sir Stanley Unwin, speculated that "The Lord of the Rings" would be more likely to live beyond his and his son's time than any other work he had printed. ∎

NOVEMBER 6, 1973

NUANCES OF WOMEN'S LIBERATION

Christopher Lehmann-Haupt

FEAR OF FLYING. By Erica Jong. 340 pages. Holt, Rinehart & Winston. $6.95.

A DIFFERENT WOMAN. By Jane Howard. 413 pages. Dutton. $7.95.

I'm on the side of books like these two from the start. Ever since Midge Decter, in her polemic, "The New Chastity," conjured out of a few tiny theories an entire universe of anti-feminism, I've been hoping for books that would explore the subtlety and variety of the women's liberation movement, and for writing that would be sensitive to the ambiguities of growing up intelligently female these days. And both Erica Jong's first novel, "Fear of Flying," and Jane Howard's combination autobiography and report, "A Different Woman," are nothing if not alert to the nuances of contemporary feminism. Moreover, both these books won me over with their strong beginnings.

Yet to varying degrees they are eventu-

SOVIET FORMALLY ACCUSED SOLZHENITSYN OF TREASON

Hedrick Smith

MOSCOW, Feb. 14—Friends of Aleksandr I. Solzhenitsyn's family reported tonight that before his deportation Soviet prosecutors had presented him with a formal indictment accusing him of treason. The crime carries penalties ranging from 10 years' imprisonment to death.

The 55-year-old Nobel Prize laureate refused to acknowledge the charge and he declared that he would not cooperate in any way with the investigation. According to the account by friends of the author's family in Moscow—based on what Mr. Solzhenitsyn told his wife in telephone calls yesterday and today from West Germany—he was given no choice whether to accept the expulsion order.

As the detailed reports of Mr. Solzhenitsyn's ordeal in detention emerged today, with the assertion that the Soviet people "unanimously" support his expulsion and that, in the words of one writer of a letter to the editor, "It serves the traitor right."

Privately, some Russian citizens expressed bewilderment at the sensational turn of events and shock at some crude wording in the exile decree. And yet they consider exile itself relatively lenient treatment, in view of the Government's hostility toward Mr. Solzhenitsyn.

Several prominent dissidents spoke out against the deportation. Mr. Sakharov demanded that Mr. Solzhenitsyn be allowed to return to publish his books in his own country. ∎

> ## The 55-year-old Nobel Prize laureate refused to acknowledge the charge . . .

ally disappointing. True, of the two, Mrs. Jong's "Fear of Flying" holds together longer, and even after it falls apart, it remains unusual in several respects. I can't remember ever before feeling quite so free to identify my own feelings with those of a female protagonist—which would suggest that Isadora Wing, with her unfettered yearnings for sexual satisfaction and her touching struggle for identity and self-confidence, is really more of a person than a woman (which isn't to deny in the least Mrs. Jong's underlying point that it's harder to become a person if you're a woman than it is if you're a man). Though "Fear of Flying" isn't meant to be an autobiography, it certainly has the ring of candid confession.

As for the appealing Midwesterner we meet at the beginning of Jane Howard's autobiographical report: she goes every-where, and gets nowhere; she reports everything, and tells us nothing. In her travels back and forth and around America to find out how the liberation movement has touched different woman, Miss Howard is forever asking questions and scribbling down answers; but, with few exceptions, the people she talks to aren't all that interesting, and the manner in which she runs together everything they say makes them even less so (one often wonders if Miss Howard's assiduous scribbling didn't make her subjects ill at ease).

Pretty soon, the vignettes begin to seem pointless and precious. Tedium sets in. We start to squirm. Certainly it's interesting to hear the movement has touched all American women—including Jane Howard. But for 400 pages? No thanks. ∎

The Motorcycles of Your Mind

Christopher Lehmann-Haupt

ZEN AND THE ART OF MOTORCYCLE MAINTENANCE. An Inquiry Into Values. By Robert M. Pirsig. 412 pages. Morrow. $7.95.

I'm not certain at what point I stopped reading this peculiar book with the special boredom and disdain I have come to feel for philosophical discourses that attempt to wed the technology of the Occident with the spiritualism of the Orient. It may have been as early as the Author's Note, in which Mr. Pirsig informs us that his "Zen and the Art of Motorcycle Maintenance" is neither in any way to "be associated with that great body of factual information relating to orthodox Zen Buddhist practice" nor "very factual on motorcycles either." Or it may have been when I learned that Mr. Pirsig hasn't written what might be expected from his subtitle, "An Inquiry Into Values"—an autobiographical account of a cross-country motorcycle trip he once took with his 11-year-old son, Chris.

In any case, when I discovered that the narrator is being haunted by a ghost from his past named Phaedrus, I grew mildly curious about what was going on. When I caught on that this ghost is stalking the narrator and his son much as the goblin pursues the father and child on horseback in Goethe's famous ballad "Erlkönig," I began to read with active interest. When I realized that this ghost named Phaedrus is actually an earlier personification of the narrator that was driven insane by some philosophical quest he once undertook and who was "killed" by electric-shock therapy, I utterly forgot that I was reading a book called "Zen and the Art of Motorcycle Maintenance." And when I began to see that all this was merely preparation for an account of Phaedrus's philosophical quest, and that this quest would be nothing less than an attempt to wed the technology of the West to the spiritualism of the Far East—just as the book's title had originally threatened—I couldn't have stopped reading Mr. Pirsig's "Inquiry Into Values" even if I'd recalled my

(cont'd. on next page)

209

ARTS & ENTERTAINMENT

(cont'd. from previous page)
special boredom and disdain.

And yet however impressive are the seductive powers with which Mr. Pirsig engages us in his motorcycle trip, they are nothing compared to the skill with which he interests us in his philosophic trip.

It all sounds a little baffling, I know, but take my word for it: it makes almost perfect sense as you read it. In fact, I now regret that I lack the expertise in philosophy to put Mr. Pirsig's ideas to a proper test, for this book may very well be a profoundly important one—a great one even—full of insights into our most perplexing contemporary dilemmas. I just don't know.

But whatever its true philosophical worth, it is intellectual entertainment of the highest order. Why, when I came down off the philosophical mountain that Mr. Pirsig climbs (naturally, he and Chris climb a literal mountain at the same time), I had even grown interested in motorcycle maintenance and the author's homely little talks on how to tinker with machines without losing one's philosophical cool. And now I even see what he means when he writes, "The study of the art of motorcycle maintenance is really a miniature study of the art of rationality itself….The motorcycle is primarily a mental phenomenon…. The real cycle you're working on is a cycle called 'yourself.'" Go, philosopher, go! ■

Criminals at Large

Newgate Callendar

Maybe, strictly speaking, it is not a mystery book. But it does have action, suspense and, at the end, a holocaust. And it is exceedingly well-written. So don't miss "Carrie" by Stephen King (Doubleday, $5.95), a first novel and one guaranteed to give you a chill.

King does more than tell a story. He is a schoolteacher himself, and he gets into Carrie's mind as well as into the minds of her classmates. He also knows a thing or two about symbolism—blood symbolism especially. That this is a first novel is amazing. King writes with the kind of surety normally associated only with veteran writers. This mixture of science-fiction, the occult, secondary-school sociology, kids good and bad and genetics turns out to be an extraordinary mixture. ■

ALL THE PRESIDENT'S MEN

Doris Kearns

By Carl Bernstein and Bob Woodward
Illustrated. 349 pp. New York: Simon & Schuster. $8.95.

At first reading, "All the President's Men," the third-person narrative by the two Washington Post reporters whose investigative reporting earned their paper a Pulitzer Prize, is a detective story. It turns Watergate into a fast-moving mystery, a whodunit written with ease, if not elegance.

It begins, as mysteries do, with a crime—the burglary on June 17, 1972, of the Democratic National Committee headquarters. As the author-sleuths retrace the crime their investigation leads from a simple break-in to a massive strategy of spying and sabotage—from five petty criminals to all the President's men. Woodward and Bernstein have rigorously reduced their tale to essentials, stripped it of introspection, philosophizing and background detail.

But the narrative form imposed upon the material obscures important themes in a book whose subject is, after all, history not fiction. We urge the young detectives on, forgetting that the scene is not Perry Mason's courtroom where justice triumphs and order is restored, and that the sleuths are not Holmes and Watson, but two young reporters left by default to play the hero.

A daily newspaper can't wait for the definitive account of events, competition demands taking risks. Yet, inadequate, misguided or wrong information hastily printed, can ruin careers or damage a reputation beyond repair. Integrity and professionalism demand accuracy. Competition created an energy of pursuit, and of course, the pleasure of breaking new ground played a role in deciding how to handle the story. But the pleasure was joined by a deeply-felt consciousness of the story's importance and significance for the country. Individual interests and public interest coincided.

"We stand by our story," Washington Post editor Ben Bradlee wrote, at a time when the reporters themselves were in despair. Discussing the subpoenas the Committee to Re-elect the President issued for the reporters' notes, Bradlee said: "Of course we're going to fight this one all the way up." ■

Bob Woodward (left) and Carl Bernstein in the Washington Post newsroom in 1973.

Inside Look at People Magazine

Philip H. Dougherty

The first People magazine staff meeting, February 1974.

The first publication from that giant company planned for only newsstand sale; the first weekly magazine since 1955 to reach a paid circulation of one million, and the first magazine in publishing history to attempt to start out with an initial single-copy circulation of one million, People is also a magazine whose goals were set before its name, content or editorial thrust were decided on.

The parameters for People, Malcolm B. Ochs, Time's marketing director for the magazine development group, told his audience in Chicago, were not only that it be a weekly with a starting rate base of one million and have single-copy sales only, but that it also operate with "a stringent editorial budget," reach a high female audience with reasonably high demographs primarily through supermarket sales and also have a good pass-along audience.

It is a "relaxing" magazine, Mr. Ochs said, one that can be picked up for 10 minutes or an hour, thumbed through, started anywhere. "An impulse usage, analogous to its impulse purchase."

A total of 100,000 copies of an actual issue were distributed to 10 markets.

"I won't bore you with statistics," said Mr. Ochs, "but when we got through tabulating them, it was clear that we had a hit on our hands."

Writers and Politicians

E. L. Doctorow

Norman Mailer during a Democratic rally in 1970 in New York City.

Watching all the candidates compete in the Presidential primaries, I see curious likenesses between politicians and writers. In the first place both normally address themselves to populations rather than individuals. Writers and politicians are one person speaking to many. Of course a difference is that we writers take office first and then we create our constituencies. That is to be a shade more arrogant than the politicians. But we have a saving grace: The power we assume is of no practical use to ourselves. If we are lucky we have our greatest influence when we are dead.

Powered by the media, politicians have an outsized mythological identity, or a capacity to bemuse. Writers however invariably disappoint their constituents when shaking hands, being not in their persons as charged with life as in their books.

Of course there are those outsized personalities in the republic of letters who have had a few media infusions of their own. But they are stars of the aesthetic rather than the real, and so their power is only a kind of mimicry of the practical power that politicians have.

Norman Mailer, a writer who has always been fascinated by political power, actually tried once to be a politician. He ran for Mayor of New York. He failed. Gore Vidal, a writer from a political family, once ran for Congress. He failed. Some years ago Upton Sinclair ran for Governor of California. In all cases these writers failed. The reasons for their failure are worth investigating. Perhaps in this country there is a public conviction that literature is play and that those who practice it cannot be taken seriously. Or that even if literature is serious, it can be taken only before the onset of responsible adulthood. After that there's no time.

Politics in this country used to have a literary quality, at least insofar as rhetoric was practiced on the campaign trails in the 19th century. Today's politicians are dreary malapropists who have such a low regard for the English language that even when they are demagogues they can't infuriate us. They are instinctive masters of doublespeak, however, of self-serving euphemism.

Writers, by contrast, have such high regard for language that they believe it is an instrument for tearing people out of their ordinary perceptions and forcing them to see and feel in ways that are genuinely alarming.

Nevertheless politicians are born knowing exactly what writers know about language: that it can change reality. They know that history does not exist except as it is composed, that good and evil are construed, that there is no outrage, no monstrousness that cannot be made reasonable and logical and virtuous, and no shining act that cannot be turned to disgrace.

W. H. Auden complained that poetry never changed anything, and said that all the anti-Fascist poems written in the 1930's did nothing to stop Hitler. So our proposition comes to focus: Writers and politicians are mirror nations of each other. It may not hold for some countries of one socialist persuasion or another—we can point to the poet Chairman Mao or the poet Ho Chi Minh, for example—but for the most part double citizenship in power and poetry will mean treason to one or to the other. ∎

AWARD BRINGS U.S. A SWEEP OF HONORS

Robert B. Semple Jr.

STOCKHOLM, Oct. 21—Saul Bellow won the Nobel Prize for Literature today, giving Americans a clean sweep of all five Nobel Prizes awarded this year.

No Peace Prize was given. Even so, this was the first time in the 76 years in which the awards have been made that all recipients have been citizens of the same country.

Mr. Bellow is the first American to win the prize for literature since John Steinbeck, in 1962. Mr. Bellow was cited, in the words of the Swedish Academy, "for the human understanding and subtle analysis of contemporary culture that are combined in his work."

In a statement accompanying the two-line citation, the academy said that Mr. Bellow's style had gone through two distinct stages, the first representing an "emancipation" of American writing from the "hard-boiled" but increasingly "routine" style of the 1930's, the second representing Mr. Bellow's improvement on himself.

The academy singled out "Henderson the Rain King" as "the writer's most imaginative expedition." It went on to say that that book showed as did most of Mr. Bellow's works a fascination with a variety of settings—in the case of "Henderson," the jungles of Africa—as well as a continuing, lively interest in his most identifiable subject, the "man with no foothold."

Yet the academy stressed that what had given the Bellow "anti-heroes" their "lasting stature" had been their courage, the courage of a man "who keeps on trying to find a foothold during his wanderings in our tottering world, one who can never relinquish his faith that the value of life depends on its dignity, not its success."

"A primitive part of me," Mr. Bellow said at a news conference, "the child in me is delighted. The adult in me is skeptical." ∎

A Taut Novel of Disorder

A BOOK OF COMMON PRAYER

Joyce Carol Oates

By Joan Didion. 272 pp. New York: Simon and Schuster. $8.95.

Joan Didion (right) with her husband, John Gregory Dunne, and daughter, Quintana Roo Dunne, in 1976.

In the title essay of her superb collection, "Slouching Towards Bethlehem" (1968), Joan Didion draws back briefly from her painful study of the Haight-Ashbury dropouts to comment on the possible meaning of the "social hemorrhaging" she has been observing at close range. The drifting, inarticulate children of the 1960's, drug-besotted and prematurely aged, take on for Didion an almost allegorical significance. They are the pitiful casualties of an immense and perhaps inexplicable social change—an "atomization" prophesied by such visionary poets as Yeats, who wrote in "The Second Coming," "Things fall apart; the center cannot hold;/Mere anarchy is loosed upon the world." Such apocalyptic murmurings have always been with us, the complacent or indifferent are quick to say; what genuine evidence have we for making such statements? Joan Didion's books offer the evidence. Her third and most ambitious novel, "A Book of Common Prayer," investigates the consequences of this breakdown over the past two decades, particularly on parents and children.

Charlotte is an attractive woman in her early 40's who is married to an attractive and very successful San Francisco lawyer involved, in ways not directly explored, with the international sale of weapons. She insists that she is not "political"—and it is, ironically, her refusal to see that she is political that brings about her death; she knows that something is always going on in the world but "believed that it would turn out all right." On a blank map of the world she would have difficulty matching names with countries.

So it is appropriate that Charlotte Douglas, cut adrift and searching for her daughter, comes to Boca Grande, a Central American country that is as close to a blank as a country can be. Rather like the Southern California Didion has explored so relentlessly in "Slouching Towards Bethlehem" and her second novel, "Play It as It Lays" (1970), Boca Grande admits of no past. In a state of shock, Charlotte Douglas arrives in this nullity of a country and, after a series of comic and grotesque misadventures with its leading citizens, she dies abruptly and senselessly—shot in the back during one of the colorful revolutions.

Joan Didion is not, of course, alone in her passionate investigation of the atomization of contemporary society. But she is one of the very few writers of our time who approaches her terrible subject with absolute seriousness, with fear and humility and awe. Her powerful irony is often sorrowful rather than clever; the language of "A Book of Common Prayer," like that of "Play It as It Lays," is spare, sardonic, elliptical, understated. Melodrama is the nature of Didion's world, but very little emotion is expressed, perhaps because emotion itself has become atrophied.

Some of the best parts of "A Book of Common Prayer" are incidental to the plot, but typically Didion: an asinine conversation between Charlotte, her former husband and an F.B.I. man who questions them about their daughter; a brilliant description of the Boca Grande airport and of the queer opaque light of Central America. The doomed elopement of Charlotte and her alcoholic former husband involves a dizzying succession of scenes in cities in the South—Birmingham, New Orleans, Greenville—which unfold in a surreal, diffracted manner.

Has the novel any significant flaws? I would have wished it longer, fuller: I would have liked to know more about the daughter, for instance. But Joan Didion's art has always been one of understatement and indirection, of emotion withheld. Like her narrator, she has been an articulate witness to the most stubborn and intractable truths of our time, a memorable voice, partly eulogistic, partly despairing; always in control. ■

213

Anaïs Nin, Author Whose Diaries Depicted Intellectual Life, Dead

C. Gerald Fraser

Anaïs Nin, the French-born novelist and diarist, died Friday night of cancer at Cedars-Sinai Hospital in Los Angeles. She would have been 74 years old next month.

Miss Nin began writing in the early 1930's and produced criticism, essays and fiction. But her literary reputation blossomed with the publication of the six volumes of her diaries.

The first, "The Diary of Anaïs Nin, 1931-1934," was published in 1966. Miss Nin had been working on the seventh volume at the time of her death.

Other prominent works included "Ladders to Fire," "Children in the House of Love," "Under a Glass Bell," "The Novel of the Future" and "Collages."

She began writing her diaries when she was 11 years old as letters to her father, from whom her mother was estranged. In addition to the diaries' pictures of the Bohemian and intellectual life of Paris in the 1930's and of New York during and after World War II, her journals became widely known for their view of the perspective of a Western woman and artist struggling to fulfill herself.

Miss Nin also lectured often in her last decade at colleges and universities. "The young recognize me as a precursor," she said. "They identify me with my struggles, with my self-liberation, with the kind of writing I do."

She had no children, but she wrote in her diary: "Nature connived me to be a man's woman. Not a mother to children, but to men."

And in an interview in 1975, she said: "My maternal feelings were never an unlived part of me. I placed them instead on helping young artists."

Some of the artists and nonartists she encountered included Marguerite Young, Timothy Leary, Lawrence Durrell, Jack Kerouac, Allen Ginsberg and James Leo Herlihy. ■

VLADIMIR NABOKOV, AUTHOR OF 'LOLITA' AND 'ADA,' IS DEAD

Alden Whitman

Vladimir Nabokov, a giant in the world of literature, died Saturday at the age of 78. The author of such works as "Lolita," "Pnin" and "Ada" succumbed to a virus infection in the suite at the Palace Hotel in Montreux, Switzerland, where he and his wife, Véra, had lived for the last 18 years.

Mrs. Nabokov, who was with him when he died, disclosed the death yesterday and said that her husband "had been very sick for the past year and a half. He had some good moments but was very ill," she said, adding that the exact virus that killed him had not been identified.

Mr. Nabokov was born in Russia and settled in the United States in 1939, living here until 1959. With the publication of "Lolita" in 1958, he received popular recognition. His later works, combined with the publication of earlier novels in translation from the original Russian, saw him elevated to the first rank of world authors.

Readers recognized Mr. Nabokov's technical brilliance and mastery of form, but were frequently baffled by his irrepressible sense of flippancy and his penchant for parody. Was he, it was asked, a gifted artificer entranced by fun and games, or was he a creative and profound artist?

The perplexity sprang in part from the fact that Mr. Nabokov possessed such a cultivated mind (he was Cambridge-educated and a Cornell professor) and had such a cosmopolitan upbringing ("I was a perfectly normal trilingual child") that he tended to emphasize the paradoxes and humor of life rather than its congruities and dolorousness. "Every artist," he once remarked, "sees the comic and cosmic side of things."

Indeed, his explosion to prominence was based on a paradox, the public reaction to his novel "Lolita," which was published in the United States in 1958, when he was 59 years old. Intended as a metaphor for the eternal quest for innocence that is resolved in satiric terms, the book sold in the thousands as an erotic story of Dolores Haze, a 12-year-old nymphet (the authors coinage) and Humbert Humbert, her middle-aged pursuer.

The serious novel succeeded for salacious reasons, which, of course, amused its author, but it also cost him many hours of explanation. "My knowledge of nymphets is purely scholarly," he was obliged to say. Ironically, the royalties gave him long-sought freedom to devote himself wholly to writing.

"Lolita," like most Nabokov stories, can be read on several levels: as a narrative, as an exercise in logodaedaly, as a search for meaning and truth, as a tantalizing flight of imagination, as an exploration of a dreamlike confusion of time and place, and as an elaborate spoof. "He is not the kind of novelist whom you sit down to with a Scotch or an apple," Anthony Burgess, the British critic, declared. ■

Author Toni Morrison in 1977.

SEPTEMBER 6, 1977

TO RIDE THE AIR TO AFRICA

John Leonard

SONG OF SOLOMON.
By Toni Morrison. 337 pages.
Alfred A. Knopf. $8.95.

Sometimes you get lucky. Of the 20 years or so I've spent pretending to be an adult, only five have been devoted to book reviewing. And yet I was permitted to review Vladimir Nabokov's "Lolita" for my college newspaper; to review Joseph Heller's "Catch-22," Doris Lessing's "The Golden Notebook" and Günter Grass's "The Tin Drum" for a radio station in California; and to review John Cheever's "Bullet Park," Gabriel Garcia Marquez's "One Hundred Years of Solitude" and Maxine Hong Kingston's "The Woman Warrior" for The Times. That's luck. These are special books. About them, a reviewer tends to feel touchy and possessive—as if, together, they constitute much of what I know and think, and to give away their magic to strangers is somehow to give away my advantage in moral and esthetic realms.

Toni Morrison's "Song of Solomon" belongs in this small company of special books that are a privilege to review. It may be foolishly fussed over as a Black Novel, or a Women's Novel, or an Important New Novel by a Black Woman. It is closer in spirit and style to "One Hundred Years of Solitude" and "The Woman Warrior." It builds, out of history and language and myth, to music. It just takes off. If Ralph Ellison's "Invisible Man" went underground, Toni Morrison's Milkman flies.

Unlike her first two novels, "The Bluest Eye" and "Sula," most of "Song of Solomon" is written from a male point of view. (All three novels, by the way, have very little to do with the white world. It is there, of course, a condition and an oppression, but she won't be deflected from the truths of her characters to score a political point. They must work themselves out according to what they know and feel. They are not allowed merely to be victims.) So it's into the bars and barbershops, and out on the streets at riot-time, and inside Milkman's head for sex.

All this, in tone and detail, is fine. The talk is a marvel of bravura and nuance. And black men may be relieved to hear that Miss Morrison isn't as hard on their case as, for instance, Ntozake Shange has been.

Milkman goes South, thinking he looks for secret gold, actually plunging into family history and racial memory, into dream and myth, walking with his city shoes where the rocks talk and the sweet gum trees are full of bobcats and Sugarman becomes Solomon becomes Shalimar, and you can ride the air to Africa.

From the beginning, when Robert Smith of the North Carolina Mutual Life Insurance Company can't fly on the day Macon Dead Jr., is born, to the end, when Milkman "fleet and bright as a lodestar" wheels in the night sky, Toni Morrison is in control of her book, her poetry. Out of the decoding of a children's song, something heroic is regained; out of terror, an understanding of possibility and a leap of faith; out of quest, the naming of our fathers and ourselves. The first two-thirds of "Song of Solomon" are merely wonderful. The last 100 pages are a triumph. ∎

OCTOBER 16, 1977

BYWAYS OF A RUNNER

J. Herbert Silverman

GREENWICH—James Fixx, a chronicler of running and a former senior editor on Life magazine, has written what may be the definitive book on the subject, "The Complete History of Running." Published by Random House, it is due out on Oct. 24, the day after the running of the New York Marathon. Participants in that taxing race will include 4,000 contestants, including the author, competing over a traditional 26-mile course through the five boroughs of New York City.

Joggers tend to run in groups, whether along the beaches of Long Island Sound, the reservoir paths of Central Park, or even at sea. Mr. Fixx, who recently sailed to Europe aboard the Queen Elizabeth 2, covered 10 miles, or 50 laps, a day circling the deck in company with other passengers and a few crew members.

Mr. Fixx's book takes in running's major components. In addition to history, health effects (sometimes in dispute), equipment (rapidly becoming more sophisticated and expensive), it offers sidelights on the cultural aspects and social amenities of the sport.

Jogging is a demanding sport, in which endurance, not speed, is the goal. But it has its lighter side and some social attributes with connections to weight-watching, concern with the environment and recreation.

"If it's raining," Mr. Fixx said, "you have to beat off well-wishers who are worried that you'll get soaked to the skin, not realizing that this can be half the fun. But most people just wave. Women runners sometimes are the target of sexist remarks, but after a while tend to shrug them off."

As for how Mr. Fixx got started running, he said:

"Some years ago when I was about 35 and weighed 220, I pulled a tendon playing tennis. Someone prescribed running, something I had only done in service wearing combat boots. I entered the Greenwich five-mile race on Memorial Day in 1970 and came in last in a field of 50. The winner was a man in his late 60's. I guess that did it."

Since then he has brought his weight down to 159 pounds.

NOBEL PRIZE TO I.B. SINGER

Christopher Lehmann-Haupt

Isaac Bashevis Singer, the Yiddish master of storytelling, was awarded the 1978 Nobel Prize for Literature. Singer, who was born into a Polish rabbinical family on July 14, 1904, emigrated to America in 1935, the year that his first major novel, "Satan in Goray," was published. Since then, always writing in Yiddish and publishing much of his work in serial form in The Jewish Daily Forward, he has produced a dozen novels, the best known of which make up his family-chronicle trilogy, "The Family Moskat" (1950), "The Manor" (1967), and "The Estate" (1965); numerous short-story collections; a memoir, "In My Father's Court" (1966); and several children's books. The Swedish Academy cited Singer for his "impassioned narratives which, with roots in a Polish-Jewish cultural tradition, bring universal human conditions to life," which is another way of saying what admirers have always observed about Singer; that he has made of the East European Jew, especially the Hasid, an exemplar of the suffering modern man who has been exiled from his divine inheritance.

But if influence and appeal are standards of Nobel excellence, then Singer is a worthy choice. For he has carried on the tradition of such Yiddish story-telling masters as Mendele, Aleichem, Peretz and Asch, and he has influenced a generation of American-Jewish writers now thriving in his wake. As for his appeal: one need only note that any writer who can command such a following in such disparate publications as the Jewish Daily Forward, the New Yorker, Commentary and Playboy can scarcely be accused of cultural parochialism. ∎

Joan Crawford with daughter Christina in 1944.

Books of The Times:
MOMMIE DEAREST

Christopher Lehmann-Haupt

MOMMIE DEAREST. By Christina Crawford. 286 pages Illustrated. Morrow $6.95.

JOAN CRAWFORD: A Biography. By Bob Thomas. 314 pages Illustrated. Simon & Schuster $10.95.

They wear matching velvet jumpers and flowers in their hair. Christina later wrote a tell-all book entitled, "Mommie Dearest," about her unhappy childhood.

One difference between Hollywood children and the rest of us is that they go ahead and write the exposés of their parents that we only dream of doing in fits of adolescent transport. But who is to say: Perhaps Christina Crawford is justified in committing "Mommie Dearest" against her late adoptive mother, the movie queen Joan Crawford.

It is one thing that Miss Crawford beat her incessantly and visited upon her cruel and unusual punishments for minor childhood transgressions; all too many children have faced and survived gusts of parental rage, whatever the cause.

(cont'd. on next page)

(cont'd. from previous page)

It is quite another thing that in her last will and testament, Miss Crawford cut off her daughter without a cent "for reasons which are well known to [her]," after Christina had thought they had achieved a reconciliation.

That was punching from beyond the grave, and there's a certain poetic justice in seeing "Mommie Dearest" atop the bestseller list, earning for Christina and her brother what her mother's last gratuitous slap denied them. And never mind all Christina's blather about forgiving Joan and loving her despite all.

This book is Gretel's revenge on the ugly old witch, and one might just as well read it as such.

Still, there's something about "Mommie Dearest" that leaves a bad taste in the mouth. What am I saying? Everything about the book tastes bad—from its whining, self-dramatizing tone to its seizures of preposterous stuffiness.

Everything about the book tastes bad

Moreover, it's hard to escape the feeling that if Christina had been as severely damaged by her childhood as she claims to have been, then she would never have been able to achieve such successes at the schools in which she was imprisoned as making high grades and getting elected to the student council.

"Mommie Dearest" is scarcely a recommendation for corporal punishment, but there is something curiously Dickensian about the pluck with which Christina keeps bouncing up and fighting back.

But what finally sinks the book is Miss Crawford's refusal to see her mother whole—to understand what it was about Joan Crawford's life that impelled her to beat and degrade her children.

To forgive requires understanding—if I may heave up a cliché—and understanding Joan Crawford requires considerably more than perceiving that she wanted children merely for the sake of show, to summon forth with a clap of the hands so that they might bow and curtsy and simper, "I love you, Mommie dearest." ∎

JANUARY 28, 1979

Poet's Prose
JOHNNY PANIC AND THE BIBLE OF DREAMS

Margaret Atwood

Short Stories, Prose and Diary Excerpts. By Sylvia Plath. 313 pp. New York: Harper & Row. $10.95.

When a major work by a major writer is published posthumously, no one bats an eye. Minor works by minor writers presumably don't get published until the author has been dead long enough to have become quaint. "Johnny Panic and the Bible of Dreams" is a minor work by a major writer and it's the contrast that causes niggling. Whom does such a publication benefit? Not the author, and not the author's reputation, which is doing very well without it. Not the general reader hitherto innocent of the Sylvia Plath opus and myth who may stumble upon it and wonder what all the shouting is about. I suppose the answer is "the student," if by "student" is meant any reader sympathetic enough to Plath's work to have read most of it already and to be interested in foreshadowings, cross-references, influences and insights. And this is the kind of audience "Johnny Panic" assumes. It's a prose catch-all, composed of short stories, short prose essays and journal entries, and as such it ought to round out one's knowledge of the writer and, perhaps, offer some surprises. Luckily it does both.

It was a shock akin to seeing the Queen in a bikini to learn that Sylvia Plath, an incandescent poet of drastic seriousness, had two burning ambitions: to be a highly paid travel journalist and to be a widely published writer of magazine fiction, either of The New Yorker or—can it be?—of the Ladies' Home Journal variety. (Poetry she considered a mere escape, a self-indulgence, an indulgence in self, and as such unreal, because she was not totally convinced of her own worth or even of her own existence.)

On one level "Johnny Panic" is the record of an apprenticeship. It should bury forever the romantic notion of genius blossoming forth like flowers. Few writers of major stature can have worked so hard, for so long, with so little visible result. The breakthrough, when it came, had been laboriously earned many times over. But there's more to "Johnny Panic" than juvenilia. The writing varies widely in quality and interest, or rather in the quality of the interest; for although the young Sylvia Plath squeezed out some fairly dismal stories, as most young writers do, all the pieces presented here are revealing.

Even when she was trying to be trite, Sylvia Plath could not conceal the disconcerting insights into her own emotional mainsprings that characterize her poetry. The unevenness of the stories is often the result of a clash between the chosen formula and the hidden message that forces its way through, seemingly despite the writer.

The stories are arranged chronologically but in reverse order. This creates an archeological effect: the reader is made to dig backward in time, downward into a remarkable mind, so that the last, earliest story, "Among the Bumblebees" (a wistful story about a little girl's worship of her father who dies mysteriously), emerges like the final gold-crowned skeleton at the bottom of the tomb—the king all those others were killed to protect. Which it is. ∎

MARCH 22, 1970

DON'T CALL HER BOGEY'S BABY

Tom Burke

She isn't even mildly fatigued. For eight nerve-shredding weeks in Detroit, Lauren Bacall has been trying out her first musical, "Applause," nightly belting a dozen songs in her big applejack-brandy alto and swooping through complex dances with such campy insouciance that houses full of taciturn auto magnates forget all about Bette Davis and "All About Eve," on which the show is based, and end up at curtain calls on their feet, cheering as if the Tigers had just won the pennant. But in a few days, she will have to make New York forget Davis, too. And in a few hours, she will have to learn a whole new final scene. And room service is late with her breakfast. And none of it fazes her in the least.

Clearly, she is exhilarated, flying high, and she talks nonstop. She sounds tough; but the growl is chastened by her unmistakable intelligence, her boundless good humor, her great, grudging good will. Twenty-five years ago, the Warners flacks thought up her professional name, but she is still Betty Perske of the Bronx to anybody who has known her more than an hour, and she isn't about to let you forget that.

"Listen," she begins, folding herself into a velvet sofa, "do me a favor, do not give me that old thing about 'Tell me the story of your life,' or 'How was it you were discovered?' or 'How did you first meet Bogey?' Because I will upchuck, right here. I mean, who cares any more, what does it matter?

"I'll tell you what does interest me: that this show has begun a whole new cycle in my life. No, it's more than a cycle; it's literally a second life. It's as though the last 25 years never happened. I mean, I lived one complete life that had a beginning, a middle and an end, and has nothing whatever to do with my life now.

"First there was my career, which began well, I had great impact, and then nothing but obstacles, never the best parts at the best times. Jack Warner convinced me very early that I was no good, worthless, rotten to the core. He

Lauren Bacall in "Applause."

was terrific at that. What I learned about acting, I learned from Mr. Bogart. I learned from a master, and that, God knows, has stood me in very good stead.

"I think I've damn well earned the right to be judged on my own," she says evenly. "Just a few days ago, there's Earl Wilson, writing a column about Bogart's 'Baby.' Jesus! I mean, is it ever going to stop? What have I lived on for, if I can't have something that's mine? Even when I'm out with a man, people come up and start talking about Humphrey Bogart!

"Anyway, with this show, I will hopefully be given that great gift at last—freedom. It doesn't seem very much to ask, somehow." She is smiling again, speaking almost girlishly. "For the first time, I'm working at full functioning capacity. The part came along at precisely the moment I was best able to cope with it, fully able to understand it. I feel so damn right on that stage! I think I'm finally fulfilling the promise I showed and then never realized.

"From the time I was 15, I had one heroine, Bette Davis. She was everything to me, I literally worshiped that woman. And now, that I am playing a part that she played, and was so marvelous in—I tell you, it is too peculiar. They haven't got me an understudy yet. They must think I'm Man Mountain Dean. Well, that's all right, because nobody's gonna get this part away from me! Over my dead body they'll get it!"

During this, a waiter has brought breakfast, and Bacall has managed to clear a place for the tray, tip generously, and consume half a plate of eggs and sausages with only five small breath-pauses. She has also briefly discussed Adlai Stevenson, whom she considers the second greatest man of our time, and Bobby Kennedy, whom she considers the greatest ("When he went, I went, I will never recover from that, never"), dissected the sixties ("The crappiest decade in history, all our best men murdered, what's fascinating about it?"), dismissed pot and nudity ("okay for others, but they're not for me"), and ground a firm heel into Washington, D.C. "I've seriously thought of living there. It's where everything that affects all our lives happens. But right now, baby, it's a wasteland.

"What matters," she suddenly announces, "is to live your life. To press on and live your life. And that goes for me, and you, and . . . and your goddam cat, if you've got one!" Then she is gone, grinning, down the hall to the elevator and the theater, to live hers.

'The Most Striking New American Play'

Walter Kerr

I wish to record a sin of omission. I happened to miss John Guare's "The House of Blue Leaves" when it opened and have only now got down to the Off Broadway Truck and Warehouse Theater to check it out. That was not only remiss of me, it was masochistic of me. Here I was sitting through dozens of plays that seem to have taken tedium as brides, and there was this enchantingly zany, desperately sad, thoroughly original little farce waiting for the fortunate all the time.

Mr. Guare makes mistakes in the play, true; though that is scarcely surprising considering the unexpectedness of what he is doing. For one thing, he doesn't know when to shut up. He makes a very inventive series of jokes, for instance, about a girl who will sleep with a man before marriage but will not cook for him, on the theory that she's bad in bed but great in the kitchen and is naturally holding out on the best. He is wrong to pursue the conceit, which has a certain perverse sense to it, to the point where the man demands she make his breakfast and the wench replies, "I'm not that kind of girl." He corrupts his own inventiveness when he turns it into vaudeville.

But forget that. Mr. Guare has an exceptional gift for the bizarre phrase, antic gesture, improbable stage picture that will turn, with a slight twist of one or another brainlobe, into plausible and sometimes distressing reality. There are few funnier sights available today than the spectacle of three savagely determined nuns clambering all over the locked grillwork that protects Harold Gould's apartment. Mr. Gould is playing a defeated song-writer ("Where is the devil in Evelyn/What's it doing in Angela's eyes?") who looks as though he'd been spun around in an automatic washing machine without any water in it, who is tied to a mad wife and unable to unload her (his wife refuses to leave the apartment because her fingernails are all different lengths), and who is passionately auditioning for an emissary from a Hollywood friend (the emissary is an ecstatically benevolent kewpie-doll brunette who, unfortunately, keeps losing the batteries to her

hearing-aid and is too embarrassed to say so; she is deaf throughout the proceedings). Each of the creatures who invades the disintegrating composer's pad is pumped to the size of a comic balloon yet keeps some link to the bitter earth, even the nuns are reasonably accounted for, though two of them do come to untimely ends.

What is most impressive about the charade, for all its frayed edges, is that its greatest extravagances somehow reinforce the real pain at its center. The buffoonery swerves like a boomerang and heads straight for the ache; I don't know when I have felt so keenly for a stage figure as I did for Mr.

Gould, brilliant in the part, at evening's end. Anne Meara, a loving girl with a lower lip like a lunging cash-register drawer, is splendid as the sleep-in but cook-out; Katherine Helmond is both amusing and affecting as the mad wife; Margaret Linn is delightfully impervious with all her batteries gone dead; and there are others nearly as good hustling in and out. This is not merely novel work. It is a new kind of double vision, Mr. Guare's own, and it not only represents a kind of quantum leap forward from his previous work but is, in my opinion, the most striking new American play of the season. Accept its occasional gaffes, and admire, admire. ∎

Sondheim Explains Craft of Lyricist

John S. Wilson

Stephen Sondheim in 1970.

Stephen Sondheim, composer and lyricist of "Follies" and "Company," gave a compact seminar on the art of lyric writing Sunday evening, as part of the Lyrics and Lyricists series at the 92nd Street Y.

Although he spent most of the evening seated at a table, talking, he moved to a piano to play and sing from time to time where he managed to range from a reading of his first lyric, written for a school show at the George School ("excruciatingly dull"

was his adult view of the lyric) to three versions of an ending for "Company," all of which were abandoned.

"I tend to sing very loud," he said when he sat down at the piano, "always right in pitch, and I tend to write in keys that are just out of my range."

Mr. Sondheim described lyric writing as "an elegant form of puzzle." "And I'm a great puzzle fan," he noted.

The major influences on his writing, he said, were Oscar Hammerstein II, who put him through a six-year course of writing for the musical theater while he was in school and college; Burt Shevelove, with whom he wrote "A Funny Thing Happened on the Way to the Forum"; and Arthur Laurents, with whom he has written four shows.

He touched on the need to consider the actor's tongue and teeth when writing lyrics, the importance of last lines and last words, the uses and danger of rhyme and humor.

When he wanted to cite examples of what not to do in writing lyrics, Mr. Sondheim went to his own work as readily as he did to demonstrate how it should be done. Rhymes, he said, are useful when you have nothing to say.

"And anytime you hear alliteration in a lyric, get suspicious," he warned, quoting from his score for "West Side Story": "'I feel pretty, I feel fizzy and funny and fine.'"

"Somebody didn't have anything to say," he emphasized. ∎

WHY MAKE ST. MATTHEW DANCE?
FOR THE FUN OF IT

Walter Kerr

Why make St. Matthew dance? Specifically, why make St. Matthew St. Vitus dance? Well, surely, for the obvious reason that after all these years of hearing and rehearing, of exegesis and apologia and conceptualization, we need some sense of a man—whether Matthew or Jesus—who moved, who put his feet against the earth with a push, who knew wheat as wheat and not as a noun in a parable, who took pleasure in the tangible, the muscular, the rhythmic, even in the giddy. Did no one in Galilee ever hum a little song to himself, snap his fingers, as he walked the roads?

I mustn't make the show sound self-important or woozily prophetic, things it almost never is (not until the last 15 minutes). But composer Stephen Schwartz and adapter-director John-Michael Tebelak, in conceiving of the return of the Prodigal Son as the occasion for a maddened polka determined to turn itself into a cake walk, in cockily arranging an exultant "Let's hear it for the master!" when the master—in a patter-song parable—remits a debt due him from a servant, and in using ventriloquists' dummies and magicians' exploding flowers and vaudevillians' sandpaper slithering to underscore beatitudes, are restlessly on the prowl for a visual vocabulary, and a scattershot of song, that will make the too-familiar become active again, alive on its toes and happy to be up there.

Jesus, a red heart painted between his eyebrows and a modest but genuine grin spreading wide beneath a red-tipped nose, is surrounded by girls in pantalettes and patches, pompons and appliquéd ice-cream cones. The carnival is innocent, busy and, above all, an uprush of doing.

Mr. Tebelak is an inventive director, never at a loss for a pantomime trick that will separate the sheep from the goats, a slapdash cross between Paul Sills and Peter Brook, maybe with bells on. What he does is fun, neither reverent nor irreverent, just fun; it suggests that somewhere in the Gospels there was meant to be some good news.

True, the Jesus of the revel is a bit too sweet, too naïve. Every once in a while you begin to yearn for the toughness in Matthew that Pier Paolo Pasolini got into his film. When you are given it, though, at the end of the second half, it's not good. The occasion becomes serious for the Last Supper (with paper cups) and the Crucifixion, and the seriousness is simply straight, with some of the lightning streaks wiped off the clowns' faces. The trouble here is that the seriousness has no stylization of its own, is not formally related in any way to the antic puppetry of what has gone before it. "Godspell" isn't "Jesus Christ, Superstar," a much more ambitious, musically complex, in fact, superior piece of work. It can't change its spots—or the tips of its noses—at the last moment without becoming awkward. But I'd go for the rest of it.

A London production "Godspell," 1972.

A Psychiatric Detective Story of Infinite Skill

Walter Kerr

LONDON—If there is one thing more than another that a contemporary playwright would like to do, it is to make a myth. We feel a desperate need these days for new icons, images, clothed symbols that will help us come to terms with the "dark cave of the psyche," the cave that thousands of years of reasoning haven't quite lighted after all.

But, it turns out, myths are extraordinarily hard to make, just by the willing of it. We are used to thinking now, used to explaining before we really see, and it's not easy to wheel about and go back to magic.

The closest I have seen a contemporary play come—it is powerfully close—to reanimating the spirit of mystery that makes the stage a place of breathless discovery rather than a classroom for rational demonstration is Peter Shaffer's remarkable "Equus," now in repertory at the British National Theater.

He's done it by using reason to despair of reason. A doctor is waiting for a patient, one he doesn't want to take on. He is weary and wary of tampering with the psyches of children, though that is his job. The patient is 17, a part-time stable boy. He has rammed a metal spike through the eyes of six horses. It is the gratuitous, unfathomable horror of the act that leads the doctor to accept the charge.

At once we are lured, with infinite skill, into a psychiatric detective story, the tensions of which account for half the evening's force. Clues are grudgingly, suspensefully come by. The defiant boy, blond curls framing a face of stone, won't speak. At last tricked into speech by adroit maneuver, he strikes a sly bargain he means to hold to. For every question of the doctor's that he answers, the doctor must answer one of his. Candor for candor, if we're going to get anywhere.

The process yields tantalizing bits of information. But all the while that we are fitting bits and pieces together, still far from the sight of any answer, the questioning process has turned up something else: the hopelessly chained soul of the doctor himself. Alec McCowen plays the role: I doubt that he has ever done anything half so brilliant.

He is jealous of the boy he means to cure, jealous of his madness. While he, with his pallid fondness for all things Greek, has leafed drawings of centaurs, the boy has become one. There is a bit between his own teeth that will never come out.

Civilization and its discontents again. Yes. And, as we move into the equally arresting second half of the play, on our way to the metal spike, we are not only aware that the theme is a common enough one in our time, we are also inclined—out of our restless logical impulses—to challenge, or at least think twice about, certain of the icon's ambiguities. Wishing for sex with a girl, the boy is temporarily impotent: "The Lord thy God is a jealous God." Only if the all-seeing god is blinded can the boy take a second step. But that is logic at work again—really work for the next day, not while the second act is actually exerting its spell—and it is to be at least temporarily dismissed in view of the fact that the structure, the two terrible tensions pulling in contrary directions, the sense of myth slowly disclosing itself, all do really function in the theater. They function in part because Mr. Shaffer has done his own work with the precision of Agamemnon's scalpel, in part because Mr. McCowen commands us to believe without reserve in the agony and honesty of his man (Peter Firth, as the boy, keeps pace perfectly with his mentor), and in part because director John Dexter has been able to make the experience intensely visual.

The boy, with his dangerous creativity, is forever driven, forever blocked. The doctor is feverishly unwilling to do what he must do. The two fit together at unpredictable angles, like differently colored pieces in a stained-glass window, but they fit and use up all the space that there it. Any move either makes destroys the other. Locked horns, both right, no escape. The play is perfectly proportioned to its mutual pain.

We have been looking for craftsmanship like this for a long time. ∎

Mikhail Baryshnikov in 1974.

BARYSHNIKOV, DEFECTING DANCER, SAYS DECISION WAS NOT POLITICAL

TORONTO, July 6 (AP)—Mikhail Baryshnikov, the Soviet dancer who defected a

'THE WIZ' (OF OZ)

Clive Barnes

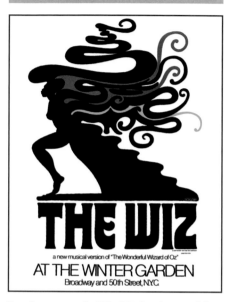

Broadway poster for "The Wiz," with artwork by Milton Glaser, 1974.

Criticism is not objective. This does not mean that a critic cannot see qualities in a work that does not evoke much personal response in himself. A case in point is "The Wiz," a black musical that opened last night at the Majestic Theater. It has obvious vitality and a very evident and gorgeous sense of style. I found myself unmoved for too much of the evening, but I was respectfully unmoved, not insultingly unmoved. There is a high and mighty difference.

L. Frank Baum's "The Wonderful Wizard of Oz" has been a standard children's story almost since its first publication in 1900. A year later Baum himself made a theatrical adaptation of the piece, and there have been other stage versions. But it was in Victor Fleming's 1939 movie, starring Judy Garland as the little Kansas girl whisked away on a cyclone along the yellow brick road to the Land of Oz, that the story received what was really its definitive treatment.

The idea of the present staging appears to have been that of the producer, Ken Harper, and one can easily see his line of thought. With a musical mixture of rock, gospel and soul music, written by Charlie Smalls, who provided both score and lyrics, "The Wiz" is intended as a new kind of fantasy, colorful, mysterious, opulent and fanciful. It was also obviously meant to be a fantasy for today—very modern, a dream dreamed by a space-age child.

The concept is very good in theory, but the practice is not made perfect. Mr. Smalls's music—vastly overamplified by the way—sounded all too insistent and oddly familiar. It had plenty of verve but it lacked individuality.

It is the over-all style of "The Wiz" that gives it its overrising impact. It has all been very carefully conceived and shaped. Not only is Mr. Smalls's music all of a piece but the visual aspect of the production—with handsomely stylized settings by Tom H. John and vibrantly colored and wackily imaginative costumes by Geoffrey Holder—offers a fresh and startling profile. This is first-rate and highly innovative.

Unfortunately, with the blaring, relentless rhythms of Mr. Smalls's music and the visually arresting but rather tiring scenic spectacle, the total result is a little cold. This is not helped by a somewhat charmless book by William F. Brown.

It is eventually the story, or more correctly the treatment of the story, that I found tiresome. A fairy tale, to work, has to have magic. We have to give ourselves up to it, to suspend our cynical disbeliefs and, to some extent, identify with the characters. To me, this proved impossible in "The Wiz." The little girl in the film played by Miss Garland was an utterly real person. The Dorothy in "The Wiz" never for a moment has those dimensions. And the Scarecrow, the Tinman and the Lion (who, in memory, must always be Bert Lahr), while fantastic, are rarely amusing.

None of this was the fault of the performers. Stephanie Mills, however, who plays Dorothy, while having a really wonderful voice, unusually mature for a 15-year-old, did not have a very persuasive personality. The singing throughout was first-class, particularly from Mabel King and Dee Dee Bridgewater, who both have big and beautiful voices.

When so much is individually good it is difficult to justify a personal sense of disappointment. Perhaps it is, at least for me, that fantasy is enthralling only when it is rooted in experience. Also the stylistic unity of the show, which may prove very exciting to many Broadway theatergoers is, of course, familiar to me from years of going to the ballet and the opera, so its originality is diluted. There are many things to enjoy in "The Wiz," but, with apologies, this critic noticed them without actually enjoying them. ∎

---

week ago after a Bolshoi Ballet performance here, has described his defection as an artistic, not a political act.

"When I was in Toronto, I finally decided that if I left the opportunity of expanding my art in the West slip by, it would haunt me always," the 26-year-old Kirov Ballet star said yesterday in an interview with The Globe and Mail. "What I have done is called a crime in Russia...But my life is my art and I realized it would be a greater crime to destroy that.

"I want to work with some of the West's great choreographers if they think I am worthy of their creations."

Mr. Baryshnikov, who has been in hiding since he defected, spoke at a secret location in Mississauga, just west of Toronto. The dancer had been on loan from the Kirov Ballet of Leningrad for the Bolshoi tour.

The dancer left no doubt about wanting to remain free to travel and pursue his career freely throughout the Western world. He said he had no intention of permanently joining the National Ballet of Canada or any other company immediately. ∎

> "I want to work with some of the West's great choreographers . . ."

A Flashy 'Rocky Horror Show'

Clive Barnes

The British invasion of Broadway continues. The latest arrival is "The Rocky Horror Show."

It is a kind of mixture between a horror and science-fiction movie, a rock show and a transvestite display. So you see there should be something for everyone to like. Or dislike if it comes to that.

In London serendipity played a large part in the show's charm—it was unexpected, unpretentious, and the cinema where it was staged, from the peeling walls to the grubby seats, provided it with a perfect ambiance. Something of this ambiance has been conscientiously attempted at the Belasco Theater, and a brave pretense is maintained that we are in a cinema in the initial throes of demolition. But we know we are not—we know that we are sitting in a comfortable cabaret theater, with obliging girls serving drinks, and the atmosphere is totally different and far grander.

The show stopped on the way in Los Angeles, and this was almost certainly a mistake. It is smarter now, but nothing like so crazy or, if one were in a mildly tolerant mood, so endearing. It now looks flashy, expensive and overstaged. The cast is better, the lights are brighter, the noise is more loudly amplified. But jokes—sick jokes, silly jokes, or even dirty jokes—are rarely improved by shouting them down a megaphone. More is often less.

The original idea of a modest spoof was both sophomoric and ingenious. It was just a romp, but there was some nice fantasy in its solemn Vincent Price-style narrator solemnly turning the pages of a dusty

Tim Curry as Frank N Furter in "The Rocky Horror Picture Show."

volume and in sepulchral tones telling of the fate and future of the young hero and heroine Janet and Brad, when one rainswept night their car breaks down and they ring the broken bell of an awfully gothic castle.

The idea of Frankenstein as a bisexual transvestite, with a baritone voice, fish-net tights and black lipstick, was also perversely attractive. One forgave the music that was bright but not especially original—

hard-rock-candy, bubble-gum and popcorn—and the performances that were camp and dreadful. The style provided the enjoyment.

The cast is fair enough. They sing better than did their London counterparts. They probably even act better. Yet why did not someone understand—before the Los Angeles paint job—that the entire point of "The Rocky Horror Show" in London was that it was tacky? Tacky, tacky, tacky! ■

ARTS & ENTERTAINMENT

'Chicago' Comes On Like Doomsday

Walter Kerr

"Chicago's" problem is one of atmospheric pressure. It's altogether too heavy to let the slender, foolish story breathe.

I am sure that Bob Fosse, who is co-author, director, and choreographer of the severely styled new musical at the 46th Street, is sick to death of hearing about its resemblance to "Cabaret." It's he, though, who has put so many of those garish, deliberately seedy, images back on the stage: the black stockings, one rolled beneath the knee, the other hiked above it to meet a blood-red garter; the perfect circles of rouge that make manipulable puppets of the wicked chorus girls; the virtual umbrellas of blue eye shadow that make lids hang heavy, heavy over bored, impertinent faces; the black netting, the black fringe, the tweaked fedora-brims, the spiked heels and the occasionally polka-dotted legs that seem to belong to underweight lady bugs.

And the format is "Cabaret's" format: the earlier enterprise introduced its narrative steps as reflections of a floorshow, with a decadently grinning compère masterminding the proceedings. "Chicago" calls itself a vaudeville bill, with an M.C. telling us that the evening is to be filled with murder, adultery, greed, treachery "and all those things near and dear to our hearts," while a 1920's band wails and thumps overhead on a filigreed gold balcony.

But, "Cabaret" had a nasty, glowering, lowering weight hanging over it to account for its black-sick humors up front: the threat, and then the presence, of Nazi Germany. "Chicago" has no such evil genie in the wings to dictate its insistent darkness, its grotesquerie. Al Capone wasn't Hitler and Cicero wasn't Munich. The original play on which the present fandango is based was a satirical comedy having to do with blondes who could shoot their husbands or lovers with impunity. It was "Front Page" territory, complete with sob-sisters, and all it wants is enough air, wait, and dimpled wickedness to make its light-minded lechery extravagantly jolly.

Mr. Fosse, of course, is a man without peer when it comes to making navels undulate, hips quiver, toes stutter, white spats and white gloves create succulent patterns against the night sky. But his undue insistence on the tawdriness of it all crowds wit to the wall. And lyricist Fred Ebb has mysteriously reduced his couplets to a fearful plainness: "Give them an act that's unassailable/They'll wait a year till you're available," that sort of thing.

When a joke is wanted, it's most often a heavily underlined pun. The delectable Gwen Verdon, as a Roxie singing one of those Helen-Morgan-out-of-Fanny-Brice salutes to her absent man, must chortle something to the effect that on the whole "he's greater than the sum of his parts."

I suspect that the greatest damage is done, though, by the imposed "vaudeville" routining. Indeed, the story-line with its built-in satire has been lost altogether, sacrificed to stunts and soft-shoe. If the satire has been blurred—very nearly blotted out—by manufactured devices and a cultivated aura of doomsday, there's plenty of good dancing left over. "I can be an awfully good sport," the ginger-haired Miss Verdon volunteers with a sweet urgency at one point, and she sure as hell can be. The entertainment not only co-stars Chita Rivera, it is constructed so that the two duplicate function—both are killers, both want show-biz careers—which means that neither comes emphatically into focus.

Miss Verdon is particularly enchanting while becoming so enraptured by her own life-story—as lawyer Jerry Orbach tells it—that she must threaten to take wing again, and co-star Rivera dances both halves of a sister-act all by herself with jackknife precision and breathtaking élan. Mr. Orbach, hair patent-leathered and sporting a sneaky mustache, is forced into the rather thankless job of pacing the neglected narrative: but he is droll indeed as he sheds vest and tie, rumples his thatch and caresses red suspenders, turning his shady presence into a homespun Clarence Darrow on the spot.

"Chicago" is a very sleek show. It just seems to be the wrong one. ∎

How 'A Chorus Line' Was Born

Robert Berkvist

"There is truth on that stage—nothing monumental or astounding, but truth nonetheless. The audience starts believing in those chorus dancers right away."

Michael Bennett, who conceived, choreographed and directed the new musical that is the surprise hit of the season downtown at the Public Theater, was responding to the critics who had almost unanimously hailed

(cont'd. on next page)

One singular sensation.

(cont'd. from previous page)

his show as a new-style musical. "I'm trying to keep myself in check," he admitted. "I could spend the rest of my life chasing this show, trying to top myself, and that's a trap I want to stay out of."

A line in the playbill reads, "This show is dedicated to anyone who has ever danced in a chorus or marched in step…anywhere." Bennett says he included that tribute as a measure of respect and affection for the dancers who give life and form to his art. At 32, Bennett, a former chorus "boy" himself, is quick to acknowledge his roots and debts.

The show is staged like an audition. Twenty-four dancers are crying out for eight openings in the chorus line of an upcoming musical. The director sizes them up, immediately cuts their number to 18 and then invites the rest to step forward, one by one, and tell him something true about themselves. This they do, telling stories that range from broken homes to homosexuality to dreams of glory. Finally, the director rejects all but four boys and four girls. The others pack up their rehearsal clothes, and their hopes, for another audition.

The intensely personal responses of the candidates to the director's cold interrogation are, of course, a gimmick, a hook upon which to impale the audience's concern. At a real audition, there is neither time nor money for on-stage psychotherapy. But, says Bennett, the dancers' revelations have the effect of a collective biography.

Bennett himself had lots of practice rejecting hopefuls in the course of casting his show, looking for "the best dancers I could find, who could also act." He estimates that more than 300 dancers tried out for fewer than a dozen roles—truly a case of life reflecting art reflecting life.

"You may not believe this," Bennett says, "but the show grew out of my feelings as I watched the Watergate hearings; it's my reaction to the falsehood and apathy that seemed to grip the country during that period. I was sick of it. I wanted to do something on stage that would show people being honest with one another."

Bennett had also been thinking of creating a show solely with dancers, and the two impulses came together one weekend in January of 1974 when he invited 24 first-rate dancers to join him at an East Side studio for a midnight workout and rap session. "I brought along a tape recorder and we talked for hours about what we were doing, what we were after, that sort of thing. I asked everybody to tell me the whys and hows of their careers, as truthfully as they could.

"That session was so long and fruitful that we met for another one. We all walked out of those talks feeling that it had been a special time."

Only about half of the dancers who attended the original discussions are in the cast today. "We were paying only $100 a week," Bennett says. "Now that the show has opened, the kids are making something over $200 a week. I hope to be able to pay back these people for all the time they've invested in the show."

What's next in the way of boundary-crossing for Bennett himself? "I'd really like to do a movie," he said dreamily. "On the other hand, I might do a ballet for Robert Joffrey, another choreographer whose work I admire and respect. Or…maybe I'll just rejoin life for a while; I tend to tune out everything when I'm working on a show." ∎

JANUARY 28, 1976

Mamet's 'American Buffalo'

Mel Gussow

David Mamet has a feeling for the contradictions that make up everyday conversation, and, as a playwright, he knows how to convert what he hears into stage speech. His dialogue is not simply overheard, but it has the glow of reality.

The author also knows the disparity between words and emotions, how tempers flare and words fail. The comedy in "American Buffalo" comes not just from the accuracy of the dialogue but from the delivery. The Mamet plays we have seen so far this season (what other new American playwright has had three plays produced here this season?) have all been blessed in their choice of actors.

In "American Buffalo" Mike Kellin and Michael Egan have an air of undeniable authenticity as a seedy pair of friends and pretenders, the first edgy and excitable, the second more amiable (but explosive when talking to an unresponsive telephone).

These two are pretending to be rascals and planning to be thieves. Mr. Egan owns a junk shop, and in Leo Yoshimura's wonderfully cluttered set, his "stuff" is hanging and leaning all over the place—chairs and violins from the ceiling, lampshades stacked on shelves and a cabinet stocked with curios. A garage sale at St. Clement's might pay for the next production.

Before this play begins, a customer has come in and bought a buffalo nickel for $90. So much for a nickel? Mr. Egan was ready to sell it for a quarter. But, now, seeing a good bet, he instantly becomes a numismatist, consulting price lists and, at the same time, he and his friend begin planning to rob the nickel buyer.

In his previous, very funny, character comedies, "Sexual Perversity in Chicago" and "The Duck Variations," both presented at St. Clement's, Mr. Mamet did almost entirely without plot. "Duck Variations," which co-starred Mr. Egan, had conversational arcs and transitions but no story (a lot of amusing talk about ducks).

In "Buffalo," Mr. Mamet tries to do more—and the effort shows. The junk shop seems airless and at times the dialogue seems predictable (we predict punchlines). The second act is sharper than the first, until the two men harass nice young Bobby, played by J. T. Walsh. The final outburst of violence seems to have strayed from a different work.

The play is tightly staged by Gregory Mosher and acted with conviction. Actors, as well as ordinary theatergoers, should be interested in Mr. Mamet. He is a writer to be encouraged.

ARTS & ENTERTAINMENT

'Annie' Finds a Home

Clive Barnes

To dislike the new musical "Annie," which opened last night at the Alvin Theater, would be tantamount to disliking motherhood, peanut butter, friendly mongrel dogs and nostalgia. It also would be unnecessary, for "Annie" is an intensely likable musical. You might even call it lovable: it seduces one, and should settle down to being a sizable hit.

It is based on the famous cartoon character Little Orphan Annie, but not all that seriously. The idea apparently was Martin Charnin's—he also wrote the lyrics and directed the show—but the book is by Thomas Meehan, and against my expectations I found it whimsically charming.

The story starts with Annie caught in an orphanage of Dickensian horrors, presided over by a formidable, liquor-swilling tyrant, Miss Hannigan, a blowsy harridan without an unmalicious thought in her head. Annie, convinced that somewhere in the wide world her parents are alive and wanting her, tries to escape from the orphanage only to be captured and returned to the deadly embrace of Miss Hannigan.

Fate clumps in when Oliver Warbucks, one of the richest men in the world, wants an orphan to spend Christmas with him. His secretary chooses Annie and the rest is history—or at least a long-running comic strip.

The show has a rare kind of gutsy charm. It takes what could be the pure dross of sentimentality and turns it into a musical of sensibility. It presumably owes most to Mr. Charnin's concept of the musical as pop-social document. Mr. Meehan's script abounds with cute but appealing references to the period, and the historical detail of the show—from the search for Dillinger to the villainess smoking Lucky Strike Green—seems formidably accurate.

The music by Charles Strouse is tuneful and supportive. It is neither unduly inventive nor memorable, but the overall impression is distinctly pleasing. The worst aspect of the show is Mr. Charnin's lyrics, which are bland to the point of banality: but even this could have been intentional, for obviously nothing is intended to disturb the show's air of amiable nostalgia. It is meant to be a show to experience, not a show to think about.

One of the problems of "Annie" must have been simply the casting of Annie herself. Imagine a Shirley Temple in a red fright-wig, tippy-tapping through the Depression with a brave little smile. Andrea McArdle seems first and foremost refreshingly normal and not at all waiflike.

As the wicked Miss Hannigan, Dorothy Loudon, eyes bulging with envy, face sagging with hatred, is deliciously and deliriously horrid. Reid Shelton, as Daddy Warbucks, looks a little like an avuncular Otto Preminger and exudes a nice brand of gruff good nature.

"Annie" really works on all levels. It is that now rare animal—the properly built, handsomely groomed Broadway musical. And leapin' lizards (Sorry, one had to say it somewhere!), you're welcome. ∎

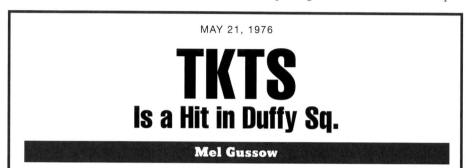

TKTS
Is a Hit in Duffy Sq.

Mel Gussow

One day last week 200 people arrived in New York from Cleveland, Tenn. They went over to the Times Square Theater Center (TKTS) in Duffy Square and—at half the box-office price—purchased 150 seats to the musical "Shenandoah" and 50 tickets to other shows, primarily "The Norman Conquests."

For TKTS, this was an unusually large single sale—mostly the center sells one or two tickets at a time—but every day at the ticket booth business booms. Once mocked by theater owners as, in Broadway parlance, "that pushcart," TKTS is now a permanent part of the Broadway landscape.

Surveying the activity, Anna Crouse, who, as president of the Theater Development Fund, founded TKTS in June 1973, says, "Just to see all those people standing in line—the theater is alive!"

Almost every show is available at one time or another at the discount center with the exception, at present, of the big hits, "A Chorus Line," "Chicago," "The Wiz," "My Fair Lady" and "Bubbling Brown Sugar" and the two current entries at Lincoln Center, "Streamers" and "The Threepenny Opera." In addition, the producers of "Pippin" and "Same Time, Next Year" refuse, on principle, to sell tickets at the center.

All tickets sell at half the advertised price, plus a service charge (50 cents for tickets under $10, a dollar for tickets over $10). The average ticket price, including surcharge, is $6.95.

When TKTS started, producers were concerned that cut-rate tickets would take away from box-office sales. TKTS officials thought otherwise and commissioned a survey in 1973, which stated that "no more than 25 percent of the half-price tickets sold at the Times Square booth would have been bought from other sources."

TKTS benefits Broadway, says Mrs. Crouse, who offers as an example "The Wiz." When the show was in previews, thousands of tickets were sold in Times Square. After opening, the show gradually became a hit. Now only rarely do tickets turn up at TKTS.

The ticket center has transformed barren Duffy Square into a gathering spot. People begin conversations, and even relationships, while waiting to buy theater tickets. Strangers find themselves buying seats to the same show, discover they are sitting next to one another, and then meet again as friends in line or elsewhere.

"The line, socially, is a great success," says Hugh Southern, executive director of the development fund. "It's a better place than singles bars to meet people."

Dramatic Wit and Wisdom Unite in 'Uncommon Women and Others'

Richard Eder

Wendy Wasserstein has satirical instincts and an eye and ear for the absurd, but she shows signs of harnessing these talents to a harder discipline.

Her play "Uncommon Women and Others," which the Phoenix Theater opened last night at its Marymount Manhattan stage, is exuberant to the point of coltishness. Miss Wasserstein, who is young, uses her very large gift for being funny and acute with a young virtuosity that is often self-indulgent.

But there is more. Unexpectedly, just when her hilarity threatens to become gag-writing, she blunts it with compassion. She blunts her cleverness with what, if it is not yet remarkable, is setting out to look for it. She lets her characters—some of them, anyway—get away from her and begin to live and feel for themselves.

"Uncommon Women," is about women in a time of changing traps: new ones, set and hidden in the same current of feminine consciousness and liberation that is springing the old ones. Although the play deals with feminist ideas, it is not so much interested in the traps as in the women. It does not disassociate itself from the march but it concerns itself with blisters.

The women are a group of friends at Mount Holyoke, one of the Seven Sisters colleges. We see them in flashbacks that take off from a reunion they hold six years after graduation. Only a small part of the focus is upon the changes that have taken place since; the time has not been long enough for them to be very great. The main emphasis is upon the lacerations, hopes, despairs and confusions that the times inflict upon these students at a hatchery for "un-common women," where walls have turned porous and let all the winds blow through.

A terror of choices and the future afflicts all of the characters, and Miss Wasserstein has made this anguish most movingly real, amid all the jokes and the knowing sophistication.

If the women, in their outlines, represent familiar alternatives and contradictions, Miss Wasserstein has made each of them most real. They do not stay within what they represent: In the reunion scene, set in the present, each has softened or shifted and they will go on doing so. Miss Wasserstein's is an interim report and a convincing one.

Her gifts for characterization are supported by Steven Robman's supple and inventive direction, and by splendid acting.

"Uncommon Women" contains enough specific sex talk to cover the walls of every women's lavatory in the World Trade Center. It is believable, sometimes funny and sometimes touching, but it becomes excessive. One has only to imagine this to be a play about men to realize just how excessive. ■

Have Pinter and Stoppard Turned to Naturalism?

Benedict Nightingale

Harold Pinter in the 1970s.

No British playwright presently stands higher than either Harold Pinter or Tom Stoppard in the stockmarket of taste; and so it is natural that the coincidental opening of a play by each man within a week should have provoked avid comparisons among the cultural brokers. Both present a somewhat conservative view of their subjects; in the case of Mr. Stoppard's "Night and Day" trade unionism; in that of Mr. Pinter's "Betrayal" marriage and adultery.

Mr. Stoppard first. It is perfectly true that his work has of late become more sober in tone as well as more specific in subject-matter. He has moved from the droll exoticism of "Jumpers," which concerned the possibility of believing in moral absolutes in the age of Noam Chomsky and B. F. Skinner, to the cool outrage of his recent television play, "Professional Foul," which was about the abuse of human rights in Czechoslovakia. This trend continues with "Night and Day," which spirits its audience off to an African nation on the brink of civil war and uses the presence of two wrangling newsmen from the London "Globe" to mount an elaborate debate on British journalism.

There are several things here to trouble a critic. First, Mr. Stoppard may tend to side too wholeheartedly with dread and paranoia. Second, the arguments don't always emerge naturally from character and seamlessly from situation. Third, and not least, some of the discussion is likely to sound parochial to an American visitor.

All true; and yet there is deft humor, sly wit, and sheer verbal mischief. And there is much to admire in the acting, especially that of Diana Rigg.

Mr. Pinter's "Betrayal" has an end, a

(cont'd. on next page)

(cont'd. from previous page)

middle and a beginning, in that order. It closes in 1968, just after a lover-to-be has made a first pass at his best friend's wife, and it opens in 1977, by which time the affair has burned itself out and the wife is divorcing her husband for his own longstanding but unadmitted infidelities. And not only does this addiction to the counterclockwise concentrate the audience's minds on the how and why of events rather than on the much cruder "what next?"; it adds emotional nuance and a wry sense of doom to a dramatic texture some might think rich enough already.

By the final curtain we've experienced the politics of betrayal in all their shoddy complexity: the instinctive evasions, the slips hastily corrected, the hollow questions, the fake offhandedness, the maneuvering and manipulation, and, interestingly, the guileful tolerance of other people's guile.

And out of this mosaic of deceit come some marvelous scenes, packed with suppressed tension, torn loyalties and confused, unspoken feelings. Even more interestingly, the play leaves one with the sense that, however magnetic the woman, it is the bond between man and man that is the more potent and profound. ∎

DECEMBER 10, 1978

SAM SHEPARD—WHAT'S THE MESSAGE?

Walter Kerr

Sam Shepard's "Buried Child" made its appearance in a makeshift auditorium so tiny that the author's devotees quickly used up the available seats and settled for hunched-up positions in the center aisle; as a result, it has now moved to the somewhat larger, though still intimate, Theater de Lys. Question: Why, approximately 15 years after his debut, and at a time when workshop productions often find it easy to move into ample theaters uptown, is Shepard still confined to the theatrical fringes?

Certainly the writer has had encouragement: he's been regularly praised by a reviewer for whom I have a healthy respect, even when I've been helplessly unable to agree. He's also an enormously productive man, ready with a play whenever an institutional or repertory or Village theater needs one, and everyone's got to admire his steadfast insistence on pursuing the vision in his head. Furthermore, he has an audience. It's a cult audience, neither large enough nor varied enough to help him make that move (if he wants to move) toward bigness, toward a general understanding. But it's a devoted one, prepared to laugh uncertainly at his uncertain humors (is the situation as grisly as it seems, is it being derided, is it half-and-half?), prepared to accept his symbols of decay as freshly prophetic (we are bartering away the earth we live on, putting a brutal end to the bloodlines that gave us birth). Still, there's a block—certainly for me.

I keep trying to analyze it. Why, as I listen attentively to the family quarrels of "Buried Child" (the quarrels are mainly between the crippled and maimed), do I feel shut out from the passion, unwarmed by the heat? I can see the outlines of what is being said and done but they are made remote by a nearly inarticulate grunt and stammer or by a muddied or bloodied appearance that serves as a mask. (In an earlier piece, "Suicide in B-flat," the principal character is literally a taped outline on the floor.) Mr. Shepard writes an opaque play. Whether deliberately or not, he places one last glass wall between what is happening and what I am perceiving of it. I cannot pass through it, come inside.

Certainly one of Mr. Shepard's virtues is his strong visual sense. If anything of his earlier work leaps vividly to mind it is never language, or any odd turn of the oblique narrative, but something graphic: the gigantic uncoiling snake on the desert of "Operation Sidewinder," a woman maniacally hurling endless artichokes out of a Frigidaire in "Curse of the Starving Class," that taped outline on the floor. In "Buried Child" it is the abrupt staircase that seems to vanish into nothingness, and the further curious nothingness of a useless corridor at the rear of the stage. Anyone entering or leaving must pass through a void. If the precise meaning of the added space is less than clear, a suggestive dimensionality is created—not in the characters, who remain cut-outs, but in the planes that extend their world. Provocative.

But as Mr. Shepard pursues the symbolic mystery of an infant once drowned in a sink and buried in the back garden, we recognize other things, disturbingly. A younger member of the family, many years away, brings his girlfriend home to meet his relations: the spectral fellow who husks corn in the living room, the savage brother whose leg has been amputated by a chain saw, the dying, cantankerous old man. We now must think of Pinter; such shape as the play begins to take on is worrisomely like the shape of "The Homecoming."

Overall, a thought forms. Is the play's opacity essentially a means of concealing or justifying a random mix of visual gimmickry, corkscrew narrative, insecure comedy, buried borrowings and a portentous symbolism that seems almost an afterthought? If I could make my way through the barrier that has been so resolutely set up, if I were permitted to dig deeper into the cloaked psyches confronting me, what would I find? I suspect I would find a posture that has not yet grown into a cohesive play, a conceit congratulating itself on its own artful dodging. There is playfulness on the stage, yes, and some pretty (and pretty macabre) pictures; I am not certain there is disciplined purpose, a mind dead set on making its inspiration clear. Evasiveness seems to me a weak form of theatrical life. ∎

228

stage

BROADWAY DISCOVERS RICHES OFF (OFF) THE BEATEN TRACK

Henry Popkin

Nell Carter in the Broadway show "Ain't Misbehavin.'"

Broadway has found a new and, at first glance, extremely unlikely source for plays—the Off Off Broadway theater. Consider that the Tony voters and the New York Drama Critics Circle found their favorite musical of last season, "Ain't Misbehavin',' and their favorite straight play, "Da," among the imports from Off Off Broadway; that playgoers have found "Eubie," another Off Off Broadway import, to be their favorite new musical thus far this season, and then consider that when the first Off Off Broadway theaters started up in the late 1950's they were by choice and virtually by definition outrageous and iconoclastic. They deliberately catered to minority tastes. After all, the majority already had Broadway and Off Broadway, and it was not expected to seek out Off Off Broadway to puzzle over strange experiments in dramatic form.

As usual, Broadway, the Fabulous Invalid, is desperately looking for ways to cut costs and still stay in business. The Broadway producer who simply looks up from a manuscript and says, "I like this play, and so I've decided to put it on," has virtually disappeared.

Moreover, producers find themselves increasingly reluctant to trust their own taste and creativity in finding shows and packaging them for Broadway. They would rather see the plays on stage first.

Once, Broadway discovered London's West End. But the royal stream of British hits may be drying up. Last season, not one new British play reached Broadway, and although some British imports are planned this season, most producers are simply looking elsewhere.

After London, Broadway turned to the regional theaters, which began to blossom in the 1960's. Plays from the regional theaters have become a common sight on Broadway. But this new source has also been drying up. Last season had only the Long Wharf's "The Gin Game," which won the Pulitzer Prize, and "A History of the American Film," which had triumphed at three regional theaters, but flopped on Broadway.

(cont'd. on next page)

(cont'd. from previous page)

Now Broadway producers have found Off Off Broadway. Why fly to London or Washington, or even take the train to New Haven? They can find the play they want all staged and ready for purchase, without a single British expression or inflection to hamper full comprehension.

And, best of all, the reviews are in. The New York press now pays close attention to the Off Off Broadway theater.

In the 1950's and 1960's, producers believed that no one could be persuaded that a play could be worth bargain-basement Off Broadway prices one week and much higher Broadway prices the next. By the end of the 1960's, however, the prices of tickets Off Broadway had made notable advances, and that helped to make Off Broadway respectable.

The economics of Off Off Broadway, though now caught up in protracted negotiations between Equity and the Off Off Broadway Alliance, means that productions are still done on a shoestring. What has changed is that the newer Off Off Broadway theaters are closer to the mainstream of public taste and are more deeply rooted in their communities.

There does not seem to be much reason to knock the new system that has emerged. "Da" (which is not a new play but needed Off Off Broadway to be discovered) and "Ain't Misbehavin'" are raising the standards of Broadway, giving employment to actors, earning revenue for their creators and the theaters whence they came. ∎

JANUARY 28, 1979

'A RIVETING NEW SERIOUS PLAY'

Walter Kerr

Bernard Pomerance's "The Elephant Man" is easily the most riveting new serious play we've had to contend with all season. You don't want to miss the musically precise staging of Jack Hofsiss (literally musical, since the evening's horrors and gratifications are linked together by an accomplished cellist), the piercingly intelligent performances of Carole Shelley, Kevin Conway and Philip Anglim, and the emotional and imaginative challenges the author so cruelly, so blood-curdlingly, offers his listeners.

I'm using words suggesting contention and challenge because Mr. Pomerance has constructed his 21-scene montage out of materials that are formally grotesque, delightfully and then disturbingly ambiguous, ultimately unresolved—leaving us, no matter how engrossed we are, with work of our own to do. The grotesquerie begins with the very existence of one John Merrick, a sideshow freak with a mind sealed off beyond a hideously deformed façade. In 1896, a program note tells us, Merrick was rescued from his degrading exposure in penny-cheap carnivals and given refuge in London Hospital by a remarkably perceptive surgeon names Frederick Treves. The evening, then, is factual at root; but fantasy is the tool that gets its work done.

Kevin Conway, as Dr. Treves, establishes this curious duality by whipping down a projection screen onto which slides are flashed—for our benefit, and for that of his medical colleagues. The slides are actual photographs of "elephant man" Merrick. If Merrick is not precisely an "elephant man," he is a monster, one revolting enough to cause Mr. Conway's associates to recoil in disgust and decree his banishment from sight. Enraged by their behavior, Mr. Conway rips the screen from its moorings and crumples it in his hands.

We are done with literalism now. In fact, even as we have been looking at the factual photographs at one side of the stage, we've also been looking at Mr. Anglim, as Merrick, bathed in a spotlight at the other. Mr. Anglim's torso, stripped to a loincloth, is spastically, symbolically, atwist. But he is otherwise unmarked. The theater is asserting itself here, insisting upon its power of suggestion. Anything too literal would function as a barrier between us, as it did for so long between Merrick and a callous world. Our imaginations can superimpose it on actor Anglim anytime we need reminding. In the meantime, thanks to the theater's silken slipperiness, we can attend directly to the man, the person, the mind so long locked away.

We are led through a remarkable series of episodes in which life and the theater—the "real" look of things and the deeper look into them—are examined, entangled, questioned.

The play is tricky, tough and fascinating. In a way, the stage is being defied on the stage, with the ultimate outcome of the contest between the literal and the implied unconcern.

Kevin Conway is first-rate in his part: abruptly honest, curt and Victorian-starchy even in his generosity, behaving in his more genial moments like an intelligent Nigel Bruce. We are puzzled when he first murmurs to himself, "To become more normal is to die," not fully persuaded as he berates himself for having helped create not a true man but an anomaly ("Past perverted, present false, future nil").

Even so, the occasion does not lose its hold on us. There is a strong bond between audience and Mr. Anglim, an understanding of his need for society, of his natural desire for sex, of his determination to complete the model of a church he's designed. Complimented on having fashioned it so expertly, he accepts his due, and something more. "God should have used both hands, shouldn't he?" he asks without malice.

"The Elephant Man" is more than an arresting experiment, it's a strikingly original theatrical achievement. The author, by the way, is American-born, though it would seem that all of his plays to date have been first produced in London. Do you suppose that somewhere along the way we can claim him? ∎

230

JANUARY 16, 1970

DIANA ROSS A SINGLE NOW

LAS VEGAS, Jan. 15 (AP)—Diana Ross parted from the rest of the Supremes early today after the trio sang their last song together, a tearful "Someday We'll Be Together." Miss Ross sang brief duets with members of the audience at the Frontier Hotel. Steve Allen, Hugh O'Brien and Bill Russell, the former basketball star, joined her.

MARCH 27, 1970

Woodstock Ecstasy Caught on Film

Vincent Canby

"Woodstock" is a record of an extraordinary event, the rock festival that last August drew nearly half a million young people to a 600-acre farm near Bethel, N.Y., for three days of music, mud, grass, love, milk, skinny-dipping, acid, Cokes, hot dogs, love, meth, music and, for those who would stand in line, Port-O-San sanitary facilities.

The movie, directed by Michael Wadleigh, produced by Bob Maurice and photographed by Wadleigh and 12 other cameramen, is somewhat less extraordinary than the event it preserves—that is, in comparison with a documentary that transforms its subject into cinematic art that is its own justification.

"Woodstock," I think, couldn't care less about such considerations. It is designed, as an entertainment film, to present the performances of its stars in the context of the event. To this end, it uses a lot of fancy optical effects, including split screens and superimpositions, in aggressive, largely superfluous attempts to interpret performers who are themselves interpreters.

The movie spends, I'd estimate, not quite a third of its time recording the off-stage events at what comes to look like Calvary (minus the last act, of course) as it might be staged by a stoned Cecil B. De Mille. An interviewer listens as one totally drenched young man castigates "the fascist pigs" in the helicopters for having seeded the clouds. A pretty little girl, with a face as blank as a pancake, marvels at how beautiful it all is, though she hasn't seen her sister in 24 hours and she must find her to get her to court on Monday morning.

I can only assume that the film follows the chronology of the festival in the presentation of its stars, who come on for compara-tively brief sets in endless procession. Some are better than others. Joan Baez is treated beautifully, without cinematic distortions, singing "Joe Hill" and "Swing Low, Sweet Chariot," as is Jimi Hendrix, who manufactures his own optical effects as he rocks "The Star-Spangled Banner" to close the festival.

The sheer length of the film (3 hours, 4 minutes), as well as the monotony of its visual rhythm, eventually produces a kind of fatigue that is, I suspect, as close to the feeling of being at an almost nonstop, three-day, togetherness orgy as can be prompted by a film.

Although the film never really gave me a sense of experiencing the public ecstasy experienced by those who were at Woodstock, it did make me feel comparatively benign. When a woman sitting in my row got up for the third time to go to the ladies' room, and stepped squarely on my toe with a high heel, I said simply: "Peace." ■

231

SO YOU THOUGHT JAZZ WAS DEAD

Albert Goldman

Through the club's door they come, two by two by two— Oh, no!—20 giggling, chattering, squeaky-bright college girls looking as though they're on a whacked-out field trip. Making straight for the bar, they hop up to the rail—eenie, mini, midi, maxi—order up frothy alcoholic confections, then start slipping from stool to stool, as if the leatherette were burning their bottoms.

Scenting a story, I approach the chief bustler and ask the logical question: "What's a nice girl like you doing in a place like this?" "I'm a regular here," she smiles back, "and these girls are friends I'm introducing to jazz. I feel jazz is ready for a great revival, it just needs a good shove!"

As for the lady's prediction of a jazz revival, there is something of the kind going on at this very moment. Let's put it this way: if you were to drop a sampling scoop into the ocean of pop music at this time, you would find the count of jazz particles was extremely high; much higher, in fact, than at any point in the past 20 years. Though nobody is using that dirty old word "jazz" damn near everybody in the commercial music business is making use of jazz licks and jazz sounds, jazz soloists and jazz soul. Ever since Blood, Sweat and Tears struck gold with their plastic Bop 'n' Basie, rock bands have been dropping chunks of jazz into their arrangements.

Some major jazz figures have tried to get with the times by developing private brands of psychedelic music. Miles Davis created on "In A Silent Way" a subliminal flow of soft celeste-colored sounds on which he floats his customary smears and sneers like paper boats down a stream. Taking the opposite tack in "Bitches Brew" and at a recent appearance at the Fillmore, Davis sought to match the energy of the rock bands with an electric rhythm section that sounded as though it was playing the hectic holes on computer punch cards. Whatever one thought of the performance—which equated for this listener with the hot flashes of musical menopause—it was obvious the flamboyant jazz star was out to woo the youth audience with something they would not dismiss as merely "jazz."

The greatest irony of this jazz revival is that it comes just when the art has been declared dead. This past winter was the severest in the 80-year history of jazz. A handful of veteran players working a narrowing circuit of tired, old rooms was all that remained. Put through the ordeal of working for $20 a night to virtually empty rooms, the last great jazzmen sipped their drinks, made their grim jokes and kept right on playing.

Today this genealogical succession has been broken. A whole generation of young jazz musicians has been throttled by adverse social and cultural conditions. Without younger men to add their thoughts to the accumulated store, jazz will inevitably fossilize and fall into the condition of the blues, which is now the property of a handful of middle-aged or elderly men who have no true successors.

The responsibility for this condition is usually laid on rock, which has had, it must be conceded, a blighting influence on every competing form of cultural life. Yet most of the blame should lie on the generation over 40, which grew up with jazz and often developed considerable knowledge of the art and a true taste for its authentic values. Abandoning jazz along with virtually every other trace of its youth as part of a process of premature aging that saw most of its members lapse into middle age before they were out of their 30's, this generation gave millions to the arts out of guilt but would not part with a penny for the pleasure of jazz.

Today, instead of resting secure on the basis of a mature public that has kept step with it, jazz must look for its survival to youth, which has been denied the opportunity to hear and enjoy the music in its most accessible forms. One can hope that the revival of pop jazz styles will provide the listening education needed to appreciate the more difficult but more rewarding hard-core styles. One can hope that enough mature musicians of integrity will survive to teach the young players the skills and tastes upon which our finest music is built. But despite many favorable signs of renewed interest and vitality, the final issue of this crisis of passage is far from certain.

SEPTEMBER 16, 1970

LED ZEPPELIN SUPPLANTS BEATLES IN BRITISH POLL

LONDON, Sept. 15—A poll printed today in Britain's most widely read pop-music newspaper shows that Led Zeppelin has replaced the Beatles as the nation's most popular group—the first time the Beatles have not been No. 1 in eight years.

The Beatles placed second in the Melody Maker poll, with the Rolling Stones sixth. ■

Led Zeppelin performing in New York City, 1970.

OCTOBER 12, 1970

Makarova to American Ballet Theater

Anthony Lewis

Russian dancers Rudolf Nureyev and Natalya Makarova in 1970.

LONDON, Oct. 11—Natalya Makarova, the Russian ballerina who defected here last month, agreed tonight to join the American Ballet Theater.

Miss Makarova signed a contract to be a principal dancer in the company for a year beginning in November. It was a coup for Ballet Theater to attract her because she had numerous other offers—some, she said tonight, "financially better."

"I thought their [Ballet Theater's] artistic aspirations coincided with my own," she explained. "What I particularly like is that the American Ballet Theater's repertory includes classical as well as modern ballets."

The ballerina, who left the Kirov Company suddenly on Sept. 4, and won asylum here, said the reason for her defection was a desire for artistic freedom. She wrote in The Sunday Telegraph of London that Soviet rules prohibited experiments in choreography. Much as she loved the Kirov Company and the superb Soviet Ballet School, she said, she could not go on just dancing "the same old parts" in "Giselle," "Swan Lake" and the like. "For me it was artistic death."

With the American Ballet Theater, she will begin with one familiar role—in "Les Sylphides." But she expects from the beginning to do some modern works as well.

There has been talk here about the possibility of the ballerina's joining Rudolf Nureyev and the two appearing as guest artists. Mr. Nureyev left the Kirov in Paris nine years ago, and she knows him well.

Leaving London will be "sad," she said. "It's very like Leningrad in many ways, architecturally and in the bad climate!

"I'm not sure whether I'd like actually living in New York, but what I do like is the artistic atmosphere, the audiences and all that."

It would be "lovely" to be able to visit Leningrad again some time, she said, but for the moment "it is an unattainable dream." ■

233

ARTS & ENTERTAINMENT

OVERDOSING ON LIFE

Jacob Brackman

Jimi Hendrix in 1970.

Most likely, neither Jimi Hendrix nor Janis Joplin meant much of anything to you. Jimi died on September 18th, Janis on October 4th, both, it was said, in connection with drugs. They were young rock stars. A little over three years ago, only the most ardent music buffs had heard of either of them.

Maybe—if you have kids, or know any—you felt surprise at how much feverish talk they inspired. Or maybe you overheard no post-mortems. They went on, I know, only in certain neighborhoods, among street people, hill people, students, fellow travelers of the New Consciousness, many of whom, having just lately grown old enough for mourning, lack proportion. Lack, you might say, an adult sense of who is worthy of being mourned.

To those who don't feel connected with, thankful for, sustained by statesmen, Hendrix and Joplin were a more grievous loss than any statesmen could be.

Both of them became overnight sensations at the Monterey Pop Festival, in 1967. Hendrix was the ruffled dandy freaky-ass black electric bluesman from London, making his American debut. In truth, he had grown up in Seattle, almost middle-class, dropped out of high school, dropped out of a handyman's apprenticeship with his father, dropped out (injured parachuting) of the 101st Airborne Division, and sat in with dozens of R&B bands all across the country. Eventually, he moved from Greenwich Village to England, changed the spelling of his first name ("to be different"), went on a sellout European tour, and returned with his own three-man group, the Experience. His sensual, savage presence and electric howly feedback music burst him, right there at Monterey, where he finished by burning his guitar on stage, into superstardom.

Janis was as insolent, as intensely theatrical, as up front low down sexy, as Jimi. She had grown up painfully out of it, in Port Arthur, Texas, tried college a few times, tried a job programming computers, wound up in Haight-Ashbury in time for the hippie explosion there. She dressed outlandishly, sweat profusely, swore freely and—although she'd never sung professionally before—achieved local celebrity belting out old-timey blues for a group, since disbanded, called Big Brother and the Holding Company.

After Monterey, they became national figures, at least to a segment of the population, and that segment followed their every development as closely and fervently as anyone ever followed the Mets or the Market or the Democrats. Following them was difficult and rewarding. They were completely serious about their art, and usually dissatisfied with it. They were determined to conduct their lives by nobody else's lights. They loved their audience, loved performing, performed with ferocious, exhausting energy, conserving nothing. Like all the great rock stars, they went through nearly perpetual changes, pulling their fans along: new musical bags, new back-up

Janis Joplin in 1970.

men, new clothes, new watchwords, new forms of intoxication.

It was common knowledge that Jimi blew every kind of dope invented and that Janis, along with her famous Southern Comfort, harbored a sometime penchant for downers and hard-stuff. Both were too passionate, too excited—in need of cooling out—and both were willing to try anything.

Now Hendrix and Joplin are dead, back to back, shocking and scary like the deaths at the end of "Easy Rider." And yet in a crazy way, also like those Easy Rider deaths, it feels absolutely unsurprising. Right in with our present scheme of things. It feels as if a great many of us have been overdosing, in one way or another; as if it's nip and tuck who'll make it into his thirties intact. ∎

NOVEMBER 24, 1970

Rock Music Turns to Spiritual Ideas

George Gent

It is perhaps too much to say that rock music is getting religion, but a large number of current records are dealing sympathetically with religious and spiritual ideals.

At the same time, rock music's once fashionably intense flirtation with drug lyrics appears to be abating in the face of industry disapproval. Some observers of the rock scene view both trends as interrelated. Here are some of today's bellwethers:

•Decca Records has just released "Jesus Christ, Superstar," a rock opera based on Christ's Passion and Death by two young Englishmen, Andrew Lloyd Webber and Tim Rice.

•Mylon LeFevre, formerly a member of the LeFevre gospel singers, is turning to gospel rock.

•SSS International and Plantation Records is investing heavily in what it calls Jesus Rock, with a full slate of disks on the religious theme being readied. A single by the Sweet Revival is titled, "Will the Real Jesus Please Stand Up?

•Among current records on Billboard's chart are Dorothy Morrison's rendition of "Spirit in the Sky" and Neil Diamond's recording of "He Ain't Heavy…He's My Brother."

There are various reasons for this apparent trend, but many observers see it as simply one more manifestation of American youth's search for values.

There are skeptics who view the swing to religious themes as little more than a timely tapping of another commercial spring, but these are in a minority. Most agree that the search is sincere, but how deep the impulse runs is a matter of conjecture.

Some persons expressed a belief that the religious lyrics might be a rebuttal to the drug lyrics of the recent past.

"They could be a reaction to the recent deaths by drug overdose of Janis Joplin and Jimi Hendrix," one observer maintained, "or it could be the rock stars' anti-drug campaign." ∎

235

ARTS & ENTERTAINMENT

ELTON JOHN: A NEW SUPERSTAR?

Don Heckman

The advance word on Elton John was so adulatory that I sat down to listen to this new release with my "show-me" hackles extended to their fullest. John already has had his songs recorded by Three Dog Night, Odetta, Dorothy Morrison and Rod Stewart. The reviews for his first American tour earlier this year were almost universally ecstatic, and his appearance at the Troubador in Los Angeles attracted the attendance of most of the city's resident rock stars. In short, John appears to be another potential superstar for an industry that was, at the beginning of the year, looking rather desperately over its collective shoulder to see if the big, bad wolf of the recession was catching up.

With the arrival of such major talents as James Taylor, Randy Newman, Loudon Wainwright III and now Elton John, the music industry is not going to have much to worry about—not this year, at least. John is authentic, all right, but at least half the credit for the superb quality of his recorded work must go to his lyricist, Bernie Taupin. John writes the music and performs the songs (in a voice that often is distressingly reminiscent of Jose Feliciano's), but it is the combining of these elements with Taupin's sensitive lyrics that suggests that a potentially influential new song-writing team has appeared, one that might eventually come to rival Lennon & McCartney.

Like so many of the other new writers, Taupin focuses his attention mostly on small, highly personal matters. He seems to be suggesting that of all potential confrontations, the most significant one is the one that takes place between you and one other person.

Unlike the other new composers, however, John does not take the predictable musical pathway through gentle melodies and flowingly simple chord progressions; he shouts when one expects a whisper, he surprises and challenges, and then suddenly becomes quiet and soft. His tunes have the curiously ambivalent qualities of newness and familiarity that always seem to be present in the truly memorable stuff of popular music.

Needless to say, my hackles were drawn back quickly enough. For once, the advance word was right. Elton John and Bernie Taupin have given us some songs we are going to remember. ■

Photo above: Elton John performing at the Hammersmith Apollo in London, early 1970s.

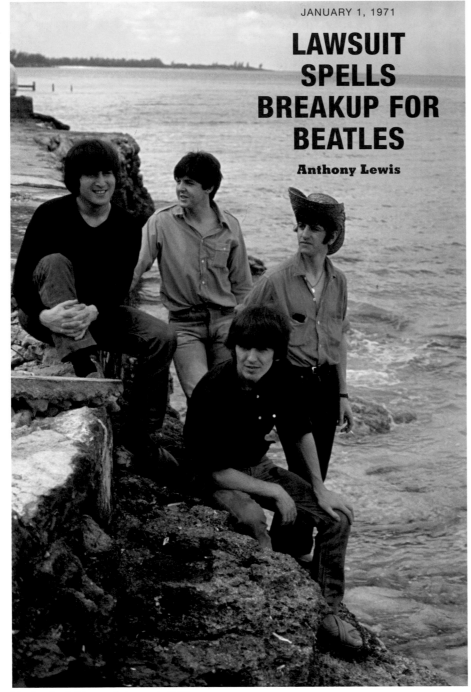

LAWSUIT SPELLS BREAKUP FOR BEATLES

Anthony Lewis

The Beatles in Nassau, Bahamas in 1968.

LONDON, Dec. 31—The Beatles, collective folk heroes of the nineteen sixties, finally broke apart today.

Paul McCartney brought suit in the High Court here to end the partnership. He named as defendants the other members of the pop group: John Lennon, George Harrison and Ringo Starr.

The writ claimed that their relationship as "The Beatles and Company" should "be dissolved." It asked for an accounting of assets and income, still thought to be running to $17 million a year.

For many months there has been talk of a final Beatle bust-up. The four have long since given up personal appearances together.

They did release a record, "Let It Be,"

last May, and a movie of the same name followed, but they have increasingly operated as individuals.

The legal conflict that began today makes it unlikely that the Beatles will again perform as an entity. In a way, the fact that one of the four should go to law against the other symbolized the end of an innocent pop age.

When the Beatles first emerged from Liverpool to world fame, in 1963, they had longish hair and funny, round haircuts. Their faces and their manner had a winning innocence that enhanced their genuinely fresh musical style.

Now all four have beards, and all have married. They have lost the teenage look—their ages range from 28 to 30. They have been involved in political protest and mysticism and business.

Mr. Lennon and Mr. McCartney wrote the songs for the Beatles, and they were always regarded as closest to each other personally. They first met at a village fair outside Liverpool 14 years ago.

But Mr. Lennon has gone off on his own in recent years. With his Japanese wife, Yoko Ono, he has made a splash with nudity on record sleeves, with public "bed-ins" and with campaigns against the Vietnam war.

The musical world has tended to regard Mr. McCartney as the most gifted of the four, or at least the most creative musically. He has played a leading part, along with the Beatles' arranger and recording manager, George Martin, in the often novel instrumentation and chords.

Early in 1970, Mr. McCartney was interviewed by a London expert on the pop-world, Ray Connolly. He said then: "The Beatles have left the Beatles—but no one wants to say the party's over. John's in love with Yoko, and he's no longer in love with the other three of us."

Mr. Lennon, for his part, said in an interview in the magazine Rolling Stone that Mr. McCartney was to blame. He accused Mr. McCartney of trying to "take over" after the death of their manager, Brian Epstein, in 1967.

In the seven years of their collaboration, Beatles records are estimated to have sold more than 250 million copies. They made three movies—"Hard Day's Night," "Help" and "Let It Be"—and lent their names and voices to a fourth, "Yellow Submarine." ∎

ARTS & ENTERTAINMENT

James Taylor, a New Troubadour

Susan Braudy

Singer/songwriter James Taylor performing on-stage at the Mariposa Folk Festival in 1970 in Orillia, Ontario, Canada.

"Five minutes to concert time," a stagehand in Columbus, Ohio, nods to James Taylor, who shoots him a fast jittery look and starts transforming his street costume into his stage costume. He yanks his white Mexican shirt over his head, pulls off the vest knitted for him by his girlfriend and fellow songwriter—performer Joni Mitchell. He tucks his undershirt inside his leather belt, a fan's gift, on which the words "Sweet Baby James" are carved.

A year and a half ago, James Taylor was singing his lulling autobiographical folk-blues to intimate coffeehouse audiences. In the past 11 months, the response to his country-tinged melodies and unpretentious, poetic lyrics has taken even his managers by surprise.

His concerts sell out months in advance, and he turned Manhattan into a James Taylor festival with concerts at Philharmonic Hall and the Fillmore on one January weekend. His second record, which cost a low $7,000 to make, "Sweet Baby James," slowly climbed the charts for six months until it became a gold record, a million-dollar grosser, in October. He is probably the hottest new performer-writer leading the trend toward soft pop music. Critics call him "the first superstar of the seventies."

Nearly 23, James Taylor has already lived a long life. After 10 years of musical obsession, a dramatic discovery by the Beatles, two short years of solo performing, three records, a recent battle with hard drugs, two self-commitments to mental institutions and a starring role in a Hollywood movie, "Two-Lane Blacktop," James is being hailed by critics and audiences as the best of the charismatic musician-performers such as Joni Mitchell, Neil Young and Elton John. Critics call them the new troubadours—composers who sing their own sweetly simple, but musically adroit songs.

James, perhaps the most innovative of these solo performers, is very different from the overamplified hard rock singers who dominated popular music in the last sixties. He sounds like a kid sitting by himself on his bed singing his lonely interior monologues.

The young fans who make up his growing cult concentrate on his musical and acting talents as well as on James Taylor the doomed romantic figure. Hollywood publicists, who as usual aren't far behind, are hyping him as the "new James Dean."

Even without rumors about his personal life, James's fans would find themselves responding to the feelings of desolation in his songs. ∎

IGOR STRAVINSKY, THE COMPOSER, DEAD AT 88

Shook Music World in 1913 with 'Sacre du Printemps'

Donal Henahan

Igor Stravinsky, the composer whose "Le Sacre du Printemps" exploded in the face of the music world in 1913 and blew it into the 20th century, died of heart failure yesterday.

The Russian-born musician, 88 years old, had been in frail health for years but had been released from Lenox Hill Hospital in good condition only a week before his death, which came at 5:20 A.M. in his newly purchased apartment at 920 Fifth Avenue.

Stravinsky's power as a detonating force and his position as this century's most significant composer were summed up by Pierre Boulez, who becomes musical director of the New York Philharmonic next season:

"The death of Stravinsky means the final disappearance of a musical generation which gave music its basic shock at the beginning of this century and which brought about the real departure from Romanticism.

"Something radically new, even foreign to Western tradition, had to be found for music to survive, and to enter our contemporary era. The glory of Stravinsky was to have belonged to this extremely gifted generation and to be one of the most creative of them all."

Planning began immediately for memorial programs. The New York Philharmonic, although unable to change its rehearsal schedules to include Stravinsky music this week, announced that the concerts would be dedicated to his memory. The New York City Opera dedicated last night's performance of "Don Rodrigo" to the composer.

With Stravinsky at his bedside were his wife, Vera; his musical assistant and close friend, Robert Craft; Lillian Libman, his personal manager; and his nurse, Rita Christiansen. Mr. Craft, according to Miss Libman, was too shaken by the death to speak to callers, but wished it known that he had "lost the dearest friend he ever had." ∎

Louis Armstrong, Jazz Trumpeter and Singer, Dies

Albin Krebs

Louis Armstrong, the celebrated jazz trumpeter and singer, died in his sleep yesterday morning at his home in the Corona section of Queens. He had observed his 71st birthday Sunday.

Death was attributed to a heart attack. Mr. Armstrong had been at home since mid-June when he was discharged from Beth Israel Medical Center after 10 weeks of treatment for heart, liver and kidney disorders. He seemed in good health during an interview June 23, in which he played his trumpet and announced his intention to return to public performances.

Tributes to Mr. Armstrong came from a number of leading musicians, including Duke Ellington, Gene Krupa, Benny Goodman, Al Hirt, Earl (Fatha) Hines, Tyree Glenn and Eddie Condon.

Mr. Ellington commented: "If anybody was Mr. Jazz it was Louis Armstrong. He was the epitome of jazz and always will be. He is what I call an American standard, an American original."

"He could play a trumpet like nobody else," Mr. Condon said, "then put it down and sing a song like no one else could."

Mr. Hines, who frequently said he had taken his piano style from Mr. Armstrong's trumpet style, remarked: "We were almost like brothers. I'm so heartbroken over this. The world has lost a champion."

In Washington, the State Department, noting that Mr. Armstrong had toured Africa, the Middle East and Latin America on its behalf, said:

"His memory will be enshrined in the archives of effective international communications. The Department of State, for which he traveled on tours to almost every corner of the globe, mourns the passing of this great American."

The entertainer's final appearance was last February, when he played a two-week engagement at the Waldorf-Astoria Hotel.

Last month, noting that his legs were weak from his hospitalization, he said, "I'm going back to work when my treaders get in as good shape as my chops."

A master showman known to millions as Satchmo, Mr. Armstrong lived by a simple credo. Putting it into words a couple of years ago, he said:

"I never tried to prove nothing, just always wanted to give a good show. My life has been my music, it's always come first, but the music ain't worth nothing if you can't lay it on the public. The main thing is to live for that audience, 'cause what you're there for is to please the people."

Mr. Armstrong was first and most importantly a jazz trumpet player without peer, a virtuoso soloist who was one of the most vivid and influential forces in the development of American music.

But he was also known to delighted millions around the world for his ebulliently sandpapery singing voice, his merry mangling of the English language and his great wide grand-piano keyboard of a smile.

Jazz music, probably the only art form ever wholly originated in America, and Louis Armstrong grew up together in New Orleans. It was in a seamy slum there that Mr. Armstrong learned to love and play jazz in the company of gamblers, pimps and prostitutes.

But in time he was to play his trumpet and sing in command performances before royalty and, through his numerous worldwide tours, to become known unofficially as "America's ambassador of goodwill." ∎

JIM MORRISON, 25, LEAD SINGER WITH DOORS ROCK GROUP, DIES

LOS ANGELES, July 8—Jim Morrison, the 25-year-old lead singer of "The Doors" rock group, died last Saturday in Paris, his public relations firm said today. His death was attributed to natural causes, but details were withheld pending the return of Mr. Morrison's agent from France.

In his black leather jacket and skin-tight vinyl pants, Jim Morrison personified rock music's image of the superstar as sullen, mystical sexual poet.

(cont'd. next page)

239

(cont'd. from previous page)

The Doors, a quartet founded in 1964 in and near the film school at the University of California at Los Angeles, became by 1967 one of the most popular groups in the country, attracting the attention of serious critics who discussed their music's origins and meanings, as well as screaming, hysterical teenagers who sometimes had to be peeled off the performers by stage hands at the group's frenzied concerts.

Their performances were invariably treated by reviewers as events of theater, for the Doors helped to take the electronically amplified rock music that bloomed on the West Coast out of the sound studio and into the concert hall.

Their music was loud and distinctive, but perhaps the most attention was paid to the lyrics, written by Mr. Morrison, which were filled with suggestive and frequently perverse meanings abetted by Mr. Morrison's grunts, sneers and moans on stage.

One critic echoed others when he called Mr. Morrison's presentations "lewd, lascivious, indecent and profane." Indeed, in one of his most famous episodes, he was arrested and later found guilty of indecent exposure at a rock concert in Miami in March of 1969.

Mr. Morrison's first two hits were "Light My Fire" and "People Are Strange." One of his most important works was "The End," an 11½-minute "extended pop song" that ended with a vision of violent death. ∎

AUGUST 2, 1971

40,000 Cheer 2 Beatles in Benefit for Pakistanis

Grace Lichtenstein

Two of the four Beatles, the rock group that came out of Liverpool to make musical history in the nineteen sixties, were reunited on stage for the first time in more than four years yesterday. Over 40,000 people acclaimed them at two sold-out concerts at Madison Square Garden for the benefit of East Pakistani refugees.

Performing some of the hit songs they had never played before a live audience, George Harrison and Ringo Starr thrilled more than 20,000 cheering, well-behaved fans at the afternoon concert when they brought out an unannounced guest: Bob Dylan.

Those who had hoped for an appearance by a third Beatle, John Lennon, were disappointed. But most of the concertgoers seemed more than satisfied by the 2-hour-and-15-minute show, which featured some of the most famous musicians on the pop music scene.

The performers, all of whom donated their services, hoped to raise at least $250,000 from the concerts for the refugees.

Mr. Harrison, slender, bearded and dressed in a luminous white suit, then led the band right into "Wah-Wah," a number from his three-record solo album that has sold a reported total of 3 million copies.

The band, which included such stars as Leon Russell on piano and Eric Clapton on guitar, next did "Something," a Beatles number written by Mr. Harrison, which had been recorded on the album "Abbey Road" but never done in live concert.

Then, at 4:24 P.M., after Leon Russell had led the group through a pounding version of the Rolling Stones' hit "Jumping Jack Flash," and Mr. Harrison had done an acoustic-guitar rendition of the Beatles' "Here Comes the Sun," a slight, curlyheaded young man wearing a dungaree jacket wandered out to join Mr. Harrison and Mr. Russell at the front of the stage.

"I'd like you to meet Bob Dylan," Mr. Harrison said with a grin, as the audience went wild.

Mr. Dylan had not appeared in concert since his date on the Isle of Wight two years ago and he had never performed live with any of the Beatles. The audience buzzed about the historic significance of the moment. With Mr. Harrison and Mr. Russell as his back-up guitars and later with Mr. Starr providing some tambourine rhythm, Mr. Dylan sang and played some of his most famous songs, including "A Hard Rain Is Gonna Fall," "Blowing in the Wind" and "Just Like a Woman," during a 23-minute set.

As the crowd struggled out into the rain, there were murmurs of "fantastic," "wonderful," and "oh wow."

George Harrison and Ringo Starr at Madison Square Garden in 1971.

JIM MORRISON AT THE END, JONI AT A CROSSROADS

Don Heckman

Joni Mitchell in 1970.

With Jim Morrison gone, the Doors presumably will fade into the vague anonymity that always drifted just below the surface of their music. In their own unique fashion, the group did create a kind of classic, and highly fragile, rock style. In it, musical elements were reduced to almost brutal simplicity, and Morrison's self-consciously hoarse, look-I'm-a-man voice dominated all.

In songs like "Love Her Madly" and "Riders on the Storm" the effect is wearily hypnotic, like a Los Angeles musical smog settling into our senses. But when Morrison tries to sing the blues in "Been Down So Long," "Cars Hiss By My Window" and "Crawling King Snake," his musical failings are obvious. What it comes down to—and the evidence is on the recording—is the fact that theater was Morrison's true medium, and he knew it well.

Writing 10 or 12 original songs for a record album is a more difficult accomplishment than most people realize. Writing the material for four albums in a period of two and a half years or so, as Joni Mitchell has done, is enough to boggle the mind—especially since she has managed to sustain, in that time, a relatively persistent artistic momentum.

This latest release represents a more enigmatic step forward than any of the others. The songs on "Blue" reach out in all directions. Touches of the old whimsy remain in songs like "A Case of You" and "The Last Time I Saw Richard," but for the most part the mood is introspective and somber—sometimes passionately so.

I suspect this will be the most disliked of Miss Mitchell's recordings, despite the fact that it attempts more and makes greater demands on her talent than any of the others. The audience for art songs is far smaller than that for folk ballads, and Joni Mitchell is on the verge of having to make a decision between the two. ∎

Classical Music Dwindling on City's Radio Stations

George Gent

Classical music, which only a few years ago was virtually synonymous with the New York radio scene, is being done in by economics and the Federal Communications Commission, and today Bach and Beethoven are rapidly giving place to the Beatles and the Byrds.

The decline of classical music broadcasting paradoxically coincides with the emergence of FM radio as an economic success. For many years FM was lightly regarded as the playground of the hi-fi freaks and held little attraction for advertisers. Now, as the classical music stations surrender to news and pop-music formats, FM radio threatens to become the tail that wags the dog of commercial broadcasting.

The move from "good music" to more news and pop music on radio can be traced back to Jan. 1, 1967, when the F.C.C.'s regulation requiring separate programming on AM and FM outlets with a common owner went into effect.

The F.C.C.'s announced intention was to stimulate greater programming diversity, and many "good music" buffs uncritically assumed that what the agency really meant was more classical music. As it turned out, they were right—but only for the short term.

Instead of simulcasting as before, some of the major stations either turned their FM outlets into classical music stations or simply programmed entirely different music on their AM and FM outlets. In either event, the immediate result was a notable increase in the variety of classical music available. Shortly after, however, a contrary trend began to appear. With the emergence of new classical-music FM stations, the older ones began to feel the pinch of competition. One by one they abandoned, partially or entirely, their classical formats for something else.

SEPTEMBER 7, 1971

Kennedy Center: at Last, the Performances Begin

Nan Robertson

WASHINGTON, Sept. 6—After 171 years, the public finally heard the sounds of music tonight in the first proper opera house ever built in the capital of the richest nation on earth.

About 3,200 people streamed into the John F. Kennedy Center for the Performing Arts for the initial preview of Leonard Bernstein's Mass. Mr. Bernstein had been asked to compose an original work for the center's opening by the assassinated President's widow, now Mrs. Aristotle Onassis.

Mr. Bernstein himself wandered in seconds after the lights dimmed to signal the 9 P.M. opening of the performance. But he, like the rest of the capacity crowd, seemed swallowed up by the vastness of the center. In the great spaces of red-carpeted halls, the knots of waiting, arriving and entering guests never seemed to create a crush or raise a fuss, and their voices also seemed swallowed up by the immense height and breadth.

It was a casual audience, comfortably dressed, with few in evening clothes, and there were few celebrities. Danny Kaye, the actor, entered almost unnoticed.

In a facetious comment, one guest was heard to remark: "This is the first new railroad station built in the United States in the last 50 years."

The Kennedy Center, the nation's only formal tribute to that President, at least gives Washington a showcase for the performing arts after a history of embarrassingly makeshift facilities dating back to the city's beginnings.

Thirteen years after Congress approved funds for a National Culture Center, seven years after the name was changed to honor Mr. Kennedy and ground was broken by President Lyndon B. Johnson, the center, almost unbelievably, was open today for business and pleasure.

And tonight it reverberated with a thunderous, 20-minute ovation for Mr. Bernstein when the performance of his Mass ended. Wiping tears from his eyes, the composer acknowledged the audience's tribute from where he sat in the Presidential box, and then he went to the stage and embraced the performers and the conductor, Maurice Peress.

The week to come will see the world premiere at the Kennedy Center of Alberto Ginastera's opera "Beatrix Cenci"; the American Ballet Theater performance of Duke Ellington's only commissioned ballet score, "The River," never given in Washington before; a concert by Eugene Istomin, Isaac Stern and Leonard Rose; and Beverly Sills heading the cast of Handel's "Ariodante" in its first staged American performance. ■

SEPTEMBER 19, 1971

Survival of the Hippest

Don Heckman

John Lennon's new recording "Imagine" has something to say about adaptation. Along with Paul McCartney's "Ram," and the earlier Lennon-McCartney solo efforts, it helps provide a fairly accurate perspective on the individual components that once came together to make Beatle music.

I don't suppose it will surprise anyone if I say that McCartney is the stronger composer, and Lennon the stronger lyricist. The question of each artist's survival as a solo performer, then, is dependent upon his ability to strengthen the aspects of his music that were weakened by the split. So far, neither has succeeded particularly well. McCartney's music continues to be superb, but his lyrics are either obscure or cutesy; Lennon, on the other hand, has become almost totally verbal—at the cost of his music.

Cover of the John Lennon album "Imagine," released in 1971.

ROD STEWART A LASTING ROCK STAR

Don Heckman

At a time when pop music superstars seem to be arriving and disappearing with revolving-door frequency, Rod Stewart is beginning to look very much like the real thing. The English performer, currently the lead singer with a group called Faces, appeared Friday night before an enthusiastic capacity audience at Madison Square Garden.

Stewart's credentials are especially apparent after hearing him work with Faces. The group is a mildly competent English rock band that is rhythmically shaky, improvisationally uncertain and texturally vague. The support it provides the lead singer is only minimally effective.

But Stewart doesn't need much help. He has the almost hypnotically appealing

---

A couple of exceptions on this new album: "Oh My Love"—a beautiful love song attributed to Lennon and Yoko Ono; "Jealous Guy"—a typically Spectorish rock & roll ballad; "Imagine"—classic Lennon optimism. Other tunes are less pleasing. "Crippled Inside" uses the now overdone, and essentially cheap technique of juxtaposing disturbing lyrics with lighthearted, rag-timey melody; the same is true of "I Don't Wanna Be A Soldier Mamma, I Don't Wanna Die." "It's So Hard" is the sort of blues-based material Lennon shouldn't mess with, and his message to Paul in "How Do You Sleep" should have been sent in a personal letter.

Clearly, Lennon is having trouble getting it together. I'm much more bothered by the too-obvious production activities of Phil Spector than I am by Spector's less intrusive production involvement with George Harrison's recordings. Does that say something about Lennon, Harrison or Spector? Probably about all three, but specifically it suggests to me that Lennon's musical point-of-view is vague enough for Spector to have a major effect upon its perspective. John Lennon is too heavy a talent to allow so much influence from sources outside himself—whether from Spector or Yoko Ono—to persist. Or at least I hope he is. The continued importance of his music depends upon it. ∎

stage presence of a Mick Jagger; one watches his strutting, cock-o'-the-walk antics even while he isn't singing. And his voice—slightly hoarse-sounding, but ringing with a crackling masculine authority—is an unmistakably original expression.

I suspect Stewart is at his best as an interpreter. His most attractive numbers, with the exception of his own "Maggie May," were almost all by other composers.

The material from his current hit album was understandably familiar, but it did little to stretch his skills.

At the moment, of course, Rod Stewart can do no wrong. But the time is rapidly approaching when he will have to find both accompanists and musical material that will more energetically stimulate his extraordinary powers. ∎

Mahalia Jackson, Gospel Singer and a Civil Rights Symbol, Dies

Alden Whitman

Mahalia Jackson and Louis Armstrong at the Newport Jazz Festival in 1970.

Mahalia Jackson, who rose from Deep South poverty to world renown as a passionate gospel singer, died of a heart seizure yesterday in Little Company of Mary Hospital in Evergreen Park, Ill., a Chicago suburb. She was 60 years old, and had been in poor health for several years.

Closely associated for the last decade with the black civil rights movement, Miss Jackson was chosen to sing at the Rev. Dr. Martin Luther King Jr.'s March on Washington rally at the Lincoln Memorial in 1963.

"I been 'buked and I been scorned/I'm gonna tell my Lord/When I get home/Just how long you've been treating me wrong," she sang in a full, rich contralto to the throng of 200,000 people as a preface to Dr. King's "I have a dream" speech.

The song, which Dr. King had requested, came as much from Miss Jackson's heart as from her vocal cords. The granddaughter of a slave, she had struggled for years for fulfillment and for unprejudiced recognition of her talent.

She received the latter only belatedly with a Carnegie Hall debut in 1950. Her following, therefore, was largely in the black community, in the churches and among record collectors.

Although Miss Jackson's medium was the sacred song drawn from the Bible or inspired by it, the words—and the "soul" style in which they were delivered—became metaphors of black protest, Tony Heilbut, author of "The Gospel Sound" and her biographer, said yesterday. Among blacks, he went on, her favorites were "Move On Up a Little Higher," "Just Over the Hill" and "How I Got Over."

Singing these and other songs to black audiences, Miss Jackson was a woman on fire, whose combs flew out of her hair as she performed. She moved her listeners to dancing, to shouting, to ecstasy, Mr. Heilbut said. By contrast, he asserted, Miss Jackson's television style and her conduct before white audiences was far more placid and staid. ∎

Scott Joplin Renaissance Grows

Harold C. Schonberg

Scott Joplin is in the news again. The Joplin renaissance started about two years ago with the recording by Joshua Rifkin of a group of Joplin's piano rags. Suddenly everybody woke up to the fact that Joplin was a real composer with something to offer. Those bittersweet rags, with their syncopations and evocative turn-of-the-century melodies, and with their astonishingly imaginative harmonies, and with their recreation of a period in American life, and as the work of a black composer—all this added up to a phenomenon that was greeted with admiration and delight. In short order came more ragtime recordings, including a disk of Joplin himself in some pianola rolls he had cut in 1916. There were Joplin concerts, and the pianist Alan Mandel has been touring Europe with a Joplin group on his program.

When I wrote an article about Joplin in this column some time ago, I received from a nice reader a copy of a letter that the American pianist-composer John Powell had written from Vienna in 1902. Powell at that time was studying with Theodor Leschetizky, the teacher from whose classes had come such great pianists as Paderewski, Howszowski, and many others. One night at Leschetizky's home there was a dinner party.

"Then," he writes, "came one of the greatest shocks of my life. Everybody asked the Prof. to play. I heaved a sigh of contentment and settled myself in my chair, closed my eyes and awaited the strains of Beethoven or Chopin. Suddenly I started up. Pandemonium had broken loose. Everybody had crowded around the Prof. singing and shouting at the tops of their voices and dancing like maniacs. When the clamor subsided a little I managed to distinguish the strains of 'The Honeysuckle and the Bee.' I almost fainted. 'Smoky Moses,' 'Rastus,' 'My Coal Black Lady,' and a mass of others followed in quick succession."

It is pleasant to think of the stout, bearded, dignified Prof. banging out "Rastus" and other rags. What he would not have played was any part of "Treemonisha." Nobody knew it, and that was the despair of the latter part of Joplin's life.

He worked on it for some years. Nobody would publish it, much less stage the work. In 1915 Joplin arranged for a run-through in Harlem, with singers grouped around a piano. "Treemonisha" was a flop. Two years later Joplin was dead.

If "Treemonisha" is accepted as the period piece it is, the score is full of delights. Joplin, no matter how hard he tried to be "operatic" in the European sense, could not evade his background. And his background was Afro-American—the world of folk tunes and spirituals, of ragtime and syncopation, of sad melody and revival-meeting outbursts, even of barber-shop quartets and popular ballads. It is a genuine folk opera and it breathes a quality that could have come from nowhere but turn-of-the-century America as seen through the eyes of a minority member.

In any case, there is more than enough in "Treemonisha" to show that its composer spoke in a unique voice. There are varieties of genius; and in his modest way Joplin was one. ■

CAROLE KING WINS 4 GRAMMYS

Don Heckman

Carole King performing in 1971.

For the first time in the history of the Grammys (short for gramophone), major presentations were made on a live television show, of which Andy Williams was the host.

The big winner of the evening was Carole King, the singer and song writer, who captured four of the top awards. She was unable to be on hand for the presentations, having recently had a baby.

Many of the major names in pop music turned out for the show. Among those presenting awards were Ed Sullivan, the Fifth Dimension, the Temptations, Richard Harris, Anthony Newley, Roberta Flack and the Carpenters.

Once again, however, there was a notable absence of rock music in the major citations. If anything, both the nominees and the winners were dominated by representatives from what can best be described as the music business Establishment.

A Special Trustees Award was bestowed on the absent, and no longer unified Beatles. But this gesture, so far after the fact of the English group as a significant musical force, was virtually meaningless. The names of other major rock performers—the Kinks, the Who, Joe Cocker, the Rolling Stones, to name only a few—were conspicuously missing. ■

DYLAN:
Reluctant Hero of the Pop Generation

Craig McGregor

Bob Dylan in 1975.

I suppose Bob Dylan is the closest thing to a culture hero this generation has. He's no prophet; apart from the fact that he's disclaimed the role, you'd have to be desperate for discipleship to follow Dylan anywhere. He has never been a profound thinker; he is, if anything, both anti-political and anti-intellectual. But he is a hero, in the John P. Marquand sense of someone who does something superlatively well.

Dylan writes good songs. Wilfrid Mellers, the English musicologist, thinks Dylan is the one 20th-century pop artist who may have the folk-like capacity to go on creating ("The Beatles have disbanded, Gershwin died young, Irving Berlin, Crosby and Sinatra remained permanently adolescent, Cole Porter survived by becoming exclusively deflatory. . . ."). We admire him for that.

But Dylan's role as hero has been less to lead anyone anywhere or point out new directions than to somehow enact the dilemmas and crises of the generation which he

represents. Dylan has managed to act out in his art the blind-man's-bluff search of young Americans for an alternate order in politics, drugs, transcendentalism, communes and love.

At exactly the time hip kids in California were turning from acid to Jesus for transcendental kicks, Dylan was displaying an arm free of trackmarks to self-appointed Dylanologist A. J. Weberman and recording lines like "Father of minutes, Father of days, Father whom we most solemnly praise." No modern hero has been less set on martyrdom than Dylan. Which is as it should be. Frail, fallible, fame-contorted, he's the sort of hero we deserve.

Dylan is a master of masks. If any proof were needed, his skillful manipulation of the mass media and his deliberate choice of public images provide it. More important: Dylan uses masks in his songs as well. In many of them he seems to be writing about himself in the second or third person, so that the "you," "he" or "she" is really "I"; and the alternative persona Dylan creates for himself is sometimes a woman.

Finally, it's worth emphasizing again the personal nature of Dylan's music. That he's a hero is sort of accidental; he's always insisted that he writes only for himself. Throughout his career he's shrugged off old roles and adopted new ones like (strait) jackets; those who hunger after his old declamatory songs of dissent, or the apocalyptic visions of the mid-sixties, are demanding from him a consistency which he has never claimed.

This capacity for growth is one of Dylan's strengths as an artist, yet it's one which critics and admirers alike have found difficult to accept. They're asking him to stand still, and he never has.

As well as being a truly great artist, one of the few of our time whom one can justly call a "genius," Dylan is also, simply, someone who has been through many of the changes we have been through ourselves. He is still going through them. The difference is that he has been able to write songs about what has been happening to him along the way.

Which is what, finally, makes him a hero. Like Achilles, he does something better than anyone else. He is a Three-Minute-Twelve-track-Super-acrylic-Longplay-Hero with an automatic cut-off at the song's end. No more, no less. What the hell else have we the right to ask for him? ∎

Zappa Creates Musical Magic

Don Heckman

Frank Zappa proved again Friday night that he is a master of musical sleight-of-hand. Dealing with a Felt Forum audience that clearly expected to hear a medley of old Mothers of Invention hits like "Son of Suzy Creamcheese," "Are You Hung Up?", "Nasal Retentive Calliope Music," "Brown Shoe Don't Make It" and other similar provocatively titled tunes, Zappa gave them instead a mixed bag of jazz-rock-classical music from a 20-musician ensemble. It is to his credit—or perhaps to the persistence of memory—that the audience loved what it got.

Zappa's knack for building a word imagery that penetrates to the center of the teenage psyche (the foundation of his commercial success) was missing; there were no vocals.

Only the tune titles recalled the marvelous inanity that Zappa conjures up to mask his serious musical intentions: "The New Brown Clouds," "Low Budget Dog Meat (A Medley)," "For Calvin & His Next Two Hitch-Hikers," "The Adventures of Greggery Peccary."

He seems to have settled comfortably into his role as the Leonard Bernstein of rock. Like Bernstein, Zappa has mastered the elements of one musical discipline (pop-rock, in his case) and attempts to ally them with elements from another (for Zappa, classical music). The results are often curiously parallel to Bernstein's—creations that are neither fish nor fowl, that survive almost as a result of sheer will rather than because of their intrinsic vitality.

Fascinating? In places, although one can think of composers who, given the resources of this excellent 20-piece group, might have done considerably better. Yet Zappa is undeniably a true original, and one of the pop-rock movement's first composers with a genuine esthetic overview of the music's enormous potentials. When he gets over his fascination with decades-old classical devices, he might produce some powerful music. ∎

Glass's Reich's New Music Is Likened to Art

John Rockwell

The music is new and not likely to be heard in conventional concert halls. One can more often encounter it in lofts, or Greenwich Village galleries, or museums uptown. For its admirers, it sounds hypnotic and highly colored; for its detractors, it is maddeningly repetitive and simplistic. Amplification is screwed up to the point of pain. Two electric organs and three wind players sustain a steady drone and a reiteration of simple rhythmically charged patterns. Melodies and seductive cross-rhythms twist and turn in the aural flux, like flotsam on a wave.

The composer is Philip Glass. His music and that of an outwardly similar composer, Steve Reich, is being heard more and more these days. But traditional musical audiences on the whole continue to resist music of this sort. Mr. Glass and Mr. Reich have been sustained for years by the support and patronage of the art world.

Trained musicians generally recoil from this "primitism," and critical response has tended to range from the puzzled to the hostile. A sizable minority, outraged at the repetitiveness and aggressive loudness, can be counted on to walk out of a Glass or Reich concert before it is half over. But for those who stay to the end, the typical reaction is wild enthusiasm, with an emotional expression of pleasure more suggestive of a rock concert than of the typical new-music event, coldly and politely received. Those who love this music find it totally engulfing, akin to Indian ragas but peculiarly American in its energy, amplitude and clarity.

Artists, unlike musicians, have embraced Mr. Glass's and Mr. Reich's works from the first, not least because of the obvious esthetic similarities between this music and recent New York art.

The simplicity of structure and initial bareness of materials in both men's music suggests a kinship to minimalism and structuralism in the visual arts. The very fact that theirs is a performing art is another reason that it may appeal to visual artists, who are themselves now reaching beyond conventionally discreet categories. "The definition of art today is much broader than old notions of painting or sculpture," says Sol LeWitt, the sculptor. "People do art—it could be sound as well as anything else." ∎

PINK FLOYD OFFERS ROCK IN MUSIC HALL

John Rockwell

Time apparently has no meaning for New York's rock 'n' roll audience. Radio City Music Hall was full yesterday morning from 1:30 to 4:15 as Pink Floyd, a British group, went through its audio-visual paces.

Pink Floyd itself is a quartet that has hung together for a long time (since 1964) with relatively high stability in terms of personnel. The result is one of the tightest acts in the business, precisely organized, musically together and neatly coordinated with a plethora of intriguing visual effects.

Yesterday's program began with a varied group from earlier albums and continued, after a break, with the band's latest release, "Dark Side of the Moon." The first half was the more interesting, full as it was of Pink Floyd's characteristic "sci-fi rock," with a predominance of long, brooding instrumentals highlighted by Rick Wright's inventive work at piano, electric piano, electric organ and synthesizer, plus a clever 360-degree sound system. The second half was more fragmented and conventionally rock in its roots.

Visually, things were dominated by a huge sphere hung above the stage on a futuristic light-tower scaffolding. The ball emitted steam in a way that suggested photographs of the sun and its corona, cast dappled mirror-dots throughout the hall, and even came forth with a few needle-like red lasers. In combination with the Music Hall's own fog effects, it all looked pretty spectacular.

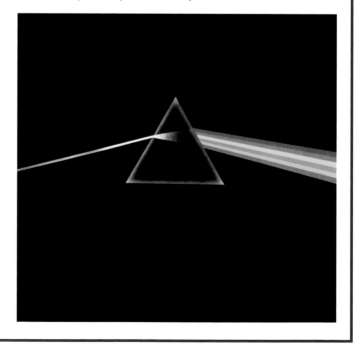

Album cover of Pink Floyd's Dark Side of the Moon released in 1973.

WHO (OR WHAT) IS DAVID BOWIE?

Henry Edwards

David Bowie onstage during his "Ziggy Stardust" era in 1973.

David Bowie's best known lyrics are knotty, surrealistic "sci-fi" cryptograms that conjure up people with "space faces" and "electric eyes." These dehumanized creatures swallow "protein pills," daydream "moonage daydreams," endure names like "Ziggy Stardust," and are an intrinsic part of a songbook that could pass for a rock musical version of Stanley Kubrick's "2001."

If Kubrick's cinema epic of a seared tomorrow has influenced Bowie in his role as composer, the futuristic look of Kubrick's "A Clockwork Orange" has tellingly influenced the unorthodox physical appearance that Bowie brings to his stage act. The composer's hair is dyed a startling reddish-orange; his costumes are the very definition of overwrought unisex fashion; his soft features are highlighted by generous amounts of delicately hued lipstick, rouge and eye shadow. Bowie not only has an epicene air about him but also looks as if he had been plated with a chromium alloy.

The David Bowie of the "Aladdin Sane" record jacket is not the David Bowie of "Aladdin Sane." Bowie has always been a lilting melodist, a quirky and not uninteresting lyricist and an expert arranger and studio producer. While these skills have always manifested themselves on his five prior disks, Bowie's oh-so au courant songs have always proved an effective disguise for the song writer's wellspring of morbidity. In "Aladdin Sane" Bowie allows that morbidity to gush forth without inhibition and, in the process, he has created the most expressive, if still uneven, album of his recording career.

The selling of Bowie, however, has been such an efficient example of the popular culture power plant in full-scale operation that one can't help wondering if this disk's ripened contents, as well as its jacket, aren't more computerized gimmicks whose function is to tantalize anew Bowie's easily manipulated horde of fans.

Six of "Aladdin Sane's" 10 selections are annotated with the names of cities Bowie visited during his first tour of the United States, a one-month excursion during the fall of 1972 which took Bowie to 15 different destinations. Using this tour as source material, Bowie crash-landed his flying-saucer-to-the-future into the heartlands of contemporary America and then borrowed Jack Kerouac's free-form literary style to create an "On the Road" of his own.

Expect no other pop or rock album this year to so ferociously envision this country as a devitalized landscape whose only signposts are violence, cruelty, turpitude, disillusionment, sexual frustration and drug and alcohol abuse. Expect no other pop or rock album this year to mate its festering contents to a series of musical effects totally dedicated to unhinging an already dislocated listener. ∎

ARTS & ENTERTAINMENT

DUKE ELLINGTON, A MASTER OF MUSIC, DIES AT 75

John S. Wilson

Duke Ellington, who expanded the literature of American music with compositions and performances that drew international critical praise and brought listening and dancing pleasure to two generations, died here yesterday at the age of 75.

The noted jazz critic and historian Ralph J. Gleason called Mr. Ellington "America's most important composer...the greatest composer this American society has produced," and summed him up as a "master musician, master psychologist, master choreographer."

"Ellington has created his own musical world which has transcended every attempt to impose category upon it and has emerged as a solid body of work unequalled in American music," Mr. Gleason wrote.

Mr. Ellington, whose innate elegance of manner won him his nickname of Duke while he was still a schoolboy in Washington, was a tall, debonair, urbane man with a vitalizing sense of the dramatic and an ironic wit that often served as a protective shield.

Amid the protests voiced in 1965 when a unanimous recommendation by the Pulitzer Prize music jury that Mr. Ellington be given a special citation was rejected by the Pulitzer advisory board, the only comment by the composer, pianist and orchestra leader was "Fate is being kind to me. Fate doesn't want me to be famous too young." He was then 66 years old.

But beneath a suave, unruffled exterior, Mr. Ellington had a fiery appreciation of his worth and style. When he was conducting a public rehearsal of his orchestra at the University of Wisconsin in 1972, he took his musicians through a first attempt at his latest composition.

"Letter E," he said to indicate where they were to start playing. But when only half the band began at the proper place, he shouted, "No! E! E as in Ellington! E! E as in Edward! E! E as in Ellington! E as in excellence! E as in elegance! E as in Edward and Ellington! E! E! E as in all good things! Edward...Ellington...excellence...elegance! E!"

Mr. Ellington combined his musical talents, his excellence and his elegance in a manner that transcended the usual connotations of "jazz," a word that he consistently rejected in relation to his work.

"In the nineteen twenties I used to try to convince Fletcher Henderson that we ought to call what we're doing 'Negro music,'" Mr. Ellington said in 1965. "But it's too late for that now. The music has become so integrated that you can't tell one part from the other so far as color is concerned. Well, I don't have time to worry about it. I've got too much music on my mind." ∎

APRIL 6, 1975

Superstar Sills makes Met debut at 46

Joan Barthel

Tomorrow night, Beverly Sills superstar soprano with the New York City Opera for 20 years, will make her debut at the Metropolitan Opera. Next month, she will be 46 years old.

"I don't consider it a sad occasion just because it should have happened 10 years ago. In those 10 years I've been singing in New York, in opera. I've been doing everything that the public has wanted to hear. I've sung thousands of performances, so I

Beverly Sills walks off the Metropolitan Opera's stage following her sellout debut.

SPRINGSTEEN'S ROCK POETRY AT ITS BEST

John Rockwell

Bruce Springsteen in 1975.

Bruce Springsteen's third album, "Born to Run," should be all he needs to push him over the top.

The trouble with Mr. Springsteen's career, as anyone who has followed rock music at all recently already knows, is that his records haven't matched the astonishing impact of his live performances.

The first record, which came out in late 1972, was called "Greetings From Asbury Park, N.J." It's an inconsistent disk, which Mr. Springsteen attributes to the fact that Columbia Records thought of him as a conventional singer-songwriter and thus blunted the rock impact of his style. Even so, with memories of his live performances fresh in one's ears, the best songs ("Growin' Up" and "Spirit in the Night," for instance) work wonderfully well.

The second album came out a year later and was entitled "The Wild, the Innocent and the E Street Shuffle." This is really a great record already, but it's not quite as consistently fine or as consistently rock-oriented as the third. However winning the songs sound, they really function as rough models for the fully formed versions one hears live.

"Born to Run" gets us closer still to what Bruce Springsteen is all about. The range is as wide as either of the earlier albums, from poignancy to street-strutting cockiness to punk poetry to quasi-Broadway to surging rock anthems. But all of it (except "Meeting Across the River," which works superbly on its own terms) is solidly rock 'n' roll.

Mr. Springsteen's gifts are so powerful and so diverse that it's difficult even to try to describe them in a short space. Sometimes his lyrics still lapse too close to self-conscious myth making but generally they epitomize urban folk poetry at its best— overflowing with pungent detail and evocative metaphors, but never tied to their sources in a way that is binding. This is poetry that attains universality through the very sureness of its concrete imagery. And Mr. Springsteen's themes perfectly summarize the rock experience, full of cars

(cont'd. on next page)

---

don't feel I'm correcting any oversight. It's just a nice joyful occasion that I'm now going to sing at the Metropolitan.

"I'm past the stage of singing for approval. It's no longer a question of 'How well does she do what she's doing?' When Rubinstein plays, you don't ask, 'Did Mr. Rubinstein play all the notes?' It's just a matter of enjoying what I'm doing. I don't have to prove anything. I don't have to worry about whether I look older. I am older.

"Why I haven't sung at the Met until now comes down to basically, a clash of personalities between Rudolf Bing and myself, partly because of the pressures of what he was doing, partly because of the pressures that were put on him to bring me in when I could no longer be called his discovery. But as Mr. Bing made it quite obvious that he didn't need me, I was also able to make it quite obvious that I felt I didn't need the Met.

"I think it's a mistake for any opera impresario to decide he doesn't need a singer that the public wants to hear. A great impresario gives the public what it wants.

And I sense from him now the feeling that he could have handled this a little better. But it has all worked out the way it should have, I think. In a sense, I revolutionized the operatic scene, because I proved you can make a great international career without the Metropolitan."

She looks wonderful, as dramatically attractive as she's been described, with that famous head of coppery hair, shining pink skin, all rosy and glowing today in a rust-colored sweater and slacks; 40 pounds lighter than she was a year ago, though she still counts carbohydrates. She says she feels wonderful too, knock wood, after her surgery last fall.

She sang her first coloratura role, "Mignon," for Erich Leinsdorf in 1956. A year later Julius Rudel became the director of the City Opera and, eventually, one of her most intimate friends. In 1963, she sang Donna Anna to Norman Treigle's Don Giovanni, and attracted considerable attention, but it wasn't until 1966 and "Julius Caesar" that she was noticed by the world at large.

By 1969, though her appearance at La Scala was as a last-minute substitute for Renata Scotto, she was secure enough to cut a costume into several pieces when her request for a more becoming dress was consistently ignored. She was a superstar; in 1970 she traveled a quarter of a million miles, singing on three continents in three weeks. Finally her husband imposed a travel limit and gave her a gold ring engraved "I DID THAT ALREADY."

She says she is the highest paid opera singer in the world, though her fee at the City Opera is $1,000 a performance, a figure she shrugs off. "I don't sing there for the money; it's a labor of love."

All her money goes into a trust fund for her daughter Muffy. "She'd have been a well-off little girl, from her father," Sills says quietly, "but this will be a present from her mama. I feel that of all the people who have made any sacrifices for this career, Muffy has made the most. It's a way of assuaging my guilt, I suppose.

She is contracted at the Met through 1978, at the City Opera through 1979. ■

ARTS & ENTERTAINMENT

(cont'd. from previous page)

and love, street macho and desperate aspiration. Hearing these songs is like hearing your own life in music, even if you never lived in New Jersey or made love under the boardwalk in Asbury Park.

Mr. Springsteen's music is both a compendium of rock influences and absolutely personal. And the tunes, the hoarse, fervent singing, the arrangements and their instrumental execution and above all the sheer feeling for what rock is about simply pour out of the speakers.

At any given moment the sound stays true to its essential simplicity and directness, even if the textures can approach almost orchestral richness. But the real diversity lies in the many different sorts of popular music that he and his wonderful E Street Band can do so well.

All this observer can say is that on repeated hearings and after seeing him perform again this summer, "Born to Run" seems one of the great records of recent years. If Mr. Springsteen has to perform more to get his message across, let him perform away—he seems to enjoy it enough. No doubt he will make still greater studio albums than this someday. But in the meantime, you owe it to yourself to buy this record. ∎

JANUARY 22, 1976

THE POP LIFE
Disco Forum Disseminates a Craze

John Rockwell

The exhibition rooms on the mezzanine of the normally sedate Roosevelt Hotel are echoing with sounds of the midnight hour this week. Billboard magazine is sponsoring the First Annual International Disco Forum there, and the Roosevelt is awash with flashing lights, Ivesian collages of disco instrumentals, hustling dancers, coolly hip disco disk jockeys, beaded and bearded record executives and a fiesta of equipment displays.

What it all amounts to is the most tangible sign yet of the packaging and dissemination of a disco craze that can legitimately count New York as its center. The current disco boom comes about from the unique mix of blacks, Latins, whites, homosexuals, heterosexuals, cafe society, drugs and media that New York combines more volatilely than anywhere else. The Roosevelt convention shows us the way the American entertainment industry moved in to market it all to the masses.

The masses should love it; to judge from disco record sales, they already do. Because if the discos of the 1970's started here, they really epitomize modern life as well as anything else—loud, noisy, tacky-stylish, energetic, thoughtless and fun. Which in turn makes many rock critics' rejection of disco music, in print or in private, rather fascinating.

One would think that disco music, representing as it does one demonstrably popular strand of pop music, would appeal to pop-music critics, on theoretical grounds alone, if nothing else. But instead, one reads of "formulas" and "mechanical" music drowning out the noble sounds of rock. It all sounds rather like the paranoid-élitist defenders of classical music on radio.

Of course, disco music is formula-ridden; all pop music is popular in part because it reinforces the familiar. And certainly there is a lot of garbage among the disco records; there is a lot of garbage in most things. But disco music has its heroes and its evolving specialist critics and its fan magazines, and no doubt it will eventually produce artists on a par with those that came out of older forms of soul and rock. The critical resistance now reflects in part the music's own embryonic state. But it also hints of a hardening of rock-critical arteries.

JANUARY 9, 1977

DARK SONGS BY CALIFORNIA'S EAGLES

Penelope Ross

It is almost impossible to talk about the Eagles without mentioning California—dream and reality—not just because the state figures in the title of their newest album, "Hotel California," but because, more than any other group since the early Beach Boys, they are so firmly rooted in that territory, exploring its myths, way of life, pleasures and perils. If the American population is inevitably heading south and west, as statistics indicate, the Eagles, in five albums over five years, have been sending out reports of the fantasies and realities that will be found there.

In that time, their vision of the world they chose (like so much of the state's population, none of the five men currently in the band is a native) has darkened considerably, becoming progressively tougher, more cynical, and still in many ways irresistible. Whatever the drawbacks, they are writing about a place that has struck a responsive chord in a lot of people for many different reasons and, in so doing, they have become one of the most commercially successful American rock bands now working, with each of their albums (including "Their Greatest Hits") selling over a million copies and holding concerts in arenas to accommodate their audiences.

They have also along the way gone from their original designation of a "country-rock" band to one more closely aligned to mainstream rock, California style, smoother than its eastern or English counterparts and highlighted by elegantly polished high harmony singing.

Through the first four albums, the Eagles were rapidly developing as musicians and songwriters, exploring the various possibilities of several kinds of collaboration. Their drift has always been toward dual or multiple authorship, with surprisingly good and varied results. From their first, tentative attempts at harmony, they have become the best harmony singers in rock, and perhaps in popular music, with the ability to do multiple

The Eagles performing in 1979. From left, Glenn Frey, Don Henley, Joe Walsh and Don Felder.

harmonies perfectly in the studio, and much more rare, on stage, to breathtaking effect. And in Henley and Frey, they have two of the best and most distinctive voices in rock, each capable of singing lead or harmony as the music dictates.

In "Hotel California," their newest album, many of the images they have been working with through the years recur. Cars and highways, rock star as outlaw, confusion between the emotional hold of success and personal relationships are all reworked to good effect in an album that is circular (rather than cyclical) in structure, with the last song forming a natural segue back to the first. The outlaw rock star and his confusion between love and success is re-interpreted in "New Kid in Town," a pretty ballad ballasted by a new cynicism that includes themselves and with a dash of irony in the title. For while the band has been musically describing California, they have also been talking about themselves. Nobody in this group is a kid anymore and they all know it.

The most ambitious song, which succeeds admirably, is "The Last Resort," which in its detailing of the destruction of the land, has taken the band out of their usual subject range. Like their best work, the lyrics are simple, but structured in a complex way that allows for repetition of words and phrases in several contexts that give them a new meaning each time they appear.

The Eagles have their flaws. They can sometimes be silly and self-pitying and take themselves much too seriously. There is the added curiosity that in a band of five writers, no one has managed to come up with an even remotely happy love song or anything intentionally funny. But that is really beside the point. The Eagles make good music which is no less stylish and intelligent for being straightforward, which is sometimes the hardest style of all. ∎

Boston Pops conductor Arthur Fiedler at an organ keyboard.

Fiedler Goes Full Tilt at 82

John Rockwell

When someone is 82 years old and going full tilt, when he has led the same orchestra for 47 years and been associated in one capacity or another with its parent body for 62 years, it is time to step back and consider what he has accomplished.

Certainly Arthur Fiedler's schedule seems more hectic than ever. "I haven't had a vacation for six or seven years," he complained good-naturedly the other day from Atlanta, in the midst of a round of guest appearances in the Southeast. "I think I'm ready for one."

The Boston Symphony Orchestra was founded in 1881, and the Pops came into existence just four years later—coincidentally the same year that Emanuel Fiedler

(cont'd. on next page)

(cont'd. from previous page)

Arthur's father, joined the orchestra. "My father played with the Boston Symphony for 25 years," Fiedler explains, "but his ambition was always to go back to the old country, and he achieved that."

Fiedler was born on Dec. 17, 1894, in South Boston. After high school he went to Berlin to continue his violin studies with Willy Hess, who had been concertmaster of the Boston Symphony. In 1915 he joined the Boston Symphony himself as a violinist and during his twenties played several instruments in the orchestra. By the late 1920's he was stepping in for the regular conductors of the Pops, and—after founding the free Esplanade concerts in 1929—he became the Pops conductor in 1930.

Since then he has solidified his position as America's premiere conductor of light-classical music. Some people complain that today Fiedler has fallen into a formula—Pops concerts almost always begin with a warhorse or light-classical selection, proceed to a standard concerto and end up with arrangements of popular or show tunes. There are criticisms that he is a rigid or perfunctory conductor. A few Bostonians wonder at the slowness of his recovery from pneumonia the past two winters, and hint that age may finally be catching up to him. ■

Billy Joel Offers Rock From Middle of Road

John Rockwell

Given the idolatrous reactions of his admirers Thursday night at Carnegie Hall, Billy Joel looked like one of America's most beloved pop-music stars. But he is actually a rather more curious case than that. He had a genuine national hit in "Piano Man" four years ago, and he has enjoyed intermittent success since with other songs.

But mostly now he is beloved by pockets of enthusiasts and by FM disk jockeys who propagate their enthusiasm, and he is especially beloved in the New York area—his Thursday night performance was the first of three, all long sold out.

Mr. Joel offers a rhetorical brand of middle-of-the-road rock—emphatic, yet mellowed by a concern for instrumental niceties and declamatory phrasing in the vocals. His busy piano figurations, lush textures and peremptory drum punctuation can sound bathetic at their worst.

But Thursday night, with his excellent band honed by a long tour and augmented by three backup singers and a small orchestra, Mr. Joel's music sounded tight and convincing. The energy overrode the softness, and the singing had a commendable warmth and sensitivity. And his songs struck an evocative chord without lapsing too far into the corny or the sentimental.

It's nice to see Mr. Joel plugging steadily away between his big hits, cultivating and rewarding his loyal audience. Certainly he deserves mass success as much as many similar, less worthy artists who attain it. ■

THE NEW DISCOS:
Life Begins at Midnight

Enid Nemy

It's midnight and the night people are out, ready for action. The discothèque scene in Manhattan has not only revived but exploded.

The new discothèques, multiplying like amoebas, differ from their counterparts of a decade ago in a number of ways. The décor and accoutrements are more sophisticated, with such features as totem poles of light intersecting a dance floor, beams of light falling as thickly and irregularly as snowflakes and swirling vapors of fog, achieved with dry ice.

The fashion scene has also changed. There is no longer a uniform, comparable to the jeans and silk shirts and rows of chains of less than a generation ago. Now it's dressing according to mood, from elegant crepe de chine and miles of fringe to workmen's overalls, jumpsuits, sailor outfits, gold lame, knotted scarves and long blouses pretending to be dresses. The result is less costume than far-out individuality.

Not unexpectedly, most of the crowds—and crowds there are—are young. More surprisingly, most of them are not gilded playgirls and boys, but workers, toiling in offices, design studios, publishing companies, television studios, artists lofts and chic shops, from 9 to 5. After 5, the routine is to climb into bed, sleep four or five hours, have dinner and arrive at New York, New York or Studio 54, both in midtown, or Infinity on the border of SoHo, at midnight or 1 A.M. At sunrise, another hour or two of sleep and the workday begins.

For diversification, the trend-setters, most of whom had already made the Manhattan discothèque scene at least once, recently journeyed to Brooklyn on school buses. There they decamped at the Empire Rollerdome to frolic and dance on skates, for the benefit of the Institute for Art and Urban Resources.

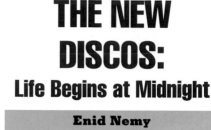

Pop

A Chicago nightclub in 1978.

And, of course, there's the new "in" dancing, which appeals to the ham in everyone. The dancing itself is not much different from what's going on anywhere else, but the idea now is to pause every so often, freeze into an exaggerated pose for 20 to 30 seconds, and then continue on normally—until the urge comes to freeze again.

Dance, dance, dance until the feet are numb and the room spins, and then on to the mezzanine or balcony, banquettes or edge of the room to weigh the talents and appearance of others. For this time round, action is not the only name of the game. Watching is just as much fun. ∎

Fleetwood Mac Finds the Combination

John Rockwell

The singer, who is wearing a backless dress, black top hat and witchy, translucent black "wings" attached to her bare arms, leans dreamily into the microphone. She begins the seductive, hypnotic song in a nasal, confidential tone, like the crooning of some ancient rite. Before long she'll be weaving about the stage, almost oblivious to the lanky, earnest guitarist to her left, the hard-working keyboard player to her right, the dour bassist or the angular, industrious drummer behind her.

This is Stevie Nicks singing her song, "Rhiannon," which was one of three No. 1 singles last year from one album (itself a No. 1) called "Fleetwood Mac." The band of the same name now has another No. 1 LP in its current "Rumours." It's been No. 1 or 2 for over four months, and a unanimous No. 1 on all the sales charts for the past month. In turn, it has already spun off two more hit singles, with more to come.

After a decade of honest but unspectacular success with steadily shifting personnel, Fleetwood Mac has found the right combination. The quintet may well wind up regarded as the most characteristic, important rock act of the late 1970's. Not only is Fleetwood Mac's music excellent on subjective terms, but it epitomizes in the best and freshest sense the late-70's tendency toward stylistic eclecticism. Even more crucially, this is a band that is both massively popular and widely respected.

Fleetwood Mac's music is a blend of London and Los Angeles, the respective centers of pop music in the 1960's and 70's. "London" means a residual flavor of the hard-rocking, blues-based energy that underlay all the great British bands of the past decade, from the Beatles to the Rolling Stones to the Who. "Los Angeles" means both the country-rocking, slick folkishness of the Byrds that has flowered today with the Eagles, Jackson Browne and Linda Ronstadt and the all-American pop escapism of the Beach Boys.

(cont'd. on next page)

ARTS & ENTERTAINMENT

John McVie, Christine McVie, Stevie Nicks, Mick Fleetwood and Lindsey Buckingham of the rock group Fleetwood Mac.

You Love Me") and introspective ballads ("Over My Head," "Songbird"), and her womanly mezzo underscores the maturity of her music. Nicks, for all the trippy occultism of some of her lyrics, projects a younger, sexier, slinkier image. And her husky, nasal, sensuously confidential soprano balances Christine's earthiness. The third writer and singer, Buckingham, is the most overt exponent of California folk-pop. Fleetwood Mac's penultimate single, "Go Your Own Way," is a fine example of his work, buoyant and clever. And his boyish tenor is strong and distinctive on its own terns.

Underlying all of the songs is the danceable, pointed rhythm work of the band's veterans—John McVie, the bass player, and Mick Fleetwood, the drummer. Fleetwood may not be a subtle, jazzish drummer like the Stones's Charlie Watts or a feverish virtuoso like the Who's Keith Moon, but his playing is always rhythmically alert and catchily individual, and he and McVie do much to anchor the others' more fanciful inspirations by underpinning them with the verities of British blues. ■

(cont'd. from previous page)

There are three active songwriters in the current Fleetwood Mac lineup, and they all bring something different and complementary to the band's repertory. Christine McVie supplies both bluesy rockers ("Say

---

ELVIS PRESLEY DIES; ROCK SINGER WAS 42

Molly Ivins

Elvis Presley in Milwaukee, on April 1977.

Elvis Presley, the first and greatest American rock-and-roll star, has died at the age of 42. Mr. Presley, whose throaty baritone and blatant sexuality redefined popular music, was found unconscious in the bedroom of his home, called Graceland, in Memphis yesterday at 2:30 P.M. He was pronounced dead an hour later at Baptist Memorial Hospital, after doctors failed to revive him.

Mr. Presley was once the object of such adulation that teenage girls screamed and fainted at the sight of him. He was also denounced for what was considered sexually suggestive conduct on stage.

Mr. Presley's early hit songs are an indelible part of the memories of anyone who grew up in the 50's. "Hound Dog," "Heartbreak Hotel" and "Blue Suede Shoes" were teenage anthems. Like Frank Sinatra in the decade before and the Beatles a decade later, Mr. Presley was more than a singer—he was a phenomenon, with 45 gold records that sold more than one million copies each.

Mr. Presley was a show-business legend before he was 25 years old. At the age of 30 he was the highest-paid performer in the history of the business. He made 28 films, virtually every one of them frivolous personality vehicles and nearly all of them second-rate at best, but they grossed millions.

A recently published book called "Elvis, What Happened?" by three of his former bodyguards alleged that the singer was given to using amphetamines.

At his death, Mr. Presley had been an indelible part of the nation's musical consciousness for 20 years. ■

BING CROSBY, 73, DIES IN MADRID AT GOLF COURSE

MADRID, Oct. 14—Bing Crosby, whose crooning voice and relaxed humor entertained millions around the world for half a century, died of a heart attack today after a round of golf outside Madrid. He was 73 years old.

Mr. Crosby, an avid golfer, collapsed after finishing a game at the La Moraleja club with three Spanish champions. He was taken to the Red Cross hospital, where a spokesman said he was dead on arrival.

A few hours after learning of her husband's death, Kathryn Crosby told a news conference in Hillsborough, Calif., "I can't think of any better way for a golfer who sings for a living to finish the round."

The singer, actor and businessman had come to Spain primarily for relaxation after a tour of Britain, which he described as a test of his recovery from a back injury he suffered in a fall earlier this year. The accident occurred while Mr. Crosby was taping a television show to celebrate his 50th year in show business.

Bob Hope, whose running gag feud with Mr. Crosby was a trademark of both their careers, was "too devastated" to comment on the death of his old friend, according to a spokesman. Mr. Hope, who was in New York City, canceled a benefit appearance at the Governor Morris Inn in Morristown, N.J., and flew home to California.

William S. Paley, chairman of CBS Inc., who signed Mr. Crosby to a national radio contract in 1931, called his death "a great loss to the entertainment world," and said in a statement. "He will be remembered as one of the best-loved and most highly respected figures in theatrical history."

Harry Lillis Crosby parlayed a burbling baritone voice, a relaxed manner and a sense of business acumen into millions of dollars and a place in the front rank of world-famous entertainers.

A star performer for almost five decades, he delighted millions on radio, television, and in motion pictures and near World War II battlefields, where he entertained countless servicemen. His records sold worldwide by the millions,.

Of more than a score of his recordings that sold above the million-disk mark, the most popular was "Silent Night," with "White Christmas" second. It has been said that there was not a moment during the year that the Crosby voice was not being heard somewhere in the world—on radio, phonograph or jukebox.

Mr. Crosby won a movie Oscar in 1944 as the year's best actor for his role as a priest in "Going My Way." Among the most popular of his half a hundred films were the "Road" comedies—"The Road to Singapore," "The Road to Zanzibar" and others—

with Bob Hope and Dorothy Lamour.

His acting style was an embellishment, in a sense, of Mr. Crosby's own personality as a performer—relaxed, low-key and quietly charming. He almost never played a heavy, even as the spineless alcoholic husband opposite Grace Kelly in the film of Clifford Odets's "The Country Girl," released in 1954, in which Mr. Crosby gave one of his most compelling performances. ∎

Bing Crosby with David Bowie on the TV special "Bing Crosby's Merrie Olde Christmas" in 1977.

Live Classical Music Soothes Bellevue Prison Ward Inmates

Robert McG. Thomas Jr.

The cello seemed somewhat out of place, and, for that matter, so did the piano, even though it was a battered old upright that had been banged in the psychiatric prison wards long enough to become slightly out of tune.

But the piano was only for accompaniment. It was the cello that carried the music—selections from Mendelssohn, Benjamin Britten and Rachmaninoff that were played last week at two afternoon recitals in the unconventional setting of two Bellevue wards where criminal suspects are held for psychiatric

observation that may or may not help explain the often violent crimes with which they are charged.

The unusual recitals were sponsored by the Pro Musicis Foundation, an international organization that arranged for selected young musicians to perform in just such unlikely institutional settings in conjunction with conventional public recitals that allow them to become better known.

It would be hard to imagine a more unlikely setting for a

(cont'd. on next page)

(cont'd. from previous page)

classical music recital than the stark Bellevue dayrooms, where prisoners slouched on hard-edged folding chairs while the musicians played against the backdrop of barred and pad-locked windows.

It was Sharon Robinson, a striking 27-year-old cellist wearing a long dress with décolletage, who riveted the attention of the prisoners and created apprehension among the uniformed guards, who stood ubiquitously with hands on hips, keeping a wary eye at each performance of the dozen or so young suspects.

The guards would have done better to follow their charges' lead and sit back to enjoy the music, which, after all, has been known since Shakespeare for its powers to soothe, not stir.

Miss Robinson was no stranger to such audiences, besides, and at previous recitals, at the Women's City Jail in Houston and at California's San Quentin prison, where she has performed a number of times, she had learned to appreciate what she described as the "immediate, unschooled reaction, of these hope-less, hopeless people."

"My most emotional experiences have occurred at prisons," she said afterward. "You're sharing. It's not to impress them. It's not to show that you have faster fingers. You begin to realize that's what it's all about with an audience—the sharing."

When the recital began with the lyrical melodies of Men-delssohn's "A Song Without Words," there was just enough ner-vous fidgeting among the prisoners, a number of whom shuffled in and out of the day room in their hospital gowns, beltless street attire and slippered feet, that the guards remained on edge. When Miss Robinson followed Mendelssohn up on a high A harmonic, a man in the front row propelled himself to the front of his seat with an audible "Um-ummm."

The cellist merely smiled. "I liked that," she said later, "you wouldn't hear that at Carnegie Hall."

When it was over, a young man asked why Miss Robinson had closed her eyes during the selection.

It was her way of responding spiritually to the music, she ex-plained.

The young man nodded.

"It seemed like you loved that music," he said.

JANUARY 6, 1978

DOYENS OF PUNK ROCK, IN THE BIG TIME

John Rockwell

The Ramones at CBGB's in 1977.

In a world in which teenage tastes seem gratified by the fancified likes of Queen and Emerson, Lake and Palmer, it's hard not to love the Ramones. The New York punk rockers first burst onto the CBGB's circuit in 1974. By the following year they had established their style. Jostling one another on stage in black leather jackets, torn T-shirts and jeans, they began every song with Dee Dee Ramone, the bass player, bellowing out "1-2-3-4." The songs themselves were short and aggressively simple, strung together in a mostly unin-terrupted chain of howling feedback and twanging dissonance into one mosaiclike, half-hour set.

If you have a penchant for Mad Maga-zine-type humor, their stuff seems both funny and cute, and that's how more and more audiences are finding the Ramones, in this country and especially in Britain, where the band is a solid concert attraction. It hasn't always been that way, however. There was a time not so long ago when the Ra-mones had bottles thrown at them.

The Ramones helped create their own image by playacting their "dumb" role to the hilt. Their manager, Danny Fields, says now that in fact: "Everyone in the group has a good sense of humor, and everyone is pretty smart. In no way is it dumb."

The Ramones—all together there are Joey, the singer; Johnny, the guitarist; Dee Dee, the bassist; and Tommy, the drum-mer, and even they concede their common "Ramone" surname is assumed—say they're in their mid-20's and come from the Forest Hills section of Queens.

When they first banded together three years ago, they were an integral part of the New York art-punk-rock scene pioneered at CBGB's by Television, with clear debts back to the Velvet Underground, the New York Dolls and Patti Smith.

Tommy Ramone, the drummer and original manager of the group before Mr.

When the Soundtrack Makes the Film

John Rockwell

Movie soundtrack albums have been around for a long time. But they have traditionally been of music composed in the post-Tchaikovsky symphonic idiom, and most of them have been little more than aural reminders of the movies.

Now rock and other contemporary styles are invading the screen. The result is a bunch of albums that pop-music fans might well find interesting to hear whether or not they see the movies. And besides that, these al-

---

Fields took over, says freely that the band had serious esthetic ambitions from the start. "We had kind of an artistic vision of rock music," he said. "We wanted to take the heart of it and then simplify it. But as soon as I understood that our songs could appeal to the general public, I figured we could try to reach everybody. Our music didn't really change; we realized we could be successful by being avant-garde."

Apart from their own success, the Ramones take credit for sparking the whole British punk-rock scene, and their claim is worth taking seriously. The Ramones first played London on the Fourth of July, 1976— "On the 200th anniversary of our liberation from England, we went back and gave 'em something in gratitude," says Mr. Fields.

For all their miming of punk hostility, and for all the upbeat energy of their tunes, what sticks in this observer's mind after a Ramones concert is the innocent, sweet good humor of it all, and it is this good humor that the British punks have pushed to an angry dead-serious extreme.

"Everything's kind of a joke with us," adds Joey. "You can't take things too seriously, or it doesn't pay to live." ∎

"We wanted to take the heart of it and then simplify it."

bums will make so much money that they've become almost as important in putting deals together as the movies themselves.

Since three-minute numbers in an aggressive rock or disco idiom are generally thought to be too obtrusive for a conventional story line, more and more movies are being shaped specifically around the music. There are films about the early days of rock ("American Hot Wax"), about growing up with rock ("American Graffiti"), about the present day of rock ("FM") and about discos ("Saturday Night Fever," "Thank God It's Friday").

Conglomerate executives, their eyes on the potential profits of both their record and film divisions, have come to realize that the prime moviegoing audience is just the same age as the prime record-buying audience, so that if people like a given singer or a given musical style, they may well turn out to see a film based on that music or starring that singer.

The very nature of the film may be altered depending on which singing stars the producers have been able to obtain, or which clearances of pre-existing rock or disco hits the producers have been able to negotiate for.

This new kind of soundtrack almost in-

variably functions as a sampler package, offering a wide range of hit or potential hit songs by a variety of artists. On that criterion, the success of the "FM" sound track comes as no surprise. This amounts to a genuine "greatest hits" compendium by a wide range of successful pop and rock artists of the mid-late 1970's—the kind who could be expected to appear on the hit-oriented, quasi-AM sort of FM that is so common today.

The bulk of the songs here are studio-recorded numbers already available as singles and on the respective artists' albums, although their appearance on a compendium is new. Thus, one has songs like Steve Miller's "Fly Like an Eagle," Foreigner's "Cold as Ice," Billy Joel's "Just the Way You Are," the Eagles's "Life in the Fast Lane," Boz Scaggs's "Lido Shuffle," Boston's "More Than a Feeling," James Taylor's "Your Smiling Face" and Queen's "We Will Rock You."

The result is not a full picture of 1970's rock, to be sure, or even of what's available on big-city FM stations. There's nothing overtly experimental (except possibly the Queen track), no hint of punk or new-wave rock, no black music and no jazz-rock. But for what it is, it's very pleasant, and whatever people think of the movie, they're clearly responding to the records. ∎

Sid Vicious Dies, Apparently of Drug Overdose

John Kifner

Sid Vicious performing with the Sex Pistols in their last concert, in January 1978 in San Francisco.

Sid Vicious, the punk-rock musician, died yesterday, apparently of an overdose of heroin, about 13 hours after he was freed on bail in the stabbing murder of a friend, Nancy Spungen.

The police said he died after taking drugs at a party celebrating his release, held at the Greenwich Village apartment of Michelle Robinson, a 22-year-old actress. At first, detectives were inclined to view the death as a suicide—he had cut his wrists with broken light bulbs in a previous attempt—but later they said they believed it was caused by an accidental overdose.

(cont'd. on next page)

GUITAR ENTERS MUSIC'S MAINSTREAM

Allan Kozinn

In the last five years, the classical guitar world has seen the beginning of a quiet revolution. It is a revolution in performance standards, programming philosophies, contemporary repertory expansion and, most significantly, it is the start of a kind of musicological exploration the likes of which the instrument has not seen since the early 1920's when Andrés Segovia and Emilio Pujol began searching Europe's libraries for the lost music of the lute and vihuela composers.

In a sense, all this activity is a somewhat belated way of facing an artistic dilemma that has long haunted guitarists: While on one hand the guitar is an extremely popular instrument—it fills concert halls and it sells plenty of records—it is also an instrument that has generally been looked down upon by the musical establishment. Not that players in the Segovia-Bream-Williams league lack for the respect of their colleagues who play more accepted instruments; but the guitarists who have reached that level are few. And it has been largely due to certain self-imposed limitations that guitarists have found it so difficult to enter the musical mainstream.

Chief among these restraints has, until recently, been that of the repertory. The common myth is that the body of literature available to guitarists is extremely small and comprised primarily of miniature pieces which, charming though they may be, lack the depth one finds in the major keyboard and string literature. Here Andrés Segovia, for all his magnificent achievements on behalf of the guitar, is partly to blame, for it has been largely his approach to programming, both in concert and on disk, which has been the standard for the last 50 years. Guitar students who lack the technique, curiosity and musicianship to learn programs of full-length works have seen in Segovia's programming a rationalization for presenting miscellaneous Bach movements rather than full suites, or a group of Sor minuets and studies rather than his longer, more demanding concert works.

On record, most major guitarists have lately taken a more conceptual approach, one pioneered by Julian Bream and John Williams in the 1960's, in which large scale works and/or works related by composer, national origin or era are packaged together, leaving the "grab bag" approach behind. In the concert hall, the old-style program prevails. And as a result, music critics in major cities (where guitar concerts are the most frequent) have with some justification all but refused to attend guitar recitals at which the standard warhorses are constantly paraded.

Guitarists are aware of this, and with the help of a new breed of guitar musicologists such as Brian Jeffery, Thomas F. Heck and Frederick M. Noad, they are finding stacks of long-lost music composed by the great virtuosos of the early 19th century. These musicologists—all British, by the way—have not only helped fill a huge gap in the literature with their well-researched critical editions, but they have turned up quite a few previously unknown works by Fernando Sor and Mauro Giuliani, most notably, which stand head and shoulders above the current standard fare.

(cont'd. from previous page)

Born John Simon Richie, the performer had, at 21, achieved brief fame as a member of the now-defunct British punk-rock group called the Sex Pistols. But he was also known for violent outbursts, drug addiction and what one music reviewer described in The New York Times as "a particularly rabid series of offstage carryings on."

Last Oct. 12, he was arrested in a blood-spattered room in the Chelsea Hotel, on 23rd Street between Seventh and Eighth Avenues, and charged with the murder of Miss Spungen, a 20-year-old go-go dancer from a Philadelphia suburb, who was acting as his manager.

Among the most notable exponents of punk rock were the Sex Pistols, who, under their lead singer, Johnny Rotten, insulted their audiences and sang that they had been turned into "morons" by Queen Elizabeth II. Sid Vicious played electric bass and vomited.

The group disbanded last year after an American tour that did not live up to its advance publicity.

The day after his arrest, Sid Vicious was freed on $50,000 bail, part of which was posted by a record company, on condition that he report daily to the homicide detectives and to his methadone clinic.

The bail was revoked last on Dec. 8 after he allegedly assaulted Todd Smith, the brother of the rock singer Patti Smith, with a broken beer bottle.

At a bail hearing on Jan. 16, Judge James Leff of State Supreme Court reinstated the $50,000 bail, adding $10,000 bail for charges growing from the disagreement with Mr. Smith, after the defendant's attorney, James Merberg, contended that his client had been completely detoxified during his stay at Rikers Island.

Dr. Michael Baden, the Medical Examiner, said that if he had been detoxified, a drug dosage of the strength he had once been used to could be fatal because his body would have lost its tolerance. There are a number of such deaths each year, he said. ■

APRIL 11, 1979

Nino Rota, 68, Writer of 'Godfather' Music

Nino Rota, who wrote the music for Francis Ford Coppola's "The Godfather" and for nearly all of the films of the Italian director Federico Fellini, died yesterday of a blood clot in a Rome clinic. He was 68 years old.

Mr. Rota composed prodigiously and was known for the melodiousness of his music. He wrote symphonies, operas and church music, but won fame and wealth for his movie scores.

When Mr. Rota's contemporary opera, "The Italian Straw Hat," had its American premiere at the Sante Fe Opera in New Mexico two years ago, Peter G. Davis, writing in The New York Times, said that he thought American audiences would be "delighted" with the opera.

The Fellini films for which Mr. Rota composed the scores included "The White Sheik" and "The Clowns." He also composed music for other Italian films, including Luchino Visconti's "Rocco and His Brothers" and Franco Zeffirelli's "Romeo and Juliet."

Mr. Rota was born in Milan and studied music composition and conducting at the Curtis Institute of Philadelphia from 1930 to 1932. He directed the Conservatory of Bri, in southern Italy, for 28 years until his retirement last year. At the time of his death, he was working on the music for Mr. Fellini's new film, "Women's City." ∎

MAY 18, 1979

THE POP LIFE

DONNA SUMMER FUSES ROCK AND DISCO

John Rockwell

Donna Summer's two-disk album, "Bad Girls," is an exhilarating set, her best yet, and the first single from it, "Hot Stuff," is the best commercial single of the year so far. The disk represents a new triumph for the production team of Giorgio Moroder and Pete Bellotte, and in its own way, it's as much a fusion record as the Summer-Moroder-Bellotte "I Feel Love" single was. But most of all, "Bad Girls" represents a breakthrough for Miss Summer as a singer.

Miss Summer's earlier records were often wonderful, but there always lurked the suspicion that the real stars were Mr. Moroder and Mr. Bellotte. Miss

(cont'd. on next page)

Donna Summer performs onstage in 1978.

DECEMBER 4, 1979

11 Killed in Crush Before Rock Concert

Robert McG. Thomas Jr.

Eleven persons were killed and at least eight others were severely injured last night when thousands of young people waiting to attend a rock concert by The Who suddenly rushed the doors of the Riverfront Coliseum in Cincinnati.

"It was mayhem—bodies were all over," said Norman Wells, Assistant Fire Chief, one of scores of rescue workers summoned to the white concrete arena on the banks of the Ohio River, where an estimated 20,000 fans had gathered for a concert by the Who.

According to Chief Wells and other officials, the incident began just before the 8 P.M. scheduled start of the concert, when some of the fans managed to open one of the arena's doors, touching off a stampede.

Officials at the Hamilton County Morgue said that those who died apparently had been crushed to death.

Despite the deaths and injuries, the concert proceeded as scheduled.

"We figured it would be better to let it go than create another panic situation," Chief Wells said.

The victims were among thousands of fans who had purchased general admission tickets and begun lining up as early as 1:30 P.M. in an effort to be assured a good seat.

At the time of the incident, eight of the coliseum's many doors had reportedly been opened, creating consternation among the fans lined up outside one door at the southwest corner, which remained shut.

The police later said coliseum officials failed to open enough doors to handle the crowd.

"I was in the middle," said one fan, 17-year-old Michael Jordan. "It was crazy. You had to fight to save your life."

Another fan, Suzanne Sudrack, 15, said, "You could see people getting hurt. People were flailing elbows and smashing noses. You could see people going down."

Although there have been larger disturbances at other rock concerts, and incidents involving more injuries, none has resulted in so many deaths. ∎

(cont'd. from previous page)

Summer attempted all manner of styles, but aside from a big voice and a lot of eager personality, she didn't really convince this listener at least that she had mastered the idioms involved. But on "Bad Girls" and particularly "Hot Stuff," she sails into the vocals with a gospel-based, rhythm-and-bluesish rock passion that is really thrilling. There hasn't been such confident, all-stops-out vocalism of this sort since the best days of Aretha Franklin.

Here she gets a chance to sing what amounts to rock-and-roll with a disco beat, and she comes into her own. The only nagging doubt is that the obligatory soft side (side three in this case) seems to be the one on which she's contributed the most as a songwriter, and it's the shlockiest part of the record.

As a fusion disk, "Bad Girls" stakes a most suggestive claim. "I Feel Love" showed the links between disco and the sort of European, synthesized, progressive rock of such groups as Tangerine Dream and Kraftwerk. "Bad Girls" makes it suddenly clear that the supposed gulf between disco and rock isn't really so wide. Both have black roots, and both deal in heavy volume and a steadily reiterated beat. The nice irony of all this is that the rock that "Hot Stuff" is closest to is heavy metal, which is precisely the kind of rock prized by the most rabidly antidisco fanatics. It seems all that was needed to sweep aside these partisan bickering between the rockers and the disco dancers was one good, exciting record that answered the needs of both. "Hot Stuff" is that record.

APRIL 15, 1979

THE RESOUNDING IMPACT OF THIRD-WORLD MUSIC

Robert Palmer

The Mongolians started it, and now it's all over town. No, it isn't a new strain of influenza, it's a peculiar singing technique, developed by Mongolian nomads, that allows a vocalist to sing a duet with himself. The vocalist sings a primary tone, then tenses his throat and adjusts the shape of his mouth cavity, thus producing a delicate, flute-like overtone high above the original tone. On a recent weekend, one could hear the Harmonics Choir using this technique in concert at the La Mama theater, the Natural Sound Workshop using it in a loft concert on Eighth Avenue, and the composer and choreographer Meredith Monk using it in one of her "Songs From the Hill" in a performance at The Kitchen.

An avant-garde thrives on new techniques and new source materials, but the American and European avant-garde aren't the only musical sectors that have been heavily influenced in recent years by what used to be called "primitive" cultures. Our popular music, especially disco, our jazz and our concert music are increasingly drawing their inspiration from Africa and Asia; traditional Western modes of playing, writing and perceiving music are being challenged and in many cases supplanted, and the trend is accelerating.

When younger composers name their influences these days, they are as likely to say "Indian music" or "West African drumming" as they are to mention John Cage or Karlheinz Stockhausen (composers who were themselves profoundly influenced by non-Western music). Indeed, the number-one pop hit at any given moment is likely to be a pulsing, repetitive chant, with conspicuous African or Afro-Latin rhythms—overlaid in polyrhythmic counterpoint and played on African or Afro-Latin percussion instruments.

Non-Western influences are sometimes present even where they are not immediately discernible. Recently I had a brief backstage conversation with Leonard Bernstein and was surprised to hear him say how very profoundly he had been influenced, beginning in his student days, by the classical music of India.

Some people will fret that in accepting musical internationalization, we are accepting the decline of the West, that we are rushing to embrace the "primitive" because we are not so sure that "civilization" is necessarily a good thing. But we should do more than accept this internationalism; we should welcome it. The world is changing and so is our music, and in welcoming fruitful new ideas, whatever their source, we can only be enriched. ∎

JULY 25, 1971

A BLACK MOVIE FOR WHITE AUDIENCES?

Clayton Riley

Richard Roundtree in "Shaft," 1971.

Hollywood, of course, has always been a primary contributor to our tranquilizing mythologies, and in its newest dream sequence—The Hip Black Movie—we see a splendid example of that cracked ethic. And if HBM's are in this year, can a Puerto Rican Elliott Gould be far behind? The beauty of this particular deception is that the Hip Black Movie doesn't have to deal in any real fashion with what Black life is actually all about. (Of course, American films have never had to deal with anything real, and certainly they shouldn't be expected to start now.) The HBM, for as long as it lasts, will only be required to have Blacks participating in its preparation.

"Shaft," a film directed by Gordon Parks, is the current front runner in the Hip Black Movie Sweepstakes. Unfortunately, there will be others moving along; "Son of Shaft" and "Shaft's Brother-in-Law" come immediately to mind.

Parks, the director, is a Black man whose gifts are many, and whose intelligence I greatly admire. He is a giant among the world's outstanding still photographers. He has also composed music and is a skilled novelist and nonfiction writer. He does so many things so very well; directing films, however, is not one of them.

To be blunt about it, "Shaft" is a disaster. Technically mediocre and, for the most part, poorly acted, it is a film that lacks both style and substance. Nothing is really examined—the lives of the characters and the texture of the Black experience go unexplored—and what we are left with finally is an extended lie, a distortion that simply grows larger and more unbelievable with each frame. Shaft, the private detective, is patently unreal from the time we meet him until the time he leaves us. Unreal because the private investigator was exposed by the films and film critics of the late sixties as a champion of nothing but his own petty interests. The Sam Spade syndrome crumbled before our eyes as the private dicks of the world were revealed as a hairy tribe of conniving shysters and sadistic, drunken bullies.

Films like "Shaft" will be well received in this city because they provide Whites with a comfortable image of Blacks as noncompetitors, as people whose essential concern in life is making Mr. Charlie happy. It's about that big, Black, historically delicious breast of Mammy being stuffed into the collective mouth of America's White Kids of All Ages. It's about Saturday night diversions being provided by the darkies, the plantation boss striding through the cabin rows to check out some of those plump and dusky belles.

Shaft, played by newcomer Richard Roundtree, entertains. He dresses expensively, lives downtown in a renovated plastic brownstone, and, of course, he sleeps around. All of this is a lie, in fact. Private investigators, real ones, work hard at full jobs for small pay. Collecting dirt for shabby divorce cases and grabbing stray hands out of petty cash boxes is what that life is actually about—"Shaft," then, is twice removed from any acceptable truth.

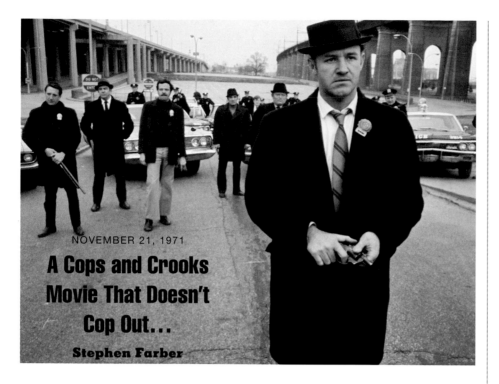

NOVEMBER 21, 1971

A Cops and Crooks Movie That Doesn't Cop Out...

Stephen Farber

Gene Hackman, as Detective Jimmy "Popeye" Doyle in "The French Connection."

Most of the genres that American movie-makers have relied on over the years—the western, the musical, the situation comedy, the war movie, the family soap opera—seem thoroughly exhausted by now; the truth is that the great majority of these genre movies have always been undistinguished, utterly conventional and banal, the cultists' inflated claims for them notwithstanding. Of the classic American genres, only the thriller seems to me to have ever had any real vitality.

"The French Connection" (directed by William Friedkin, written by Ernest Tidyman, produced by Philip D'Antoni) is a creditable addition to the list, the best American thriller since "Point Blank," and just possibly the best American movie released this year. It is, first of all, a stylish and exciting melodrama about a $32-million heroin exchange, but, beyond that, a hellishly precise vision of the disintegration of modern urban life and of the ambiguous role of the police in an increasingly polarized and corrupt society.

Like "Point Blank," John Boorman's surrealistic gangster movie with Lee Marvin as a zombie-like avenger in Los Angeles, "The French Connection" has a marvelous sense of place. Friedkin has managed to find real New York locations that look almost preternaturally eerie, sinister and fantastic.

In this urban inferno, where abrupt flashes of violence are all that disturb the desolation, it is almost impossible to find our bearings. Throughout the film, appearances prove deceptive. The most defiant black in a bar turns out to be a police informer; the affluent society matron whom the cops spot in a fancy nightclub returns home to a seedy little diner, and a moment later has become a skinny teenage waitress combing out an expensively coiffure wig—Cinderella after the ball. The film's disorienting network of impersonations suggests something about the erosion of any clear sense of identity under the pressures and confusions of urban life, the blurring of traditional moral distinctions, the rootlessness and anomie that contribute to the peculiar desperation of the modern nightmare city.

In discovering a new kind of policeman hero, the film makes its most significant contribution to the detective genre. Steve McQueen's Bullitt and Sidney Poitier's Virgil Tibbs were still superheroes, cops with a code. Gene Hackman's Popeye Doyle is a cop of a different order—brutal, racist, foulmouthed, petty, compulsive, lecherous. But even at his most appalling, he is recognizably human, something more than the one-dimensional "pig" of current liberal folklore. ■

NOVEMBER 28, 1971

Don't Believe They Didn't Know About Hitler

Alfred Kazin

Marcel Ophuls's "Le Chagrin et la Pitié" (The Sorrow and the Pity), a documentary film of France under the Nazi occupation, runs four hours and twenty minutes. This was not too long for me and the rapt, racked audience the night I saw it at the New York Film Festival. Though the period the film covers is at most five years, Nazism has so occupied and embittered our minds—those for whom it has more and more become the central yet most mystifying event of the 20th century—that it hardly seems 31 years since France was defeated and occupied.

Films are made to communicate. And though a camera dwelling on a face, a street, a wedding party, takes in more than the orderly processes of the mind can handle, all that raw footage is so cunningly edited, cut, dubbed, spliced, voiced, synchronized, music-filled, that the effect of communication, the instant effect on the audience, is obviously at variance with what the camera cannot help dwelling on in the shot of a face, of an actual street, of the unsynchronized faces at a wedding party. The final product is a fascinating hodgepodge, unresolved—often fortunately—in a way that no book can afford to be. But films are graphic, they are on the surface, they present. And one terrible effect of Nazism is that though the pain is everlasting, the cruelty still seems too improbable for books, just real enough—when caught in the flesh—for film.

What Marcel Ophuls and his crew, to begin with, have so amazingly captured for interviews are so many of the significant leaders and significant types. For me, surely for most in the spellbound audience, but above all for the people on the screen, telling their stories now, everything pertaining to the occupation of all Europe is still, in 1971, a thing of passionate breathtaking emotion. History, this history above all, has made our individual lives more intense. A tension is created, between the people on the screen and the audience, between the audience and its memories and private fears, that gives certain anecdotes and confessions in the film the effect of explosion. ■

'A CLOCKWORK ORANGE' DAZZLES THE SENSES AND MIND

Vincent Canby

"A Clockwork Orange" is Stanley Kubrick's adaptation of Anthony Burgess's perversely moral, essentially Christian novel about the value of free will, even if the choice exercised is to tear through the night robbing, raping and battering the citizens until they lie helpless, covered with what its antihero, Alex (Malcolm Macdowell) described happily as "the real red vino," or krovvy.

"A Clockwork Orange" is a great deal more than merely horror show. It is brilliant, a tour de force of extraordinary images, music, words and feelings, a much more original achievement for commercial films than the Burgess novel is for literature, for Burgess, after all, has some impossibly imposing literary antecedents, including the work of Joyce.

The film is cast in the form of futurist fiction, but it is no spinoff from Mr. Kubrick's "2001," nor is it truly futurist, if that means it is one of those things-to-come fantasies. More correctly it contemplates the nightmares of today, often in terms that reflect the 1950's and 1960's, out of which the Burgess novel grew. It is also—at least it seems to me—an essentially British nightmare (while "2001" was essentially American) in its attentions to caste, manners, accents and the state of mind created by a kind of weary socialism.

Alex is a terrifying character, but also an intelligent, funny and pathetic one, whose spiritual crucifixion comes when, having been jailed for murder, he is subjected to the Ludovico Treatment, which involves the conditioning of his responses, via the nonstop viewing of sex, horror and atrocity movies. At the end of two weeks, he is left as dumb and defenseless as a defanged, declawed animal.

Alex's eventual return to his original "free" state becomes an ironic redemption, yet not much attention is paid to the fact that Alex the hood is as much a product of conditioning as was the denatured Alex, the product of aversion therapy.

However, I won't quibble over the point. "A Clockwork Orange" is so beautiful to look at and to hear that it dazzles the senses and the mind, even as it turns the old real red vino to ice.

At one point in his therapy, Alex says: "The colors of the real world only become real when you viddy them in a film." "A Clockwork Orange" makes real and important the kind of fears simply exploited by other, much lesser films. ∎

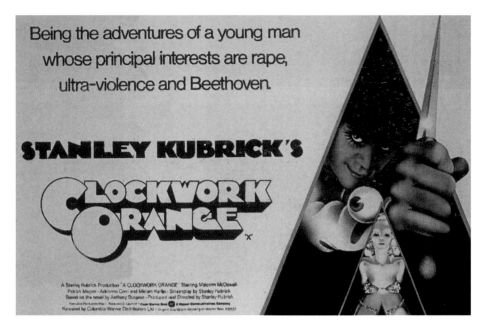
The movie poster for Stanley Kubrick's, 'A Clockwork Orange.'

> It is brilliant, a tour de force of extraordinary images, music, words and feelings

'Harold and Maude' and Life

Vincent Canby

Harold is 20, very rich and very suicidal. Maude is 79¾, very poor and so full of a sympathetic life-force that she grieves for a small tree, suffocating in the city's pollution. Harold and Maude meet at one of the anonymous funerals they like to attend, fall in love while transplanting the tree, and marry on the eve of Maude's birthday.

Even if this idea strikes you as immensely comic, you might well want to miss Hal Ashby's "Harold and Maude," a comedy that pretends to be as thoroughly in favor of life as "You Can't Take It With You," whereas it's quite as much about death as it appears to be.

As Harold and Maude, Bud Cort and Ruth Gordon are supposed to appear magnificently mismatched for the purposes of the comedy. They are mismatched, at least visually. Mr. Cort's baby face and teenage build look grotesque alongside Miss Gordon's tiny, weazened frame.

Yet, as performers, they both are so aggressive, so creepy and off-putting, that Harold and Maude are obviously made for each other, a point the movie itself refuses to recognize with a twist ending that betrays, I think, its life-affirming pretensions. ∎

BRAVO, BRANDO'S 'GODFATHER'

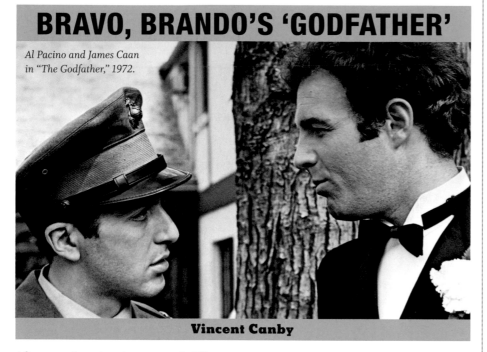

Al Pacino and James Caan in "The Godfather," 1972.

Vincent Canby

Putting the Hex on 'R' and 'X'

Stephen Farber and Estelle Changas

After a very long time, in too many indifferent or half-realized movies, giving performances that were occasionally becalmed but always more interesting than the material, Marlon Brando has finally connected with a character and a film that need not embarrass America's most complex, most idiosyncratic film actor, nor those critics who have wondered, in bossy print, what ever happened to him.

The film is Francis Ford Coppola's screen version of Mario Puzo's "The Godfather," the year's first really satisfying, big commercial American film, a movie that describes a sorrowful American Dream as a slam-bang, sentimental gangster melodrama.

Brando's role is that of Don Vito Corleone, the aging Mafia chief who remains a fearsome, rudely magnificent creature even though his hair has thinned, his jowls have thickened, his belly has dropped and his walk is not always steady, like a man searching for firm footing across a swamp. The role is not big enough for Brando to dominate the film by his physical presence, but his performance sets the pitch for the entire production, which is true and flamboyant and, at unexpected moments, immensely moving.

"The Godfather" rediscovers the marvelous possibilities existing in the straightforward narrative movie that refuses to acknowledge it's about anything more than its plot, and whose characters are revealed entirely in terms of events. It moves so quickly, in

such a tightly organized series of interlocking events, that the film, like its characters, doesn't have time to be introspective.

In this respect the film is very much like the novel, which Coppola and Puzo have adapted for the screen with extraordinary fidelity—yet the film has a life that completely eluded me in the novel.

To suggest—as I'm sure many people will—that "The Godfather" glorifies crime is to take the film both too seriously and not seriously enough. It is to deny the elation that one can experience through great storytelling, no matter what the bloody point of the story may be. It is also to confuse the movie's romanticized view of crime (to which some small part of us always responds) with a seductive view of crime, which the film does not have.

"The Godfather" does, however, honor its characters, and the coming-of-age experience that has been unique to one small group of first and second generation Americans who receive, according to the members of the Italian-American Civil Rights League, much more publicity than they have ever honorably deserved. That's a topic I'm not qualified to discuss. "The Godfather," however true or false to specific facts, is as dark and ominous a reflection of certain aspects of American life as has ever been presented in a movie designed as sheer entertainment. Now, as then, when the system doesn't work, the system will be by-passed. ■

Last November the Los Angeles International Film Exposition held a panel discussion on the subject of artistic freedom; one of the participants was the recently appointed chief of the MPAA's Code and Rating Administration, Long Island psychiatrist Aaron Stern. This was one of Dr. Stern's rare public appearances, and he was bombarded by angry criticisms from the audience.

The first obvious problem with the 3½-year-old rating system is the overly harsh restrictions it imposes on movie attendance; these restrictions deny teenagers access to many of the films they might find particularly meaningful. But the brief period we spent on the board made us aware of a more disturbing problem that outsiders often ignore.

The board actually has several secret duties in addition to classifying films. As in the days of industry censors Will Hays and Joe Breen, board members participate in re-editing films and even in reshaping scripts. In other words, the board circumscribes the rights of adults as well as those of minors; it restricts the creative freedom of filmmakers, and the adult audience's freedom to see what it chooses. Films are emasculated before shooting even begins.

More tampering takes place after the film is completed. Approximately 50 percent of all films in release today were first reedited at the direction of the rating board in order to make them more "suitable" for mass consumption. Among the recently censored films are "Little Big Man," "THX-1138," "Gimme Shelter," "A New Leaf," "Marriage of a Young Stockbroker," "The Last Movie," "The Hospital," "The Gang That Couldn't Shoot Straight," "Diamonds Are Forever," "Straw Dogs" and "Dirty Harry." At its worst, the board's censorship can alter the meaning of a film.

The predominantly male board had no objections to total female nudity in R films. The male genitalia, more sacred, remained X material—out of bounds even for teenagers. Rape was sometimes approved in GP films (the unrestricted category recently re-designated PG); normal, pleasurable sex—never. Since no blacks or representatives of other ethnic minority groups have ever served on the board, it is not surprising that rating is based on narrow white middle-class, middle-aged biases.

The too-willing cooperation of the studios may encourage the board in its censorship, but there is one simple reason for all the meddling that takes place: The board members believe they are charged with the responsibility of cleaning up the screen. Although they do not represent the creative film community—or the contemporary movie audience—they feel qualified to sit in judgment on the industry. Since they enjoy permanent appointments, their power is virtually unchecked.

Despite these attempts at intimidation, filmmakers could have more power than they think. The rating system could not survive without the support of the creative community. Most filmmakers have up to now been content to complain privately about the Stern office, while meekly acquiescing in its decisions. Until American writers and directors begin to protest the rating board's arbitrary intrusion on their freedom, and demonstrate that they respect their own work, they are foolish to count on respect from anyone else. ∎

Maria Schneider and Marlon Brando in "Last Tango in Paris," directed by Bernardo Bertolucci.

'TANGO'—EROTIC OR EXOTIC?

Vincent Canby

Bernardo Bertolucci's "Last Tango in Paris" is a beautiful, courageous, foolish, romantic and reckless film and Bertolucci is like the diving champion, drunk on enthusiasm, who dares dive from the high board knowing well that the pool is half empty. The stunt comes off, but the dive is less grand than we might expect from what we've heard and read, and especially from what we know of Bertolucci. I mention this at the outset because the film is being so overpraised (and overpriced) that many disappointed people may be reluctant to indulge its failures, thus to miss its achievements, which are considerable.

"Last Tango in Paris" is the movie romance of the 1970's, at least of that portion of the 1970's we have seen so far. It carries its ideas of love and sexuality not to the limits of conceivable time, but to the limits of last year—the era of Norman Mailer, Germaine Greer, "J," airplane goggles, porno films and revolutionary semantics. It's not the film's boldness that shocks, amuses and fascinates us, but its topicality, which, when we stumble upon it in films, has the practical effect of a vision of the future—movies, which take up to two years to make, being usually and fundamentally out-of-date. It's a movie for the breathless weekly news magazines that discover, analyze and embalm trends when the trends are still in nascent states.

It's what in the 1960s (a decade not great for jargon) would have been called, lamely, a Now film. It's so Now, in fact, that you better see it quickly. I suspect that its ideas, as well as its ability to shock or, apparently, to arouse, will age quickly. This is not true, I think, of the superlative production by Bertolucci, nor of the extraordinary performance by Marlon Brando who, following his fine, sentimental triumph in "The Godfather," now plays a role that does not simply identify him with his own time, as did his roles in "A Streetcar Named Desire" in the 1940s and "On the Waterfront" in the 1950s. It also makes him a Pop spokesman, tough, irreverent, mocking, as well as an incurable sentimentalist, a guy who still thinks it's possible to exorcise nothingness by embracing it, who chooses exile in a super-fascist state of mind where the only love allowed is sexual.

The sex scenes, not so incidentally, simply extend the limits of the sort of prudery that conventional films have always practiced. The sex is, of course, simulated. Only Jeanne (Maria Schneider) is seen nude, front view, full-figure, while Brando, more often than not, is wearing his pants while making love to Jeanne. This is not important to the film, but only to its reputation as a breakthrough movie, which it isn't.

However, the finest things about "Last Tango in Paris" are these scenes, riotous, furious, frenzied celebrations of the differences between men and women. Oddly enough, I found them more funny, occasionally more embarrassing, even more philosophical, than erotic. The intensity of Brando's anger and humor, and the desperation with which he sets out to insulate himself from the world through this affair, are very special to behold. His language—crude, witty and magnificently vulgar—and the stories that tumble out in the form of random monologues are unlike anything we've ever heard on the screen before. It sounds tough as hell, which explains, I think, why the film's full-blown, almost old-fashioned romanticism goes unnoticed.

To be crudely commercial about it, the film will also be helped by the fact that at the Trans-Lux East, where it opens next Thursday, the price of admission will be $5 a seat at every performance. The only other straight dramatic films to get away with those prices are the porno films. I have reservations about the ultimate point of the film, but "Last Tango in Paris" is too fine to be associated with the porno junk, even if only through the cost of tickets. ∎

'Graffiti' Ranks With 'Bonnie and Clyde'

Stephen Farber

Film poster for "American Graffiti."

Superlatives are dangerous, but sometimes hard to resist. George Lucas's "American Graffiti" is easily the best movie so far this year. Beyond that, I think it is the most important American movie since "Five Easy Pieces"—maybe since "Bonnie and Clyde." The nostalgia boom has finally produced a lasting work of art.

The film takes place in 1962, in Modesto, California, on the night before two high school graduates are scheduled to set off for college in the East. There is no conventional "story"; the movie has a freer musical rhythm, interviewing the adventures of four teenage boys as their paths crisscross during the night. Lucas uses all the resources of the medium to build his mosaic of impressions of small-town life.

Great films absorb the audience in a distinctive world, and the garish night world of "American Graffiti" is vividly detailed, sometimes claustrophobic. But the film represents more than a technical triumph. The stunning screenplay by Lucas, Gloria Katz and Willard Huyck is rich in characterizations, full of wit and surprise.

All the characters burst out of stereotype; they seem to have an independent life, and by the end they are so real that it's painful to leave them. The whole movie is brilliantly cast and performed. Lucas's technical flair was already visible in his first movie, "THX-1138," but his work with the actors in "American Graffiti" is a revelation. His gifts are prodigious; at 28 he is already one of the world's master directors.

It seems as if several years are compressed into one night—a series of comic, terrifying, romantic adventures that represent the most hypnotic possibilities of small-town life. The film isn't meant to be a naturalistic record; it's a carnival fantasy, a pageant of wonders, seen through the eyes of kids who don't want to leave.

The film has the spirit of rock music—bold, confident, colloquial, casually lyrical, unpretentious but evocative; it is a tribute to the beauty of American graffiti. Although it is a highly personal film, drawn from Lucas's own experience (he grew up in Modesto and was graduated from high school in 1962), it has the universality of the greatest popular art.

"American Graffiti" connects with an audience in a way that few movies every have. The only thing that worries me is the thought of all the exploitative fifties nostalgia pix that this movie may spawn. "American Graffiti" happens to reflect the public's yearning for the innocent contentment of the fifties, but the special excitement of the film is that it takes us beyond nostalgia—into a rediscovery of the past, and of memories that might have been lost forever. For those of us in Lucas's generation, watching "American Graffiti" is like going home; it's a primal experience, and the deeply conflicting feelings that it stirs cannot possibly be resolved. ■

'The Exorcist' Comes to the Screen

Vincent Canby

"The Exorcist," the story of the attempts to save the life of a demonically possessed little girl named Regan (Linda Blair), is a practically impossible film to sit through but not necessarily because it treats diabolism with the kind of dumb piety movie makers once lavished on the stories of saints.

It establishes a new low for grotesque special effects, all of which, I assume, have some sort of religious approval since two Jesuit priests, who are listed as among the film's technical advisers, also appear in the film as actors.

Among the sights to which the audience is treated are Regan, her face contorted and parched by the devil inside, vomiting what looks to be condensed split-pea soup onto an exorcising priest, and her paroxysms of fury as she jabs a crucifix into herself and shoves her mother's head down under her bloodied nightgown. In the context of this kind of spectacular nonsense, a carefully detailed sequence showing the child undergoing an encephalogram is almost therapeutic.

"The Exorcist" is not an unintelligently put-together film, which makes one all the more impatient with it.

The cast is made up of some excellent actors: Ellen Burstyn (who is becoming America's answer to Glenda Jackson), Max von Sydow as the old Catholic priest who also functions as chief exorcist, the late Jack Mac-Gowran as the director of the film within, Jason Miller as the priest who attains success through imitation of Jesus, and Lee J. Cobb as a kindly Jewish detective.

The care that Mr. Friedkin and Mr. Blatty have taken with the physical production, and with the rhythm of the narrative, which achieves a certain momentum through a lot of fancy, splintery cross-cutting, is obviously intended to persuade us to suspend belief. But to what end? To marvel at the extent to which audiences will go to escape boredom by shock and insult.

According to trade reports, "The Exorcist" cost about $10 million. The money could have been better spent subsidizing a couple of beds at the Paine-Whitney Clinic. ■

SEPTEMBER 1, 1973

John Ford, the Movie Director Who Won 5 Oscars, Dies at 78

Albin Krebs

John Ford, one of the greatest directors the American motion-picture industry has produced, died of cancer yesterday at his home in Palm Desert, Calif. He was 78 years old.

Imaginative, daring, sensitive, courageous, craftsmanlike, tough and, above all, durable, Mr. Ford was the only person to win Academy Awards for four feature films, of which he directed more than 130 in a four-decade career. He also won a fifth Oscar for his direction of a documentary during World War II.

With his classic "The Informer," released in 1935, less than a decade after the movies had learned to talk, Mr. Ford almost singlehandedly made the sound motion picture come of age.

Most of Mr. Ford's films had merit, but particularly excellent were those for which he won the director's award of the Academy of Motion Picture Arts and Sciences— "The Informer," plus "The Grapes of Wrath," "How Green Was My Valley" and "The Quiet Man." He was also the only director to be cited four times by the New York Film Critics.

Other Ford movies that have won positions on lists of important films worldwide were "Stagecoach," "The Lost Patrol," "Young Mr. Lincoln," "The Fugitive" and "Arrowsmith."

In stamping on his films his own personal trademark of quality, Mr. Ford became known as a meticulous, tough taskmaster who fought with producers, studio presidents, writers and performers.

("All actors," he once fumed, "are children—unborn children.")

The director was a nervous, twitchy man given to biting handkerchiefs. A six-footer, in recent years he appeared quite thin, almost frail. His once sandy hair had grayed and become wispy, but his still jaunty, arm-swinging gait belied his years. He always had a cup—often filled with a brew stronger than coffee or tea—and a cigar near while he worked.

He was probably the only director, at least until recently, whose name was often known better than those of stars in his pictures. In the forties and fifties, exhibitors booked his films sight unseen simply because he was the director. ■

JUNE 21, 1974

POLANSKI'S 'CHINATOWN' VIEWS CRIME OF '30S

Vincent Canby

Jack Nicholson and Faye Dunaway in "Chinatown," 1974.

There's nothing wanton, mindless or (with one exception) especially vicious about the murders and assaults that J. J. Gittes (Jack Nicholson), a private detective who has heretofore specialized in matrimonial disputes, sets out to solve in Roman Polanski's "Chinatown." No senseless massacres, no rapes, no fire-bombings of innocents.

In that far-off time—midway between the repeal of Prohibition and the inauguration of lend-lease—murderers, swindlers and blackmailers acted according to carefully premeditated plans. These plans, in turn, were always there for the uncovering by a Sam Spade or a Philip Marlowe or, in this case, a J. J. Gittes, a man whose name is repeatedly mispronounced as Gibbs, which is one of the burdens he learns to live with, along with a vulnerable nose.

This fixed order of things, of a cause for every effect, explains the enduring appeal of fiction like "Chinatown," but it also is something of a test for the writer who

(cont'd. on next page)

267

ARTS & ENTERTAINMENT

(cont'd. from previous page)

comes after Dashiell Hammett and Raymond Chandler and who doesn't hesitate to evoke their memories and thus to invite comparisons.

Robert Towne is good but I'm not sure he's good enough to compete with the big boys. When Robert Altman set out to make Chandler's "The Long Goodbye," he had the good sense to turn it into a contemporary film that was as much a comment on the form as an evocation of it.

Mr. Polanski and Mr. Towne have attempted nothing so witty entertaining, being content instead to make a competently stylish, more or less thirtyish movie that continually made me wish I were back seeing "The Maltese Falcon" or "The Big Sleep." Others may not be as finicky.

Among the good things in "Chinatown" are the performances by Mr. Nicholson, who wears an air of comic, lazy, very vulnerable sophistication that is this film's major contribution to the genre; Faye Dunaway, as the widow of the film's first murder victim, a woman too beautiful to be either good or true, and John Huston, who plays a wealthy old tycoon whose down-home, sod-kicking manner can't quite disguise the sort of fanaticism displayed by Sidney Greenstreet in Mr. Huston's "Maltese Falcon."

The plot is a labyrinth of successive revelations having to do with Los Angeles water reserves, land rights, fraud and intra-family hanky-panky, climaxing in Los Angeles's Chinatown on a street that seems no more mysterious than Flatbush Avenue. ∎

JUNE 21, 1975

ENTRAPPED BY 'JAWS' OF FEAR

Vincent Canby

Richard Dreyfuss (left), as marine biologist Hooper, and Robert Shaw, as shark fisherman Quint, fight the great white.

"Jaws" is the film version of Peter Benchley's best-selling novel about a man-eating great white shark that terrorizes an East Coast resort community, which now looks very much like Martha's Vineyard, where the film was shot.

It's a noisy, busy movie that has less on its mind than any child on a beach might have. It has been cleverly directed by Steven Spielberg ("Sugarland Express") for maximum shock impact and short-term suspense, and the special effects are so good that even the mechanical sharks are as convincing as the people.

"Jaws" is, at heart, the old standby, a science-fiction film. It opens according to time-honored tradition with a happy-go-lucky innocent being suddenly ravaged by the mad monster, which, in "Jaws," comes from the depths of inner space—the sea as well as man's nightmares. Thereafter "Jaws" follows the formula with fidelity.

If you think about "Jaws" for more than 45 seconds you will recognize it as nonsense, but it's the sort of nonsense that can be a good deal of fun if you like to have the wits scared out of you at irregular intervals.

It's a measure of how the film operates that not once do we feel particular sympathy for any of the shark's victims, or even the mother of one, a woman who has an embarrassingly tearful scene that at one point threatens to bring the film to a halt. This kind of fiction doesn't inspire humane responses. Just the opposite. We sigh with relief after each attack, smug in our awareness that it happened to them, not us.

Characters are simply functions of the action

In the best films characters are revealed in terms of the action. In movies like "Jaws," characters are simply functions of the action. They're at its service. Characters are like stage hands who move props around and deliver information when it's necessary, which is pretty much what Roy Scheider (the police chief), Robert Shaw (the shark fisherman) and Richard Dreyfuss (the oceanographer) do.

It's not their fault if they are upstaged by the mechanics of the fiction. That, too, is the way "Jaws" was meant to be. Mr. Spielberg has so effectively spaced out the shocks that by the time we reach the spectacular final confrontation between the three men and the great white shark, we totally accept the make-believe on its own foolishly entertaining terms. ∎

'Nashville,' Lively Film of Many Parts

Vincent Canby

Robert Altman's "Nashville" is the movie sensation that all other American movies this year will be measured against. It's a film that a lot of other directors will wish they'd had the brilliance to make and that dozens of other performers will wish they'd had the great good fortune to be in.

It should salvage Mr. Altman's reputation in Hollywood as a director who makes movies only for the critics.

"Nashville" is a panoramic film with dozens of characters, set against the country-and-Western music industry in Nashville. It's a satire, a comedy, a melodrama, a musical. Its music is terrifically important—funny, moving and almost nonstop. It's what a Tennessee granddaddy might call a real toe-tapper of a picture.

There are so many story lines in "Nashville" that one is more or less coerced into dealing in abstractions. "Nashville" is about the quality of a segment of Middle American life. It's about ambition, sentimentality, politics, emotional confusion, empty goals and very big business, in a society whose citizens are firmly convinced that the use of deodorants is next to godliness.

The film has a well-defined structure, while individual sequences often burst with the kind of life that seems impossible to plan. I have no idea where the director and the writer leave off and the performers take over.

Whoever is responsible, "Nashville" comes across as a film of enormous feeling. At the end, Barbara Harris, as a perpetually disheveled, very unlikely aspirant to country and Western stardom, almost tears the screen to bits with a gospel version of a song heard earlier ("It Don't Worry Me") that concludes the narrative in a manner that is almost magical.

Ronee Blakley, a composer singer who came to Mr. Altman's attention when she attempted to interest him in some of her songs, dominates the film, as much as it can be dominated by any one performer, as Barbara Jean, Nashville's beautiful, fragile, country and Western princess—a rural girl who's hit it big and throughout the film, sinks deeper and deeper into emotional panic. ∎

LUMET'S QUINTESSENTIAL NEW YORK FILM

Vincent Canby

John Cazale and Al Pacino in "Dog Day Afternoon," 1975.

"Dog Day Afternoon" is not only the most accurate, most flamboyant of Sidney Lumet's New York movies, which include "Serpico" and "The Pawnbroker," it is the best film he's ever made, with the exception of "A Long Day's Journey Into Night," and that one had the advantage of the Eugene O'Neill play and three great roles superlatively acted by Ralph Richardson, Katharine Hepburn and Jason Robards.

"Dog Day Afternoon," is an original. The events are based on a real-life Brooklyn bank robbery, yet the point of view, the tone, the focal area of the narrative are the decisions of Mr. Lumet and his screenwriter. They had no pre-sold or tested literary sources to fall back on. It is not cluttered with big themes that, more often than not, don't fit easily onto the movie screen. It's an action film in that almost everything it has to say grows spontaneously out of the confrontation of characters prompted by one bizarre event. This narrative method leaves a lot of psychological questions unanswered. Action movies, by definition, have no time for introspection, which is one of the reasons it took so long for critics to judge them seriously.

In fact, the film may be more "serious" than anything Lumet has done before. It's full of thoughts, feelings and questions about the quality of a certain kind of urban civilization. That sounds like a terrible load to drop onto any movie, much less one about a bank robbery, but these are the things about "Dog Day Afternoon" that continue to nudge the memory long after one has seen it, not the details of the attempted heist itself.

It's edge of cruelty, and the way the movie allows—and even encourages—the audience to laugh at desperate characters driven to lunatic endeavors, are as much the method of the film as its message. The film's New York is a cruel, desperate, lunatic place. I don't want to frighten moviegoers away from "Dog Day Afternoon" by mentioning things like messages; I only want to emphasize that it is a movie that knows what it's up to even when it's being ambiguous.

Lumet keeps the time of the narrative to that of the hold-up itself, 14 hours, and seldom allows the action to get very far from the bank and the Brooklyn neighborhood. In fact, the only times the film falters are when he cuts away briefly to scenes with Sonny's wife and parents at home, watching Sonny's show live on television. It looks as if Lumet wanted to explain Sonny in some way, which is patently impossible in this sort of film.

The movie's concentration of time and place adds terrific intensity to the melodrama, though it limits the psychological territory that can be covered. This, however, is a perfectly honorable artistic decision to have made and, indeed, it's a part of the content and style of this quintessential New York film. ∎

NOVEMBER 23, 1975

A SANE COMEDY ABOUT PSYCHOTICS

Vincent Canby

Jack Nicholson as Randale Patrick McMurphy in "One Flew Over the Cuckoo's Nest."

In a certain kind of sentimental fiction, mental institutions are popular as metaphors for the world outside. The schizoids, the catatonics, the Napoleons and the Josephines inside the hospital are the sanes, while all of us outside who have tried to adjust to a world that accepts war, hunger, poverty and genocide are the real crazies.

It's a comforting concept, and a little like believing in Santa Claus, to think that if we just give up, if we throw in life's towel, and stop thinking rationally while letting our wildest fantasies take hold, that we'll attain some kind of peace. No fear. No pain. No panic. The world becomes a garden of eccentric delights.

The thing that distinguishes "One Flew Over the Cuckoo's Nest," Milos Forman's screen version of the 1962 Ken Kesey novel, is its resolute avoidance of such nonsense. Although the film is not without its simplicities and contradictions, its view of disconnected minds is completely unsentimental. The mental hospital in "One Flew Over the Cuckoo's Nest" is, I suppose, a metaphor, but it is more important as the locale of one more epic battle between a free spirit and a society that cannot tolerate him.

Randle Patrick McMurphy (Jack Nicholson), the fast-talking hero of "One Flew Over the Cuckoo's Nest," more or less has his non-conformism thrust upon him, out of bravado and ignorance and the demands of this sort of fiction. After two months on a prison farm for the statutory rape of a 15-year-old girl, Randle has gotten himself transferred to the hospital for psychiatric observation, figuring that the loony bin would be a softer touch than picking peas.

Once Randle is in the hospital, however, the world shrinks to the size of his ward, which is the private domain of a singularly vicious character named Nurse Ratched (Louise Fletcher), a woman of uncertain age who is capable of understanding and sympathy only when they reinforce her authority.

The story of "One Flew Over the Cuckoo's Nest" is the duel between Randle and Nurse Ratched for the remnants of the minds of the other patients in the ward, a contest that starts out in the mood of a comedy on the order of "Mr. Roberts" and winds up, rather awkwardly, as tragedy.

"One Flew Over the Cuckoo's Nest" is indecently sentimental and simplistic if you take it as a serious statement on the American condition, which is much too complex to be represented by this mental ward. However, if you can avoid freighting it with these ulterior meanings—and Forman and his screenwriters have had the good sense not to bear down too heavily on them—"One Flew Over the Cuckoo's Nest" is a humane, loose-limbed sort of comedy containing the kind of fine performances that continually bring the film to explosive, very unsettling life.

There are some troublesome things in "One Flew Over the Cuckoo's Nest" that I'm not sure can be alibied by saying that it is, after all, a fiction and not a documentary. The ward that we see in the film is (most of the time) so spic and span that it seems to give the lie to horror stories we all know about the filth and overcrowding in so many mental hospitals. Also, can it be possible that shock treatments are (or were until recently) given out so arbitrarily as punishments, and could a single ward nurse ever have authorized a lobotomy without some second opinion?

These can be major factors in the way one responds to the film. But another is the extraordinary way that Forman has been able to create important, identifiable characters of psychotics, people who are most often represented in films as misfit exotics, creatures as remote from our experience as members of a Stone Age tribe in the Amazon.

CONNERY AND CAINE FLEE KIPLING INDIA

Vincent Canby

The setting is India in the late 19th century when the British raj was in its glory. In the upland territories British soldiers guard the frontiers to places of which someone will say, quite seriously, "No white man has ever gone in there and come out alive."

The most pleasant surprise about "The Man Who Would Be King" is that although it is about as romantic and implausible an adventure as you're likely to see, it's not an anachronism. It's neither a silly update of an entertainment designed for pre-World War II Saturday-afternoon America, nor is it one of those films that are wise with hindsight about earlier eras, like John Milius's "The Wind and the Lion."

"The Man Who Would Be King" manages to be great fun in itself while being most faithful to Kipling, whose story, written in the 1890's, is a kind of raffish metaphor for the British colonial experience that did not end for another half century. But this really isn't what "The Man Who Would Be King" is about. It's a tall tale, a legend, of steadfastness, courage, camaraderie, gallantry and greed, though not necessarily in that order.

It's about two former English soldiers turned con artists, Danny Dravot (Sean Connery) and Peachy Carnehan (Michael Caine), who decide that Victoria's India is no longer big enough for them (and their growing reputations as blackmailers and forgers). They decide to carve out their own kingdom in Kafiristan, now a part of Afghanistan but then an undiscovered territory not visited by a known tourist or king since Alexander the Great.

Danny gets himself crowned king and recognized as a god, the legitimate son of Alexander, and Peachy becomes chief of the armed forces and the treasure chamber. But while Peachy keeps his eye on the main chance, that is, an opportunity to abscond with the gold, Danny begins to like the divinity business and to take his re-sponsibilities seriously, which is their downfall.

Not in a very long while has Mr. John Huston, who wrote the screenplay with Gladys Hill and also directed the film, been so successfully lighthearted and so consistently in command of his subject. Small-time frauds who get in over their heads have always appealed to him, and Danny and Peachy, as played by Mr. Connery and Mr. Caine, are two of his nicest discoveries—larger-than-life, robust, sometimes curiously prim but suddenly stalwart in the crises.

The movie, which was shot in Morocco, looks lovely and remote (how did we ever once settle for those black-and-white Hollywood hills?) and has just enough romantic nonsense in it to enchant the child in each of us. ∎

New German Movie Directors Are Winning Acclaim

Craig R. Whitney

MUNICH—A new and promising generation of young movie directors is struggling to rise from the ashes of the German film industry, which has not seen their like since the pre-Hitler days of Fritz Lang, Ernst Lubitsch and Josef von Sternberg.

The Munich directors are self-taught, left-wing and low-budget. They are neither polished nor slick, and they are without a real tradition.

But their work has been acclaimed at international festivals in Paris, Cannes and New York; it has been packing young crowds into German theaters and some of it has even been shown commercially in the United States. "The Lost Honor of Katharina Blum," by Volker Sohlöndorff, 37 years old, and "Every Man for Himself and God Against All," by the 33-year-old Werner Herzog, played in New York late last year.

The new directors do not belong to a single formal movement. They include such different people as the leftist theater director Rainer Werner Fassbinder, who has worked in both Munich and Frankfurt, and Wim Wenders, one of the few new figures with formal training in cinematic art. Both are 29.

The new German directors are not inhibited like their predecessors from making clear statements about some central themes of German politics and history. The cult figure among them is Werner Herzog, a self-taught man who looks like a younger Vincent Price.

"I make my films as if there were no history of the cinema," he said in an interview. "I am trying to define a new image of what it means to be a human being."

"These people are making films about the German experience," said Peter Buchka, the film editor of the respected Süddeutsche Zeitung. "Herzog's penetrating philosophical explorations, and use of dream sequences in film—these are pictures that have never been seen on the screen before."

"Jaws" will make $4 million in Germany, and Werner Herzog's 'Kaspar Hauser' might make $120,000," said Hansjorg Kopp, one of the seven staff members of the Filmverlag. "But we are enjoying a success by our own standards."

The new German films have not yet done well commercially in America. "The renaissance of the German film is a fragile thing," Mr. Herzog says. "The reputation of German culture was destroyed by the Nazis, and it will be a long time before it is accepted again in the United States. You still haven't forgotten your Civil War, and that was more than 100 years ago." ∎

films

ARTS & ENTERTAINMENT

Scorsese's Disturbing 'Taxi Driver'

Vincent Canby

Robert De Niro as Travis Bickle in "Taxi Driver."

Several hours after I'd seen Martin Scorsese's new film, "Taxi Driver," last week, someone said to me with the kind of smugness with which pronouncements about the weather are made, "Well, it's the sort of film you either love or you hate. There's no middle ground." As I remember, my answer was non-committal but the more I thought about the remark, the more uneasy I became. There is—or should be—a very large middle ground surrounding this vivid and violent film, about a Manhattan cabbie who finds salvation through slaughter, made by one of our more talented young filmmakers ("Mean Streets," "Alice Doesn't Live Here Anymore"). Either to love or to hate it is not to pay attention to it. Rather it's to gulp it down whole, without chewing. Mindlessly.

With increasing frequency film critics, myself included, appear to be slipping into the use of hyperbole, the syntax of the copywriter who, in the interests of commerce, makes a complex world comprehensible by reducing everything to good or bad. It may be time that we attempted to retake the qualified middle, though not by making aggressive declarations to the effect, say, that "'The Hindenburg' is junk and I loved it," which is just an aggressive way of straddling the same old fence.

Our eagerness to express enthusiasm, and the uses that producers make of it, can mislead the public. I'm sure that Robert Altman's "Nashville" eventually suffered from all of its terrific praise, in which I was a willing participant, because no film could possibly measure up to the expectations that we had created.

I hope that "Taxi Driver" is not thus oversold. Though it is much more flamboyant and much more elaborate technically than "Mean Streets," it is a smaller film.

Until the penultimate sequence of the film, which is of a violent intensity that is not easily supported (for me, anyway) by what has gone before, "Taxi Driver" is one of the most compelling portraits of a lunatic personality I've ever seen on film. Robert De Niro, who played the simple-minded Johnny Boy in "Mean Streets," is superb as Travis Bickle, the taxi driver of the title. He manages to display both pathos and lethally dangerous charm as Travis goes about the city slowly and methodically preparing for his one-man Armageddon. As long as the film maintains its picaresque form—confrontations with assorted Manhattanites and tourists—it is a sort of crosstown epic, but when it demonstrates its more serious interests, in violence as a kind of catharsis, it goes suddenly schematic and didactic, but the scheme and the didacticism aren't up to the complex, contradictory observations of the rest of the film.

It's not necessary to identify with a character to find him fascinating but where Scorsese and Schrader go wrong in "Taxi Driver" is in attempting to make Travis Bickle in some way politically and socially significant. But he's not. He is an aberration, and the only way we respond to the character is in De Niro's display of himself as an actor of bravura unique among young American actors today. Nobody in the rest of the cast gets a chance to come near him, but there are some fine contributions, including those of Cybill Shepherd as a pretty, self-assured campaign worker who gives every indication of having a sense of the ridiculous, Harvey Keitel as an East Village pimp, and Jodie Foster as a pre-teenage prostitute of terrifying self-assurance.

I can't truly say that I either love or hate "Taxi Driver," though it has some dazzling moments. It's a movie that one should discover for himself. ■

HOLLYWOOD HAS SEEN THE FUTURE— AND HOPES IT WORKS

Robert Lindsey

Director Steven Spielberg on the set of "Close Encounters of the Third Kind," in 1977.

LOS ANGELES—Steven Spielberg, the young director who made "Jaws," the 1975 hit that was the most financially successful motion picture ever, is now filming his next project—"Close Encounters of the Third Kind"—and instead of focusing on a killer shark, it is about Unidentified Flying Objects.

George Lucas, who directed "American Graffiti," the movie about teenage life in a California town in the 1950's, is shooting his next film—"Star Wars," about galactic combat in the distant future. It stars Alec Guinness and simulated robots.

Jerry Zeitman, the producer, is working on "Damnation Alley," a movie about people trying to survive on earth after a nuclear war has shifted the planet's axis, and he is making ready another movie about an experiment to shrink humans to one-half inch high because the world is running out of food, energy and space.

These projects are only a sample of a curious resurgence here of science-fiction films, and represent a big gamble by Hollywood that the public wants to see them. More than a dozen science-fiction films are now in the works by major studios and independent producers.

For the most part, they are not low-budget ventures, but relatively expensive projects, and starting this summer, moviegoers will begin looking at the future through the eyes of a variety of different filmmakers.

There isn't any consensus among the moviemakers over why there is a renewed interest in "sci-fi." But their theories range from a belief that they reflect heightened public apprehension over the future because of energy shortages and slower economic growth, to a supposed alienation and disillusionment about today's world among some young people, to a profit-motivated, collective search for something different at a time when the public is saturated with cops-and-robbers stories.

Some moviemakers, such as Mr. Spielberg, don't even like the term science fiction and deny they are part of an easily definable trend. "I know people are going to classify it as science fiction because it's an easy handle to latch on to," he said to his new film about U.F.O.'s. "But it really won't be science fiction; I prefer to think of it as preternatural contemporary science fact.

"In reality, it will be about reality," he said a bit mysteriously, adding that it would encompass some elements of an adventure story, but otherwise refusing to disclose any details of the movie, which is scheduled for release late this year.

Other filmmakers, however, do see a trend. "I think they are today's westerns," said Mr. Zeitman. "They give you action, they take you into new territory and new terrain; and there are no limits on what you can do; creatively, you don't have to worry about reality." ■

"In reality it will be about reality,"

ROCKY ROAD TO 'ROCKY'

Guy Flatley

Sylvester Stallone as Rocky Balboa (left) and Burgess Meredith as his manager, in "Rocky."

Sylvester Stallone himself may be taken aback if he is not proclaimed a star when "Rocky" opens, since stardom was his goal when he sat down to write the role, an inarticulate, tender-hearted bum of a boxer who dominates virtually every scene of the drama.

"It took about three and a half days to write 'Rocky,'" said Mr. Stallone, an impressively muscled Italian-American decked out in a vivid shirt, jeans and boots. "I'm astounded by people who take 18 years to write something. That's how long it took that guy to write 'Madame Bovary.' And was that ever on a best-seller list? No. It was a lousy book and it made a lousy movie."

Mr. Stallone's childhood in Hell's Kitchen reads like a page out of Zola. "I don't want to say I was mistreated, but the first thing my parents ever bought for me was a leash. I was not an attractive child; I was sickly and even had rickets. My personality was abhorrent to other children, so I enjoyed my own company and did a lot of fantasizing.

"I was told by my teachers that my brain was dormant, and I took it to heart and channeled a tremendous amount of energy into my physical development, using the extra weights my mother brought home from the gym."

The weight-lifting paid off when he won an athletic scholarship to the American College in Switzerland, and it was there that he first dipped into drama, playing Biff in "Death of a Salesman." Disastrous as it was, the slapstick "Salesman" sold him on acting.

Yet it was a rocky road to "Rocky," the most calamitous pothole being his nervous participation in the nude Off Broadway drama "Score," a role which he won by walking across the stage and expanding his chest on command. Although he does not wish to disrobe on stage or screen again, Mr. Stallone, who is 5 feet 10 inches tall and weighs 185, feels that physical fitness is of prime importance. "An actor is what he looks like," he said. "I exercise religiously every day. So does my wife. And so does my dog."

Still, the flesh is not so sacred as the spirit, and that, according to Mr. Stallone, is why "Rocky" does not have a fashionably downbeat ending. "I wanted the human spirit to triumph for once," he explained. "This nihilistic idea that the only way to end a story is in the death of the human spirit has gone too far. There are no heroes anymore, only anti-Christs and hatchet murderers. Bring back comedies, bring back mirth and dreams. If you want realism, cut a hole in the wall of your living room and charge people $3 to sit and watch what's going on in your front yard." ■

273

Chayefsky's 'Network' Bites Hard

Vincent Canby

After a long and rewarding career with the UBS Television network as one of America's most respected news commentators, Howard Beale (Peter Finch) is being given the sack. He's obsolete. The night after receiving the bad news, Howard signs off the air by urging his viewers to tune in to his final show next week. He will, he says cheerily, commit suicide on camera.

Howard Beale has just catapulted himself into a new career as television's biggest new star. He's also flipped, being certifiably insane.

"Network," written by Paddy Chayefsky and directed by Sidney Lumet, is about the fall, rise and fall of Howard Beale and about television's running amok. It's about dangerous maneuvers in the executive suites and about old-fashioned newsman like Max Schumacher (William Holden), who have scruples and are therefore impotent. It's also about Arab oil, conglomerates and new-fashioned hucksters like Diana Christensen (Faye Dunaway), a television executive whose sensitive reading of the viewing audience prompts her to promote the lunatic coming-apart of Howard Beale as America's most popular personality since Will Rogers.

"Network" is, as its ads proclaim, outrageous. It's also brilliantly, cruelly funny, a topical American comedy that confirms Paddy Chayefsky's position as a major new American satirist.

Which leads me to wonder what it will mean when "Network" becomes—as I'm sure it will—a huge commercial hit with, one assumes, the same audiences whose tastes supposedly dictate the lunacies that Mr. Chayefsky describes in "Network." Could it be that Mr. Chayefsky has not carried his outrage far enough or that American audiences are so jaded that they will try anything once, say, "Network" or Russian roulette? I'm not sure.

"Network" can be faulted both for going too far and not far enough, but it's also something that very few commercial films are these days. It's alive. This, I suspect, is the Lumet drive. It's also the wit of performers like Mr. Finch, Mr. Holden and Miss Dunaway. As the crazy prophet within the film says of himself, "Network" is vivid and flashing. It's connected into life. ∎

'ANNIE HALL,' ALLEN AT HIS BEST

Vincent Canby

Diane Keaton as Annie talks to Woody Allen as Alvy Singer in "Annie Hall."

Woody Allen's fine new film, "Annie Hall," is a comedy about urban love and incompatibility that finally establishes Woody as one of our most audacious film makers, as well as the only American film maker who is able to work seriously in the comic mode without being the least bit ponderous.

Because Mr. Allen has his roots as a writer of one-liners and was bred in television and nightclubs, standing up, it's taken us quite a while to recognize just how prodigiously talented he is, and how different he has always been from those colleagues who also make their livings as he once did, racing from Las Vegas to the Coast to Tahoe to San Juan, then back to Las Vegas. Among other things, he's the first major American film maker ever to come out of a saloon.

For all of Mr. Allen's growth as a writer, director and actor, "Annie Hall" is not terribly far removed from "Take the Money and Run," his first work as a triple-threat man, which is not to put down the new movie but to upgrade the earlier one. "Take the Money and Run" was a visualized nightclub monologue, as freely associated as an analysand's introspections on the couch.

This also is more or less the form of "Annie Hall," Alvy Singer's free-wheeling, self-deprecating, funny and sorrowful search for the truth about his on-again, off-again affair with a beautiful young woman who is as emotionally bent as he is. The form of the two films is similar, but where the first was essentially a cartoon, "Annie Hall" has the humane sensibility of comedy.

As Annie Hall, Diane Keaton emerges as Woody Allen's Liv Ullmann. His camera finds beauty and emotional resources that somehow escape the notice of other directors.

One of Mr. Allen's talents as a director is his casting, and "Annie Hall" contains more fine supporting performances than any other American film this year, with the possible exception of "The Late Show" and "Three Women." Most prominent are Paul Simon as a recording industry promoter, Carol Kane as Alvy's politically committed first wife, Tony Roberts as Alvy's actor-friend, Colleen Dewhurst as Annie Hall's mother, and Christopher Walken as Annie's quietly suicidal brother. That's to name only a few.

There will be discussion about what points in the film coincide with the lives of its two stars, but this, I think, is to detract from and trivialize the achievement of the film, which, at last, puts Woody in the league with the best directors we have. ∎

Not since 'Flash Gordon Conquers the Universe'...

David Prowse as Darth Vader (voice by James Earl Jones) in "Star Wars."

Vincent Canby

It may well be true, as some of my colleagues apparently fear, that the immense success of "Annie," the Broadway musical incarnation of Harold Gray's "Little Orphan Annie," and George Lucas's "Star Wars," a gigantic comic-strip of a sci-fi movie, are the seminal works of a new age of Non-Think, an anti-intellectual reaction to plays and films that go out of their way to insult, shock, provoke and disturb, that question everything including the system that allows the artist to express his outrage. One can easily make a case for this argument.

Among other things, "Annie" virtually reduces the first term of Franklin Delano Roosevelt to one cabinet meeting at which Annie gives FDR the inspiration for his New Deal. The show doesn't seem to have a thought in its head, being composed of a series of sure-fire stimuli that call forth the sort of preconditioned responses that everyone who is not a card-carrying ogre has to orphans, stray dogs, mean overseers, kindly benefactors and tap-dancing toddlers.

At the same time "Star Wars" is the first science-fiction film since "Flash Gordon Conquers the Universe," a 12-episode 1940 serial, that makes absolutely no meaningful comment on such contemporary concerns as nuclear war, overpopulation, environmental pollution, depersonalization and sex. Reduced to their lowest common cliche, "Annie" and "Star Wars" are escapist entertainment. Each is guaranteed not to disturb the tired businessman who wears his fatigue like a battle ribbon.

This is, I think, quite true, but to leave it at that is to miss the point of what is too glibly described as escapist entertainment, as if everybody's escapist entertainment were the same thing and as if there weren't effective escapist entertainment and escapist entertainment to which one can be allergic, like penicillin. "The Sound of Music," which soothed the ragged nerves of almost everybody else, brought me out in spots. It depressed me as much as if I'd been listening to Dr. Martin Abend talking about Red China.

"Star Wars" pretty much defines what most people mean when they speak of escapist entertainment. It isn't about anything at all in any serious way, though it is so beautifully and cheerfully done, and it is so full of references to the literature of one's childhood, that the escapism is of a particularly invigorating sort. The movie's cinematic and literary richness are such that it cannot honorably be associated with other film and theater works that, by their blandness of subject and safe, unimaginative treatment, describe themselves as artifacts of the Age of Non-Think.

If, as I believe, the works of the Age of Non-Think can be identified as much by their lack of style as by their lack of substance, then "Star Wars" escapes such classification by a mile. "Annie" I'm not so sure about.

In "Star Wars" Lucas has created a jumbo-sized fantasy that pays homage first to those movie serials of our youth—including the "Flash Gordons," "Buck Rogerses" and "Captain Marvels"—that, in spite of their tackiness, liberated the imagination of millions of children around the world.

Lucas populates his galaxy with all sorts of curious beings, including nasty, pint-sized Sand People, hybrid animals that must be seen to be appreciated, talking griffons, a wino who looks like the Creature from the Black Lagoon, and one Wookie, Han Solo's first mate, a fellow who is supposed to be a hairy anthropoid but who looks more like Lucas's version of the Cowardly Lion.

Not since "The Wizard of Oz," I think, has a moviemaker so successfully created such a series of original monsters, some less nice than others.

The movie is full of extraordinary action but the action is anything but violent. No one is harmed in any believable or frightening way. This is not the sort of film that will send a child screaming for shelter under his seat. He may be pleasantly scared but he won't dare look away for fear of missing some further pleasure.

The chances are that parents will share that pleasure most of the time. It does go on a bit long, but those of us over 8 will appreciate the film's remarkable techniques, including the miniatures, and camera tricks, as well as the wit that never becomes facetious. This is not a film of the Non-Think Age. Actually, I may have to see it again. A friend of mine had to point out something I missed the first time—that the last scene is a direct quote from Leni Riefenstahl's "Triumph of the Will." Is Lucas, in that last scene, making some comment on the totalitarianism inherent in so many fairy tales and visions of extraterrestrial life? I suppose so. I also suppose he was having a terrific time thinking it all up, anticipating just such comments. ∎

DECEMBER 16, 1977

THE PRINCE OF BAY RIDGE

Janet Maslin

Tony is a handsome, big-hearted guy with a lot more style than he knows what to do with. His job in a paint store doesn't call for much élan, but Tony supplies that anyway, charming the customers and strutting gamely down the street as he makes his deliveries. Even so, things can get him down—but just when they do, another week is over and it's time to hit the local disco. On the weekend, and on the dance floor, Tony is king.

Tony's whole life, as somebody else in "Saturday Night Fever" manages to point out, is "a cliché." But John Travolta is so earnestly in tune with the character that Tony becomes even more touching than he is familiar and a source of fierce, desperate excitement. The movie, which spends mercifully little time trying to explain Tony, has a violent energy very like his own.

This is best demonstrated during the dancing sequences, which take up much of the film's time. Though the dancing is set to a blaring, contemporary score and often photographed in a red glow, the movie owes a lot more to "West Side Story" than it does to "Mean Streets."

Mr. Travolta dances with a fine arrogance that follows naturally from the rest of his performance, and he has one solo number that stops the show. But John Badham isn't always content to let the simple energy of the music or the performances suffice. Too often, he cuts distractingly in the middle of a routine, and his efforts to aggrandize characters by shooting them at angles or from below are superfluous.

"Saturday Night Fever" begins to flag when, after an initial hour filled with high spirits and jubilant music, it settles down to tell its story; the effect is so deflating that it's almost as though another Monday has rolled around and it's time to get back to work.

Ten minutes into the movie, you can be sure that its ending will be at least partly upbeat and that whatever happens will be blunt. But that is still no preparation for all the gruesome tricks Norman Wexler's screenplay uses to get Tony out of Brooklyn.

Mr. Travolta is deft and vibrant, and he never condescends to the character.

Among the movie's most influential principals—although they never appear on screen—are the Bee Gees, who provided the most important parts of its score. It could be argued that the Bee Gees have been turning out the kinds of jaunty, formulaic disco hits that punctuate the movie for so long that they've lost any trace of originality. But it could also be argued that the group now has this kind of music down to a science, and that originality is not exactly a key ingredient in the disco mystique. In any case, at its best, the music moves with a real spring in its step, and the movie does too. ■

John Travolta with Karen Lynn Gorney in "Saturday Night Fever."

Chaplin's Little Tramp, an Everyman Trying to Gild Cage of Life, Enthralled World

Alden Whitman

No motion picture actor so captured and enthralled the world as did Charles Spencer Chaplin, a London ragamuffin who became an immortal artist for his deft and effective humanization of man's tragicomic conflicts with fate. In more than 80 movies from 1914 to 1967, he either portrayed or elaborated (he was a writer and director as well as an actor) the theme of the little fellow capriciously knocked about by life, but not so utterly battered that he did not pick himself up in the hope that the next encounter would turn out better.

His harassed but gallant Everyman was the Little Tramp, part clown, part social outcast, part philosopher. He was "forever seeking romance, but his feet won't let him," Chaplin once explained, indicating that romance connoted not so much courtship as the fulfillment of fancy.

Stumble Chaplin's Everyman might, but he always managed to maintain his dignity and self-respect. Moreover, he sometimes felled a Goliath through superb agility, a little bit of luck and a touch of pluck. There was pathos to the Little Tramp, yet he really did not want to be pitied.

The essence of Chaplin's humor was satire, sometimes subtle as in "The Kid" and "The Gold Rush," sometimes acerbic as in "The Great Dictator" and "Monsieur Verdoux." "The human race I prefer to think of as the underworld of the gods," he said. "When the gods go slumming they visit the earth." And what they saw mostly was uncelestial folly.

In ridiculing that folly Chaplin displayed a basic affection for the human race. He was serious and funny at the same time, and it was this blend of attitudes that elevated his comedy beyond film slapstick into the realm of artistry. ■

FEBRUARY 5, 1978

A Celebrity Turns Fugitive

"I don't want to sound pompous, but in a way I'm actually a moralist," Roman Polanski said a few years ago. Last March, the film director was arrested and charged with raping and drugging a 13-year-old girl. After long plea bargaining, five sex and drug charges were dismissed, and Mr. Polanski pleaded guilty to a charge of unlawful intercourse. with a minor. That offense carries a maximum penalty of 50 years in prison, and last week, on the day that had been set for sentencing, Mr. Polanski's lawyer told a Santa Monica, Calif.

Roman Polanski outside a Los Angeles courtroom in 1977.

Judge that he did not believe his client was in the United States. "I suspect he is in a country where a plea of un-lawful sexual intercourse would not be an extraditable offense," the deputy district attorney said. "It could be in France." It was; Mr. Polanski had flown to Paris. French citizens cannot be extradited from France under any circumstances, and it so happens that Mr. Polanski is a French citizen .■

FEBRUARY 19, 1978

The Five-Year Struggle to Make 'Coming Home'

Kirk Honeycutt

HOLLYWOOD—"Movie making is like fighting a war," says Jane Fonda. "Soldiers are good when they believe in what they're fighting for. The same is true for an artist: You must really want to express some dream or vision. Without that, eventually all the juices begin to dry up."

The actress's military analogy is particularly apt in light of the campaign fought to bring a five-year-old dream, "Coming Home," to the screen. A collaborative effort by several ambitious, strong-minded individuals, the movie finally emerged last week only after battles to control their vision, creative conflicts within the group itself, casualties (one director and two writers), sudden changes in strategy and even legal arbitration.

A Vietnam War story developed at a time when the popularity of the subject in Hollywood was equal to that of a documentary on dysentery, it evolved out of extensive research with disabled Vietnam veterans and improvisational work by the actors until the final day of shooting.

Five years ago, Miss Fonda was heavily involved with the anti-war movement, pregnant with her second child, boycotted by some theater exhibitors, "gray listed" by the film industry and seriously considering leaving the entertainment field. But nagging at her mind was the possibility of doing a movie about the war and its impact on Americans. She formed a film company with fellow activist Bruce Gilbert, and the two began kicking ideas around.

"A close friend of mine, a Vietnam vet who is a paraplegic, said to me, 'I've lost my body, but I've gained my mind,'" says Miss Fonda. "The process of his coming home to the morass of V.A. hospitals and his growing disenchantment with the war capped his innate, supple intelligence." The story, they decided, would focus on the war's effect on three people: a paraplegic vet, a "classic Marine officer" and the officer's wife who has an affair with the vet while her husband is in Vietnam. ■

DECEMBER 15, 1978

SCREEN:
'The Deer Hunter'

Vincent Canby

Michael Cimino's "The Deer Hunter" is a big, awkward, crazily ambitious, sometimes breathtaking motion picture that comes as close to being a popular epic as any movie about this country since "The Godfather." Though he has written a number of screenplays, Mr. Cimino has only directed one other movie (the 1974 box-office hit, "Thunderbolt and Lightfoot"), which makes his present achievement even more impressive. Maybe he just didn't know enough to stop. Instead, he's tried to create a film that is nothing less than an appraisal of American life in the second half of the 20th century.

I don't mean to make "The Deer Hunter" sound like "War and Peace" or even "Gone With the Wind." Its view is limited and its narrative at times sketchy. It's about three young men who have been raised together in a Pennsylvania steel town, work together in its mill, drink, bowl and raise hell together, and then, for no better reason than that the war is there, they go off to fight in Vietnam.

The three friends, all of Russian extraction, are Mike (Robert De Niro), Nick (Christopher Walken) and Steve (John Savage).

Mr. Cimino has described his treatment of the three friends' war experiences as surreal, which is another way of saying that a lot of recent history is elipsized or shaped to fit the needs of the film. What is not surreal is the brutality of the war and its brutalizing effects, scenes that haunt "The Deer Hunter" and give point to the film even as it slips into the wildest sort of melodrama, which Mr. Cimino plays out against the background of the collapse of Saigon and the American withdrawal from Southeast Asia. It's Armageddon with helicopters.

More terrifying than the violence—certainly more provocative and moving—is the way each of the soldiers reacts to his war experiences. Not once does anyone question the war or his participation in it. This passivity may be the real horror at the center of American life, and more significant than any number of hope-filled tales about raised political consciousness. The big answers elude them, as do the big questions.

Director Michael Cimino (left) confers with actor Robert De Niro on the set of "The Deer Hunter."

Deric Washburn's screenplay, which takes its time in the way of a big novel, provides fine roles for Mr. De Niro, Mr. Walken and Mr. Savage, each of whom does some of his best work to date. Meryl Streep, who has long been recognized for her fine performances on the New York stage, gives a smashing film performance as the young woman, who, by tacit agreement among the friends, becomes Nick's girl but who stays around long enough to assert herself.

"The Deer Hunter" is both deeply troubling and troublesome (for the manner in which Mr. Cimino manipulates the narrative), but its feelings for time, place and blue-collar people are genuine, and its vision is that of an original, major new film maker.

FEBRUARY 18, 1979

OUT OF THIS WORLD

Harlan Kennedy

LONDON—"Alien," is yet another science fiction tale. For since the premiere 21 months ago of "Star Wars," the biggest grossing film of all time, Hollywood has been flinging up more space vehicles than NASA.

This year will witness a film recounting the exploits of comic-strip hero Buck Rogers; a Canadian production of H. G. Wells's "The Shape of Things to Come," with Jack Palance; "Battlestar Galactica," from the TV series; a new version of "Close Encounters of the Third Kind" which Steven Spielberg is editing, and a film based on the TV series "Star Trek."

On top of these, at least two more expensive space operas will presently enter production—Dino de Laurentiis's "Flash Gordon" and the first "Star Wars" sequel, "The Empire Strikes Back," in which Darth Vader will presumably return to menace Luke Skywalker and friends.

And then there is "Alien." Budgeted at $9-million, it stars Sigourney Weaver, Tom Skerritt, John Hurt, Veronica Cartwright, Yaphet Kotto, Harry Dean Stanton, Ian Holm and a cat named Miss Jones.

How does it plan to orbit above the glut of science-fiction films?

The nature and the appearance of the Alien have been cloaked in secrecy since shooting began. What can be deduced, from stray hints, is that it is a chameleon-like creature that can change form and color at will.

Photography on the film is now complete, and Mr. Scott is busy editing the footage. Time is short, for 20th-Century Fox wants very much to open it this May 25. Why that date? Perhaps superstition is out of place in both today's corporate world and the space age that "Alien" depicts—but May 25, 1979, just so happens to be the second anniversary of another Fox release: "Star Wars." ∎

'Norma Rae,' Mill-Town Story

Vincent Canby

When the issues dividing labor and management can be clearly drawn, there is nothing quite as satisfying as collective effort to fight oppression.

These are sentiments that Martin Ritt, the director, and Irving Ravetch and Harriet Frank Jr. (Mrs. Ravetch), his screenwriters, understand and fervently evoke in their often stirring new film, "Norma Rae." The movie also provides Sally Field with the plum role of her career, an opportunity to demonstrate once and for all that she is an actress of dramatic intelligence and force, someone who no longer need be referred to in terms of her television credits.

As Norma Rae, a small-town Southern mill worker, a resilient young woman of no great education but a lot of common sense, Miss Field gives a performance that is as firm and funny as the set of her glass jaw—and just as full of risk. The performance, which gives dimension to the film, may well be the one that those of other actresses are measured against this year.

"Norma Rae" is about the efforts of one young New Yorker, a glib, fast-talking Jewish organizer names Reuben Marshasky (Ron Leibman) to bring justice to the tiny town where Norma Rae, her father (Pat Hingle), her mother (Barbara Baxley), her husband-to-be, Sonny (Beau Bridges), and virtually everyone else are dependent upon the cotton mill, the town's only industry.

The film's principal appeal, though, is not the manner in which this uphill struggle is fought and won, but in the way that Mr. Ritt, his writers and his cast reveal the natural resources of the characters—their grit, their emotional reserves and their complex feelings for one another.

The film, which was shot in Alabama, places its characters in a recognizable social contest that neither parodies nor patronizes them. In short, swift, effective scenes "Norma Rae" dramatizes the limits imposed on imaginations by both poverty and tradition.

"Norma Rae" is not without blemish. Mr. Ritt and the Ravetches persist in equating the awakened social conscience with literature not always of the highest order. When Norma Rae is having her consciousness raised, it's signaled by the report that she's reading Dylan Thomas—offscreen. The platonic affair between Norma Rae and Reuben is given more time than her rocky, equally interesting relationship with her husband, a role that Mr. Bridges invests with more heft than seems to have been written into the script.

These are small objections. "Norma Rae" is a seriously concerned contemporary drama, illuminated by some very good performances and one, Miss Field's, that is spectacular. ■

NOTES ON WOODY ALLEN AND AMERICAN COMEDY

Vincent Canby

American actor and film director Woody Allen.

Alvy Singer, the fellow played by Woody Allen in "Annie Hall," is depressed by live lobsters and almost everything else you can think of, including the concept of the expanding universe.

All is change. Nothing can be forever—neither beer bottles nor Buicks nor universes. Whether or not it's the way things are, it's the way we see things, especially in a capitalist society in which the expanding universe is exemplified by the expanding economy and its needs. To hang onto what one has is to lose ground. It's our rule of thumb. We identify movement and call it progress.

There's a terrible tendency in the popular arts to describe movement as progress when it's only change. What we tend to overlook and to underrate is fulfillment.

Like Alvy Singer, I'm a worrier. I worry when people insist that Woody Allen's fine, funny, sorrowful, brilliantly realized new film, "Manhattan," is a breakthrough American film comedy, the last word in films about the 70's. Would these same people have dismissed Woody if he'd made a film that was "only" as good as "Sleeper" or "Love and Death"? I worry not only for Woody but for all the rest of us. When we say that Woody continues to top himself, we are acknowledging the right phenomenon in the wrong way. We are emphasizing movement over fulfillment and we are describing the creative process as if it were something to be followed linearly, like a dog race.

Neither Woody nor American film comedy is really changing. They are discovering what's always been there. When we understand this, our lives and those of our artists may become slightly more serene.

What makes a movie like "The National Lampoon's Animal House" so popular?

I've no idea, though because "Animal House" has grossed more money than any single Woody Allen film, I'd like to hazard a guess. When "Animal House" first came out, it was roundly criticized by some reviewers, including me, as being an especially sloppy movie, one in which there was scarcely a sequence or a single gag that might not

(cont'd. on next page)

(cont'd. from previous page)

have been improved by better editing and timing. Yet the film is often very funny and, in retrospect, it seems to be funny at least partially because its sloppiness is a reflection of the sloppiness and sloth of its characters. Though the film is set in the not-so-long-ago 60's, its irreverence is as much a rebellion against the orderliness and conformity of the late 70's as it is against the uptight campus administration it means to lampoon.

Who are the two brainiest funnymen in America today?

That's easy. Mel Brooks and Woody Allen, both of whom began their careers with (I assume) their ears glued to the radio, listening to Bob Hope, Jack Benny, George Burns and Gracie Allen, Joe Penner, Ed Wynn, Eddie Cantor and "It Pays to be Ignorant." Both Brooks and Allen started as comedy writers, peddling their gags to established comedians. The word, or the gag, was of paramount importance, and each man was in need of some discipline by which the word could be channeled for maximum effect.

Woody became a stand-up comic, the monologue his medium. When Brooks began making movies, it was clear he was one of the funniest men alive, yet his first movies were either chaotic, like "The Producers," or too formal, like "The Twelve Chairs." It wasn't until Brooks began his parody films that he found the discipline he needed in the limitations set by the genre being parodied. He still makes films as if they were Christmas stockings to be filled with everything available, from diamond watches to walnuts, with good gags and bad.

We laugh in "Manhattan" when Isaac Davis (Woody) says, "I've never had a relationship with a woman that lasted as long as Hitler's with Eva Braun." It's something that, conceivably, Virgil Starkwell might have said. Yet this time there's anguish within the self-realization.

"Manhattan" is a most serious as well as most funny movie. There are great swatches of the earlier Woody Allen in it, but the view now is longer, wider. With this film he stakes his claim to a kind of comedy that, though marvelously verbal, seems to have very little to do with the stand-up comic of nightclubs. But has Woody changed? Not—I think—for a minute. I suspect that once we have understood what he is capable of, we'll go back and see things we never before noticed in "Bananas," "Sleeper" and "Love and Death." Not the least invigorating thing about Woody Allen these days is the way he has demonstrated the possibility of fulfillment within the confines of the commercial film industry. Hollywood (the generic Hollywood) doesn't always strangle its best talents. Sometimes it liberates them.

MAY 21, 1979

'APOCALYPSE NOW' STUNS CANNES

Susan Heller Anderson

CANNES, France, May 20—Tension mounted last week for what was surely the main event of the 32nd Festival International du Film: the first public showing of Francis Coppola's eagerly awaited blockbuster, "Apocalypse Now." Thousands of onlookers jammed the street in front of the Palais du Film last night when the picture was shown to an audience of show-business personalities and executives, many of whom were more interested in making the scene than in watching the screen.

For what flashed on the screen for two hours and 20 minutes was a rare cinematic experience. On the surface it has a plot: A career army officer, played by Martin Sheen, is sent on a mission to kill a high-ranking commander, portrayed by Marlon Brando, who has gone insane and has taken the war into his own hands.

Using Vietnam, the all-American war, as a framework, Mr. Coppola begins his epic as a war film. But as Mr. Sheen progresses on his journey up a river into the soul of the jungle, the picture becomes increasingly mystical. It ends on a question mark: after killing Mr. Brando, does Mr. Sheen stay to replace him as the deity of the jungle tribe? Or does he return to the society that sent him?

Inspired by Joseph Conrad's "Heart of Darkness," the film, on its most global level, is a mind-shattering trip up the river of society along whose banks lie peace and war, right and wrong, innocence and corruption, good and evil and, finally, the freedom to choose between life's alternatives. On a less abstract level it shows the madness of war fought by freaked-out youths commanded by men who ultimately go crazy. What it is surely not about is Vietnam, a fact that seems to have elided many of the foreign critics bent on interpreting it as an American catharsis.

The reaction of critics who viewed it yesterday morning was mixed. One American magazine editor found it "too weird" to make the cover of his news weekly. Another complained that it was "two films and they both fell apart at the end." One New York spectator was repelled by the violence. The evening industry crowd clapped politely, but several movie executives stated that it was "not commercial" and "too long."

"It was a very brave and original work and a very good one," said the Pulitzer Prize-winning critic Roger Ebert. "You can take it to a very deep place." That this film is so heavily larded with literary and musical allusions makes it even more opaque to an audience whose primary cultural reference is movies.

Mr. Coppola has retained Conrad's name for Colonel Kurtz, the Brando character who recites poetry from T. S. Eliot's "The Hollow Men." This poem is itself prefaced by a line from the Conrad novel: "Mr. Kurtz he dead." When Mr. Sheen finally finds Mr. Brando living like the king of a primitive tribe of worshippers, the scene is reminiscent of the opening of Puccini's opera "Turandot," strewn with the decapitated heads of the princess's unsuccessful suitors. Nude bodies dangle on ropes from trees as in a Hieronymus Bosch canvas.

"This film is operatic," Mr. Coppola said at a news conference yesterday. "My film is in a different world. I tried to make it more of an experience than a movie. At the beginning there's a story. Along the river the story becomes less important and the experience more important." ∎

'DUKE,' AN AMERICAN HERO

Richard F. Shepard

John Wayne in the western, "Chisum," 1970.

In more than 200 films made over 50 years, John Wayne, who died yesterday at 72, saddled up to become the greatest figure of one of America's greatest native art forms, the western.

The movies he starred in rode the range from out-of-the-money sagebrush quickies to such classics as "Stagecoach" and "Red River." He won an Oscar as best actor for another western, "True Grit," in 1969. Yet some of the best films he made told stories far from the wilds of the West, such as "The Quiet Man" and "The Long Voyage Home."

In the last decades of his career, Mr. Wayne became something of an American folk figure, hero to some, villain to others, for his outspoken views. He was politically a conservative and, although he scorned politics as a way of life for himself, he enthusiastically supported Richard M. Nixon, Barry Goldwater, Spiro T. Agnew, Ronald Reagan and others who, he felt, fought for his concept of Americanism and anti-Communism.

But it was for millions of moviegoers who saw him only on the big screen that John Wayne really existed. He had not created the western with its clear-cut conflict between good and bad, right and wrong, but it was impossible to mention the word "western" without thinking of "the Duke," as he was called.

By the early 1960's, 161 of his films had grossed $350 million, and he had been paid as much as $666,000 to make a movie—although in his early days on screen, his salary ran to no more than two or three figures a week.

It was rarely a simple matter to find a unanimous opinion on Mr. Wayne, whether it had to do with his acting or his politics. Film critics were lavish in praise of him in some roles and shrugged wearily as they candled his less notable efforts; one critic, apparently overexposed to westerns, angered him by commenting, "It never Waynes, but it pours."

Mr. Wayne was co-director and star of "The Green Berets," a 1968 film that supported the United States action in Vietnam. The movie was assailed by many major critics on all grounds, political and esthetic, but the public apparently did not mind; in only six months, it had earned $1 million above its production cost of $7 million.

He had a handsome and hearty face, with crinkles around eyes that were too lidded to express much emotion but gave the impression of a man of action, an outdoor man who chafed at a settled life. He was laconic on screen. And when he shambled into view, one could sense the arrival of coiled vigor awaiting only provocation to be sprung. His demeanor and his roles were those of a man who did not look for trouble but was relentless in tackling it when it affronted him. This screen presence emerged particularly under the ministrations of John Ford and Howard Hawks, the directors.

Mr. Wayne made his last public appearance at the Academy Awards ceremony in April, where he drew an emotional standing ovation when he strode out on stage to present the Oscar for best picture. ∎

DECEMBER 19, 1979

'Kramer vs. Kramer'

Vincent Canby

"Kramer vs. Kramer" is a Manhattan movie, yet it seems to speak for an entire generation of middle-class Americans who came to maturity in the late 60's and early 70's, sophisticated in superficial ways but still expecting the fulfillment of promises made in the more pious Eisenhower era.

Ted Kramer (Dustin Hoffman) is a self-described take-over guy who left Brooklyn for Manhattan's East Side and is speeding to the top at his advertising agency. Everything in his life is working out as planned.

It is with some surprise, then, that he returns home to find his wife, Joanna (Meryl Streep), jaw-set and teary-eyed, determined to depart forever, leaving Ted with their six-year-old son, Billy (Justin Henry), to take care of.

"Kramer vs. Kramer" is one of those rare American movies that never have to talk importantly and self-consciously to let you know that it has to do with many more things than are explicitly stated. It's about fathers and sons, husbands and wives, and most particularly, perhaps, about the failed expectations of a certain breed of woman in this day and age.

Though much of "Kramer vs. Kramer" is occupied with the growing relationship between the abandoned father and son, through tantrums and reconciliations and playground accidents, the central figure is that of the movingly, almost dangerously muddled mother, played by Miss Streep in what is one of the major performances of the year.

Mr. Hoffman is splendid in one of the two or three best roles of his career. It's a delicately witty performance, funny and full of feeling that never slops over into the banal, which is the greatest danger faced by an actor who must play most of his scenes with a small boy who is as down-to-earth and pragmatic as Justin Henry. ∎

ARTS & ENTERTAINMENT

TELEVISION

TV Will Drip Social Significance

George Gent

Youth and contemporary relevance are the targets of the new television season, which starts next Sunday, but the bearers of those hopes for the most part will be dressed in the traditional garb of lawyers, doctors, policemen, adventurers, career girls and young marrieds.

To be sure, there will be some new wrinkles in the old clothes. The doctors, lawyers and policemen will be dripping with social consciousness, some of the young marrieds will be black, and the career girl has been cast as a TV newswoman.

There will also be comedies about a pair of housekeeping males, based on Neil Simon's "The Odd Couple," and about a blue-collar worker at sea in a white-collar world. There are no new Westerns, although there are plenty still around from other seasons less concerned with relevance.

An innovation will be Monday night professional football, which the American Broadcasting Company is introducing. Movies, both those produced especially for TV and the regular theater variety, will occupy a large portion of the evening schedules. Specials are expected to be down, except at the National Broadcasting Company.

"The Odd Couple," which stars Jack Klugman and Tony Randall as a mismatched pair of housekeeping males, interests because of the quality of the cast, while "Barefoot in the Park," another adaptation of a Simon comedy—the story of a young Manhattan couple who set up housekeeping in a one-room apartment—has drawn attention because its principal players will all be black.

Two of the series will center on psychiatrists—A.B.C.'s "Matt Lincoln," which stars Vince Edwards as a new-breed practitioner, and N.B.C.'s "The Psychiatrist," which stars Roy Thinnes as a hospital-based therapist. The latter show is part of N.B.C.'s "Four-in-One" program, which features four different

series, each of which will run for six weeks on Wednesday nights.

The others in the series will be "Mc-Cloud," with Dennis Weaver as a Western law officer assigned to New York; "San Francisco International," a suspense drama set in a major airport, which stars Lloyd Bridges; and "Rod Serling's Night Gallery," an anthology series.

Situation comedy continues to rule the evening schedule, with eight new series beginning this month. Mary Tyler Moore will

have her own show as a TV newswoman, Danny Thomas will be a new granddad and Andy Griffith "The Headmaster." Herschel Bernardi tops "Arnie," a C.B.S. comedy series about the problems of a man who is promoted from the loading dock to an executive office.

Finally, comedy and variety will have three new entries in Tim Conway on C.B.S. and Flip Wilson and Don Knotts on N.B.C. Red Skelton, long a fixture on C.B.S., has moved over to N.B.C. this season. He will occupy a half-hour spot on Mondays. ∎

TV REVIEW
PRO FOOTBALL KICKS OFF IN A.B.C. PRIME TIME

Jack Gould

Monday Night Football commentators, from right, Howard Cosell, Don Meredith and Frank Gifford.

The American Broadcasting Company introduced professional football last night as a regular Monday evening prime-time attraction, presenting Joe Namath and the New York Jets against the Cleveland Browns. The innovation will be watched carefully by media students. They are curious to see how sports does in the ratings against a movie on the National Broadcasting Company network and the regular situation staples on the Columbia Broadcasting System.

Heretofore the lady of the household, presumed to be in control of the set on weekday evenings, has asserted her preference for filmed stories and comedies after deferring to her spouse's selections on Sunday afternoons. What remains to be reported, however, is the increasing prevalence of multiple-set households, where divided interests can be accommodated on two or more sets in different rooms. With the one-set home, domestic harmony presumably now will be put to one more TV test.

Whatever the outcome of evening football, A.B.C. is hardly likely to be a loser. The network has had formidable troubles putting together a Monday night schedule of entertainment and, at least until January, football would seem almost certain to improve the chain's competitive position, if not necessarily outdrawing its rivals in total number of viewers. Should evening network sports give entertainment a serious challenge, last night could be remembered as marking one more change in the course of television.

Before the Browns-Jets engagement, the A.B.C. network unveiled two premieres, neither of great dramatic sturdiness. The first, at 7:30 P.M., was "The Young Lawyers," which featured law students coming to the aid of an intern whose efforts to help an automobile accident victim resulted in a malpractice suit. It is almost a duplicate of the crisper "Storefront Lawyers" on C.B.S.

A.B.C.'s second premiere, at 8:30, was "The Silent Force," a sort of "Mod Squad" in business suits. Ed Nelson, Lynda Day and Percy Rodrigues made up a special Federal unit—the F.B.I. can't do everything, after all—that is committed to uprooting organized crime.

Their maiden accomplishment was to thwart the framing of a deputy sheriff and bring down a district attorney with political ambitions and mob connections, A.B.C. helpfully told the whole story at the installment's outset, which may be television's distinctive contribution to the conservation of electricity. ∎

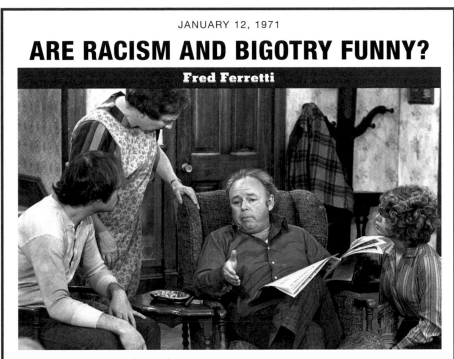

JANUARY 12, 1971

ARE RACISM AND BIGOTRY FUNNY?

Fred Ferretti

Archie Bunker surrounded by his family.

Tonight the Columbia Broadcasting System Television Network will find out if Americans think bigotry and racism, as the prime elements of a situation comedy, are funny.

(cont'd. on next page)

JANUARY 11, 1971

Bawdy B.B.C. 'First Churchills' Bows

Fred Ferretti

Even if "The First Churchills" weren't coming at us with humor, bawdiness and taste and with equal amounts of petticoat and epée—which they are—the return of Alistair Cooke as a weekly TV visitor would be enough reason to rejoice at the British Broadcasting Corporation's latest export.

The series, which will trace the 17th-century history of John Churchill, first of the line that led to the last Sir Winston, begins in bed. The Duchess of Cleveland is on the bedcovers, John is straightening his jabot. He smiles, drops his hat 20 feet to a straw-covered court below the Duchess's window and follows it with himself just before Charles II stalks into the Duchess's bedroom. It is only the first of the night's bawdy episodes.

As Mr. Cooke, slightly jowly, but as calm and tempered as in his "Omnibus" days, tells us, "it was hard in those days of Charles II, who had 29 illegitimate children, to always know who did what to whom."

In last night's episode, John, played with elan by John Neville, fought his way up through Army ranks so that by the hour's end he was a colonel.

Also by that hour's end, he had met Sarah Jennings, touched her, been called "an idle lecherous rogue…who ogled me black and blue," danced with her, and seen her curtsied to by the King. Not bad for an hour.

The series is photographed in color of a yellowish cast, which reminds one of so much parchment. The acting is broad and stylized, perhaps deliberately. It seems ideally suited to the elegance of the court. The actors swagger convincingly, women are wenches, and the halls and rooms of Whitehall Castle are filled with such things as "drunk as an alderman's whore" and "love in a carnal way," to mention some of the milder lines.

As Mr. Cooke told us as the camera faded out on John Churchill holding hands with Sarah Jennings, "We hope, as you did with 'Forsyte Saga,' that each week you'll see people you love to hate and whom you hate to love." ∎

(cont'd. from previous page)

Is it funny, for example, to have the pot-bellied, church-going, cigar-smoking son of Middle America, Archie Bunker, the hero of "All in the Family," fill the screen with such epithets as "spic" and "spade" and "hebe" and "yid" and "polack"? Is it funny for him to refer to his son-in-law as "the laziest white man I ever seen"? Or to look at a televised football game and yell, "Look at that spook run…It's in his blood"?

The answer, I say, is no. None of these is funny. They shock because one is not used to hearing them shouted from the television tube during prime-time family programs. They don't make one laugh so much as they force self-conscious, semi-amused gasps.

They are not funny because they are there for their shock value, despite C.B.S.'s protestations that what are being presented are "familiar stereotypes" with "a humorous spotlight on their prejudices…making them a source of laughter," so "we can show how absurd they are." What is lacking is taste.

"All in the Family" could have been funny; in fact it was funny when it was "'Til Death Do Us Part," a four-year hit on British Broadcasting Corporation television. It was offered to networks here and rejected.

And it was funny when it was "Those Were the Days," a pilot half-hour made for the American Broadcasting Company in 1969 by Norman Lear and Bud Yorkin. A.B.C. rejected it out of hand, and it was bought by C.B.S.'s Michael Dann as his last program decision before leaving C.B.S.

That first pilot, which I saw last week, was funny. Vulgar, suggestive, coarse, but funny.

Carroll O'Connor as Archie and Jean Stapleton as his wife, Edith, were, despite the vulgarity, amusing and, oddly enough, sympathetic. Mr. O'Connor so warmed to his role of blue-collar bully that he came off as well as Jackie Gleason ever did as Ralph Kramden. Miss Stapleton as his whining, wise-cracking wife was the perfect foil, saying with utmost sweetness, after Archie referred to blacks as "black beauties," that the reference was "nicer than when he called them coons."

But what happened to that pilot on its way to a network showing was a complete rewriting by Mr. Lear under network pressure; deletion of several remarks, and insertion of a remark wherein Archie calls his son-in-law "a Polish joke."

The shock lines were left in, but a rather amusing scene where son-in-law and daughter are surprised in deshabille by the Bunkers was written out. Sex is out, it would appear, but bigotry stays.

In the next couple of weeks we'll see episodes in which Archie writes a letter to President Nixon; he has an auto accident with a "yenta" but asks to be represented by a Jewish lawyer; in which a friend of his son-in-law turns out to be a "birdie…queer as a three-dollar-bill."

It will be an interesting 13 weeks, for C.B.S. as well as for the viewing public.

C.B.S. and A.B.C. Overhaul Schedules

The Columbia Broadcasting System and the American Broadcasting Company announced yesterday their plans for a second season, beginning in January.

C.B.S. is giving the ax to three programs and introducing four new shows, while A.B.C. is canceling four, temporarily dropping another and introducing a quartet of new shows. Both networks also plan extensive changes in their current time schedules.

Among the programs being dropped by C.B.S. is "Funny Face," which stars Sandy Duncan, who is recovering from a recent operation for the removal of an object behind her eye.

The other shows being dropped by C.B.S. are "The Bearcats" and "The Chicago Teddy Bears."

The new programs will be "The Sonny and Cher Comedy Hour," "Me and the Chimp," starring Ted Bessell, and "The Don Rickles Show," a situation comedy.

MOVES BY A.B.C.

A.B.C. is killing "Nanny and the Professor," "Shirley's World," with Shirley MacLaine, "Man and the City," with Anthony Quinn, and "Getting Together," with Bobby Sherman. In addition, "The Smith Family," starring Henry Fonda, will go off the air until April because A.B.C. must return a half-hour it "borrowed" from its local affiliates in September to put on pro football and "The Mod Squad."

In their place, it is introducing "Show of the Week," an hour series devoted to comedy, variety, music and sports, on Mondays at 8 P.M.; "The A.B.C. Comedy Hour," which alternates on Wednesday nights at 8:30 P.M. with "The Kopy Kats," which features leading comedians; and "The Sixth Sense," a one-hour Saturday series exploring extrasensory perception, which will be shown at 10 P.M. ■

Sonny and Cher in their "Comedy Hour," 1971.

Waltons Are People We Can Care About

Robert Berkvist

A Christmas episode of "The Waltons."

"The Waltons," C.B.S.'s gift to viewers who were hoping for one, just one, different show this season, seems strangely out of place until you realize what makes it different: you're being asked to care. Caring is an emotional muscle that seldom gets flexed prime time, thanks to the cutouts that pass for people on the tube. The wonderful and unusual thing about the Waltons is that they come across as real people.

Add to that a bit. The really unusual thing about the Waltons is that they're poor. All right, let's concede that these aren't the ghettoized victims of today's prosperous poverty. The Walton family lives in Virginia's Blue Ridge country and the time is the Depression, so the show can't boast the relevance of…well, what's your favorite relevant TV show? "Bridget Loves Bernie"? No, the Waltons relate to something else, something important.

The series is based on novelist Earl Hamner's recollections of his own upbringing under similar circumstances, in a large, close-knit family beset by economic hardships but getting by, making family life the anchor against all winds. Hamner's TV family, introduced last year in a well-received film special called "The Homecoming," has its budding writer too, in the person of 17-year-old John-Boy Walton, sensitively portrayed by Richard Thomas. John-Boy's reminiscences (he does leave home to become a successful writer—and doesn't that sound curiously old-fashioned?) are the framework in which each episode is set.

The Waltons' adventures, if they can be called that, are pretty mild stuff next to some of TV's improbable happenings. On one recent episode, the children—there are seven in all—were on the verge of attending the local fair, having counted up their hard-earned pennies and calculated there might even be enough for some cotton candy, when grandma broke her eyeglasses. The money, all agreed (the children with a gulp), would have to go for granny's new specs.

A nice twist in the plot led to the presence in the Waltons' barn of several carny performers left behind when the fair moved on. The slightly raddled troupers, one of whom, much to ma's and grandma's dismay, is a brazenly spangled tightrope walker, turn out to be decent sorts whose concern is the same as the Waltons'—how to earn their bread in a world gone awry. John Walton, the hard-pressed but open-handed head of the household, invites the castaways to share what the family has. The troupers, in turn, repay in their own coin by staging a show for the Waltons before moving on. Simple? Yes. Sentimental? Sure.

"we were richer than we knew"

Another episode found the Walton kids becoming so attached to their cow's newborn calf that they spirited the animal away from the farmer it had been sold to. Seems the calf had to be sold to pay for a new axle for the family jitney, without which there would be no way for John Walton to haul wood to market. "We live by the lumber we cut," he explains to one of his tear-stained daughters.

Well, one thing leads to another, the kids and the kidnapped calf are found, the irate farmer is soothed and a few lessons are learned along the way. Simple? Sure. Old-fashioned? Wow.

Most of us will never know what it's like to live in a sprawling old house with a screen door that slams and cocks that crow in the barnyard. Most of our children won't have run through grassy fields alight with wildflowers. Few of us would give a stranger the time of day, let alone shelter. Family life, for many, is a temporary prison en route to…what?

The Waltons, I think, remind us of where we have been and suggest there was value there. There's respect here, and affection openly displayed, and both young and old have their own dignity.

"It was a poor time," reflects John-Boy, looking back, "but in it, we were richer than we knew."

Watching "The Waltons" now, we know it too. ∎

An American Family Lives Its Life on TV

Stephanie Harrington

All too infrequently does television offer us a slice of life without first embalming it in a solution of predictable packaging and preconceptions. But starting this Thursday at 9 P.M., WNET/13 will present a series of 12 weekly episodes called "An American Family," surveying seven months in the life of the William C. Louds. The series chronicles the trivia of the Louds' daily routine as well as their crucial failures to reach out to each other across the empty spaces that make this affluent middle-class family such a fragile composition of fragments.

Unlike most documentaries, "An American Family" does not proceed from a premise and then marshal the evidence to dramatize that premise. Its only starting point was the intention to record on film the daily life of an American family. There was no predetermined structure into which the daily life of the Louds was squeezed; the failures to communicate, the strands of discontent were allowed to weave themselves into an inevitable denouement.

As a result, despite the fact that we know how it ends—the first episode, the only one in which the chronology is tampered with, shows us the Louds after the parents have separated—the tension builds, and you find yourself sticking with the Louds with the same compulsion that draws you back day after day to your favorite soap opera. The tension is heightened by the realization that you are identifying, not with a fictitious character, but a flesh and blood person who is responding to personal problems of the kind you yourself may face.

The idea for the series originated with Craig Gilbert, who produced "Margaret Mead's New Guinea Journal." He wanted to find out how the enormous technological, social and cultural changes of the past half-century have affected the daily life of an American family. Gilbert spent two months looking for the "right family," which meant one that "would put up with a major invasion of privacy...one that was composed of attractive, articulate [to minimize the need for narration] people who came close to the realization of the vaguely-defined American Dream."

Gilbert also wanted a family with teen-age children rather than toddlers, since they would be old enough to have ideas, relationships, problems and dreams of their own and friends whose presence in the household would broaden the scope of the film. Gilbert centered his search in California because it is the mecca of the "new life," the center of the new technology, a seed bed of fads. In short, it is the last ersatz frontier for the sons and daughters of the pioneers.

In the two senior members of the Loud family—Bill, 50, the owner of a firm that sells replacement parts for strip-mining equipment, and Pat, 45, an attractive woman with a striking resemblance to Jackie Onassis—Gilbert found two people whose forebears had moved west with the country and who themselves moved from Eugene, Ore., south to the lush life of Santa Barbara, Calif., and their approximation of the American Dream—an eight-room ranch house, a horse, three dogs, a pool, a Jaguar, a Volvo, a Toyota and a Datsun pick-up. Their five children—Lance, 20; Kevin, 18; Grant, 17; Delilah, 15; and Michele, 13—are fashionably into mod clothes and rock music. And all of the Louds—except Bill, who comes off as more of a square—are a combination of sophistication and provincialism that expresses itself in glib patter full of one liners that enables them to talk to each other without ever saying anything.

The viewer is at once absorbed in the Louds' unfolding drama, aching to tell them what they're not telling each other or admitting to themselves and, at the same time, suffering little shocks of self-recognition, identifying with one or the other of the Louds.

Margaret Mead has said that "An American Family" "may be as important for our time as were the invention of drama and the novel for earlier generations: a new way to help people understand themselves." This form of cinema verité may never be so ubiquitous a form as the novel or the drama, but we can at least hope (although it might inspire the Administration to try to cut off funds for public television completely) that Craig Gilbert and others will get their cameras inside as many doors as possible. ■

It Wasn't All Ponytails

Cyclops

You may not believe this, but it's true: Ten minutes into the first episode of the new "Happy Days" series on A.B.C., my 11-year-old son left the living room to go upstairs and read Low's abridgement of Gibbon's "Decline and Fall of the Roman Empire." Whether he's precocious or just suggestible, he knows what he doesn't like.

My 7-year-old daughter, on the other hand, stayed to the bitter end. She's the one in our house who listens to Donnie Osmond records all day long. It is for moon children like my daughter—as well as the usual substratum of catatonics who are afraid to do anything else on Tuesday nights except watch television—that "Happy Days" apparently has been concocted.

"Happy Days," of course, is a sitcom about the ostensibly innocent fifties. The decade itself is presumed to be a sitcom. We have the ubiquitous Ron Howard—he cruised around in the film "American Graffiti"; he ran away to Cincinnati on C.B.S.'s "The Migrants"; he died of leukemia on "The Waltons"—as a high school teenager, Richie. We have Tom Bosley as his father, which is like using the Koh-i-noor diamond to feed a parking meter. And we have Potsie (Anson Williams) and Fonzie (Henry Winkler).

Richie, Potsie and Fonzie are fixated on ponytails. They spend one half-hour wondering how "to go all the way" with a ponytail. They spend another half-hour wondering whether, if they had a car, they would automatically get a ponytail. They spend a third half-hour getting drunk with some Marines, in order to make themselves more worthy of ponytails. Tom Bosley chuckles philosophically in the kitchenette. (Most fifties philosophizing, you will recall, took place in the kitchenette; the bedroom was not invented until Dick Van Dyke.) And there are snippets of popular songs and jokes about Milton Berle.

If all this strikes you as "Ozzie and Harriet" with hair on their palms, you're right. Come back, Ricky Nelson, all is forgiven.

Having graduated from high school in

1956, I have my own teeth to grind. Yes, indeed, the ponytails seemed inaccessible. I wanted to bury my head in their miracle fabrics. It never, however, occurred to me that you could make a TV series out of a glandular disturbance.

Now the Pill has become, for the sixties and seventies, what radioactive fallout was for the fifties: an invisible menace to innocence. In the fifties, before our children became strangers, drugs were class-conscious and color-coded; they stayed out of white suburbs. Glue-sniffing in the garage was as far as it went. Drain the oil out of these kids' hair and they'll be normalized, ready to embark on the paper route of life.

What's forgotten is that the fifties were also a time when Joe McCarthy's jugendbund ran around firing the teachers in our schools and the actors on our screens; when Egypt and Israel had another war; when the Soviet Union invaded Hungary; when Adlai Stevenson was ridiculed by Richard Nixon for proposing an end to A-bomb and H-bomb testing. Happy days!

And yet my daughter sits mesmerized, with her hair in her eyes, playing with her emotions as though they were blind puppies. For this happy day, A.B.C. canceled "Adam's Rib" and "Room 222"? ■

Henry Winkler as Arthur " The Fonz" Fonzarelli in "Happy Days."

'Jane Pittman' Fulfilled My Deepest Expectations

Nikki Giovanni

Not everyone had a grandmother they adored, or remembers warmly the little old ladies with their pillbox hats and shaggy sweaters thrown around their too-frail shoulders, so it is not surprising that not everyone loved "Miss Jane Pittman." What disappoints me about Stephanie Harrington's review is her lack of knowledge of blacks as well as her almost total inability to relate to the television show.

If Cicely Tyson isn't one of the best actresses on screen, then "grits ain't groceries, eggs ain't poultry, and Mona Lisa was a man," to quote Little Willie John.

The New York Times isn't our local bridge club or bowling league, it's an opinion-making body, and although it may not disturb the editors that they are running a piece for which the homework was only partially done, it disturbs me. C.B.S. presented a drama, a fiction, a story. The facts and their subtleties are for us to fill in. I hope Mrs. Harrington explains slavery to her children better than she explained drama to me.

Do we really expect Jane Pittman or Big Laura to discourse on the economic institution of slavery? Do we really expect Jane, née Ticey, to tell the soldier, "I am from a great tribe in Western Africa and my real name is Wangari so put me down, you honkie"? Jane is the name Ticey picked and it was freedom to her. Who picks our names now and are we any less enslaved?

Mrs. Harrington probably also missed the scene with a poor white woman screaming, "Look what you've done to me!" and the scene of the plantation where Jane spent "12 long years," falling apart without black labor. It was very evident that blacks were the backbone. You didn't see the former owners throwing parties and singing, "Happy Days Are Here Again," did you?

(cont'd. on next page)

287

(cont'd. from previous page)
You saw the mistress when Ticey was getting water for the Yankee troops, saying, "don't you dare tell them where the master is hiding." You saw a scraggly bunch of slaves walking away from what had to have been a flourishing plantation. I'm afraid Mrs. Harrington doesn't know the history of blacks or America, or she would have known that by looking at the plantation.

If the movie had talked about an obscure period in American history, perhaps more than a scene or a word would have been required, but the Civil War is one of two most written about periods in American history. I don't think either C.B.S., Xerox or Ernest Gaines, who wrote the original novel, had to be more explicit. The Klan rising against the school, the man hanged while the woman screamed with the baby in her arms, Ned and Jimmy being murdered. Being displeased with the image is no excuse for pretending it does not exist.

"The Autobiography of Miss Jane Pittman" was not intended to be anything other than what it is, a novel much like Margaret Walker's "Jubilee," letting another point of view into our consciousness—bringing a different and much welcomed drama to the screen.

If Mrs. Harrington would like to see blacks treated with the time and format that Alistair Cooke received for "America," then so would I, but that does not, cannot, and will not change in any way the complete validity of "Jane Pittman." From Joe Pittman dying in his attempt to break a wild white stallion, to the sheer absurdity of blacks being unable to get a decent drink of water while a man is going into outer space. America can explore outer space but not inner feelings.

"Miss Jane Pittman" fulfilled my deepest expectations. I did not look for a miracle nor did I view it with malice. That the show will spawn another film depicting other blacks in other experiences is unquestioned. That it was a triumph of and for the enduring strength of black people is also beyond doubt. ■

Cicely Tyson as Jane Pittman drinks from a "whites only" water fountain to the consternation of the local authorities in the made-for-televison movie "The Autobiography of Miss Jane Pittman," 1974.

TAKE ONE COVERED WAGON, ADD SUGAR...

John J. O'Connor

Sometimes it's just a matter of packaging. If "The Little House on the Prairie," shown on the National Broadcasting Company network a couple of Saturdays ago, had been presented as a 90-minute after-school special for young people, the program and the network might have been praised for doing something good in an area begging for something good. Instead, the production was stretched to two hours and run in the adult prime-time slot of 9 to 11 P.M., demanding a different evaluation and considerably less praise.

Based on a novel by Laura Ingalls Wilder, the script contained enough family warmth and struggle to make "The Waltons" look like a pack of pampered snobs. Charles (Michael Landon) and Caroline (Karen Grassle) had only three daughters, the required adorable dog, a covered wagon and lots of faith when they settled in Kansas.

Laura (Melissa Gilbert) did the narrating, pointing out such things as "this is a fair land" and generally monopolizing attention as daddy's precocious pet. Her older sister stood around a lot and smiled, with an occasional and understandable hint of sibling strain. Ma managed to look and sound just like Miss Michael Learned, the Ma in "The Waltons." And, throughout, everybody remained incredibly well-scrubbed.

Script difficulties appeared early on. In getting the family wagon across a river, Charles forgot to include the dog, which was promptly swept downstream. A day or so later, as the family sat around the campfire, what should greet their ears but the sound of doggie whimpering. "How did he find us?" asked Laura. "Instinct...love," replied Pa.

There was also much, however, of purely historical value: the building of the

The cast from "The Little House on the Prairie."

Fall Programming Cuts Down on Violence

Les Brown

The television networks next fall will cut back in programs that deal with violence and stress series concerned with family life and personal relationships. That is evident from the new prime-time schedules for September disclosed yesterday.

According to industry sources, programs are being discarded for both rating inadequacy and in response to the recent hearings on television violence by the Senate Communications Subcommittee. While three new police and private-eye shows have been added by the two networks, all have been assigned late-evening time periods, at 10 o'clock, and several others from the present schedule have been moved to a later hour.

Many of the new one-hour dramatic shows will eschew law-enforcement story lines and gunplay for situations involving truck drivers, schoolteachers, forest rangers and game wardens.

The American Broadcasting Company network is expected to release the final draft of its fall schedule early next week, but the advance information is that it too will favor less violence in the peak viewing hours.

The reduction in violent programs has been made easier by the demonstrated viewer interest in family-oriented series such as "The Waltons," "Happy Days" and "Apple's Way," a network official pointed out.

In the most sweeping change in its regular programming since the three-network competition began in the early nineteen fifties, N.B.C. yesterday canceled almost half the programs on its present schedule for next season and will introduce 12 new series in September.

Among the programs being dropped by N.B.C. for inadequate ratings are the Flip Wilson and Dean Martin shows, "Lotsa Luck," "The Girl With Something Extra," "Music Country, U.S.A." and "The Brian Keith Show."

C.B.S. has canceled "Sonny and Cher," "Here's Lucy," "Dirty Sally" and "The Dick Van Dyke Show." ■

small, windowless log cabin; the threat of wild wolf packs and prairie fires; the hunting for fox, muskrat and beaver; the diet of rabbit stew and biscuits "the way you like them," according to Ma.

And then there were the Indians, despised and feared by Ma although they were the ones being driven off the land being settled. Pa was more tolerant. And, of course, little Laura was positively radical chic, observing that "it's not fair—they were here first."

In the end, Mr. Ingalls made his peace with the Indians, neatly blowing the historical fact that the plains of Kansas had been generously seeded with the bodies of murdered Indians. Although ominous Indian drums occasionally left family nerves frayed, the Ingallses and the Indians concluded matters on a handshake of friendship.

Not surprisingly, "The Little House on the Prairie" was a pilot for a possible weekly TV series. And the idea does have some promise. The pilot, though, as directed by Michael Landon, never rose much above the level of those Americana commercials for "natural" cereals insisting that they contain no artificial ingredients. It is not mentioned that the cereals are chock full of sugar. The kids would have loved it. ■

ARTS & ENTERTAINMENT

GOOD TIMES FOR THE BLACK IMAGE

John J. O'Connor

The "invisible man," this country's black population, has at long last achieved a remarkable degree of visibility in the powerful machine of mass communications. The gradual, but startlingly steady, emergence can be traced directly to the civil-rights movements of the sixties and the subsequent formation of black pressure groups demanding a fair share of the image-making pie.

The revolution has been quiet but immensely significant. Unquestionably, the civil-rights movement triggered more coverage, in both print and electronic journalism, of black America. Subsequent pressure began opening some job opportunities for blacks and, eventually, black viewpoints in newsrooms. And, on a purely practical but crucial level, whites began discovering blacks as a key element in a consumer economy.

In TV entertainment, the tightly proscribed world of the black superstar performer (Sammy Davis, Jr.) or superstar comedian (Flip Wilson) has been expanded to include black characters and themes on major dramatic specials and even weekly series.

A scene from the television series "The Jeffersons."

Curiously enough, the new black visibility can be most noticeably traced to the unsophisticated world of situation comedy. Three comedy series built around black characters are among the most popular programs currently on TV, and all three come out of the phenomenal Norman Lear factory. N.B.C.'s "Sanford and Son," based on a British series, features a junk dealer and son. CBS's "The Jeffersons," the latest spin-off from "All in the Family," follows the fortunes of a family well on its way up the economic ladder. And "Good Times," also on C.B.S. (Tuesdays at 8 P.M.), has an upper-poor- or lower-middle-class family struggling for a measure of respectability in a Chicago housing project.

"Good Times" provides some fascinating examples of what can be slipped into a situation comedy in the form of old-fashioned middle-class morality and values.

Florida Evans (Esther Rolle) used to be the maid on "Maude." Here, she has her own family: husband James (John Amos), older son J. J., or Junior (Jimmie Walker), daughter Thelma (BernNadette Stanis) and younger son Michael (Ralph Carter). Much of the comedy runs true to familiar form. Mom and Pop have their misunderstandings, spats and reconciliations. Junior is the family comedian, always good for a put-on or put-down turn, particularly in insult battles with his sister.

But lurking behind the required quota of laughs, there are regular intimations of a reality that is not quite so funny. The message is survival and advancement in the golden "land of opportunity." Mr. Evans keeps searching for that better job. His wife holds the family together with the constant reminder that the father is "the head of the house." J. J., the comedian, is serious about becoming an artist. Michael writes "my-favorite-person" school essays on Malcolm X or Jesse Jackson.

On one side, black viewers are being afforded material that provides immediate personal and psychic identification. They no longer have to be content with only "Father Knows Best," which was unreal even for many white Americans.

On the other side, whites are being given glimpses of black life that, however simplified, can't help but weaken artificial racial barriers. When more than 18 million American households tune into "Good Times" each week, when an ordinary black family becomes a mass-public favorite, at least one change is no longer in the wind. It's here, right in front of our eyes.

Admittedly, it is easy to inflate the significance of a TV series. Racial tensions still exist on the national scene. But the changes that we have been seeing are substantial enough to resist their being dismissed as mere "lip service."

Of course, the rewards of this new visibility are not without their dubious aspects. In a sense, breaking into the arena of situation comedy merely gives blacks an equal opportunity to be as silly or banal or "unrealistic" as their white counterparts. But never underestimate the power of being silly on television. Aside from being lucrative, it can be more influential than all the "brotherhood" sermons delivered in several months of Sundays. ∎

NATIONAL PAY TV PLANNED FOR 1976

Les Brown

A national pay-television network may be in operation next year, by means of a domestic communications satellite, if the Federal Communications Commission approves the plans of a pay-TV programming service and two major cable television systems.

Home Box Office, Inc., a wholly owned subsidiary of Time Inc., which has been providing a single channel of pay-TV service in Northeastern states since 1972, has entered into an agreement with RCA Global Communications for use of its satellite facilities. The satellite will distribute the channel, carrying 70 hours a week of programming, to all parts of the mainland United States.

From a central studio and transmission control center in Manhattan, Home Box Office has been sending out a daily program package to cable systems in New York, New Jersey, Pennsylvania and Delaware. But it has been restricted to the region by the need to distribute its programming by land lines and microwave.

For the program package—a mixture of current motion pictures, live sports events and special-interest shows—subscribers pay monthly fees ranging from $6 to $9, in addition to the regular charge for cable service.

The company expects to begin satellite transmissions in October, initially to cable systems in Florida but eventually also to other sections of the country where earth stations are installed.

In the four Northeastern states, Home Box Office claims about 100,000 subscribers, and Florida earth stations potentially would make the service available to 250,000 more cable households in the state.

"This will provide the framework for a nationwide pay-TV system," said Gerald M. Levin, president of Home Box Office. He indicated that it would expand as agreements were reached with other cable television companies to become affiliates of Home Box Office, agreements that entail the building of earth stations.

The proposals of Home Box Office and the two cable companies are all subject to approval by the F.C.C., which must determine whether they conform to its rules for pay-TV and satellites.

Sprightly Mix Brightens NBC's 'Saturday Night'

John J. O'Connor

The new "Saturday Night" is a live, late-night comedy variety series carried on N.B.C. weekly (except for the first Saturday of each month, when N.B.C. News's "Weekend" magazine gets the 90 minutes). In the beginning, several weeks ago, the "Saturday Night" format didn't quite work. George Carlin, the comic, turned uncharacteristically heavy. Paul Simon and Art Garfunkel, briefly back together again, sang nicely but added little else to the proceedings. About 75 percent of the surrounding material seemed to meander pointlessly. In more recent weeks, however, at least 75 percent has proved to be sharply and sometimes wickedly on target. N.B.C. has found itself a source

(cont'd. on next page)

Jane Curtin, left, Dan Aykroyd and Laraine Newman, as the Coneheads on Saturday Night Live, 1975.

(cont'd. from previous page)

for legitimate pride, a commodity in scarce supply at any network these days.

On "Saturday Night," producer Lorne Michaels, still hovering around the age-30 mark, is putting together a form of comedy that he conceives is reflective of his "peers," most of them shaped by the 60's and 70's, by Vietnam and Watergate. A couple of years ago, the producer says, he and some friends, including Lily Tomlin, whom he'd worked with on "Laugh-In," vowed to change the content complexion of TV—not forward to something like "The Age of the Documentary," but backward to something approaching defined styles. As a "TV baby" and an unabashed admirer of television, Mr. Michaels insists that, while growing up, he could recognize immediately when a comedy skit was written by, say, Mel Brooks. He seeks a rebirth of both that definition and that recognition.

His writers carry offbeat credits ranging from the National Lampoon to "The Great American Dream Machine" to docu- mentaries on Buckminster Fuller and Anaïs Nin. His "Not Ready for Prime-Time Players" company (John Belushi, Gilda Radner, Jane Curtin, Garrett Morris, Laraine Newman and Dan Aykroyd) has been recruited from Off Broadway productions and improvisational revues. One of Mr. Michaels's best performers is one of his writers, Chevy Chase. And two of his regular features are mini-movies by Albert Brooks and skits with a batch of new Jim Henson Muppets.

The mix is held together and, to some extent, shaped by the program's guest host, who works closely with the company in frantic rehearsals. That "Saturday Night" attracts "name" talent to work for scale salaries indicates the impressive lure of the program's conception for performers. Robert Klein, the comedian, was good, although his stand-up routines interfered somewhat with the overall pacing. Candice Bergen was better, blending easily and attractively into the company. And Miss Tomlin was, of course, best, her sustained characterizations fitting the format brilliantly.

The fact of live transmission does create an element of nervous tension. Mr. Michaels insists that panic can be glimpsed in the eyes of hosts as they open the show. But the permanent repertory company is proving incredibly adept in using the liveness to full advantage. Chevy Chase's "Weekend Update" uses breaking news stories as the base for some outrageous reports.

The future of "Saturday Night" is uncertain—intentionally so. Mr. Michaels and company are especially anxious about avoiding the pitfalls of being slick, coy or predictably routine. Mr. Chase is already wondering if the "Weekend Update" has run its course. The modus operandi seems to be that if it works, drop it, try to develop something else. For however long it lasts, "Saturday Night" is the most creative and encouraging thing to happen in American TV comedy since "Your Show of Shows." ∎

APRIL 23, 1976

BARBARA WALTERS ACCEPTS A.B.C.'S MILLION

Barbara Walters with Harry Reasoner in 1976.

Robert D. McFadden

Barbara Walters yesterday accepted an offer of $1 million a year over the next five years to become a major personality of A.B.C. News and the co-anchor, with Harry Reasoner, of "The Evening News."

She will thus become the world's highest-paid newscaster and the first woman ever to present the evening news over a major television network.

Miss Walters, who has been co-host of the N.B.C. "Today" show for the last two years and a writer and personality with N.B.C. for 12 years, has a contract with N.B.C. that runs until next September.

It was unclear yesterday whether that contract would be canceled early or allowed to run its course, but William Sheehan, the president of A.B.C. News, said that A.B.C. would put her on the air soon after any cancellation, or in the autumn, at the latest.

Broadcasting-industry sources yesterday called Miss Walters's decision to switch networks a coup for A.B.C. It was expected to boost the ratings for A.B.C., not only of the evening news program but also of the network's "Good Morning, America" show, which appears opposite "Today" on weekday mornings—because of her affiliation with the network, though she will not appear on the early program.

"The Evening News," A.B.C.'s entry in the prime-time news programming, will

JUNE 27, 1976

A Saga of Slavery That Made the Actors Weep

Michael Kirkhorn

On Sept. 29, 1767, a 17-year-old African named Kunta Kinte was brought ashore from the filthy hold of the slave ship Lord Ligonier to be sold at auction at Annapolis, Md. His name was changed by his master to Toby. As an old man, limping around the plantation on a maimed foot, chopped off across the arch when he tried to escape, he still called himself Kunta Kinte. His children inherited this single keepsake—his name—and they passed it along to their children until it reached Alex Haley. With the name and a few other African words providing the flimsiest of clues, Haley managed to retrace his ancestry.

be expanded to 45 minutes from a half-hour when Miss Walters joins the program, broadcast sources said.

In addition to her major spot on the evening news program, Miss Walters's contract, which is expected to be signed in a few days, stipulates that she will anchor four hour-long prime-time "special" programs that will be produced each year by her own production company and paid for by A.B.C.

Both A.B.C. and N.B.C. had been in negotiations with Miss Walters in recent weeks and had offered her approximately the same financial terms, although the N.B.C. offer did not include a job as co-anchor of the network's major news program, "The Nightly News" with John Chancellor.

It appeared yesterday that Miss Walters's departure from N.B.C. might be effected on something less than amicable terms.

Miss Walters scoffed at the N.B.C. spokesman's contention that a "circus atmosphere" had crept into negotiations between her representatives, the William Morris Agency, and N.B.C. "It was done with great dignity," she contended.

Mr. Reasoner said that a woman co-anchor "may well be an idea whose time has come, and if it is, there's no better candidate."

As for billing on the program, Mr. Reasoner declared, "I suggest we just do it alphabetically by last name." ∎

Haley's "Roots," which will be published by Doubleday in October, tells this laboriously authenticated story. It will be retold beginning next January on ABC-TV in a 12-hour-long "novel for television," three hours of which were filmed this past May along the Georgia coast by Wolper Productions. Network executives are enthusiastic about "Roots" because its miniseries format resembles last season's serialization of "Rich Man, Poor Man," which drew a large audience and won four Emmy awards. They also are nervous because the resemblance between the two productions stops there.

"Roots" is a risky enterprise, both artistically and commercially. Because it is a saga, beginning in 1750 with Kunta Kinte's birth and ending 117 years later in Henning, Tenn., with a grateful prayer to Kunta Kinte, the departed forebear, no one character remains in the film from start to finish. Furthermore, the filmmakers' insistence on authenticity requires some female nudity. Finally, there is the possibility that the unsparingly accurate depiction of slavery could prove repugnant to home viewers.

If these are disadvantages for a prime-time program, the filmmakers are doing their best to anticipate and offset unfavorable reactions. The writers have concentrated on pivotal characters and key events that carry the action from episode to episode, and well-known performers are used strategically: Cicely Tyson plays Kunta Kinte's mother; Maya Angelou portrays the grandmother; the captain of the slaver is Ed Asner (who won an Emmy for his performance in "Rich Man, Poor Man") and the cruelly pragmatic first mate is played by Ralph Waite, "The Waltons" kindly father.

More than the brief nudity, producer Stan Margulies seems concerned about the starkness of the scenes in the hold of the slave ship, where Africans were chained hip to hip in their own waste, breathing air so fetid that a candle would not burn. It is an item of faith with Margulies, director David Greene and others involved in the making of "Roots" that they are depicting in uncringing detail scenes of shameful degradation never before truthfully revealed to Americans in films and certainly not on television. In a warehouse outside Savannah, the film crew constructed a slave hold set so depressingly authentic that when it was crammed with chained

LeVar Burton as Kunta Kinte in the miniseries "Roots."

extras for a day of shooting some members actually wept.

"The scene on the slave ship is as strong a scene as ever has been shown on prime-time commercial television," Margulies said. "It's so strong that some people might tune out. Our fervent hope is that the audience will care so much about LeVar Burton [a University of Southern California theater student who plays young Kunta Kinte] and about the slaves in general that they will stay and see. Our ultimate purpose is to be as faithful as possible to Alex's story. One of the things that intrigued A.B.C. is that we didn't invent this, any more than Buchenwald was invented."

Burton said that the first day of shooting in the hold of the slaver was an overwhelming experience: "They told me that I was trembling when I came off the set."

Haley considers "Roots" to be a universal story. Its significance is not limited to the fact that those who suffered slavery were black people; slavery was degrading to oppressors as well as victims. The Shanghaied waterfront dregs that made up the crew of slave ships died, Haley said, in about the same proportion as the slaves during the three-month crossing and certainly the moral dilemma has weighed heavily on white and black Americans. ∎

OVERDOSING ON THE BICENTENNIAL

John Leonard

The flag goes up and down, with a rattle and a snap, like a window-shade on the TV screen. Behind the eyes, between the ears, is a highway. No grass grows. No grass grows because it has been trampled out by 10,000 drum majorettes: amber waves of thighs. No bird sings. No bird would dare to compete with the gurgling of Mike Douglas and Lorne Green, Ed McMahon and Paul Anka, Kate Smith and Anita Bryant. Inside Kate Smith, an Anita Bryant is trying to get out. Why is Anita Bryant singing "The Battle Hymn of the Republic" instead of Dionne Warwick? Why don't they let Dionne Warwick do all the singing? Why did the Fifth Dimension give up after singing only half of the Declaration of Independence? Explain Sammy Davis Jr. Go ahead, explain him. Who invited Roy Rogers, Evel Knievel and Mark Spitz to my 200th birthday party? Inside Bob Hope, General Westmoreland is trying to get out. Walter Cronkite and Valerie Harper are co-anchorpersons.

Of what significance is it that the Strategic Air Command has an orchestra? Debbie Reynolds—Debbie Reynolds?—is "Martha Washington, Martha Washington" in a parody of something or other, perhaps David Susskind. Viking, alas, has yet to find a parking place on Mars. On the other hand, five million people—lining the banks of the Hudson River to see 16 windjammers and a Loch Ness monster—capsize Manhattan Island, hurling Bloomingdale's into the middle of New Jersey's uncommitted delegation. Inside Paul Lynde, Donny and Marie Osmond are trying to get out. Inside Donny and Marie Osmond, nothing is trying to get out.

Well, were you uplifted?

It's not nice to be queasy about the Bicentennial—Thomas Jefferson, after all, kept his birthday a secret from the nation so that a celebration of him wouldn't interfere with a celebration of the Republic for which he stood, or sat, Mr. Jefferson having invented the swivel chair—but, as Thomas Fuller put it in 1732, "As long as I live I'll spit in my parlor," which is where the TV set is, of course.

It was necessary that the Bicentennial be televised in order to assure us that it has, indeed, taken place. No fooling. Anita Bryant and Ed McMahon say so, not to mention a 1,870-voice student chorus and a 2,010-piece band in Los Angeles Memorial Coliseum, and the Mormons who took over the Lincoln Memorial, and President Ford and Jim Nabors and the British Broadcasting Corporation and Andre Kostelanetz and Arthur Fiedler and Phyllis Diller and Queen Elizabeth II and Yankee Doodle Cricket. Only David Brinkley seems skeptical.

Yankee Doodle Cricket? "Yankee Doodle Cricket," inspired by George Selden's splendid children's book, was the best Bicentennial program I saw on television the week of the overkill. The animated cricket is the brainchild of Chuck Jones, the man who gave us "Bugs Bunny" years ago, a Walt Disney with a sense of humor. I await his "Moby Duck."

Next to "Yankee Doodle Cricket," I liked the movie version of "1776." Its night on TV was the only night of the week when one didn't hear "The Battle Hymn of the Republic," "America the Beautiful" and "God Bless America" badly rendered. As for the rest, John Chancellor bravely admitted patriotism. Howard K. Smith sermonized on democracy and bureaucracy. Walter Cronkite maundered. Disney overproduced the fireworks. Everybody but President Ford and the rain stayed away from Philadelphia.

Finally, it was a week of some of the worst singing and dancing I've ever seen on television; an almost unparalleled confusion of purposes and perspectives; a long march of vulgarians; and a profound, relentless insult to the memory and meaning of Woody Guthrie, whose "This Land Is Your Land" was over and over again expropriated by plastic bunny rabbits, peppy zipperheads, majoring in suntan lotion, dental hygiene, necking and Ripple. The dispossessed are not perceived through contact lenses. I hope that you went out-of-doors last weekend to do your Whitmanesque yawping. In the parlor where I spit, the pieties of Las Vegas were observed.

> It was a week of some of the worst singing and dancing I've ever seen

patriotic

NOVEMBER 21, 1976

SOFT-CORE PORN SNEAKS INTO PRIME TIME

John J. O'Connor

Charlie's original Angels, from left, Farrah Fawcett, Kate Jackson and Jaclyn Smith.

There are those of us who have always found certain TV material obscene, particularly in the area of humiliating game shows. But the increasing amount of material that could be called genuinely pornographic is a new development, at least during the carefully monitored hours of evening prime time.

As is known by any lawyer or by any theater operator showing "adult" movies, it is virtually impossible to define pornography, especially in an era noted for its new permissiveness. But the court definition of an "appeal to prurient interest" will do as well as any other. In hard core, that appeal is direct and explicit. Soft core can be merely suggestive to varying degrees. And, in a sense, television thrives on the power of suggestion.

On television, the first reflection of society's new permissiveness could be detected on a soap opera.

Several years ago as I was concluding a visit with Julia Child, I was advised by the noted cooking authority not to miss several of the afternoon soaps. "You wouldn't be-lieve what's going on," she said with her inimitable gusto. "Drugs, prostitution, lesbianism, and all sorts of other goodies." Today, all of those items have become standard daytime commodities, and it seems impossible to flip around the dial haphazardly without finding at least one instance of a youngish bare-chested man bedding down some youngish attractive woman, either voluntarily or, not infrequently, forcibly.

These same subjects and situations have also become commonplace on the evening schedule, usually in the sincerity-laden guise of social concern. But ever since the TV programmers discovered that the subject of rape, for instance, does well in the ratings, the veneer of concern has been replaced with blatant exploitation.

Consider A.B.C.'s "Charlie's Angels," the runaway hit among this season's new series. In effect, the program is a girlie show, starring three beautiful women in a succession of splendidly revealing costumes. The angels would obviously do anything for their boss, Charlie, and their conversations, via an intercom system, are heavy with suggestive smirking.

Recently, A.B.C. offered "Nightmare in Badham County," posing rather nervously as an exposé of women's prisons in the South. "Slavery is not a thing of the past!" screamed the ads. "The sadistic sheriff knows it. The psychotic warden knows it. But two girls learn it the hard way." So did the innocent viewer, who was treated to two hours of relentless sado-masochistic titillation, overseen by tough woman guards decked out in halters and high-powered rifles. Broad hints of lesbianism were added for good measure.

Perhaps the evolution of electronic porn is inevitable within society's current cycle of permissiveness. The compulsion to break the next taboo is apparently irresistible. Book publishing has profitably mined the field with best-selling "how to" books on sex and novels on demonic possession, with their customary sexual explorations. A number of quite prominent publishers are now certain that the next major "breakthrough" will involve incest. Onward and upward with the arts, evidently. ∎

Power, Lust and Revenge Texas-Style

John J. O'Connor

The cast of "Dallas" in 1979. From left, Steve Kanaly, Patrick Duffy, Victoria Principal, Jim Davis, Larry Hagman, Charlene Tilton and Linda Gray, with Barbara Bel Geddes seated.

"Dallas" is daytime soap opera gussied up with some on-location Texas settings and innumerable scenes of people getting into, driving or getting out of cars. At the center of this tall tale of power, lust and revenge is the Ewing family, powerful oil barons. Last Sunday, Bobby Ewing (Patrick Duffy, formerly the hero of "The Man From Atlantis") was suddenly discovered to be married to Pamela Barnes (Victoria Principal), daughter of his father's longtime enemy.

Bobby's father (Jim Davis) is incensed. His brother (Larry Hagman) is suspicious and worried about holding onto his own corporate position. And Pamela's father (David Wayne) is struck speechless in the middle of his drunken ramblings. In the background are such savory types as young Lucy (Charlene Tilton), sulking sexily through what appears to be an audition for a remake of "Baby Doll," and the range foreman Ray (Steve Kanaly), Lucy's current favorite and the former boyfriend of Bobby's new wife ("You and me," he reminds her, "it was good, real good").

Last week, Bobby's brother and Ray were foiled in a plot to discredit Pamela, while she held her own trump card, prompting her proud husband to declare, "She's my wife, J.R., and she's going to stay that way." This week, sassy Lucy, determined to get out of school, nearly destroys the career of an innocent instructor. And so, presumably, it will go for several more weeks. Wandering around among the players, with about three lines of dialogue, is the fine stage actress Barbara Bel Geddes, who plays the Ewing matriarch. The show is enervating. ∎

W
hat was the greatest sports moment of the 1970s? There's a question to get a spirited barroom debate going.

Contenders are many, starting early in the decade with what was routinely called "the fight of the century." This was the 1971 match at Madison Square Garden between the heavyweight champion, Joe Frazier, and Muhammad Ali, continuing his comeback from exile. In the late 1960's, he had been stripped of his title for refusing to submit to the draft in protest against the Vietnam War. On this March night in 1971, the electricity in the Garden could be felt all the way to the upper reaches. Frank Sinatra was at ringside taking pictures for Life magazine. Everyone sensed that this was far more than a boxing match. America's cultural values seemed on the line.

Ali, still called Cassius Clay by some sports writers who stubbornly refused to acknowledge his chosen Muslim name, lost to Frazier in a 15-round unanimous decision. That was in the ring. In spectators' hearts, Ali was clearly a winner. The fight left no doubt that he was back and indeed the men would battle twice more, with Ali turning the tables.

Baseball lovers might put their money on the April night in 1974 when Henry Aaron of the Atlanta Braves hit his career 715th home run, breaking a record held by Babe Ruth for four decades. As with Ali, more was at stake than a sports stat. On his road to glory, Aaron endured vicious threats from racists, angry that a black man, of all people, was about to eclipse a white man's achievement that some deemed sacred. Aaron absorbed the malice with characteristic poise. Baseball, and the republic, survived.

The 1972 Summer Olympics in Munich, Germany, provided grandeur and horror. Grandeur lay in Mark Spitz's swimming excellence, which earned him seven gold medals, a record

Joe Frazier, left, on his way to beating Muhammad Ali to retain the title. The epic fight ended with Frazier winning unanimous on points.

that lasted into the new century. The horror was unspeakable. Palestinian terrorists broke into the Olympic Village and took Israeli athletes hostage. Eleven Israelis were ultimately killed. Intensifying the outrage was the tone-deaf response of Avery

A general view of the Opening Ceremony in Munich's Olympic Stadium in 1972.

Hank Aaron talks during a press conference after he hit his 715th career home run on April 8, 1974.

Billie Jean King raises her hands in triumph after defeating Bobby Riggs in the "Battle of the Sexes" Challenge Match at the Astrodome on September 20, 1973, in Houston, Texas.

Brundage, president of the International Olympic Committee, who acted as if he were the wounded party. At a memorial service, he managed to bemoan the impact of this outrage on his Games, without once mentioning terror's victims.

In that decade, Eastern European stars in separate Olympics, Nadia Comaneci and Olga Korbut, sparked mass interest in gymnastics. Bobby Fisher, the strange American loner who defeated the Russian Boris Spassky, did the same for chess in 1972. Billie Jean King showed grit in beating the tennis hustler Bobby Riggs in a 1973 match in which feminist aspirations loomed as large as the $100,000 prize.

There was nobility in the baseball star Roberto Clemente, killed in a plane crash on New Year's Eve, 1972, while on a humanitarian mission to earthquake-scarred Nicaragua. Nobility also defined Jackie Robinson, who integrated Major League Baseball in 1947, and died in 1972.

But the greatest athlete of the decade? A case could be made for one who wasn't human. That would be Secretariat, winner of horse racing's Triple Crown in 1973. In the last of those three races, the Belmont Stakes in New York, he and the rest of the field were barely in the same time zone. Secretariat won by an incredible 31 lengths. And he did it with grace — no gloating, no denigrating the opposition. How many athletes can you say that about, then or now?

Secretariat, winner of horse racing's Triple Crown in 1973.

MISS CRUMP GETS DERBY BERTH ON FATHOM

Joe Nichols

Jockey Diane Crump exercising horse at race track in 1970.

LOUISVILLE, Ky., April 30—The 96th running of the Kentucky Derby on Saturday has attracted 18 entrants, the largest field for the 1¼-mile test in 19 years. The turnout was a surprise; it included at least two horses that had been considered quite unlikely starters.

When all the fees are in, it will be the richest Derby with a gross value of $171,200 and the winner getting $128,000. Moreover, it will have Diane Crump participating as the first woman jockey to ride in the race.

With so many entrants, the race will offer a mutual betting field made up of Dr. Behrman, Rancho Lejos, Robins's Bug, Native Royalty, Action Getter and Fathom. The strong horse in this group is Dr. Behrman. Fathom will be ridden by Miss Crump, the 21-year-old native of Woodmont, Conn., who now lives at Oldsmar, Fla. She has won stakes races in Florida.

Earlier in the week Don Devine, the trainer, had said Fathom would not go if he performed unimpressively in the one-mile Derby Trial. But he changed his mind even after Fathom had finished seventh.

The 1951 Derby had 20 starters and the race was won by Count Turf. The previous richest Derby was in 1956, when gross worth was $165,950. Needles, the best of a field of 17, earned $123,450. ∎

OBITUARY

SEPTEMBER 4, 1970

VINCE LOMBARDI, FOOTBALL COACH, DIES

William N. Wallace

Vince Lombardi being carried off the field in 1966.

Vince Lombardi, the professional football coach who symbolized toughness and dedication in sports, died of intestinal cancer yesterday in Georgetown Hospital in Washington. His age was 57.

Lombardi guided the Green Bay Packers to the premier position in the National Football League in the 1960's. Under his direction the Packers won six division titles and five National Football League championships in nine seasons between 1959 and 1967. This was professional football's best winning record and Lombardi was acclaimed as the sport's best coach.

Lombardi was a symbol of authority.

"When he says 'Sit down,' I don't even bother to look for a chair," one of the Packer players explained.

"He's fair. He treats us all the same—like dogs," said Henry Jordan, another Packer.

"He coaches through fear," said Bill Curry, a sensitive player Lombardi let go.

Most of his athletes accepted his demanding ways and biting criticisms. His primary target was a player named Marvin Fleming, who said in reflection, "I didn't mind. When I came to him I didn't have anything. He taught me how to be a winner."

Another Packer, Jerry Kramer, said, "His whippings, his cussings and his driving all fade; his good qualities endure."

Lombardi admitted that scoldings sometimes were merely for effect. During last season at Green Bay, when he was goading an aging team to another championship, he said, "I have to go on that field every day and whip people. It's for them, not just me. I'm getting to be an animal."

Lombardi was always a hard man when it came to football.

In college, at Fordham where he graduated with honors in 1937, he played guard on a famous line called the Seven Blocks of Granite. He was smallest of the group at 5 feet 8 inches and 175 pounds. "But he hit like 250," a teammate said.

During his span of nine seasons as head coach of the Packers, Lombardi saw his team win 141 games, lose 39 and tie 4. He insisted that the Packers never lost. They merely ran out of time. ∎

SUPER BOWL:
ONLY A GAME?

Robert Lipsyte

H istorians have written that the weeks leading up to that ancient American religious spectacle, the Super Bowl, were filled not only with song and celebration, but with mass national seminars. In 1967, before the event was officially called Super Bowl (supposedly after a child's high-bounce black ball), the entire country was divided into two antagonistic factions, called the National Football League and the American Football League. N.F.L. fans believed it essential that the Green Bay Packers win to uphold tradition, orderly change and basic national values. A.F.L. fans came to believe that if the Kansas City Chiefs won, all mankind would realize that youth, new money and inferior talent were no handicaps in the battle for the top. After Green Bay won, N.F.L. fans, with noblesse oblige, said: "It's only a game." A.F.L. fans, realizing there would be always youth, new money and inferior talent making life tense for everyone else, seemed willing to wait for success until they got older. They, too, said: "It's only a game."

In 1969, a long-haired, weak-kneed, booze-loving, active young man said: "And we're going to win Sunday—I'll guarantee it." The national seminars were very troubled. N.F.L. fans argued that the crewcut, tight-lipped, grim-visaged Baltimore Colt quarterbacks would uphold the values and decency by beating the Jets, while their defensive line beat up on Joe Namath. Some A.F.L. fans also hoped this would happen although they felt it was time for the leagues to merge as equals. When it was all over, everybody agreed that the habits of American adolescence were much too important to be dependent on the outcome of a 60-minute sporting event. After all: "It's only a game."

Super Bowl IV, the last before the A.F.L.-N.F.L. rivalry was blurred by reorganization, was very complex. A broader ideology began to appear in the seminars, although it was masked by football metaphors: Would the basic brute strength and rote execution of Minnesota, the fundamentalists, be able to withstand the new technocracy, K.C.'s stream-lined formations? But it all worked out and the metallic voice of K.C.'s computer said, after: "It's only a game."

Super Bowl V, played in 1971, provided a glimpse of the genius of the game's managers. The teams that met that year were both from the old N.F.L. The only celebrity on either team was the Colts' quarterback, Johnny Unitas, who, when asked if chills ran up and down his spine when thinking about playing again in the Super Bowl, kept answering: "It's only a game."

Former football players infiltrated the mass national seminars to bring up the question: Is this game a moral event? A philosophy professor at the University of Guelph, John McMurtry, who played linebacker for the Calgary Stampeders, looked southward and wrote in The Nation: "The connections between the politics of fascism and the mania for football are too many to be ignored: both ground themselves on a property-seizing principle, apotheosize struggle and competition, publicly idolize victory and the powerful, make authority absolute and relate to opposing groups by violent aggression."

A former St. Louis Cardinals' linebacker, Dave Meggyesy, published the book, "Out of Their League," just before Super Bowl V and stumped the country saying such things as: "The fan in the stand is saying to the players, 'I'm hostile and angry, you get it off for me.' Football acts as a bread and circus and ultimately cheats the public of really getting down to the basis of what is bothering them."

Historians of the times fail to appreciate the extraordinary scheme: If McMurtry and Meggyesy prove right, pro football would say, "They're our boys," and if they prove wrong, "Well, weren't you listening? It's only a game."

compete

FRAZIER OUTPOINTS ALI AND KEEPS TITLE

Dave Anderson

In a classic 15-round battle, Joe Frazier broke the wings of the butterfly and smashed the stinger of the bee last night in winning a unanimous 15-round decision over Muhammad Ali at Madison Square Garden.

Defying an anonymous "lose or else" death threat, Frazier settled the controversy over the world heavyweight championship by handing Ali his first defeat with a savage attack that culminated in a thudding knockdown of the deposed titleholder from a hammerlike left hook in the final round.

During the classic brawl, one man in the sellout throng of 20,455 died of a heart attack.

When the verdict was announced, Ali, also known as Cassius Clay, accepted it stoically.

Hurried to his dressing room rather than the postfight interview area, Ali remained there for about half an hour. Suddenly, he departed for Flower-Fifth Avenue Hospital for X-rays of the severely swollen jaw. He was released from the hospital after 40 minutes and left unbandaged.

Ali's defeat ended his winning streak after 31 triumphs, with 25 knockouts. "I always knew who the champion was," Frazier, his brow swollen above each eye, said later with a smile.

During his uncharacteristic postfight silence, Ali sent this word to newsmen through Drew (Bundini) Brown, his assistant trainer: "Don't worry, we'll be back, we ain't through yet." But regarding a possible return bout, Frazier said, "I don't think Clay will want one."

Ali had predicted Frazier would fall "in six rounds" and he had maintained that there was "no way" the recognized champion could outpoint him. But the swarming Philadelphia brawler, battering his Cherry Hill, N.J., neighbor, ended the 29-year-old Ali's credibility as a prophet.

Joe Frazier knocks down Muhammad Ali in the 15th round at Madison Square Garden in 1971.

In the final round, Frazier landed a wild left hook that send Ali sprawling onto his back in a corner. But the 6-to-5 betting underdog was up almost instantly and took the mandatory eight-count on unsteady feet. Moments later, Frazier jolted his 215-pound rival with another left hook.

With a minute remaining, Ali desperately tried for a knockout, but his punches had virtually no effect. With the crowd roaring in the final seconds, the bell rang and Frazier playfully cuffed Ali across his head, bowed in apparent defeat.

When the decision was announced, a patter of boos erupted, but the cheers soon thundered above them.

Claiming exemption as a Muslim minister, Ali refused induction in the armed forces on April 28, 1967. He promptly was stripped of his title and license to box by the New York State Athletic Commission and the World Boxing Association, which governs boxing in most of the other states.

Not long after that, Ali was convicted of draft evasion. His sentence was five years in prison, plus a $10,000 fine, but an appeal currently is before the Supreme Court.

While his exile matured Ali's physique, it sabotaged his speed. During the early rounds, Frazier pounded his left hook into Ali's midsection, but several times the deposed champion shook his head in the clinch as if to reassure his idolators.

Ali's knockdown was only his third in a decade of competition, but it was the final embarrassment for the deposed champion, the sixth ex-heavyweight champion to fail in an attempt to regain his title. ∎

"Don't worry, we'll be back, we ain't through yet."

BIGGEST NAME IN N.B.A.:
JABBAR

Terence Smith

WASHINGTON, June 3—For Oscar Robertson, it will be a chance to "listen and learn"; for Lew Alcindor, a "return to the fountainhead."

These were the terms in which the two basketball stars today described their upcoming tour of six African countries on behalf of the State Department.

At each stop they will conduct clinics, give exhibitions and meet the national basketball teams. Basketball is the fastest-growing sport in each of the countries on their itinerary.

"For me, this is a return to the fountainhead," Alcindor said. He explained that he had studied African history at the University of California, Los Angeles, and long wanted to go to Africa.

"My grandfather was from the West Indies," he said, "but he spoke Yoruba (the language of Western Nigeria) and I think he came from Nigeria."

Twice during the short news conference Alcindor asked to be called by his Muslim name, Kareem Abdul Jabbar, correcting newsmen who called him Lew or Mr. Alcindor.

He said Kareem translates to "noble or generous." Abdul is "servant of Allah" and Jabbar means "powerful."

Unlike the former heavyweight champion, Muhammad Ali, Alcindor is not a black Muslim, he said, but a Sunni Orthodox—"like the religion practiced in Pakistan." ■

SEVEN GOLD MEDALS FOR SPITZ

As usual, the current Olympic Games in Munich are producing a new crop of sports heroes and forcing a wholesale revision of the record books. But nothing that has happened in Munich so far this summer can compare with the awesome feats of Mark Spitz, swimmer extraordinary. It seems ridiculous a few weeks ago when some observers suggested that Spitz would win seven gold medals and thereby set a new Olympic mark in this respect. But that is exactly what the dentist-to-be from Carmichael, Calif., has done. His is clearly the outstanding individual performance of the 1972 Olympics, and his record bag of gold medals will not soon or easily be surpassed. Mark Spitz, like Bobby Fischer, provides a useful reminder that old fogies inclined to denigrate Americans under thirty need to take a better look at this new and very promising younger generation. ■

American swimmer Mark Spitz shows five of his seven Olympic gold medals.

BASEBALL PLAYERS TO STRIKE OVER PENSION

DALLAS, March 31—The Major League Baseball Players Association voted today to strike against Organized Baseball, effective with exhibition games scheduled to be played tomorrow.

Marvin Miller, executive director of the association, said in a terse prepared statement, issued after a 3-hour 15-minute meeting, that the strike would continue until there was "an appropriate resolution of the dispute" between the players and major league owners. The regular season was scheduled to start Wednesday.

The vote was 47-0 for the strike, with one abstention, but Mr. Miller declined to identify the one player representative who did not vote.

At issue is the amount of money the owners will contribute to the players' pension fund as well as the length of the pension fund agreement.

Commissioner Bowie Kuhn said in New York that "obviously the losers in the strike action taken tonight are the sports fans of America."

"I don't think anyone really wants a strike," said Don Mincher, player representative of the Texas Rangers. "But we've made no progress in our demands for a 17 percent cost of living increase in our pension fund payments. And that's what it's all about."

"I want to play," said Brooks Robinson, the Baltimore Orioles player representative. "I think all the fellows do. It all boils down to whether the owners are willing to make some concessions. I think our fellows are willing to make some, too. And that seems to be the best chance."

Under the old contract, the owners paid about $5 million a year to the players association. They have offered a $400,000 raise that would keep health and medical benefits up to date. But the players seek another $800,000—or a total increased payment from owners of $1.2 million. ■

JACKIE ROBINSON, FIRST BLACK PLAYER IN MAJOR LEAGUES, DIES

Dave Anderson

Jackie Robinson, who made history in 1947 by becoming the first black baseball player in the major leagues, suffered a heart attack in his home in Stamford, Conn., yesterday morning and died at Stamford Hospital. He was 53 years old.

Mr. Robinson, who was honored at the World Series in Cincinnati a week ago Sunday, had been in failing health for several years. He recovered from a heart attack in 1968 but then lost sign of one eye and the partial sight of the other as a result of diabetes.

For social impact, Jack Roosevelt Robinson was perhaps America's most significant athlete. As the first black player in major-league baseball, he was a pioneer. His skill and accomplishments resulted in the acceptance of blacks in other sports, notably professional football and professional basketball.

His dominant characteristic, as an athlete and a man, was a competitive flame. Outspoken, controversial, combative, he created critics as well as loyalists. But he never deviated from his opinions.

In his autobiography, "I Never Had It Made," to be published next month by G. P. Putnam's, he recalled the scene in 1947 when he stood for the National Anthem at his debut with the Brooklyn Dodgers. He wrote: ". . . but as I write these words now I cannot stand and sing the National Anthem. I have learned that I remain a black in a white world."

Describing his struggle, he wrote: "I had to fight hard against loneliness, abuse and the knowledge that any mistake I made would be magnified because I was the only black man out there. Many people resented my impatience and honesty, but never cared about acceptance as much as I cared about respect!"

His belligerence flared throughout his career in baseball, business and politics. "I was told that it would cost me some awards," he said last year. "But if I had to keep quiet to get an award, it wasn't worth it. Awards are great, but if I got one for being a nice kid, what good is it?'

To other black ballplayers, though, he was most often saluted as the first to run the gantlet. Monte Irvin who played for the New York Giants while Robinson was with the Dodgers and who now is an assistant to the commissioner of baseball said yesterday: "Jackie Robinson opened the door of baseball to all men. He was the first to get the opportunity, but if he had not done such a great job, the path would have been so much more difficult." ■

Jackie Robinson in 1950.

Fischer Captures Chess Title As Spassky Resigns by Phone

Harold C. Schonberg

REYKJAVIK, Iceland, Sept. 1—Bobby Fischer, who for years has been saying he is the greatest, proved it today by becoming the chess champion of the world, the first American ever to hold the title.

He won it and the $156,000 victor's share of the $250,000 purse when Boris Spassky of the Soviet Union did not show up for the adjourned 21st game. Instead, Spassky, who had held the title for three years, telephoned his resignation to the referee, Lothar Schmid.

The 29-year-old champion from Brooklyn, whose demands for more money and haggling over playing conditions nearly wrecked the match, thus captured the crown he had sought from childhood, combining 7 victories with 11 draws to gain the 12½ points he needed. He will formally receive the title on Sunday at a banquet in Exhibition Hall, where the match began nearly two months ago.

The match, which could have run to 24 games, drew thousands of players, many of them masters and grandmasters, to Reykjavik, while it lifted chess into the realm of mass appeal in the United States.

Fischer, who at first refused to come to Exhibition Hall today until he had obtained a written statement of resignation from Spassky, was prevailed upon to go. When he came on stage at 2:47, Schmid addressed the audience of 2,500 people.

"Ladies and gentlemen," he said. "Mr. Spassky has resigned by telephone at 12:50. This is a traditional and legal way of resignation. Mr. Fischer has won this game, No. 21, and he is the winner of the match." The final score was 12½ to 8½.

The audience burst into rhythmic applause and rose. Fischer, still busying himself at the chessboard, again nodded, looked uncomfortable, glanced at the audience from the corner of his eyes, and rushed off to his hotel.

Thus ended a battle for chess supremacy that had its moments of glory and its moments of slapstick comedy. Almost forgotten today were the hectic, even delirious, days when Fischer did not arrive as originally scheduled and little hope was given for the match. Almost forgotten were the charges and countercharges, the last-minute negotiations, the wheeling and dealing.

It was a meeting of temperamental opposites—two minds and ways of life that touched only at one point: mastery of the 32 pieces and the 64 squares. It was billed as "the Match of the Century," and in many ways it was.

The two best players in the world, one a Russian and the other an American, were meeting face to face. As for politics, Spassky was not even a member of the Communist party, and Fischer may well be the least political figure who ever lived.

"I am a chess player and not a politician," Spassky said.

"I believe only in the best moves," Fischer said. ∎

PIRATES STAR DIES IN CRASH

SAN JUAN, P. R., Jan. 1—Roberto Clemente, star outfielder for the Pittsburgh Pirates, died late last night in the crash of a cargo plane carrying relief supplies to the victims of the earthquake in Managua.

Three days of national mourning for Mr. Clemente were proclaimed in his native Puerto Rico, where he was the most popular sports figure in the island's history. He is a certainty to be enshrined in Baseball's Hall of Fame. He was only the 11th man in baseball history to get 3,000 hits, and his lifetime batting average of .317 was the highest among active players.

Mr. Clemente, who was 38 years old, won the National League batting championship four times in his 18-season career, was named to the All-Star team 12 times and in 1966 was named the league's Most Valuable Player. He was also one of the finest defensive outfielders with a very strong throwing arm. He led the Pittsburgh Pirates to two world championships, in 1960 and 1971, the latter time being named the Most Valuable Player in the World Series.

Mr. Clemente was the leader of Puerto Rican efforts to aid the Nicaraguan victims and was aboard the plane because he suspected that relief supplies were falling into the hands of profiteers.

The plane, carrying a crew of three and one other passenger, came down in heavy seas a mile and a half from shore. The wreckage was not found until 5 p.m. today in about 100 feet of water. There was no sign of survivors.

Mrs. Clemente said she was concerned that the plane seemed old and overloaded, but her husband assured her that everything would be all right. When the pilot did not show up until late, she said he told her, "If there is one more delay, we'll leave this for tomorrow."

Mr. Clemente had been asked to take part in the collection of funds by Luis Vigoraux, a television producer.

"He did not just lend his name to the fund-raising activities the way some famous personalities do," said Mr. Vigoraux. "He took over the entire thing, arranging

Roberto Clemente of the Pittsburgh Pirates holding the 3,000th ball he hit on September 30, 1972.

for collection points, publicity and the transportation to Nicaragua."

Mr. Clemente's interest in Nicaragua may have been heightened by his experience in managing the Puerto Rican team that participated in the amateur world series held in Managua in late November and December. Sixteen teams participated. The Puerto Ricans took fifth place.

News of Mr. Clemente's death plunged Puerto Rico into mourning. ∎

American League to Allow 'Designated Pinch-Hitter'

Joseph Durso

The owners of the 24 major league baseball teams took a radical step yesterday to put more punch into the game. They voted to allow the American League to use a "designated pinch-hitter," who may bat for the pitcher without forcing him from the game.

The plan will be tried experimentally for the next three seasons by the American League, which has been hurt financially in recent years and has been searching for ways to ener-

Designated hitter Frank Howard of the Detroit Tigers awaits the next pitch during an at bat in 1973.

gize baseball. But it will not be used in the National League, which has resisted the change, or in the World Series, the All-Star Game or interleague exhibition games.

The action was voted at a joint meeting of the major leagues in Chicago yesterday, with Commissioner Bowie Kuhn breaking an impasse between the leagues. As a result, for the first time since the American League was organized in 1901, the two big leagues will play under differing rules.

Another proposal to dramatize baseball—regular games between teams from the rival leagues—was turned over to a study committee, with expectations that it might be approved for 1974.

By approving the experiment, which was tried in the high minor leagues three years ago, the club executives made the most basic change in the rules since foul balls were ruled strikes in 1903. Since then, the spitball was banned in 1920, the "lively" ball was introduced in 1930, the strike zone was enlarged in 1962 and reduced again in 1969 and the pitcher's mound was lowered the same year.

But none of those changes revolutionized the rules that were essentially followed since the days of the old New York Knickerbockers baseball club a century and a quarter ago.

Under the change forced yesterday by the American League, 8 of whose 12 teams lost money last season, the manager would follow this procedure if he wished:

- He would give the umpires a line-up card before the game with the nine regular players listed by position and the 10th player listed as the "designated pinch-hitter." His only job would be that. When it came time for the pitcher to bat, the designated man would swing for him. The pitcher, though, would stay in the game and the pinch-hitter would go back to the bench until the next time round.

- If the starting pitcher was replaced later by a relief pitcher; the designated pinch-hitter would bat for him.

- If the manager decided to replace the designated pinch-hitter with another pinch-hitter, he could do that at any time. But the second man then could be used only for that purpose and could not play in the field, while the first pinch-hitter would be out of the game.

- Except for the "designated" man, all the other players customarily used as pinch-hitters would follow the old rules. They could bat for a player, then stay in the game at any position the manager wished.

JUNE 10, 1973

SECRETARIAT SWEEPS TO TRIPLE CROWN BY 31 LENGTHS

Joe Nichols

Secretariat won the Belmont Stakes yesterday with a finality that was incredible. The Meadow Stable star flashed to success in the 1½-mile event by the improbable margin of 31 lengths over Twice a Prince, his runner-up, and, even with the big margin, he set a track record time of 2:24.

The performance was executed under a splendid ride by Ron Turcotte, and was most noteworthy in that it enabled Secretariat to become the ninth winner of the Triple Crown for 3-year-olds.

A crowd of 69,138, the second largest turnout to see a Belmont Stakes, attended the 105th running of the race. It had five contestants, and the advance indications were that it would turn out to be a duel between Secretariat, whose payoff at the end was $2.20 for $2 to win and $2.40 to place, and Sham, who competes in the silks of Sigmund Sommer.

Sham was in there for a while, but he found the going too tough as the contest went on, and he wound up in the most unlikely spot—last place. The colt that finished back of Twice a Prince was Arthur Appleton's My Gallant, who was a half-length out of second place and 13 lengths ahead of C. V. Whitney's Pvt. Smiles. Sham trailed that one by three-quarters of a length.

The exacta of Secretariat and Twice a Prince returned $35.20 for $2. The OTB letters were A and E.

The race had a gross value of $150,200, with the five starters, and the share to the winner, who is trained by Lucien Laurin, was $90,120.

In the day or two preceding the Belmont, Sham's trainer, Frank (Pancho) Martin, had said he would send a "rabbit," Knightly Dawn, into the race, to test Secretariat with an early pace, but yesterday morning Martin changed his mind and withdrew Knightly Dawn.

The race, as regards tight competition, was hardly a tingle, considering the huge margin of victory. But it held continuous excitement because of the superequine achievement of Secretariat.

At the start he went to the front with Sham, who was ridden by Laffitt Pincay, and for a spell the pair raced together, the others being "nowhere."

AMERICAN RECORD SET

The occasion of the Belmont Stakes was one of complete joy, glory and accomplishment for Mrs. John (Penny) Tweedy, who directs the activities of the Meadow interests founded by her late father, Christopher T. Chemery; for Turcotte, who had ridden Secretariat in all but the first two of the colt's 15 races, and for Lucien Laurin, Secretariat's trainer for Meadow interests.

Secretariat is a Virginia-bred son of Bold Ruler and Somethingroyal, and now has a record of 12 victories in his 15 races. His share of yesterday's gross purse was $90,120. This sum raised his season's earnings to $438,838, and his career earnings, over the last two years total $895,242. ■

Jockey Ron Turcotte sits atop of Secretariat racing to win the Triple Crown at the Belmont Stakes June 9, 1973.

Billie Jean King and Bobby Riggs during the "Battle of the Sexes Challenge Match" at the Astrodome in Houston, Texas, on September 20, 1973.

SEPTEMBER 21, 1973

Mrs. King Defeats Riggs Amid a Circus Atmosphere

Neil Amdur

HOUSTON, Sept. 20—Mrs. Billie Jean King struck a proud blow for herself and women around the world with a crushing 6-4, 6-3, 6-3 rout of Bobby Riggs tonight in their $100,000 winner-take-all tennis match at the Astrodome.

In an atmosphere more suited for a circus than a sports event, the 29-year-old Mrs. King ended the bizarre saga of the 55-year-old hustler, who had bolted to national prominence with his blunt putdowns of women's tennis and the role of today's female.

Mrs. King, a five-time Wimbledon champion and the most familiar face in the women's athletic movement, needed only 2 hours 4 minutes to reaffirm her status as one of the gifted and tenacious competitors in sport, female or male.

A crowd of 30,492, some paying as much as $100 a seat, watched the best-three-of-five-set struggle, the largest single attendance ever for a tennis match. Millions more viewed the event on national television. The match also was seen in 36 foreign countries via satellite.

Mrs. King squashed Riggs with tools synonymous with men's tennis, the serve and volley. She beat Bobby to the ball, dominated the net and ran him around the baseline to the point of near exhaustion in the third set, when he suffered hand cramps and trailed, 2-4.

Most important, perhaps for women everywhere, she convinced skeptics that a female athlete can survive pressure-filled situations and that men are as susceptible to nerves as women.

Mrs. King, the biggest money-winner in the history of women's athletics and the foremost spokesman for equality in sport, is certain to reap even greater financial returns from tonight's victory. But as she said yesterday, "pride matters a lot more than money."

"She was too good," said Riggs, the 1939 Wimbledon singles champion. "She played too well. She was playing well within herself, and I couldn't get the most out of my game. It was over too quickly."

DOLPHINS ROUT VIKINGS TO WIN 2ND SUPER BOWL IN ROW

William N. Wallace

HOUSTON, Jan. 13—On the scoreboard it was not the most one-sided Super Bowl victory of all, the Green Bay Packers retaining that distinction for their 25-point triumph over the Kansas City Chiefs in the first of pro football's extravaganzas seven years ago. But the flow of the play on the artificial turf of Rice Stadium today was the most decisive in Super Bowl annals as the Miami Dolphins annihilated the Minnesota Vikings, 24-7, to win the championship of the National Football League for the second year in a row.

The Dolphins followed exactly the formula for success devised by their coach, Don Shula, who has walked off the field a winner 32 times in the last 34 games, including successive Super Bowls.

The Miami offense ground out the yards, led by that astounding 238-pound former farmboy, Larry Csonka, who set a Super Bowl record by rushing for 145 yards. Bob Griese, the quarterback, threw only seven no-risk passers, completing six, and the Minnesota attackers were left standing on the sideline waiting for a chance to try their stuff.

By the time Francis Tarkenton, the Minnesota magician, had some room in which to maneuver, the Dolphins were ahead, 17-0, and smug. That was midway through the second quarter.

Following the Shula formula further, the Dolphins made no mistakes—no lost fumbles, no intercepted passes and only one penalty for a loss of 4 unimportant yards. They tackled in teams of twos and threes. They covered receivers in group fashion and left Tarkenton with only one type of play that worked at all. That was the pass to the tight end, of which there were four completions.

Are the Dolphins the best team of all time? Shula said, "It's not my job to say, although I feel that way." ■

Aaron Hits 715th, Passes Babe Ruth

Joseph Durso

ATLANTA, April 8—Henry Aaron ended the great chase tonight and passed Babe Ruth as the leading home-run hitter in baseball history when he hit No. 715 before a national television audience and 53,775 persons in Atlanta Stadium.

The 40-year-old outfielder for the Atlanta Braves broke the record on his second time at bat, but on his first swing of a clamorous evening. It was a soaring drive in the fourth inning off Al Downing of the Los Angeles Dodgers, and it cleared the fence in left-center field, 385 feet from home plate.

Skyrockets arched over the jammed stadium in the rain as the man from Mobile trotted around the bases for the 715th time in a career that began a quarter of a century ago with the Indianapolis Clowns in the old Negro leagues.

It was 9:07 p.m., 39 years after Ruth had hit his 714th and four days after Aaron had hit his 714th on his first swing of the bat in the opening game of the season.

Hank Aaron hitting home run No. 715, breaking Babe Ruth's record.

The history-making home run carried into the Atlanta bull pen, where a relief pitcher named Tom House made a dazzling one-handed catch against the auxiliary scoreboard. He clutched it against the boards, far below the grandstand seats, where the customers in "Home-Run Alley" were massed, waiting to retrieve a cowhide ball that in recent days had been valued as high as $25,000 on the auction market.

So Aaron not only ended the great home-run derby, but also ended the controversy that has surrounded it. His employers had wanted him to hit No. 715 in Atlanta, and had even benched him on alien soil in Cincinnati.

The commissioner of baseball, Bowie Kuhn, ordered the Braves to start their star yesterday or face "serious penalties." And tonight the dispute and the marathon finally came home to Atlanta in a razzle-dazzle setting.

The stadium was packed with its largest crowd since the Braves left Milwaukee and brought major league baseball to the Deep South nine years ago. Pearl Bailey sang the national anthem; the Jonesboro High School band marched; balloons and fireworks filled the overcast sky before the game; Aaron's life was dramatized on a huge color map of the United States painted across the outfield grass, and Bad Henry was serenaded by the Atlanta Boy Choir, which now includes girls.

Gov. Jimmy Carter was there, along with Mayor Maynard Jackson, Sammy Davis Jr. and broadcasters and writers from South America and Britain.

Head slightly bowed and elbows turned out, Aaron slowly circled the bases as the uproar grew. At second base he received a handshake from Dave Lopes of the Dodgers, and between second and third from Bill Russell.

The game was interrupted for 11 minutes during all the commotion, after which the Braves got back to work and went on to win their second straight, this time by 7-4. ∎

Skyrockets arched over the jammed stadium . . .

OCTOBER 18, 1974

A'S WIN WORLD SERIES FOR THIRD STRAIGHT TIME

Joseph Durso

OAKLAND, Calif., Oct. 17—The Oakland A's, fussing and feuding to the end, swept to their third straight baseball championship tonight when they defeated the Los Angeles Dodgers, 3-2, and won the 71st World Series.

Only one team in baseball history has won more World Series in consecutive years than the controversial and frequently rowdy American League champions—the New York Yankees. The Yankees won four straight starting in 1936 and five straight starting in 1949, but tonight the A's moved right behind them into the record book.

"Their record speaks for itself," conceded Manager Walter Alston of the Dodgers, whose team won 102 games this summer with the best performance in the major leagues. "They play the game the way it should be played. They don't make any mistakes."

They didn't make any tonight before 49,347 fans in the Oakland-Alameda County Stadium as they stopped the Dodgers for the third night in a row and took the series, four games to one. ∎

Sal Bando of the Oakland Athletics jumps on top of teammates after defeating the Los Angeles Dodgers in Game 5 of the World Series on October 17, 1974.

After winning an unprecedented fifth Master's tournament, Jack Nicklaus receives the green jacket from Gary Player, who won the previous year.

APRIL 14, 1975

40-Foot Birdie Putt Helps Nicklaus Win 5th Masters

John S. Radosta

AUGUSTA, Ga., April 13—Jack Nicklaus, who likes to live dangerously and has a sense of show business, set up one of the most exciting finishes today in the history of the Masters gold tournament.

It came down to the last two putts on the last green, and when the delirious shouting was over, Nicklaus has fended a thrilling charge by two of the best players in the game, Johnny Miller and Tom Weiskopf—and he beat them each by a shot. And the shot he beat them with was a 40-foot putt that broke two ways before dropping for a birdie on the 16th green.

Nicklaus, widely accepted as the greatest golfer in history, became the first man to win the symbolic green jacket a fifth time. To get there he shot a final round of 68 for a 72-hole total of 276. Only two other scores have been better—Nicklaus's record 271 in 1965 and Ben Hogan's 274 in 1953.

But what a finish! Miller, in a drive that he himself calls "berserk," shot a six-under-par 66 to finish at 277. Weiskopf shot a 70 for his 277.

No finish could have been more theatrical. The lead had swung between Nicklaus and Weiskopf three times. Twice they shared the lead. At no time was Miller in front, but with birdies at the 15th and 17th holes, he came to within one shot of the lead.

So there was Nicklaus on the 18th green—on in two, with a 10-foot putt that had to break left about 18 inches. Nicklaus misgauged the amount of break, and the ball slid past the hole. A tap-in for par-4, and Nicklaus was in, 12 under par for the tournament.

"I wanted to end the tournament right there," Nicklaus said, "but I just couldn't get that putt in. I figured a break of about a foot, and it broke at least a foot and a half."

As Nicklaus watched from the scorer's tent near the 18th green, Weiskopf and Miller marched up the hill, each 11 under. Miller hit a 9-iron 20 feet from the hole; Weiskopf's shot was about 8 feet away.

Miller knew it was a hard putt. He missed. There was no way Weiskopf could understand how he missed. Even watching a replay on television, he was convinced his ball would go in—but it didn't.

Any time Jack Nicklaus wins a Masters, the question comes up: Can he win the other components of the grand slam—the United States and British Opens and the championship of the Professional Golfers' Association—all in one year? ∎

ASHE TOPPLES CONNORS FOR CROWN AT WIMBLEDON

Fred Tupper

WIMBLEDON, England, July 5—Jimmy Connors, the man everybody thought unbeatable, was thrashed by Arthur Ashe in the Wimbledon men's final today.

Before a stunned center-court crowd, Ashe won, 6-1, 6-1, 5-7, 6-4, over 125 minutes and became the first black man to take the highest honor in tennis. Althea Gibson, a black, won the women's title in 1957 and 1958.

For many years Ashe had waited in the wings, his best efforts here having been a losing semi-finalist in 1968 and 1969. He will be 32 next week, and had set two objectives for this year—to win the World Championship Tennis and Wimbledon crowns. Amazingly, he has achieved both.

Connors was a 3-to-2 favorite to win the title for the second straight time. Three times he had beaten Ashe, never having lost to him. Jimmy had waded through the draw without dropping a set, and his massacre of Roscoe Tanner, the huge server in the semifinals, was thought to have contained the hardest hitting ever seen at this historic shrine.

Ashe took the pace off the ball and gave the slugger little to bang at, and he served wide to the backhand to pull Connors off balance.

This match brought alive what had been a dull Wimbledon. On the changeovers Ashe sat still, eyes closed, meditating, relaxing for the task ahead. He had nine games in a row, leading by 3-love in the second set.

"Come on, Connors!" a voice yelled in the distance.

"I'm trying, for crissake!" replied Jimmy, tearing around the court, mop of hair flying.

Deliberate and careful, Ashe stuck to the battle plan.

Arthur Ashe holding up the championship trophy for men's singles of the Wimbledon Lawn Tennis in 1975.

The winner received $23,000 and the loser $13,800.

"I just didn't have it today," said a crestfallen Connors, but the bravado was still there. He had played a wonderful Wimbledon.

"I came here with my head high and I'll walk out that way, and I'll be back with my head even higher," he added. ■

For many years Ashe had waited in the wings.

SPORTS

ALI RETAINS TITLE AS 'THRILLA IN MANILA' IS STOPPED AFTER 14TH

Dave Anderson

MANILA, Wednesday, Oct. 1—In the most brutal confrontation of their five-year rivalry, Muhammad Ali retained the world heavyweight boxing championship today when Joe Frazier's manager, Eddie Futch, surrendered from the corner moments before the bell was to ring for the 15th round.

Frazier, dominating the middle rounds with the fury of his youth, had been battered by the champion throughout the three rounds prior to Futch's merciful decision.

"I stopped it," Futch explained, "because Joe was starting to get hit with too many clean shots. He couldn't see out of his right eye. He couldn't see the left hands coming."

Ali was far ahead on the scoreboards of the three officials. Using the 5-point must scoring system, referee Carlos Padilla Jr. had the champion ahead, 66-60. Judge Alfredo Quiazon had it 67-62 and Judge Larry Nadayag had it 66-62. On a rounds basis, Quiazon had Ali ahead 8-3, with three even. The others each had it 8-4-2.

Ali's victory was recorded as a knockout in the 14th round since the bell had not rung for the final round.

"My guy sucked it up," said Ali's trainer, Angelo Dundee. "When he looked completely out of gas, he put on another gas tank. I thought we were in front. My guy was hitting him better shots."

"Joe had two bad rounds in a row," Futch said. "Even with three minutes to go, he was going downhill. And that opened up the possibility in that situation that he could've been seriously hurt."

"I didn't want to be stopped, I wanted to go on," Frazier said, "but I'd never go against Eddie."

Frazier dismissed questions about retirement, saying, "I'm not thinking that way now." But the weary champion indicated

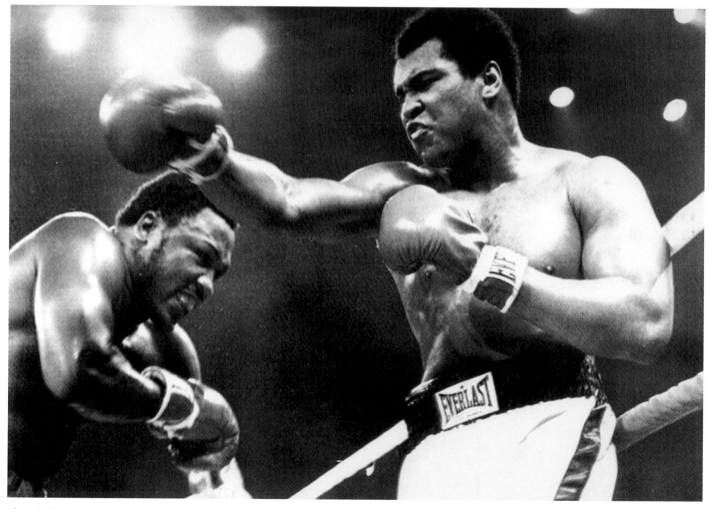

The "Thrilla in Manila" Heavyweight Champion Muhammad Ali, right who beat challenger Joe Frazier on a TKO in the 14th round.

that the "Thrilla in Manila" might have been his last fight.

"You may have seen the last of Ali," the champion said. "I want to get out of it. I'm tired and on top. What you saw tonight was next to death. He's the toughest man in the world."

They resembled two old bull moose who had to stand and slam each other because they couldn't get away from each other.

Unlike their first two fights, Ali-Frazier III maintained a level of boxing violence seldom seen. During their 1971 classic, Frazier earned a 15-round unanimous decision and undisputed possession of the title with a relentless assault as Ali often clowned. In their 12-round nontitle bout early last year Ali's holding tactics detracted from his unanimous decision.

But from the opening bell in the Philippine Coliseum, the estimated crowd of 25,000, including President Ferdinand Marcos and his wife, realized that Ali had not come to dance.

At the bell, Ali came out, hands high in a semipeekaboo. He stood flat-footed rather than dancing, as if looking for the early knockout he had predicted. Frazier, in contrast, moved in aggressively, trying to unload his left hook but the champion tied him up effectively in two clinches.

In the second round, Ali remained flat-footed, using his pawing jab to keep Frazier at bay.

In the third round, Ali landed a series of hard punches to the head, but Frazier burrowed through them to land a left. Ali covered up against the ropes, and when Frazier stepped back, Ali waved his right glove at Frazier, as if inviting him to return.

But in the fourth round Ali's tempo slowed as Frazier's increased. By the fifth round, a chant of "Frazier, Frazier" filled the round arena. As the struggle continued, the crowd sounded as if it favored Frazier, one of the few times that Ali hasn't converted the live audience into cheering for him.

Ali, at 224½ pounds at last Saturday's weigh-in, had been the 9-to-5 betting favorite in the United States but he was a 6-to-5 choice here. Frazier had weighed 214½ at the ceremonial weigh-in.

Ali's won-lost record is now 49-2 with 34 knockouts. He has lost only to Frazier in 1971 and to Ken Norton, who broke Ali's jaw in winning a 12-round decision that Ali later reversed. Frazier's record is now 32-3.

In the decades to come, Ali and Frazier will be remembered as two of boxing's classic rivals through 42 rounds. As memorable as their first two fights were in Madison Square Garden, their masterpiece developed halfway around the world from where their rivalry began. ■

MARCH 16, 1976

MESSERSMITH
Open To Bidding Today

Murray Chass

Fifteen months after Catfish Hunter immersed himself in Yankee gold, Andy Messersmith goes on baseball's auction block today. Indications are, however, that the pitcher won't attract the bids that got Hunter a $3.75 million contract.

Messersmith played for the Los Angeles Dodgers last season without signing a contract. He becomes a free agent today, the stipulated seven days after the United States Court of Appeals for the Eighth Circuit upheld a district court order declaring that major league rules did not "inhibit, prohibit or prevent" other clubs from negotiating with the 30-year-old pitcher.

The 24 clubs, who had been forbidden by the league presidents from negotiating with Messersmith while the case was in the courts, were notified yesterday by the league offices that the former Dodger was free to deal with any of them as of today.

Messersmith will leave most of the preliminary work to his agent, Herb Osmond, who is also his neighbor. Osmond might find the bidding slower and less lucrative than Hunter experienced for several reasons: the possible availability in the near future of many more free agents; the clubs' desire to avoid establishing high-payment precedents for them, and their regret that they had let the Hunter bidding soar so high.

"We're interested in Messersmith and we're looking forward to meeting him," said Ted Turner, the new owner of the Atlanta Braves. "However, this situation is different than with Catfish because the supply of superstars available as free agents probably will be a lot higher than in the past."

George Steinbrenner, the principal Yankee owner, said he hadn't discussed Messersmith with Gabe Paul, who runs the club's baseball operation. But Steinbrenner added: "You have to be interested in a pitcher like that. I am, but I leave it up to my baseball people."

Messersmith, who won a total of 39 games the last two seasons and rejected a Dodger offer of $540,000 for three years just before the arbitration hearing, said he had no preference for league, team or location. ■

Janet Guthrie's crew working her Lightning 76 1/Offenhauser TC during the 1977 Indianapolis 500 on May 29, 1977.

MAY 11, 1976

WOMAN FINALLY DRIVES AT INDY

INDIANAPOLIS, May 10 (UPI)—Janet Guthrie, on her third try, finally made her debut on the track at the Indianapolis Motor Speedway, but her rise was cut short by mechanical problems in her car.

The first woman nominated to compete in the Indy 500-mile auto race drove seven laps at moderate speeds before a burned piston in the Rolla Vollstedt machine forced her off the track.

The same thing had happened yesterday to her teammate, Dick Simon, while he was shaking down the car for her. As a result, Miss Guthrie never got a chance to make her track debut.

On Saturday, the opening day of practice for the May 30 race, mechanical problems, while Simon was test-riding the car, prevented Miss Guthrie from making her first trip around the 2½-mile race course.

Today she logged six laps at a speed of about 152 miles an hour before she was brought in for instructions. She went out again, but after one lap lost power, shut off the engine, stopped between the first and second turns and climbed from the cockpit.

"It's not a problem of whether she can go fast enough," said Simon, who is also acting as the team's spokesman. "It's just a question if we can keep it [the car] together. She was just playing around at 150."

A burned piston meant a teardown of the engine—a time-consuming task.

Eighteen cars had made practice runs by mid-afternoon of the third day of practice, including initial appearances on the track of Al Unser, Bill Vukovich and Mike Hiss.

Tom Sneva, who was seriously burned in a spectacular crash during last year's race, was clocked at a speed of 185.223 m.p.h. Unser, utilizing a British Cosworth engine, was timed at better than 184. ■

. . . she logged six laps at a speed of about 152 miles an hour . . .

JUNE 18, 1976

BASKETBALL LEAGUES MERGE; NY TO RETAIN TWO TEAMS

Sam Goldaper

HYANNIS, Mass., June 17—The National Basketball Association and the American Basketball Association finally merged today into a 22-team league.

Four of the A.B.A.'s six teams—the New York Nets, the Indiana Pacers, the Denver Nuggets and the San Antonio Spurs—have been absorbed into the N.B.A. and will play in the 1976–77 season.

Each of these franchises will pay $3.2 million in cash to the N.B.A., with the first payment of $1 million due on July 15 and the remainder on Sept. 15.

Since the A.B.A. began as an 11-team league for the 1967–68 season, it had 22 different franchises, seven commissioners and had been involved in countless lawsuits. The league contends it has lost $40 million.

The A.B.A. started the 1975–76 season as a 10-team league, but in rapid succession the Baltimore Claws folded on Oct. 20 and the San Diego Sails dropped out Nov. 10, followed by the Utah Stars on Dec. 3 and the Virginia Squires May 10.

The Kentucky Colonels and Utah Rockies, who were to take over the Spirits of St. Louis franchise next season, were left out of the consolidation and they will be paid about $3 million each by the four teams accepted into the N.B.A.

The Kentucky and Utah players will be dispersed in a special draft in which the 18 N.B.A. teams, plus the four newcomers, will participate. The Chicago Bulls will have the first pick because they had the worst record in the league. They are expected to select Artis Gilmore, the 7-foot-2-inch Kentucky Colonel center. Several other outstanding players will be available, among them Moses Malone, Maurice Lucas and Marvin Barnes.

There could be a lot of trading or selling of draft picks. The Knicks are almost certain to bid for at least one of those stars to fill their need for an overpowering big man. The Knicks are scheduled to pick sixth in the dispersal draft.

Intensive merger negotiations between Larry O'Brien, the N.B.A. commissioner, and Dave DeBusschere, his A.B.A. counterpart, began at the suggestion of Federal Judge Robert L. Carter of the Southern New York District Court. He asked both sides to attempt an out-of-court settlement of the A.B.A. antitrust suit against the N.B.A.

Although many problems may still develop in future negotiations, nothing is expected to hinder the ultimate agreement. Especially since each N.B.A. owner will receive almost $700,000 and there is an almost additional $5 million awaiting them in the third year of their television contract with CBS. The television network had promised the extra money if the N.B.A. would accept at least four teams into the league.

The vote for the consolidation was 17-1, with the unexpected dissenting vote cast by Sam Schulman, the owner of the Seattle SuperSonics. Schulman had been a leading proponent for the merger for almost eight years.

When the $3.2 million cash settlement was finally substituted yesterday for the original $4.5 million five-year payout plan, Prentice Yancey, the general counsel of the A.B.A. Players Association, was summoned from Atlanta.

During the all-night negotiations, Yancey entered into an accord that included the honoring of all present A.B.A. contracts, including those of players who may not make it to the N.B.A. A pool was also set up that would pay off the contracts of those players whose teams had folded.

As for the new N.B.A. teams, their rosters were frozen as of May 1. They will not share in any television monies for the next four years and, should the league decide to share gate receipts in the future, they would be excluded from the vote. In the N.B.A. the home team keeps all the receipts.

Larry Fleisher, the general counsel of the N.B.A. Players Association, said, "It's better to have two teams disbanded rather than six. I don't think the A.B.A. would have been able to survive another year."

handoff

PERFECT SCORES IN GYMNASTICS PUT JUDGES ON TRIAL

Neil Amdur

MONTREAL, July 23—Judges in women's gymnastics were under considerably more pressure than in any previous Olympics, several members of the international panel disclosed today.

"It's more difficult to differentiate between one-tenth or one-half of a tenth," said Mrs. Jackie Fie of Jefferson, Iowa, the only American on the 25-member judging panel. "It doesn't make me more nervous. I know what I'm going to do. It's just a more tense situation because there are so many good ones."

Ursel Baer of Britain was among the four judges in last night's floor exercise final in which Nelli Kim of the Soviet Union registered a perfect score en route to one of her three gold medals.

"Nobody's perfect," Miss Baer said, although at least three of the four judges would have had to approve to reach a perfect mark. "You must judge according to the first routine. There may be slight imperfections, but you may have to go to a 10 because it's better than anything that's been before."

"There's been a fantastic improvement in the standards," said Miss Baer. "We, as judges, need more in the code to differentiate from them. We know these things need revisions and we have members to work with the countries and revise the standards. Hopefully, this will be achieved in the near future."

Politics continues as a major problem in gymnastics. Soviet coaches complained about some of the perfect scores received by Nadia Comaneci of Rumania, who wound up with three gold medals and seven perfect marks after last night's individual events. Two women's judges also reportedly were replaced before the finals, only to be reinstated after a hastily arranged meeting and formal protest.

"The top-class gymnasts are taught to train different routes through exercises," Mrs. Fie said. "If they miss something, they have auxiliary exercises to follow. The trick is being good enough to do it without letting the judge think you've done anything wrong." ■

Nadia Comaneci, age 14, performs during Olympic beam event on July 21, 1976, in Montreal, Canada.

"There's been a fantastic improvement in the standards"

3 STEROIDS USERS ARE BANNED

MONTREAL, July 30 (AP)—The International Olympic Committee announced today that three athletes had been disqualified from the Olympic Games for use of anabolic steroids (muscle-building drugs).

The three were Mark Cameron of Middletown, R.I., and Peter Pavlasek of Czechoslovakia, weight lifters, and Danuta Rosani of Poland, a women's discus competitor.

None won medals. Cameron was in the heavyweight division and Pavlasek in the superheavyweight division.

The steroids, illegal under Olympic rules, apparently showed up in tests given to randomly selected athletes.

Pavlasek finished sixth in his division. Cameron, 24 years old, finished sixth, fifth and fifth in three competitions.

The United States Olympic Committee issued a statement saying it was "shocked and appalled" by the disqualification of Cameron. Philip O. Krumm, the U.S.O.C.'s president, criticized the I.O.C. Medical Commission for announcing the decision without informing the U.S.O.C.

The U.S.O.C. said Cameron would not be dropped from the team and would be permitted to remain in Olympic Village.

AUGUST 31, 1976

CONTROVERSY OVER RENEE RICHARDS ADDS DIMENSION TO SEX ROLE IN SPORTS

Robin Herman

Before she underwent a sex-change operation last November, Dr. Renee Richards was known as Dr. Richard Raskind, an amateur tennis player who in 1974 ranked third in the East and 13th nationally in the men's 35-and-over division. Last week, before curious crowds buzzing with debate, the 42-year-old ophthalmologist reached the semifinal round of a women's tournament in South Orange, N.J.

When Dr. Richards was accepted into the Tennis Week open by the tournament director, a longtime friend, 25 women players withdrew in protest. They argued that Dr. Richards's presence was unfair, that despite her operation and resulting feminine appearance, she still retained the muscular advantages of a male and genetically remained a male.

Dr. Richards questions the validity of sex identification through genes, and insists that bodily, psychologically and socially she is female. Under her new name and sex, she has been given new official papers, such as a passport, certificate to practice medicine and other licenses. "In the eyes of the law," she said, "I am female."

Dr. Richards had planned to enter the United States Open, which begins tomorrow. But she was thwarted by the United States Tennis Association, which for the first time instituted a chromosome test as a prerequisite for women entries. Dr. Richards has refused to take the test and is considering legal action against the U.S.T.A.

By instituting the sex test, the U.S.T.A. is belatedly following the lead of the International Olympic Committee. At the 1968 Olympics in Mexico, the I.O.C. made the chromosome test mandatory for competitors in women's events. In most cases a male will show an XY pattern of chromosomes, a female XX.

(cont'd. on next page)

Renee Richards hits a return during the Women's 1977 U.S. Open.

(cont'd. from previous page)

The only athlete known to have failed a femininity test was Ewa Klobukowska, a Polish sprinter. She was ruled ineligible for the European Cup women's track and field competition in 1967. A year later the I.A.A.F. took away the gold and bronze medals she had won in the 1964 Olympics.

Although Dr. Richards had a sex-change operation just last year, she emphasizes that she does not belong to the imposters against whom sex tests were first meant to guard.

Dr. Richards entered and won her first women's tournament last month in La Jolla, Calif. At that time she did not make it known that she was a transsexual. Reporters investigating her background subsequently discovered her former identity.

"I'm not a fulltime major league tennis player," she said at South Orange. "I'm here to make a point. It's a human rights issue.

"I want to show that someone who has a different lifestyle or medical condition, has a right to stand up for what they are. They don't have to hide from the press, their family and friends. I'm not making the issue for transsexuals in tennis. It's just that tennis is my vehicle."

At first she was upset when her background was revealed. She had obtained a divorce and moved to California to preserve her anonymity after the operation.

As in the Karen Quinlan case, which demonstrated that there can be varying definitions of death, Dr. Richards says that sexuality can be defined in many ways. Dr. Richards argues that her phenotype—her primary and secondary physical sex characteristics—is female. As a result of the sex-change operation, she says, her body characteristics are those of a female and she has a female blood hormone level. Her body no longer produces testosterone, the male hormone, she says.

She suggests that in determining an athlete's sex all factors be taken into consideration, including chromosomes, bodily characteristics and the psychological state.

Kathy Harter, whom Dr. Richards defeated at South Orange, was among those who supported her entry in the tournament as a legal and human right. Aside from the strictly medical debate, a question of humanitarianism and rights has been raised. Dr. Richards speaks of a right to compete. "I can't do without it," she says. ∎

Howe Mulls Retirement

"I'll probably retire, but I always leave 10 percent open." So said Gordie Howe, the 49-year-old grand old man of hockey on Wednesday night as he contemplated plans for after the season. He had just scored the 1,000th goal of his career in a 6-3 victory by his New England Whalers over the Birmingham Bulls. "I'll be a grandfather soon," he said, "and not many grandfathers play hockey." Maybe so, but Howe, who is in his 31st year as a professional hockey player, has changed his mind about retiring several times before, most notably when his two sons Mark and Marty, both also with the Whalers, turned pro. ∎

JANUARY 22, 1979

BRADSHAW HURLS 4 SCORING PASSES IN SUPER BOWL XIII

William N. Wallace

Terry Bradshaw throws a pass against the Dallas Cowboys during Super Bowl XIII on January 21, 1979, at the Orange Bowl in Miami, Florida.

It was a game with everything a football fan could want. It had the excellent passing of Terry Bradshaw, the Pittsburgh quarterback who set Super Bowl records for most passing yardage, 318, and most touchdowns thrown, 4. It had the utter frustration of Jackie Smith, the Dallas reserve tight end—a veteran of 16 professional seasons—who dropped a certain touchdown pass in the end zone that would have given his team a 21-21 tie in the third period. It had the acrobatic catches of Lynn Swann and John Stallworth. It had the running of the cagey Tony Dorsett and stubborn Franco Harris. It has a lost fumble by the Cowboys on a kickoff. It had a penalty call— Benny Barnes interfering with Swann—that will be debated endlessly.

The 66 points scored at the Orange Bowl were exactly double the average number of points scored in the previous 12 Super Bowl

It was a game with everything a football fan could want.

games. Neither team could establish a dominating running offense, so they both resorted to passing, an attack that went a lot of places, good places for Pittsburgh.

Rocky Bleier, the Steeler running back who caught Bradshaw's third touchdown pass on the next-to-last play of the first half, summed up the game witnessed by 78,856 fans in the stadium and by uncounted millions who watched on television.

He said: "The Steelers and the Cowboys have played the two most exciting games ever in the Super Bowl. I give credit to Dallas because they didn't quit. They kept our defense out there in the fourth quarter. They really gave us a scare."

Bleier was referring to the Pittsburgh victory over Dallas here three years ago, also by 4 points, 21-17, and to the Cowboys' late comeback today from an 18-point deficit that the Steelers had accumulated suddenly in the middle of the last period.

"They played their hearts out," said Tom Landry, the Dallas coach, of his team.

But they wound up 4 points short.

Those 4 points were lost when Smith, the 38-year-old second-string tight end, failed to catch a pass from Roger Staubach in the Pittsburgh end zone in the third period. Smith slipped on the damp, yellow-painted grass and the pass, low and wobbly, hit him in the shoulder pads and fell to the turf. Dallas had to settle for a field goal.

"I was wide open and I missed it," said Smith. That play cost the 45 Cowboy players $405,000 because each of the 45 Steelers received $18,000 for winning the game and each of the Cowboys $9,000.

Staubach said later, "I could have thrown Jackie a lot better pass." The Dallas quarterback, playing in his fifth Super Bowl game, was good. Bradshaw was better. Staubach completed 17 of 30 pass attempts for 228 yards and three touchdowns, and had one intercepted pass as did Bradshaw. Staubach was dropped five times by the Steelers and fumbled once. Bradshaw fumbled twice, one bobble resulting in a Dallas touchdown.

Bradshaw seemed unfazed by his record performance. When told of his record day he said, "Did I do all that?"

Records broken included most points scored, 66; most touchdowns, 9; most touchdown passes, 7; most yards gained by passing in one game, 467; most yards by passing, Bradshaw, 318; most touchdown passes thrown, Bradshaw, 4. ■

Earvin (Magic) Johnson playing against Larry Bird during the 1979 N.C.A.A. tournament.

MARCH 27, 1979

MICHIGAN STATE DEFEATS INDIANA STATE FOR N.C.A.A. TITLE

Gordon S. White Jr.

Special to The New York Times

SALT LAKE CITY, March 26—Michigan State grounded The Bird with a touch of Magic and a magnificent zone defense tonight to win its first National Collegiate basketball championship and end Indiana State's chance to achieve an unbeaten season.

Despite a heavy load of personal fouls that created serious problems down the stretch, the Spartans held fast to an early lead and beat the Sycamores, 75-64, in the final of the 41st National Collegiate Athletic Association tournament before 15,410 persons in the Special Events Center of the University of Utah. The loss was the only one for Indiana State in 34 games this season. Michigan State finished with a 26-6 record.

Earvin (Magic) Johnson, who played the entire second half with three personal fouls, was his usual spectacular self, scoring 24 points for the winners. Larry Bird, the big man for Indiana State with a three-year career average of more than 30 points a game, was kept to only 19 points, his lowest scoring game in five N.C.A.A. tournament contests.

As a result, Indiana State, the eighth undefeated team to reach the final, became only the second of them to lose in the championship game. Ohio State was the first when the Buckeyes were losers to Cincinnati in 1961.

Michigan State had been to three previous N.C.A.A. tournaments and only one previous Final Four, a semifinal loss to North Carolina in 1957. With tonight's victory, the Spartans gave the Big Ten Conference a sweep of the two major post-season college tourneys. Indiana won the National Invitation Tournament last Wednesday.

In winning the title, Michigan State became only the second team to do so with as many as six losses for the season. Kentucky did it with six losses in 1958 and Marquette with seven in 1977.

But there was no beating the Michigan State defense during this tournament and there was little any team could do to stop the fast offense triggered by the magic of Johnson's passing.

(cont'd. on next page)

(cont'd. from previous page)

This defense stopped Bird after no other team could do so in this tourney. The 6-9 senior had scored 22, 29, 31 and 35 points in his four previous tourney games. What's more, Michigan State closed down the Indiana State passing lanes, and held Bird to only two assists.

"We defended him with an adjustment and a prayer," coach Jud Heathcote said.

A couple of times during the first half Bird got to the top of his jump and could not decide whether to shoot or pass off. This led to missed shots and missed passes as the Bird hit only 7 of 21 field-goal at-tempts—33 percent. He had hit 53 percent before tonight.

Although it was the defense that turned the tables on Indiana State, Michigan State got off to another of its spectacular offensive shows early in the game. This enabled the Spartans to go in front by 16 points in the first two minutes of the second half.

Through it all, Heathcote was obviously concerned about Bird. "I thought every shot the Bird took would go in," the Michigan State coach said.

Indiana State's man-to-man defense didn't appear to bother Johnson. He made one of the game's most exciting moves when he drove the baseline around Alex Gilbert only to be facing Bird, standing his ground under the basket.

Kelser was coming down the lane to Johnson's left and the Michigan State sophomore faked a pass to Kelser. Bird took the fake and moved just a bit to defend Kelser coming into the basket. Johnson kept the ball and made an easy layup.

Such spectacular play may have been Johnson's last for Michigan State. It is expected that the Lansing, Mich., athlete who stayed home to play college ball will declare hardship and be drafted into the pros for next season. ■

Yankees' Thurman Munson Killed Piloting His Own Small Jet in Ohio

Jim Naughton

Mourners for Thurman Munson at Yankee Stadium on August 4, 1979.

Thurman Munson, the 32-year-old catcher and team captain of the New York Yankees, was killed yesterday when the plane he was piloting crashed short of the runway while trying to land at the Akron-Canton Airport in Ohio.

Two passengers who were flying with him were taken to local hospitals where they were reported in fair condition.

Munson's Cessna Citation twin-engine jet crashed outside the perimeter of the airport and came to rest 200 feet north of runway 19 at 3:02 p.m., Eastern daylight time, according to the Akron police.

Federal Aviation Administration officials said that the plane had lost its wings and burst into flames after the crash, resulting in injuries to two occupants and the death of the third.

One of the two passengers, David Hall, 32, of Canton, who first taught Munson to fly, was reported in fair condition with burns on his arms and hands at the Akron Regional Burn Center at Children's Hospital. The other passenger, Jerry D. Anderson, also of Canton, was reported in fair condition with burns of the face, arms and neck at Timken Mercy Hospital in Canton.

Munson, a native of Akron, often flew home during home stands and road trips to be with his family. A Yankee coach, Elston Howard, said Munson told him he was interested in running a commercial commuter airline and was studying for a special license.

The coach said Munson wanted to stay as close to his family as possible. "That's why he told me he was flying home on his own plane on off days. He just said, 'Ellie, I want to see my family.' That's what he told me."

Munson, who batted over .300 five times and played on three Yankee pennant winners and two world championship teams, was the first Yankee captain since Lou Gehrig.

News of the death shocked the baseball world.

The Yankees' principal owner, George Steinbrenner, said in a statement: "There's very little I could say to adequately express my feelings at this moment. I've lost a dear friend, a pal and one of the greatest competitors I've ever known. We spent many hours together talking baseball, and business. He loved his family. He was our leader. The great sport that made him so famous seems so very small and unimportant now."

Billy Martin, the Yankee manager, said: "For those who never knew him and didn't like him, I feel sorry for them. He was a great man, for his family, friends and all the people who knew and loved him, my deepest sympathy. We not only lost a great competitor, but a leader and a husband and devoted family man. He was a close friend, I loved him."

Commissioner Bowie Kuhn called the crash "an almost indescribable loss."

Munson was an all-America catcher at Kent State in 1968. He came to the Yankees in 1969 and was rookie of the year in 1970. He won a Gold Glove Award in 1973, 1974 and 1975. He won the American League Most Valuable Player Award in 1976 and was named captain of the Yankees that year. ■

Index

INDEX

INDEX